INSIDE EUROPE

INSIDE EUROPE

by

JOHN GUNTHER

1940 WAR EDITION

HAMISH HAMILTON
90 GREAT RUSSELL STREET LONDON

First Published   January 1936
New and Revised Edition (Fifteenth Impression)   October 1936
Revised Illustrated Edition (Twenty-fifth Impression) November 1937
War Edition (Thirty-third Impression)   February 1940

PRINTED IN GUERNSEY, C.I., BRITISH
ISLES, BY THE STAR AND GAZETTE LTD.

To

MY WIFE

IN LOVE AND FRIENDSHIP

CONTENTS

CONTENTS—*continued*

PREFACE

THIS book is written from a definite point of view. It is that the accidents of personality play a great role in history. As Bertrand Russell says, the Russian revolution might not have occurred without Lenin, and modern European development would have been very difficult if Bismarck had died as a child. The personality of Karl Marx himself has powerfully influenced the economic interpretation of history. Important political, religious, demographic, nationalist, as well as economic factors are not, I believe, neglected in this book. But its main trend is personal.

The fact may be an outrage to reason, but it cannot be denied: unresolved personal conflicts in the lives of various European politicians may contribute to the collapse of our civilisation. This is the age of great dictatorial leaders; millions depend for life or death on the will of Hitler, Mussolini, Stalin. Never have politics been so vital and dynamic as to-day, and so pervasively obtrusive in non-political affairs. The politicians usurp other fields. What fictional drama can compare with the dramatic reality of Mussolini's career? What literary craftsman ever wrote history as Trotsky both wrote and made it? What books in the realm of art have had the sale or influence of Hitler's *Mein Kampf*?

These men and their lesser contemporaries—French politicians like Daladier and Blum, crude and boisterous adventurers of the type of Goering, nationalist officers like General Franco, British leaders like Chamberlain and Churchill, Balkan kings like Carol—are playing decisive roles in the stupendous drama of Europe at war. It is very difficult to explore usefully the private lives of these men. This is not a peep-hole book. It contains no gossip for gossip's sake. But it tries to tell the intimate story of these leaders, the personal sources of their power, the reasons for their impact on history. Who are these men who dominate our lives?

The book begins with Hitler, then makes a tour around him. I have tried to note the impingement of Hitler's Germany on every European country, and to include an analysis of every important European crisis and situation. We visit, in a counter-clockwise

circle, France, Spain, Italy; make a detour upward to that dominant island, England; proceed through the deceased states of
Central Europe and the battered survivors of the Balkans; finish
the circle around Germany with what was once Poland; visit Scandinavia and the neutral states briefly; inspect what we have seen
of Western Europe at Geneva; and emerge finally in the Soviet
Union.

J. G.

BIBLIOGRAPHICAL NOTE

Inside Europe was first written in the summer and autumn of 1935, and published in both England and the United States in January 1936. Since that time it has been revised and republished so frequently that a word of explanation is perhaps necessary.

In March 1936 I wrote a new preface, carrying on events; oddly enough I finished this preface on the very day that Hitler marched into the Rhineland. Soon thereafter—in May 1936—another new preface became necessary.

In the late summer of 1936 my publishers suggested that I rewrite considerable portions of the book, so as to bring it up to date more comprehensively. This was an adventurous undertaking to which I gladly agreed. So in October 1936 the first *completely* revised and reset edition appeared. I eliminated some material that had already become outdated, made numerous minor changes, added new sections on the Rhineland crisis and the Ethiopian War, and wrote two entirely new chapters, one on Léon Blum, one on de Valera.

In March 1937 a new chapter was inserted in this edition, dealing with the Simpson crisis and the abdication of King Edward VIII.

The pressure of European events increased, the march of the groaning continent continued. In the autumn of 1937 I undertook another complete revision, which was published in November of that year. This was called the 'Revised Illustrated Edition'. It was the twenty-fifth English printing since first publication. This Edition was fully reset and published anew. It contained a map, 800 textual revisions and about 30,000 new words, with new chapters on the Russian treason trials, the neutral states (which I had hitherto neglected), the war in Spain, and Neville Chamberlain.

Various minor changes were made during 1938, while I was absent in Asia. In the spring of 1938, after the seizure of Austria, my publishers added footnotes here and there.

After the Munich crisis, in October 1938, I wrote two new chapters, which were promptly incorporated into the book. One was a discussion of the Austrian and Czechoslovak crises, called 'The

Fascist Offensive'; one was a new introduction summarising the events of the year.

From that time until the present, events came so quickly that a new comprehensive revision was impossible. Now, after the outbreak of war, I have attempted it. The present edition, known as the '1940 War Edition', is again—for the third time—completely rewritten and reset. I have made multitudinous additions and subtractions, with about 2,000 textual changes and perhaps 20,000 new words. (When *Inside Europe* was first published in 1936 it was 180,000 words long; it now runs to about 260,000.) I have included new sections on Daladier and Churchill, new material on almost every country, and a new chapter on the events from Munich to the invasion of Poland. There is also a brief introduction summarising events since the outbreak of war.

Despite all these changes, insertions, subtractions, revisions, and additions, the essential structure and point of view of *Inside Europe* have remained unchanged. It still begins with Hitler, it still ends with Stalin. During the unprecedented turbulence and dynamism of the last five years, I have naturally had to modify some early opinions, but basically the book conforms still to the structure I first gave it.

As I write this I feel that I will never revise *Inside Europe* again. The war brings new perspectives. I hope, however, to add a brief preface or introduction each year. But the present edition will be the last, I think, to be completely rewritten and reset.

Since its first appearance *Inside Europe* has been published in fourteen countries. It has been translated into French, German, Spanish (two Spanish editions exist), Chinese, Japanese, Dutch, Swedish, Norwegian, Danish, Czechoslovak, Hungarian, Jugoslav, and Esthonian. Parts of it have appeared in other languages.

J. G.

INTRODUCTION TO THE 1940 WAR EDITION

I N September 1939 the catastrophe of war again descended on
shaken Europe. No one wanted this war. In the tremendous
week from August 21 to August 27 I flew from Moscow to London,
stopping off in the Baltic and Scandinavian states. I kept watching the frontiers. From the air you can't tell where Russia stops,
where Latvia starts. You can't tell the difference, crossing from
Sweden to Denmark to Germany to Holland, between one country
and the next. The greenish brown fields, the red brick houses, the
slate roofs, are the same. They all seem part of a common whole, a
common organism. You can't tell frontiers apart—from the air.
But you certainly have to learn to tell them apart, on earth.

In the stormy summer of 1939 I visited eighteen European
countries. I circumnavigated Germany, which means going to
thirteen different states, and I spent some time in Germany itself,
in the Soviet Union, and in Great Britain. Everywhere the
common people wanted peace. The shopkeepers in Amsterdam
and Cologne; the peasants harvesting wheat from Belgium to
Esthonia—they wanted peace. In Latvia and Poland I talked to
housewives, to telegraph clerks, to waiters in the coffee houses;
they wanted peace. Flying across the Baltic I stopped for a moment
in a Finnish town; the pretty girls on that golden beach wanted
peace; so did the shipmasters in their old schooners. Everywhere,
in every country, the common people wanted peace. They didn't
want war. But war was what they got.

Nor did any European Government want war. The British
Government certainly did not want war. Nor did the French
Government. Nor did the Polish Government. Nor, I think, did
the German Government. Up to the very last moment,[1] it seems
reasonably clear, Hitler thought that he could—once more—manufacture an enormous crisis, bluff his way through it, and emerge
with victory without having to fight. He thought that by the
Russo-German pact he could frighten the British off, nip Danzig
away from Poland, and retire triumphantly without conflict.

[1] The Polish crisis and events leading up to the outbreak of the war are described in Chapter IX below, a new chapter in this edition.

Hitler did not want war. He must know that, by all the imperatives of reason, war will destroy him. What he wanted was victory
without war. His whole prestige rested on the concept of victory
without war.

Why, then, did war come? First, because Hitler made his
colossal miscalculation. Such a miscalculation was, however,
inevitable from the nature of the Nazi movement. Hitler became
a prisoner of forces stronger than he was. He had to expand, or
burst. He built his own dynamics; they swept him on.

Second, war came because the British decided to resist. They
decided to resist, I think, for three main reasons: (*a*) 'fedupness'
with the recurring Hitler crises, a feeling that even warfare was
better than the intolerable assault on nerves and the disruption of
all normal activity that each fresh crisis brought; (*b*) realisation
that, if Hitler took Danzig, the whole of Poland would go next,
and after that whatever Hitler chose to grab, until all Europe
might be his; (*c*) former British weakness. Because the British had
previously been weak, it was doubly necessary to be strong.

The war was not popular though the British faced it with stubborn grimness. No war can be popular nowadays. People know
too much. They remember the last war, which ended only twenty-
one short years ago. They remember slogans like 'Save the World
for Democracy' and 'The War to End War'. They cannot so
readily believe in slogans this time. Almost the most astonishing
thing I saw in London during the first weird month of war was a
brass band—astonishing because its martial music, normally something to be taken for granted, seemed strangely out of place. There
was no Rupert Brooke in 1939. There was no glamour left to
warfare.

The British are a decent, a kindly, a humanitarian, an intensely
civilised folk; they know that war costs much, and that it may
settle little; they abhor the pain, the suffering, the tremendous
human dislocation that this war—or any war—must bring. Nevertheless, they had to fight. They fought with grim and even bitter
determination. Germany was unified by the feeling that Britain
sought to destroy Germany. Britain was unified by the conviction
that no peace, no law and order, no fruitful development of
national life, no security for small or big states, no decency in
international relations, was possible until Hitlerism was destroyed.

   .   .   .   .

So war began—and surely it was the strangest war ever fought anywhere, at least in its first few months. Inspect the picture: massive armies were locked in naked embrace on the Western Front, and scarcely moved an inch. Enormous masses of men, with their inordinate cargoes of munitions, tiptoed towards action as if on eggshells. The great capital cities were blacked out against air raids that did not come.

The reason for this sombre inactivity in the west was surely not far to seek. Neither side dared to attack the other frontally, with artillery and infantry in the conventional manner, because of the terrible losses a major offensive would entail. The Maginot and Siegfried lines are probably the strongest positions any army ever faced. General Gamelin could have smashed through the Westwall if he had been willing to lose a million men. But no nation nowadays can risk such appalling casualties. Again, one should point out that new principles of strategy rule the military world. The old principle was that attack is the best defence. But now most military experts, like Captain Liddell Hart, whose influence on British war strategy has been profound, believe that defence is the best attack. Finally, there was the question of man power. Late in 1939 the British and French were still outnumbered in the west. But a big offensive, to have even a remote chance of success, needs an infantry superiority of at least three to one. Therefore the French and British had to wait.

London expected catastrophic and cataclysmic air raids almost at once. The first sirens blew twenty-two minutes after Mr. Chamberlain declared that a state of war existed. In London alone, the hospitals were cleared to take care of 300,000 casualties in the first week. But neither side bombed the great western cities. Indeed the war in the air was fought, in the first few months at least, with extraordinary politeness, with gloves on as it were. British aviators mapped the entire Siegfried line, at times flying for miles at a very low altitude indeed, without being molested. In fact German troops waved them on cheerfully. German pilots, who took part in raids on British naval bases in Scotland, said that they were subject to court-martial and the death penalty if—by some error—they bombed open towns.

There were several reasons why the great cities were not bombed. From the British side one may mention three. First, the early raids on military objectives, like that at Kiel the second night of the war, caused severe losses. It became clear that in a major raid the attacking force would lose between twenty and thirty per cent of its planes. The British could not risk such losses, since the German air force has about a ten to seven superiority over British and French air fleets combined. But time will, it is presumed, redress this disadvantage; therefore it was good sense on the part of the British to wait. Second, the British did not want to risk bombing civilians, and they knew that in a big bombardment some women and children were bound to get hit. Third, the British feared retaliation. They did not bomb Germany because they did not want to get bombed themselves.

The Germans did not begin serious assaults on British cities for similar reasons. They too hated to risk precious planes. They too hesitated to provoke retaliation. Besides, during the first months of the war, German plans were based on the idea of a 'peace offensive'. They hoped to persuade the British to call off the war. Therefore they would not risk inflaming Britain by severe raids. They used the *threat* of attack as a weapon with which they hoped to force peace.

I cannot, at this date (December 20, 1939) pretend to make any detailed or exhaustive history of the first months of the war. That task must await better perspective. It may, however, be useful to sketch briefly some main events. The body of this edition of *Inside Europe* is completely revised up to and including the outbreak of the war. It carries the story of each country into the autumn of 1939. In this addendum I wish merely to say a further word about the war itself.

· · · · · · · ·

The German invasion of Poland began at dawn on September 1. The campaign was fierce and brilliant. It was a real *Blitzkrieg*. For years we had heard of the professional skill and competence of the Reichswehr, and of the tremendous potentialities of Marshal Goering's huge air fleet. We now saw what it could do. What it did was plenty. The Poles were badly led, isolated from all assistance, and pitifully incompetent; nevertheless, the German campaign was a masterpiece. Nothing quite like it has ever been seen in military history.

First, the Germans attacked by air power the chief aerodromes in Poland, all but obliterating them in the first forty-eight hours. This meant that the Poles had practically no liaison, no opportunity to counter-attack, no communication. Second, the German air fleet unmercifully bombed Polish railway stations and lines, which frustrated Polish mobilisation. Third, three highly-mechanised German armies attacked from three directions. General von Kluge with twenty divisions nipped off the Corridor from the north-west and presently met a second army which struck towards Warsaw from East Prussia. Meantime, von Runstedt's force of thirty-five divisions hammered towards Kattowitz, Cracow and Tarnow in the south. This triple pincers movement was perfectly successful. The Polish Army as a whole never got a chance to fight. By September 8, German forces had reached the outskirts of Warsaw; by September 12, they had wiped up Poland—except for Warsaw which was isolated—west of the Vistula. They continued to advance and clean up what resistance remained. Warsaw held out bravely and hopelessly, and capitulated on September 27. In a month, the war was over.

Why did not the British and French help the Poles? Certainly the Poles, in those terrible first days, anticipated prompt assistance —as the British pledge called for—and felt very badly let down. According to the British Blue Book, Colonel Beck, the Polish foreign minister, was hoping for British 'action of a military character to relieve the pressure' on Poland as early as September 1, the first day of the war. The British Ambassador in Warsaw telegraphed Lord Halifax on September 2, 'I trust I may be informed at the earliest possible moment of our declaration of war and that our air force will make every effort to show activity on the Western Front with a view to relieving pressure here.'

The ambassador's hopes were dashed by events. To say nothing of Polish hopes. But it was impossible from any practical point of view for either the British or French to send direct help to Poland. There was no way to get troops there. Nor could they send aircraft to Poland in any considerable number. We know now that the Germans used at least ninety per cent of their first line planes in the Polish campaign. But no one knew this then. The British, in those first furious and uncertain days, had no guarantee that the Germans might not make a terrific assault on Paris and London. They had to keep every plane at home. Nor was a frontal attack on the Siegfried line possible. All the British could do was say to the Poles, in effect, 'Wait. Your only hope of resurrection is that we win the war in the west. If we risk anything to help you now, we may both lose. Wait. Your time will come.'

Great Britain meantime had declared that a state of war existed with Germany as from 11 a.m., Sunday, September 3. The Saturday had passed in final desperate manœuvres to save the peace. When, on September 2, Chamberlain postponed the declaration of

B

war, he came near to being shouted down in the House of Commons. The French followed the British declaration of war on Sunday, September 3, at 5 p.m. Both countries immediately set about the fullest co-operation and co-ordination. Events took place almost at once that had taken years to achieve in the first World War. The principle of a unified command had already been accepted; a Supreme War Council comprising both French and British began to function. By September 12—an astonishingly quick perform-ance—British troops were landing in France.

The major attention of the British was, however, devoted to air and sea. On September 4 occurred the first big air raid of the war in the west, a British attack on the German fleet at Wilhelmshaven. On the following nights the British sent planes over Germany drop-ping millions upon millions of propaganda leaflets. Churchill became First Lord of the Admiralty on September 4, and a Ministry of Economic Warfare was set up, with the veteran treasury official Sir Frederick Leith-Ross as director-general. This ministry was in essence a ministry of blockade. It became clear that the major British strategy would be what it turned out to be in the last war, an attempt to starve Germany out. To this blockade the Germans responded with counter-blockade. The British sank or interned German ships, and set up a severe contraband control. The German U-boats sought to torpedo and sink British merchantmen. As early as September 29, the British had the convoy system in full operation. This checked the U-boats.

During the first weeks of the war almost everyone expected a French offensive on the Western Front. But—for reasons I have adduced—it did not materialise. General Gamelin began a process of infinitely slow and careful nibbling. He sent scouting parties to mop up the No Man's Land between the two great western walls. By September 9 most of the Warndt forest fell to the French. But the advance, severely limited in objectives, was severely cau-tious in procedure. By the end of September the French stood on a thin line of German territory along the whole Rhine-Moselle front, without however attempting to penetrate the Siegfried line proper. When Polish resistance collapsed, the French withdrew. Stalemate then set in. It lasted months, almost without activity. Each side sat deep in concrete, kept warm, and waited. There were very few casualties. Probably from September to December 15, fewer men were killed and wounded on the Western Front than perished in a single minute's advance in the great offensives of 1914-18.

Meantime extraordinary events were taking place in the east. Russia watched the Polish campaign warily. On September 14, when it was already clear that the Poles could not survive, an ominous Press campaign against Poland began in the Russian Press.[1] On Sunday, September 17, a Sunday never to be forgotten by journalists in London, Russian troops invaded Poland along the whole length of the frontier. This was a staggering event. It seemed to reverse the whole process of Soviet history. Everywhere people had been disillusioned by the Russo-German pact of August 24. Now came this sequel. The Soviet Union, which had for so many years declaimed against aggression, became an aggressor itself. The Russian invasion of Poland was a severe blow to friends of the U.S.S.R.; it was a severer blow to Poland. It was the *coup de grace*. The Poles, trapped between two enemies, could not possibly continue fighting. On September 17 the Polish Government fled. Rydz-Smigly and Beck were interned in Rumania. They ought, one might say, to have been interned somewhere else before.

The Russians encountered very little resistance and reached Vilna on September 18 and Lwow on the 20th. Then Russian and German armed forces met for the first time, and greeted one another, in of all places Brest-Litovsk, where twenty-one years before they had signed a pregnant peace. The two dictator states then carved Poland between them. The fourth partition of Poland took place, and Poland as an independent state disappeared. Provisionally the new Russo-German frontier was drawn through Warsaw. The knife went through the unhappy country's heart. Subsequently the Russians agreed to recede to the line Grajev-Brest Litovsk-Prsemysl, roughly equivalent to the Curzon line of 1919. They retained White Russia and a substantial share of the Ukraine. On September 29 came a second Russo-German friendship treaty, which delimited and confirmed the new frontiers.

But the Russians had by no means finished their adventures. On the same day, September 29, the Soviets concluded a 'Pact of Mutual Assistance' with the small Baltic state, Esthonia. The Esthonian foreign minister had been summoned to Moscow; he could not resist the Soviet demands placed before him. Similar treaties, following similar diplomatic pressure, came very promptly with Latvia (October 5), and Lithuania (October 10). The treaties were cut

[1] It is sometimes forgotten that, significantly, the Russians concluded an armistice with Japan on September 16. This released them from any preoccupation with the Far East, and provisionally gave them a free hand in the west.

to the same pattern. They gave the U.S.S.R. the right to establish naval and aerial bases in each country, and to maintain garrisons there. Presently Red Army troops marched into Esthonia, Latvia, and Lithuania, about 30,000 in each country. The Baltic became, in part, a Russian lake. Stalin extended the power if not the actual territory of the Soviet Union to the old Czarist frontier. These events staggered the western world. The great unknown quantity was the position of Germany, and the degree of association between Hitler and Stalin. Their co-operation in regard to Poland was manifest. But whether Hitler approved of Soviet penetration into the Baltic is far from certain. At once Hitler summoned Baltic Germans back to Germany. An unprecedented forced migration took place of thousands of German families, some of whom had lived in the Baltic area for centuries.

Soon after the Latvian pact, and before the Lithuanian pact was concluded, the Russian Government opened negotiations with Finland. Their eyes turned north. Finland alone of the Baltic states remained outside their new sphere of influence. The Russians were more polite to the Finns—at first—than to the other Balts. The negotiations were protracted. They began on October 7, and broke off on November 15 with the return of the Finnish delegation to Helsingfors. The Finns refused to accede to the Russian demands. What the Russians wanted was, so far as we know now, certain islands and headlands in the Gulf of Finland for use as naval bases, as well as a territorial rectification in the extreme north. The Finns would not give this territory up. A few days of uneasy tension followed. Then—again ominously!—came the familiar Press campaign, then mass meetings in Russia against the Finns, and finally that well-known diplomatic cure-all, a frontier 'incident'. It was as clumsy and obviously fabricated as all such 'incidents' have been since Mukden in 1931. On November 30, 1939, the Russian invasion of Finland began.

Seldom has a more callous and brutal attempt to browbeat and club a nation into submission taken place. But to the astonishment of everyone the Finns, with a total population of 3,667,067, with only insignificant and outdated equipment, isolated from outside help, fought back. They attempted to repel the giant Russian invader, with his 170,000,000 people, his army of not less than 15,000,000 men. The war opened with an aerial bombardment of Helsingfors. The Russians then attacked with tanks and infantry on three fronts; in the extreme north, near the Finnish nickel mines, where they sought to cut Finland from the sea and establish a common frontier with Norway; in the middle, where they hoped to cut the 'waist of Finland' and reach the Gulf of Bothnia, which would bring them very close indeed to Sweden; and in the south, on the Karelian Isthmus, between Leningrad and Helsingfors. On all three fronts, Finnish resistance was stubborn. Late in December the war was still bitterly fought.

Meantime events in the west were largely confined to diplomacy, propaganda, the air, and the sea. On October 6 Hitler made his most important speech of the war to date, in which he summarised the results of the Polish campaign, and outlined—not too specifically—his conditions for peace. This was the culmination of the so-called 'peace offensive'. The British replied that they could accept no peace proposals which did not 'effectively free Europe from the menace of aggression', that Hitler had 'open aspirations for world domination', and that no trust could be put in his word.

Early in November it seemed that the Germans, to break the deadlock in the west, might attempt a flank movement on the 1914 pattern and invade France through Holland and Belgium. Fear of invasion was particularly acute in Holland. On November 7 came a joint peace offer by the Netherlands Queen and the Belgian King. It was rejected. But because the Belgians associated themselves with the declaration and emphasised their 'solidarity' with the Netherlands, it may have saved Holland from war. To attack Holland, and thus get precious air bases for the campaign against England, was one thing for the German general staff to consider. But to attack Belgium too, if the Belgians gave permission for British and French troops to enter their territory, was quite something else again.

During October and November air raids in the west were incessant but seldom successful. The Germans on several occasions reached the Firth of Forth and Scapa Flow, but their bombers did comparatively little damage. On October 25 British reconnaissance planes flew over Berlin for the first time. In mid-December British squadrons reached Wilhelmshaven, and the fiercest air battle of the war was reported, with several score of planes engaged.

At sea the British were almost completely successful in maintaining their communications and keeping the Germans locked up. Sea power was the great British contribution. On September 18, however, the aircraft carrier *Courageous* was sunk, and on October 14—the single most extraordinary feat of the war so far—a

German submarine managed to penetrate Scapa Flow, and torpedo
the battleship *Royal Oak*. On November 26 the converted cruiser
Rawalpindi was sunk in a naval engagement near Iceland by one
of the German pocket battleships that still roamed the Atlantic.
Meantime, by dropping magnetic mines from the air, the Germans
destroyed considerable amounts of British and neutral shipping
on the east coast of England. On December 17 the pocket battleship *Graf Spee* was caught by three smaller British ships near
Montevideo, and forced into harbour after a brilliant action.
Rather than endure internment or risk destruction, the *Graf Spee*
killed itself.

By mid-December the Germans claimed that they had destroyed
more than 800,000 tons of British and allied shipping. On the
other hand, the British blockade was becoming more efficacious
and damaging to the Germans day by day.

.   .   .   .

The position of the neutral states remained of the greatest possible importance during the early months of the war. Almost the
most interesting thing about the struggle was the number of
countries not in it. Belgium, Holland, Spain, Hungary, Rumania,
and the Balkan and Scandinavian states maintained a precarious
neutrality. On October 19 came a vitally important treaty between Britain, France, and Turkey, binding the three states to
co-operation and mutual defence. This seemed to assure Turkish
benevolence to the allies, though the Turks are not obliged to
take action against Soviet Russia. As to Italy, Mussolini very carefully set about and maintained a policy of 'non-belligerence'.

What kept the neutral states neutral was, of course, self-interest
and the desire for self-preservation. Everybody wanted to dig in
and avoid the storm.

INSIDE EUROPE

CHAPTER I

HITLER

'The union of theoriser, organiser, and leader in one man is the rarest phenomenon on earth; therein lies greatness.'

—ADOLF HITLER.

ADOLF HITLER, irrational, contradictory, complex, is an unpredictable character; therein lies his power and his menace.
To millions of honest Germans he is sublime, a figure of adoration;
he fills them with love, fear, and nationalist ecstasy. To many other
Germans he is meagre and ridiculous—a charlatan, a lucky hysteric,
and a lying demagogue. What are the reasons for this paradox?
What are the sources of his extraordinary power?

This paunchy, Charlie-Chaplin-moustached man, given to
insomnia and emotionalism, who is head of the Nazi party, com-
mander-in-chief of the German army and navy, Leader of the
German nation, creator, president, and chancellor of the Third
Reich, was born in Austria in 1889. He was not a German by birth.
This was a highly important point inflaming his early nationalism.
He developed the implacable patriotism of the frontiersman, the
exile. Only an Austrian could take Germanism so seriously.

The inside story of Hitler includes many extraordinary and
bizarre episodes. Before discussing his birth and childhood and
outlining his career, it may be well to present a broad detailed
picture of his character and his daily routine and his attitudes and
habits, his personal characteristics and limitations.

Hitler the Human Being

His imagination is purely political. I have seen his early paint-
ings, those which he submitted to the Vienna art academy as a boy.
They are prosaic, utterly devoid of rhythm, colour, feeling, or
spiritual imagination. They are architect's sketches: painful and
precise draftsmanship; nothing more. No wonder the Vienna

1

professors told him to go to an architectural school and give up
pure art as hopeless. Yet he still wants deeply to be an artist. In
1939 during the crisis leading to the Polish War, he told Sir Nevile
Henderson, the British Ambassador, that his only ambition was to
retire to the Berchtesgaden hills and paint.

His schooling was very brief, and by no stretch of generosity
could he be called a person of genuine culture. He is not nearly so
cultivated, so sophisticatedly interested in intellectual affairs as is,
say, Mussolini. He reads almost nothing. The Treaty of Versailles
was, probably, the most concrete single influence on his life; but it
is doubtful if he ever read it in full. He dislikes intellectuals. He
has never been outside Germany since his youth in Austria (if you
except his War experiences in Flanders and two brief visits to Mussolini), and he speaks no foreign language, except a few words of
French.

To many who meet him, Hitler seems awkward and ill at ease.
This is because visitors, even among his subordinates, obtrude personal realities which interfere with his incessant fantasies. He has
no poise. He finds it difficult to make quick decisions: capacity for
quick decisions derives from inner harmony, which he lacks. He is
no 'strong, silent man'.

Foreigners, especially interviewers from British or American
papers, may find him cordial and even candid but they seldom have
opportunity to question him, to participate in a give-and-take discussion. Hitler rants. He orates. He is extremely emotional.[1]
He seldom answers questions. He talks to you as if you were a
public meeting, and nothing can stop the gush of words.

Years ago, before signing his short-lived friendship pact with
Poland, he received a well-known American publicist and editor.
He asked a question: What the American would think if, for example, Mexico were Poland and Texas were cut off from the
United States by a 'corridor' in Mexico. The American replied,
'The answer to that is that Canada is not France.' Hitler had
intended the question rhetorically, and he was so shocked and upset
by the little interruption that it took him some time to get in full
voice again—on another point.

For a time it was said commonly that Hitler's best trait was loyalty.
He would never, the sardonic joke put it, give up three things: the
Jews, his friends, and Austria. Nobody would make that joke to-day,

[1] He told one astonished group of interviewers that they could 'crucify' him if
he did not keep his promises.

now that Captain Roehm is dead. Nor would anyone of knowledge and discernment have made it even before June 30, 1934, because the scroll of Hitler's disloyalties was written in giant words.

One after another he eliminated those who helped him to his career: Drexler, Feder, Gregor Strasser. It is true that he has been loyal to some colleagues—those who never disagreed with him, who gave him absolute obedience. This loyalty is not an unmixed virtue, considering the unsavouriness of such men as Streicher, the Nuremberg Jew-baiter. Nothing can persuade Hitler to give up Streicher and some other comrades. Unsavouriness alone is not enough to provoke his Draconian ingratitude.

His physical courage is doubtful. When his men were fired on in the Munich *Putsch* of 1923, he flung himself to the street with such violence that his shoulder was broken. Nazi explanations of this are two: (1) linked arm in arm with a man on his right who was shot and killed, he was jerked unwittingly to the pavement; (2) he behaved with the reflex action of the veteran front-line soldier, that is, sensibly fell flat when the bullets came.

Hitler has told an acquaintance his own story of the somewhat mysterious circumstances in which he won the Iron Cross. He was a dispatch bearer. He was carrying messages across a part of No-Man's-Land which was believed to be clear of enemy troops, when he heard French voices. He was alone, armed only with a revolver; so with great presence of mind he shouted imaginary orders to an imaginary column of men. The Frenchmen tumbled out of a deserted dug-out, seven in all, hands up. Hitler alone delivered all seven to the German lines. Recounting this story privately, he told his interlocutor that he knew the feat would have been impossible, had the seven men been American or English instead of French.[1]

Like that of all fanatics, his capacity for self-belief, his ability to delude himself, is enormous. Thus he is quite 'sincere'—he really believes it—when in an interview with the *Daily Mail* he says that the Nazi revolution cost only twenty-six lives. He believes absolutely in what he says—at the moment.

But his lies have been notorious. Heiden[2] mentions some of the more recondite untruths, and others are known to every student.

[1] This story is not the official version, which is more grandiloquent. Some mystery attaches to the exact circumstances. cf. *Heil*, a bright anonymous book about Germany, p. 9.

[2] *A History of National Socialism*, by Konrad Heiden, a book indispensable for the study of the new Germany.

Hitler promised the authorities of Bavaria not to make a *Putsch*; and promptly made one. He promised to tolerate a Papen government; then fought it. He promised not to change the composition of his first cabinet; then changed it. He promised to kill himself if the Munich coup failed; it failed, and he is still alive.

The Man Without Habits

Hitler, nearing fifty-one, is not in first-rate physical condition. He has gained about twelve pounds in the past few years, and his neck and midriff show it. His physical presence has always been indifferent; the sloppiness with which he salutes is, for instance, notorious. The forearm barely moves above the elbow. He had lung trouble as a boy, and was blinded by poison gas in the War.

In August 1935, it was suddenly revealed that the Leader had suffered a minor operation some months before to remove a polyp on his vocal cords—penalty of years of tub-thumping. The operation was successful. The next month Hitler shocked his adherents at Nuremberg by alluding, in emotional and circumlocutory terms, to the possibility of his death. 'I do not know when I shall finally close my eyes,' he said, 'but I do know that the party will continue and will rule. Leaders will come and Leaders will die, but Germany will live. . . . The army must preserve the power given to Germany and watch over it.' The speech led to rumours (quite unconfirmed) that the growth in Hitler's throat was malignant, and that he had cancer.

Nowadays Hitler broods and talks about death a good deal. One reason for his prodigious expansionist efforts in 1938 and 1939 was fear of death before his work was complete.

He takes no exercise, and his only important relaxation—though lately he began to like battleship cruises in the Baltic or North Sea—is music. He is deeply musical. Wagner is one of the cardinal influences on his life; he is obsessed by Wagner. He goes to opera as often as he can, and he was attending the Beyreuth Festival when, on July 25, 1934, Nazi putschists murdered Chancellor Dollfuss of Austria. Sessions of the Reichstag, which take place in the Kroll Opera House, sometimes end with whole performances of Wagner operas—to the boredom of non-musical deputies! When fatigued at night, in the old days, his friend Hanfstaengl was sometimes summoned to play him to sleep, occasionally with Schumann or Verdi, more often with Beethoven and Wagner, for Hitler needs music like dope.

Hitler cares nothing for books; nothing for clothes (he seldom wears anything but an ordinary brown-shirt uniform, or a double-breasted blue serge suit, with the inevitable raincoat and slouch hat); very little for friends; and nothing for food and drink. He neither smokes nor drinks, and he will not allow anyone to smoke near him. He is practically a vegetarian. At the banquet tendered him by Mussolini he would eat only a double portion of scrambled eggs. He drinks coffee occasionally, but not often. Once or twice a week he crosses from the Chancellery to the Kaiserhof Hotel (the G.H.Q. of the Nazi party before he came to power), and sits there and sips—chocolate.

This has led many people to speak of Hitler's 'asceticism' but asceticism is not quite the proper word. He is limited in aesthetic interests, but he is no flagellant or anchorite. There is very little of the *austere* in Hitler. He eats only vegetables—but they are prepared by an exquisitely competent chef. He lives 'simply'—but his house in Berchtesgaden is the last word in modern sumptuousness.

He works, when in Berlin, in the palace of the Reichskanzler on the Wilhelmstrasse. He seldom uses the president's palace a hundred yards away on the same street, because when Hindenburg died he wanted to eliminate as much as possible the memory of Presidential Germany. The building is new, furnished in modern glass and metal, and Hitler helped design it. Murals of the life of Wotan adorn the walls. An improvised balcony has been built over the street, from which, on public occasions, the Leader may review his men. Beneath the hall—according to reports—is a comfortable bomb-proof cellar.

Hitler dislikes Berlin. He leaves the capital at any opportunity, preferring Munich or Berchtesgaden, a village in southern Bavaria, where he has an alpine establishment, Haus Wachenfeld. Perched on the side of a mountain, this retreat, dear to his heart, is not far from the former Austrian frontier, a psychological fact of great significance. From his front porch he could almost see the homeland which repudiated him, and for which he yearned for many years.

Above the Berchtesgaden house—where he came in 1938 and 1939 to spend more and more time, often neglecting Berlin for weeks on end—is an amazing lookout or eyrie his engineers have built on a mountain top, near Kehlstein. A special, heavily guarded, looping road leads to bronze gates cut into a sheer wall of rock; inside the solid mountain, an elevator shaft rises four hundred feet. Here, on top, is a large circular room walled with windows. And here, when he really wants to be alone, Hitler comes.

Another peculiar point about Hitler is his passionate interest in astrology. It is widely believed that he set the date for the Sudeten crisis by advice of astrologers.

Friends

By a man's friends may ye know him. But Hitler has very few.

The man who is probably closest to Hitler since Roehm's death is his chief bodyguard, Lieut. Brückner. Another close associate is Max Amman, who was his top-sergeant in the Great War. For a time his former captain, Fritz Wiedemann, now German consul-general in San Francisco, was also close. Politically his most intimate adviser is certainly the foreign minister, Herr von Ribbentrop, who is one of the very few people who can see him at any time, without previous arrangement. He is bewitched by Ribbentrop's 'wisdom'. His chief permanent officials, like Dietrich, his Press secretary, may see him daily, and so may Hess, the deputy leader of the party; but even Hess is not an *intimate* friend. Neither Goering nor Goebbels, as a rule, may see Hitler without appointment.

He is almost oblivious of ordinary personal contacts. A colleague of mine travelled with him, in the same aeroplane, day after day, for two months during the 1932 electoral campaigns. Hitler never talked to a soul, not even to his secretaries, in the long hours in the air; never stirred; never smiled. My friend remembers most vividly that, in order to sneak a cigarette when the plane stopped, he had to run out of sight of the *entourage*. He says that he saw Hitler a steady five or six hours a day during this trip, but that he is perfectly sure Hitler, meeting him by chance outside the aeroplane, would not have known his name or face.

He dams profession of emotion to the bursting point, then is apt to break out in crying fits. A torrent of feminine tears compensates for the months of uneasy struggles not to give himself away. For instance, when he spent a whole night trying to persuade a dissident leader, Otto Strasser, from leaving the party, he broke into tears three times. In the early days he often wept, when other methods to carry a point failed.[1]

Hitler does not enjoy too great exposure of this weakness, and he

[1] Compare to Stalin, for instance. Can one imagine Stalin weeping after a hard day, or summoning a comrade to play him music?

tends to keep all subordinates at a distance. They worship him: but they do not know him well. They may see him every day, year in year out; but they would never dare to be familiar. A man quite close to him told me once that in all the years of their association he had never called Hitler anything except 'Herr Hitler' (or 'Herr Reichskanzler' after the Leader reached power); and that Hitler had never called him by first name or his diminutive. There is an inhumanity about the inner circle of the Nazi party that is scarcely credible.

An old-time party member, to-day, would address Hitler as 'Mein Führer'; others as 'Herr Reichskanzler'. When greeted with the Nazi salute and the words 'Heil Hitler', Hitler himself replies with 'Heil Hitler'. Speechmaking, the Leader addresses his followers as 'My' German people. In posters for the plebiscites he asks, 'Dost thou, German man, and thou, German woman—etc.' It is as if he feels closer to the German people in bulk than to any individual German, and this is indeed true. The German *people* are the chief emotional reality of his life.

Let us, now, examine Hitler's relation to the imperatives which dominate the lives of most men.

Attitude Towards Women

He is totally uninterested in women from any personal sexual point of view. He thinks of them as housewives and mothers or potential mothers, to provide sons for the battlefield—other people's sons.

'The life of our people must be freed from the asphyxiating perfume of modern eroticism,' he says in *Mein Kampf*, his autobiography.[1] His personal life embodies this precept to the fullest. He is not a woman-hater, but he avoids and evades women. His manners are those of the wary chevalier, given to hand-kissing—and nothing else. Many women are attracted to him sexually, but they have had to give up the chase. Frau Goebbels formerly had evening parties to which she asked pretty and distinguished women to meet him, but she was never able to arrange a match. Occasional rumours of the engagement of the coy Leader to various ladies are nonsense. It is quite possible that Hitler has never had anything to do with a woman in his life.

Occasionally young English or American girls, ardent Aryans,

[1] Most of my quotations from *Mein Kampf* are from the English edition. (Hurst and Blackett, Ltd., 1933.)

come to see him, and sometimes they are received, like Miss Unity Mitford. But Hitler does little but harangue them. At the top of his voice he talks politics and after a time subsides, as if limp and exhausted. Even these occasions are not tête-à-tête. For Hitler is very fond of the little daughter of Dr. Goebbels, and, fantastic as it may seem, she is often in the room, sometimes on the Leader's knee.

Nor, as is so widely believed, is he homosexual. Several German journalists spent much time and energy, when such an investigation was possible, checking every lodging that Hitler, in Munich days, had slept in; they interviewed beer-hall proprietors, coffee-house waiters, landladies, porters. No evidence was discovered that Hitler had been intimate with anybody of any sex at any time. His sexual energies, at the beginning of his career, were obviously sublimated into oratory. The influence of his mother and child-hood environment, which we shall examine in Chapter II, contributed signally to his frustration. Most of those German writers and observers best equipped to know think that Hitler is a virgin.

Attitude Towards Money

Hitler has no use for money personally and therefore very little interest in it, except for political purposes. He has virtually no financial sophistication; his lack of knowledge of even the practical details of finance, as of economics, is profound.

Nowadays what would he need money for? The state furnishes him with servants, residences, motor-cars. One of his last personal purchases was a new raincoat for the visit to Mussolini in June 1934. Incidentally, members of his staff got into trouble over this, because on their advice he carried only civilian clothes; when he stepped from his aeroplane and saw Mussolini and all the Italians in uni-form, he was ashamed of his mufti nakedness: and even suspected his advisers of purposely embarrassing him.

Hitler takes no salary from the state; rather he donates it to a fund which supports workmen who have suffered from labour accidents; but his private fortune could be considerable, if he chose to save. He announced late in 1935 that he—alone among statesmen—had no bank account or stocks or shares. Previous to this, it had been thought that he was part-owner of Franz Eher & Co., Munich, the publishers of the chief Nazi organs, *Völkische Beobachter*, *Angriff*, etc., one of the biggest publishing houses in Europe. Its director,

Max Amman, Hitler's former sergeant, was for many years his business manager.

If Hitler has no personal fortune, he must have turned all his earnings from his autobiography, *Mein Kampf*, to the party. This book is obligatory reading for Germans and at a high price (RM 7.20 or about twelve shillings) it has sold 5,200,000 copies since its publication in 1925, now being in its 494th edition. If his royalty is fifteen per cent, a moderate estimate, Hitler's total proceeds from this source at the end of 1939 should have been at least £600,000.

Nothing is more difficult in Europe than discovering the facts of the private fortunes of leading men. It is sacrosanct and thus forbidden ground to questioners in all countries. . . . Does any dictator, Hitler or Mussolini or Stalin, carry cash in his pocket, or make actual purchases in cash? It is unlikely.

Attitude Towards Religion

Hitler was born and brought up a Roman Catholic. But he lost faith early and he attends no religious services of any kind. His catholicism means nothing to him; he is impervious even to the solace of confession. On being formed, his government almost immediately began a fierce religious war against Catholics, Protestants, and Jews alike.

Why? Perhaps the reason was not religion fundamentally, but politics. To Hitler the overwhelming first business of the Nazi revolution was the 'unification', the *Gleichschaltung* (co-ordination) of Germany. He had one driving passion, the removal from the Reich of any competition, of whatever kind. The Vatican, like Judaism, was a profoundly international (thus non-German) organism. Therefore—out with it.

The basis of much of the early domestic madness of Hitlerism was his incredibly severe and drastic desire to purge Germany of non-German elements, to create a hundred per cent Germany for one hundred per cent Germans only. He disliked bankers and department stores—as Dorothy Thompson pointed out—because they represented non-German, international, financial and commercial forces. He detested socialists and communists because they were affiliated with world groups aiming to internationalise labour. He loathed, above all, pacifists, because pacifists, opposing war, were internationalists.

Catholicism he considered a particularly dangerous competitive force, because it demands two allegiances of a man, and double allegiance was something Hitler could not countenance. Thus the campaign against the 'black moles', as Nazis call priests. Several times German relations with the Vatican have neared breaking point. Protestantism was—theoretically—a simpler matter to deal with because the Lutheran Church presumably was German and nationalist. Hitler thought that by the simple installation of an army chaplain, a ferocious Nazi named Müller, as Reichbishop, he could 'co-ordinate' the Evangelical Church in Germany, and turn it to his service. The idea of a united Protestant Church appealed to his neat, architect's mind. He was wrong. The church question has been an itching pot of trouble ever since. All through 1937 and 1938 it raged.

It was quite natural, following the confused failure to Nazify Protestantism, that some of Hitler's followers should have turned to Paganism. The Norse myths are a first-class nationalist substitute. Carried to its logical extreme, Naziism in fact demands the creation of a new and nationalist religion. Hitler indicated this in a speech at Nuremberg in September 1935. 'Christianity,' he said, 'succeeded for a time in uniting the old Teutonic tribes, but the Reformation destroyed this unity. Germany is now a united nation. National socialism has succeeded where Christianity failed.' And Heiden has quoted Hitler's remark, 'We do not want any other God than Germany itself.' This is a vital point. *Germany* is Hitler's religion.[1]

One of Hitler's grudges against God is the fact that Jesus was a Jew. He can't forgive either Christians or Jews for this. And many Nazis *deny* that Jesus was Jewish. Another grudge is nationalist in origin. The basis of the Nazi revolution was the defeat of Germany in the War. Thus religion had to be Nazified because no God who permitted the French and other 'inferior' races to win the War could be a satisfactory God for Germany.

Hitler's attempt to unify religion in Germany may lead to one danger. He himself may become a God. And divinity entails difficulties. Gods have to perform miracles.

Vividly in *Mein Kampf* Hitler tells the story of his first encounter with a Jew. He was a boy of seventeen, alone in Vienna, and he had never seen a Jew in his life. The Jew, a visitor from Poland or the Ukraine, in native costume, outraged the tender

[1] In 1937 a special prayer was chanted over all German radio stations calling Hitler 'God's revelation to the German people' and their 'redeemer'.

susceptibilities of the youthful Hitler. 'Can this creature be a Jew?' he asked himself. Then, bursting on him, came a second question: 'Can he possibly be a *German?*'

This early experience had a profound influence on him, forming the emotional base of his perfervid anti-Semitism. He was provincially mortified that any such creature could be one with himself, a sharer in German nationality. Later he 'rationalised' his fury on economic and political grounds. Jews, he said, took jobs away from 'Germans'; Jews controlled the Press of Berlin, the theatre, the arts; there were too many Jewish lawyers, doctors, professors; the Jews were a 'pestilence, worse than the Black Death'.

No one can properly conceive the basic depth and breadth of Hitler's anti-Semitism who has not carefully read *Mein Kampf*. This book was written almost fifteen years ago. He has changed it as edition followed edition, in minor particulars, but in all editions his anti-Jewish prejudice remains implacable.

Long before he became chancellor, Hitler would not allow himself to speak to a Jew even on the telephone. A publicist as well known as Walter Lippmann, a statesman as eminent as Lord Reading, would not be received at the Brown House. An interesting point arises. Has Hitler, in maturity, actually ever been in the company of a Jew, ever once talked to one? Possibly not.

'*Am I My Brother's Keeper?*'

Extreme precautions are, naturally, taken to guard Hitler against assassination. When he rides out in Berlin, he travels in a Mercédès-Benz as big as a locomotive. Lieut. Brückner, his chief aide, usually sits beside him. SS men with rifles may stand on the running-boards. If the occasion is ceremonial and large crowds are present, the route is lined with SS men (Black Shirts) alternately facing inward and outward.

Brückner is of great importance politically because he serves to block Hitler off from normal contacts. The complaint frequently is heard that Hitler is badly informed on even vital matters, because Brückner so isolates him from wide acquaintance; even advisers with the best intentions may have little chance of seeing him.

Not long ago Hitler broke his new rule against social affairs by visiting informally a diplomat and his wife who had been useful to him in earlier days. The diplomat talked to Hitler frankly and told him some honest truths. Hitler was upset. Then, the story

C

says, Brückner descended on the diplomat, warning him under no circumstances to dare talk frankly to Hitler again.

Insurance rates on Hitler's life are quoted in London. A man with important business in Germany, which might be ruined by the terror and revolution which would very likely follow Hitler's assassination, paid £10 10s. per month for each £200 of insurance against Hitler's death.[1]

Personal Sources of Power

Now we may proceed to summarise what might be called Hitler's positive qualities.

First of all, consider his single-mindedness, his intent fixity of purpose. His tactics may change; his strategy may change; his *aim*, never. His aim is to create a strong national Germany, with himself atop it. No opportunistic device, no zigzag in polemics, is too great for him; but the aim, the goal, never varies.

Associated with his single-mindedness is the quality of stamina. All dictators have stamina; all need it. Despite Hitler's flabbiness and lack of vigorous gesture, his physical endurance is considerable. I know interviewers who have talked to him on the eve of an election, after he has made several speeches a day, all over Germany, week on end; they found him fresh and even calm. 'When I have a mission to fulfil, I will have the strength for it,' he said.

Unlike most dictators, he has no great capacity for hard work, for industry; he is not the sloghorse that, for instance, Stalin is. He is not a good executive; his desk is usually high with documents requiring his decision which he neglects. He hates to make up his mind. His orders are often vague and contradictory.

Yet he gets a good deal of work done. 'Industry' in a dictator or head of a state means, as a rule, ability to read and listen. The major part of the work of Hitler or Mussolini is perusal of reports and attention to the advice of experts and subordinates. Half their working time they spend in receiving information. Therefore it is necessary for a dictator (*a*) to choose men intelligently—many of Hitler's best men he inherited from the old civil service, (*b*) to instil faith in himself in them. Hitler has succeeded in this double task amply. And when his men fail him, he murders them.

Hitler's political sense is highly developed and acute. His calculations are shrewd and penetrating to the smallest detail. For

---

[1] cf. *News Chronicle*, London, May 21, 1935. The charge for similar insurance against Mussolini's assassination were £4 on £100 for three months.

instance, his first three major acts in foreign policy, Germany's departure from the League of Nations, the introduction of conscription, and the occupation of the Rhineland, were all deliberately set for Saturday afternoon, to ease the shock to opinion abroad. When he has something unpleasant to explain, the events of June 30 for instance, he usually speaks well after eight p.m. so that foreign newspapers can carry only a hurried and perhaps garbled account of his words.

He made good practical use of his anti-Semitism. The Jewish terror was, indeed, an excellent campaign manœuvre. The Nazis surged into power in March 1933 with an immense series of electoral pledges. They promised to end unemployment, rescind the Versailles Treaty, regain the Polish corridor, assimilate Austria, abolish department stores, socialise industry, eliminate interest on capital, give the people land. These aims were more easily talked about than achieved. One thing the Nazis could do. One pledge they could redeem—beat the Jews.

Hitler bases most decisions on intuition. Twice, on supreme occasions, it served him well. In the spring of 1932 his most powerful supporters, chiefly Roehm, pressed him to make a *Putsch*. Hitler refused, *feeling* absolute certainty that he could come to power in a legal manner. Again, in the autumn of 1932, after the Nazis had lost heavily in the November elections, a strong section of the party, led by Gregor Strasser, urged him to admit defeat and enter a coalition government on disadvantageous terms. Hitler, with consummate perspicacity, refused. And within three months he reached power such as the maddest of his followers had not dreamed of.

Another source of Hitler's power is his impersonality, as Frances Gunther has pointed out. His vanity is extreme, but in an odd way it is not personal. He has no peacockery. Mussolini must have given autographed photographs to thousands of admirers since 1922. Those which Hitler has bestowed on friends may be counted on the fingers of two hands. His vanity is the more effective, because it expresses itself in non-personal terms. He is the vessel, the instrument, of the will of the German people; or so he pretends. Thus his famous statement, after the June 30 murders, that for twenty-four hours he had been the supreme court of Germany.

Heiden says that Hitler's power is based on intellect, and his intellect on logic. This would seem a dubious interpretation because Hitler's mind is not ratiocinative in the least: he is a man of

passion, of instinct, not of reason.   His 'intellect' is that of a chame-
leon who knows when to change his colour; his 'logic' that of a
panther who is hungry, and thus seeks food.   He himself has said—
proudly—that he is a 'somnambulist'.   Strange giveway!

His brain is small, limited, vulgar, sly, narrow, and suspicious.
But behind it is the lamp of passion, and this passion has such
quality that it is immediately discernible and recognisable, like a
diamond in the sand.   The range of his interests is so slight that any
sort of stimulus provokes the identical reflex: music, religion,
economics, mean nothing to him except exercise n German
nationalism.

Anthony Eden, when he visited Berlin in the spring ᶜ 1935,
and talked with Hitler seven hours, was quoted as saying   ᵗt he
showed 'complete mastery' of foreign affairs.   This is, of ᴄ ᵗse,
nonsense.   Hitler does not know one-tenth as much about forᴄ ᵔ
affairs, as say, H. R. Knickerbocker, or F. A. Voigt, or Hamiltoᴏ
Fish Armstrong, or Dorothy Thompson, or Mr. Eden himself.
What Eden meant was that Hitler showed unflagging mastery of
his own view of foreign affairs.

Demosthenes in Brown Shirt

Then there is oratory.   This is probably the chief external
explanation of Hitler's rise.   He talked himself to power.   The
strange thing is that Hitler is a bad speaker.   He screeches; his
mannerisms are awkward; his voice breaks at every peroration; he
never knows when to stop.   Goebbels is a far more subtle and
accomplished orator.   Yet Hitler, whose magnetism across the table
is almost nil, can arouse an audience, especially a big audience, to
frenzy.

He knows, of course, all the tricks.   At one period he was accustomed to mention at great length the things that 'We Germans' (*wir*)
had, or did not have, or wanted to do, or could not do.   The word
'*wir*' drove into the audience with the rhythmic savagery of a pneu-
matic drill.   Then Hitler would pause dramatically.   That, he
would say, was the whole trouble.   In Germany the word '*wir*' had
no meaning; the country was disunited; there was no 'we'.

Recently Hitler told a French interviewer about an early oratorical trick and triumph, fifteen years ago in a communist stronghold
in Bavaria.   He was savagely heckled.   'At any moment they might
have thrown me out of the window, especially when they produced
a blind War invalid who began to speak against all the things that

are sacred to me. Fortunately I had also been blind as a result of the War. So I said to these people, "I know what this man feels. I was even more bewildered than he at one moment—but *I* have recovered my sight!" '

Hitler's first followers were converts in the literal sense of the term. They hit the sawdust trail. Hitler might have been Aimée Semple McPherson or Billy Sunday. Men listened to him once and were his for life—for instance, Goebbels, Brückner, Goering, Hess.

'Ruin Seize Thee, Ruthless King'

Hitler never flinched from the use of terror, and terror played a powerful role in the creation of the Nazi state. From the beginning he encouraged terror. The only purely joyous passage in *Mein Kampf* is the description of his first big mass meeting, in which the newly-organised SA pummelled hecklers bloody. The function of the SA was rough-house: first, rough-house with the aim of preserving 'order' at public meetings; second, rough-house on the streets, to frighten, terrorise and murder communists.

He gave jobs, big jobs, to confessed and admitted terrorists and murderers, like Heines. When a communist was murdered at Potempa, in Silesia, in circumstances of peculiarly revolting brutality, Hitler announced publicly his spiritual unity with the murderers. When, in August 1932, he thought that Hindenburg might appoint him chancellor, he asked for a three-day period during which the SA could run wild on the streets, and thus revenge themselves upon their enemies.

And we shall see presently what happened on the 30th June, 1934. To say nothing of what happened to the Jews in 1938 and 1939.

Führer Prinzip

Hitler's chief contribution to political theory was the *Führer Prinzip* (Leader Principle). This means, briefly, authority from the top down, obedience from the bottom up, the reversal of the democratic theory of government. It was, as Heiden points out, a remarkably successful invention, since almost anybody could join the movement, no matter with what various aims, and yet feel spiritual cohesion through the personality of the leader. The Nazi movement gave wonderful play to diverse instincts and desires.

Then again, Germans love to be ruled. 'The most blissful state a German can experience is that of being bossed,' a friend of mine put it in Berlin. And Edgar Ansel Mowrer has recorded the shouts of Nazi youngsters on the streets, 'We spit at freedom.' A German feels undressed unless he is in uniform. The *Führer Prinzip* not only exploited this feeling by transforming the passive character of German docility, German obedience, into an active virtue; it gave expression also to the bipolar nature of obedience, namely that most men—even Germans—associate with a desire to be governed a hidden will to govern. The *Führer Prinzip* created hundreds, thousands of sub-*Führers*, little Hitlers, down to the lowest storm-troop leader. It combined dignified submission with opportunity for leadership.

Mein Kampf, for all its impersonality, reveals over and over again Hitler's faith in 'the man'. After race and nation, personality is his main preoccupation. It is easy to see that the *Führer Prinzip* is simply a rationalisation of his own ambition; the theory is announced on the implicit understanding that the 'man' is Hitler himself. 'A majority,' he says, 'can never be a substitute for the Man.'

Another Hitlerite doctrine is, of course, that of race. But Hitler did not invent the concept of Aryanism; he took it over from Gobineau and Houston Chamberlain. Most—if not all—neutral authropologists think that Hitler's 'racist doctrine' is nonsense. They do not believe that 'pure' races exist.

Opposition

Hitlerism in its first stages was the process of 'unifying' Germany. Yet the Nazis struck at Protestants, Catholics, Jews; they mortally affronted the working classes; they could not put any serious programme of economic amelioration into effect without offending the industrialists; they alienated, by brutality and terror, the republicans, democrats, socialists, communists.

Hitler has held three major plebiscites so far. One asked vindication of Germany's departure from the League, and he received a 92.3 per cent vote of confidence. The second sought acceptance of his combination of chancellorship and presidency after the death of Hindenburg; the affirmative vote was 38,362,760 out of 43,529,710 ballots cast. The third followed the Rhineland crisis in March 1936; his vote was no less than ninety-eight per cent. Of course none was a fair vote in the Anglo-Saxon sense of the term. The plebiscite in the Saar gave him ninety per cent, but it probably would have been the same under any other chancellor. The last general election in Danzig, where every effort was made to bring out the vote and which was a better indication than the Saar of public feeling on a straight for-or-against-Hitler issue, brought him 139,043 votes out of 234,956—good enough, but not the two-thirds majority he hoped for.

The last reasonably fair German election, on March 5, 1933— even though it took place under the shadow of the Reichstag fire —gave Hitler thirty-seven per cent. I believe in an election to-day he would better this considerably. Even so, the total Marxist (communist-*cum*-socialist) vote in 1933 was 11,845,000. This number has probably receded, but just the same there is still a large opposition submerged in Germany. What has happened to these millions of hidden voters?

They are terrified. They are hounded by the police and by spies. They vote Yes in plebiscites because they are frightened of their skins. Some few of them have sought cover actually by joining the SA. Most simply swallow their opinions, their feelings, their inward decency—and wait. They are waiting for their Day. But are they an active political force? No.

The reason is that revolution is a profoundly difficult matter in a police state like Germany, Russia, or Fascist Italy. It is almost an axiom these days that no revolution can succeed until the equipment in arms and ammunition of the revolutionaries is equal or superior to that of the government. And this margin of superiority is transcendently difficult to achieve.

The Nazis, to their own disadvantage, discovered the *essential* necessity of arms in the Austrian civil war of July 1934. They neglected to arm their Austrian adherents, out of carelessness or over-confidence; they assumed that once the signal for the revolt was given the Austrian army and police would mutiny and turn over their arms to the Nazis; this did not happen. The army and police of Dr. Dollfuss remained, by and large, loyal. Therefore we had the spectacle of thousands upon thousands of potentially revolutionary Nazis inhibited from any decisive or direct action simply because they did not possess arms. This lesson is cardinal. You cannot fight a machine-gun by saying 'Boo' to it.

If the people riot, Hitler can simply shoot them down. He has the Reichswehr (regular army) to do this, not merely the SA and SS. The Reichswehr (the ranks are mostly peasant boys) might not shoot at a rising in the agrarian districts, but the farmers are the most tractable people in Hitler's Reich. An urban population would get short shrift. But, one may say, no man, not even Hitler, could shoot down tens of thousands of unarmed or roughly armed rebels. The answer to this is that it is not necessary to shoot down tens of thousands. A few hundreds will be enough.

What is more likely to happen than open rebellion is the slow pressure upward of mass discontent, grumbling, and passive resistance, sabotage caused by growing privation, until the *morale* of the government cracks, and the government, panicky, does foolish things. Discontent may corrosively simmer to the top, disorganising the headship of state, causing new rivalries between sub-leaders, creating fissures between, say, Ribbentrop on the left and Goering on the right, so deep and so unbridgeable that Hitler is powerless to compose the conflict. But there are no signs that this is happening yet. The 1939 war, moreover, served to unify Germany, at least provisionally.

Succession to the Purple

If Hitler should die to-morrow his successor would certainly be Goering, bitterly as he is disliked and feared by many members of the party. The Leader might himself prefer Hess, his deputy, as successor, but in the rough-and-tumble that might follow his death, Hess would have small chance against such a doughty character as Goering. The general is the logical choice. Therefore when the Polish campaign began Hitler formally named Goering to the succession, with Hess as second choice. After Hess, the Nazi Party is to choose the 'strongest' man.

Goering has force, colour, ambition; he is a figure of great popular appeal. The quality and quantity of his uniforms are highly attractive to Germans; his marriage may produce a dynasty. What is more important, the army likes him because he stands for the same thing as it stands for: a strong Germany. Moreover, in the SS and remnants of SA, Goering has a considerable armed force behind him. Finally, he has the courage to grab the job, if grabbing is necessary, which it probably won't be.

Goebbels would be impossible as successor to Hitler; he is the cleverest of all the Nazis, but everybody hates him. Frick is important, but too colourless; Ribbentrop too limited; Ley and Darré out of the running as 'radicals'; Schacht is of the greatest importance in economics and finance, but impossible as a popular leader. In fact, the only alternative to Goering would seem to be a complete

Reichswehr ministry formed by an army *coup d'état,* such as the one Schleicher might have headed. Or a dark horse.

Rumours, however, to the effect that Goering is *now* actively intriguing against Hitler are nonsense. There are many virtues that Goering lacks, but loyalty is not among them—at least not yet. Besides, Hitler could eliminate Goering to-day almost as easily as he eliminated Roehm. Hitler is all-powerful. Real rivals do not exist. Goering, Goebbels, and all the rest of them, as H. R. Knickerbocker once expressed it, are no more than moons to Hitler's sun. They shine—but only when the sun shines on them.[1]

---

[1] Sir Nevile Henderson, the British Ambassador to Berlin, stated in October 1939 that Goering told him, 'When a decision has to be taken, none of us counts more than the stones on which we are standing. It is the Führer alone who decides.'

CHAPTER II

PSYCHO-PATHOLOGY OF DICTATORS

'The German has not the slightest notion how a people must be misled if the adherence of the masses is sought.'

—ADOLF HITLER.

Nот only Hitler but several modern leaders were born in border-zones or actually different countries from those they came to rule. Mustapha Kamal Ataturk, though you would hardly have called him a Greek, was born in Salonika, Greece; Pilsudski was Lithuanian in origin; Schuschnigg, the former Austrian chancellor, was born in Italy; and Stalin, as everyone knows, is not a Russian at all, but a Georgian.

I have visited Braunau, in Austria, and seen the house where Hitler was born. The legend has grown of a rustic dwelling, the Teutonic equivalent of our country cottage, where, in stern but idyllically bucolic circumstances, the Leader first saw daylight. Of course this is inaccurate. The house is a three-story structure on the main street of Braunau, and for twenty years it has been a *Gasthaus* (saloon, village pub) owned by a local worthy named Josef Pommer. Where a bronze tablet may one day mark the Leader's birth-place an enamelled metal sign now says, 'Spekl beer on draught.'

The house to-day is painted bright ochre brown, the colour of the brown-shirt uniform. It was padlocked by the Austrian authorities in July 1933, because it was a natural focus for the local Nazis. Hitler's parents never owned it; they lived in furnished rooms rented from the landlord. On the other hand, his father was not a poor man, and the legend that Hitler all but starved as a boy is nonsense.

The whole region around Braunau is Hitler country. Dozens of people who are still alive remember him as a young man. In the village of Spital, near Weitra, I met his mother's sister and two of his first cousins; in Leonding, near Linz, I talked to his *Vormund* (godfather), the son of his old schoolmaster (who had been one of his classmates), the proprietors of the pub where his father died, and—interesting old woman!—the midwife who hauled his infant body from his mother's womb.

Family Tree

The Hitler family springs from a section of Austria known as the Waldviertel, billowing Danube country near what is now the Czechoslovak frontier. The peasants living there are humble folk, blanched by poverty and gnarled by work; honest, God-fearing, illiterate, and heavily inbred. Populations of whole villages are first and second cousins. They live by tilling the soil, working in mills, or practising some humble trade like carpentry.

In the Waldviertel village Spital a man named Johann Georg Hiedler was born in February 1792. This was Adolf Hitler's grandfather. He was a wandering miller's helper. By him, a woman named Maria Anna Schicklgruber had a son, born in a near-by hamlet Strones in 1837. Five years later the parents were married, but the son took his mother's name—Schicklgruber—and was not legally legitimised till he was forty years old, in 1877. Then he became known as Alois Hitler—Adolf Hitler's father.

The change from 'Hiedler' to 'Hitler' is easily explained. The peasants could scarcely read and write; names were hardly ever written down, except at birth and death. Hiedler's father, in fact, called himself 'Hüttler', according to the records I saw in the village church. And Paula Hitler, Adolf's sister, to this day signs herself 'Hiedler'.

Alois Hitler, Adolf's father, was a cobbler. He married three times. His first wife, Anna Gläsl-Horer, was born in the Waldviertel town of Theresienfeld in 1823, and died in Braunau in 1883. This Anna, a moderately rich woman, treated the young cobbler, then known as Schicklgruber, almost more like a mother than as a wife; she sent him to school, then purchased him a job in the Austrian civil service. She was fourteen years older than he. Thanks to her, he became a solid citizen, and the education of his son Adolf, born years later by another wife, was made possible.

Anna died in 1883; Alois waited only six weeks to marry again, this time to a woman named Franziska Matzelsberger. Their marriage lasted only a year. She died in 1884. Only three months after her death, Alois married once more, this time to Adolf's mother, Klara Poelzl, a distant cousin. This was on January 7,

1885. Four years later, in Braunau, on April 20, 1889, Adolf Hitler, creator of the Third Reich, was born. His father was fifty-two at his birth, his mother twenty-nine.

Klara Poelzl, Adolf's mother, was a woman of enterprise and courage. Her father was a peasant in the village of Spital, and her mother was Johanna Hüttler, a cousin of Alois Hitler's father. When Klara was ten years old (in 1870), she got her first job—as maid in the home of Alois Hitler's first wife, Anna Gläsl-Horer. Here Alois first saw the little girl, a distant relative, whom fifteen years later he was to marry—his first wife's servant.

Presently Klara ran away to Vienna. This was an unprecedented thing to do. Few other girls in the Waldviertel had shown such initiative. No one knew the reason for her flight. I have asked her sister (living to-day) about it. She has no explanation. Klara lived in Vienna—her circumstances a complete mystery—for ten years. Then in 1885 she returned to her native village, Spital. She was a tall, nervous girl now, not as strong as most of the peasant stock she came from. She lived with her parents in a house adjacent to the one—I have seen them both—wherein Alois was brooding over the loss of his two wives. He remembered the girl who had been his first wife's servant—and married her.

By the first wife, Anna, Alois had had two children. A son, Alois Junior (Adolf's half-brother) became a waiter and subsequently the proprietor of a Berlin restaurant. A daughter, Angela, went to Vienna where she married a man named Raupel and earned a living as a cook in a Student's Charity Hall in Vienna. Some years ago Adolf brought her to Germany and installed her as housekeeper in his Berchtesgaden villa.

Klara had two children besides Adolf. Paula, born in 1897, is unmarried (another spinster in this neurotic family) and lives to-day in Vienna, an anonymous and forgotten figure. The local Nazis tried to make a heroine of her, but she was too retiring. Hitler apparently has nothing to do with her. The third child, Edouard, died in infancy.

Alois, a customs inspector, and Klara, with the boy Adolf growing up, lived in Braunau,[1] an important frontier town, until 1896, when Alois retired on pension. Then he moved to a village near Linz named Leonding, bought a house, and lived in it with Klara and Adolf till he died in 1903.

[1] Interestingly enough two of the most famous clairvoyants of modern Europe were born in Braunau, Willi and Rudi Schneider.

Father and Mother

I have seen the tombstone of Hitler père. It reads:

HIER RUHET IN GOTT HERR

ALOIS HITLER

K.K. Zollamts Oberoffizial I.P.

und Hausbesitzer

Gest. 3 Janner 1903, in 65 Lebensjahre

Dessen Gattin Frau

KLARA HITLER

Gest. 21 Dez. 1907 i. 47 Lebj.

R.I.P.

As is common in Austria, a small photograph of the dead man is attached to the stone. A skull big and round and hairless like a melon; small, sharp, wicked little eyes; a pair of bicycle-handle moustaches, and a heavy tyrant's chin. The mother's picture we saw later in a relative's house. A tall woman, with a narrow, sensitive face and arching eyes over sunken cheek-bones; her yellow braids now a grey mat at the back of the neck; large, luminous eyes.

Young Adolf detested his father and loved his mother. This difficult parental relationship, on which the villagers with whom I talked and the surviving relatives agreed, was obviously a cardinal point in the development of Hitler's character. He had an Oedipus complex as big as a house.

Hitler père was truculent and overbearing; he died over a bottle of wine in a public-house, of a sudden stroke. The father thought that Adolf was a weakling and a worthless idler and dreamer; he called him 'moonstruck', and bullied and beat him. So young Hitler identified himself with his mother in opposition to the father. His jealousy of the father produced an extreme divergence in his character. Old Hitler was a drunkard; young Hitler never touched alcohol. Old Hitler married three times in quick succession; young Hitler never had any love life at all. Old Hitler was besotted with indulgence; young Hitler feared it.

Adolf loved his mother passionately. When he was about six she developed cancer, and it took her almost ten years to die. From her he got his impulse to ambition, his sense of historical mission, because she, too, wanted him to be different from his father. The mother encouraged him to be an artist. Throughout his life, Hitler has been subconsciously proving to his mother, the only woman he has loved, his right to independence, success, power.

In Spital, a country hamlet about an hour's journey from Leonding, I met several surviving members of the family, among them Hitler's aunt, Theresa Schmidt (Klara's sister) a bouncing old woman, and her two sons, Edward and Anton, Hitler's first cousins. One of them, Edward, is a hunchback with an impediment in his speech—a pitiable creature. They are miserably poor.

These people are Hitler's blood relatives. Their plaster huts seem a million miles from the shining roofs of Wilhelmstrasse, where the Leader rules. Hitler has never returned to visit the district since he left it as a boy. He sends these cousins no letters, no money, and seems totally unaware of their existence.

Authority Complex

All dictators are abnormal. This may be accepted as an axiom. No man perfectly normal can take it upon himself to rule a nation dictatorially, if only because the vanity of the normal male is not capacious enough to accept such supreme responsibility. Aside from this, most dictators are profound neurotics. Kamal Ataturk had a wildly disorderly personal life; Dollfuss had a dwarf-complex; Pilsudski's breathless rages were pathological; Mussolini is something of a megalomaniac. Of the lot, Stalin is probably the nearest to a normal human being, but one should not forget that he was a criminal, viz. bomb-thrower, in his youth.

The great Viennese psychiatrist Dr. Wilhelm Stekel has a theory which accounts handily both for the neuroticism of dictators and for the supine willingness of most people to submit to dictatorial rule. He calls it the Authority Complex.

One must begin with the child. In every child, says Stekel, there is a struggle between his own instincts and the lessons he derives from the outer world. Children like, for instance, to be dirty. But they are taught by external education to be clean. Education is largely an effort to mould a child in opposition to his original instincts. Education is effected by authority. And authority becomes the child's enemy, because it means renouncement of his own instincts.

The first authority is that of the parents. If the parents are too weak and the child is overtly defiant, then other authorities come into play. The authority of older children. The authority of the teacher. In some cases, the authority of the law. The authority, above all, of religion. The final weapon in the hands of adults teaching authority to children is the phrase, 'God will punish you.'

Since about 1914 the authority of parents has tended to break down. It is obvious that the family is no longer the sacred unit it once was. 'Parents,' Stekel puts it, 'did not respond themselves to the moral standard which they demanded of their children.' Inevitably children revolted at this unfairness. Parents sought stupidly or blindly to impose on children the moral imperatives which they ignored, which left the children no alternative but to revenge themselves by overthrowing parental prohibitions.

As with parents, so with teachers. School and university were taken less and less seriously. The Great War undermined authority internationally, and presently law and order within national boundaries suffered: a flood of criminality deluged the world, especially in America. Then too, religion had been displaced by modern science as a vital authoritarian factor. Finally, young men and women asked how they could longer believe in a God who permitted the War and the butchery therein of some ten million men. Thus the principle of authority became discredited, and the old belief and faith in authority collapsed.

Following this came the wave of dictators. The Hitlers and Mussolinis were essentially father-substitutes. People may resent authority but they cannot easily live without it in some form; children have revolted against their fathers, and Hitler, Mussolini, Pilsudski, Alexander of Jugoslavia, Dollfuss,.Kamal Ataturk, Stalin, replaced them. The modern child thought his parents unworthy and thus sought an external leader. The sphere of authority was moved outside the home.

How Dictators Rule

Fundamentally all government is a subtle combination of the forces of fear and love. Dictators increase the dynamics of this process. Alexander of Jugoslavia tried to win over the rebellious Croats at the same time that he dragooned them to submission. Little Dollfuss murdered the socialists by artillery fire and then begged them to forgive him. Hitler is beloved by many of his followers; just the same, the St. Bartholomew of June 30 was necessary.

Why does the individual not resent the authority of the dictator, or leader, just as he resented parental authority? The reason, according to Stekel, is that individual doubt of the fallibility of the dictator is lessened as more and more people come to follow and worship him. The greater the number of followers, the less the necessity for doubt. 'A psychic epidemic of adoration' floods the country, engulfing the whole nation which prostrates itself at the dictator's feet.

Moreover, Stekel says, as more and more people join the leader, their merged inferiorities become a superiority. The people identify themselves with the leader. They partake of the flesh of his authority. They become part of his soul and substance, and he of theirs. They share in his Authority Complex. Germans, for instance, say that they don't fight for Hitler, but that Hitler fights for them. Mussolini does not want power for himself, many Italians believe, but only for the sake of Italy, viz., other Italians, viz., themselves. 'Obedience and defiance, love and hate, finally combine,' says Dr. Stekel, 'and the dictator becomes the saviour.'

In olden days new leaders were usually the founders of new religions. Now they are political. Many present-day leaders are jealous of religion; they fear the implacable rivalry of the Authority of God. Thus, very often, they try to kill religion, their strongest competitor, by seeking to destroy the religious faith of their people: Kamal Ataturk disestablished Islam, Stalin tried to root out the Orthodox Church.

Dictators are themselves usually neurotics because they too suffered from the iron circumscription of the Authority Complex; *they* too revolted against authority in childhood. But they were persons of superior mentality and will-power, and, after a miserable childhood, their revolt was successful; they revenged themselves on their parents by imposing authority on others. They became fathers, not of a family, but a nation.

Almost all the modern dictators (Alexander of Jugoslavia was an exception) were born in poverty. Mussolini and Stalin were wretchedly poor. Moreover several dictators, like Hitler, underwent childhood experiences of the most disastrous sort; Dollfuss, for instance, was of humble origin. The dictators compensated for their bitter youth by search for power and glory afterwards. Power and glory, even achieved, may not be anodynes enough. Thus Hitler seeks refuge in music, Mussolini in a strenuous physical life, and Kamal Ataturk sought it in dissipation.

Dictators reach power so easily, Stekel believes, because we, the common people, seek to blame something for every crisis, and the nearest and biggest and easiest things to blame are our institutions. So the institutions fall, to give way to dictatorship. Dictators keep power so easily because the force of arms is inherent in their systems, and we, the common people—speaking broadly—like to be afraid.

Début

Hitler entered political life as a spy. The fact is unpleasant. The story is fully told by Heiden. Hitler was a non-commissioned officer in the German army, which had just become the Reichswehr, and he was detailed early in 1919 as a sort of intelligence officer to attend labour meetings, mingle with workers groups, and report to his superiors the state of popular opinion. Fulfilling one of these missions, he heard a man named Gottfried Feder speak. He was impressed by Feder's violent economic theories, including the distinction between *raffendes* (grasping, hence Jewish) and *schaffendes* (creative, hence Aryan) capital; he came again to hear him, and joined excitedly the discussion following the meeting, squelching an opposition speaker.

Feder was closely in touch with an ex-locksmith, Anton Drexler, who had formed a minuscule group of riffraff called the German Workers Party. Presently, Hitler was invited to join this party. He records his two days of 'agonised meditation and questioning' before giving assent. Then he became No. 7 not in the party itself (which at the time numbered about sixty members) but in its council. This was in July 1919. Officially, however, until the next June, Hitler remained in the service of his regiment.

The rise of the party under Hitler is history. He changed its name to N.S.D.A.P (*National Sozialistische Deutsche Arbeiter Partei*), which, usually shortened to 'Nazi' is still its official name. He spoke first to audiences of twenty, then to twenty thousand. He founded his private army, the SA, the Brown Shirts. He was ill-advised enough to attempt a revolution in Munich in 1923 and was defeated and sentenced to jail for high treason. This was the celebrated 'Beer-hall *Putsch*'. He emerged—Germany's potential 'saviour'.

It is well to underline two subsidiary but important points. One was that Hitler began to equivocate almost from the moment he seized control of the party, so that he might win as many adherents as possible. He stretched his net very wide. But it should not be forgotten that Naziism began as a predominantly Left-socialist movement, and the party programme, written by Feder and pronounced unalterable by Hitler, was a distinctly anti-capitalist document. Hitler shed some socialism as he marched towards power, but essentially his movement was *radical* in political and economic beliefs. It appealed to the Have-Nots, to the underpossessed. It

D

was not merely, as the Marxists say, a 'front' for capitalism. It was itself definitely revolutionary.

The second point is Hitler's intimate association with army influences almost from the beginning. He, as well as anyone, knew that the Reichswehr would in time wield decisive influence in Germany. As much as he dared, cautiously, cleverly, he cultivated the Reichswehr. It is not generally known that he was enabled to purchase control of the *Völkische Beobachter*, which became the principal Nazi organ, through use of Reichswehr funds. And gradually the army became his weapon.

Hitler took over the party from Drexler and Feder, but essentially it was his creation. He cozened it, nurtured it, watched it grow, and controlled it. The party came out of his own blood and heart. He was helped, and not inconsiderably, by industrialists, by gangsters, by smart bureaucrats and organisers; but his was the feeding spirit, the dominating pulse. He was himself responsible for the smallest details. He designed the Swastika flag, for instance, and he shaped the general propaganda methods, the like of which were never before seen in Germany—or anywhere. The party was everything to Hitler. It was his wife, mother, mistress, and all his children—at the end thirteen million of them.

Miracle of Nationality

Hitler became a German citizen only by virtue of machinery remarkably devious. He could not run for President against von Hindenburg while still technically an Austrian subject. But the Reich Government of the day had no intention of conferring statehood on its chief opponent. Therefore the Nazis had to resort to guile.

Dr. Frick, one of the earliest Hitlerites, the first Nazi to hold electoral office in the Reich, was minister of education and the interior in Thuringia. Citizenship would come automatically to Hitler if he became a German official, and Frick therefore decided to appoint him commander of gendarmerie in the inconspicuous hamlet of Hildburghausen. But news of this forcible 'naturalisation' leaked out and when all Germany laughed at the picture of Hitler as a Hildburghausen policeman the plan was given up.

Subsequently another Nazi who held a governmental post, Dietrich Klagges, the minister of justice in Brunswick, appointed Hitler to be Counsellor of the Brunswick Legation in Berlin.

Scarcely anyone in Germany knew that such a post existed. Hitler took oath to be loyal to the constitution—which he was openly threatening to destroy—and the Austrian village boy became at long last—a German.

CHAPTER III

WHO KILLED THE GERMAN REPUBLIC?

'Everything has a cause, and the cause of anything is everything.'
—W. J. TURNER.

PERSONAL qualities alone would not have brought Hitler power. But they contributed to one of the main factors that did—his feat in identifying himself with a large percentage of the German nation. He became a demigod, a prophet, because with great mesmeric ability he persuaded so many Germans that he, and he alone, represented their renascent Germanism. People love Hitler because they love Germany. And Hitler and Germany—to Nazis—are one.

Germany was a loose aggregation of quarrelling states until the dawn of yesterday. Literature in a German language that can be read easily to-day did not exist till the seventeenth century. England and France unified themselves, constituted themselves homogeneous nations, in the Middle Ages; but even Bismarck did not make Germany a nation in the sense that England and France had been nations for five centuries.

Germany, the Nazi apologists say, is now at long last growing up. Adolescence produces pangs in children as well as nations, and no one becomes mature without suffering. The frightfulness of the Nazi terror, the confusions in personnel and administration, the lies and disingenuousness of foreign policy, the war-mongering and finally the outbreak of the war in 1939, the extraordinary capacity to blunder and irritate everybody in the outside world (i.e. grown ups)—these are evidences of a period of puberty.

Germany lost the war of 1914. It was an honourable defeat and in fact Germany came within a hair's breadth of beating the entire world; nevertheless the Germans felt 'humiliation'; they felt degradation and shame. The Nazis invented the legend of having been stabbed in the back by the Jews, socialists, pacifists—to excuse defeat. Hitler made immense capital of this unconscionable distortion of the facts. And he progressed to another deduction, equally false, that Germany had *not*, in fact, lost the War at all.

His technique was something like the following. He suggested to the German people first that they were sick, second that he alone could make them well. His argument was passionate and direct: 'You are humiliated. You are degraded. Germany is a sick nation. Admit it. Concede the extent of your misery. You have been trying to persuade yourselves that you are content with this miserable republic. . . . Those who stabbed you in the back, the Jews and the Marxists, are ruling you to-day. They prevent you from recovering your self-respect. They are the spiritual death of your nation. And your own spiritual death too. For *you* are Germany. *We* are Germany. Be men! Out with the traitors, the Jews, the pacifists, the republicans. . . .' (And so on, in the early speeches, often for two hours and a half.)

These speeches had an immense emotional effect. Women, especially, were overcome by them. If the audience was full of women, Hitler would shriek out, 'You are mine, and I am yours, as long as I live!' So Hitler presented the Germans, who are idealists, who are exceptionally sensitive, who had had a very rough time, with their lost 'self-respect'. Suppression of liberty was the price they were willing to pay for his leadership.

The same technique is manifest in *Mein Kampf*. Compare this book with, say, the autobiographies of Trotsky or Henry Adams. It is vapid, vain, rhetorical, diffuse, prolix. But it is a powerful and moving book, the product of great passionate feeling. The theme is stated twenty times, slowly arising out of clouds of circumlocution and confusion, that Germany has been disunited, mortified, crucified, by the peace treaties, and that it must and will arise, a new, powerful, united, regenerated, national state.

One can well imagine hundreds of thousands of honest Germans, from dispossessed shopkeepers to General Blomberg, conscientiously, dutifully picking their way through this turbulent ocean of print, sinking back from it exhausted, but with its message, if only by the ceaseless repetition of the argument, left impregnably in their minds, fecund and germinating.

A number of elements quite outside Hitler's own character contributed, of course, to his meteoric, incredible career. What set the course of that savage, swooping arrow, Brüning-Papen-Schleicher-Hitler? One should keep in mind the following items:

1. The German inflation which was the result of passive resistance to the French invasion of the Ruhr, because it ruined the

lower middle class, the *petite bourgeoisie*, and caused it to seize on Hitler's extravagant promises.

2. The deflationary policy of Brüning which helped to crush the upper middle class, already hard hit by the world economic crisis. Hard times bred both the violence of Hitler and the apathy of his opponents. The Nazis fed on other people's hunger.

3. The support of the great industrialists, chiefly the steel magnate Fritz Thyssen, who from 1930 on helped finance the Nazi party. This support was important. It was not, however, decisive. Hitlerism was a tremendous national movement, before the industrialists, seeing how the road led—years late—jumped on the bandwaggon. The idea that Thyssen manufactured the Nazi movement by giving Hitler thousand-mark bills in a back room is simply monstrous, as Raymond Gram Swing has pointed out. As soon as the industrialists belatedly got round to seeing that Hitler was dangerous, and also might turn to be useful, they sought to buy him up. They hoped to make Hitler their puppet. But they were mistaken.

4. Sabotage of the republic by its own officials, army officers, and government administrators; coupled with the extremely democratic character of the Weimar constitution whereby demagoguery got every chance to express itself in votes.

5. Finally, personal considerations. A great number of personal imponderables helped blow Hitler into port. The first of these was the mind and character of the old president, Field-Marshal Paul Ludwig Hans von Beneckendorf und von Hindenburg. His mind and character—plus the coruscation of intrigue blazing around him as he aged.

To understand properly Hitler's seizure of Germany and his establishment of power we must tell the story of three great episodes: the Papen-Schleicher-Hindenburg conspiracies, the Reichstag fire, and the events of the 30th of June. Let us begin with Hindenburg. To be blunt, it is quite possible that Hitler would never have become chancellor had not Hindenburg been senile.

The Squire of Neudeck

In the critical year, 1932, Hindenburg was already eighty-five and not in full possession of his faculties. He was 'all right', people said, until about the beginning of the morning, and those rare personages who could get to him at breakfast, or even earlier, could do something with him. This was the great strength of Franz von Papen, for a time his chancellor.

In Berlin at the time the health of the Old Man was of paramount interest, and a marvellous and cruel miscellany of jokes grew up at his expense, hinging on the question of his competency. It was no joking matter; the person of the President was the most powerful constitutional force in the country. But no one could talk or write openly on such a delicate matter: thus the retreat to an apocrypha of legend.

One of the Hindenburg stories had him turning in puzzled recollection to his son Oskar and asking, 'Where *has* that chap with glasses (Brüning) gone to?' Another alleged that he confused Brüning with Schleicher when Schleicher was dismissed. And once, the story goes, he received General von Hammerstein, the chief of the Reichswehr; the general had some pretty important business on his mind but Hindenburg began and ended the interview by shouting, 'Herr General, I was not satisfied with the autumn manœuvres!'

When Hitler finally became chancellor, the Old Man—watching the immense parade of Nazi storm-troops celebrating the occasion—carefully unhinged his old knees to sit down and said to Oskar, 'Son, I did not know we had captured quite so many Russian prisoners.'

A favourite story, while Hindenburg was alive, detailed the alleged circumstances of his death. Kneeling at the bar of heaven, he was received by St. Peter who, glancing at him in surprise, asked him his identity. 'I am Hindenburg,' the field-marshal replied. 'But why are you here?' continued St. Peter. 'Because I am dead,' replied Hindenburg. St. Peter shook his head saying, 'There has been an error: you are not dead, but alive.' Hindenburg retreated in confusion: 'Ha! That rascal Meissner has misinformed me again!'

Meissner, the state secretary to the President, wielded influence on the Old Man, because next to Oskar he was nearest to his person. Meissner was, and is, a remarkably subtle politician. He has continuously been state secretary to all three German presidents—Ebert, the socialist, Hindenburg, the field-marshal, Hitler, the Nazi—an office-holding feat of no small quality. It is said that Hindenburg, knowing that his health and mind were failing, appealed to Meissner to be a super-efficient watchdog, to 'protect' him from breaking his oath, that is, the oath to preserve the Weimar

constitution. It is also said that the Nazis 'got to' Hindenburg—
through Meissner.

Meissner's influence was always palpable, but it diminished
towards the end, as the Old Man, adrift in a perpetual maelstrom
of crises and appeals to the German nation, unable to understand
the intrigues going on, more and more hesitant to trust anyone,
came inevitably to supreme dependence on the one person so close
to him that question of faith did not arise—the flesh of his own
flesh, Oskar, his son.

Oskar was no stripling. He was a veteran officer. He had no
taste for politics. But politics were all around him. General von
Schleicher, later to become chancellor, was a fellow-officer in his
regiment, the Third Potsdamer Foot Guards, and gradually, with
Schleicher's connivance, a palace *camarilla* rose, with Oskar a
member. The chief business of the *camarilla* was 'protection' of
the aged President. Soon he was practically isolated from other
contacts.

Every politician who wanted to see Hindenburg—the supreme
repository of power—had to penetrate the wall of the *camarilla* first.
The power of the *camarilla* grew. The Nazis did their best to gain
the President's isolated ear. For a long time, however, Oskar and
Schleicher and their crowd, aristocrats and Junkers, distrusting
Hitler as a parvenu and a corporal, fended them off. In 1928 a
group of Prussian notables had presented Hindenburg with an
estate at Neudeck, thus fulfilling the Old Man's dearest dream: to
become a landowner, a country squire. Immediately after Hitler
became chancellor, the Government of Prussia presented him with
an additional five thousand acres of land. The title was made out
in Oskar's name, in order to avoid inheritance tax, since it was clear
that Hindenburg père could not possibly live much longer.

(Acquisition of the Neudeck estate promptly produced a new joke
when the Hitler government began to function. Q. 'What is the
newest and smallest concentration camp in Germany?' A.
'Neudeck.')

The *camarilla* exerted power chiefly because the Reichstag
parliament met only stertorously and for short intervals (in the two
years between December 1930 and November 1932 it did not pass
a *single* law) and because the President, and the President alone,
possessed the power of appointing a chancellor and giving him
authority to dismiss the Reichstag if it were unruly. Intrigue
reached a Borgia-point. Between the palace camp, the army camp,

with this formidable mutiny? He did not dismiss Strasser from the party, as Stalin or Mussolini might have done. Instead he summoned a meeting of all the Nazi deputies. Strasser himself was present. Ignoring him, Hitler began to speak, somewhat as follows:

'In every group of men there is likely to be a Judas. One of the things about a Judas is that he believes there are other Judases too. We have a Judas in our midst. This Judas of ours has spread reports of growing disaffection. But is he right? *Do* others share this baseness, this treachery of character?' Hitler paused. All eyes were turned on Strasser. Hitler pulled a piece of paper from his pocket. His secret service, *within* the party, was of the best.

'Apparently our other Judases do exist,' Hitler proceeded. 'Not only do they exist; I have their names. Do you want to hear the names of these other Judases, who would destroy our unity, disrupt our party?' Consternation. Hitler began reading names. Deputy A. Deputy B. And so on. All the names of those deputies who he knew sympathised with Strasser. As each name was read, Hitler turned sharply to the man, saying, 'Is it correct? Is it true that you are a Judas?' One and all, naturally, leapt to their feet, screaming denunciation on Strasser, loyalty to Hitler. It was only necessary to read the first few names. The meeting exploded into a pandemonium of violent fidelity.[1]

The Strasser interlude was over. What next? The Nazis were still a tidal wave of almost twelve million voters and no bulwark in a democratic system could withstand the pressure of such a torrent. It was impossible to suppress the Nazis, impossible—so it was thought then—to give them *carte blanche*. The Nazis had to be seduced into the government or they might destroy Germany in civil war involuntarily. Yet Hitler, still smarting from the rebuff in August, steadily refused to enter any coalition save on prohibitive terms. Something had to be given him—but what?

'A Mighty Maze—But Not Without a Plan!'

Hitler might have made a civil war, but his whole policy was based on getting office by legal means. He was nicknamed, contemptuously, 'Adolf Légalité'. Perhaps his fear of risking a fight was

---

[1] A few days later Hitler was returning to Berlin from Munich. His chief lieutenants met him at the station. Strasser, contrite, was among them. Hitler slowly greeted each man, shook his hand; and cut Strasser dead. Strasser, agape, was left standing on the platform. He was murdered, the penalty for his rebellion, on June 30, 1934.

patriotic; perhaps it was cowardice derived from the cold steel of 1923. His vanity, moreover, was supreme enough to suggest dictatorship of a type new to history, a dictatorship chosen voluntarily by the people, *voted* into power. But he did not have quite the necessary votes. He was too timid to use force. Therefore—intrigue.

The details are confused, a violent explosion of tangled plot and counter-plot.

First, Papen, who was Schleicher's creature, turned against him. He subtly began to influence Hindenburg against him too. Having tasted glory, Papen wanted more. Partyless (he had been expelled from the Centre), thirsting for position, he joined the Nationalists of Dr. Hugenberg, the industrialist publisher, and leader of the big-capital reactionaries. Second, Papen, turning on all his charm, contrived to meet Hitler secretly in the home of the banker Schroeder in Cologne. He succeeded in persuading Hitler —at last—to envisage the possibility of coalition.

The Hitler forces were summoning new strength. Hitler rightly regarded Schleicher as the last hurdle between himself and power. Worried, Schleicher called a secret meeting in the Reichswehr ministry. It is said that creation of a military dictatorship was discussed, with the arrest of Papen and Hugenberg. Received by the Old Man, Schleicher cautiously informed him that the situation was serious, that the Reichswehr might have to go into the streets against the Nazis. Schleicher's threat was probably a bluff. He wanted to frighten Papen and Hugenberg. But the threat didn't work.

For hearing that Schleicher planned to call out the army, Papen and Hitler met again. The situation had developed beautifully to Papen's hand. He was now in a position to say to Hitler, 'If you don't join us now—on our terms—we are both lost. Schleicher will set the army on both of us. We *must* make a coalition.' Hitler agreed and accepted terms that hitherto had been impossible for him—three seats in the Cabinet as against Papen-Hugenberg's eight.

Schleicher, disastrously out-Schleichered, was victim of his own intrigue, because Hitler and Hugenberg presented Papen's plan for a Nazi-Nationalist government, and the Old Man accepted it. He appointed Hitler chancellor, Papen vice-chancellor. Then he rolled round and fell back to sleep. This occurred, an amazing point before Schleicher, who *was* chancellor, had been dismissed.

It was not till next morning that the general, to his bewildered stupefaction, discovered himself out of office. When he heard the news, he walked in a long oval around his room, whispering to himself, head half bent.

(Brüning said, 'I was badly treated—but poor Schleicher—five times worse.')

Hindenburg thought that he had thoroughly safeguarded himself by drawing Hitler's sting. It was established that Hitler should never be received by the Old Man except in Papen's presence. So did democracy die in the Reich. So did Adolf Hitler, who had become a German citizen only a year before, find himself chancellor of Germany.

And little did Papen, Hindenburg or anyone reckon on the next bizarre development—the Reichstag fire.

CHAPTER IV

THE TRICK BY FIRE AND THE PURGE BY BLOOD

'Goering discloses the fact that the late Kurt von Schleicher plotted a coup against the Reich in 1933. We knew the Nazis would find out some day what they shot him for.'

—Howard Brubaker.

O N the night of February 27, 1933, a few days before the March 5 elections which were to confirm Hitler's chancellorship, the building of the German Reichstag in Berlin was gutted by fire. This fire destroyed what remained of the German republic. It not only burned a public building; it incinerated the communist, social democratic, catholic, and nationalist parties of Germany. It was discovered at about nine-fifteen on a winter evening back in 1933; but its embers are burning yet.

The Reichstag fire ruined a couple of million marks' worth of glass and masonry. It also ruined some thousands of human lives. Logically, inevitably, the fire produced the immense Nazi electoral victory of March 5, the savageries of the subsequent Brown Terror, the persecution of the Jews, the offensive against Austria, the occupation of Czechoslovakia, the invasion of Poland, and the enormous process of *Gleichschaltung,* or forcible assimilation, which steamrollered over Germany.

The fire turned an imposing edifice to dust and ashes.   Also it turned to dust and ashes the lifework of many thousands of pacifists, liberals, democrats, socialists, decent-minded people of all sorts and classes.   But for the fire the Nazis would never have gained so sweeping and crushing a victory.   In the flames of the Reichstag fire disappeared the old Germany of Bismarck, William II, and the Weimar constitution.   In its smoke rose Hitler's Third Reich.

'When Germany awoke,' Douglas Reed wrote, 'a man's home was no longer his castle. He could be seized by private individuals, could claim no protection from the police, could be indefinitely detained without preferment of charges; his property could be seized, his verbal and written communications overheard and perused; he no longer had the right to forgather with his fellow countrymen, and his newspapers might no longer freely express their opinions.'

The actual course of events of the night of February 27 is quickly told. Smoke and flames were seen from the windows of the Reichstag, in the heart of Berlin near one end of the Unter den Linden, at about nine-fifteen p.m. The fire brigade was there by nine-twenty-five. The main hall was already a roaring cauldron. The ramparts of the building were saved but the interior was gutted. Incendiarism was soon suspected. The fire had started simultaneously in a great number of places—between twenty and thirty in all, according to a subsequent official report. Goering and Hitler arrived within an hour and at once said the fire was the work of communists. 'A sign from Heaven!' Hitler exclaimed, as he surveyed the ruins.

The background of these events may also be briefly sketched. Hitler as we know, had become Reichskanzler. He had only three Nazis in the cabinet as against eight belonging to Papen-Hugenberg, but he had not the faintest thought of playing second-string to them. To accomplish supremacy a great increase in Nazi votes in the March 5 elections was necessary. Hitler desperately needed what he had never had before, a clear majority of Reichstag seats. Papen-Hugenberg were equally determined to prevent this. There was much bad feeling between Hitler and the nationalists. Fighting on a common front, they were fighting each other in reality, because each wanted to dominate the ensuing government.

Things were not going too well with Hitler. Hindenburg still distrusted him. There were wild rumours that Hitler would seek to depose him by force. The Nazis feared that they were going to lose votes. Only one thing might save them by giving them a clear majority. There would be, it was estimated, about six hundred deputies in the new Reichstag, and the communist party was bound to get about one hundred of them. The Nazis claimed about two hundred and fifty. Well, two hundred and fifty is not a clear majority of six hundred; but is half of five hundred. Therefore suppress the communist party and wipe out those critical one hundred seats, and all was won.

At first the Nazis decided to raid the Karl Liebknecht house, the communist party headquarters in Berlin, incriminate the communists in conspiracy to revolt, and thus obtain a pretext to suppress them. The raid was carried out, but it was a failure. The date for the elections was rapidly approaching. Tension between Hitler

E

and Papen-Hugenberg increased. The Nazis had to think of something else—in a hurry. They did.

The fire produced exactly what the Nazis hoped for. This we have seen.

The one hundred communist deputies were arrested. A state of virtual siege was proclaimed. The provisions of the constitution guaranteeing individual liberty were suppressed. Plans for a communist outbreak were 'revealed'. Germany rose with a roar. There was intense public excitement. The Nazis stormed the country, and Hitler was able to manœuvre himself into a dictatorship for four years, affix himself to power immovably, unshakably.

Arson de Luxe

The true story of the fire is not so well known to-day as it might be. The Nazis did their job so expertly that, whereas everyone well informed instantly suspected them of complicity, there was much puzzlement as to details. Even to-day there are mysteries, subsidiary mysteries, not entirely clear. Let us deal with them.

During the night of the fire a Dutch half-wit named Marinus van der Lubbe was arrested when police found him in the burning ruins. There were no witnesses to his arrest except the police. The first statements about the Dutchman, issued by Goering, were false. It was said that he had a membership-card of the communist party on his person, a leaflet urging common action between socialists and communists, several photographs of himself, and a passport. Obliging fellow! He did possess the passport, but not the other documents, as the trial subsequently proved.

His career and movements were closely traced. He had set three other fires—minor ones—in Berlin just before the Reichstag fire. In 1929 he had joined something called the Dutch Communist Youth Organisation, a secessionist group. Two years later he was expelled from this as a worthless and stupid fellow. He never belonged to the communist party itself. Van der Lubbe's itinerary the few days before the fire was well established. As late as the night of February 17–18 he slept at Glinow, near Potsdam. He could not have got to Berlin before the 19th or 20th. Yet within a week he, an unknown tramp, either (a) so insinuated himself into the graces of the rigidly articulated communist party as to be given the dangerous and delicate job of firing the Reichstag, or (b) was hired to do it by someone else.

When it became clear, even in Germany, that the Van der Lubbe explanation simply would not hold water, the mystery thickened. The police got to the point of having to admit that Van der Lubbe had confederates. But how, carrying incendiary material, could enough of them possibly have penetrated the Reichstag walls, doorways, or windows in the middle of Berlin without being seen?

The German authorities themselves let the cat out of the bag, and an astounding cat it proved to be. It was announced that the incendiaries had presumably entered and escaped from the building by means of an underground tunnel leading from the Reichstag basement to the palace of the speaker of the Reichstag—Goering—across the street. Originally this tunnel was part of the Reichstag's central heating system. Until an official communiqué revealed its existence not a dozen persons in Berlin had ever heard of it. So one aspect of the mystery was solved. The incendiaries, whoever they were, got in and out of the Reichstag building—through Goering's back yard. Incredible information!

An ostrich sticks its head in the sand—well-meaning but stupid ostrich. There is an obverse of the ostrich process. A man may naïvely and stridently call attention to something he wishes to conceal, hoping thereby to lessen interest in it. A squirrel hides a nut under a tree. Then he squats and points at it, showing where it is. Disingenuously a man may reveal what is embarrassing to him, hoping thus to modify the terms of the embarrassment.

Long before the trial opened the accusation that the Nazis themselves had burned the building had impressed the world. A mock trial was held in London. The *Brown Book*, telling part of the story—but inaccurately—was published by *émigrés* and widely circulated. Moreover, a secret nationalist memorandum, written to the order of a prominent deputy named Oberfohren, was passed from hand to hand. Oberfohren was a nationalist, a Junker, one of Papen's men. He asserted flatly that the Nazis were the incendiaries. In June, a Nazi detachment searched his flat; mystery for some time surrounded Oberfohren's whereabouts. Then it was announced that he had 'shot himself'.

The half-wit Van der Lubbe was not the only person arrested. Ernst Torgler, chairman of the communist *bloc* in the Reichstag, gave himself up to the police when he heard the announcement incredible to his ears that he was accused of complicity; subsequently three Bulgarian communists, Dimitrov, Popov, and Tanev were arrested, when a waiter who had served them in a Berlin café told the police that their activities had been 'suspicious'. Dimitrov was

in Munich, not Berlin, on the night of the fire, as an incontrovertible alibi proved; nevertheless he was held for five months until
the trial, without a scrap of evidence against him.

Trial

I reported the trial in Liepzig and Berlin during its first six
weeks. The court sat for fifty-seven days, and provided superlative
drama. The trial was neither a farce nor a frame-up. The behaviour of the police and judicial authorities before the trial was
outrageous, but once the proceedings reached the court-room there
was a difference. The court got itself into a curious dilemma, of
having to pretend to be fair even while exercising the greatest
animus against the defendants, and little by little this necessity—
caused mostly by the pressure of foreign opinion—to stimulate justice led to some modicum of justice in the court-room.

When the trial opened, I think, the judges like many people in
Germany genuinely thought that Van der Lubbe was a communist
and that the communists were guilty. The prosecution thought so
too and, assuming that the trial would be quick and easy, it made
no serious effort to fabricate a 'good' case. As the hearings went on
it became evident even to the judges that there was no case at all.
The evidence of the prosecution was a mystifying confusion of in-
accuracies, contradictions, and plain lies. But once the trial started,
it couldn't be stopped. With dreadful pertinacity, with true Teutonic thoroughness, the court plodded on, deeper every day in a
morass of evidence that ineluctably proved just what it didn't want
proved—the innocence of the accused. The prosecution, panicky,
began to produce incredible cranks as witnesses, whom even the
judges couldn't stomach; the judges turned Dimitrov out of court
whenever his questions became too intolerably pointed—which
was often.

No one, of course, counted on the brilliant gallantry of Dimitrov.
This Bulgarian revolutionary had, moveover, brains. Unerringly
he picked every flaw in the testimony of a dishonest witness; unerringly he asked just those questions most damaging to the prosecution. He turned the trial into a public forum. The trial started as
an attempt to pin the guilt of the Reichstag arson on the defendants.
Dimitrov turned it before long into an action precisely opposite:
one seeking to clear the Nazis of the same charge.

Also Dimitrov, if only because he is the only man in recorded
history to have made Goering turn publicly red in the neck, con-

tributed deeply to the pure joy of living. When a witness could not be found, he asked: 'Have you looked for him in a concentration camp?' When the judge rebuked him for making communist propaganda, Dimitrov pointed to Goering—on the witness-stand—and said with a subtle combination of impudence and perfect courtesy: 'But he's making National Socialist propaganda!' No one who saw him will ever forget Dimitrov pointing to Lubbe and exclaiming, in his picturesque Balkan German: 'This miserable Faust! Who is his Mephistopheles?' Nor the climax to his final speech when, imperturbable as ever with the executioner's axe or Goering's private vengeance facing him he demanded of the court 'compensation for his wasted time!'

Once the court was forced into calling every relevant witness, like porters and workmen in the Reichstag building, the flood-gates were open. Important little clues came out. Lubbe, inert, apathetic, testified—in one of his few lucid moments—that he had been 'with Nazis' the night before the fire. A gateman testified that a Nazi deputy, Dr. Albrecht, left the burning building, in great excitement, as late as ten p.m. A servant in Goering's house, Aldermann, testified that he heard, on several nights before the fire, mysterious sounds in the underground tunnel. Thus the fire—got hot.

Mystery

The court had no option but to acquit Torgler, Dimitrov, Popov, and Tanev; Van der Lubbe was sentenced to death and presently decapitated. (Torgler, one should interpolate, was held in 'protective custody' for two years after the trial, though the court declared him innocent.) The Dutchman died with his lips sealed, and with him to the grave went one secret—how exactly he and the incendiaries had worked together.

It was quite clear that he could not have set the fire alone. He was armed with household fire-lighters only; the expert evidence proved that some self-combustible chemical, phosphorous and sulphur, besides large quantities of petrol, which Lubbe could not possibly have carried, were used in the central hall of the Reichstag chamber. He was half blind; he shambled rather than walked; the Reichstag was a dark, unfamiliar building, composed of stone and heavy wood; yet two minutes five seconds (the re-enactment proved) after he entered the building, the central hall was fiercely burning.

It was also quite clear that Van der Lubbe was not an overt *agent provocateur* hired by the Nazis. This theory, for a long time popular, had to be given up immediately Lubbe took the stand. The Nazis could not possibly have deliberately picked an agent so inept and witless. Lubbe was an obvious victim of maniacal depressive psychosis. He could hardly have been acting. Nor was he drugged. He was no friend of the Nazis, and the court was terrified every time he opened his mouth.

Thus this mystery; if Van der Lubbe acted independently of the Nazis, how could the fire have been so physically successful. If he acted with the Nazis, why did he all but give them away in court?

The answer is, first, according to the only theory that will fit the facts, Van der Lubbe was not an *agent provocateur*, but a dupe; second, according to expert testimony at the trial, which can hardly be gainsaid, there were *two* fires, not one, in the Reichstag building that night.

Van der Lubbe, a typical enough unfortunate by-product of modern civilisation, was not only weak-minded; he had a deep grievance against society and authority, which his feeble brain sought to remedy by pyromania. He was a genuine arsonist. A homeless vagrant, wandering in the Berlin slums, he set several fires, and in his thick manner boasted about them. And Nazis heard him. So much is fact.

Entering the Reichstag building, Van der Lubbe ignited his miserable smudges of tablecloths and curtains, using his shirt for tinder. The fires, like the acts of arson he had committed on previous days, were not fires but failures to set fires; feeble puddles of smoke and soot, nothing more. He proceeded—and must have seen, bursting ahead of him, a mighty cauldron of vivid flame! This was the other fire. It was the chemical fire set by the Nazis, who carried their material through the Goering tunnel, and timed it to go off at just that moment. But Lubbe thought it was *his* fire! He retreated, proud, triumphant—and was arrested by the police.

This was just what the Nazis planned. They wanted a scapegoat —any kind of scapegoat—so that they could blame the communists. The link between Lubbe and the Nazis is quite clear. He said in the Berlin underworld that he was going to burn the Reichstag. It was a matter of a moment—so honeycombed was Berlin with spies, tools, agents—for this information to reach high quarters.

The Nazis knew that Lubbe was going to be there. But they did not tell him that *they* were going to be there. *He* thought that he was alone. He never knew the Nazis were acting on his words. Thus his peculiar behaviour in the court. He was proud of his fire; he resented it deeply when anyone was put forward to share the credit. With impenetrable obstinacy, he insisted that he had no confederates, and set the fire alone—and really believed it. This is the only combination of theory and fact which accounts for all the circumstances of the Reichstag fire. It is the theory which Dimitrov, when I saw him in Moscow in June 1935, accepted as the best explanation of the events.

Explanation?

Karl Ernst, one of those extraordinary characters tossed up from obscurity to flitting eminence by the turmoil of the Nazi revolution, was murdered on June 30. He had been a waiter in a night club in the west end of Berlin. He was Roehm's chief protégé, and consequently his promotion was very rapid; at the age of twenty-seven he became *Obergruppenführer* (a rank corresponding to major-general) of the Berlin-Brandenburg SA, numbering sixty-five thousand men. Before June 30, Ernst was aware of impending dissension within the party. He wrote a letter, dated June 3, 1934, and sent it abroad, with instructions that it be published if his fears became true.

This Ernst letter purports to be a full description of the Reichstag fire plot. It gives a brilliant and terrible picture of the attitude and manners of the Nazi leaders just before the fire and after. They were (except for Hitler, who is mentioned reverently only as 'He'), vulgar, lusty, cruel, courageous, and having a marvellous time. They sound like a group of Capones in politics for the fun of it. And the fire was plotted almost like a bit of deviltry.

Ernst says that he lit the actual fire. His comrades were two SA men, Fiedler and Von Mohrenschild.

All three were 'executed' in the clean-up of June 30. Dead tongues tell no tales.

The Ernst letter may not be genuine. Even so, if Ernst didn't set the fire, someone like him did.

Blood Bath

The events of June 30, 1934, were an historic inevitability. They were indeed a necessity. Hitler was poised between two mutually exclusive armies, the Reichswehr (regular army), and the SA, his private Brown Shirt force, led by Roehm. Events made it imperative for him to give undisputed authority to one or the other. He chose the Reichswehr. The SA therefore had to be liquidated. This, in plain language, is the secret of June 30.

A secondary consideration, almost as important, was the nature of the Nazi party itself. The party, as Heiden put it, was a unity not of aims but of causes; it was founded on no coherent body of doctrine; its personnel was of the most various. The *Führer Prinzip* was its only structural bastion, and when sub-leaders became jealous of one another and thus undermined it, even though Hitler himself was not attacked, there was nothing to do but eliminate them—forcibly.

Third, it is necessary to remember that what began as a terrible administration of discipline to Roehm's men degenerated uncontrollably into a violent situation which leaders seized as a priceless opportunity to settle old-standing party or *private* grudges. Admit terror as a principle, as Hitler did: and there was no telling where it would end.

The deaths occurred mostly on the night of June 30–July 1. Hitler, in his speech justifying the executions, admitted to seventy-seven slain. This was certainly an underestimate. The full toll may never be known. Probably it reached two hundred and fifty, possibly three hundred.

The dead fall into several groups. First, the SA men:

> Captain Ernst Roehm, Reichs minister without portfolio and chief of staff of the SA; Hitler's best friend; organiser of his private army.
> Karl Ernst, SA *Obergruppenführer*, Berlin and Brandenburg.
> Three other SA *Obergruppenführers* (major-generals). Edmund Heines, boss of Silesia; August Schneidhuber, police president of Munich, and Fritz von Krausser.
> Hans Hayn, SA *Gruppenführer* for Saxony, and other *Gruppenführers* (brigadier generals).
> SA *Standartenführer* (colonel) Uhl, named by Hitler as the man appointed to assassinate him.

Second, a 'Catholic' group, composed mostly of men close to Vice-Chancellor von Papen:

> Dr. Erich Klausner, leader of the 'Catholic Action,' an important and distinguished political leader.
> Adelbert Probst, leader of the Catholic Youth movement.
> Fritz von Bose, Papen's state secretary.
> Edgar Jung, Papen's private secretary.
> Dr. Beck, of the International Students Exchange.

Third, victims of private or semi-private vengeance:

> Gregor Strasser, brilliant theoretician of the Nazi party, formerly Hitler's first assistant, in virtual retirement since November 1932.
> Gen. von Kahr, the dictator of Bavaria in 1923, whom the Nazis said 'betrayed' the first Hitler *Putsch*.

Fourth, in a special group:

> Gen. Kurt von Schleicher, former chancellor.
> Elisabeth von Schleicher, his wife.
> Gen. von Bredow, his former assistant in the ministry of war.

Finally, those killed purely by accident, like the Munich music critic Willi Schmidt, who was executed by an SS squad despite his protests that he was not the Willi Schmidt, a Munich SA man, whom it sought. The proper Willi Schmidt was found and duly shot—later.

Former Chancellor von Papen, after his secretaries were killed, barely escaped with his life, and former Chancellor Brüning would certainly have been killed, had he not fled the country, against his will and on the urgent advice of friends, twenty-seven days before. Brüning slipped over the Dutch frontier partially disguised, in the company of Dutch priests.

Why was Schleicher killed? Why did these other former chancellors narrowly escape death? Because (*a*) they *were* former chancellors, and Brüning and Schleicher were the only two men in Germany who could conceivably have succeeded Hitler if intrigue of the same kind that brought him to power should presently unseat him; (*b*) Papen was still at his own game of palace manœuvres, and had deeply shocked and annoyed Nazi extremists by a speech at Marburg on June 17, attacking them; (*c*) Brüning was the man who had dared take the Nazi Brown Shirts off the streets, and they never forgave him for it.

Additionally, Schleicher was murdered because many leading Nazis thought him dangerous. The allegation that Schleicher had intrigued with a foreign power was nonsensical. He was a friend of Roehm's, but no evidence has been adduced that he and Roehm were actually plotting. Schleicher was a great diner-out; he was called the 'Social General' and had friends in the foreign embassies; that was all.

Fellow officers in the Reichswehr deeply resented Schleicher's murder, and they demanded that his name be cleared. The Nazis hesitated. The documents in the case were in the hands of

Himmler, the SS chief. The Reichswehr obtained the documents
—no one knows how. Himmler tried to get them back. He failed.
A group of four hundred Reichswehr officers met in a semi-public
ceremony, with the old Field-Marshal von Mackensen in the chair,
and drank a toast to Schleicher's memory, inscribing his name and
that of Bredow in the regimental honour-roll. This frightened the
Nazis. A secret meeting was called by Goering, attended by a handful of prominent Nazis and all Reichswehr officers above the rank of
captain, at which, it is believed, Goering confessed that Schleicher's
death, like that of Willi Schmidt, was a 'mistake'.

Could any 'plot' (by talking of a plot, Hitler justified the
clean-up)[1] have united Roehm, Strasser, Schleicher, Von Kahr, Willi
Schmidt, Fritz von Bose, Klausner. The idea is, of course, fantastic.
But was Roehm alone, as boss of the SA, considering subversive
action? Most of those who were in Berlin at the time think not.
But it is just possible.

Background of the Killings

Berlin was very tense in May and June, 1934, and economic distress was sharp. The revolution had taken place, i.e. the Nazis had
seized power. But where were the rewards of victory? Why had
not the Nazi economic programme been converted to reality? The
radical Nazis, the rank and file, the men in the street, felt that
Goering and the Reichswehr and the industrialists had grabbed
the plums. They were tense with dissatisfaction, and they appealed
to Hitler—in vain. The Leader announced that no 'second revolution' would occur.

Discontent was concentrated, among Nazis, in the SA. The SA
considered itself the chief instrument of the party. It was Hitler's
army of the streets, that had brought him office; Hitler was a Brown
Shirt, first and last. The SA was the pedestal of the movement; the
submerged mass and reservoir of man power; it contained many
honest Leftists, eager for the promised land of economic reform.

---

[1] German apologists have been hard put to it to explain both the killings and
Hitler's explanations of them. The most novel excuse I heard came from a highly
nationalist German. Roehm and the others were shot, he said, because the
Treaty of Versailles deprived Germany of colonies. Other countries may rele-
gate unpopular or fallen heroes to distant places; for instance, Mussolini sent
Balbo to Lybia to cool his heels. But Germany has no colonial posts available.
Roehm might easily have gone to Tanganyika as administrator. But Tanganyika
is no longer German, and therefore nothing could be done with Roehm except
shoot him.

The SA had swollen to the immense number of 2,500,000 men, and with the revolution complete, there was nothing for them to do. They were all dressed up—in their nice brown shirts—with no place to go. Hitler, having created a private army, didn't know what to do with it. They were a fearsome burden on party finance; they had been replaced for guard duty by the SS; and they were an ocean of restlessness and undirected energy.

The leader of the SA was Roehm. He was a remarkable man. He had the blunt energy of Goering, the sharp ruthlessness of Goebbels, and an organising talent like none in Germany. A brusque character, a man of limited imagination, who hated peace, loved disorder, Roehm was second only to Hitler in the affection of the Brown Shirts. Hitler owed more to Roehm than to anybody. Hitler created the SA, but Roehm was the disciplinarian, the executive. And Hitler loved him.

Roehm's solution of the SA problem was quite simple. Ambitious, he wanted to feed the SA into the Reichswehr,[1] convert the Reichswehr into an immense national army, and become head of the armed forces of the German state. Thus he became the personification of two tendencies. He was (a) the chief of the Leftist tendencies of the régime, since the SA were the Have-Nots in Germany, and (b) the competitor of the Reichswehr for basic authority in the nation.

The Reichswehr naturally opposed him with bitterness and vigour. The generals, first, had no intention of giving up their jobs to Roehm; second, they had built the 100,000 men of the Reichswehr into a beautifully precise and tempered military instrument, and would have committed suicide rather than see it drowned, inundated, with two and a half million hooligans, clerks, half-trained boys, *Lumpen Proletariat* off the streets. Merger with the SA meant death to the Reichswehr. And the general staff told Hitler so—in no uncertain terms.

The Leader sought about him warily. He hated to give up Roehm; but on the other hand the 100,000 men of the Reichswehr were infinitely more valuable to him than the 2,500,000 virtually unarmed SA. Assiduously he had cultivated the Reichswehr higher officers, especially General von Blomberg, who was minister of defence. Blomberg, an important point, became deeply devoted to Hitler. Actually on June 29, the day before the clean-up,

[1] He had had this idea as far back as 1922, and went to exile in South America when he previously split with Hitler on the same issue.

Blomberg in a significant speech expressed his contentment with the Nazi régime. This was enough for Hitler. If he could be absolutely sure of the Reichswehr, the most powerful force in Germany, the SA lost its *raison d'être*.

Hitler called Roehm to see him. They talked for five hours. Roehm asked him once more to enlarge the Reichswehr by inclusion of the S.A. Hitler told him that the general staff of the Reichswehr insisted on selective recruiting, when and if conscription was introduced. Roehm departed, beaten. Sulking, he went to Munich. It was announced that, beginning July 1, the SA would take two months' leave, during which period they were not to wear uniforms. The SA off the streets! The revolution betrayed!

At this point should be mentioned another factor. We have not till now discussed the SS. These, the *Schutzstaffel*, were the *Black* Shirts, about three hundred thousand strong. They were the *élite* of the fighting forces of the party, founded originally as a bodyguard to Hitler and the other leaders. The SA was a mob. The SS was a pretorian guard, smart, well-fed, armed. The SA was loyal to Roehm. The SS, with which Roehm had nothing to do, was loyal to Hitler. The chief of the SS was a man who hated Roehm, Himmler. And Hitler could count on the SS absolutely.

The Reichswehr was sufficiently alarmed by this crisis to undertake unusual precautions. For ten days before the clean-up, Reichswehr staff officers in Berlin carried service revolvers, keeping them at hip even in their offices. A Reichswehr regiment was mobilised at Doebritz, near Berlin. This followed rumours—apparently without substantiation—that Karl Ernst, the most devoted of Roehm's followers, intended to defy the SA dispersal order and occupy Berlin. It was even said that Ernst intended murdering the general staff!

Precautions by the Reichswehr do not prove the existence of a plot. It is even possible that the Reichswehr, to serve its own ends, might have invented a plot, so as to be rid of Roehm. Certainly young Ernst seemed remarkably innocent of any political intentions, let alone mutiny. He had recently married and he was arrested *en route* to Bremen, where he was boarding ship for a postponed honeymoon in Madeira. Hitler had been best man at his wedding, not six weeks before.

'Spake The Grisly Terror'

Possibly to allay suspicions by Roehm that he was aware of

treason, if any existed, Hitler left for south Germany to inspect a labour camp. He took Goebbels with him, and also a man named Lutze, who when Roehm was dead was promptly named new SA chief of staff. Goering had been charged with the clean-up in Berlin. That was why Goebbels was with Hitler. Goering, running wild, was capable of anything. In the middle of the night (June 29), Hitler records that he heard news of 'such serious character' that he must take action at once.

Goebbels had described the occasion picturesquely:

> 'I still see the Leader standing on the terrace of the Godesberg Hotel. The Leader looks seriously into the dark sky. Nobody knows yet what threatens. The Leader is true to his own principles. The Leader is full of determination regarding the reactionary rebels who have cast the nation into unlimited disturbance.
> 'Reports come to him from Berlin and Munich. After only a few minutes' conference, the decision is made not to wait until the next morning. We start at two in the night. At four we are in Munich.
> 'On the aerodrome the Leader receives reports. Then he decides to go into the lions' den. He rushes by car to Wiessee. Without resistance he manages to get into the house of Roehm. With incomparable courage Hitler carries out the arrests. Soon after the arrest of Roehm his staff arrives from Munich. Hitler confronts them and tells them in one sentence to go back to Munich. They obey.'
> —(*Manchester Guardian*, July 2, 1934.)

Now if Roehm was planning an outbreak in Munich on the 30th, why was he in bed at Wiessee, twenty miles away, at six a.m. of the morning that the action was alleged to have begun? Why, if Munich was rising in revolt, was it quite peaceable when Hitler, the same morning, arrived there?

An official Nazi *communiqué* describes the raid at Wiessee in more detail:

> The Führer entered, and in person arrested Chief of Staff Roehm, who yielded 'silently and without resistance' in his bedroom. In Heines's room immediately opposite 'a shameful picture' met the Führer. Heines was in bed with a youth; the repulsive scene which accompanied their arrest cannot be described. It pitilessly reveals the conditions reigning in the circles around the former Chief of Staff.
> —(*The Times*, July 2, 1934.)

The unofficial story is that Hitler, far from being alone, was accompanied by a squadron of SS gunmen, and that Roehm, far from accepting arrest silently, bawled insults at the Leader, denouncing him as a traitor to the revolution, and that Hitler shouted in return until the SS men took Roehm away.

Roehm was brought into Munich. Heines and his *Lustknabe* were apparently dispatched on the spot. Hitler did not know what to do with Roehm. The chief of staff was clapped in prison and told to shoot himself. He refused, saying that if anyone shot him, it would have to be 'Adolf himself'. He was not killed till five p.m. the next day, about thirty-six hours after his arrest. No one knows the precise circumstances. Probably the jailers came to Hitler again and again, with the words, 'He won't kill himself. . . . What shall we do. . .?' And one can imagine Hitler's final, irritated, desperate order to get rid somehow of the man who was his only friend, get him out of the way, shoot him, kill him. . . .

The others did not matter to Hitler so much—personally. There were plenty of others. He made a clean sweep of the allegedly disaffected SA leaders in Munich and the vicinity. Then early in the morning he apparently sent Goering a message to go ahead in Berlin. Goering waited till about eleven a.m. before cutting loose. Then he commenced action, 'expanding the original scope of his instructions', as he admitted later.

It is a moot point whether Goering had talked over with Hitler those whom he wished to kill. Possibly not. Hitler's 'executive' orders were often extremely vague.[1] At any rate the death squads got to work. Himmler superintended them. Annihilation, quick and terrible, began.

Schleicher was shot in his home. He was completely unaware that any action against him impended. He was, in fact, talking to a friend on the telephone when the SS men arrived. He said into the telephone, 'Excuse me just a moment; someone is in the room.' He turned and saw his executioners. They opened fire. Frau von Schleicher, hearing the shots, rushed into the room. She was killed so that there would be no witness to her husband's death.

The SS men were divided into two groups. Those who did the shooting were full-time veterans, members of Hitler's *Leibstandarten* (bodyguard). The executions, as apart from downright assassinations, took place in the Lichterfelde barracks. The cul-

---

[1] The story goes that Hitler, some months later, was asked by a foreigner the whereabouts of a friend. A Nazi at the luncheon table stammered explanation that he had 'disappeared on June 30'. Hitler paled, not knowing the man was dead.

prits were given a one-minute 'trial' before a drum-head court martial. The procedure in most cases was simply a statement by the officer in charge, 'You are accused of treachery and condemned to death.' As each man was brought out to face the firing squad, a blinding searchlight was turned into his eyes and drums rolled. Then the volley.

Several of the condemned SA leaders, including Sander, Ernst's chief of staff, were shot with 'Heil Hitler' on their lips. They thought that a mutinous group of SS men had revolted against Hitler and that they were dying loyal to the *Führer* and the Nazi movement! 'Traitors', indeed!

It took Hitler from July 1 to July 13 to recover his shaken nerve. At first the announcement was made that only a few ranking SA leaders and General von Schleicher and his wife had been killed. Fearing that the plot theory would not receive credence the propaganda ministry also called attention to the homosexual character of Roehm, Heines, and their closest friends. The party had always been split on the homosexual issue. Hitler spoke on July 13 and tolled off the names of the seventy-seven whom he admitted to be dead. He looked like a broken man. The first part of his speech was received in almost complete silence, though Nazi deputies (some thirty seats were significantly vacant) were the audience.

In great detail, according to habit, Hitler first sketched the history of the Nazi revolution. Then he recounted his differences with Roehm. About details of the 'plot' he was far from precise. Referring to Schleicher's alleged meeting with a foreign diplomat, he made the remarkable statement that if 'German traitors met a foreign statesman and gave strict orders to conceal it from me, I will have such men shot, no matter whether this clandestine discussion had been devoted only to the weather, old coins, and the like.' Then he concluded with his passionate outburst that for twenty-four hours he had been supreme court of the German people—and the audience broke into wild applause.

Modern Monte Cristo

As extraordinary as some of the murders on June 30, were some of the escapes. Take the case of Gottfried Treviranus. He had been a submarine commander during the War and as a cabinet minister under Brüning had taken a nationalist point of view almost as strong as that of the Nazis. But he was on the death list for several reasons: (1) he was Brüning's closest friend, (2) he was a strong influence in the fighting services, (3) he had always despised Hitler and never concealed it.

On June 30, just after lunch, Treviranus was playing tennis in his back yard. A lorry containing a dozen SS men, with drawn revolvers, ground to a stop athwart his house. One of his children met them and they shouted 'Where is Treviranus?' A voice from upstairs, attracted by the commotion, called 'Here I am.' But this was Treviranus's father! Rushing upstairs the SS men saw him, realised their mistake, and asked where his son was. Meanwhile the child ran out and told Treviranus, in the tennis court, what was happening. Instantly he jumped the garden wall and leapt into his car, parked outside. The SS men, now downstairs, saw him drive off, shot at him and missed.

Very intelligently Treviranus drove straight into town instead of trying to get into the country; the truck full of SS followed him but could not shoot on account of the heavy traffic, then lost him. Treviranus stopped at the home of a friend and borrowed street clothes. He then went to Schleicher's house to find out what was happening. There was a crowd outside. He got out of his car and *asked* an SS guard what had occurred. Hearing that Schleicher had been shot, Treviranus jumped back into his car with considerable alacrity but outward calm, and drove into the country, where he smashed the car against the edge of the road, to give the impression he had sought further escape into the fields. He returned to inner Berlin by taxi and took refuge in the house of a friend, where —incredible detail—he kept cool by reading Macaulay's *History of England*.

End of Hindenburg

On August 2, Hindenburg died. The bloodshed of June 30 may have been a shock to his aged frame; on the other hand the Old Man seemed to have been well satisfied with Hitler and Goering, because he sent telegrams of congratulation to each.

Even the day before the death the most competent of Berlin correspondents and diplomats considered that the event must be a crisis of the gravest sort for Hitler. Who would be President? Could he appoint himself President? If he did so, who would become Chancellor? Above all, what would the Reichswehr do?

Now, with better perspective, we know that Hitler had bought off the army on June 30. Even so, wise after the event, one is bound to be impressed at Hitler's cleverness and daring.   No one at the time dreamed of the simple and subtle scheme long up Hitler's sleeve, of *combining* the office of President and Chancellor.

As to the Reichswehr, Blomberg took care of that.   The very morning of Hindenburg's death, all Reichswehr garrisons in Germany took a new oath, and one of the most extraordinary in military history.   Usually armies swear allegiance to the crown or head of state.   This was an oath of fidelity, and a thorough one, to Hitler personally:

> 'I swear by God this sacred oath, that I will render unconditional obedience to the Leader of the German Reich and people, Adolf Hitler, the Commander-in-Chief of the *Wehrmacht* (armed forces) and that I will, as a valiant soldier, at all times be ready to stake my life for this oath.'

Each soldier and minor officer swore the oath two words at a time, repeating them after the commandant with hand upraised. Some officers, hating Hitler, took sick leave that day.   The general staff was not perturbed.   Each absent officer was forced to take the oath personally on his return to service. . . . After the oath all sang not only Deutschland Über Alles, but the Horst Wessel song, which is the Nazi anthem.

As long as Hindenburg lived, there was some possibility, although it was remote, that he might dismiss Hitler from the Chancellorship.   With his death this possibility passed.   Hitler was now Head of State.   He could only dismiss himself.   His undeviating path had reached its natural end.   Only God could remove him now.   And God, he claimed, was on his side.

F

CHAPTER V

THE TWO G-MEN

'Be my brother, or I will bash your head in.'
—GERMAN PROVERB.

SURROUNDING Hitler are fantastic congeries of sub-Hitlers. In the early days in Berlin I heard one of the shrewdest observers of German affairs say: 'No top Nazi is perfectly normal or perfectly sincere. They are either cynics, on-the-make, or hysterics.' Every national revolution, it is true, convulsively stirring the depths of a great nation, may bring strange fish to the surface. And I do not say that hundreds and thousands of decent Germans, some of them in important administrative posts, are not forthright and honest men.

Several of the more notorious misfits perished on June 30. Many remain. It is not only that they remain, but they hold jobs extraordinarily appropriate to their weakness and failings. Who should be director of 'popular enlightenment' in the Third Reich? Who, indeed, but Dr. Goebbels, whose power of enlightenment is that of a cripple, a man maimed and dwarfed! Who should have almost supreme police power over eighty million Germans? Who, indeed, but General Goering, a man of the most violent and unstable passions!

Hitler once told an interviewer that he did not like Yes-men. Deliberately he chose to surround himself with bold and blustering spirits who often disagreed among themselves. He has, in fact, made a definite policy of playing one sub-leader against another; he keeps them guessing, gets out of each his best. Also, it is believed, he has something against most of them in his dossiers. The leaders, jealous of each other, and knowing Hitler the all-powerful arbiter of their destinies, compete with one another for his favour.

Hitler takes good care that none of the sub-leaders approach his own supremacy. When Goering got too powerful, he took the secret police away and gave them to Himmler.

Party posts more or less correspond to posts in the government.

60

Dr. Goebbels, for instance, is *Reichsleiter* for propaganda in the party and also Reichs propaganda minister; Darré is party leader for agriculture, and also minister of agriculture. If party and state were perfectly co-ordinated, as in Russia, this correspondence of posts would be complete. But it is by no means complete. Dr. Schacht, for instance, for a long time had no party rank at all, though he was economic minister. And whereas Rosenberg is party chief for foreign affairs, he is very far from being foreign minister in the government, which is Ribbentrop's job.

Germany is divided into a series of party districts or *Gaus*. Dr. Goebbels is *Gauleiter* for Berlin. When the *Gauleiter* is also the SA leader of the district, a condition which Hitler seeks to prevent as far as possible, he becomes a personage of enormous local power. Heines was both *Gauleiter* and SA commander in Silesia. Julius Streicher, the worst of the anti-Semites, is both *Gauleiter* and SA leader in North Bavaria.

The rivalries between these men are formidable. That between Goering and Goebbels is the best known. That between Goebbels and Rosenberg is no less vicious. It would be a complex task to draw a chart of the mutual hatreds within the party. Goebbels and Schacht are far from being friends; Goering and Ribbentrop; Goebbels and Himmler; and everyone dislikes Rosenberg. The only two men on fairly good terms with everyone are Hess and Frick; neither is ambitious, and both have pleasant personalities.

This unnatural *mélange* of hatreds produces friction and discordance and also inefficiency. Beyond that, it indicates what may be a serious weakness of Hitlerism. The party, founded on emotion, based on no fixed and stable ideology, held together only by the Leader Principle, is not indissolubly part of the structure of government and society, as is Fascism in Italy or communism in Russia. Hitler's three principal advisers for years were not Nazis at all: Schacht, Neurath, and General Blomberg. Imagine a Soviet Government in which the ministers of economics, foreign affairs, and war were not communists!

There are these sub-Hitlers then. Let us begin with Marshal Goering.

Public Clothes-horse No. 1

'Adolf Hitler is the greatest German of all time.'
—MARSHAL GOERING

Though he stands above all for the entity of Prussia—his great air force aside—the gusty Goering is a Bavarian; he was born in Rosenheim, Bavaria, on January 12, 1893. He came of a good family—his father was governor-general of German South-West Africa—and his schooling was good. He spent his holidays climbing the Austrian Alps. He too, like Hitler, has strong emotional affiliations with Austria, and this may be one of the contributory factors accounting for the Nazi assault on Austria in 1933 and 1934. Hitler's sister still lives in Vienna, and so does Goering's brother. And his two sisters married Austrians.

At twenty-one, Goering enlisted in the German Air Force. By the autumn of 1915 he was leader of No. 5 Pursuit Squadron. He was awarded the highest German decoration, the *Pour le Mérite* (equivalent to the Victoria Cross) and in 1918 he succeeded to the command of the celebrated Richthofen Squadron. He shot down twenty-three planes during the War, as against fifty-four for Udet, the second German pilot, and eighty-odd for Richthofen.

Two incidents which contributed deeply to the evolution of his life came in 1918, just after the Armistice. First, Goering refused to demobilise and surrender his planes. He was ordered to do so by the German General Staff, but, deliberately insubordinate, he refused to obey, until he was finally brought to ground near Darmstadt. He said farewell to his fellow officers, toasting the day when Germany would be supreme in the air. His planes were then destroyed.

He never got over this. The destruction of his precious aircraft, by men whom he considered his infinite inferiors, was a psychological shock from which he did not recover; his present passionate energy to build a new German air fleet is compensation.

Secondly, after he had returned to Berlin, a socialist mob saw him in uniform and forcibly tore his officer's insignia from his coat lapels. Foaming with rage, he swore vengeance. His hatred of socialists, which is psychopathic in intensity, dates from that day. It is not entirely fanciful to assume that much of the Brown Terror had its inner sources in this incident.

Goering went to Sweden in 1919 and got a job as a commercial flyer. There he fell in love with a woman who profoundly influenced his life, his first wife, Baroness Karin Fock. He met her, in almost Wagnerian fashion, after a forced landing on her estate at Rockelstad, in North Sweden. He was severely wounded in the Munich beer-hall *Putsch* of 1923, having become one of Hitler's leading followers the year before. He escaped to Italy and then returned to Sweden. His health broke down.

Frau Goering died in 1932, just before her husband became President of the Reichstag, his first big job. Thereafter, when Gregor Strasser was disgraced, Goering succeeded to much of his influence with Hitler and the party. At this time memory of the dead Karin seemed the most important personal factor in his life. He brought her body to Germany (she had died in Sweden) and built a sort of shrine in his Berlin home, where her portrait stood between lighted candles and tinted by reflections from a stained-glass window built into the wall. There Goering knelt daily and prayed—until he met Frau Emmy Sonnemann.

This massive lady, an actress, won his favour and a gargantuan wedding took place in Berlin in April 1935. The ceremony was practically a Roman feast. Hitler was best man. The newly-weds got £80,000 worth of wedding gifts. On the same day two communists, Epstein and Ziegler, who had been condemned to death on the charge of complicity in the murder of the Nazi hero, Horst Wessel, were executed by the axe. Many Nazis admired the symbolic inference—a blood sacrifice to propitiate fertility in the married couple. The Goerings, incidentally, called their first daughter Edda, after Edda Mussolini.

Goering holds an imposing galaxy of jobs. He is President of the Reichstag, General of Reichswehr, General of Police, Reichs Minister of Aviation, Prime Minister of Prussia,[1] Master of the Hunt, Chief Forester of the Reich, and Director of Television—— this last because television may be applicable to aerial warfare. In 1936 he became superintendent of the German 'Four-Year Plan' and as such the nominal economics dictator. Above all, he is Marshal of the Air Force. It is Goering who built and runs Germany's terrific air fleet.

He is famous for the variety and flamboyance of his uniforms, but legend has got the better of fact, and in reality he wears only about a dozen. Usually he carries a hilted sword, like that of a crusader. Behind the desk in his principal residence, a colossal headman's sword is suspended perpendicularly on a velvet curtain. He has a mania for display not only in dress but houses.

Mostly he lives in a large structure on Liepziglerplatz. A sizeable swastika is designed in tile above the main fireplace. In one

[1] But he won't cross the threshold of the Prussian Ministry because it was formerly the stronghold of the socialists.

room the wallpaper is said to be blood-red and the carpet pitch-black; a marble bust of Hitler stands on a pedestal, illumined by a spotlight. Another room, an immense and richly-decorated hall, may be transformed into a movie theatre; at the touch of a button the tapestry on the wall rises into the ceiling, disclosing a movie screen.

In Bavaria Goering has a country house, near Hitler's chalet, on a five thousand acre estate presented to him by the local government. His most ambitious project, and the one dearest to him, is the tremendous air ministry in Berlin, with two thousand five hundred rooms, so big that aeroplanes can land and take off from the roof.

His ambition as well as his vanity is enormous. On March 6, 1933, exactly one day after the elections which confirmed Hitler's accession to office, he ordered his portrait painted—with a book in his lap conspicuously entitled *Life of Napoleon*. His pets are lion cubs. All of them, male or female, are supposed to be named Caesar.

He is as carnivorous as Hitler is frugal—brusque, impulsive, cruel. Testimony after the Munich *Putsch* of 1923 recorded his orders to 'beat in the skulls' of his opponents 'with rifle butts' (*Heil*, p. 19). His famous order to the police in February 1933 to shoot 'enemies' without question, really signalled the beginning of the Nazi terror. His ruthlessness is unthinking, spasmodic, hot-blooded. He is not a plotter, a conspirator, like Goebbels. He has great executive ability, and this serves to make him doubly dangerous. He knows how to listen. He gets things done. Oddly enough, he has great charm—when he wishes to be charming.

Since Goering came to symbolise the police power of the Third Reich, 12,863 people have been sterilised, some of them forcibly. Several hundred thousand Jews have been forced out of the country. In the year between June 1933 and June 1934, 212 men and women were beheaded out of 214 sentenced to death, the great majority for political offences which in no other country would entail the capital penalty. The number of persons sentenced to imprisonment was 280,308; they were to serve an aggregate of 129,421 years. In addition, 184 persons were shot 'while attempting to escape', 13,000 were deprived of citizenship, and 49,000 sent to concentration camps.

Goering is a good Aryan. For instance, he greeted the conclusion of the Anglo-German naval agreement of June 1935 as 'a victory for race law'. But he is the only leading Nazi who is not an outspoken anti-Semite. As to economic affairs, he is with the Rightists in the party. He cared nothing for the 'socialist' part of Hitler's programme. He became a Nazi because Naziism meant a strong national Germany with a new army and a powerful air force.

The jokes about Goering are, of course, legion. Most of them are predicated either on the resplendence of his uniforms or his abnormal size. He is not merely fat: he is fat on top of an immensity of muscle. He moves with the vigour of a man a hundred pounds lighter; there is nothing torpid about him; his energy is terrific. But the story goes that he is so obese that he 'sits down on his own stomach' and that he wears 'corsets on his thighs'.

One story is that he dons an admiral's uniform whenever he takes a bath, with rubber duplicates of all his medals. A new unit of weight has been established in Germany—a 'goering'—to signify the aggregate displacement of his decorations. Once he visited a steel factory and his companions were horrified to see him suddenly leave the floor and move horizontally upward to the ceiling. Reason: an electro-magnet above had caught his medals.

Another little story has him arriving late at a luncheon in Berlin where he is to meet an eminent (and doubtless mythical) visiting Englishman. Goering apologises for his tardiness, and says that he has been out shooting. The Englishman turns to him with lofty words, 'Animals, I presume?' Goering, incidentally, is said to be fond himself of all the stories about him.

Once, the legend has it, Hitler fell into a doze during a performance of *Lohengrin*. The Führer was too tired to keep fully awake. His eyes opened suddenly as the figure of the shining knight in armour took the stage. Hitler thought it was Goering. 'Hermann,' he shouted, 'you are going too far.'

Goering's basic importance, now that war has come, is not his blood lust, not his position in Prussia, not his command of the Prussian police. What matters is his association with aviation. At the beginning at least the war was largely fought in the air, and Goering, with his immense drive and ruthlessness was directing it on the German side. His work helped make the dazzling Polish campaign possible.

As befits his character, the general can use doughty language on occasion. 'Anyone who writes against Germany,' he has said, 'must have filth in his brains.' He is exceptionally forthright. When he first met Mussolini he smiled and said, 'The last time I was in Italy I bombed Verona.'

The Doctor

'A Jew is for me an object of physical disgust. I vomit when I see one. . . . Christ cannot possibly have been a Jew. I don't have to prove that scientifically. It is a fact. . . . I treasure an ordinary prostitute above a married Jewess.'

—Dr. Goebbels.

Dr. Joseph Paul Goebbels was born with a club foot. This was the most important event in his life. It explains much of his personality and career. Crippled, as Heiden puts it, 'a dwarf among giants', he had to make his way by skill, by cleverness, by conspiracy. When his classmates went away to war—he was born in the Rhineland in 1897—he had to stay at home on account of his deformity. His crippled foot sharpened his ambition, and also his hatred of the healthy. He is the most vicious man in the party, the most virulent —and the best educated. He took his Ph.D. at Heidelberg. The doctorate, alleged often to be spurious, is quite genuine.

The Goebbels family was devoutly Roman Catholic, but he is a ferocious anticlerical. His father was a teacher, the grandfather a peasant; his mother's family were handicraft workers, and all were poor. He worked his way to a scholarship at Heidelberg, after attending several other schools. As a youth he wanted to be a literary figure, and indeed he has written much: his published works fill fourteen volumes.

His wife, who married him after divorcing her first husband, was an important influence in his career. Enemies said that the first husband was Jewish; this was not true—he was a quite Aryan lawyer named Quandt. Hitler liked Frau Goebbels and, in the first years of his chancellorship, went often to her musical parties. This was highly advantageous to the political plans of the little doctor. For a time Frau Goebbels was director of the *Deutsche Moden-Amt*, a sort of fashion ministry supposed to create truly Aryan styles for German women; but it didn't last long.

The little doctor—he is scarcely five feet five inches—entered a meeting-hall in Munich in 1922; the speaker was Adolf Hitler. Goebbels says that pure chance brought him there. Converted instantly to Naziism, he went to the Rhineland to organise party groups. Hitler soon came to appreciate his quick tongue, his soaring words; next to the Leader he became the most valuable orator in the movement. In 1926 Hitler sent him to organise the party in Berlin, where it had made comparatively little progress. Goebbels founded a newspaper, the *Angriff*, and inside four years, by great feats of journalistic and organisational skill, he was leader of a powerful machine: next to Munich Berlin became the chief stronghold of the Hitlerites.

Goebbels's violence in oratory and journalism exceeded that of anyone in Germany. He was completely unscrupulous, reckless, and vindictive. At one time there were one hundred and twenty-six libel suits pending against him. Once, long ago, he printed a headline in the *Angriff*, IS HINDENBURG STILL ALIVE? The President brought suit for libel and collected eight hundred marks damages. Retaliating, Goebbels wrote that Hindenburg was surrounded 'by Jews and Marxists'. (*Time*, August 13, 1934.)

At the end of 1939 Goebbels was still Reichsminister of Propaganda and Public Enlightenment. As such he was undisputed ruler of the Press in Germany and, something almost as important, ruler of the radio. He likewise controlled the theatre and the cinema, as well as most musical, artistic, cultural, and even scientific activities; he made the Reich a cultural prison, a Nazi vacuum, a country in a mental strait-jacket, for eighty million Germans.

Goebbels is also stage manager to the Nazi party. He invented the technique of the great mass meetings which helped so cardinally to bring Hitler votes. His tactics were simple. 'Propaganda has only one object,' he wrote, 'to conquer the masses. Every means that furthers this aim is good; every means that hinders it is bad.' He planned the strategy of incessant and unremitting attack. Thus the flaming decorations, the loud-speakers, the careful 'build-up' for Hitler's appearance, the marching, the uniforms.

Then, when Hitler was chancellor, he engineered the first incredible mob displays which so vehemently aroused the Nazis. He suggested the burning of the books; he organised the May Day and Harvest festivals; he superintended the *Winterhilfe* relief campaign. His supreme achievement was, however, the creation of the Horst Wessel legend. Out of a procurer he made a hero.

The youthful bravo named Horst Wessel, son of a Lutheran pastor, was one of the many rowdies who disfigured the Berlin streets before Hitler came to power. He became an SA troop commander, active in largely communist districts, and the communists hated him. Three hooligans, moved by personal as well as political reasons, went up to his room and shot him as he lay in bed. He refused to have a Jewish doctor who was summoned, and died of his wounds.

Goebbels saw in Horst Wessel's funeral, a perfect opportunity for propaganda on a large scale. But the police (this was way back in 1930) refused to permit an expansive demonstration. So Goebbels had to think of something else. Horst Wessel had written words to a street song, based on an old Bavarian tune, which was sung by Nazis and communists both. Goebbels decided to make capital of this song; and a good rousing tune it indeed is. Before a month had passed, the song was the unofficial Nazi hymn. Soon it was official. And Horst Wessel became, and still is, the first Nazi martyr.

Outwardly relations between Goebbels and Goering are correct, but they seldom miss opportunity for surreptitious digs at one another. Goering, as prime minister of Prussia, ruled the *Staatsoper* in Berlin. So Goebbels, undaunted, organised another opera in Berlin as a rival to Goering's opera. Goebbels is very jealous of his prerogatives. Putzi Hanfstaengl, late in 1933, was charged with the preparation of a film depicting the life of Horst Wessel. Goebbels succeeded first in temporarily banning the film, then in having its treatment altered and title changed, even though it was able Nazi propaganda as it stood.

Some Goebbels *obiter dicta*:

> 'I know it is a sacrifice for us not to have a new war.'
> 'Our Brown Shirts saved France from Bolshevism, and even now with its Stavisky scandal and Paris street riots, things are not in order there.'
> 'Hitler's attack on the democratic spirit is merely the opening act of a development the end of which will be a National Socialist Europe.'
> 'War is the most simple affirmation of life. Suppress war, and it would be like trying to suppress the processes of nature.'
> 'Germany marches with Hitler's *Mein Kampf* in one hand and the sword in the other. Book and sword shall be the symbols of our national life.'

Control the Press of a nation and half the job of dictatorship is done. Goebbels has given living strength to the authority of this maxim. As supreme dictator of the printed word in the Third Reich, nothing may be published in Germany without his consent. He is at liberty to censor even the words of fellow cabinet ministers.

In June 1934 he prevented full publication of Papen's Marburg speech; in August 1935 he censored Dr. Schacht's similar warning to extremists at Königsberg; in the same month he forbade the broadcasting of Streicher's Jew-baiting rally in Berlin. No journalist may find employment in Germany till Dr. Goebbels certifies his acceptability; no newspaper may publish anything without his consent. Incidental result: 1,400 German newspapers, about *one-third* of the total number in the Reich, have perished since 1933.

Goebbels has kept his footing partly because Hitler needs him, partly because of his supernal shrewdness. His nose is sharp, and his instinct for self-preservation immense. He flatters those who, he thinks, are of use to him, and he never says anything against those who at the moment are powerful. When crisis brews, as on June 30, Goebbels will be found on Hitler's shadow.

Dr. Goebbels is the spiritual source of such a medley of violent nonsense as the modern world has seldom seen. For instance listen to Professor Herman Gauch, author of the Nazi tract, *New Bases of Racial Research*:

'In non-Nordics, the teeth, corresponding to the snout-like narrowness of the upper jaw, stand at a more oblique angle than in animals. The grinding motion of chewing in Nordics allows mastication to take place with the mouth closed, whereas men of other races are inclined to make the same smacking noise as animals. . . .

'The Nordic mouth has further superiorities. Just as the colour red has a stirring effect, the bright red mouth of Nordics attracts and provokes kisses and courtship. The Nordic mouth is kiss-capable. On the other hand, the non-Nordic's broad, thick-lipped mouth together with his wide-dilated nostrils displays sensual eagerness, a false and malicious sneering expression and a dipping movement indicative of voluptuous self-indulgence.

'Talking with the aid of hands and feet is characteristic of non-Nordics, whereas the Nordic man stands calmly, often enough with his hands in his pockets.

'Generally speaking, the Nordic race alone can emit sounds of untroubled clearness, whereas among non-Nordics the pronunciation is impure, the individual sounds are more confused and like the noises made by animals, such as barking, sniffing, snoring, squeaking.

'If non-Nordics are more closely allied to monkeys and apes than to Nordics, why is it possible for them to mate with Nordics and not with apes? The answer is this. It has not been proved that non-Nordics cannot mate with apes.'

No detail is too small for Dr. Goebbels's men. For instance, this attack on the alien lemon:

'Farewell, lemon, we need thee not! Our German rhubarb will take thy place fully and entirely. He is so unpretending that we overlooked and despised him, busy with infatuation for foreign things. In all our shires we can have him in masses, the whole year round. We get him almost for nothing; his tartness will season our salads and vegetable dishes. Slightly sweetened he provides us with delicious refreshment, and, what is more, he is a blood-purifying and medicinal agent true to German type. Let us make good with German rhubarb the sins we have committed with the alien lemon.'

—(*The Times*, July 29, 1935.)

But it is unspeakable tragedy rather than racial or citric nonsense that Goebbels, above all, stands for. He is the organiser of the worst excesses of Nazi anti-Semitism.

When Austria fell to Germany, 300,000 Austrian Jews fell to the Nazis. A series of drastic measures thereupon implemented the Nuremberg laws. Jews were barred from being real estate agents, travelling salesmen, or accountants; they were forbidden to enter the Stock Exchange or visit their safety deposit vaults—if any— without police escort. Landlords had to expel Jewish doctors, and in most cities Jews could not live in apartments facing main streets. Jews were excluded from state schools and universities, from park benches, from bathing beaches, even from shops at certain hours. Jewish children in particular suffered revolting tortures. One law obliged every Jew to adopt the name Sarah or Israel, and Jews were restricted in future to a short list of given names. This list, incidentally, did not include Mary. Nor did it include Joseph or Paul —which are Dr. Goebbels's own given names.

In November 1938 came the shooting of the German diplomat Von Rath by the Jewish boy Herschel Grynszpan. Again terrible outrages against Jews occurred. The Jews were barred from all economic activity in the Reich, and at the same time collectively fined 1,000,000,000 marks. They were ordered to make good all the damage done by the rioting Nazis, damage estimated at some 13,000,000 marks; meantime their insurance claims were cancelled. In February 1939 all Jews in Germany were ordered to give up their jewellery and similar valuables. Later—strange detail—they were forbidden to own carrier pigeons!

Goebbels is not a Jew, but his appearance is un-Aryan, to say the least. His enemies in the party have often pointedly but in circumlocutory fashion referred to the dangerous racial aspects of lame or deformed men, those with club feet in particular. Goebbels's reply was a minor masterpiece. He found an anthropologist who invented a classification in Aryan ethnology to apply to himself alone—*Nachgedunkelter Schrumpfgermane.* This is hard to translate. An approximate rendering: 'A dwarf-like German who grew dark.'

CHAPTER VI

THE OTHER LITTLE HITLERS

'We interpret treaties as we think right. We do not submit to the judgment of others.'

—ADOLF HITLER.

'The methods by which a people forces its way upwards are of no moment. Only the goal is important.'

—DR. GOEBBELS.

The Perfect Bureaucrat—Frick

LESS publicised than either, Dr. Wilhelm Frick is, after Goering and Goebbels, the most powerful Nazi office-holder. He was appointed minister of the interior for the Reich in Hitler's first cabinet, and he has held this office ever since. Thus he controls the civil administration of Germany, and his influence is strong in the schools, the public services and the police.

Born in the Palatinate in 1877, Frick studied law and became a *Beamter*, an official. He is a bureaucrat through and through. Hitler is not intimate with him, but he respects him. He became minister of the interior because he was the only important Nazi with civil service training. Precise, obedient, uninspired, he turned out to be a faithful executive; he has been called the 'only honest Nazi'.

Yet no one should think that this dry, so-typical German *Beamter* is not capable of great, exhilarating Nazi words and deeds. It was Frick who drafted the Aryan law defining Jewishness unto the third generation. It was Frick, a cabinet minister in Thuringia, who enforced compulsory prayers on all school-children: hate-prayers for the destruction of the Treaty of Versailles. And in the Reichstag, as the senior Nazi deputy, Frick once introduced a law for the castration of homosexuals (cf. *Heil*, p. 69). Frick has always been on the side of the conservatives in the party, like Goering.

A fierce intra-party battle for the control of cultural affairs has been waged. Goebbels asserts that all art is propaganda and therefore belongs to him. Rosenberg holds that art is *Weltanschauung* and should thus be in his province. Goering, as boss of Prussia, feels that art is the prerogative of the executive authority, and therefore his. Rust, minister of education, would like culture as part of his domain, but being only a lion of the second magnitude, he is silent while the others roar. And Frick, the while, holds on to all he can.

His seven precepts for the education of the young are powerfully nationalist. And German school books—a profoundly important point—are compact with an appallingly militant, aggressive, pan-German propaganda.

Hess The Indispensable

Rudolf Hess, born in Alexandria, Egypt, in 1896, is the Führer's personal deputy, the deputy-leader of the party, and Reichsminister without portfolio. When Goering, after the murder of Schleicher, underwent a temporary period of severe unpopularity with the Reichswehr, Hess—had he been bold and assertive enough—might have taken his position. But the talents of Hess lie otherwise. He is the private secretary *par excellence,* the watchdog, the faithful servant. Hess, like so many others, was converted to Hitlerism on first hearing the Leader speak; like Goering and Ley, he was a flying officer during the War. He was the first 'gentleman' to join the Nazi party, and he became Hitler's secretary in 1923. For a time he had been secretary to the influential and mysterious Professor Haushofer, the geographer.

The strength of Hess lies in his closeness to Hitler. He has no government department, but, a cabinet minister himself, he acts as a co-ordinator between the other ministries. Hitler has given him several thankless jobs: for instance the onus of making the first public apologia for the murders of June 30. It is very difficult to get to Hitler on any political or party business except through Hess. His office is thronged with office-seekers and it has been nicely termed the *Klagemauer* (Wailing Wall) of the Third Reich. When the Polish campaign began Hitler said that Hess, after Goering, would be his successor.

Hess has recorded that in Alexandria he became a nationalist, during the War a socialist, and in Munich after the War an anti-Semite. Therefore his soul was ripe for Hitler's seed. His anti-Semitism is rigorous and extreme. During his Egyptian years, incidentally, he came very much under Arab influence.

Hess is retiring in character, genuinely modest, and very popular.

At every *Parteitag* in Nuremburg (annual Nazi congress) he receives the biggest applause next to Hitler: far more from the Nazi rank-and-file than Goering, Goebbels, Rosenberg, or Frick. His whole life is devoted to Hitler. His only outside interest is faith-healing, and he has founded a hospital in Dresden devoted to cures by means that scientific medicine does not recognise.

Hitler appointed him to become the head of the political section of the Nazi party in the fall of 1932, after the disgrace of Strasser. Previously, except in Hitler's intimate circle, he had been little known. The appointment was sound politics. With his usual perspicacity, Hitler chose as his deputy the one man in Germany who was not ambitious for a better job. Yet Hess's control of the party *machine* is an important political factor.

Hess was named as the German official who collaborated with Trotsky for the overthrow of the U.S.S.R. in the Moscow treason trial of January 1937. Strange as it may seem.

Boss of the Black Shirts

Heinrich Himmler wears pince-nez and looks like a schoolmaster. He is one of the most sinister personalities in the new Germany. He is two things, first Reich commander of the SS (Black Shirts), second, head of the entire German police, including the Gestapo, or secret police. He is the Boss of Terror, despite his mild appearance. He has informally told the world that in the event of an attempt on Hitler's life, even if it is unsuccessful, there will be chaos in Germany and 'a great pogrom'.

Born in Munich in 1900, Himmler, like so many of his colleagues, belonged to a nationalist gang of guerilla fighters; like Brückner, Goering, Streicher, Hess and other prominent leaders, he took part in the *Putsch* of 1923. In 1927 he became deputy leader of the SS, which was being formed by Hitler as a counterweight to the SA of Roehm. In 1929 he became Supreme leader of the SS, and in 1934 chief of the political police.

The SS, as we have seen, are the picked Nazi forces. Himmler himself has said, 'The SA is the Line, the SS are the Guards.' Every SS man must obey especially strict standards of discipline; he must be of satisfactory height and appearance; he may not marry until he and his bride are certified by Himmler's Eugenics Bureau as irreproachably Aryan and healthy potential parents.

This man, holding in his person the double job of policeman and SS ruler, fulfils an important function. The Gestapo and SS between them are invincible. The police arrest people. The SS guard them in concentration camps. Himmler is all-powerful at each end. He is policeman, judge, guard, and—if necessary— executioner. Besides, he is a convenient instrument for the civil side of the party, in that he can obey secret orders and fulfil them, while the government officially disclaims 'knowledge' of what he does.

Himmler almost never makes speeches. Of all the Nazi luminaries he is the least known. The man 'behind' him is said to be an even more sinister character, by name Heydrich, an ex-naval officer.

Bodyguard

Lieut. Brückner, the chief bodyguard, officially known as Adjutant to the Führer is, as befits his post, one of the huskiest men in Germany. He is at least six foot four and a tremendous specimen of agile muscularity. Brückner is never far from Hitler. He sleeps just outside Hitler's room. He was born in Baden-Baden in 1884 and, like Himmler, joined a corps of nationalist volunteers after the War. He and the Leader, as we have noted, are inseparable; Brückner was the man at Hitler's side when he arrested Roehm. He is in the SA not SS, with the rank of brigadier-general.

Nuremberg Jew-Fancier

Of all the leading Nazis, Julius Streicher is the most notorious. This rapacious anti-Semite, the Reichscommissar for Franconia, is a man of fifty-four, barrel-chested, shaven-headed, in appearance the incarnation of brutality. According to *Heil*, in July 1933 he ordered two hundred and fifty Jews who had been arrested to pluck grass out of a field with their teeth.

Streicher organised the anti-Jewish boycott held in Berlin in April 1933 just after the Nazis came to power. This was one great show that Dr. Goebbels did not put on. It was not repeated. Streicher publishes a weekly newspaper, *Der Stürmer*, solid with viciously revolting and pornographic anti-Semite propaganda. Once he issued a special 'Ritual Murder' issue. It caused such a storm of protest in the outside world—by the Archbishop of Canterbury for instance—that it had to be suppressed in Germany.

Streicher is quoted by the American magazine *Time* (April 8, 1935) as follows:

'With my riding-whip, I sometimes give it to prisoners I have had

G

taken into protective custody to save them from the mob. Take that school-teacher Dr. Steinruck who used to talk so big! I went with several Party members into his cell. He began to talk with a weeping voice and acted like a schoolboy. He did not act like the man I had expected after so much big talk, so I gave him a good thrashing with my whip.'

On his fiftieth birthday the local authorities made him a picturesque gift—the dossier in the archives of the Nuremberg police which 'formerly might have been used against him as incriminating material'. Streicher's proudest boast is that he has cleared one Franconian district, Hersbruck, comprising thirty-six villages and 22,000 inhabitants, entirely of Jews. Not a single Jew remains. Everywhere in Franconia the terror against the Jews proceeds with miserable ferocity. Streicher's ultimate solution of the Jewish problem is to castrate all Jews.

His general culture is not too brilliant. When he came to Berlin in August 1935 to speak at the Sport-Palast meeting he said: 'The great Jew who lived in England, Benjamin Disraeli, became Premier. Later he was elevated to the peerage under the name of Lord Gladstone.'

It is no use, as some sympathisers do, saying that Hitler personally 'deplores' Streicher's blood-thirsty brutality. Hitler does not deplore it. He has been given every opportunity to get rid of Streicher. He refuses to do so. Streicher is one of his oldest supporters. Streicher joined him in 1923, having first formed a rival 'workers' party. Hitler has commended him highly and in public. Only *two* Nazis are mentioned by name in the whole of *Mein Kampf*: Hess and—Streicher. And when Streicher turned fifty, Hitler specially flew to Nuremberg from Berlin to pay him a surprise birthday visit.

Two Lesser Lights

Count Wolf von Helldorf, appointed police chief in Berlin during the second wave of Nazi terror against the Jews, in July 1935, has a peculiar qualification for his post: he was himself sentenced to jail in 1931 for leading a violent anti-Semitic demonstration on the same street, Kurfürstendamm, where the new riots, which he was appointed to 'clean up', occurred.

Baldur von Schirach is the leader of the Youth Movement. He was born in 1907, and is married to the daughter of Heinrich Hoffman, who is Hitler's personal photographer. He is fanatically devoted to Hitler, given even to writing verses to him. He is interested in religion. Recently he said, 'The Nazi party has been proved to have better relations with the Lord of the Heaven than had the Christian parties which disappeared.' And note well: Von Schirach, like several other Nazis who mingle religion with nationalism, has become a pagan.

Two Radicals

These, though their names are seldom heard outside Germany, are among the most important Nazis. They are Dr. Robert Ley, chief of the trade unions and leader of the German labour front, and R. Walter Darré, 'Peasant Leader' and Reichs minister for agriculture. Both are known as 'radicals'.

Darré, born in Buenos Aires[1] in 1895, is something of a scholar. He entered the inner ranks of Nazi nobility not by way of freebooting and brawls in Munich but—very late from the hierarchical point of view—as an agrarian expert. He had been a civil servant in the ministry of agriculture. He was hoisted into office after Hugenberg faded out. Promptly he initiated an ambitious series of agricultural reforms, and to him credit is due for almost all the 'socialist' measures the Nazi government has undertaken. Darré arranged a price-fixing scheme for grain, and he inaugurated the Hereditary Farms Act, by which old-established peasant holdings may not be sold or mortgaged, but must pass in entail to descendants of the owners.

Darré was a little too quick for his superiors. And they frowned at what they called his lack of modesty and tact when, a few months after taking office, he caused a monument to be erected to himself at Wiesbaden, marked 'Blood and Soil', and himself made a speech at its dedication. The party, however, has no cause to complain of his racial zeal. Darré is the author of the celebrated scheme to divide all the women of the Reich into eugenic classes, like cattle, for breeding purposes.

Dr. Robert Ley, the leader of the trade unions, somewhat unbridled in character, went to Geneva, before Germany left the League, to attend a meeting of the International Labour Office, and before an audience partly composed of South Americans made a remarkable speech denouncing inhabitants of several South American republics as uncivilised 'idiots'. He was a pilot during the War, and entered the party early. When Strasser was disgraced,

[1] Another chieftain—like Hess—not German by birth. Also Rosenberg.

in November 1932, Ley and Hess together succeeded to his posts. To Hitler he is unswervingly loyal, and so the Leader keeps him.

Ley's grandiloquence is notable. Listen: 'We begin with the child when he is three years old. As soon as he begins to think, he gets a little flag put in his hand; then follows the school, the Hitler Jugend, the SA and military training. We don't let him go; and when adolescence is past, then comes the *Arbeitsfront* which takes him again and doesn't let him go till he dies, whether he likes it or not.'

The Warriors

The immensity of German military strength, both material and spiritual, is no longer news to anybody. Rearmament was covert until October 1933, when Germany left the League; an open secret until March 1935, when Hitler tore up the military clauses of Versailles and introduced conscription; since March 1935 the Reich has been an enormous military camp, with no disguise about it.

As well as anything else, a little joke best summarised the covert period. Frau X asks her husband, a worker in a perambulator factory, to procure her a baby-carriage. He promises to filch the parts, piece by piece, from the factory. Some months later they have all been stolen, and Herr X sets to work putting them together. He turns finally to his wife in puzzled despair: 'I have put the thing together three different times, and each time it turns out to be a machine-gun.'

This era is long past. For a time, it is true, the Germans laboured under certain disadvantages. There was difficulty in the import of essential raw materials. The air force grew enormously but even as late as 1937 there were severe shortages of heavy guns and tanks. On the other hand, marvellous technical proficiency plus a centralised direction of effort produced extraordinary results. The navy expanded. The Reichswehr was enlarged to a 'peace' strength of 850,000 men. According to Winston Churchill, the country by 1938 was spending the stupendous sum of £800,000,000 annually on armament.

The minister of war until early 1938 was Col.-General Werner Eduard Fritz von Blomberg. Born in 1878 at Stargard in Pomerania, he came of a distinguished officers' family. He entered the army and for a long time his promotion was very slow. He was second lieutenant in 1897, first lieutenant in 1907, captain in 1911, and only colonel in 1925. After 1928 his rise was extremely rapid. He was major-general in 1928, lieutenant-general in 1929, full general in 1930, minister of defence in 1933, colonel-general (the highest German rank except field-marshal) in 1934.

He was by no means a typical Prussian officer. Pleasant, cordial, calm, rather soft in manner, he seemed the last remove from a martinet, a goose-stepper. He spoke languages and has travelled widely; in 1930 he took a vacation in the United States.

The importance of Blomberg was that he was deeply, passionately devoted to Hitler. He was a *begeisterter Nazi*, quite different from those officers who, granting that Hitler is a convenience, found much that was offensive in his fanaticism. Blomberg was an ardent, convinced, *personal* Hitlerite.[1]

He had known Hitler well only since 1933. His appointment as minister of war came in odd fashion. There was some difficulty in finding a man, on account of the sharp clash between Schleicher and the Nazis. One of Hitler's best friends was, and is, Ludwig Müller,[2] then a military chaplain in the division which Blomberg was commanding. He recommended Blomberg to Hitler, and through this priestly intermediary Blomberg got the job. Then Müller, as reward, was made Reichsbishop of the Protestant Church in Germany!

Under Blomberg for a long time was General Werner Freiherr von Fritsch, the chief of army direction (*Chef der Hereesleitung*), i.e. commander-in-chief. Fritsch was a quite different type from Blomberg. He was the complete army man. Nothing meant anything to him except the army. He represented exclusively the army point of view. Blomberg, it was said in Germany in the old days, was 'Hitler-loyal'; Fritsch was 'Fatherland-loyal'. Fritsch did not want the Reichswehr to be increased to as many as 850,000 men. He thought this was too much. He was a firm believer in the Seeckt principle: of an army like a flail, a sword; an army not too big, but

[1] For Blomberg's sudden dismissal from the Ministry of War see Chapter VIII below.

[2] One of Müller's feats was production of a new Nazi version of the Sermon on the Mount. In the King James Bible, for instance, Matthew v. 9, reads as follows: 'Blessed are the peacemakers; for they shall be called the children of God.' The Nazi 'translation' is: 'Happy are they who keep the peace with *their fellow-nationals* (italics mine); they do God's will.'

perfectly tempered, perfectly trained, superlatively supple, swift, sure.

When Blomberg went, Fritsch went too—though for a different reason. For a time he lived in strict retirement, nursing his grievances. He was such a valuable officer, however, that he was rehabilitated in August 1938, and given a small command. But other generals had taken control of the army as a whole, like the redoubtable Ludwig Beck (who, however, subsequently followed Fritsch into retirement). In the fighting before Warsaw Fritsch was mysteriously killed. His friends say that he was so heartsick that he wanted death. But rumours have not been lacking to the effect that Nazis murdered him.

Hitler reorganised the army command with himself as supreme leader. There is no minister of war. He is like the Kaiser, the all-high chief. Then comes Colonel General von Keitel, a kind of administrative officer in charge of liaison to the three heads of the fighting services, Marshal Goering for air, Admiral Raeder for the navy, and Colonel General Heinrich Walther von Brauchitsch for the army. Brauchitsch was born in 1889, the son of a general. He served on the General Staff in the Great War, and has had a routine career. He has never played an important political role, as have so many German generals.

Hitler and the Reichswehr

Is Hitler dependent on the Reichswehr for support? Yes. But is not the Reichswehr loyal to Hitler? Again yes. Indeed, the question that is so often asked is rather pointless, viz. which, as between Hitler and the Reichswehr, is really boss in Germany. The fact is that both rule Germany. And so long as their aims are identical little chance of conflict between them exists.

The Reichswehr is a necessity to Hitler, but also Hitler is a necessity to the Reichswehr. Each needs the other. They are complements. The Reichswehr wants a strong, united Germany and Hitler is incomparably the strongest man in the country. The alternative to him is either an overt military dictatorship or chaos. The Reichswehr has no need of an overt military dictatorship, which would be unpopular, as long as Hitler does its job. And it certainly does not want chaos.

Moreover, one should not forget the oath that every officer and soldier in the army swore to Hitler personally. Prussian officers and soldiers do not break their word of honour lightly.

On the other hand, should the Reichswehr betray Hitler, he is doomed.

Do not, finally, forget that the Reichswehr, from the very beginning, supported Hitler. Reichswehr money made the first party organisation and the early *Völkische Beobachter* possible. And Hitler began 'public' life as a Reichswehr spy.

CHAPTER VII

WAR, PEACE, POLICY, AND CASH

'The Germans do not want a war; all they want are the rewards of victory.'
—JULES CAMBON.

ON March 7, 1936, with flamboyant suddenness, Hitler sent his troops into the Rhineland, provoking what was in a sense the greatest European crisis since 1919. By terms of the peace treaties the Rhineland zone was to have been demilitarised in perpetuity. Germans—with much justice—resented bitterly the 'inequality' thus symbolised between themselves and the other powers. But Hitler not only invaded the Rhineland; by so doing he automatically tore up the Treaty of Locarno, which had been a bastion of European peace since 1925, through its guaranty by Britain and Italy of both sides of the Franco-Belgian-German frontier. Inviolability of the Rhineland zone was part of the Locarno Treaty. And Hitler's destruction of this treaty split Europe open like a rotten melon.

Some of the French wanted to march; and didn't quite have the nerve. Most of the British wanted to temporise—and did. The Italians, annoyed by sanctions in the Abyssinian crisis, refused to join Britain, France, and Belgium in a united Locarno 'front'. As was inevitable, Italy and Germany—long separated by their quarrel over Austria—tended to come together. The Belgians,[1] led by a man who quickly gained great respect through Europe, Paul van Zeeland, were especially exasperated by the crisis. Not only was Belgium virtually defenceless, as in 1914, against the enormous might of Germany, but Hitler had defended the Rhineland coup on the pretext that the Franco-Soviet pact of mutual assistance, which was about to be ratified in Paris, was itself a violation of the Treaty of Locarno. But Belgium was as much endangered by the new situation as was France, and with the Franco-Soviet pact Belgium had nothing whatever to do.

A great concourse of statesmen met in London to patch up the matter. They were confronted, of course, with the ancient and

[1] For Belgium see Chapter XXXV, below.

honourable problem of how to lock the stable door after the horse
had fled. For ten days they wrangled to find a formula for settlement. British opinion, at first sharply pro-German, veered to
realisation of the future disasters implicit in Hitler's treaty
breaking. In the end Herr von Ribbentrop, then the German
ambassador-at-large, accepted an academic rebuke by the League
Council in return for consideration of a 'peace' plan which the
Leader had announced. Hitler, that incredible creature, meantime publicly told the world what he really was—a somnambulist!
—and received a 98.81 per cent vote of confidence from the German
people.

The Peace Plan proposed (a) a twenty-five years non-aggression
pact between Germany, France, and Belgium, (b) a western air
pact, (c) 'moral' disarmament, (d) an eastern security pact including Lithuania but excluding Soviet Russia, (e) return to the
League by Germany if these and other conditions were fulfilled,
(f) abolition of heavy tanks and heavy artillery. There was also an
amazing incidental Hitlerism—a suggestion that not only Germany but *France* should hold a plebiscite on these issues. Also
included was a reference to colonial equality within a reasonable
time.

Careful scrutiny of the Plan showed at once that its face value
might be high, its inner value dubious. Non-aggression pacts—
there have been some two hundred in the post-War years—have not
proved effective. Mutual assistance pacts Hitler eschewed—because they might be effective. The pacts he proposed, it seemed,
would have two effects, to allow him to take on enemies one by one,
and to freeze the western frontiers so that his hands would be free
for the East. Hitler's enmity to the Soviet Union—at that time—
seemed subcutaneous and ineffaceable. Suggestions for 'moral
disarmament', including suppression of publications and educational books making for bad feeling between France and Germany,
came strangely, to say the least, from the country where the
Stürmer is published and where implacably nationalist militarism
is hammered daily into the young. A western air pact on a quanti-
tative basis was, most experts considered, a technical impossibility,
and Hitler's proposal for it a mere gesture. As to tanks and heavy
artillery, these were precisely the weapons in which Germany was
weakest; therefore let them be abolished! Above and beyond
all this was the question of Hitler's good faith. What, in effect,
he was doing was to promise not to violate any more treaties

immediately after flagrantly tearing one up—and at the same time denying that he had done so.

A tedious and nerve-wracking period of diplomatic jockeying and bargaining ensued. Hitler's victory was complete in that he got what he wanted, the militarisation of the Rhineland. But an emphatic White Paper of the Locarno powers told him, to his annoyance, that Britain and France were provisionally bound by what amounted to a defensive military alliance against German aggression, and talks between the General Staffs of the two countries began. Mr. Eden then sent a questionnaire to Berlin, and a highly important document it was. As a manifest of Hitler's good faith it asked—politely but very firmly—if he were prepared to include Soviet Russia in his eastern pact, and what assurances he could give of the sanctity of future treaties. The questionnaire put Hitler in a tight spot, and rudely he never answered it.

Meantime, the thoughtful sought to digest a sentence from his March 14 speech: 'I do not believe that there can be peace among the nations until they all have the same law and system of law. That is why I hope that National Socialism will one day extend over the world. That is no fantastic dream, but an achievable object.'

Rome-Berlin Axis and Anti-Comintern Pact

In September 1936 the British tentatively suggested conversations towards a new Locarno; the German answer was indecisive. Again in January 1937 Mr. Eden sought to open negotiations; again the Germans quibbled and delayed. Two events of major importance meantime occurred, serving to push Hitler to different tangents. Both gave the democracies of the world cause for legitimate alarm.

1. On November 25, 1936, Germany and Japan announced suddenly the conclusion of what was soon known at the Anti-Comintern Pact. The agreement, directed 'against the communist international', was to last five years; it bound Germany and Japan to consultation and collaboration and established a permanent committee, 'both investigative and defensive', against the Comintern; Ambassador Ribbentrop who signed it on behalf of Germany called it 'an epoch-making event, a turning-point in the defensive struggle of all nations loving order and civilisation'. The Pact was, of course, short-lived. Though we did not know this then.

The Russo-German agreement in the summer of 1939 killed it deader than Cheops.

2. Something that came to be called the 'Rome-Berlin axis' evolved. This was not a formal treaty between Hitler and Mussolini, but a gradual approximation of their policies. Germany and Italy commenced a period of very close co-operation; they intervened in Spain together and they recognised the Franco 'government' in identical notes sent the same day. Goering, Blomberg, Neurath, visited Rome; Mussolini presently went to Germany, and Hitler later repaid his visit.

Soon the axis became a triangle, when Italy joined the Anti-Comintern Pact as an original signatory. But for further developments in this direction we must await Chapter VIII.

Before the Deluge

It was said in pre-1939 days, on the basis of several arguments, that war was impossible for Hitler. Let us explore in retrospect.

First, it was said that Germany was too poor to make a war. But poverty has never prevented conflict. It may make the war hard to carry on, but a desperate country, already poverty-stricken, has less to lose by war than the rich countries which oppose it.

Second, it was argued that Germany didn't have raw materials enough to make a war. The answer to this is she probably had as good an equipment of war materials in 1939 as in 1914 when, despite the blockade, she managed to fight a very good war for four long years.

Third, it was said that opposition to Hitler within the Reich was too strong; that the workers would not mobilise; that they would shoot in the wrong direction. But the lesson of the totalitarian state is that each year it stays in power the strength of opposition lessens. Look at Soviet Russia. And look at Mussolini's success in Abyssinia. 'Good propaganda,' Frances Gunther expressed it, 'can make anything popular—even death.'

On the other hand, Germany's will to war was shown by an impressive list of factors. For one thing, the creation of the new German army and air force. For another, the fact that essential German ambitions to expand in the East or in Central Europe could only be achieved by war. Underground aggression in Austria, threats against Lithuania, agitation and intrigue among Germans everywhere—in Switzerland, Holland, Czechoslovakia, Jugoslavia, Scandinavia, the Baltic states—indicated the latent explosive force of the Nazi revolution. All the frontiers of Germany tingled from the aggressive strain inside.

Again, Naziism, essentially a militarist creed, produced in Germany a renascence of incorrigibly belligerent Wotanism that was apt to burst outward whether Hitler so desired or not. This factor was intensified by the possibility of economic breakdown. The lesson of the Abyssinian war seems to have been that dictatorships, if they are in danger of breaking down, break out. Thus the steady German advance against Austria, the Sudetenland, and Poland.

Post-War Germany is one of the Have-Nots, since Germany lost the War. But her policy was not only to regain what she lost, which would have been fair enough, but much more. It is a paramount item in the Nazi creed that all contiguous Teutons should be incorporated into the Third Reich. This meant Austria, and then the Germans of Czechoslovakia, Poland, Denmark, Holland, and perhaps—eventually—the Italian Tyrol. For Naziism stands for renascent pan-Germanism or nothing.

Germany's will to expand is to be explained not so much by increase in the birth-rate but by 'moral' factors: Germany's right to a place in the sun, Germany's bursting energy demanding outlet. The birth-rate is not, in long perspective, increasing but actually decreasing; according to present estimates the population of Germany (within 1938 frontiers) will be only about 49,000,000 in 1975. As to the necessity of expansion it is illuminating to recall that in 1914 the total population of Germans in the German colonies was only about 25,000, which was fewer than the number of German residents in, of all places, Paris.

Hitler, confronted by a hostile world, had to survey his objectives with great caution. One should remember that Germany had gone a long way towards redressing the injustices of Versailles before he came to power. Foreign military control was abolished early in the Weimar republic. The Rhineland was evacuated of foreign garrisons under Stresemann. Reparations disappeared under Brüning and Papen. And the allies accepted Germany's theoretical right to military equality under Papen-Schleicher.

Hitler continued the process, by introducing conscription, reacquiring the Saar, occupying the Rhineland with troops, and denouncing the war-guilt clauses of the Versailles Treaty. Concurrently, he left the League of Nations and gave up German claims on the Polish Corridor for ten years (because it was temporarily essential for him, hemmed in, to come to terms with Poland). His progress cost him a good deal. He was, for a time, about as popular internationally as smallpox. He alienated Mussolini, who might have been his friend; he frightened and annoyed Denmark, Holland, Switzerland; he united France, 'because the French Right hates Germany, the Left hates Hitler'; he temporarily knit the Soviet Union, the Little Entente, and France into an alliance against him. He thought to counter-balance all this by gaining British friendship. His whole plan was that England should cover the German rear. But his plan—failed.

Hitler himself has said:

> 'It must be understood that in general the will of the German nation should no longer be limited to mere passive defence, but, on the contrary, should be steeled for a final, active settlement with France in a death grapple for the realisation of German aims.
>
> 'In the annihilation of France, Germany sees merely the means for our nation to obtain full development in another direction. Our foreign policy will only have been correct when there are two hundred and fifty million Germans, not crowded like coolies in a factory, but free peasants and workers.
>
> 'Almighty God, bless our weapons! Judge if we have merited freedom. Lord, bless our combat!'[1]

The dilemma for the rest of the world was obvious, and like all obvious dilemmas perplexing in the extreme—to allow Germany to become strong but not too strong. Germany should, manifestly, have been allowed recovery of her self-respect. But Germany grew so strong that promptly it demanded a new war as price for former defeat. The situation was maddening. Germany had been 'unjustly' treated. Granted. The Germans had a perfectly good case, in that the allies foisted on the world the myth of exclusive warguilt, invaded the Ruhr, and themselves refused to disarm in accordance with the terms of the treaty which they imposed on Germany. Granted. But it is interesting to note that Germany was just as militaristic in 1914 when it could not complain of 'unjust' treatment.

The analogies between the international situation in the summer of 1914 and, say, the autumn of 1934 were, indeed, astounding. A homosexual *camarilla* surrounded Wilhelm II as it did Hitler.

---

[1] These passages are expurgated from the foreign editions of *Mein Kampf*. It may be argued that Hitler wrote them, in hot blood, twelve years ago. But he has steadily refused to repudiate them. And new editions of the book—inside Germany—continue to include them.

Wilhelm II talked of 'shining armour'; Hitler talked of 'race renascent'. Wilhelm II challenged Britain with a fleet; Goering challenged Britain with an air force. Lord Haldane went to Berlin in 1912 on a mission somewhat analogous to that of Sir John Simon in 1935. For Agadir, read Dollfuss; for Sarajevo, read—lots of things!

How difficult it is for a nation, like an individual, to keep from being itself!

Foreign Minister von Ribbentrop

I think we all have had a drop
Too much of Herr von Ribbentrop;
The name by which he'd better go
Is Herr von Ribben Trop de trop . . .

—MAURICE BARING.

In the early 30's Herr von Ribbentrop, the German foreign minister and in 1939 the man, who, on the whole, has more influence on the Führer than any living person, was virtually unknown. By 1938 he was certainly one of the most conspicuous public men in Europe and many lovers of peace thought that he was probably the most dangerous man alive. This was because he persistently told Hitler that Great Britain would not, under any circumstances, fight. Hitler trusted him—and on this basis pursued his adventures, confident that the British were only bluffing. And Ribbentrop was wrong.

Ribbentrop's first great coup in foreign policy was the Anglo-German naval treaty of 1935, which led him to believe that the British would always be easy to handle. This treaty was important for a variety of reasons: (1) It legalised German naval rearmament and permitted Germany to build a fleet one-third as great as the British fleet, which meant virtual naval parity between Germany and France. (2) It came directly after the declaration of an alleged 'united front' between Britain, France, and Italy at Stresa and helped to shatter it. (3) Britain, condemning Germany with one hand for creating an illegal army, with the other immediately gave permission for her to build a legal fleet—indication, the Germans said, that Britain was at long last on their side.

Joachim von Ribbentrop was born in 1893 in the Rhineland, the son of a colonel. He had an excellent education, partly in England, partly in Switzerland; he speaks French and English almost flawlessly. (This, incidentally, was something Hitler admired and it helped bring him close to Hitler; most of the men around the Leader are monolingual.) Young Ribbentrop emigrated to Canada at

eighteen. He had decided to make his own way in the new world.
For a time he worked, so the story goes, as a manual labourer in
steel construction; for a time it seems he was a clerk in a Montreal
bank.

The War came; Ribbentrop fled to avoid internment; on a
Dutch boat returning to Europe he hid in the coal bunkers to
escape arrest; he reached Germany and joined the army. He was
an officer on the eastern front and later on the staff of the war
ministry. After the War, he served in a minor capacity on the
German delegation to Paris, and then, deserting public affairs, he
went into the wine business. In 1920 he married Anna Henkel,
the heiress of Germany's biggest champagne manufacturer. His
'von' came, curiously enough, through adoption; some years after
his marriage he was adopted by a titled aunt, Fräulein von Ribbentrop of another branch of the family, who had no heirs.

His political importance began about 1930. Though not a Nazi
at first, he was an ardent nationalist; he met Hitler and the Führer
liked him. And this wealthy and polished young man, widely travelled and with such a knowledge of the world, might be useful.
He was. It was Ribbentrop, indeed, who helped engineer the meeting between Hitler and von Papen in the Cologne home of the
banker Schroeder in January 1933, which, as we have seen, made
Hitler's chancellorship possible. Hitler, grateful, began to be
attached to Ribbentrop.

In 1934 he began to use him on confidential diplomatic errands
and to sound out opinion in other countries. Gradually the 'Buro-
Ribbentrop' came into being, a sort of shadow foreign office behind
—or in front of—the official foreign office of von Neurath. Ribbentrop became first special commissioner for disarmament questions,
then ambassador-at-large. In 1936 he became ambassador to London, where he had a difficult and trying time. He had to explain
the extremities of German behaviour to the British, and perhaps
through misguided zeal he committed curious blunders—for instance giving the Nazi salute to King George VI. His too-forthright
raising of the colonial issue was rebuffed, and though he was ardently
taken up in pro-German circles, his mission as a whole failed.
Nevertheless, on the theory that he 'understood' the mysterious
British, Hitler promoted him to be foreign minister.

Ribbentrop has four children. For relaxation he plays the violin.
In general, his personality is amiable.

.   .   .   .

There should also be a word about Ribbentrop's predecessor as foreign minister, Baron Constantine von Neurath, who is now president of Hitler's state council. When Hitler became chancellor, President Hindenburg insisted that Neurath remain in the foreign ministry as a safeguard against Nazi extremism. Hitler learned to like him and respect his judgment. And he, apparently, learned to like Hitler. Curiously enough, he had also, like Ribbentrop, once been German Ambassador to London. Hitler cannot get over being fascinated by people who presumably 'know' the mysterious British.

Neurath was born in 1873 of a noble family in Württemberg. He studied law, then entered the diplomatic service, and experienced the normal promotions of a professional diplomatist. Always an arch-conservative—and spiritually at one with the Nazis even when he was not a Nazi—he made no pretence of deeply admiring the German republic when he served it at the Court of St. James's. It was Neurath, in a congress at Stuttgart in September 1937, who formulated a pan-German programme for Germans living outside the Reich. He denied the right of foreign governments to interfere with Nazi organisations abroad.

The Incredible von Papen

The influence of Franz von Papen, 'the breakfast chancellor',[1] who is Hitler's ambassador to Turkey, is still considerable. For a time he was in sharp eclipse. No wonder. His fundamental policy, the conception that he and the nationalists could control Hitler and keep him in order, had been a terrible error. His two closest associates, Jung and von Bose, were murdered in his own office. Glad to be rid of him (and Papen himself must have felt a certain relief to get outside of Germany!) Hitler dispatched him to Austria after the Dollfuss murder in July 1934. He 'came back' by negotiating the new Austro-German Agreement of July 1936.

Edgar Jung was a Munich lawyer, and Papen's dependence on him was extreme. Papen seldom had ideas of his own. Jung wrote most of his speeches, including the celebrated Marburg speech. This not only warned the Nazis to avoid extremism; it said that 'those who threaten with the guillotine are the first to fall under the axe'; naturally the Nazis were annoyed—and two weeks later Jung was dead.

[1] So called because of his 'diplomatic breakfasts', during which he did most of his business.

What is one to say about a man who can see his two best friends murdered for service on his behalf and then accept new office under the government that murdered them?

Papen's Marburg speech was not his only blunder in technique. Only a person of extreme lack of perception could have appointed Goering as his first assistant, as Papen did, and expect Goering—of all men!—to be a milksop.

Papen has, it is well known, a great reputation for poise, for grace, for suavity. But suavity in Papen reached a degree where it was a kind of blind incompetence, a self-assurance so monstrous that all reason, all caution, were obliterated.

He was born in 1879 in Werl in Westphalia. He was a lieutenant in a cavalry regiment. He married the wealthy daughter of Boch-Galhau, owner of a Saarland ceramics firm, and was transferred to a better regiment. In 1913 he went to Washington as military attaché. Promptly, as his job demanded, he engaged in espionage; but the job did not demand the terribly suave carelessness, the persistent 'charming' blundering, that distinguished him. In December 1915, before the United States entered the War, he and his colleague, Captain Boy-Ed, were expelled from the United States.

It was bad enough for Papen to be caught. But he let everyone else be caught. Captain von Rintelen, the well-known German agent, describes vividly, in a book called *The Dark Invader*, his horror at Papen's carelessness. The American secret service found in the desk of one of his secretaries the key to the German code. Thus the Americans were able to read German foreign office messages, for instance the one from Zimmerman suggesting an alliance between Germany and Mexico.

Papen had sailed for Germany. The ship was searched by the British authorities at Falmouth and his papers were seized—he thought a *laisser-passer* rendered him immune to search! The young German military attaché had most meticulously retained his cheque-books. In neat black ink, on stub after stub—one hundred and twenty-six in all—were found the names of German secret agents in America. Papen was pay-out man. The cheques linked him to dynamiters and saboteurs.

'No man has ever been caught so comprehensively, so drastically. Papen had recorded—and *preserved*—the most precise details of his transactions. He kept not only the cheque stubs but the cancelled cheques themselves, so that all the endorsements were available

H

for scrutiny and investigation. In addition, dozens of his semi-official letters were found, carefully filed and assorted in his baggage. One is aghast at the effrontery of a man who could tempt fate so.

Once bitten, twice shy. For ordinary mortals this adage may hold true, but not for Junker officers of the imperturbable suavity and self-confidence of Franz von Papen. On arriving in Berlin he was assigned to service as a liaison officer to the Turkish Army. The British captured Jerusalem. Captain von Papen fled—leaving his trunks behind! Here was discovered another treasury of documents, including more papers incriminating agents in America, which Papen *still* had not destroyed.

One great service to Germany, from the nationalist point of view, Papen performed; in basic importance it may outrank his preparation of the way for Hitler. Early in his chancellorship the German Steel Trust (*Vereinigte Stahlwerke A.G.*), the agglutination of heavy industry that is one of the most powerful industrial forces in the world, suffered a severe financial crisis. Friedrich Frick, the owner of the largest block of stock, dumped them on the market. It seemed at first that French steel interests might acquire them. This was intolerable to the industrial patriotism of the Germans. The Papen Government stepped in and took over Frick's shares; the German Government became—and still is—the largest shareholder in the greatest industrial concern in Germany.

Philosopher Rosenberg

From the point of view of underlying and eventual realities in foreign affairs, Alfred Rosenberg, 'the philosopher with the sour stomach', was for a time almost as important as Neurath, Ribbentrop, or Papen. Rosenberg is the *Nazi* specialist in foreign policy. He is one of Hitler's closest and most intimate associates; he is editor of Hitler's newspaper, the *Völkische Beobachter*; he heads the foreign political bureau of the Nazi party, and is 'director of philosophical outlook'[1] for the Reich.

Rosenberg is probably the most disliked man in Germany, next to Dr. Goebbels. His personality is unpleasant. He is a prude and a prig. He is suspicious, close-minded, arrogant, ingrown. Like Hitler, he is a bachelor and 'a moral athlete'. The Leader got probably fifty per cent of his ideology from him, so that it is important to

---

[1] The full title is imposing: *Beauftragter des Führers Zur Überwachung der weltanschaulichen Erziehung der nationalsozialistischen. Bewegung.*

see exactly what he stands for. He was born on January 12, 1893, in
Reval, which was then in Russia and which is now capital of the
border-state Esthonia. He is thus a Balt. Rosenberg's whole
philosophy, ideology, and career are based on a psychopathically
intense hatred of the Soviet Union. He studied architecture (as
Hitler wanted to) and for a time was an instructor in draftsmanship;
he went to school first in Riga, then in Moscow. The revolution
intervened and a period of mystery followed: some say Rosenberg
was drafted into the Russian army; others have it that he got across
the frontier, enlisted with German troops, and took part in the campaigns in East Prussia.

He arrived in Munich in 1919 where so many riff-raff of the wars
assembled. He was at that time more Russian than German; he
seemed to be just another White Russian refugee. He met Dietrich
Eckhart, the first 'poet' of the Nazi movement, and then Hitler.
Promptly he intoxicated Hitler's imagination by his dream of a
German empire in the East, and became the chief prophet of
German expansionism and imperialism.

Rosenberg is the nightmare dreamer of Naziism. When he
attempts to put his dreams into practice, he is a miserable, grotesque
failure. His only adventure into practical politics occurred in May
1933, when he took it upon himself to make a good-will visit to
England. One of his first acts was to lay a Swastika flag on the Ceno-
taph! The British, sensitive about such things, were indignant;
Rosenberg scurried back to Berlin, and has not been outside Germany since.

Rosenberg's major opus is an enormous book *Der Mythus des
Zwanzigsten Jahrhunderts* (Myth of the Twentieth Century). It is
a torpid, florid, gusty, grandiloquent discourse on race, politics, and
Germanism.

Goering's dislike of Rosenberg is notorious. At a party meeting
in Hamburg in 1925, he said to Gregor Strasser: 'Let that damned
Rosenberg tell us what he *did* do in Paris during the War.' In 1935
Rosenberg decided to erect a monument to the four thousand Saxons
slain by Charlemagne. For each Saxon he wanted to provide a
granite block of a peculiar sort, very old and pure geologically, found
only in North Prussia.[1] Goering heard of the plan and promptly
ordered that no stone of this kind might be quarried.

Rosenberg's strength is, like that of so many Nazis, his undeviating single-mindedness, his obsessive devotion to an *idée fixe*. With

[1] The Aryan principle applied to petrology!

Goering, it is the air force; with Streicher, the Jews; with Rosenberg, anti-Sovietism. Since the twin pacts between Germany and Russia in 1939, Rosenberg has had, of course, to keep quiet on this issue.

Unpopular as he is—except with Hitler—Rosenberg's influence is considerable. He is a party force of almost first magnitude. It was, for instance, his private bodyguard of SA, mostly composed of White Russian guardists, which Hitler chose for the delicate honour of standing guard on the dying Hindenburg. His strength is founded on Hitler's great affection for him and the Leader's dependence on his 'ideas'.

Cash and Credit

'Germany is Hitler, and Hitler is Dr. Schacht.'

—BERLIN SAYING.

Superficially it seemed that by the end of 1938 the Nazi régime had produced a considerable degree of economic recovery. This was caused mostly by the spur to industry of war preparations. Unemployment had practically disappeared; and the volume of industrial production was back almost to the 1929-30 level. But this not very substantial boom was only achieved at frightful cost. The economic fabric of the country stretched and sagged.

In 1929 German exports amounted to approximately 13,000,000,000 Reichsmarks. By 1933 they had fallen to a value of scarcely 5,000,000,000 Reichsmarks, and in 1934 to only 4,187,000,000. Germany had a passive trade balance for the first time in years in 1934, when it amounted to 400,000,000 marks. German industry, normally, lives by its foreign trade. Its foreign trade began to disappear on account of the high gold value of the Reichsmark, the increase of import restrictions abroad, and the international boycott.

Yet Germany had to continue to pay for imports. It needed imports of raw material desperately. It needed silk, rubber, nickel, manganese, chromium, tungsten, raw textiles, tin, copper, gasolene. Using every available facility of cash and credit, Germany bought immense stores of these goods. Purchases of such commodities as Swedish iron ore by the German Steel Trust mounted year by year. German imports of raw nickel—an essential war material—tripled between 1932 and 1935. And every effort was made to produce agricultural self-sufficiency, so that the Reich could feed itself despite blockade.

The search for *Ersatz* (substitute) materials was unceasing. Sugar from sawdust; flour from potato meal; gasolene from wood and coal; clothes from chemical fibre; tyres out of 'reclaimed' rubber; margarine from coal—these were some of the substitutes inflicted on hapless but patriotic Germans.

Wages were mercilessly deflated by means of forced payments to relief, the labour front, the air defence league, and so on. A bank clerk's salary, for instance, became 241.90 RM per month instead of 290.25 RM, purely as a result of 'voluntary' contributions. H. R. Knickerbocker found that a skilled workman, such as an expert joiner, earning 39 RM per week, very high for Germany, had to pay out no less than 10.95 RM in taxes.

Even so, where did Dr. Schacht get all the money from? He had the quadruple job of paying for imports, financing public work projects to relieve unemployment, meeting the cost of rearmament, and maintaining the ordinary budget of the government. His gold reserve dwindled almost to nothing; in 1939 the cover was 1.59 per cent. He defaulted on his foreign debt. He seemingly sucked the last cent out of the German taxpayer. Yet he needed money, money, money. The cost of the arms programme was estimated abroad at £600,000,000 per year. How meet such staggering bills?

It seemed, roughly speaking, that Schacht adopted two general courses. Internally, he juggled by financing the current business of the government with internal loans, from banks, insurance companies, and the like, which were bled almost empty. They were practically forced loans. He gave in return government I.O.U.s worth no more—and no less—than the government's promise to pay. These forced loans—together with minor items such as conversion at lower interest rates of former public loans—amounted, of course, to nothing less than the compulsory mobilisation of the wealth of the German people. What were the German people promised in return for their savings? Prosperity and peace. Yet the money went to finance a colossal war machine.

Externally Dr. Schacht performed even greater feats of financial jugglery. He seems to have been the first financier of the period to have seized on the idea that the position of a big debtor was better than that of creditor. He made immense capital out of the fact that Germany owed money. Schacht, beyond any doubt, is one of the ablest financial experts alive. He really understands money. What he did may have been unscrupulous, but it was brilliant. He made Germany 'the most successful fraudulent bankrupt in the history of the world'.

This happened because he contrived to pay for imports by getting his creditors to foot the bill. German firms owe money, of course, to England, France, Scandinavia, the United States. Exporters in these countries do business with Germany. Dr. Schacht said to them in effect: 'Buy from us, and then we can pay our debts. If you don't buy, we cannot pay.' He promulgated partial moratorium after moratorium; and at the same time threatened to cease payment entirely unless he got more business. He was saying: 'Buy from me, or you will get nothing at all, since I cannot finance my debts unless you lend me more.'

There are always people willing to throw good money after bad, and the situation became that Germany was in reality expanding its armament industry by new borrowings. The potential enemies of Germany in the next war, France, the small succession states, Great Britain, and even Soviet Russia, were financing the effort that Germany was making to destroy them. The process reached its most extreme phase when, in December 1934, the Bank of England granted a £750,000 credit to Germany in order 'to facilitate the mobilisation of German commercial credits', i.e. so that Germany might have means (new credit) to meet old debts—and build aeroplanes that can cross the English Channel in seven minutes.

Also Dr. Schacht performed complex miracles in the field of barter. He needed raw materials from the Balkans, for instance, and finally the last gold to pay for them was gone. This deterred Dr. Schacht not at all. He visited the Balkan capitals, and made arrangements whereby he paid for tobacco, cotton, minerals, with *goods*. The Balkan exporters (exporters in many other countries too, for instance South America) had large credits in frozen marks in Berlin; Dr. Schacht proposed to liquidate these marks by payment in German manufactured goods, particularly munitions. So Greece, for instance, traded a tobacco crop for a crop of guns. Naturally this increased German political as well as economic influence in the Balkan regions. Eventually Schacht added a final fillip to this remarkable process; he 'bought' raw materials actually at a loss, had them shipped not to Germany but to a re-export point in, say, the Netherlands, and then *sold* them—for gold or foreign exchange. With this foreign exchange he was able to import material from countries which would not subscribe to the barter deals.

Schacht—The Former Money Bags

It took Hitler a long time to find Schacht. He tried and discarded several economic experts. There was no financial Rosenberg, no economic Goering, on hand from the beginning. Hitler's first choice as economic adviser was a certain retired captain, by name Wagner; for the past three years he has been in concentration camp. Following Wagner, a minor industrialist Wilhelm Keppler had decisive influence. When Keppler fell, a new and ambitious economist, Albert Pietsch, president of the Munich Chamber of Commerce, advanced; he had insinuated himself into the post of 'economic adviser' to Hess, Hitler's deputy. But meantime Schacht was ready.

He was born in January 1877 at Tingleff in Schleswig. His father was a great admirer of the American democratic tradition; thus the name he gave his son, Hjalmar Horace Greeley Schacht. The Hjalmar came from the mother, who was a Dane. Schacht is very proud of his Viking ancestry. His children have Danish names.

He studied at several universities in Germany, obtained a doctorate, and went to work as an archivist clerk in the Dresdener bank —one of the lowest posts. Clever and ambitious, he rose very quickly. One of his jobs was to prepare the routine trade bulletins; he did them so well—combining vigorous unorthodoxy with sly good sense—that presently the directors of the bank used them as a guide to policy. So, by 1908 he was deputy director. In 1916 he went to a rival bank, the Darmstaedter and National, as director.

In 1923, when the mark collapsed, he was appointed Reichs currency commissioner and he saved Germany from utterly chaotic conditions by inventing the Rentenmark, which stabilised the currency. As reward for this coup, he was appointed president of the Reichsbank; he had already refused the finance ministry, which he thought not big enough. He was Reichsbank president till 1930, when he resigned in protest at the Hague agreements which implemented the Young Plan. In March 1933, Hitler appointed him to the presidency of the Reichsbank again.

He is a man of utterly boundless ambition. Until he hitched his star to the Hitler waggon, he wanted to be president of Germany. He is a complete opportunist. He was one of the founders of the democratic party, in 1919, and the socialists supported him as the man who saved the mark. The campaign slogan went, *'Wer hat die*

Rentenmark erdacht? der Demokrat, Herr Dr. Schacht!' But early
in 1930 Schacht saw on which side Germany's bread was buttered,
and he turned to Hitler. He had met Hitler through Goering.

Dorothy Thompson interviewed Schacht early in 1931. He told
her he was going Nazi. She asked him why. He replied, 'Because
I believe in everything that encourages German Nationalism.' Miss
Thompson said, 'But if Hitler comes to power, the Nazis can't run
the country financially, economically. Who will run it?' Schacht
replied, 'I will.'

Like many Hitlerites, Schacht has no discernible private life.
He owns an estate in the country, but he preferred living in the
bank itself in town. He wears extraordinary collars, high and jaw-
breaking. He likes good conversation. He is cool, shrewd, witty.
His power is based first on tremendous ability, second, absolutely
ruthless and calculating opportunism. As a boy Schacht had ambitions to be a poet, and one of his songs, incorporated in a musical
comedy, survives:

> 'I am a musician, very well known,
> and loved in the whole country.
> When I arrive in a little town
> everybody cheers, the grown-up and the children.
> For I play upon my fiddle
> first a dance and then a song.
> And when people are happy together
> I am welcome everywhere.'

Not only was Schacht Hitler's keeper of the purse for years, but
he contrived to make himself indispensable as a link between Hitler
and the whole of German economic life. Schacht dominated, for
instance, the newly-created Reich economic chamber. Theoretically, this organisation embraces the labour front, with its fifteen
million members, whose dues amount to 100,000,000 RM per year.
Then he became minister of economics.

Naturally Schacht has no fondness for Goebbels and the 'Left'
extremists. He knows full well that anti-Jewish nonsense hurts
German export trade. At Königsberg, in August 1935, he denounced the lunatic rabble, and Goebbels suppressed his speech.
Schacht told friends that his course would lead him to a monument
or the scaffold, he did not know which. Such conflicts, quarrels like
these within the party, are bound to continue; they rise from the
very nature of the Nazi movement.

The industrialists influence Schacht, as they influence Hitler, but he is by no means under their thumb. He is under no one's thumb. It may be said that Hitler 'protected' capitalism, saved capitalism for his industrialist friends. But this is not quite the truth. Hitler is no friend of orthodox finance capital. If private profits interfere with the security of the state, out private profits will go. The industrialists disapproved of much of Schacht's jugglery, and they have found that although Naziism serves to perpetuate capitalism, it also demands heavy sacrifices of the capitalists.

Schacht began to slip in 1937, when he was replaced by Goering as economics dictator. He was too conservative for the radicals in the party; he was too proud to remain merely a figurehead. In January 1939 he gave up his stronghold, the presidency of the Reichsbank, to become minister without portfolio. He left at once for a long holiday in India. He was succeeded both as minister of economics and president of the Reichsbank by Dr. Walther Funk, a much lesser man. Funk was a journalist for many years, specialising in economic affairs, and for a time was Hitler's Press chief. He was born in 1891. His job is one of the most difficult in Germany.

Hitler has no interest in economics (which was one of the sources of Schacht's strength) but economics may be his ruin. The permanent realities of the economic situation in Germany wait upon no Hitlers, no Schachts, no Thyssens. When Schacht failed, Hitler found another would-be Schacht. But the fundamental difficulties remain. Germany must feed eighty million people; it must borrow or export enough to pay for imports; it lives by the manufacture of raw materials, and no financial hocus-pocus can alter the inexorable law that goods, somehow, must be paid for.

The day of reckoning will come for Hitler—in gold as well as guns.

CHAPTER VIII

THE FASCIST OFFENSIVE

'Who overcomes by Force
Hath overcome but half his foe.'
—JOHN MILTON.

IN November 1937, Lord Halifax went to Berlin and saw Hitler,
though ostensibly he visited Germany merely to attend a 'Hunting Exposition'. The visit was in effect another of the several
attempts since 1933, when Germany left the League, to make a
general European settlement, to bring the Reich into a scheme of
what was then still optimistically called 'collective security'. The
visit was a failure as regards practical results, but it had value in
that Hitler at last defined his terms, told Halifax what he wanted.
Halifax, who was then Lord Privy Seal, returned to London
shocked at the extremity of the German demands. Nor was Hitler
boasting. Almost immediately began the Fascist Offensive which
culminated in the acquisition of Austria by Germany and the
assault on Czechoslovakia.

Perhaps when the pious Halifax met the Führer he thought that
he might patch up a compromise like the celebrated compromises
he, as Lord Irwin, had made with Mr. Gandhi. But he found Hitler
much less pliable than the Mahatma.

According to the *Manchester Guardian* Hitler presented Halifax
with a series of points as follows:

First, Germany agreed to rejoin the League, provided that the
Covenant was redrafted, the machinery for sanctions scrapped, the
League divorced from the peace treaties, and the war guilt clause
cancelled.

Second, Germany insisted on the reorganisation of Czechoslovakia
on a cantonal system, with something like autonomy for the Sudeten
Germans.

Third, Germany asked Great Britain to refrain from any political
or diplomatic assistance to Austria.

Fourth, Germany pledged itself to refrain from raising the issue
of colonies for six years, if Britain would in return promise to assist
German colonial claims after that period.

100

Fifth, Germany asked that Britain recognise the Italian conquest
of Ethiopia and the Franco government in Spain, in return for which
the Germans would work for the restoration of peace in Spain.

Revelation of the bold candour and comprehensiveness of these
demands staggered opinion in England. But what was to come was
much more staggering. The next act was the acquisition of Austria
in March 1938. This extraordinary event, which shook Europe
like nothing since Sarajevo, but which could have been forecast
with certainty by anyone who really knew Hitler's mind, was
assisted by three factors aside from German single-mindedness and
will. We must touch briefly on the three. First was the development of the Rome-Berlin Axis, second was the purge of the German
army high command, third was the resignation of Mr. Eden as
British Foreign Secretary.

The Axis had been brought sharply to the limelight by Mussolini's visit to Hitler in September, which repaid—three years late—
Hitler's visit to Venice in 1934. Community between the Fascist
states had meantime become so close as to be tantamount to an
alliance. German generals, German politicians, incessantly visited
Italy, and Count Ciano went several times to Berlin. Mussolini
said: 'German-Italian solidarity is a living and active solidarity, the
expression and result of national homogeneity and common interests.'

(Mussolini's nine hours in Munich gave observers a curious side-
light on the extreme and rigorous protective devices necessary when
modern dictators travel. According to the *New York Times*
[September 25, 1937], every train entering Munich was searched,
and every motor-car halted. Every piece of baggage arriving in the
Munich station was 'segregated and minutely searched'. All the
cellars and attics of buildings along the triumphal route were
sealed, and no front windows were allowed to be opened during the
procession. All foreigners were drastically checked upon, and
householders had to submit lists of people in their abodes. No
chances to be taken—despite the vast and unprecedented popularity
of the Fascist idols!)

In November 1937 the anti-Comintern pact which had been
signed the year before between Germany and Japan was extended
to include Italy. The Italians adhered to the protocol as original
signatories, and Hitler announced that the Axis had become a
triangle—he said that a 'great world-political triangle' had been
formed. Ostensibly the pact had no object except opposition to

communism, but in Italy Signor Gayda, the Duce's well-advertised mouthpiece, said that it gave the three signatories 'vast objects of collaboration'. Its second anniversary, late in 1938, was resoundingly celebrated both in Berlin and Rome.

Now the important thing about this new Fascist International or Fascintern, as it came to be called, was Hitler's position in the centre between Tokyo and Rome. Hitler was the pivot. Straightway it became clear that Hitler, not Mussolini, was the dominant partner. This made the acquisition of Austria possible, even though Mussolini strongly opposed it. Hitler contrived to get the Duce as an ally, so that it was difficult for him to denounce Hitler without breaking the alliance, which was essential to him while he was grappling with England. Hitler made the Duce climb down on the hitherto vital Austrian issue which had separated them.

Mussolini should have read *Mein Kampf* more carefully. Listen: 'The binding force of an alliance decreases the more it confines itself to maintaining an existing condition. On the other hand, an alliance waxes stronger the more the individual contracting parties are able to hope they will gain definite, tangible aims of expansion; in which case, as always, strength lies not in defence, but in attack.'

Hitler writes muddily as always; his language is a fumbling jargon; it is extraordinary that his behaviour in action so belies his style.

Next came the strange episode of the Marshal Blomberg's mesalliance and his consequent departure as German minister of war.

.   .   .   .

Rumours of friction between the Nazi party and the army command were rife early in January. Berlin buzzed with uncertainty, and the atmosphere came almost to resemble that which preceded the great blood bath of June 30, 1934. Then, on January 12, 1938, came a brief announcement that Marshal Blomberg, 59 years old and for five years a widower, had married 23-year-old Erika Gruhn, who was presently discovered to be the daughter of a carpenter and a masseuse. Hitler and Goering, it was announced, had been witnesses at the ceremony.

This would seem to have given the marriage all the official sanction it needed, but a storm of repressed excitement rose among Blomberg's colleagues and subordinates. They were gunning for Blomberg because he was considered to be too completely under

Hitler's thumb. His marriage, which violated the strict Prussian code of eligibility for officers' wives, was no more than a convenient pretext. What really worried some of the higher officers was Hitler's policy. Part of the army disapproved of the extent of German intervention in Spain; they were distrustful of the value of an alliance with Mussolini; they feared that Hitler's activism might bring a war for which they were not prepared. But Blomberg, an ardent Hitlerite, prevented expression of these discontents. So on January 28, Colonel General von Fritsch, the chief of staff and for a long time Blomberg's rival for supreme military authority, went unprecedentedly to Hitler and demanded that Blomberg be dismissed, since his marriage violated the army code.

Hitler took advantage of this situation with one of his miraculously effective double-strokes. He fired *both* Blomberg and Fritsch! Apparently he considered that Blomberg's usefulness was at an end. As for Fritsch he had never been as close to Hitler as Blomberg and his enemies accused him of Hohenzollern sentiments and monarchist flirtations. Behind the story was the familiar picture of bitter rivalries among the Nazi leaders. Goering was ambitious for more power; Himmler and Ribbentrop, representing the left wing, wanted to 'get' the conservative generals.

But if anyone thought that he would succeed to the high command of the army he was wrong. With the dramatic statement, 'Henceforth I, personally, will exercise direct command over the entire armed establishment,' Hitler took over the army himself. No new minister of war to succeed Blomberg has ever been appointed.

The shakeup was peaceable, but it struck in several directions. Thirteen generals besides Blomberg and Fritsch were shelved (the official story incidentally said no more than that their resignations were accepted on account of 'ill health'), and many others were shifted. Goering became a Field Marshal. Three ambassadors known to be 'moderates' were recalled, and Ribbentrop succeeded Neurath as foreign minister.

On February 4, Hitler announced the creation of a new cabinet council. This became the inner citadel of German power. Its president was Neurath,[1] and its members were Ribbentrop, Goering, Hess, Goebbels, Dr. Hans Lammers (chief of Hitler's chancellery staff), the new commander-in-chief of the army Colonel-

---

[1] Herr von Neurath later became 'Protector' of Bohemia-Moravia when Czechoslovakia was seized in 1939.

General von Brauschitsch, the new chief of staff General Wilhelm Keitel, and the commander-in-chief of the navy Admiral Raeder. This group of nine men, under Hitler, became the composite ruling power of Germany.

.   .   .   .

Mr. Eden resigned as British foreign minister on February 21, 1938. The immediate issue was the angry one of negotiations with Italy. Anglo-Italian relations had been severely strained since the great sanctions crisis in 1935, and an attempt to patch them up with an agreement in January 1937 had not been successful, largely because Italy subbornly refused to withdraw its troops from Spain. The British prime minister, Mr. Chamberlain, desperately wanted a settlement with Italy; in July he had sent a personal letter to Mussolini, urging resumption of negotiations. But the Italians continued to pinprick Britain with radio propaganda in the Near East and with intrigue in Egypt and Palestine. The Spanish sore still festered with Italian troops.

It seemed that the prime minister, in writing to Mussolini direct, had gone over his foreign minister's head. Similarly by dispatching Halifax to Berlin he seemed to be neglecting Mr. Eden, who disapproved of the trip. In fact the gap between Chamberlain and Eden was gradually widening. Chamberlain gave very clear indication that he intended to be his own foreign secretary. He wanted an agreement with the dictators at almost any price, if it should lead the way to peace in Europe; Eden wanted an agreement too, but not at the sacrifice of vital British interests. The Italian Press kept howling and bleating that Eden must go if negotiations were to be reopened. Eden said that the Italians should at least make some gesture first, such as the withdrawing of troops from Spain. Finally Mr. Chamberlain took matters in hand and received Count Grandi, the Italian Ambassador, at 10 Downing Street to push a settlement. Promptly Eden resigned.

Lord Cranborne, Eden's parliamentary under-secretary, resigned also. He said in parliament: 'I am afraid that if the government enter on official conversations it will be regarded not as a contribution to peace but as a surrender to blackmail.'

Eden's resignation was vastly important because the Fascist powers deduced from it the apparent factor that the British were not willing to stand up longer against the dictators. His departure showed them clearly that no strong opposition to their course existed in England. Eden was the symbol of the collective system.

When he went, the Fascists knew that the door was open. And the invasion of Austria promptly took place.

One other factor made it convenient for Hitler to strike when he did; a severe cabinet crisis in France deprived France of a government that fateful week-end.

Hitler and Schuschnigg[1]

The world, and not only Austria, was electrified on February 12, 1938, to hear that Chancellor Kurt Schuschnigg, the Austrian chancellor, devout Catholic and inheritor of the Dollfuss régime of Austrian independence, had gone suddenly to Berchtesgaden to meet in conference that other Austrian, Adolf Hitler. This was the opening wedge. Schuschnigg delivered himself into the lion's den. He thought presumably he was going to get a breathing spell; what he got was extinction.

First the strange story of an intrigue and a plot that miscarried. Since July 1936 the Austro-German relations had been 'regularised'; Germany promised to respect the independence of Austria and in return the Austrian Nazis were to be absorbed into Schuschnigg's patriotic organisation, the Fatherland Front. But of course the Nazis were not content with this. They were impatient for full power. Ringleaders among the extremist group decided to make a *Putsch*, thus giving the German army pretext for immediate invasion. Nazi *agents-provocateurs* were to surround the German embassy in Vienna and to make an attempt on the life, according to one version of the story, of General Muff, the military attaché, and, according to another, of Von Papen, the ambassador. The Austrian Government got wind of this plan, and several of the conspirators were arrested. The *Putsch* was scheduled for January 30, the anniversary of Hitler's accession to power as Chancellor. News of the failure of the *Putsch* got to Berlin; officers of the Reichswehr protested in alarm at the idea; and Hitler suddenly cancelled the great annual speech he customarily delivers on January 30.

The moderate Reichswehr generals did not want an invasion of Austria; the two armies had close sympathies, and Fritsch feared international repercussions. Thus the *Putsch* plan had a very important bearing on the German army purge. Hitler had to get rid of those officers who thought the Austrian adventure dangerous.

Papen found himself out of a job in the February shake up.

[1] There are detailed chapters about Austria below, Chapters XXIV—XXVII, inclusive.

That slippery and debonair gentleman had, moreover, no fondness
for the role he was scheduled to play if the *Putsch* went through.
He got Hitler's ear and presented an alternative plan. Let Hitler
invite Schuschnigg to Berchtesgaden and *talk* him out of Austria.
Previously Hitler, in high horror, had always refused to have anything to do with Schuschnigg or any of the other Austrian 'traitors',
i.e. loyal Austrians. Hitler, for want of anything better, accepted
Papen's scheme.

Why did Schuschnigg consent to go? First, he knew that the
position was untenable; an explosion was predictably imminent.
To keep the Germans out was like trying to withstand Niagara with
a barn door. Since the development of the Rome-Berlin Axis he
was no longer sure of Mussolini's help, and since Halifax's visit to
Germany he was dubious of the value of Franco-British aid. Both
France and Britain were, of course, pledged to the theory of Austrian
independence; but the year of our Lord 1938 was yet another year
when pledges were torn up like tickertape. Schuschnigg went to
Berchtesgaden because he thought that somehow, *somehow*, he
might come to terms with Hitler and save something from the
wreck.

Disillusion smote him instantly. He was treated at Berchtesgaden not only with personal rudeness, but as a political puppet
beneath contempt. He was forced to give up his own bodyguard at
the Salzburg frontier, and accepted a 'guard of honour' led by enemy
Austrians. In eleven hours of strident talk and listening, he was
given exactly one meal; he is a heavy smoker, but not once was he
allowed respite for a cigarette.

Hitler raged and shouted; he threatened immediate armed
invasion of Austria unless Schuschnigg succumbed to his demands.
The first demand was for the inclusion of a man named Arthur
Seyss-Inquart as minister of interior and public security—which
meant control of gendarmerie and police—in the Austrian cabinet.
The phenomenon of one dictator demanding the right to compose
the cabinet of another is a strange one even for these times. Schuschnigg compromised by agreeing to offer Seyss-Inquart the ministry
of justice. Seyss-Inquart—incidentally an old friend of Schuschnigg's—though not officially a Nazi, was of course the Nazi's
man.

Hitler introduced the new German commander-in-chief, General
Keitel, to Schuschnigg, pointedly reinforcing his threats to cross the
frontier. Hitler screamed at Schuschnigg: 'Understand that I con-

sider myself the Führer not only of the Germans in the Reich, but of all Germans throughout the world!'

Schuschnigg went back to Vienna, shaken and tormented; hardly had he returned when an ultimatum came from Berlin, demanding again that Seyss-Inquart be given control of the police. Schuschnigg agreed. This—at 2.30 a.m. on February 16—was the first ultimatum. The next day Seyss-Inquart became head of 'all the pacification departments in Austria'—a charming word 'pacification'—and immediately flew to *Berlin*, there to make contact with Hitler and receive instructions. Meantime Nazi passion rose all over Austria; there were riots and demonstrations in Graz and throughout the country; Nazi political prisoners were released.

Schuschnigg had one last desperate card. He played it. On March 9 he announced that a plebiscite would be held on March 13 wherein the people of Austria might freely vote whether or not they wished to remain independent.

Mussolini, when he heard of this, is reported to have said: 'The plebiscite will go off like a bomb in his hand.' It did. Hitler was enraged. He flew into one of the wildest tantrums of his career. The reason was obvious: if the plebiscite were held, he, Hitler, would lose it. The best authorities in Austria at the time agree that, even then, the Nazis would not have received better than a forty per cent vote. So it was absolutely imperative for the Germans to prevent the plebiscite at all costs. Hitler has recorded that he could not believe his own ears when word of the plebiscite reached him. He decided that Schuschnigg had betrayed him. 'I determined to act at once.' So, through Seyss-Inquart, an ultimatum—the second ultimatum—was presented to Schuschnigg, demanding that he call off the plebiscite and resign. This was at 4 p.m. on March 11. The Austrian chancellor was given, first till 6 p.m. then to 7.30 p.m. to accede, or German invasion of Austria would begin. This from Hitler, who had told Schuschnigg at Berchtesgaden that any threat of bloodshed, of fighting between Germans and Germans, was intolerable and unthinkable! At 6 Schuschnigg duly called off the plebiscite, and at 7.50 he resigned.

Schuschnigg said over the radio in a broken voice:

'I place on record before the world that all reports to the effect that disturbances have broken out in Austria and that the government can no longer control the situation are lies from beginning to end. I am instructed by the Federal President to inform the Austrian people that we are yielding to force. . . . Determined at all costs

I

even in this grave hour to avoid bloodshed, we have ordered the Austrian forces to withdraw without resistance. . . . And so I take my leave of the Austrian people. God save Austria!'

Even then few people thought that Hitler would go to the extreme limit of annexing Austria outright. They should have remembered his tactics after Hindenburg's death. He is a whole-hogger or nothing. The Nazis rose in Vienna, and the German troops soon streamed across the frontier. Hitler arrived in Linz the next day like a Roman conqueror. On the 13th he announced the Anschluss, and Austria as an independent state ceased to exist.

Schuschnigg made no attempt to run away. In fact flight was impossible. He was arrested by SS men as he left the chancellery after his farewell speech, and late in 1939 was still in custody.

Loot

The military, political, economic, and strategic gains to Hitler of the annexation of Austria were very considerable. The population of the Reich increased overnight to almost 75,000,000, making Germany without doubt the most powerful country on continental Europe. At least eight new divisions were made available to the German army, and they were consolidated into the Reichswehr at once.

Germany got Austria's Alpine Montangesellshaft, the biggest iron works in Central Europe, capable of producing at least 2,500,000 tons of iron ore a year. It got the munitions industries in Steyr and Hirtenberg, and the biggest deposits of magnesite—a mineral useful in aeroplane manufacture—in the world. It got a great reservoir of electric power, dairy industries, and above all, timber, which Austria had in profusion and which Germany badly needed. And not inconsiderable was the £18,000,000 in gold found in the Austrian national bank, a quantity of gold incidentally almost quadruple that possessed by the entire Reich. (And promptly, of course, Germany repudiated the Austrian external debt.)

But the chief gains were political. By acquiring Austria, Hitler won his supreme triumph in foreign policy to date. 'On March 12, 1938, Germany won the World War of 1914,' it was nicely said. The German frontiers were extended to the Brenner Pass, and Czechoslovakia—ominous!—was virtually encircled. Germany squatted like an octopus beyond the Rhine, astride the Danube, and the countries of south-eastern Europe could not but feel the impingement of its tentacles, the pressure of its might. Germany now directly faced no fewer than eleven different countries—across some highly perishable frontiers.

Duce Infelix

When Lord Halifax received news of the conquest of Austria he is said to have buried his face in his hands, muttering 'Horrible, horrible!'[1] When Mussolini heard the news, according to one report, he sat in granite silence for some moments, then hurled a heavy paperweight through a picture frame. It is now, eighteen months after the fact, almost indisputable that neither Britain nor Italy—inconceivable as it seems—were consulted or advised in advance.

(According to Pertinax, the French commentator, the French prime minister and foreign minister saw Anthony Eden on his return from Geneva in January, and said that diplomatic steps must be taken at once if Austrian independence were to be saved. They implored him to communicate this view to Chamberlain, and promised French assistance in the event that Austria should be attacked. But apparently it was too late. Halifax had already indicated to Hitler that Great Britain was not prepared to fight for Austria. Eden did his best, and then resigned.)

The correspondence between Hitler and Mussolini during the occupation is illuminating. Hitler had just inflicted on his ally a stunning diplomatic defeat—probably the worst in Mussolini's whole career. So his telegram was defensive, rather worried, and emphatic in its pledge never to interfere with Mussolini's own frontier, the Brenner.

> 'I have now decided to restore order and tranquillity in my country (Austria). . . . Do not see in this anything more than an act of legitimate national defence, and therefore an action which any man of character in my position would perform in the same way. At a critical hour for Italy I demonstrated the strength of my sentiments to you. . . . This decision (to respect the Brenner frontier) will never be touched or questioned.'

Then Hitler made a little peroration:

> 'I did not take this decision (to acquire Austria) in the year 1938 but immediately after the Great War. I have never made a mystery of it.'

[1] But he had had 'prolonged discussions' with Ribbentrop on March 10. What on earth did they talk about?

The inflexible singleness of will of this man, his terrific cold fixity of vision, who waits patiently for twenty years until his moment comes!

Mussolini's reply could hardly have been colder:

> 'My attitude is determined by the friendship between our two countries, which is consecrated in the Axis.'

Then Hitler telegraphed again—one can practically see him almost weeping with relief—that he will 'never forget' Mussolini's answer. *'Ich werde Ihnen dieses nie vergessen,'* he proclaimed. Within six weeks Mussolini had to receive Hitler in Rome for the return visit which had been arranged in Munich the September before. The Duce couldn't wriggle out of it, and welcomed the victorious Führer with as good grace as he could muster. (But Mussolini too, probably, knew that the merger of Germany and Austria was inevitable. . . .)

Death of Austria

So Austria perished. The country which had more quality of grace, of cultivation and sophisticated charm, than any other in the world, succumbed to Nazi boot-heels. Even the name perished. Austria became a group of provinces known as 'Ostmark'. Vienna, the city of quiet and sceptical laughter, the home of individualism, of worship of art and the intellect, the wit of Schnitzler, the charm of Strauss, became a German provincial town—*gleichgeschaltet* (co-ordinated) into the despotism, the cultural aridity, the terrible uniformity of the Third Reich.

(But Austria was a German country—at least in race. Vienna was a German city—at least in speech. Hitler was, as it were, coming home.)

When he stood on the bridgehead at Linz, on March 12, he announced that it was 'the greatest hour of his life'. It was not a great hour in the lives of some hundreds of thousands of his countrymen.

Quick and merciless, the Brown Terror struck. By early summer, at least fifty *thousand* of his countrymen were in jail,[1] most of them charged with no offence except the greatest—that of being enemies of the Nazi régime. The drag-net knew no other categories. Jews of good station were made to clean streets and toilets. Those arrested included bankers like Louis Rothschild, ski teachers like

[1] According to Vincent Sheean in the New York *Herald Tribune*.

Hannes Schneider, physicians like Dr. Neumann, Catholic politicians like Dr. Ender, aristocrats like Archduke Max Hohenberg. They included social democrats, capitalists, Habsburgs, old Schutzbunders, Heimwehr Catholics, munition makers, Jews, communists.

Some few eminent Jews got out, like Professor Freud. Some seven thousand of them did not get out, and committed suicide.

A few conspicuous political opponents of the Nazis disappeared early. Baron Odo Neustädter-Stürmer, it was announced, 'committed suicide'. He was the stalwart Heimwehr man who stood outside the chancellery on July 25, 1934, and led the movement against the Nazi raiders who had imprisoned and murdered Dollfuss inside.[1] Then—curious irony!—it was announced that Major Emil Fey, who was inside the building negotiating with the Nazis that same fateful day, had also 'committed suicide'. The Germans hated Neustädter-Stürmer because he opposed them, and Major Fey, because, they said, he betrayed them. So the three chief actors of the terrific spectacle of July 25 were united at last—in death.

Fey's wife was found dead by his side, and also his dog. The sardonicism of Viennese humour finds outlet in the darkest hours. 'Dear God,' one Viennese asked another, 'do they shoot even *dogs*?' His friend replied, 'Ah, you do not apparently realise that the dog also committed suicide.'

Seyss-Inquart, his role played, was quickly subordinated to Herr Bürckel, the pacifyer of the Saar, who became Reichs commissioner for Austria. A plebiscite was held in the usual manner, and the Nazis got the usual vote. Hitler revealed that he had offered to stand alone against Schuschnigg in an election—what a single combat on what a tournament field that jousting would have been!—and that now he stood in Schuschnigg's place, with the help of Providence which had destined him for the job, because he was an abler man (which last is certainly true). The murderers of Dollfuss, who performed one of the most treacherous and cruel assassinations in history, were ennobled as martyrs and heroes—which caused even *The Times* to protest. The Press was filled with lies about the former régime—which had its faults, heaven knows—of the most flamboyant transparency. And General Goering let one cat out of the bag when he justified the terror by saying that Vienna, with 300,000 Jews, was not a 'German' city—although the whole

[1] See Chapter XXVI below.

pretext for Hitler's twenty years' campaign was Austria's Germanism.

All this being true, let us note on the other hand that the Nazis began a campaign for the economic rehabilitation of Austria quite beyond the powers of the former government. Road building and new factories were pressed forward, slum clearance was advanced, new mines and hydro-electric plants were announced, and the government took care to emphasise to the bewildered workers the 'socialist' elements of National Socialism.

A good many tears have been wept for poor Schuschnigg. And indeed his fate is lamentable. But one should not forget that he and Dollfuss (plus Mussolini) were responsible for the *débâcle* which set the whole earthslip moving—the suppression in blood of the Austrian social democrats in February 1934.

Czeching Up

Before proceeding to outline briefly the history of the German assault on Czechoslovakia it is well to underline three factors, to emphasise three important items that sometimes got lost in the shuffle of the most prodigious crisis Europe has seen in modern times.

It is true that Czechoslovakia was a composite state. (True, also that, until the crisis, it was the strongest and stablest of the succession states; a peaceable state with high national intelligence; a state not only with a powerful and authentic national tradition but with a generous sense of the needs of Europe as a whole; a state which was a pool of decency and democracy in the turbulent regions beyond the Rhine, in fact the *only* real democracy beyond the Rhine.) But the Czechs, it is undeniable, took more than their proper share in the Versailles settlements. By the census of 1931 Czechoslovakia contained something like 10,000,000 Czechoslovaks, and in addition 3,231,688 Germans, 691,923 Hungarians, and 81,737 Poles.

The business of self-determination has its tricks and pitfalls. Rationally if you believe in self-determination, and it is extremely difficult not to believe in it, you have to concede that the German minority had as much right to autonomy as the Czechoslovaks had to independence. But it was not quite so simple as all that. The peace makers of Versailles were greedy, but something more than greed is a controlling factor in the story. No frontier can ever be drawn in Central or Eastern Europe without leaving some minori-

ties on the wrong side of the border.   It is geographically impossible
to give self-determination to isolated enclaves of people, remote
from any frontier, without disrupting the state to which they belong.
The question of ultimate ends must be considered.   The nation
itself has as much right to nationhood as the fractional minorities
have to autonomy—to put it mildly.   You cannot follow the practice
of self-determination to its logical extreme without reaching an
absurdity—that of the state itself being sacrificed to its minorities.
You cannot liberate minorities if in doing so you sacrifice the possibility of the free existence of the state itself.   Thus the frontiers
of the succession states were drawn with military and strategic
as well as purely ethnological considerations in mind.   Thus
too the minority treaties were established in 1919, guaranteeing that the new states with minorities would not mistreat
them.

So far so good.   Let us proceed to three preliminary and important points.

First, the German minority in Czechoslovakia was by and large
better treated than any other minority in Central Europe, infinitely
better treated for example—there is no comparison—than such a
minority as the Jews in Germany.   The Serbs dragooned their
Croats; the Rumanians crushed their Hungarians.   But the
Czechoslovaks, certain small stubborn tactlessnesses aside, treated
the Sudeten Germans well.   The Sudetens had the right to use
their own language, they had their own schools.   They were equal
citizens in a free democracy; they were free to enter politics and
three Germans were cabinet ministers until the crisis.   From 1919
to 1933 they lived at peace with their Czech neighbours.   There
were frictions and grievances, but utterly no secessionism until
Hitler came to power.   There was no 'Sudeten question' before 1933.
The Sudetens indeed did not even include autonomy in their programme till 1938.

Second, the German thesis that the Sudeten crisis was a movement to liberate a downtrodden minority does not hold much water.
It is pretext to claim that Hitler wanted *only* to free Germans from
non-German rule.   This was part of the story.   But not all.   There
were German minorities in Poland whom Hitler sacrificed without
a qualm in order to hammer out a pact with Poland which, when
he was isolated, he desperately needed; he condemned the 750,000
good Germans in the South Tyrol to what seemed permanent servitude, when he told Mussolini after the Austrian coup that the

Brenner frontier was eternal. These Tyrolean Germans suffered infinitely more ignominiously than any Sudeten Germans ever suffered. The very names on the gravestones of their ancestors were erased. Hans Sachs became Giovanni Saccio.[1]

Third, the German Press unendingly stated that the Sudeten area had been torn from Germany by the peace treaties. This is pure fabrication. The Sudeten area was *never* part of Germany. It has never been German except in language. The Sudeten area was part of Austro-Hungary, not of Germany, and the frontier between Germany and Czechoslovakia on the north was one of the very few that the Versailles map makers did *not* change. The boundary followed without alteration the historic line that always divided the kingdom of Bohemia—since A.D. 1526 at any rate—from Germany. The Czechoslovaks did get a few square miles of German soil in Silesia— a very few square miles indeed—but not one inch from the Sudeten region.

The German point of view is simple and may be briefly put. The Reich, an overwhelmingly powerful expansionist nation, demands its proper privileges; it demands the room that its military and political significance rightly entail. If anyone suffers, it is hard luck. One can no more stand in the way of the Reich, in its irresistible march to dominance of continental Europe, than one can turn the centuries backward. One can no more deflect Hitler from his path than one can deflect an avalanche. The whole sweep of modern history is with the Germans; the modern historical process reaches its culmination in German reversal of the peace treaties. Hitler is indubitably a great man and the Jews who have to wash pavements are unfortunate victims of a cosmic explosion, forlorn by-products of a civilisation past use. Hitler is Germany's revenge not merely for Versailles but for Napoleon. Hitler *is,* in fact, the Napoleon of the twentieth century.

'Mortal Crisis Doth Portend an End!'

Events moved with dismaying swiftness and certitude after the sack of Austria. I can no more than very briefly foreshorten them here. On February 20, immediately before the Austrian adventure, Hitler referred to the Sudetens and assured them protection; on March 7 the German *Diplomatische Korrespondenz,* an official propaganda organ, suggested autonomy for them. This was something

[1] In the summer of 1939 it was announced that the Tyrolese Germans would be moved back to Germany.

quite new. Germany was jumping in the Czechoslovak arena with both feet and in effect putting forward the idea of dismemberment of the state. Quite properly, but with great dignity and self-restraint, Prime Minister Milan Hodza of Czechoslovakia replied that Czechoslovakia must oppose any outside interference in domestic affairs.

Already, trying to mend the situation, eager to forestall the storm, the Czechs had made great concessions to the minorities. In February 1937, a year before, the government had made an agreement with all the German minority parties, except Henlein's group, promising them subsidies for employment and public works, granting them jobs in the civil service in proportion to their number, and extending the use of the German language instead of Czech in official communications. The Henlein group rejected these concessions as inadequate. It must be clearly understood that the extremist Henlein party was only one of several German parties in Czechoslovakia. German clericals, German agrarians, German social democrats, although good Germans, had no special fondness for the Nazis, and were included in the Czechoslovak cabinet.

Konrad Henlein, the Sudeten leader, a puffy-faced sub-Hitler in his early forties, was first a bank clerk, then a gymnasium instructor. By 1930 he was head of the German *Turnverein*, or gymnastic association, in Czechoslovakia, and he turned to politics. Hitler's rise to dictatorship in Germany enormously stimulated his movement. But at the beginning at least he always stated unequivocally that he was a loyal subject of the Czechoslovak state, working merely for the improvement of the German minority within the country, and as late as 1936 he still asserted that he was *not* a Nazi, but a convinced democrat. In 1933 he had said:

> 'The welfare of the Sudetens is indissolubly bound up with the welfare of the Czechoslovak republic. We stand in principle and unanimously for loyalty to the state. For more than a thousand years Germans and Czechs have lived together in these lands, and always their fate has been common. . . . We feel too vividly the power of historical tradition to consider seriously *any kind of territorial revision*.' (Italics mine.)

Five years later he was to change his mind. Rather Herr Hitler (with certain aid from the British) changed it for him—with a vengeance.

By mid-March 1938, it was clearly obvious that the Germans were going to do something about—or to—Czechoslovakia, without much delay. Prague stiffened. The French Government in an absolutely categorical declaration promised on March 14 that it would fulfil its treaty obligations to assist Czechoslovakia if it were invaded; so did the Russians, though—an important detail—the shrewd Litvinov had so written the treaty between Czechoslovakia and the Soviet Union that the Russians were obligated to march only if the French marched first. Even Mr. Chamberlain in London seemed alarmed; on March 24 he issued a statement that did not give any explicit British pledge of the Czechoslovak frontiers, but which warned Germany that if war broke out it might be impossible to localise it.

Germany receded a step. Marshal Goering stated that Hitler wanted to 'improve' Czecho-German relations—ghastly joke this seems now! Within Czechoslovakia the non-Henlein Germans, however, began to desert the sinking ship. The representatives in the Prague cabinet of the three non-Henlein German parties resigned. Some of their followers merged with Henlein, which made his party the largest in the country. Henlein, still theoretically standing for the 'territorial integrity of Czechoslovakia', demanded a general election. The Prague government announced as a conciliatory measure that it would substantially enlarge its programme of concessions as outlined in February 1937 by making a totally new 'Nationalities Statute', which, it became known later, amounted virtually to re-drawing the constitution of the state in favour of the minorities.

April was an angry month. Give a Nazi an inch; he takes twenty miles. Dr. Beneš pleaded for harmony with Germany; Daladier in London again gave complete assurance that France would, in the event of war, come to Czechoslovak aid. (This assurance was once more repeated by M. Bonnet on May 21; the record of French repudiation of promises and funk is almost beyond belief.) But harmony was not what the Nazis wanted. A blasting campaign against the Czechs began in the German newspapers—officially controlled of course—a campaign as noteworthy for falsehood as for ferocity. On April 22 the Czechoslovak Government raised the ban on public meetings and promised elections in May in 11,000 communities. On the very next day, April 23, answering this retort courteous with a smash to the nose, Henlein announced his 8-point 'Karlsbad' demands:

These had best be given in full:

1. Equality of Sudeten Germans and Czechs with the Sudeten Germans no longer to be considered merely a minority.
2. Recognition of the Sudeten Germans as a legal and corporate body.
3. Determination of the Sudeten boundaries within the state.
4. Full self-government for the Germans in this demarcated territory.
5. Legal protection and guarantees for Germans living in Czechoslovakia outside this demarcated belt.
6. Removal of 'injustices' and discriminations against Germans, in the matter of language, jobs, and the like, inflicted since 1918, *and reparation for them.*
7. State and civil employees and officials in German areas to be Germans.
8. The Germans to have full liberty to profess German nationality and to proclaim allegiance to the ideology of Germany, i.e. Nazidom.

A state which accepted these eight demands would have ceased to be a state. These extraordinary points at least cleared the air. They proved one thing beyond doubt, namely that the Sudetens did not *want* a settlement, since the demands were utterly impossible from any workable or practical point of view, if Czechoslovakia was to survive. Yet the Czechoslovak Government did not immediately reject them; it simply indicated that the request that Czechoslovakia change its foreign policy was unreasonable, and that it could not grant its citizens the right to profess allegiance to another country. The demands were proof that Henlein had given up any thought of a normal solution by negotiation. But Dr. Beneš continued to urge a settlement. Instantly Henlein countered with a statement that the Karlsbad programme did not embody his 'maximum' demands!

In May came crisis. Stormingly the Sudetens began their election campaign. They complained that they were crushed and suppressed; yet they were allowed to make speeches freely! They asserted that they were victims of 'political terrorism'; but they were allowed free expression of their beliefs in a free election! The farce passed beyond reason.

It passed beyond peace, too—almost. Two Sudetens were killed in a frontier brawl on the eve of May 22 elections. The week-end very nearly brought war. Henlein saw Hitler on the 19th. German troops massed at the border, and there was every indication that the Germans planned a *Blitzkrieg*, lightning war, to destroy Czechoslovakia before the powers could—if they would—intervene. With great promptness and energy the Czechs met the threat by a partial mobilisation. The frontiers were manned, and several hundred thousand reservists called up. So Hitler receded again, and the crisis continued to grind on.[1]

The Czech Government met the Sudetens at a Round Table Conference in June. Four different plans were prepared to meet the Sudeten ultimatum during the summer, even though Henlein had refused to negotiate on the basis of the new Nationalities Statute—until 'peace and order' were restored! In other words, the bandit refused to talk with the policeman, until the policeman consented to stop committing 'crimes'. The fourth Czech plan, hammered out with infinite patience in circumstances of almost inconceivable difficulty, when every concession could be interpreted as a surrender to blackmail, and was instantly followed by more and more brutal Nazi pressure, performed the miracle of *almost* meeting the Karlsbad programme. The Germans and other minorities were promised local autonomy, and were given quasi-independent status within the state. Czechoslovakia was to be cantonised, like Switzerland; the Czech cabinet was to include 'bureaus' representing each minority; the police and gendarmes in the minority districts were to be turned over to the minorities themselves.

Finally, new laws to govern this procedure were to be drawn up by a commission consisting equally of representatives of the government and the Sudetens. Conciliation could go no further. But it was no use. A trivial incident on the frontier, when a Sudeten deputy was slapped by an angry officer—the German headlines read 'SAVAGE HORSEWHIPPING BY BESTIAL CZECH'—broke off negotiations. They were half-heartedly resumed, but it was doubly clear by this time that a peaceful settlement was impossible. Already, after a violently agitated August, it was September.

Meanwhile Lord Runciman had come to Prague as an official adviser and mediator. To date it is difficult to assess accurately or in complete detail the role that Runciman seems to have

---

[1] As a result of having been frustrated by this May crisis, Hitler decided to build the Siegfried of German fortifications in the west.

played. Most of the independent American newspaper correspondents in Prague assert that he seemingly favoured the Sudeten
case almost from the beginning. His report at any rate went far
beyond anything that even Henlein or Hitler had dared *openly* talk
about—actual dismemberment of the Czechoslovak state. *The
Times,* at a crucial juncture, also appeared with an important
editorial advocating rectification of the frontier, and territorial
cession of the Sudeten area to Germany. Obviously these events
greatly strengthened Hitler's hand.

September is the month of the Nazi congress at Nuremberg. It
met in the tumultuous shadow of impending war. Germany was
mobilised—though the operation was masked with the term
'manœuvres'—with 1,300,000 men at arms. Europe paused, tense,
to hear the Führer. He outdid himself on September 9 with a surly
and bombastic speech, full of the smoke and thunder of defiance.
He refused to believe that negotiations could bring a settlement;
he said that Germany would capitulate to no one. Germany
roared; the Czechs waited; Europe quivered; and Mr. Chamberlain
flew to Berchtesgaden. But he did not fly there to save the Czechs;
he flew there to prevent a war.

War didn't come. War was to be averted for another year.
What came instead was—Munich.

CHAPTER IX

FROM MUNICH TO WARSAW

'The heart of Poland hath not ceased
To quiver, tho' her sacred blood doth drown
The fields . . .'

—TENNYSON.

WHEN Mr. Chamberlain took off at Heston aerodrome in the early morning of September 15, 1938, to visit that well known Austrian house-painter, somnambulist, and sub-Napoleon Adolf Hitler, in his mountain retreat at Berchtesgaden, Europe knew at last, after almost twenty years of armistice, that the real crisis had come. Previously there had been other crises. When France invaded the Ruhr, when Germany invaded the Rhineland, when Mussolini invaded Ethiopia, when Hitler invaded Austria, the Press of the world pronounced in flaming headlines that the 'greatest' event since 1914 had arrived. But these other crises were child's play compared to the Czechoslovak crisis which Mr. Chamberlain was attempting to overcome. This was the real thing—war or peace—at last.

Two weeks followed of sound and fury, of agonised suspense and almost intolerable tension. The world listened with ears glued to broadcasts from London and Prague, Berlin and Rome. Europe tottered on the brink, anguished and terror-struck. The monstrous war machines plunged stertorously towards action. A war that might easily destroy what was left of European civilisation seemed starkly, unbelievably inevitable. The French manned the Maginot line, and the British fleet went into the North Sea prepared for action. Only Italy and Soviet Russia of the great powers did not mobilise. One small incident dramatised the alarm of the world as well as any other: the Great German steamship *Europa*, jammed with Americans fleeing Europe, turned about in mid-ocean, recalled by radio to home waters. It seemed as if Europe as well as the *Europa* named for Europe was going back, back, back—no one knew whither.

And this all happened in a year during which Herr Hitler had

120

promised that the 'era of surprises' in German foreign policy was over!

Mr. Masefield, the poet laureate, expressed pungently the relief that most of the world felt when it became known that Chamberlain was going to Hitler:

> As Priam to Achilles for his son,
>   So you, into the night, divinely led,
> To ask that young men's bodies, not yet dead,
>   Be given from the battle not begun.

The controlling, the dominant factor of the crisis was fear, fear of war, fear of air raids in great cities, fear that London and Paris might meet the fate of Guernica and Barcelona, destroyed by German bombs. Fear, funk, fear, paralysed, what the *New Statesman* calls the 'demo-plutocracies'. Fear, funk, fear, let Britain into such a humiliation as it had hardly known for centuries, and France into the cruellest repudiation of presumably sacrosanct pledges that modern history can record. Fear, funk, fear, accounted for the gross and sickening betrayal of the Czechoslovak nation, its assassination by its 'friends'.

Hitler's speech at Nuremberg on September 9 sounded the final phase of the great struggle. He talked once more about the 'shameless ill-treatment, the violence and torture' (this last imaginary) undergone by the Sudetens, and said flatly that Germany would not tolerate further oppression. He also asserted that Germany need no longer fear a blockade in the event of war. The speech was a signal for violent disorder. Fighting took place in the Sudeten areas, and was quickly crushed; Henlein fled to Germany and organised the Sudeten Free Corps there on German soil, and the Czechs—at long last—declared martial law.

So the situation was worsening. Something had to be done quickly. The British Ambassador to Germany, Sir Nevile Henderson, apparently found it impossible to talk to Hitler privately while the Nuremberg festival was proceeding. The British had sent several warnings to Germany, but they were unheeded. When, in fact, in August Henderson had appealed to Ribbentrop for moderation, Ribbentrop bluntly replied that British efforts for peace merely served to stiffen the Czechs. Sir John Simon's speech at Lanark, repeating a warning that Britain might find it impossible to remain aloof in the event of war, merely annoyed the Germans. Again a direct warning to Ribbentrop—'regarding the probable attitude of

His Majesty's Government in the event of German aggression against Czechoslovakia, particularly if France were compelled to intervene'—brought no reply. Germany thought England was merely bluffing. It was imperative that Hitler himself be seen.

Chamberlain in his House of Commons speech on September 28 said:

> 'One of the principal difficulties in dealing with a totalitarian government is the lack of any means of establishing contact with the personalities in whose hands lie the final decision.
>
> 'I, therefore, resolved to go to Germany myself and interview Herr Hitler and find out in a personal conversation whether there was any hope yet of saving peace.
>
> 'I knew very well that in taking such an unprecedented course I was laying myself open to criticism on the ground that I was detracting from the dignity of the British Prime Minister, and to disappointment, even to resentment, if I failed to bring back a satisfactory agreement.'

A word for Mr. Chamberlain. He has been bitterly, savagely attacked. But his motive was completely simple and of the best: to avert war. He was not, I think, so much pro-German as pro-Peace, if that is not a contradiction in terms. He was convinced that Mussolini and Hitler were permanent realities that had to be dealt with; he thought that a peaceful Europe was only possible by coming to terms with them. It is almost unforgivable that he gave the Czechoslovaks themselves no chance to negotiate; but perhaps circumstances in the form of Herr Hitler and the German air force permitted him no choice. He stood for peace and got it—temporarily—only by making someone else pay a terrible price. But in this course there is no doubt that the great mass of the British people—the French people also—stood behind him. Finally, he was forced to accept Hitler's terms because he was in no position to wage war. Both Britain and France were—still—shockingly unprepared. Hitler had all the cards—and guns—in *his* hands. Chamberlain had to make any concession, no matter how dramatic, because if war had come then, England and France might have been beaten.

The spectacular drama of the flight of this 69-year-old merchant from the Midlands to see Hitler on his mountain top was only exceeded by the spectacular quality of the 'settlement' he made. He found at once that the only solution was the cession of Czechoslovak territory to Germany.[1] The Germans were willing to risk a world war to get the Sudeten area. Chamberlain returned to London, where MM. Daladier and Bonnet met him. British and French cabinets wrestled with the details over the week-end of the 18th— very few authentic details were permitted to leak out—and finally accepted Hitler's terms. A horrified world listened to the projected lines of settlement:

1. Czechoslovakia to cede to the Reich outright all territory containing more than fifty per cent of Germans. (This territory included the mountainous barrier which was the nation's first and essential defence, as well as its tremendous fortification system and most of the key industries.)
2. Plebiscites in other German districts.
3. Czechoslovakia to give up her French and Russian pacts, and be 'neutralised'.
4. Britain and France to guarantee Czechoslovakia's new abbreviated frontiers.

When M. Oususky, the Czechoslovak minister in Paris, heard the terms, he burst into tears crying, 'Do you want to see a man convicted without a hearing? Here I stand!'

The comment of Leon Blum of France was revelatory: 'War has probably been averted, but I feel myself divided between cowardly relief and my sense of shame.' A great many people in many countries shared this sentiment.

The terms were presented to Prague. Despair struck Czechoslovakia. On the 20th the Czechs replied with an offer to submit the matter to the Hague Court under terms of the 1925 treaty of conciliation between Germany and Czechoslovakia. This treaty was not, as has been said, a forgotten document disinterred for the occasion; actually in March 1938 General Goering had referred to

[1] Lord Runciman had come to the same conclusion, though his report exonerated the Czechs of the ridiculous charges of 'Terrorism', put the responsibility of the final break on Henlein, and asserted that agreement might have been reached on the basis of the Karlsbad demands. (See Chapter VIII.) It is obscure when precisely Lord Runciman decided that dismemberment of Czechoslovakia was necessary. The whole question of his report demands elucidation. For instance, it was dated September 21, six whole days after Chamberlain's first visit to Hitler. Perhaps there was no time, but surely the report, which was to have been the basis for a settlement, should have preceded the negotiations, not followed them.

K

it as the proper basis for peaceful relations between the two countries! On the 21st Britain and France exerted pressure on Prague in the most urgent manner. If Czechoslovakia did not submit, they said coldly that they would leave it to its fate. If it did not accept partition, the terms of which were close to suicide, the German invasion would take place and the nation would be obliterated. It was a choice between self-amputation and murder. At 2.15 a.m. the French and British ministers were received by Dr. Beneš. In circumstances of unparalleled tragedy and strain the Czech cabinet stayed in session till 9 a.m., accepted the demands, and then resigned. A new cabinet under the one-eyed war hero General Syrovy was formed. And Europe relaxed—a little.

The Czech submission was in language that did the nation honour. Without rancour, without recrimination, with dignity and courage, but making it clear that they were submitting to extraordinary pressure, the Czechs gave up a great deal of their country for the sake of European peace:

> 'The government is determined to maintain peace and order and independence under the new conditions that confront it. The President of the Republic and the government could do nothing but accept the suggestions of the two powers. . . . Nothing else remained, because we were alone. . . .
>
> 'We will defend freedom, self-sufficiency, and independence under the new conditions. . . . Farmers, workers, industrialists, employers, soldiers, all remain at your posts and do your duty. . . . No violence or demonstrations on the streets. . . . Remain firm to your faith in your Republic.'

Chamberlain said—he could hardly have said less—that the British Government 'was profoundly conscious of the immense sacrifice which the Czechoslovak Government had agreed to and the immense public spirit it had shown'.

Winston Churchill said: 'The idea that you can purchase safety by throwing a small state to the wolves is a fatal delusion.'

At the time of the Czech acceptance a vast wave of relief, tinged with some sentiment of dismay, swept most people. War had been averted. The settlement was cruel, but it was not dishonourable. It seemed that self-determination for the Germans was a defensible proposition, even though it was accompanied by threat of force; it seemed that the Czechoslovaks had added a new note to history, a new definition of national honour, by consenting to a sacrifice which might be for the good of Europe as a whole. Chamberlain was praised for his courage, and Beneš for his unselfishness and nobility.

But much worse was to come. The first settlement at Berchtesgaden was only the beginning.

'Peace in Our Time'

On Thursday, September 22, Chamberlain returned to Germany to meet Hitler at Godesberg, a spa on the Rhine. He brought with him Czech acceptance. He thought the crisis was over. Instead he was directly confronted with new demands, and not only new demands, but a time limit, an ultimatum, before which they must be accepted. The new demands were worse than blackmail. They were staggering.

It all must have seemed easy to Hitler. The Czechs had been forced to accept his first demands. This meant in his view that the British and the French could be prevailed upon to exert pressure on them to accept even further demands. He had got something for nothing. Why not grab more? Mr. Chamberlain, in his House of Commons speech, quotes Hitler as saying 'that he never for one moment supposed that I (Chamberlain) should be able to come back and say that the principle (self-determination, i.e., territorial dismemberment) had been accepted.' What a cat out of what a bag! Hitler never thought that Britain would accept even his *first* demands!

Chamberlain was thunderstruck. He listened to Hitler on the 22nd, then sulked on his side of the Rhine till evening of the 23rd, just before his departure. Meanwhile notes were exchanged. The new German demands were in text and manner those that a victorious enemy humiliatingly extends to a vanquished foe. And indeed Czechoslovakia *was* a vanquished foe. The Godesberg ultimatum, expiring October 1 (whereas the Berchtesgaden agreement allowed several months for fixing the new frontiers) extended by at least a thousand square miles the territory Germany was to take; it crippled Czechoslovakia irremediably by cutting the nation virtually in two; it allowed only eight days for the removal of Czechoslovaks who did not want to live in Germany (whereas the Treaty of Versailles had given three *years* to Germans in Czechoslovakia who wished to opt for German citizenship); it made no provision for consideration of minorities in the plebiscite areas; it demanded that the Czechs, in the surrendered territory, give up all rolling stock, munitions, freight installations, utility services, radio services, foodstuffs, cattle, goods, and raw materials. In other words, Czechs or non-Nazi Germans fleeing from the new German areas would have to flee—within eight days—utterly destitute.

Chamberlain says:

> 'I declared that the language and manner of the document, which I described as an ultimatum rather than a memorandum, would profoundly shock public opinion in neutral countries, and I bitterly reproached the German Chancellor for his failure to respond in any way to the efforts which I had made to secure peace.'

He then adds:

> 'In spite of those frank words, this conversation was carried out in more friendly terms than that which preceded it.'

Wonderful giveaway! Talk sharply to Herr Hitler, and he becomes more friendly.

At this time Hitler repeated to Chamberlain that the Germans had no further territorial aims in Europe once the Sudeten area was acquired. Chamberlain believed him. Quaint it seems now.

Why, with the Sudeten Germans in his lap, did Hitler break the crisis open again? He must have known that his second demands entailed some risk. He was risking what he had always asserted to be his object, and *which he had already obtained*—the promise of the incorporation of the Sudetens in the Reich—for a further object. In other words, his argument on the basis of self-determination, if not in itself fraudulent, was certainly a pretext for something else.

The something else was of course, as we know now, power in Europe. The ultimate object was not merely the Sudeten area, but destruction of democratic Czechoslovakia as a barrier in his path. Power to break the Franco-Soviet pact, power to isolate and impenetrate Poland and the Balkan states, power to rule Europe east of the Rhine—that is what Hitler wanted. 'The master of Bohemia,' Bismarck said once, 'is the master of the continent.' That mastery was Hitler's object.[1] Let us hear no more nonsense about self-

---

[1] When I first wrote this Chapter on October 5, 1938, I included at this point the following paragraph: 'As to Hitler's promise that he does not wish more territory, one can only say that his lies have been notorious. Like Napoleon, he breaks his word any time that dishonesty is politically convenient. He promised to respect the Treaty of Locarno; and violated it. He promised not to fortify the Rhineland; and fortified it. He promised not to annex Austria; and annexed it. He promised not to invade Czechoslovakia, and invaded it.'

determination. Look at the Germans in the South Tyrol. What is Hitler doing for *those* lost Germans?

As Chamberlain flew back to London from Godesberg, two things continued to happen. One was a provocatively vicious, vulgar, inflammatory, and untruthful assault by the united (and officially controlled) German Press on Czechoslovakia—together with complete suppression of any news that Germany did not like.

The other was the presentation of demands by Poland and Hungary for Czechoslovak territory. The jackals of Warsaw and Budapest rose from their caves and followed the German Lion to the feast. Their whine unpleasantly exacerbated the crisis. Poland certainly had a legitimate claim to Teschen, and Hungary certainly lost too much territory by the Trianon Treaty, but minority assertions by either Poland or Hungary had their certain humours, to say the least. Hungary oppressed the Slovaks and Transylvanian Rumanians for generations. Poland was a composite state precisely as was Czechoslovakia, with almost 10,000,000 non-Poles in a total population of 33,000,000.

On Sunday, the 25th, Daladier and Bonnet again came to London. The Czechs, convinced now that they must perish fighting, mobilised; word had gone from Chamberlain to Prague that in view of the Godesberg demands the Czechs had best prepare themselves. The entire nation rose to arms. The French decided that the new German proposals were unacceptable; so did the Czechs. And a highly important Anglo-French communiqué was issued to the effect that, if Germany invaded Czechoslovakia, 'the immediate result must be that France will be bound to come to her assistance and Great Britain and Russia will certainly stand by France.' So finally the British, in finally unmistakable terms, did commit themselves—and Russia!—to the defence of Czechoslovakia. The French and Belgians mobilised; London got ready for Goering's raiders. Gas masks were distributed, and men frantically dug trenches in Hyde Park.

The result was what might have been expected. Hitler in his speech at the Sport-Palast the next day receded—not much—but he did recede. He assaulted Dr. Beneš and the Czechoslovaks vigorously, but he did not close the door for ever. That night President Roosevelt made his first dramatic appeal for peace, and on Tuesday, September 27, Chamberlain addressed the world by radio in a brief grave speech, saying that he would labour for peace to the end, but that Britain would have to fight if 'any nation made up its mind to dominate the world by fear of force.'

Chamberlain's most trusted adviser, Sir Horace Wilson, was shuttling by air between London and Berlin. Mr. Roosevelt sent a second appeal to Hitler, which like the first was not even printed in Germany and to which the answer was a curt statement that further correspondence would not be useful. Hitler, playing his hand with wonderful skill, pressing hard now, let it be known that he changed his ultimatum from October 1 (which first date had been disclosed not by Hitler but by Mussolini) to 2 p.m. on the 28th. Then, on Mussolini's intervention, it was advanced 24 hours till the 29th. Time was almost up. Gas masks were fitted in Buckingham Palace.

On the 29th Chamberlain addressed the House of Commons in what was certainly the most momentous session since August 1914. Chamberlain told as much of the story as he could, and was reaching his peroration with an account of the last desperate manœuvres. Hitler had assured Sir Horace Wilson that his troops would only occupy the Sudeten areas; Chamberlain wrote Hitler once more imploring him not to precipitate a world catastrophe when agreement in principle had already been established; he also revealed that he had urgently written Mussolini asking him to stay Hitler's hand.

Then a messenger arrived in the House of Commons. Chamberlain looked at the piece of paper. He announced:

> 'I have something further to tell the House. I have now been informed by Herr Hitler that he invites me to meet him in Munich to-morrow morning. He has also invited Signor Mussolini and M. Daladier. Signor Mussolini has accepted and I have no doubt that M. Daladier will also accept. The House will not need to ask what my answer will be.'

The four leaders met at Munich on September 29 and whittled out an agreement. No Czechoslovak representative was permitted to take part in the deliberations; a Czechoslovak emissary was, in fact, shown the door. It was agreed that Germany begin occupation of four Sudeten districts on October 1, that the Czechs must not remove any 'installations', that an international commission should decide future regions for plebiscites, and that Germany and Italy should join Britain and France in a guaranty of the new frontiers. So in nine hours of talk four men accomplished the dismemberment of a nation.

Chamberlain additionally signed a short bi-lateral pact with Hitler—apparently without consulting the Foreign Office or the Dominions, who ordinarily are informed about any such important diplomatic step—asserting that the Munich agreement was 'symbolic of the desire of our two peoples never to go to war with one another again', and pledging the signatories to 'a method of consultation' in dealing with questions concerning the two countries. So Hitler's victory seemed complete. And when Chamberlain returned to London, he said, 'It is peace in our time.'

On October 1 the German troops began their victorious occupation of Czechoslovakia.[1] By October 5 it was clear that they did not intend to stop at the lines originally drawn. On October 6 Dr. Beneš resigned. No man ever had a crueller trial, or sought to render greater service to his country.

Aftermath of Munich

In a day or two Europe awoke as if shattered by a nightmare. Everyone, dazed, sought to trace just what had happened; and a few prescient folk wondered if it could possibly have been as bad as the nightmare seemed. It was. Germany had won the greatest diplomatic victory of the century. Czechoslovakia was in essence destroyed, and the Little Entente collapsed. Disillusion with the democracies smote Russia sharply, and France—it seemed—became a second-rate power. The entire European system of security was burst asunder. Even in Britain there were dark forebodings. For British foreign policy had for three hundred years depended on the balance of power, a theory which in turn depends on the presumption that no single country on the Continent is too powerful. After Munich, Germany became overwhelmingly the strongest power in Europe. The British decided that they had better hurry on with their exhausting arms programme—after all.

Yet many well-informed Europeans thought that a chance, a slim but infinitely precious chance, remained that Munich might bring —not war—but real peace. Germany, they said, must obviously play its proper role in Europe. One cannot go from generation to generation knocking Germans on the head and waiting for them to rise again, in order to knock them on the head once more. The Germans are a courageous, an industrious, a supremely patriotic people, indispensable to the unity and well being of Europe.

[1] When Hitler entered Karlsbad he said astoundingly, 'I always knew that some day I would stand here, but I never knew how it would come about.'

The German problem, that of a powerful expansionist state in the heart of the Continent, must be solved somehow if Europe is to survive at all. And so it was said, with stilled and hopeful breath, 'If only, if *only* Hitler keeps his word this time, if only he will rest content with this immense victory and forswear further adventures, it is possible—just possible—that peace will come.'

But Hitler didn't keep his word. Within six months, he had absorbed the rest of Czechoslovakia. Within a year, he made war on Poland.

End of Czechoslovakia

Almost at once it became clear that Germany, in dealing with Czechoslovakia, was not going to abide by the Munich settlement. First, the promise that plebiscites would be held in the border areas was dropped; second, the projected Anglo-French guaranty of the new frontiers never materialised. The Germans insisted on using the 1910 census as a criterion for deciding who was Czech and who was German. As a result, some 800,000 pure Czechs found themselves assigned to Germany; some areas with less than ten per cent German population—by contemporary statistics—were severed from Czechoslovakia and surrendered to the Reich. All in all, Czechoslovakia lost some 19,000 square miles out of roughly 54,000; it lost 4,922,440 inhabitants out of roughly 15,000,000. Of these, 3,600,000 went to Germany, about 1,000,000 to Hungary, and about 240,000—in the Teschen area—to Poland.

Meantime a shaky and almost powerless government, terrified of the Nazis, sought to rule in Prague. Nothing except complete pro-Germanism was possible to any surviving Czech politician—if he wished to survive. By November a pro-German 'national' party was formed and a Supreme Court judge named Hacha became president of the republic. Also in November the Slovaks and Ruthenes were 'given' virtual autonomy, with Germany, of course, pulling the strings; the way was thus prepared for the final conquest. 'Czechoslovakia' shrivelled in effect to the two central districts of Bohemia and Moravia. Here too German power was potentially absolute. The Germans, by pushing a button, could turn off all Prague's electric light and water power. Then—as if this were not enough—the Germans announced their intention of building an extraterritorial highway straight across Czechoslovakia, linking the Reich proper with Vienna.

Crisis came in March. It is a very complex story about which it is still too early to write with authority. We know something; we do not know all. In Bratislava, the capital of Slovakia, a cabinet crisis was provoked by Slovak separatists. Dr. Tiso, the pro-German prime minister, was forced out; immediately he left for Berlin, accompanied by the German consul-general (this was on March 13), where he was received by Hitler. The government in Prague, under President Hacha, was desperately trying to retain some tiny fragment of Czech national dignity and independence. It could not allow the Slovaks to secede from what remained of the republic without at least protesting. But the protest was unavailing. Germany stepped in—full-force and full-weight—on the Slovak side. With greased wheels the propaganda machine, so well trained on the Austrian and Sudeten crises, went into action. There were the usual stories—all quite untrue—of disorder, violence, and murder by Czechs against Germans. On March 14— the crisis came to a head very quickly indeed—Hitler peremptorily summoned President Hacha and his foreign minister, Dr. Chvalkovsky, to Berlin.

Hacha was the Czech Schuschnigg. He was treated better than Schuschnigg. But the result was the same. Only the pace was faster. He arrived in Berlin at 10.40 p.m. on the 14th, and was received at 1 a.m. At 4.15 he broke down, and signed the independence of his country away. Hitler and Goering broke him down. Once he fainted. Alarmed, fearing he might die of heart failure, Goering gave him a stimulant. He fainted again. He read what he had signed, 'The Czechoslovak president . . . trustfully lays the fate of the Czech people and country into the hands of the Führer of the German Reich.'

Already German troops were in motion. They had started across the frontier, in fact, and occupied towns like Moravska-Ostrava and Vitkovice, on the 14th before Hacha arrived in Berlin. The Reichswehr machine moved with oiled and beautiful precision. No resistance came from stunned Prague. All of Czechoslovakia except Ruthenia (which the Hungarians took) was occupied smoothly and at once. Sullen, silent, the Czech crowds watched the Germans enter. Germans had not been in Prague since 1648. That night —the same incredible March 15—Hitler slept in the Prague palace of the old Bohemian kings.

Bohemia-Moravia was at once transformed into a protectorate; Slovakia became in theory 'autonomous' with its political 'independence' guaranteed under German guidance. Tiso was rewarded by the Slovak premiership; rather surprisingly, Hacha was permitted to remain in the Bohemia-Moravia 'presidency', though atop him—now—was the new Reichs 'Protector', Baron von Neurath. Thus Czechoslovakia disappeared.

Of all European coups this century, this probably was the most astonishing, both for its celerity and for the vast political implications it evoked. This was something new—even for Hitler. This was something *not* written in his programme. This was something *not* in *Mein Kampf*. Hitler did not merely, in the most glaring manner, violate all his Munich pledges to Chamberlain (where was that Anglo-German understanding to 'consult' that Mr. Chamberlain had been so proud of?); he violated every promise he had ever made to his own people and to his own destiny. If Hitler stood for anything, it was the integrity of German race. Over and over again, he had proclaimed that only Germans interested him. Yet here he was, calmly acquiring some seven million Czechs. Here he was, a conqueror of the old school, with all doctrines of self-determination, pan-Germanism, racism, tossed overboard. He said at Munich he had no more territorial claims in Europe. Yet here he was—with a non-German country in his bag!

Hitler's explanation was embodied in his first proclamation establishing the protectorate: 'Bohemia and Moravia have for thousands of years belonged to the *Lebensraum* of the German people. Force and unreason have arbitrarily torn them from their old historical setting. . . . Sooner or later the Reich, as historically and geographically the power most interested in the region, would have to bear the heaviest consequences. It is in accordance, therefore, with the *principles of self-preservation* (italics mine) that the Reich is resolved to intervene . . .' Thus the new slogan, *Lebensraum* (living space) was born. Thus too self-determination became transformed into self-preservation. The next motto followed soon—'encirclement'.[1]

German troops entering Czechoslovakia were armed with a German-Czech phrase book, according to the New York *Times*. Excerpts:

[1] As if as a sop to the racial theory, the laws of the protectorate, announced on March 16, differentiate between classes of citizens. Pure Germans become *German* nationals, 'for the protection of German blood and honour,' while Czechs become merely citizens of the protectorate.

If you lie you will be shot.
Are the inhabitants peaceful?
It is punishable by death, first, to go near the railway; second,
to use the telephone.
Are you the mayor? Open all the cupboards. Where is the
safe? How much money is in it? I confiscate the money.

As if still in the stride of this staggering coup, with his left hand
as it were, Hitler reached out on March 22 and took Memel from
Lithuania. He was intoxicated with success. But the Czech adventure, the obliteration of the Czechoslovak state, may not turn
out to be a Hitler victory. He announced himself after March as
the *Mehrer* (Aggrandiser) of the German Reich; it is not a title that
becomes him. The March crisis can, in fact, be interpreted as a
defeat of the first magnitude for Hitler. In one sense it was not a
victory at all; it was his first great historical mistake. Because it
brought the British into line against him.

The Polish Crisis Begins

'No one in Germany thinks of going to war with Poland over the Corridor.'
—HITLER in 1933.

I cannot propose in this book to deal with the Polish crisis comprehensively. To do so would necessitate whole chapters, if not
volumes. This book does not, after all, pretend to be a detailed
history. I can sketch only highlights. It is still too early to write
the final, definitive story.

Within a week of the acquisition of Bohemia-Moravia, on
March 21 in fact, six days later, Hitler opened his great diplomatic
offensive against Poland. He was supremely confident. He revealed, speaking to the Reichstag on March 28, that he had made
certain 'proposals' to the Polish Government. First, Danzig should,
as a Free City, return to the Reich. Second, Germany should receive
a combined road and railway across the Corridor, with extraterritorial status: in other words, a German 'corridor across the corridor'. Third, Germany would recognise the Polish frontier as
final and guarantee it for twenty-five years. The Poles replied to
this offer with a cautious and provisional negative. Presumably
they assumed that a period of bargaining was to begin. They replied—on March 26—that they were quite willing to discuss
'objectively' the German points, but that before discussion could
start they must be assured, first, of Germany's peaceable intentions,

second that Germany would adopt only peaceful methods of procedure.

Meantime the events of March 15 had been a staggering shock to Chamberlain and the great bulk of British opinion. The prime minister, bitterly disillusioned—with Munich down the chute and the whole 'appeasement' policy in ruins—rebuked the Germans. 'Is this the end of an old adventure,' he asked, 'or the beginning of a new? Is this the last attack upon a small state, or is it to be followed by others?' With alacrity the British set about mending fences. Poland—it was obvious—was going to be the next victim. The British, not merely out of disinterested regard for the Poles, but because they now realised that Hitler could not be trusted and that his march to European dominance was a vital threat to their most vital interests, determined to support Poland. On March 31 Chamberlain announced terms of a British and French guarantee to the Poles as follows:

> 'In order to make perfectly clear the position of His Majesty's Government . . . I have now to inform the House that . . . in the event of any action which clearly threatened Polish independence and which the Polish Government accordingly considered it vital to resist with their national forces, His Majesty's Government would feel themselves bound at once to lend the Polish Government all the support in their power. They have given the Polish Government an assurance to this effect.'

As Chamberlain himself said on April 3, this unprecedented and sensational pledge marked a 'new epoch' in British foreign policy. The British frontier became the Vistula. For the first time in history, Britain promised to support an eastern European power. For the first time in history, Britain pledged itself to fight for a European state other than France or Belgium. The pledge was badly drafted. It gave the Poles virtually a blank cheque. It did not specify frontiers. It was not, for a time, clear whether Danzig was or was not included in the pledge. It did not mention the putative aggressor—with the result, that when *Russia* invaded Poland (the British of course had had only Germany in mind), it seemed that the British were committed to go to war against the Soviet Union. Above all, the pledge did not take account of concrete realities—*how* the British were going to support Poland, *how* help could possibly be rendered Poland 'at once'.

Hitler's answer was sharp. On April 28 the Germans denounced both their famous non-aggression pact with Poland, which had regularised German-Polish relations on a peaceful basis since 1934, and the Anglo-German naval agreement, which had been such a feather in Ribbentrop's first cap. The British then proceeded to extend their eastern European guarantees to Rumania, Turkey, and Greece, including financial assistance. This was locking stable doors with a vengeance—after the Austrian and Czechoslovak horses had been hamstrung and kidnapped.

At about this time entered another inordinately important factor —Anglo-French relations with the Soviet Union.

It must have been obvious to a moron, a child, or even an arch-bishop that Poland was impossible of effective defence without Russian help. And at first it seemed that Russia was willing to help. On March 18, two days after the seizure of Prague, the Soviet Government suggested an immediate conference at Bucharest at which the democratic powers might hammer out a common pro-gramme. The British Government rejected this proposal as 'premature'. By mid-April, Chamberlain began to see the cardinal necessity of bringing the Russians in. Even so, he detested doing so. His attitude and that of his government was strikingly like their former attitude in regard to Spain. As politicians, as nationalists, it was imperative to work with the Bolsheviks. But from a class point of view, from the point of view of their deepest social instincts and economic prejudices, they loathed the idea. What happened as a result of this half-heartedness, this division of impulse, was inevitable—a dawdling approach to Russia, an incompetent and laggard attempt to bring Russia 'in'.

Not till June 12 did William Strang, Chamberlain's right-hand man in the Foreign Office, set out for Moscow—though Maisky, the Soviet Ambassador to London, appealed frantically for haste, and asked that the British send Halifax or some cabinet minister, not merely a subordinate official whom the Russians incidentally de-tested; not till August 10 did the joint Anglo-French military mis-sion finally arrive in Leningrad. It was amusing, meantime, to detect the sudden change in the British Press in regard to Russian affairs. *The Times* and *Observer* ceased—for a few strange weeks —to call Russians Bolsheviks; the whole stress was on the idea of Russia as a powerful and friendly national state, with a proud his-tory and a massive military machine, now an ally.

On the other hand, it must be firmly stated that the Russians— once the British got to Moscow and indeed all through the negotia-tions—behaved insufferably. The British were half-hearted, badly informed, and dull; the Russians were mendacious, double-faced, and diabolically clever. The negotiations broke down on two scores. First, the Russians asked what help the Red Army should give Poland. The British, embarrassed, referred to the Poles, who it is understood refused to countenance any military assistance, at least by infantry. So the Russians—perplexed—asked what was the object of having negotiations at all, if they were in one breath asked to render assistance, and in another breath refused the possibility of contributing it. Second, the Russians insisted on comprehensive privileges in regard to the Baltic states. They demanded the right to intervene in the Baltic area not merely if the Baltics were directly attacked by Germany, but in the event of 'indirect' aggression. In other words—and we know now only too well what the Russians were driving at—they wanted the prerogative of intervention in the Baltics even to frustrate a purely internal *coup d'état* that they might dislike. The British could not accept this Baltic proposal. They thought it was too high a price to pay for Russian help.

But we overreach our story. Let us return to Germany and Poland. By March 28 the familiar grisly Press war had begun. Dr. Goebbels unleashed all his inky guns. And progressively relations between Germany and Poland disintegrated. The central issue was of course Danzig. At this time Hitler did not openly admit that he intended to make an issue of the Corridor and Silesia also, and to grab them if he could.

Note well that the Press campaign against Poland—which culminated in the atrocity stories that, Sir Nevile Henderson believes, played a great role in finally moving Hitler to open warfare—as well as the diplomatic and political campaign, were evolved by Germany almost overnight. Since 1934 German relations with Poland had been quite cordial. Colonel Beck, the Polish foreign minister, was amicably greeted in Berchtesgaden as late as January 1939; in the same month Ribbentrop went to Warsaw, and announced unctuously, 'I can assure the Germans in Poland that the agreement of January 26, 1934, has put a final end to enmity between our two peoples.' The Danzig and Corridor questions had been 'settled' five years before. During those five years, hardly a breath of complaint was heard from Germany. Then, in twenty-four hours, the situation of Danzig and the Corridor became 'intolerable'. Overnight, the Germans found it too 'terrible' to be borne.

Danzig is, incontestably, a German city. It was, incontestably,

removed from Germany by a very stupid and shortsighted provision
of the 1919 treaties. Yet Danzig, though German, was of profound
and legitimate importance to Poland too, since it controlled
Poland's outlet to the sea. It is German; but its hinterland was
Polish, also incontestably. Danzig meant, of course, more to Hitler
than Danzig. It meant prestige, it meant a new diplomatic victory,
it meant above all power. He thought of it as a wedge into the
Corridor, which was—and still is—more Polish than German.
Danzig was to be for Poland what the Sudetenland turned out to
be for Czechoslovakia.

Again and again, as a dark spring entered into tortured summer,
the British told Hitler that they would fight for Poland, would fight
even for Danzig. As early as May 27 Henderson said to Goering
that 'if Germany attempted to settle German-Polish differences by
unilateral action such as would compel the Poles to resort to arms
to safeguard their independence', the British and French would
make war on Germany. (British Blue Book, p. xiii.) On August 15,
Henderson told Baron von Weizsäcker, the state secretary in the
German Foreign Office, that 'if the Poles were compelled by any
act of Germany to resort to arms to defend themselves, there was
not a shadow of doubt that we would give them our full armed
support'. He appealed to the Germans not to make the 'tragic
mistake' of believing the contrary. Another warning to Hitler in
person, in even firmer language, came on August 25. Still the
Germans would not listen. Until the last, they never believed that
the British would actually care—or dare—to fight.

By July the situation—centring on Danzig—had reached full
and angry crisis. The gist of it was that the Germans, who already
had complete political control of Danzig (they had Nazified it by
progressive stages since 1933), began to militarise the area. Troops
and supplies poured into Danzig from East Prussia. At the same
time—though we did not know it then—Germany began important
military movements in Slovakia; the town of Bratislava became the
headquarters of a German army command in June. The Poles
didn't know quite what line to take in regard to Danzig. It seemed
that at any moment Germany might try the ruse of an *internal*
Danzig coup, as to which they could disclaim responsibility; the
Poles, then, would have to take the onus of aggression. All through
July and early August came incidents and agitation. Colonel Beck
announced finally the three fundamental Polish desiderata: First,
Danzig must retain its status as a Free State; second, it must remain

within the Polish customs union; third, Polish shipping and railway rights must be safeguarded. Then on August 7 came a new crisis over Polish customs inspectors in the Danzig area who were dismissed by the Danzig (Nazi) authorities. Obviously this manœuvre had one intention, the removal of Polish officials who might detect and seek to halt the continued stream of German military goods entering the area. The Poles sent a fairly stiff note to Germany, warning the Germans not to interfere in Polish-Danzig affairs. Germany chose to regard this as an 'ultimatum'.

Following is part of the telegram Lord Halifax sent the British Ambassador in Warsaw on August 15:

'I have the impression that Herr Hitler is still undecided, and anxious to avoid war and to hold his hand if he can do so without losing face. As there is a possibility of him not forcing the issue, it is evidently essential to give him no excuse for acting, whether or not conversations about Danzig at some future time may be possible. It therefore seems of the first importance to endeavour to get the local issues (customs inspectors, margarine and herrings) settled at once, and not to let questions of procedure or "face" at Danzig stand in the way. It also seems essential that the Polish Government should make every effort to moderate their press, even in the face of a German press campaign and to intensify their efforts to prevent attacks on their German minority.'[1]

Meantime, on July 17, General Ironside and a British military mission arrived in Warsaw to inspect the Polish defences and presumably arrange collaboration. In August, after laborious discussion, the British gave Poland a credit of £8,000,000 for purchase of war materials. The Poles did not, however, obtain a cash advance of £5,000,000 they asked for. This produced a certain amount of ill-feeling in Warsaw. At the moment the British were spending at least £2,000,000 per day on their own armament. It seemed that they did not consider their Polish ally to be worth even two and a half days' expenditure.

By mid-August an explosion was predictably imminent. The Germans continued their onslaughts; the Poles remained restlessly defensive; the British sought to make a settlement. Then came climax in the form of an utterly unexpected surprise—the Russo-German non-aggression pact.

[1] From the British Blue Book, Documents Concerning German-Polish Relations and the Outbreak of Hostilities between Great Britain and Germany on September 3, 1939. Cmd. 6106. p. 92.

The Russo-German Pact

I happened to be in Moscow on August 19, 1939. That evening a small group of journalists and diplomats read with amazement a brief announcement in the *Pravda*. It stated that the Soviet Union had just arranged a trade agreement with Germany. The Reich agreed to lend Russia 200 million marks with which Russia should buy German goods. And Germany during the next seven years was to buy Russian goods valued at 180 million marks.

This announcement was, after all, not so surprising as it first seemed. Russo-German commercial discussions had been going on for months, it was well known. But at this precise time the announcement was unexpected if only because of Russian negotiations with the British and French delegations in Moscow. At first well-informed folk thought that the Russo-German commercial agreement was meritorious. After all Russia and Germany are, or should be, excellent economic partners. The optimists thought that the agreement might assist peace. It might give Hitler just the alternative to warfare that he needed, an opportunity to unwind economically, to transform his economy from a wartime to a peace-time basis, by a large export business with Russia.

But on August 21 news came that pushed the sensational enough commercial agreement into complete insignificance. Late that night a laconic communiqué stated that Germany and Russia had negotiated a non-aggression treaty. Nothing more unbelievable could be imagined. Astonishment and scepticism turned quickly to consternation and alarm. Promptly Ribbentrop arrived in Moscow, and on August 24 the pact was signed. It was a far reaching document, going considerably beyond the stipulations of most non-aggression treaties. It bound the signatories to consult, to refrain from any acts of force against one another, and to refuse support to any third power attacking either contracting party.

(The first comment I heard in Moscow was, 'Well, Stalin joined the anti-Comintern pact to-day. . . .')

It seemed, at the beginning, almost too much to believe—that Stalin, under the very nose of the French and British delegations, had leapt into the enemy's camp, that Russian communists should extend the hand of friendship and collaboration to German Nazis, that the Russians, who for years had feared Hitler like poison, should now join the man who for years had called *them* his mortal and implacable enemy. Yet, certain shrewd observers had seen

L

which way the wind was blowing. They had seen that Communism and Fascism were more closely allied than was normally understood. On August 16, Baron Weizsäcker significantly hinted to Sir Nevile Henderson that 'Russian assistance to the Poles would not only be entirely negligible, but that the U.S.S.R. would even in the end join in sharing in the Polish spoils'. (British Blue Book, p. 91.)

The reason Hitler negotiated the Russian pact is quite clear, even though he had no ardent desire to do so.[1] By the pact he hoped finally to frighten Great Britain off, to freeze and squeeze the British into neutrality. It was his last desperate bid to get what he wanted, Danzig and the rest, *without* warfare. The Russo-German pact isolated and in fact, as we know now, doomed Poland. It condemned Poland to death. Hitler calculated that the British would antici- pate this, and would therefore force Poland to submit to his demands. But what happened was the contrary. The Russo- German pact stiffened the British. It turned the British to stronger support of Poland than ever before.

(Sir Nevile Henderson is inclined to blame Ribbentrop for Hitler's bad information about the British. He writes in one dis- patch that the idea propounded to him by Weizsäcker—that the British would not fight—'sounded like Herr von Ribbentrop who had never been able to understand the British mentality'. On another occasion, in the New York *Times*, October 18, 1939, Hen- derson is quoted as saying that Hitler came to regard Ribbentrop more and more as a second Bismarck, 'a conviction which Herr von Ribbentrop himself probably shared to the full'.)

As to Stalin's motives for signing the pact with Hitler, they are quite clear too. The pact was an enormous diplomatic victory for Russia. It made the British angry, but for some months at least, angry as they were, the British treated Stalin more politely than previously.

1. The Russo-German pact removed in a stroke—provisionally at least—the single greatest preoccupation of Soviet foreign policy. It banished the deepest Russian fear—fear of attack by Germany. It eliminated the danger of aggression by Germany against the Soviet Union for a long time to come.

[1] Henderson telegraphed Halifax on August 24: 'In referring to the Russian non-aggression pact he (Hitler) observed that it was England which had forced him into agreement with Russia. He did not seem enthusiastic over it but added that once he made an agreement it would be for a long period.' British Blue Book, p. 101.

2. It was a wonderful manœuvre against the Russian enemy in the east, Japan, since it gave Russia virtually a free hand against Japan. The Russians felt that no longer would they have to watch both frontiers. The Japanese, stunned and frightened, immediately agreed to a truce in the Far East. A Russo-Japanese non-aggression pact may follow.

3. By isolating Poland it made the subsequent Russian attack on Poland and Russian penetration into the Baltic states possible.

4. It served to destroy the anti-Comintern pact, which had for years been the focus of Fascist designs on the U.S.S.R.

5. By making war virtually inevitable, it put the Soviet Union into a position where it could profit so long as the war lasted, no matter how the war should turn out.

One result of the pact was, of course, to end Popular Frontism, which could hardly survive such a violent ideological twist. A Popular Front against Fascism had little meaning after the Russians joined the Fascists. But Stalin was probably tired of this strategic deviation, which is what Popular Frontism was. He was tired of picking democratic chestnuts out of the fire. He began to look for chestnuts of his own.

I discuss other aspects of Russian relations with Germany as well as the general course of Soviet foreign policy in Chapter XL below. It is time now to proceed with our main story.

Grim Harvest in Poland

'The Sudetenland is the last territorial claim which I have to make in Europe.'
—HITLER, September 26, 1938.

'Germany has concluded a non-aggression pact with Poland . . . and she will adhere to it unconditionally.'
—HITLER, May 31, 1935.

'Germany is the bulwark of the West against Bolshevism.'
—HITLER, November 29, 1935.

The last tragic act came quickly. The catastrophe was now beyond control. The nerves and vitality of the Continent had been sapped by the long crisis. There was nothing to do with Hitler now except stop him by force. The last act took only twelve crowded and terrible days. On August 24 the Russo-German pact was signed. On September 1 the Germans invaded Poland.

These twelve days of body-wracking tension and suspense were occupied mainly by last-minute strenuous and dogged negotiations

between Britain and Germany. The other countries in effect
dropped out. They took to the sidelines. They watched the two
giants fight. The showdown had come finally. It was Germany
against the world, but Britain against Germany.

This is not to say that nothing happened in other countries.
Plenty happened. Belgium, Holland, France, and Italy mobilised,
as well as Germany and Poland. It was like the Munich crisis of
the year before, but much sharper, much more highly geared.
France, with three million men in arms, closed its frontier with
Italy, which had 1,700,000 men mobilised. The Mediterranean was
barred to British shipping; Germans were told to leave Great
Britain; by the thousand, American tourists scurried home. Germany filled Slovakia with troops, and a thousand German planes
landed there. The Pope appealed for peace; so did President
Roosevelt. On August 24 the Nazi leader, Foerster, became head
of state in Danzig. Frontier incidents occurred daily along the
whole Polish border. On August 27, German planes incessantly
flew over the Polish port Gdynia, and armed Germans at a dozen
points sought to enter Polish territory. On August 29 the Dutch
and Belgians made a peace offer. It was in vain. And anyway too
late.

During these tremendous days Sir Nevile Henderson saw Hitler
four times for four tremendous colloquies.

The first meeting took place at Berchtesgaden on August 23.
Henderson brought with him a last appeal in the form of a letter
from Chamberlain. (The Germans recognised that Chamberlain
could not himself come to Germany, *this* time!) The letter presented three main ideas, that the British would stand unalterably
by their pledge to Poland, that they were prepared to discuss all
matters between the two countries peaceably, and that they would
welcome direct conversations—in regard to minorities and the like
—between Germany and Poland.

Let Henderson tell the story:

'We arrived Salzburg soon after 11 a.m. and motored to Berchtesgaden, where I was received by Herr Hitler shortly after 1 p.m. I
had derived the impression that atmosphere was likely to be most
unfriendly and that probability was that interview would be
exceedingly brief.

'During the whole of this first conversation Herr Hitler was ex-
citable and uncompromising. He made no long speeches but his
language was violent and exaggerated both as regards England and
Poland. He began by asserting that the Polish question would have

been settled on the most generous terms if it had not been for England's unwarranted support. . . .

'He then violently attacked the Poles, talked of 100,000 German refugees from Poland, excesses against Germans, closing of German institutions and Polish systematic persecution of German nationals generally. . . .

'At the end of this first conversation Herr Hitler observed, in reply to my repeated warnings that direct action by Germany would mean war, that Germany had nothing to lose and Great Britain much; that he did not desire war but would not shrink from it if it was necessary; and that his people were much more behind him than last September. . . .

'I spoke of tragedy of war and of his immense responsibility, but his answer was that it would be all England's fault. I refuted this only to learn from him that England was determined to destroy and exterminate Germany. He was, he said, 50 years old: he preferred war now to when he would be 55 or 60.'

—British Blue Book, pp. 98–100,

It was in this conversation that Hitler first mentioned that Germans had been 'castrated' by Poles. He several times returned to this allegation.

Hitler answered Chamberlain's letter with a threat of full mobilisation, and on August 25 Henderson was received for the second time. Hitler said by way of introduction that 'the assertion that Germany affected to conquer the world was ridiculous. The British Empire embraced 40 million square kilometres, Russia 19 million, America 9½ million, whereas Germany embraced less than 600 thousand square kilometres. It is quite clear who it is who desires to conquer the world.' Hitler proceeded to mention Poland's 'intolerable provocations'; he said that Germany would at all cost abolish the 'Macedonian conditions' on its eastern frontier; he agreed that the war, if it came, would be long and bloody, and, speaking of Russia in warm terms, said that Germany would have to fight only on one frontier; finally, he agreed to 'accept the British Empire and pledge himself personally for its continued existence and to place the power of the German Reich at its disposal', on certain conditions. These conditions appeared to be, first, a limited colonial settlement; second, no interference with German relations with Italy and Russia.

Hitler was quite calm during this conversation, Henderson reports. 'He was absolutely calm and normal and spoke with great earnestness and apparent sincerity.' Henderson suggested that Ribbentrop and Beck meet somewhere. Hitler demurred. It was in this talk that Hitler made two extraordinary statements. First, that 'the only winner of another European war would be Japan'. Second, that he was an artist by nature, not a politician, and that when the Polish question was settled he wished to retire from politics and 'end his life as an artist'.

Henderson flew to London at Hitler's suggestion—this was on the 26th—and the British cabinet spent an agitated week-end studying the German note and preparing a reply. It accepted, without commitment as to detail, the German suggestion for a general understanding with Great Britain. But it reiterated that a settlement of the Polish problem must come first, and that this must come peaceably. It suggested direct negotiations between Germany and Poland, with Britain lending its good offices to the discussion. The Poles, the British said, would agree to talk.

Henderson flew back to Berlin with this message and was received by Hitler for the third interview on August 28. In this conversation Hitler for the first time went beyond his first demands; he now asked not merely for Danzig but for the Corridor and for a 'rectification' in Silesia. Henderson appealed to him not to raise his price. Hitler then asked if Great Britain would accept an alliance with Germany, and if the British would offer Germany 'something in the way of colonies as evidence of her good intentions'. As to the alliance, Henderson said cautiously that personally he did not exclude it as a possibility; as to colonies, he said that 'concessions were easier of realisation' in a good atmosphere. The next day, August 29, came the written German reply. And this reply brought climax.

The Führer received Henderson at 7.15 p.m. This, the fourth great interview, was 'stormy'. Poland had mobilised, and the German Press reported that five Germans had been killed by Poles. This excited Hitler violently. Later, in October, when Henderson wrote his report of the whole extraordinary episode, he stated that he believed that this report 'was probably fabricated by extremists in fear he [Hitler] was weakening'. Hitler, according to Henderson, was walled off from every advice but that of extremists. On the 28th Henderson found Hitler 'friendly and reasonable'. On the 29th he was 'upset and uncompromising'.

Hitler's note of the 29th made three points:

1. Germany was sceptical of success, but solely out of desire to achieve friendship with Britain, it would accept the principle of direct negotiations with Poland.

2. In the event of any territorial changes Germany could not participate in any guarantees without consulting the Soviet Union.

3. The Polish plenipotentiary—with whom the direct negotiations would presumably be instituted—must arrive in Berlin by the 30th of August, the next day.

Henderson's dispatch to Halifax states:

'I remarked that this phrase sounded like an ultimatum, but after some heated remarks both Herr Hitler and Herr von Ribbentrop assured me that it was only intended to stress urgency of the moment when the two fully mobilised armies were standing face to face. I said that I would transmit this suggestion immediately to His Majesty's Government, and asked whether, if such Polish plenipotentiary did come, we could assume that he would be well received and that discussions would be conducted on footing of complete equality. Herr Hitler's reply was "Of course".'
                        —British Blue Book, p. 138.

This gave the Poles from 7.15 p.m. on the 29th to midnight on the 30th, that is 28 hours and 45 minutes, to send an emissary to Berlin. The British at once said that it was unreasonable to expect that Colonel Beck or anyone else should arrive in Germany at such short notice. The official German note of the 29th then put a different complexion on the matter; it stated that 'the German Government will immediately draw up proposals for a solution *acceptable to themselves*' (italics mine) to place before the Polish negotiator. The British protested. They asked why the Germans could not submit the proposals in the normal way to the Polish Ambassador, for transmission to his government. The Poles had no intention of sending an emissary if he was going to be treated like Schuschnigg or Hacha. They did not intend to come to Berlin if coming to Berlin meant their own death sentence, if it meant cutting their own throats.

Henderson saw Ribbentrop on the evening of the 30th. Ribbentrop—it must have been an amazing scene—pulled a long document from his pocket and read it, in German, 'at top speed'. These were the sixteen points which the Germans had formulated for settlement with Poland. They included cession of Danzig and a plebiscite in the Corridor. When Ribbentrop concluded Henderson asked him for the text. Ribbentrop refused to give it to him, on the ground that the Polish plenipotentiary had not arrived. Henderson was stupefied. He inquired why, at least, Ribbentrop did not summon the Polish Ambassador and give him the proposals.

'In the most violent terms Ribbentrop said that he would never ask the ambassador to visit him.' But Ribbentrop then said that if the ambassador took the initiative in requesting the interview, 'it might be different'.

Beginning at 8 a.m. the next day, August 31, the Polish Ambassador, M. Lipski, requested that he be received. He was asked, 'Do you come as an ambassador or as a plenipotentiary?' He said he came as an ambassador. The Polish Government meantime agreed to accept the principle of direct discussions. In London Lord Halifax sent telegram after telegram appealing to both Warsaw and Berlin for moderation and a last minute settlement.

The Poles agreed to instruct Lipski to tell Ribbentrop that Poland accepted the British proposals, though they did not like the prospect that he might simply be given a document in the form of an ultimatum. Finally at 6.30 p.m. Lipski was received. Ribbentrop handed him the sixteen points. At once Lipski sought to get into communication with his government. It was too late. The Germans had already cut the lines to Warsaw. At 9 p.m. (August 31) the Germans broadcast the sixteen points, and said that Poland had rejected them. As a matter of fact the Polish Government never even saw them. Nor did the British Government. Neither the Poles nor the British knew what the German demands were till they heard them on the radio. Germany presented its programme while at the same time—a final fantastic detail—contriving that no one had a chance to consider it.

At dawn, the next morning, September 1, the German invasion of Poland began; with incredible hypocrisy Ribbentrop said that the Poles were invading Germany. So—once again—war came to weary Europe.[1] So—once again—Europe vibrated to the shock of marching men.

[1] Events of the first months of the war itself are sketched in a brief introduction to this volume.

CHAPTER X

DALADIER AND BLUM

EDOUARD DALADIER, the war prime minister of France, who rules the country with full powers of a sort unparalleled in recent French history, lives in a modest four-room apartment on the Rue Anatole des Forges, a few moments from the Arc de Triomphe. The neighbourhood, like so many in Paris, is divided sharply between a fashionable sector and one not so fashionable. M. Daladier lives on the non-fashionable side. Recently I inspected this neighbourhood. I wanted to see what the prime minister's habitat was. I wanted to see what *he* saw when he went to work in the morning, when he returned home for lunch and dinner every day.

M. Daladier is an average man. This is a central point for understanding his character. And he lives in an average—an extremely typical—French neighbourhood. First you note the rounded glistening cobbles of the Rue Anatole des Forges, then the broad pavements of the Avenue Carnot, planted with plane-trees. The young trees are protected by circular iron cages. In the balconies of the upper apartments, behind their metal grills, are bright flower boxes. Above them rise soft grey mansard roofs.

Urban France is composed pre-eminently of small shopkeepers. M. Daladier could live his whole life within a few yards of his apartment, and never lack anything. This is typical of Paris, where almost every neighbourhood is self-sustaining. Autarchy descends to the local street corner. The shops contain every necessity for a reasonable life. On the nearest corner is a big Café Tabac, advertising beer on its orange awning, with its terrace comfortably packed with orange rattan chairs. In front of the café is a good homely pissoir, and next to it an old lady selling roses from a wicker basket. She keeps her reserve flowers in a battered, rusty, iron pail.

I counted the shops. The Boucherie de l'Étoile, under a magenta awning, sells meat. You see kidneys, livers, legs of mutton, on white tile counters. Next is the Crémerie, with a truckload of empty milk bottles before it. The truck is drawn by heavy, shaggy horses, with

147

enormous thighs.   Next, in the Boulangerie Patisserie, you see windows stacked with incomparable French bread, in slim loaves, a yard long.   Then another Café Tabac, then a Pharmacie full of cheap medicines and thermos bottles.   The coiffeur, next in line, is followed—inevitably—by the dealer in antiquities, who advertises rugs and draperies, and—even more inevitably—by that standard pivot of France, the wood-and-coal merchant.   Then comes a shoe shop (advertised as a Maison de Confiance) then an electrician-locksmith (with a huge gold key over his door), then a papeterie where the newspapers are neatly folded, French-fashion, the long way, and where some weather-worn postcards are displayed outside in wire trays.   Finally comes a shop for mops, pails, and household goods, and at last another Crémerie, with a white enamel sign embossed on its shining windows.

This is the kind of neighbourhood that exists in a thousand different parts of Paris, and in ten thousand French towns and villages. M. Daladier could not have chosen a more average place to live in.

Presently I decided that I would also visit the place where the prime minister works.   His office is not the Palais Matignon, which his predecessor Léon Blum used, but the Ministry of War.   And it is typical of Daladier that he chose the Ministry of War as his headquarters, even before war broke out.   Not because he is militant by nature.   Very few Frenchmen are.   Not because he is bellicose.   But, on the contrary, because when he took office the War Ministry fittingly symbolised French preoccupation with security and national defence.   Daladier was war minister before he became prime minister.   One of his great sources of power was his close connection with the army.   He has been war minister off and on for years.

The low sweeping buildings of the Ministère de la Guerre on the Rue St. Dominique are in considerable contrast to the shops of M. Daladier's home neighbourhood.   Here, behind the Quai d'Orsay, in the heart of the Faubourg St. Germain, is the citadel of old France, the France of literate aristocracy, massive social tradition, and superb taste and cultivation.   The roads are not cobbled here, but polished, glistening asphalt.   There are few shops; instead, gracious old family mansions, and a long façade of public buildings.   The War Ministry itself stretches along the Rue St. Dominique for two or three solid blocks, flush with the street. A series of tall gates open into flowering courtyards. Officers lean from ornate windows, and the sentries stand at rather casual attention. From inside comes the soft click and hiss of type-writers.

This is the gamut that Daladier represents: the typical bourgeois small-Frenchman, a self-sufficient individualist, transported by the pressure of events and his own career to the arena of politics and military affairs, to the world of mass conflicts, extinction of the individual, and the second world war.

Personal Characteristics of Daladier

Daladier is short and stocky. He has big shoulders and heavy hands. His eyes are a very bright clear blue, below uncombed eyebrows which dart upward. The forehead is broad, the hair sparse. He smiles almost continually when he talks: a quick perceptive smile, punctuated by short bursts of rather hard laughter. His conversation is very quick and to the point. He likes badinage, but doesn't waste much time on it. He can lose temper easily: the thick shoulders bulge, the face turns red, the neck pushes against the low collar. Thus one of his nicknames: The Bull of the Camargue.

He was born in this area of southern France, in the region of the Rhone delta. His native village was Carpentras, in Vaucluse, and he sits for this constituency to-day. His father was the local baker. When the father died a few years ago, one of Daladier's brothers took over the bakery shop, and still runs it. There is no false pride in Daladier. Several of his contemporaries—Hitler for instance—resolutely ignore members of the family who still hold humble station. Not so Daladier. He is a frequent visitor to Vaucluse and his native village, and knows every stick, stone, and person by heart.

I asked one of Daladier's closest friends and collaborators what he represented most. The answer came that Daladier, a peasant, born of peasant stock, above all represented the land—the soil—of France. From this basic peasanthood other characteristics derive. As a peasant Daladier believes unalterably in private property, in personal ownership of land. As a peasant, too, he stands for hard work, for tenacious cultivation of his soil. He wants to hold what he has. Then, again, as a peasant, he is both an individualist and a democrat. He stands for himself; he stands too for equality with his fellow men. Finally, like most peasants, Daladier is a bit ingrown, a bit méfiant—suspicious. He buttons his collar close, as the French like to say.

He worked a hard day as a child; he works a hard day now. He arrives at the War Ministry early. His office is that of Clemenceau's

in the last Great War—not an uninteresting juxtaposition. There
the day's reports, interviews, correspondence, await him. Like that
of every prime minister, his range of responsibility is enormous.
He goes home to lunch, returning to the office in mid-afternoon.
Then he stays at his desk till late—usually well into the evening,
nine o'clock or later. He's not always easy to work with; basically
his humour is good, but when fatigued he may ride his collaborators hard.

A head of state, a prime minister, must listen to a great many
people, and take information and advice from a bewildering array
of friends and subordinates. But Daladier sees comparatively few
people. He has no social life at all. He isolates himself at home or
in the War Ministry, and receives nowhere near as many visitors as
did his predecessors Herriot or Chautemps. The diplomats find it
rather difficult to see him, except the American Ambassador, William C. Bullitt, whom he likes and trusts deeply. But he is very
frugal with his friendship; few people know him well. The two
members of his cabinet closest to him are Guy la Chambre, the
youthful minister of air, and Champetier de Ribes, the assistant
foreign minister. Among his confidential assistants are General
Decamp, his *chef de cabinet* as war minister, and an old friend,
M. Clapier, also a man from Vaucluse, who is *chef de cabinet* in the
prime minister's office. For political affairs his closest adviser is
Jacques Keyser, journalist and vice-president of the radical-
socialist party.

Daladier has no interest in money. He has never been rich, and
has never wanted to be. He lives on his salary, and is one of the
comparatively few French politicians never touched by any financial or other scandal. Nor has Daladier any interest in religion,
another of those basic preoccupations, like sex and money, which
dominate the lives of most people. He has never had a religious
crisis. One of his remote ancestors was what the Spanish call a
penitente, a professional mourner at village funerals, but for generations his family has been anti-clerical. Daladier is, as the French
say, very *laique.* Yet his relations with the church are cordial.

Daladier likes good food and lots of it. He smokes moderately,
mostly a pipe. He drinks as any normal Frenchman drinks, and is
very fond of a derivative of absinthe known as *pastis.* He is one of
the few French prime ministers fond of sport. Most politicians in
Paris have hardly taken five minutes' exercise in their lives. But
Daladier likes to walk, ride, and swim. He often visits Chantilly

or Rambouillet, and for a time kept two horses. When the day's work was done, he had a brief canter in whatever park was nearest. Before he could afford horses, he bicycled for exercise; even as prime minister, during his first term in 1933, he would leave the office, get his bicycle, and pedal his way across Paris or out into the country. Nowadays he swims a good deal. He likes to swim in the Oise at night, near Chantilly. His chief intellectual exercise is reading; he was a professor of history for many years, and still reads a good deal, especially on military affairs and on the history of the Middle Ages and renaissance. He speaks no language except French and his native Provençal, with perhaps a few words of Spanish and Italian.

Shortly after the War Daladier married a Mademoiselle Laffont, the daughter of a scientist, who had been his 'Marriane' while he was in the trenches; 'Marriane' was the name given during the Great War to girls back home who regularly corresponded with some soldier. Came demobilisation; immediately Daladier looked up this girl whose letters had helped carry him through four brutal years of war, but whom he had never met; he fell in love with her and married her. He was madly devoted to her. She died about eight years ago. The blow was a terrible one for Daladier. He has been a lonely man ever since. The Daladiers had two sons. One, Jean, is now 17; the other, Pierre, is 13. Daladier is very close to them. They are the core of his heart. His wife lives still in the person of the two sons. His boys mean more to Daladier than anything in France, except perhaps France itself.

The Bull of Vaucluse

Edouard Daladier was born at Carpentras in Vaucluse on June 18, 1884. Not only was his father the village baker, and his grandfather before that; his mother, whose maiden name was Moriès, was the daughter of a baker in a neighbouring village, Montmoron. Bread was the staff of the Daladier life. Young Edouard went to the village school; snapshots exist of him, a dark, pert-looking boy, sitting at his crude desk. At eleven he proceeded to another school, got a scholarship, studied in Lyons, and finally entered that holy of holies of the French rational mind, the École Normale Supérieure. He was graduated with distinction, and set out to be a teacher. Then came 1914. Daladier was called up, and became a sergeant of tirailleurs, then a captain. He won the Legion of Honour and the Croix de Guerre with three citations.

But long before this he had become interested in politics. A few yards from the ancestral boulangerie—where the Daladiers, of course, baked as well as sold their own bread—was the homely Café du Commerce of Carpentras. Its second floor was the headquarters of the local radical-socialist party. From the beginning Daladier was a radical; he has always been a radical. Unlike a great number of French politicians, he has never changed party. As a boy, he listened to the elder radicals of Carpentras; he decided to enter politics, and while still teaching at Grenoble was elected mayor of Carpentras, his first political post. A 'radical-socialist' in France, be it noted, is often not a radical, and seldom a socialist. Rather the radical-socialist party, normally the most powerful in France, corresponds roughly to the English liberals or the American democrats, covering widely divergent political beliefs.

When the War was over, Daladier turned seriously to a political career, though for some years he kept a teaching job too. He is one of the very few notables in French politics who is not a lawyer or journalist by profession. In 1919, aged 35, he ran for the Chamber of Deputies, and was elected for the Vaucluse constituency. He has been its deputy ever since.

Daladier's political career was, in a curious way, both comparatively rapid and—for a long time—comparatively undistinguished. He was a good radical wheelhorse; not brilliant, but safe; stable, not eccentric or dangerous. He continued to be the middle-of-the-road Frenchman. He was not ambitious enough to arouse jealousy in his superiors; he worked hard and was dependable for almost any kind of job.

From 1924 Daladier was a familiar figure in all radical-socialist cabinets. The variety of posts he held is worth recording:

> June 1924–April 1925—Minister of Colonies.
> October 1925–November 1925—Minister of War.
> October 1925–March 1926—Minister of Education.
> July 1926 (for three days)—Minister of Education.
> February 1930 (for three days)—Minister of Public Works.
> December 1930–January 1931—Minister of Public Works.
> June 1932–December 1932—Minister of Public Works.
> December 1932–January 1933—Minister of War.
> January 1933–October 1933—Prime Minister and Minister of War.
> October 1933–November 1933—Minister of War.
> November 1933–January 1934—Minister of War (different cabinet).
> January 1934–February 1934 (for eight days)—Prime Minister and
> Foreign Minister.
> June 1936–April 1938—Vice-Premier and Minister of National
> Defence and War.

April 1938–September 1939—Prime Minister and Minister of
National Defence and War.
September 1939 to date—Prime Minister, Minister of National
Defence and War, and Minister of
Foreign Affairs.

Note the gradually increasing power Daladier reserves for himself. Note also that, three different times, he held office for eight days or even less, and that on four other occasions, his tenure was only about a month. Daladier is a good democrat. But there is no denying that the incessant shufflings and reshufflings in parliament, the extreme brevity of life of most French Governments, and the consequent insecurity of office, have impressed him a good deal. It is significant, too, that Daladier has never been a great parliamentarian. His speeches in the chamber are seldom as effective as those he gives in the country at large; also, his popularity is much greater in the country than in the parliamentary corridors. When Daladier became prime minister in April 1938, after the collapse of the Front Populaire, it was not surprising that he soon asked for full powers. Recently he postponed the next general election from 1940 to 1942.

It would be unfair, however, to call Daladier a dictator. He is still—even in war time—the servant of the chamber. He could at any time be dismissed from office by an adverse vote of the chamber. He has made no attempt to build up a totalitarian machine, nor are the *pleins pouvoirs*, full powers, that the chamber granted him, really exceptional. In emergencies, France almost always calls for a strong hand. And all states must centralise authority in time of war. Later they get over such temporary totalitarianism as may be necessary, as a healthy boy gets over measles. Even in peace time, French prime ministers have often ruled with special powers. Poincaré and Laval both governed by decree for long intervals. Daladier may be a dictator in the sense that Clemenceau was a dictator, not in the sense of Stalin, Hitler, Mussolini.

During his early career Daladier cultivated a special intellectual interest—military affairs. He travelled a good deal (something that most Frenchmen don't do) and in the 20's visited the Soviet Union, Great Britain, Germany, always with an eye open for army matters. For a time he was deeply interested in the Near East; he specialised in Syria and Turkey, and wrote a preface to Jacques Keyser's book on Bulgaria. But military business was his main preoccupation. By 1923 or 1924, he had become the radical party's best spokesman on army affairs. He cultivated the acquaintance of army officers, and by the time he was minister of war in 1932 he was in as close touch with the French general staff as it was possible for a civilian to be. He is called the best French war minister since Maginot. He had no time to get started in 1932, but in 1933–4, when he was minister of war uninterruptedly for thirteen months, he grasped a real opportunity to overhaul the French Army, revitalise it, and above all mechanise it. Maginot built the line; Daladier built the tanks, the armoured cars, the caterpillar trucks, behind it. That the French Army is to-day the best in Europe—when it needs to be just as good as it can be—is partly Daladier's work.

Since 1927, with one or two interruptions, Daladier has been president of the radical-socialist party. When he wasn't president, his great rival Edouard Herriot (who was one of his early teachers) was. Daladier and Herriot were close friends for many years; Herriot thought of Daladier as his protégé, and in 1924 gave him his first cabinet post. Later they quarrelled, and became jealous of one another. When Daladier succeeded Herriot as prime minister in 1933, Herriot snapped that he wouldn't last ten weeks. But Daladier stuck it out ten months. Daladier represented the younger element of the radicals, the radicals who really wanted to be somewhat radical, against Herriot's conservatism. In 1939 Herriot had ambitions to become president of France, the supreme job—nominally—in the Republic. But Daladier thought he might give the job more than nominal attention, and so contrived that old Albert Lebrun should run for re-election—though presidents in France don't usually serve second terms—in order to keep Herriot out.

Front Populaire[1]

There have been two supreme crises in Daladier's life. The first came in February 1934, when he had been prime minister only a few days, and when bloody rioting forced him out after the Stavisky crisis. I tell the Stavisky story later.

Daladier spent more than a year in the wilderness. But in the summer of 1935 he sharply rose to influence again, when he brought his left wing of the radicals into the newly formed Front Populaire. In the July 14 demonstration that summer, Daladier marched to the Bastille with Léon Blum, the leader of the socialists, and Marcel Thorez, the communist chieftain. This was a sensational

[1] See also Chapter XIII below.

step. It is as if Franklin Roosevelt, say, should celebrate Washington's birthday by raising the clenched fist at Arlington in company with Norman Thomas and Earl Browder. Before July 1935 the radicals had resolutely refused any serious co-operation with the socialists and communists. Likewise the socialists had refused collaboration. When Daladier brought the radicals in, the Front Populaire was born as an effective political force. In the summer of 1936 came a general election, which the Leftist coalition handsomely won. The chamber elected then rules France still. Léon Blum became prime minister, with Daladier as vice-premier and war minister. Daladier, his enemies say, only joined the Popular Front on the understanding that, when it came to power, he would be rewarded with the war ministry. This is probably to overstate the truth. When the leader of a powerful party adheres to a coalition to fight an election, it is usually understood that he shall share in the responsibilities and rewards of power.

The Popular Front, under Blum, with Daladier's collaboration, lasted from June 1936 to April 1938, when it collapsed. In its twenty-two months of power, the Popular Front achieved a good deal. It was an attempt to put liberalism into politics on a forceful scale. The Blum-Daladier Government reduced the power of the financial oligarchy and the Bank of France, it nationalised the aviation industry, it co-ordinated the railways, it established the forty-hour week, it gave workers holidays with pay. Above all, it checked the growth of Fascism. It gave France a much-needed respite from incessant turbulence and agitation by Rightist plotters.

But the Popular Front collapsed and died because its failures were also formidable. It had to face one of the most difficult of all questions, not merely for France but for the world: Can a Left Government reform capitalism without abolishing it, can a Left Government function efficiently *inside* a capitalist structure? Blum was constantly perplexed by the problem of how far to go. The communists pushed him Left. Daladier and the radicals held him to the Right. Blum wobbled in the middle. He outlined a tremendous programme of social reform. But, ultimately, the budgeteers and bankers had him at their mercy. He had to have money. Only they could give it to him, since he had no mandate—or desire—to make a real revolution. He came into office on a platform of extreme socio-economic amelioration. But the more he gave to the Left, the more he was at the mercy of the Right. Moreover, his own Left let him down. He gave the trade unionists such privileges

M

and concessions that work almost stopped. The industrial structure all but disintegrated.

Blum and Daladier were, moreover, unceasingly pressed and harried by the international problem, the mounting international crisis. The Front Populaire Government betrayed shocking cowardice in regard to Spain, where the policy of non-intervention helped Franco—the ideological enemy—win. But Spain wasn't all. There was the pressing threat of Germany under Hitler. France needed aeroplanes and munitions, it had to inaugurate and push through a huge arms programme. Yet at the same time the government was shortening hours, tacitly encouraging strikes and making efficient production on a big scale impossible. During the last six weeks of the Blum Government, not a single aeroplane was manufactured in France.

Daladier broke away from the Front Populaire, though he still paid lip service to it. He succeeded Blum as prime minister, and began a steady, marked turn to the Right. He had always been suspicious of the communists; now this *méfiance* erupted into active hostility. Very soon after he took office, the forty-hour week was, in actual practice, dropped. Daladier began to attack the communists fiercely, and in November 1938 he crushed a general strike. In September 1939, after the Russian pact with Germany and the Russian invasion of Poland, communist deputies were arrested and the communist party suppressed.

When Daladier became prime minister in 1938, his declaration of policy sounded a special note. He said, '*La défense nationale est un bloc.*' He made national defence the basic desideratum in every field; he preached national unity, national integrity, national solidarity. He said that France, to survive, must be strong; to be strong it must be united; to unite it became his task. Yet he was risking serious alienation of the Left. The war came to his rescue, as it comes to the rescue of every competent politician in office. Daladier rules by terms of a moral authority he could not possibly have achieved in peace time. And—communists aside—he *has* united France.

But one must go back a bit to mention the other supreme crisis in Daladier's career. This was Munich.

Daladier Chez Hitler

There are reasons for believing that Daladier deeply distrusted the policies of the slippery Georges Bonnet, his former foreign minister. The story is that he had one of his own trusted aides in the Quai d'Orsay, to read and check all of Bonnet's telegrams and instructions. Yet when the Munich crisis came in September 1938, Daladier followed Chamberlain's lead. He went to Munich, he met Hitler and Mussolini, he helped sell Czechoslovakia out. From the point of view of strict ethics Daladier's behaviour was worse than Chamberlain's. The British, after all, were not pledged to defend Czechoslovakia; the French *were* so pledged. Czechoslovakia was the heart of the French security system in Europe. Time and time again, even late in that tragic summer, the French reiterated their promise to come to Czechoslovakia's aid, as we have seen. On July 12, Daladier himself said, 'The solemn undertakings we have given to Czechoslovakia are sacred and cannot be evaded.' The betrayal that came in September—after remarks such as this—is one of the harshest known to modern history.

The French put up three major excuses for the Munich episode. The first is that France was not in any position to face a showdown, to fight. The country was pervaded with defeatism; the air force was inefficient and in bad order; the national muscles were flabby with lack of exercise. Second, even if the military position had been more hopeful, the great mass of French public opinion would not have supported a war. A settlement—a settlement at any price—was what the people wanted. They did not want to fight, to risk their lives, for Czechoslovakia. Third, and most important, the French willy-nilly had to follow England. Daladier was not in any position to act independently. He had to do what the British did, and what the British told *him* to do.

Daladier flew back to Paris after Munich, not at all happy about it, glum, despondent, and vastly worried at what French reaction would be. His plane circled the airport; he saw a big crowd. He was terrified. He thought that he and his advisers might be mobbed. Memories of February 6 came to mind. He braced himself, wondered if the Gardes Mobiles would be there to protect him, and stepped off the plane. To his amazement, he was greeted with a wild ovation. Stupefied, he was led in triumph to the chamber.

.   .   .   .

It is difficult to sum up the sources of Daladier's power. He is no genius. He is no demagogue. He lacks magnetism, he lacks political 'oomph'. He is no titan, no born leader of men. He is certainly not a 'great' man, as Clemenceau was. Probably he is not even as strong a man as Poincaré. But he speaks the language of the

average Frenchman. This is his secret. Like the average Frenchman, he is resilient, an individualist, shrewd, not particularly ambitious, packed with common sense, rational, and moderate. He has
the incomparable advantage of being archtypical of the people he
represents. Therefore the people like and trust him. They understand his every accent. He is one of themselves.

I asked one of his best friends what Daladier's central faith was,
what he believed in most. The answer came, 'Three things.' I
asked what they were. 'France. The small man. And himself.'

Léon Blum—Socialist

M. Léon Blum, the socialist exquisite of the île St. Louis, was
for a few brief years a key figure in the world struggle between
Fascism and democracy. This elegant and fastidious man of letters,
surrounded by beautiful books and a few delicately chosen *objets-
d'art,* became the main counterweight in contemporary Europe to
the blackshirts, the mass propaganda, the crushing totalitarianism
of Hitler and Mussolini. The man of thought stood in opposition
to the man of action. Against the bruiser's fist was M. Blum's silver
poniard of wit and intellect. Against the loud speaker echoing the
dictated will of a nation in bulk came the thin but penetrating voice
of M. Blum, the cultivated individualist. He emerged from his
Ivory Tower to confront Hitler and Mussolini, men of the market-
place.

Blum, leader of a mass movement, was not a man of the masses.
Therein lay both weakness and strength.

Nor was he, for many years, predominantly a man of politics.
'Thank God!' exclaimed one of France's ambassadors, called to
meet Blum for the first time. 'The new prime minister is not a
politician!'

When Anthony Eden saw Blum just before he became Président
du Conseil, their conversation—about politics and the international
situation—languished. Then a change came. For an hour the
veteran socialist and the young British diplomat bubbled with
reciprocal enthusiasm. They were discussing Proust.

After he had been in power a week, one of his chief political
opponents, as if to condone Blum's momentary supremacy, sighed,
'After all, Léon *is* an aristocrat and a gentleman.'

When Blum came to London in July 1936, for vitally important
discussions with the Locarno powers, he finished his work, then
disappeared—into the British Museum. With his friend Princess

Elizabeth Bibesco he was renewing his acquaintance with the time-
less beauty of the Elgin marbles.

Blum is no demagogue. He is the last possible remove from the
man on horseback. He is utterly devoid of personal ambition.
He is no opportunist, no adventurer. He is no longer young. Yet
history called him to fulfil at least one important function. He was
the first leader of a Popular Front government in an important
bourgeois country since the War. It was historically inevitable
that the parties of the Left, sometime, somewhere, should fuse.
Blum performed their first successful fusion.

Léon Blum was born on April 9, 1872, in Paris. Very few French
politicians, it happens, are Paris-born; Blum and his inveterate
antagonist André Tardieu are exceptions. Blum's family came
originally from Alsace. His father was a manufacturer of silk
ribbon, with a well-known business which still exists on the Rue du
Quatre Septembre. The business, once prosperous, has suffered
since styles in millinery changed. Léon was one of five brothers;
when the father died the business was given to them jointly. Léon,
however, and his younger brother René, who is art director of the
Monte Carlo ballet, leave the other three in charge. The family,
as everyone knows, is Jewish, and all the Blums have a strong family
sense. Léon is not an orthodox communicant, but friends call him
a 'good' Jew. The five brothers meet piously on each anniversary
of their father's death.

Léon's maternal grandmother was a remarkable woman, a
Frondeuse, blind for many years, who nevertheless owned a book-
store on the Île de la Cité, had profound radical convictions, voiced
them on fit occasions, and held political salons twice a week.
Young Blum was devoted to her. Jules Renard, the dramatist, tells
in his invaluable *Journal* how Blum attended her. 'Graceful as
Antigone, Léon serves her, tells her what to eat, prepares her
food. Blind for thirty-six years, she looks in the direction of his
voice. . . .' In 1901 Blum took her on a holiday through Italy,
giving her sight with his lucid explanatory conversation.

Blum's mother emphasised the Jewish family tradition of unity,
loyalty, and affection. The father was a merchant; she was an
intellectual. She believed, almost too firmly, in justice, social and
otherwise. At least the story is told that when she gave apples to
her five sons, during their childhood, each got a different half
of a different apple, so that full impartiality might be attained.
Blum adores her memory, and speaks touchingly of her. He is,

however, extremely stubborn about the privacy of his non-public life. Questions about his family or home life are, with charm, rebuffed.

Blum had a first-rate education in classics and the humanities. He went first to the Lycée Charlemagne, then the Lycée Henry IV (where he studied philosophy under Henri Bergson), and finally the École Normale Supérieure. Edouard Herriot was his classmate there. Later he took degrees both in philosophy and law. He was, at this time—an odd contradiction—an experienced duellist. But challenges were few after he wounded one antagonist. A recent cinema history of Blum, tracing his career in photographs, shows him duelling—lithe, graceful, with wrists of celerity and steel.

His career progressed in concurrent phases. For many years he was both a lawyer and a literary man; he was interested in politics early, but did not emerge as a practical politician until the War, when he had reached full maturity. As a lawyer he became an 'auditeur' in the Conseil d'État, the highest organ of the French civil service. It is a sort of supreme Court of France which, though it cannot declare any law passed by the parliament illegal, may adjudicate on injustices in the application of a law. Blum reached the high post of 'Maître de Requêtes', viz., solicitor-general, in charge of the state's cases. This was the top rank he could achieve in the civil service.

But meantime he was inveterately occupied with literature and journalism. Articles, essays, books, came in subtle and distinguished prose from his pen. He was a sort of literary man-about-town; Mallarmé, Paul Valery, André Gide, Tristan Bernard, Jules Renard, Jules Lemaître, the Guitrys, Alfred Capus, Anatole France, were his friends. Passionately fond of the theatre, he was dramatic critic first of the *Revue Blanche,* an *avant-garde* literary journal, then of the *Matin,* finally of *Comoedia,* the 'official' theatrical newspaper. He wrote half a dozen books, one on marriage—in which he expressed his belief in sexual equality—one on Stenhal, one on Eckermann.

Across the life of this young lawyer-aesthete-philosopher was now flung the massive shadow of Karl Marx. Mallarmé left the boulevards for symbolism; Anatole France retreated into irony; Blum became a socialist. Two persons and one terrible fact combined to transform him into what he has been ever since. The persons were Lucien Herr, the socialist librarian of the École Normale, and the great Jean Jaurès, the terrible fact was the Dreyfus case. Convinced by Herr's 'incredible and truly unique force' (the words are Blum's) he became a Dreyfusard; through Herr he met Jaurès, the dynamic founder of modern French socialism. Blum was still a dandy, *précieux* to his slim finger-tips; Jaurès was historically uncouth, famous for spitting into his handkerchief. The two were staunch companions through all the inferno of the Dreyfus affair. Blum discovered in himself a passion not only for the theatre, but for social justice. He forgot his essays like '*En Lisant, réflexions critiques*'; he read Sorel, Proudhon, and Marx. Jaurès took him into the streets, showed him people. Delicately—at first—he fingered proletarian Paris. The enormous ebullience of Jaurès taught him much. And in 1906 Blum and Jaurès together founded a daily socialist newspaper, *L'Humanité*.

So then politics. Blum wrote the leading article every day. Jaurès with the voice, Blum with the cutting pen; this was the partnership. At first, still clinging to literature, Blum preferred purely literary participation. Jaurès asked him to stand for the Chambre; he refused. But his friends say that at that time he could, out of his head, give you the votes on any issue of every deputy, as an American baseball-fan can give batting averages. Just before the outbreak of the War Jaurès was assassinated. A month later Blum did finally become a politician, to take up the Jaurès mantle; not however in the manner of a subordinate leader carrying on, but as a friend who wished to make a gesture in memory of his friend. Blum was neither conspicuously energetic nor ambitious. But Jaurès was dead; Jaurès had wanted him to go into politics; therefore he did. Almost at once he was appointed *chef de cabinet* in the Ministry of Public works. This was Blum's only actual experience of political administration before his premiership—twenty-two years later—in 1936.

After the War he became a deputy from the Seine, though comparatively few socialists got in; it was a 'khaki' election like the one in England at the same time. He was beaten in 1928, and re-elected —for Narbonne—in 1929. The same year he became president of the parliamentary group of the French socialist party. Meantime *Humanité* had become the communist organ; Blum founded a new paper, *Le Populaire*. To this, the official socialist newspaper, he contributed a daily leading article, year in, year out. As socialist leader, he steadily and stubbornly refused participation in the various radical cabinets of the time. He would not accept power,

he said, without responsibility; he would not accept responsibility
without power.   Then in May 1936 the socialists—for the first time
—became the largest single party.   Blum was offered the premiership and accepted it.

Blum lives in the Île St. Louis, facing the Seine in the oldest
and loveliest part of Paris.   The legend that he is very rich is without
foundation.   He has many books, and everything in the apartment
is 'a very good choice', as the French would say; but the elegance is
by no means sumptuous.   Blum was supposed to own a famous silver
collection, and was, in fact, invited to lend some of it to an exhi-
bition; he could not do so because he had only enough knives and
forks for his own modest table.   The Blums were interested in
another apartment on the Quai before they took their present home;
it had once been occupied by Paul Painlevé, a former premier.   The
landlord said 'I'd be happy to rent it to you, but I don't like the
swarm of journalists and politicians who came to see Painlevé, and
I suppose you too will be *Président du Conseil* some day.'   Blum
replied that it was altogether improbable that he would ever become *Président du Conseil*, but he refused to sign a clause in the
lease saying so; and the negotiations were broken off.
Mme Blum, who died last year, was his second wife.   He was
devastated by the loss.   His first wife, a sister of the composer Paul
Dukas, died some years ago, after long illness.   By her he had one
son, now employed in the Hispano-Suiza factory.   The second
marriage was childless.   Mme Blum was a Mademoiselle Thérèse
Pereira, an important member of the socialist party and a member
of a firm of decorators.   The marriage was extremely happy, and
Mme Blum accompanied her husband everywhere.   At every political meeting, she was with him, and in the days preceding his
premiership she was practically his *chef de cabinet*.   His secretary,
nowadays, is—appropriately enough—named Blumel.
When he was prime minister Blum worked at the Hôtel Matignon,
on the Rue de Varenne, the history of which is curious.   It is one
of the most distinguished of the *hôtels particuliers* of the eighteenth-
century Paris, a stately house behind a high solid gate and gravelled
court, with wide gardens and flowering trees.   It was the Austro-
Hungarian Embassy before the War.   When Flandin was the French
prime minister in 1933, he discovered that unless the *Président du
Conseil* also held a ministerial job, he had no office, no place to
work.   So a bill was prepared making the Hôtel Matignon the

permanent headquarters of the prime minister like No. 10 Downing Street.

Blum's method of work is a combination of apparent slipshodness and actual precision. He is an inveterate note-taker. He writes everything down, not only ideas as they come to him, but notes on other people's conversation. An idea may arrive in a taxi, at a meal, during a debate, in an aeroplane, during a conference. Out of the pocket comes a notebook; the pencil cabalistically flies. If the notebook is not available, Blum uses any odd bit of paper that may be handy, even a newspaper. But everything must go down—in writing—and at once. These notes, which are voluminous, are carefully checked, filed, and preserved. Many are written at night just before he goes to bed. Out of them come his speeches, essays, arguments.

His speeches, extraordinarily lucid, and in a French of grave purity, give an impression of casualness, of extemporaneity. But behind them is much careful preparation—and the notes.

Although he represents an agricultural and mainly wine-growing constituency (Narbonne) Blum is almost—not quite—a teetotaller. He is a *convenable*, i.e. quite normal eater, not a famous gourmet like Herriot. He smokes French cigarettes '*grises Gitanes*', denicotinised—which are mild and cost Fr. 3.50 for twenty; he needs a packet or two per day. He plays good bridge, but plays it seldom. He wears a big black Latin Quarter hat. He loves conversation and his friends are legion.

Charm, fastidiousness, intellectual detachment and humanism, are not Blum's only qualities. There is, for instance, his supernal patience. I have noted his long refusal to take office—until he could take it on his own terms. Another example is the revolt of the 'Neo-socialists' in 1933. Three of his ablest associates, Marquet, Déat, and Renaudel tired of what they called his pontifical manner, his 'theorising', demanded a more active policy and the abandonment of socialist internationalism. They stormed at Blum and finally quit him. Blum said little; he was content to wait. To-day the 'Neos' are forlorn and forgotten. Marquet is still mayor of Bordeaux, but Déat is out of the chamber, and Renaudel is dead.

Blum's mind is salty, and he has great sense of phrase. Once Poincaré remarked to a group of friends, 'I smell war.' Blum said simply, 'Let him disinfect himself.' His intellectual honesty is complete. 'The free man,' he once told Jules Renard, 'is he who does not fear to go to the end of his thought.'

His manners are good, and he gets along with people, though at a certain distance; he was on thee-and-thou terms even with Laval. But no one could accuse him of being a person of the corridors. His political discernment is, however, shrewd. As long ago as 1933, quietly, almost surreptitiously he was feeling his way towards the Popular Front.

Until the summer of 1936, people invariably accused him of being doctrinaire. He is not a good mob speaker, being far too rational and precise. It is doubtful if he ever can become a popular hero, and he has yet to prove himself as supple as Briand, or as flint-like as Clemenceau. He is not, most people think, a fighter. He has no shoulders: only antennae. And most observers fear that he seriously lacks physical stamina, which prime ministers notably need.[1]

But at a time when most democratic politicians were objects of derisive laughter, when the general public in France was sick to death of the venality, the inefficiency, the opportunism, the vulgar heroics of most of the Paris politicians, Blum emerged with one supreme quality, namely that he commanded *respect*, that no one who knew him well could fail to note and admire the disinterested honesty of his career and mind.

Just before becoming prime minister Blum and Monsignor Maglione, the Papal Nuncio, crossed in the anteroom of M. Sarraut. Mgr. Maglione expressed the desire to make Blum's acquaintance. 'Soon I am leaving France,' he said (he was *en route* to Rome to become a cardinal) 'and I cannot go without having shaken hands with Léon Blum.' They talked for a minute or two. As Maglione took leave, Blum remarked, 'I don't suppose I may dare to ask your benediction.' The Nuncio reflected, then replied, 'I shall pray God to give you His.'

.   .   .   .

When Blum, on June 1, 1936, became prime minister of the Popular Front government, he was confronted at once with a first-rate crisis. The Left rose. In strikes. The strikes, most competent observers agree, were spontaneous in origin; they were neither fomented nor organised by either socialists or communists. Work-men in one industry after another downed tools, in what was a sort of spiritual epidemic, until production all over France was paralysed, with more than a million men in occupation of the factories. Hotels, department-stores, dockyards, munitions plants,

[1] Incidentally, he was badly beaten up by a royalist mob in the spring of 1936.

restaurants, mines, beauty parlours, shut down, in some cases for
a day or so, in some cases for several weeks. The Left, celebrating
its victory, seemed to be showing Blum what latent power he
represented.

The strikes were a marvellous tribute to the good sense and
restraint of the average Frenchman. In an industrial stoppage as
comprehensive and drastic as anything seen in Europe since the
War, not a tool was injured, not a machine damaged, not a person
hurt, not a single drop of blood spilt. One of the most experienced
of American correspondents in France, Edgar Ansel Mowrer,
cabled his newspaper that during the tensest days he would not
have hesitated to lead a girls' school through the slums of Paris. In
the great department-stores, men and women slept on the floors—
instead of the beds. They were underpaid and often hungry—and
never stole a cheese or opened a box of beans.

The strikes were a considerable asset to Blum, because they
demonstrated both the power and the discipline of the workers.
They were a cogent sign to the Senate if it should hesitate to pass
his flood of bills. Blum resolutely refused to use troops or government power to clear the factories. This would only, he knew, cause
bloodshed.

> 'I know the occupation is illegal,' he said, 'but is it not better to
> have the strikers sitting quietly in the shops and factories—where
> they are doing no harm—than fighting the police, and probably the
> Fascist Leagues, outside? The Garde Mobile and the troops might
> clear the factories, but what would be left of the factories when they
> had finished?'

Thus the rational mind. But after the first week, with the movement still spreading, it became necessary to show that the government could and would, if necessary, take steps to force a return to
normal. Blum could not afford to let the situation get out of hand.
Thorez sounded the word for the members of the communist unions
to resume work. Roger Salengro,[1] the minister of the interior,
announced that 'future' stay-in strikes would not be tolerated.
Quietly, with good discipline, everyone slipped back to their
machines.

What helped to end the strike so promptly was, of course, the
courage, the comprehensiveness, and the speed of Blum's reforms.

---

[1] Who committed suicide in November 1936 following a slanderous campaign
against him in the Rightist Press.

He set about an immediate realisation of the *Front Populaire* programme—which five months before had been ignored as visionary. People saw that he really intended fulfilling his political promises, and with a vengeance. On the Right, mouths gaped with resentment—and astonishment. The Left pretended that it was not astonished. Probably it was. Blum went far—and fast.

A variety of minor bills occupied the government first. (This, incidentally, included three women as under-secretaries, the first women to be given cabinet rank in French history.) The school-leaving age was raised. The cabinet was reorganised into seven 'spheres', to promote economy and efficiency in administration. The Laval wage and salary cuts were in part restored. A new régime for pensions was outlined. A comprehensive plan for agriculture was announced. And, perhaps recklessly, a bill was proposed to check the notorious venality of the Paris Press.

All this, however, merely touched the fringe. M. Blum had his eye on bigger business. And three astonishing measures were passed in record time. First, by an unprecedented majority (444 to 77), the chamber voted for the reform of the Banque de France, viz., curtailment of its feudal privileges. The new bill abolished the old Regency council of the Bank and aimed to put the Bank in its proper place as the servant not the master of the country. Second, by an even greater majority, 484 to 85, the government passed a law for the nationalisation of the munitions industry. The initial cost was to be 1,000,000,000 francs. Nothing quite like this bill has been seen in Europe before. Third, striking boldly at his chief enemies, Blum put through an act for the dissolution of those bad boys of the streets, the Fascist Leagues. Their tails between their legs—at least for the time being—the members of the Croix de Feu crawled home.

Then in October, Blum took a step of profound importance; he devalued the precious franc. For seven years France had been hamstrung by the gold standard, with industry all but ruined and the cost of living appallingly high, but no French Prime Minister had dared the plunge off gold. Blum took a deep breath and dived into the pleasant water of modified inflation. The franc eased off nearly thirty per cent. Great Britain and the United States joined to support the new figure, a good augury for future co-operation among the great democracies. French public opinion stood the shock comparatively well.

The Popular Front, as I have noted above, did not last long.

While it did last, a new energy, a new freshness, blew through France.

Camille Chautemps

Camille Chautemps, who took over from Blum, is much less a statesman; he is a professional politician, with all the vices of that ilk: a careerist, whose family has been a sort of radical dynasty since 1871. The royalists call him 'Le Ténébreux', the shadowy; he is an acknowledged Freemason. Chautemps was seriously involved in repercussions of the Stavisky scandal; he was minister of the interior in Stavisky's big days, and his brother-in-law, Pressard, was head of the Paris *parquet* (prosecutor's office) which let Stavisky off. The campaign against Chautemps in the Rightist Press in those days was one of the most virulent of modern times. A commission of inquiry subsequently cleared Chautemps of any connection with Stavisky. He was prime minister for a brief interval in 1930, and again in 1934 between the first two Daladier ministries. One thing he did may unfortunately live after him; he was the first prime minister of France to resign without being voted out by the chamber. Pressure of the February rioters forced him out. Chautemps, a native of Paris, was born in 1885; he was educated as a lawyer. Some day he will probably be prime minister again.

CHAPTER XI

FRENCH POLICY—AND WHY

'The friends of gold will have to be extremely wise and moderate if they are to avoid a revolution.'

—J. M. KEYNES.

'The only way to treat a Prussian is to step on his toes until *he* apologises.'

—BAVARIAN PROVERB.

ANY French prime minister, until the provisional victory of the *Front Populaire*, was a creature of the financial oligarchy. I have alluded to the Banque de France in the preceding chapter. France for generations has been run by a group of about 200 financial families—the celebrated *Deux Cents*—whose central pediment was the Banque de France. How this oligarchy traditionally worked should be described. France, as the French said, was no longer a kingdom, but the Third Republic was the pawn of the eighteen 'regents' of the Banque.

The Banque de France was founded by Napoleon I; although it issues the public money of France and holds its gold supply, it is a private bank, not a state bank. By terms of its basic charter, which Blum attempted to alter, only the two hundred shareholders with the most stock are permitted to vote for the regents, who up to now have controlled the Banque absolutely.

In 1933 there were approximately forty thousand shareholders in the Banque de France. 17,889 shareholders held one share each, 9,021 held two shares, 8,021 held four shares. All told, 24,931 small shareholders held 68,015 shares. The remaining 115,485 shares were held by only 6,069 persons. Of these, the top two hundred alone had voting power. They chose the regents.

These two hundred men, the cream of financial France, are an amazing plutocracy. They are as snobbish as a vintage sardine or a Rue de la Paix hat. Mere wealth cannot buy its way into this velvety inner circle. The two most flagrantly conspicuous of modern French millionaires, Coty the perfume man, Citroën the automobile manufacturer, were not members of what is customarily called merely the 'oligarchy'. The chosen insiders combine the hereditary distinction of family as well as the contemporary command of wealth.   They rise straight from pre-Revolutionary times; they were the upper *bourgeoisie* during Napoleon; they worked together, consolidated their power under Louis Philippe and Napoleon III.   The last person really 'taken in' by the oligarchy is supposed to have been Eugène Schneider, the steel and arms merchant, about thirty years ago.

Of the eighteen regents of the Banque de France, three—the governor and the two vice-governors—were appointed by the state. They had no more voting power than the other regents, but in actuality a governor of the Banque de France who disagreed with the private regents had little recourse but to resign.   By terms of the Code Napoleon, the governor must possess one hundred shares of Banque stock, each vice-governor fifty shares—and the current price of shares is 10,000 francs.   Not many civil servants of the French state had 500,000 or 1,000,000 francs to spend.   So, in practice, the custom arose whereby the other regents lent each new governor the price of the necessary shares.   When a governor retires, he is usually taken care of.   A recent ex-governor, M. Sergent, went to the board of the Banque de l'Union Parisienne, a big business bank formed to handle the commercial business of the private bankers of the regency.   Ex-governor Moreau went to the Banque de Paris et des Pays-Bas.   Ex-governor Charles Rist, like ex-President Doumergue, joined the board of the Suez Canal Company.

Three other regents of the Banque were by ancient custom civil servants representing the French treasury.   They held office primarily to oversee the treasury account.   And they represented, as a rule, an extraordinary plutocracy within a plutocracy, that of the 'Inspecteurs de Finance' of the French civil service.   These 'Inspecteurs' begin public life by passing one of the stiffest competitive examinations in the world.   They are cultivated young men of good intellect and family.   There are only about eighty of them in France, and they are at the top of the permanent civil service.   After years of training they become 'inspectors'; later they may become regents of the Banque, or they may resign to take private positions in industry or banking.   The eighty-odd 'inspecteurs de finance' comprise a sort of financial general staff, scattered—but closely knit— through the financial structure of the French republic.

The remaining twelve regents, representing private interests, were—until Blum—the actual rulers of the Banque de France. They were supposed to embody a cross-section of French finance, industry, commerce, agriculture. Six of the twelve were bankers, all of them, in the absolute sense of the term, 'hereditary' regents. Their seats were passed down, father to son. Of the six families represented, five came to France from Switzerland in the eighteenth century to assist Necker in preserving the finances of the Ancien Régime. The sixth seat was that of the Rothschilds; Baron Alfonse de Rothschild became a regent in 1855.

The six 'banking' regents were:

> Baron Edouard de Rothschild. (Rothschild bank.)
> Baron Hottinguer. (Banque Hottinguer.)
> Baron Jacques de Neuflize. (Banque de Neuflize.)
> M. Ernest Mallet. (Banque Mallet.)
> M. David Weil. (Banque Lazard Frères.)
> M. Pierre Mirabaud. (Banque Mirabaud.)

All of these banking firms are venerable private institutions, which for centuries have administered the estates of the French nobility, besides doing normal commercial business. They represent family dynasties. For instance, Pierre Mirabaud succeeded his uncle William d'Eichtal who succeeded his uncle Paul Mirabaud who succeeded his grandfather, Adolphe d'Eichtal. M. Weil succeeded to the seat of Felix Vernes, who had taken his place after father and grandfather. The Mallets have occupied a chair uninterruptedly for 109 years.

The final regents were traditionally chosen among '*manufacturiers, fabricants* (merchants), *ou commerçants*' who were shareholders of the Banque. They were:

> M. François de Wendel, steel merchant.
> M. Tinardon, industrialist.
> M. René Duchemin, chemical manufacturer.
> M. Camille Poulenc, chemical manufacturer.
> M. Robert Darbley, paper manufacturer.

Interlocking directorates among the banking and industrial regents reached a point where these eleven men had one hundred and fifty seats in ninety-five corporations, which accounted for at least sixty per cent of the industrial output of France. They sat on the boards of thirty-one private banks, eight insurance companies, nine railway companies (four of which are foreign), eight navigation companies, seven metallurgical corporations, eight electrical companies, eight mining companies, twelve chemical companies.

Above all, the regents were part and parcel of that immense industrial complex known as the Comité des Forges.

The eighteenth regent, who has not been mentioned so far, is the Marquis de Vogüé, President of the Société des Agriculteurs de France.

For more than twenty years, agriculture, the backbone of France, has been represented at the central banking institution, and it is as spokesman of the farmers and peasants that M. de Vogüé joined the Council of Regency.

The regents of the Banque de France decisively controlled French politics, because by withholding credits from the treasury they could break any prime minister they didn't like. The Banque, which more or less represents the *rentier* class, stood for complete deflation. The much maligned Chamber of Deputies, representing the man in the street—and his pocket-book—opposed this. Thus the Banque could only get its way by taking the matter out of the hands of the chamber. The way to do this was to obtain '*pleins pouvoirs*' (full powers) for a prime minister it liked. For instance the Banque persuaded old Gaston Doumergue, who headed France's 'National Government' formed after the Stavisky riots, to demand such powers. The chamber promptly threw the fatuous old gentleman out. The next prime minister was Pierre-Etienne Flandin, and the Banque squashed him in six months.

Flandin, six feet four, a man of the Centre, an honest fellow, refused to bow unconditionally to the Banque's will. He said, 'We are given a choice: deflation or devaluation of the franc. I refuse to let myself be tied up in this dilemma.' He proposed a third alternative, a policy of easier money, gradual 'reflation'. The Banque didn't like this and engineered a plot to throw Flandin out. The prime minister retaliated by dismissing Clement Moret, the governor. The bank thereupon refused to rediscount government short-term loans. Pressure on the government from the Banque became enormous. On June 15, the government had to meet a big payment of government bonds, but it was penniless; Flandin was living hand to mouth by borrowings from the post-office savings. Frenchmen, worried, fearing inflation, began to buy gold and ship their capital abroad. Blandly, the Banque let this go on. It could have stopped the drain of gold, but it wanted to beat Flandin. In a panic, Flandin appealed to the chamber for the same *pleins pouvoirs* which he had previously refused to request. The chamber was naturally incredulous and overthrew him. The Banque, victorious, then easily plugged the leak of gold. This was the inner history of the French financial 'crisis' of June 1935.

N

Laval became prime minister and obeyed the Banque implicitly in a merciless policy of deflation. He did not, however, swallow whole the programme of De Wendel, chairman of the Comité des Forges, who wanted four or five billion francs for 'economic redressment', viz. gifts to industry in the form of lightened taxation and government subsidies. Taxes went up. Everybody suffered. But it is interesting to note how De Wendel had Laval at heel when the prime minister asked the chamber for four thousand million francs for special military credits. The chamber entered two amendments, (1) to limit profits on arms manufacture to five per cent, (2) to nationalise the arms industry within a year. When Laval saw that these amendments would pass, he withdrew the bill.

The De Wendel-Laval decrees outdistanced anything in the history of the French republic for 'encroachment on the field of private enterprise'. The yield of government bonds was reduced ten per cent by fiat; the government procured the right to fix prices and profits in almost every branch of business, down to the corner *bistro*; house rents and mortgages were cut ten per cent by decree; private borrowers were permitted to reduce interest payments; official salaries, wages, and pensions were cut three to ten per cent; prices of coal, gas, electricity, were deflated. Even so, the cost of living in France remained about twenty-five per cent above the world level.

Why did the *rentiers*, the small capitalists, the peasants with savings, swallow such a programme when devaluation of the franc might much less painlessly lighten the burden? The reason is, of course, largely psychological. The terrors of deflation were comparatively unknown; those of inflation were known and doubly feared. Until the *Front Populaire* France was dominated by a stick-to-gold psychosis, much like that of the United States under Hoover. And it should not be forgotten that the French capital-owning classes lost four-fifths of their savings when the franc was re-established on gold by Poincaré.

Those who think that Fascism is exclusively a force operated for personal advantage by industrialists confront a paradox here. France is a democracy. But the industrialists of France have considerably more power over political life in France than have German industrialists in Germany. The point might well be made, were economics the only index of Fascism, that France is a more 'Fascist' country than Germany, where, by terms of a recent Hitlerite decree, no industry is permitted more than six per cent profit. Yet to say that France is Fascist would be preposterous.

Comité des Forges

François de Wendel is a good many things besides president of the Comité des Forges. He has, of course, his own steel business, 'Les Petits-fils de F. de Wendel et Cie'. The Wendels are an international family and three brothers run the business; one cousin, now dead, was a German citizen until the War, calling himself not *de* but *von* Wendel.[1] François de Wendel is a senator, the owner of the *Journal de débats*, and part owner of the semi-official French organ, *Le Temps*.

The Comité des Forges is the French steelmakers trade association, something like the Iron and Steel Institute of the United States. It neither sells nor produces steel, but it dominates the policy of the two hundred and fifty odd producers who are its members, by allotting quotas and setting prices. Of the companies in the Comité, probably the best known is Schneider et Cie, of Le Creusot, run by M. Eugène Schneider, who, like De Wendel, is of Franco-German extraction. The Schneider firm was founded by a Saarlander, the grandfather of the present Schneider, who settled in France in 1836. Schneider-Creusot does not produce much steel, but buys it from companies in the Comité that do, and then transforms it into armaments.

If I am killed in the next war I hope they will put on my white cross a notation that the bullet which killed me cost a fraction of a cent to make and sold for three cents or more. Someone, I should like it known, made a nice profit on my mouldering bones.

Bullets do not cost much. But if you shoot one million rounds an hour at £6 per thousand, the figures mount up. A rifle does not cost much—perhaps £5. But equip an army of one million men, and you have spent £5,000,000. A machine-gun costs about £128. The French have about forty thousand of them. A 37 mm. field-gun costs about £200, and each shell about £3. The famous French 75's come to about £1,600 each. They are expensive and intricate, with fuses built like watches. Their shells cost £5 each and in a single bombardment some millions may be fired. A big tank, complete, costs about £16,000. A bombing plane may diminish your

---

[1] He was Ivan Edouard von Wendel (1871–1931), a cousin of François, not a brother as is often said.

budget £20,000. A modern cruiser costs £2,200,000, an aircraft carrier £3,800,000, and a big battleship almost £6,000,000.

Thus war, as we have good reason to know, is expensive. It costs us money. We pay taxes. But war also makes money—for some— a lot of money. Thus the munitions business, one of the strangest in the world.

The world, according to the League of Nations, spent £855,360,000 on armament in 1934, about £2,800,000,000 in 1937, and at least £3,400,000,000 last year. These sums are too astronomical for ready comprehension. Suppose I had that much money and spent it at the rate of £2 per day. I should still have some left after more than a million years. Suppose it should be transformed into a piece of tape, mile for dollar; it would go around the world 172,169 times. Suppose I had it in gold pieces of £1 each and counted them at the rate of one per second; the job would take 26 years!

The root of the munitions problem is the fact that only highly industrialised countries can profitably manufacture appreciable quantities of arms. These countries sell to those less industrialised. Ninety-eight per cent of the total arms exports of the world comes from ten countries; about sixty-five per cent comes from Great Britain, the United States, France, and Sweden, the four greatest exporting nations. France, typified by Schneider-Creusot, supplied in 1932 no less than 27.9 per cent of the world's total output of arms.

Schneider-Creusot, like all great arms companies, is several things—an arms firm, a myth, a steel works, a microcosm of the munitions industry, a national institution, a nightmare to pacifists, an idol to patriots, a military necessity to more than one country, and a whale of a good business. The directors of Schneider and the other firms in the Comité des Forges which do munitions business are quite mild-mannered gentlemen. They do not seem ferocious; but their business is the invention, manufacture, and sale of implements of death.

The arms companies are as incestuous as white mice. They play together and breed. This is because they are in a signal sense noncompetitive; good business for one means good business for the others; obviously if Schneider, say, gets a big order from Country X, other companies will have better chance of business from Country Y, which is X's unfriendly neighbour. As soon as one country buys a new military invention, other countries must buy it also.

Arms firms may underbid one another for a contract in a single state; but internationally they all stand to gain. Cannon is expensive; cannon fodder cheap.

Extraordinarily interrelated and intertwined, the arms firms lace the whole world in their net. Schneider and Vickers were connected through Sir Basil Zaharoff, munitions salesman extraordinary. Schneider for years controlled Skoda, the former Czechoslovak munitions firm, through a French holding company, the Union Européenne. The Schneider interests were believed to control an Austrian bank also, which was interested in the chief Austrian steel company, the Alpine Montangesellschaft. But the Alpine concern is 'owned' by the German Steel Trust! And through a Dusseldorff firm, Rheinmetall, Schneider was formerly believed to be linked to Krupp.

It is, of course, an old story that arms firms maintain an extreme political impartiality in their business. They sell to each side in any war. They sell to friend and foe alike. Pluck a bullet out of the heart of a British boy shot on the North-west Frontier, and like as not you will find it of British make. Paul Faure, deputy in the French chamber, is in possession of photographs showing representatives of Turkey and Bulgaria buying arms at Creusot before the War which during the War were used against French troops; he has also a precious picture of Eugène Schneider on a yachting party with the Ex-Kaiser Wilhelm. French munition traffickers helped arm Abdel-Krim in his Morocco campaign against the French. The Turks used British cannon to beat the British at the Dardanelles; British battleships were sunk by British mines.

There is money in war. There is money in fear of war. Schneider and Skoda stocks skyrocketed on the Paris bourse from the time that Hitler came to power in Germany. Skoda dividends, even in 'depression' years, reached twenty-eight and a half per cent. And in times of comparative tranquillity, the arms traffickers were not above fomenting war scares. For details, one should read two remarkable pamphlets published in London by the Union of Democratic Control, the *Secret International* and *Patriotism, Ltd.*

War scares are good; real wars are better. Let there be no mistake about it. Arms dealers want war. They are hypocrites if they deny this. War is to them what milk is to a baby. They fatten on it. They fatten on it like pigs in corn.

One should not think, however, that Schneider-Creusot and the De Wendels are more noisome specimens of the arms merchant

genera than those of other lands. France has its finger in the arms
traffic pie; so have many other countries, including such pacific
states as Denmark and Sweden. Schneider-Creusot is on the whole,
slightly more savoury a company than several of its great com-
petitors. And, remembering some of the disclosures of the senate
commission in Washington, one should recall the proverb about
glass-houses.

M. Blum was the first modern statesman to tackle the arms racket.
In 1937 it was announced that Schneider-Creusot would be
nationalised.

Liberty, Equality, Fraternity—and Sterility

France is almost perfectly balanced between agriculture and industry; it needs to import only a very little food; it is infinitely less
dependent on foreign markets than Great Britain or Germany; the
backbone of the nation is the *petite bourgeoisie*, the small landowner, the peasant capitalist; industry feeds healthily on the iron
beds of Lorraine; the country is rich, even if the government is
hard-up—these are the permanent economic realities of France.

There is another reality not quite so comforting. No Chautemps, no Laval, no Tardieu, no Herriot, no De Wendel, has power
to change it. The paramount problem of France is not internal
economics or finance. It is not even the safety of the Rhine frontier,
security against the great enemy, Germany. It is a demographic
problem—the falling birth-rate.

In 1934 in France there were 677,365 births, 638,525 deaths; the
surplus of births was thus only about forty thousand. In the first
quarter of 1935 there were ten thousand fewer births than in the
corresponding period of 1934. The birth-rate in 1934 was 16.1 per
thousand, and for years it has steadily gone down; the death-rate
was 15.1 per thousand. In Germany, by contrast, the birth-rate
was 18.0, the death-rate only 10.9. The corresponding figures
for Italy are 23.2, and 13.1; for the U.S.S.R., 44.1 and 26.1. Germany, on the average—even though the German birth-rate, despite
a temporary fillip following Hitler, is also going down—has about
1,100,000 births annually. And France has only 700,000—in a
fruitful year.

No wonder France, with a population of forty-two million looks
across the Rhine at Germany, with its eighty million, in trepida-
tion and alarm. No wonder Marshal Foch, in one of his lighter
moments, suggested that the only permanent solution of the

Franco-German problem would be the castration of some twenty million Germans.

The Watchword—Security

There are arms merchants in France, but in general the French are the most pacific people in the world. The great mass of French rentiers and small shopkeepers want no more war. It is interesting, as Frances Gunther pointed out, to note the catchwords that come to mind in connection with different nationalities. Deutschland Über Alles, for instance. Germany *on top* of everything. 'Rule Britannia', for instance. The equivalent for France is '*Vive la France*', let France *live*. The Frenchman doesn't want to die: he wants to stay alive, keep his small shop, cultivate his plot of land.

The French have what Lytton Strachey, alluding to Gibbon, called the classic virtues: precision, balance, lucidity. They hate extravagance and sloppiness. They love order. Both the national habit of saving and the political desire for security are functions of the same instinct, the Frenchman puts his gold in a sock and his treaty at a frontier to satisfy the same craving—for economy, for order. By order I do not mean the compulsion to goose-step, but the inner harmony of activity in personal and political life that rises from lucid, well-balanced intelligence.

France got a good deal out of the last war. All France wants is to be permitted to keep what she has. I have written 'a good deal'; but in reality did France get so very much? In proportion to their sacrifices and to the total German losses, the share of the French was not unduly great. Alsace-Lorraine; the Saar for fifteen years; the Syrian mandate and the Cameroons; reparations. Well, Alsace-Lorraine was French anyway, at least since Louis XIV; the Saar was duly given back to Germany; the Syrian mandate has been an expensive nuisance; and where, oh where, are reparations now?

For France, the 'peace' of 1919 has not proved enough. Twenty years later France again saw the terrible weight of German militarism leaning against the fragile west frontier. The French have been invaded by Germany thrice in a little more than a century. They don't want to be invaded again.

The war-guilt topic is complex. Of course France contributed to the origins of the Great War. To say that Germany alone was guilty is a monstrous exaggeration. Nevertheless, the German *army* was the aggressor. Monsieur Briand and Herr Stresemann—it seems a long time ago—once had a brief conversation on the subject:

'Well,' the old Frenchman sighed, 'I don't, of course, know what history will say, but I am afraid you will have to agree that in 1914 Belgium did not invade Germany!'

France, a realistic nation, having suffered the loss of almost two million war dead, having suffered unparalleled devastation and destruction of property and human values, sought after the War to create a system of defence, known as 'security'. It comprised the following items:

> The most powerful army in western Europe.
> The first formidable air force.
> The greatest number of tanks and artillery.
> The line of fortifications on the eastern frontier.
> An immense munitions industry.
> The second largest gold reserve in the world.
> The League covenant and the Locarno treaties.
> The demilitarisation of Germany.
> The military and diplomatic alliances with the Little Entente (Czechoslovakia, Jugoslavia, Rumania) and Poland.
> The short-lived 'Stresa Front' with Italy and Britain.

These were among the spoils of victory, but soon they—spoiled. All these items the French had. But soon the French saw that they were not enough. And with reason. 'France,' it has been said, 'was perfectly prepared in 1914 for the war of 1871, and in 1937 France was perfectly prepared—for the war of 1914.' The League system was dealt terrible blows by the Japanese in Manchuria, the Italians in Abyssinia. The alliances with the Little Entente and Poland became a doubtful quantity. Germany, by leaving the League of Nations, ended the 'disarmament' phase of international politics, and the 'collective security' phase which replaced it was neither collective nor secure. The Russian treaty seemed valuable, but Munich killed it. Finally, the 'Stresa Front' collapsed when Great Britain signed the Anglo-German naval treaty and when Mussolini began the Abyssinian war.

During the long Briand period, the French, albeit grudgingly, were conciliatory to Germany in the main. It was obvious to Briand that Germany, a complex of sixty-five million people in the heart of Europe, couldn't be kept down permanently, that a healthy Germany was the *sine qua non* of general European stability. But what happened? Every concession redoubled German chauvinism. The French evacuated the Rhine; the answer they got was the end of reparations. They granted Germany equal military status; the answer they got was Hitler. They gave Germany back the Saar;

the answer they got was German conscription, plus Goering's tremendous air fleet. They gave Germany Munich; the answer they got was the seizure of Czechoslovakia and Poland.

Unilateral denunciation of treaties has become a bit of a bore, the French think. Suppose Spain should suddenly decide to demand the Philippines back from the United States! The French have submitted to a permanent inferiority in one branch of armament, that is, they accepted the 1.75 naval ratio vis-à-vis America and Britain. Why could not the Germans accept similar proportional inferiority? Should the Germans get back all they lost simply by asking for it? If they dislike the Treaty of Versailles, why did they sign it in the first place? What in short, was the use of winning the War anyway? Which is, of course, and the honest Frenchman will admit it, the exact point: winning the War brought little gain; no one won the War; winners were losers.

French policy to the outbreak of the war in 1939 was based, as always, on the necessities of defence. Since the Doumergue government, the general staff of the army has been actually *in* the cabinet, first in the person of Marshal Pétain, then through General Denain, the air minister. The Flandin government doubled the length of military service for conscripts. This was to counterbalance the meagre cadres of the 'lean years' during the War, when fewer men were born to reach military age.

Diplomatically, France sought to follow the Barthou tactics, to keep its allies in order through regional pacts within the League of Nations. The French allies were, as everyone knows, the 'status quo' countries, the 'Haves' of Europe, those which got what they wanted by the War, more or less: Belgium, Czechoslovakia, Jugoslavia, Rumania, Poland. The conflict between these groups and the German-led 'Have-Nots' produced a vicious circle. The security arrangements of the 'Haves' stimulated the revisionism of the 'Have-Nots', threats of revision by the 'Have-Nots' then forced the 'Haves' to stiffer standards of security. French nationalism spurred German nationalism, and vice versa. The more eager the Germans were to revise, the keener the French got for the status quo.

The new pacts France would have liked, on French terms, were the following:

1. A western air pact. This would have extended the old Locarno to immediate assistance by air to any signatory attacked, not merely France or Germany. The advantage to France was a closer tie-up to England and possibly Italy. To accompany it France

wanted a security arrangement in Eastern Europe, which Hitler—who might have signed a western air pact alone—balked at, thus bringing the whole business to nothing.

2. A Danubian pact. This, if it could have been negotiated, would have taken the form of a Franco-Italian guarantee of the present frontiers in Central Europe, plus assistance of some kind for Austria. Germany opposed it, because of course it would have tended to prevent what Germany wanted, *Anschluss* between Germany and Austria.

3. An 'Eastern Locarno', similarly guaranteeing the frontiers of Poland, Germany, the U.S.S.R., and the Baltic states. The U.S.S.R. was for a time eager for such a treaty, and made preliminary regional pacts with the buffer countries. But both Germany and Poland—when the Germans and Poles had their short interlude of working together—opposed it.

A pact which the French did succeed in signing, and which was of paramount importance so long as it lasted, was the Franco-Soviet Treaty of Mutual Assistance of 1935. It was ratified by the French chamber after furious deliberation, and became the chief bastion of French security when Locarno died. Promptly it was associated with the Franco-Czech and Russo-Czech security treaties, and it seemed that a defensive league stretching right across Europe had been formed. People came to talk about Collective Security and the 'democratic' front represented by the French, the Russians, and the Czechs, in contrast to the Fascists.

The Franco-Soviet treaty, it is interesting to note, was negotiated and signed, not by the Leftists of the *Front Populaire*, but by a highly nationalist French government of the *Right*. It was the child of such non-Bolsheviks as Barthou and Laval; on a trip to Moscow, in fact, Laval arranged it. The Germans, naturally, were furious at the Franco-Soviet pact; its signature was the pretext for the 'invasion' of the Rhineland. They countered, as we have seen, with both the Anti-Comintern pact and the 'Rome-Berlin axis'. As in 1914, conflicting treaties served to split Europe into two camps, with the difference that in 1937 the opponents were distinguished by ideological as well as national stigmata. The Spanish civil war, as everyone knows, savagely illuminated this cleavage of Europe into two mutually exclusive *blocs*.

For a time, immediately after Hitler came to power, there was some fear that France might wage a 'cold' war, a preventive war, the theory being that it was better to strike at Germany when she was comparatively weak than risk waiting for a war made by Germany when strong. The idea fell flat, for the simple reason that France wouldn't fight. No government in France could get a single Frenchman to cross a frontier in any aggressive war. But woe to the man who treads two feet inside French territory.

Brass Check in France

One of the things which makes France so hard for a foreigner to understand is the notorious venality of the French Press. There are no fewer than one hundred and two daily newspapers in Paris alone and of the lot probably few except two are honest in our sense of the term, the *Action Française*, organ of the royalists, and *Humanité*, the communist sheet. Most of the others, from top to bottom, have news columns for sale.

When the American Ambassador Walter Edge arrived in Paris at the beginning of his term, one of the editors of an important paper called on his secretary, hat in hand, sure that the new emissary would appreciate the very best in '*publicité*'. A year or so ago in Barcelona, the leader of the Catalan movement told me that he had had to pay another important paper to print a series of articles describing sympathetically Catalan aspirations.

Paris papers may be subsidised by foreign governments, for instance Japan and Italy. During the Japanese war in Manchuria the French Press was, by and large, thoroughly pro-Japanese—and for a reason. Italy, a competent authority estimates, spent about sixty-five million French francs on French newspapers in 1935. In 1939 two important editors were accused of accepting funds from Germany. The Press is subsidised by the French Government too. Both the ministry of foreign affairs and the ministry of the interior have at their disposal huge *fonds secrets*.

Esprit de France

France, above all, as Edgar Ansel Mowrer once said, is a *success*. Its language, its literature, its culture, are the envy of the intelligent in every country; France is the most civilised country in the world. But since the War the French have discovered that harmony, civilisation, are not enough. During the past fifty years the world has changed more than in history, and it has isolated the perfection of French character. The world is no longer bounded by the chaste walls of a room in the Faubourg St. Germain, or an apple orchard in Normandie, or a shopkeeper's neat, frugal premises in Lyons.

The Frenchman sees the values of his world changing, and he doesn't know what to do about it.

More important in France than the figure of M. Léon Blum or M. Edouard Daladier is the person of M. Jean Frenchman. France is a nation of forty-two million individualists. What does the average Frenchman think of the shattered world, the world slipping to a new catastrophe? M. Jean Frenchman, since his country is a success, is a standpatter. He is almost a stick-in-the-mud. His idea of a good time is to go fishing and have a well-cooked dinner. His approach to things is, above all, rational. He refused, for a long time, to believe that Hitler—for example—was anything but crazy. He knows better now. But tell him that Hitler is a prophet, and he will reply, sceptically, rationally, 'Prophète? Il n'y a plus de prophètes.'

M. Jean Frenchman has lived on a volcano all his life. Three times within living memory it has exploded. It may explode again. He grumbles, potters, and hopes—not very vigorously—for the best, meantime teaching his children, from the earliest ages, to be responsible. M. Frenchman wants above all to be let alone. He wants nothing more than to do nothing. He is no good except under pressure. 'Everything in France is at least twenty per cent better than it looks; everything in Germany is twenty per cent worse,' Mowrer says. Now that war has come, M. Frenchman will fight, and it will be hard to beat him, even if the perfection of his civilisation has sapped much of his vitality. Rather than let the Germans have what he owns, he will burn it if he cannot defend it. Maturity isn't necessarily decadence; and Germany learned that at Verdun.

CHAPTER XII

MORE ABOUT FRENCHMEN

'It is impossible to think of France except in terms of individuals.'
—ANDRÉ SIEGFRIED.

GERMANY is Hitler. But France is a whole lot of people. Six hundred and eighteen of them are members of the chamber of deputies, subdivided into bewilderingly numerous parties and groups. In the sixty-eight years of the French republic there have been one hundred and three cabinets, the average life being eight months. Living in France to-day are fifteen ex-prime ministers,[1] each of whom, as long as he lives, must be addressed officially as 'M. le Président [du Conseil]'. From one point of view, France is the *reductio ad absurdum* of democracy.

Several factors cause this extreme political fluidity. For one thing, as Siegfried says, the Frenchman wears his heart on the left, his pocket-book on the right; therefore he is a creature of conflicting impulses. Second, the parties and groups are not clearly demarcated as in America or England. Politics is largely a matter of personality; deputies are individualists rather than members of a rigid party machine, and many—thirty-one in the present chamber—belong to no party at all.

The French electoral system is a combination of the British and American, in that the chamber is elected for a stated period (four years), but that the cabinet must resign if it is outvoted; the new cabinet carries on under the old chamber, which is the source of much of the confusion. There are so many parties that no single one can command a majority, and they combine in coalitions.

'The nomenclature of parties,' Albert Guerard wrote, 'is'—he put it mildly—'perverse. The "Liberals" are dyed-in-the-wool conservatives. The "Conservatives" are revolutionary in spirit, tone, and method; the "Social and Radical Left" belongs to the Right; the "Radical Socialists" are trimmers and time-servers; and the most

[1] Paul-Boncour, Caillaux, Chautemps, Daladier, Doumergue, Flandin, Tardieu, Herriot, François-Marsal, Millerand, Steeg, Sarraut, Bouisson, Laval, Blum.

reactionary statesman of recent years, Millerand, was a socialist. French parties are not even shadows. It would tax the subtlety of a Byzantine theologian to distinguish between the Democratic Alliance, the Republicans of the Left, and the Republican Union.'

But, mystified by the whirling rotation of French cabinets, the foreign observer is likely to exaggerate its implications. The changes, the reshuffles, do not as a rule mean much. The civil service—the permanent staff of each ministry—holds the fabric of government tight and secure. The prime minister is titular rather than actual ruler of the country, and often it hardly matters who he is; behind him the bureaucracy carries on.

As a matter of fact, there have been only six drastic changes in governments in France since the War, the same number as in Britain. From 1919 to 1924 the *Bloc National* ruled, dominated by Clemenceau, Poincaré, and the financial oligarchy; it gave way from 1924 to 1926 to a Left coalition under Herriot, the *Cartel des Gauches*; Poincaré returned with the *Union Nationale* to save the franc from 1926 to 1929; a series of Left coalitions, more or less antagonistic to the oligarchy and the Banque de France, ruled roughly from 1929 to 1934; then came the 'National' period of Doumergue, Flandin, and Laval; in 1936 arrived the Popular Front.

Cutting across the political welter is one considerable issue, that of religion. France is divided into two extremes religiously, the Catholics and the Freemasons. The Catholics, the largest group, are nationalist, conservative, strong in the oligarchy and strong in the army; some, like the brilliant pamphleteers of the *Action Française*, are royalists; the bulk of the Catholics are loyal to the republic, but on the Right.

The Freemasons, on the other hand, are largely represented in the parties of the Left. Briand was reputed to be a Freemason; Herriot is supposed to be one; Chautemps is. The Freemasons are alleged to control the radical party; they are ferociously republican and anticlerical; they oppose the financial oligarchy and the banks. France is the only country in Europe where masonry is a serious political issue; the Right, for instance, exploited the Stavisky scandal as a 'masonic' plot.

'Lavaluation'

'There are five or six men in the world on whom peace depends. Destiny has placed me among them.'
                                                                                 —PIERRE LAVAL.

Pierre Laval, Mayor of the tough Paris suburb Aubervilliers,

senator for the department of the Seine, former prime minister and
foreign minister, was born in 1883 in the village of Châtelon, in the
Auvergne. He is called '*Le Bougnat*'—slang for Auvergnese—
figuratively 'coal and wood man'. The Auvergne is a deep fastness
in south-central France, made of granite as old as the earth; the
Auvergnese are the grimmest of French peasants, hard-working,
shrewd, with primitive reflexes, close to the soil. All over France
they are the coal and wood dealers. There is a strong negroid cast
of feature in many Auvergnese; Laval has thick lips, heavy, black,
oily hair.

Laval's chief characteristic is his sense of the concrete, plus wili-
ness. He is, as the French say, *malin*—a word for which there is no
precise translation; it means a sort of worthy unscrupulousness,
slyness without evil. The joke goes that Laval was clever enough
even to be born with a name which spells the same backwards and
forwards, left to right or right to left. He rose from extreme
poverty to wealth; yet he is one of the few French politicians
untouched by financial scandal. He is supple as a cat. Like a
cat, he never attempts anything he is not perfectly sure of; he
calculates every jump to the inch. He gets out of things marvellously.

The great Briand, whose protégé he was, said of him, alluding to
his slipperiness, 'Alas, it is impossible to agree with everyone *and*
M. Laval.' Yet Laval is all things to all people. His manners in
the lobbies of the chamber are the quintessence of tact. He is a
couloir (corridor) politician, a fixer, *par excellence*. He is unas-
suming, unpretentious; among his friends are men in every party,
journalists of every nation. He is on thee-and-thou terms, people
say, with more men than any personage in France.

Not only is his capacity for friendship comprehensive; he
treats one and all with an unvaryingly shrewd and watchful
eye. Laval is too sly to trust anyone too fully. His character,
in fact, embodies to a signal degree the national French trait of
suspiciousness.

His father, who is supposed to be descended from the Moorish
invaders of France, was the village butcher. Pierre did odd jobs as
a child, went to school, read voraciously, taught himself Greek.
For two years, when he was about nineteen, he was school-teacher
in the village. Then he studied law, went to Paris and entered
politics. Nominally he is still a barrister at the Paris court of
appeals. In his comparatively short period as an active lawyer he

had few conspicuous cases; mostly he was an 'inside' man on corporate work; he was an indifferent pleader. The great world of politics seized him—and here he pled well.

His career opened in 1914 when he was first elected deputy from Aubervilliers, where he chose to settle down. He has maintained the closest connection to this proletarian Paris suburb ever since. It is strongly communist, but enough communists vote for him to keep him perpetually mayor. He was up for re-election in 1935 while the government was negotiating the Moscow pact—so the communists didn't fight him very hard. His constituency knows him universally as 'Pierrot'; he gets along with everybody, and the poor people of the district like his homely manners, his bad teeth.

He began political life as a violent socialist, and until at least 1922 he was known as a man of the extreme Left. Since then he has moved steadily Right, until now he occupies a Centre position. He belongs to no political party, and describes himself as 'independent'. It is not quite fair to say that socialism brought Laval to power and that he then kicked it over, as did other notable French politicians. Laval was never an orthodox party man. He was a lone wolf, on the make.[1]

But Laval was a passionate pacifist at the beginning of his career, when pacifism took real courage. His name was in the famous 'Carnet B' of the ministry of interior; he was called a 'dangerous' anti-militarist. He refused to volunteer in the French army, and on being drafted he served as a common *poilu*—for a very brief time. His pacifism made him popular with the disaffected infantry in the black middle period of the War. In 1916 he cried out in the chamber, 'Except for [Czarist] Russia, we shouldn't be at war at all!' A year later, referring to the socialist peace congress in Sweden, he shouted, 'Stockholm is the pole-star of our hopes'.

He lost his deputy's seat in 1919, and remained in the political wilderness till 1924. Then his qualities as a negotiator boosted him suddenly to cabinet rank. The *Cartel des Gauches* (Left coalition) was undergoing one of its frequent shuffles, and Laval acted as an intermediary between Paul Painlevé and Briand and Caillaux; as reward, he became minister of public works. Caillaux lived in his house, Briand liked him, and when Briand became

[1] For a time according to Robert Dell (cf. *Nation*, October 28, 1931), he joined an abortive 'communist-socialist' party, which, however, never spread beyond the working-class districts of Paris and soon died.

prime minister, Laval was first appointed his general secretary—
a valuable key post—and later minister of justice.

Then the Left coalition crashed and during the Poincaré régime
Laval was very much out in the cold. He was far too Leftish—
still—for the harsh, legalistic Poincaré. This taught him a lesson,
and he cultivated the friendship of a man distinctly not on the
Left—André Tardieu. And when Tardieu formed a cabinet in
1930, Laval was his minister of labour. Laval played with Briand
and Tardieu both. In January 1931, he became prime minister—
at Briand's urgent intercession—and included Tardieu as minister
of agriculture by sacrificing Left support. His first premiership
lasted thirteen months—a long time for France.

Laval, among other things, went to Berlin, the first French prime
minister to visit Germany since the War. All things to all men, it
looked as if he intended to be all things to all nations too. The
Germans gave him an imposing reception.[1] In June 1931 he showed
the world his stubbornness in haggling for seventeen bitter days
before France accepted the Hoover moratorium. In October he
went to America—the first French prime minister to do so—and
talked to Hoover at Rapidan. Meanwhile, the influence of Briand
was waning. The Old Man of Peace was sick and tired, but reports
that Laval deliberately undercut him are not true. The two men
had great regard for each other, and Briand was too ill to work; when
in January 1932 he resigned, Laval naturally succeeded him as
foreign minister.

But the next month Laval himself went out of office. The
frugal French grudged him his free trip to America. And he had
angered the all-powerful Banque de France, because he insisted
that France stick to the British pound, and when the pound went
off gold (partly as a result of Laval's long haggle over the Hoover
moratorium), the Banque de France lost £20,000,000 on paper. So
he went. This taught him a lesson, as we shall see; the next time
he became prime minister he listened to the Banque more carefully.
He was 'out' two and a half years. In October 1934 he became
foreign minister after Jugoslav bullets and the lack of French first-
aid killed Barthou at Marseilles; in June 1935 he became prime
minister again, when the financial oligarchy vanquished his friend
Flandin.

[1] But the story is that Brüning, then chancellor, careful to risk no hostile demonstration at the station, filled it with several thousand detectives and their wives—
disguised as the cheering populace.

Laval is a bad speaker, and he never talks in the chamber unless it is absolutely necessary. He keeps his left hand in his trousers pocket and saws the air with his right hand. His oratorical delivery, say the sophisticated critics of the lobbies, lacks 'elegance'. But elegance is the last quality this swarthy peasant's son would pretend to. And why worry about public talk in the chamber, when private whispers just outside are more effective?[1]

Laval is probably the only important man in French public life who has never written a book, and the only one whose final ambition is not to become a member of the Academic Française. He is not like Blum or Herriot, passionately erudite. His intellect is that of an engineer, not a scholar. He dislikes abstractions, and he has little use for art, science, or pure literature. He is a lawyer, but he cares nothing for legal forms.

. . . .

But Laval, a typical Frenchman of the middle class—not a Parisian—is quick, shrewd, logical, practical, and lucid. Compare his intelligence to that of a German, for instance Rosenberg. Rosenberg is, as Dorothy Thompson once said, a man of great intelligence who is also a complete fool: like so many Germans, he is both brilliant and incredibly stupid; he is capable of erecting dialectical structures of extreme brilliance upon hypotheses which a child could knock apart. Laval is at the other extreme. He thinks not only with his head but with his finger-tips.

Every German has a sense of national mission. Every Frenchman, like Laval, has a sense of individual destiny. Scratch a German, and you find a sheep; scratch a Frenchman, and you have an anarchist. 'Remove liberty from Germany,' Frances Gunther wrote, 'and you unite the country; remove liberty from France, and you have a revolution.'

A famous *mot* is attributed to Clemenceau. 'Briand,' he said, 'knows nothing, understands everything; Poincaré knows everything, understands nothing.' Laval is in the middle ground. He knows a lot, but not everything; he understands even more than he knows, but he admits limits to his understanding. He loves to reconcile opposites. And he has one trait excessively rare among politicians: he is not vain.

Laval married a woman from the Auvergne, who, like the wives of most French politicians, takes no part in public life. The Lavals,

[1] For a background to contemporary French politics see Alexander Werth's admirable *France in Ferment*.

in Paris, live in the little impasse Villa Saïd, next door to Anatole France's old house. He prefers the country to Paris, and often returns to Châtelon, his birth-town, where, the local boy who made good, he owns an imposing château. Even during cabinet crises he tries to get out of Paris for the week-end. He has two or three country estates, including a stock farm in Normandie at La Corbière. His attractive daughter José, the wife of Count René de Chambrun, is his constant companion.

Laval has no vices—except perhaps that since his doctor told him he must cut down his cigarettes, he now smokes a mere eighty per day. He still wears the kind of white tie that he adopted in 1914—because white ties don't fade and are washable.

He had, it seems, no taste for the prime minister's job in June 1935. He much preferred to stick to his chosen field of foreign affairs where, indeed, his record was much brighter. He assumed the premiership only with great reluctance, because he knew that he could not last, while as a foreign minister his tenure would be longer. It is his life's ambition to be the great and permanent foreign minister of France, to effect French security by long-range settlement with England, Italy, and Germany.

He took the foreign office just after Barthou had been busy patching up some badly broken French fences in Central Europe, thus annoying the Germans. The Saar plebiscite was coming soon and Laval did his utmost to appease Hitler by a strictly reasonable, business-like conclusion to the Saar problem. His policy was sensible: he knew the Saar was in any case bound to go to Germany, and he decided to give it up with good grace. Generosity, in the circumstances, cost nothing.

Then Laval went to Rome, and in January 1935 concluded his famous arrangement with Mussolini, which, it was announced, settled all outstanding difficulties between France and Italy. He gave Mussolini some worthless sand in Lybia; in return he got promises of joint Franco-Italian action in Central Europe. But these celebrated conversations with Mussolini gave him plenty of trouble later, because when the Abyssinian war began, the Frenchman was torn between his promises to Mussolini—who assumed that Laval had given him a free hand in Abyssinia—and the burning necessity to keep on good terms with Britain within the League of Nations fold.[1] Laval went on, the story said, trying to save 'both his faces'.

[1] For the Hoare-Laval plan see Chapter XVII below.

Then the sanctions quarrel—plus domestic intrigue—finished him. At least for the time being.

Big Brother of Lyons

Edouard Herriot, the Mayor of Lyons, a strenuous idealist, was for years leader of the radical-socialist party, the second largest in the French Chamber. This party, as pointed out above, is neither very radical nor socialist, and Herriot, a copious enough personality, signalises well its aims, tempo, and limitations. He is always a power, because the average Frenchman is a radical.

He was born in Lyons, in 1872, and still lives there; he has been Mayor of Lyons uninterruptedly since 1905. When local opposition is serious, he descends on the town council, weeps and wails, and gets re-elected by making it ashamed of itself for even daring to consider any other candidate. He was a poor boy, largely self-educated. He became a teacher, then a professor at the University of Lyons, finally a deputy.

He is a great artist in the emotions. Sometimes this leads him to bizarre excesses of pathos. 'Gentlemen,' he said, with tears streaming down his cheeks, 'we must not quarrel over the bedside of our sick mother (France)', when he and Poincaré furiously bickered after the *débâcle* of the franc in 1926. He is very fond of placing his hand on his heart and declaiming about his warm virtues. He gets a lot of ragging for it.[1]

The antithesis of the lean, dry, acrid Poincaré, Herriot is a tower of massive flesh, given to indulgence. A friend of mine had a 'snack' with him—just a bite—recently at Geneva; he ate soup, two *truites bleues*, a partridge, considerable quantities of vegetable matter, a sweet, and cheese, washed down with two full bottles of burgundy. But he attributes his good health to the fact that he is a total abstainer from alcohol, viz., any alcohol except wine and beer.

Herriot first became prime minister in 1924, and his government set out to reverse the *revanche* politics of Clemenceau and Poincaré. Europe looked up with hope and interest. Herriot—and Mac-Donald across the channel—seemed symbols of a new and conciliatory era. Herriot in particular, robust, expansive, scholarly, benign, generous, suggested to nationalist Europe the France it had

---

[1] cf. *Not to be Repeated*, p. 259. Cartoonists like to portray Herriot as a transparent body with six or seven hearts.

forgotten, the France of the classic humanities of Jean Jacques Rousseau, the ideals of the great Revolution.

For a time he flourished on the reversal of arid Poincarism. He set about to reach an agreement with England—Franco-British relations were then severely strained—and to conciliate Germany by settling the reparations question. Two months after the formation of his ministry the Ruhr was evacuated and the Dawes Plan went into operation. This seems small potatoes now; but it was a literally tremendous achievement. Herriot gave Europe a new start. He initiated the policy which has dominated French foreign politics ever since—reliance on the League—when the League behaves itself.

Much later, in 1930, Herriot was still battling with disarmament plans which might entice the Germans into a peaceful policy. Fittingly, he was the negotiator of the Lausanne settlement, which ended reparations—and closed a gloomy post-War chapter. He was the first French prime minister to get on good terms with the U.S.S.R., and as far back as 1932 he signed a Franco-Russian non-aggression treaty. He thought that France ought to pay its debt to the U.S.A., and lost office when the frugal French, like the normally honest British, thought that this idea was nonsense.

As disillusion came to Herriot, his idealism became a little tarnished. Inevitably, like most liberals, he had made some considerable compromises. He took office in the Doumergue national government, even though his party did not. One would have expected him to denounce the gold standard and Laval's humiliating dependence on the banks. But he took office under Laval too. This, his friends say, was so that he might the better watch Laval at Geneva, keep him in proper order. His ambition is to be President of the Republic, but, as we have seen, Daladier blocked him.

Herriot can make a speech, and a magnificent speech, though his very delivery is orotund and portly, on any occasion, extemporaneously. He was crossing on the *Ile de France* after his American visit in 1933, with Paderewski a fellow-passenger, on a day that happened to be the Polish national holiday. The ship's company persuaded Paderewski to play; lights were kept low so that no one could see the old man, suffering agonies from rheumatism, too closely. Paderewski, barely able to lift his hands to the keyboard, played all his runs glissando, but he played them beautifully.   Herriot, as was inevitable, had spoken introducing him.   His speech was quite on a par with the music.   At the end, anyone in the audience not knowing him would have thought him a Pole.

He is, like many French statesmen, a man of profound erudition and very nearly first-rate literary style.   The rhythm of a sentence, the lilt of a sly adjective, the passion of an unexpected verb—these are matters almost as dear to his heart as the sauce of the *quenelles de brochet* at his favourite restaurant in Lyons.   Herriot has written several books, and they are admirable.   One was a study of Mme Recamier.   Another was one of the best biographies of Beethoven ever written.

The Former Fusiliers

Eugène Frot, a youthful lawyer with lively black eyes and a vivid black beard on his lean jaws from ear to ear, was minister of the interior in the ill-fated Daladier government that was swept from office by the February 1934 riots.   He was known, even then, to be among the young radicals heartily bored with the *crise de parlémentarisme*, with the scandalous inefficiency of the routine of the French Government.   People called him a 'Young Turk', or even a 'Fascist of the Left'.   He was the chief actor of February 6, who brought the crisis to a head by causing the discharge of Chiappe, the Corsican who was chief of police.   The royalists always call him the 'assassin'.   Once they doused him—at a public meeting—with a bucket of butcher's blood.

Another of the 'Fusiliers' was Pierre Cot, minister of air in the Daladier and Chautemps governments.   Thin, meagre, unimpressive physically, a scholar, he has considerable executive ability. The first thing he did on becoming air minister was learn to pilot a machine.   He kept office in a good many cabinets, because he had the arduous task of tidying up the Aeropostale scandal and re-organising French civil aviation on reasonably efficient lines.   He seemed indispensable at the job, but the riots of February 6 swept him away.   The Right hates him.

With Daladier Cot joined the socialist-communist United Front. On July 14, 1935, he appeared at the monster *Front Populaire* demonstration at the Place de la Bastille, sitting atop a motor-car with an enormous tricolour above him; beside him was another car flying a red flag, equally huge.   The crowds, greeting him, shouted *'Vive le dictateur!'*   Daladier, by contrast, walked in the ranks with the leaders of the march. Hundreds saw Daladier; thousands saw Cot. Even so, most folk did not think Cot would go too far.

Caillaux

Old Joseph Caillaux is seventy-seven. At the end of 1939, it was a surprise to many who recalled the scandal of 1913, when his wife killed Gaston Calmette, editor of *Figaro*, that he was still alive—and not only alive, but an important factor still in French politics. Caillaux is one of the chiefs of the radical-socialist party, as influential in his way as either Herriot or Daladier; and he is presiding officer of the important Senate finance commission.

Caillaux is arrogant, neat, vain, precise, clear-headed, and a dandy. He is either violently reverenced or violently hated by the young. He was one of the few men in France courageous enough, during the War, to assert that both vanquished and victors would be ruined; as a result, Clemenceau had him jailed for 'complicity with Germany'. He was not tried till 1920, when, adjudged guilty by the Senate of 'imprudent conversations', he was deprived of political rights for five years and of the right to enter Paris—*'interdiction de séjour'*, a judgment usually reserved for white-slavers, drug addicts, and thugs. Caillaux, a millionaire, and a man of the highest culture, was amnestied by Herriot in 1924.

Paul-Boncour and Other Radicals

When the *Action Française* does not call Joseph Paul-Boncour, the greatest lawyer in France, 'Don Juan de Lavabo', it calls him 'Paul-Arlette-Boncour'—because, it seems, the eminent jurist once had the honour of the acquaintance of Arlette Simon, the surprisingly beautiful wife of Serge Stavisky. When she was ill in hospital —before the scandal broke—he was one of two ministers who visited her.

Paul-Boncour, an old parliamentary hand, began politics as a socialist, then founded a short-lived party of his own. He looks like a Michelangelo angel—a fallen angel, perhaps. Over the massive carved head is the great mane of carved white hair. As foreign minister, he was too tender with Germany for the French general staff and almost lost his job. He made marvellous speeches at Geneva; but he forgot to meet Colonel Beck, the Polish foreign minister, at the railway station, mortally affronting him.

Of the other radicals little need be said. Albert Sarraut, former prime minister, is a communist-hater and an old-style political careerist. He gave Chiappe the job of chief of police when he was Poincaré's minister of the interior. . . . Henri Cheron, a frequent finance minister, was the man whom Philip Snowden, at the Hague, called 'grotesque and ridiculous'. And when Snowden accepted a peerage, the French papers were quick and neat to headline the story: 'Viscount Snowden—Grotesque and Ridiculous.' . . . Albert Dalimier was the minister in the radical cabinet who unwittingly caused the Stavisky explosion by recommending the Bayonne bonds. . . . The party threw him out—too late.

Tardieu Getting Old

André Tardieu, 'The Shark', born in 1876, the most representative French politician of the Right, is a Parisian; the countryside, which is the bedrock of France, has always distrusted him, and this may have something to do with the comparative failure of his career. Too ambitious, his life never quite fulfilled the promise of his exceptionally brilliant youth, though he has been prime minister three times. He was first in his class at the École Normale Supérieure; he was first in his examinations for the diplomatic service; he was *chef de cabinet* of a prime minister (Waldeck-Rousseau in 1899) at the astounding age of twenty-three.

For twelve years, 1902 to 1914, Tardieu was a journalist, principally for the *Temps*, *Figaro*, and *Revue des Deux Mondes*. It is quite possible that he was the most brilliant journalist in the history of modern France. During the same year he was professor of history at the School of Political Science and the École Supérieure de Guerre. He wrote six volumes of contemporary history. He entered politics—as a deputy—in 1914—and spent most of the early part of the War at the Front; he was wounded, poisoned by gas, cited in army orders, decorated. Clemenceau took him up. From about 1917 on he was Clemenceau's man, first in the United States as high commissioner—where his excellent manners, *chic*, good English, and brilliant social sense made him very popular—then as a delegate to the peace conference and minister for the liberated regions.

After he had tried to break up Doumergue's national government by attacking the radicals, Tardieu resigned his office as minister of state and spent most of his time in retirement. The report is that he is not well; doctors are supposed to have given

him only a limited span of life. Tardieu, on the Right, like Daladier, on the Left, is contemptuous of present parliamentary procedure. He has said that he will never accept office in a cabinet
constituted on the present basis. If France should go Fascist or
semi-Fascist, then Tardieu may become an important—and dangerous—man again.

The Grand Inquisitor

One of the most remarkable of French political characters, also
on the Right, though he calls himself independent, is Georges
Mandel, whose real name is Jeraboam Rothschild. He was Clemenceau's first assistant in 1917-1918 and since the Tiger devoted himself exclusively to the War, Mandel, those two years, practically ran
France. Until 1934 he was a sort of invisible Richelieu, an
éminence grise behind the scenes; he knew everything, he forgot
nothing, and the chamber quaked when he rose to talk. He refused
to take formal office—any premier would have been glad to have
him—until Flandin persuaded him to be minister of posts and tele-
graphs. Literally as well as figuratively, Georges Mandel could
listen-in on anything in France. As a result, he became a taciturn
and formidable encyclopedia on the secret life of the Third Republic. And his power is great.

Mandel is supposed to have entrenched himself with Clemenceau
when he first asked for a job on the Tiger's newspaper. 'You are an
ugly rat,' said Clemenceau. 'So I can see in that mirror,' Mandel
instantly replied—pointing to the glass opposite the Tiger. Clemenceau made him foreign leader-writer because he knew nothing of
foreign affairs. 'Mandel,' he said once, 'your articles are not
stupider than others. But they are complicated. Hereafter, you
may use merely one subject, one object, one verb in each sentence.
The object must be direct. If you use an indirect object, consult
me first.'

Then for fifteen years Mandel pursued many indirect objects—
but not in literature.

Paul Reynaud and the Centre

Another highly important personage in the political life of
France is Paul Reynaud, born at Barcelonette in 1879, a lawyer and
long-time deputy, who was Tardieu's minister of finance and Laval's
minister of colonies. Reynaud, able and ambitious, a son-in-law
of the great Parisian barrister Maître Robert, had a kind of double

foreign policy for a long time; he was an ardent nationalist, and at the same time wanted Franco-German *rapprochement*. In 1935 he made a notable speech opposing Laval on the Abyssinian deal; he said it was madness for France to alienate Britain for the sake of Mussolini's doubtful friendship.

Reynaud is a member of what is known as the Democratic Alliance, but he has never taken much interest in party politics. He is, and always has been, a lone wolf, though for a time he was more closely associated with Flandin than any other politician. When Flandin took a pro-Munich policy, Reynaud resigned from his group. Reynaud set about the reorganisation of French finances and economy when he became Daladier's finance minister. He sought to find a path midway between Laval and Blum. When war came in 1939, Reynaud initiated the closest possible financial and economic collaboration with Great Britain. He even talked in terms of customs union and common currency.

Reynaud is a deputy from a Paris constituency. He is one of the most brilliant living Frenchmen. Should Daladier be displaced, Reynaud is regarded as his probable successor.

The Centre in French politics, says Siegfried, is not so much a point of natural concentration in French politics, but a watershed dividing Left from Right. The most typical man of the Centre is probably Pierre-Etienne Flandin. Not a true leader, not a dynamic human being, he has commendable qualities: industry, a sense of balance, great technical proficiency in matters of economics and finance. He ruined his career, however, during the Munich crisis, when he took an extreme pro-appeasement and even pro-Hitler line.

Flandin is called the Skyscraper; he is six foot four, and solidly built, zoned almost like a building. He was—at forty-five—the youngest prime minister in the history of France. He was a flyer during the War. Though on the Centre, he is a devout republican; though his family is rich with affiliations to heavy industry, he is no warm friend of the oligarchy.

The Jesuit Warrior

General Maxime Weygand retired as inspector-general of the French army when, early in 1935, he reached the age of sixty-eight. When war came in 1939, this peppery and shrivelled little military priest, the man who in 1922 wrought the 'Miracle of Warsaw', was too old to fight again. He was active in diplomatic life, however; he helped negotiate the new Anglo-Franco-Turkish Treaty.

Weygand entered St. Cyr, the French equivalent of Sandhurst, *à titre étranger* (as a foreigner, since he was born in Belgium) and had a brilliant career. Joffre appointed him chief of staff to Foch after the first battle of the Marne, and he remained Foch's 'right hand' (as Foch called him) all during the War. Foch, like Weygand, was a devout Catholic. The two generals prayed together at mass every morning, before beginning the day's fighting.

After the War Foch lent Weygand to the Poles; he reorganised the Polish army, vitalised it, and won the battle before the gates of Warsaw which halted the Bolshevik invasion. The Poles, of course, never forgave him for having saved them; he didn't claim the credit, but they didn't like it when other people did. Weygand, contrary to habit, was frank; *both* the Poles and Russians were, he said, the worst armies in the world. This was in 1922. It makes curious reading now.

Clemenceau's opinion of Weygand is worth quoting:

> 'Weygand is somebody. Ugly—he is ugly, misshapen, tortured, twisted; he must have had a lot of kicks when he was little. But he's intelligent; he has something in him; a dark fire. He used to anger me at the Interallied Council. He is a man—how shall I say it?—dangerous, capable of going far in a moment of crisis, of hurling himself too far. . . . Dangerous but precious. . . . He has one enormous quality, that of knowing how to do his work without talking or being talked about. He went to Poland. I don't know what he did up there, but what he did had to be done. He came back, didn't say anything. You don't know what he did or what he's about. That's pretty good. . . . Foch wasn't stupid. But he had good-boy genius, simplicity. Weygand is something else, tender and profound. Of course, he's up to his neck in priests.'

Weygand's Catholicism—he is a fanatic Catholic—naturally made him suspect to the Left. They accused him of political ambitions, of having turned St. Cyr into a royalist-Catholic nest. Weygand was, before Poland and after, a bitter Bolshevik hater. When he was governor-general of Syria, Herriot succeeded in ousting him; even now, he is not a marshal of France, although this is probably because of the technical point that only supreme army commanders may be marshals, and he was only chief of staff. Weygand is, naturally, the old white hope of the Right, and the terrier-darling of the Fascist Leagues.

Gamelin and Georges

General Maurice Gustave Gamelin, born in Paris in 1872 of an

old military family—five of his relatives were generals—is commander-in-chief not merely of the French armies, but supreme
military leader of all the allied forces, British as well as French.
Like Weygand, he is an ardent Catholic, but he and Weygand,
though comrades in arms for many years, have not always been close
friends. Gamelin had an exceptionally brilliant military career.
At twenty-one, he was graduated from St. Cyr first in a class of
500. He spent years in the War College, in Algeria, and in the
colonies; he was educated by both Foch and Joffre; he became a
great expert in cartography. When the Great War came, he was
one of Joffre's staff, and he is widely credited with having devised
and pushed through the manœuvre which won the Battle of the
Marne.

Gamelin hates to spend lives. This is one secret of his power.
He is frugal with blood. When war broke out again in 1939, he
told his friends that never, under his command, would there be
another Somme, another Paschendaele, when hundreds of thousands
of lives were lost for extremely limited gains. In the battles of the
frontiers in 1914, the French lost three hundred thousand dead *in
five weeks*. Gamelin said in effect, 'Never again.' Thus the infinite
caution of his procedure in 1939, the excessively patient and wary
tactics he pursued, and the consequent stalemate on the Western
Front.

Gamelin is a small, tough, stubborn, friendly man, utterly without pretension or vanity. He is only five feet four. He married at
fifty-five. He has one hobby (like Hitler!), water-colour painting.

Gamelin will reach retirement age in 1940, when he will be
sixty-eight. But the exigencies of the present situation will probably keep him at his post. If he retires, his successor is almost
certain to be his present right-hand man, General Alphonse Georges.
This very distinguished and brilliant officer is known as a 'Weygand man'.

Monsieur le Président

Until 1946, unless death or revolution intervenes, the President
of France will be that amiable and harmless old gentleman Albert
Lebrun. Like all French presidents, he is above all *safe*: no brilliance, no eccentricity, is tolerated in the Élysée. He is supposed to
have a great capacity for tears; cartoonists usually depict him in a
puddle. He is known as 'pouh-pouh', because shortly after he
entered the Élysée, he posed for the talkies, with wife, children,

and grandchildren in considerable number. A small grandchild started to cry; the benevolent Lebrun dandled him on his knee, forgetting the sound camera, to the tune of 'Pouh-pouh-pouh'. And the unfortunate syllables resounded throughout France.

CHAPTER XIII

FASCISM AND THE *FRONT POPULAIRE*

'Democracy which cannot defend itself has no right to exist.'
—Dr. Emil Franke.

THE inner history of the Stavisky case is briefly this. He was a petty gangster who knew important people and killed himself —or was murdered—when his little fraudulent empire collapsed. The case rocked parliamentarism in France, which was not illogical. Of the six hundred and ten French deputies and three hundred and five senators, not more than ten or twelve ever knew Stavisky or had anything to do with him, and his total defalcations amounted only to about 40,000,000 francs; but the implications of the affair reached the very heart of French political life.

In France there are thousands of small-scale crooks who know people who know people who know ministers. They wait in reception-rooms and filch official letter-paper. Lawyers in France, as in America, go to the courts and say that their clients are 'sick', and the cases are postponed. The French Government itself may not be corrupt, but negligence, *piston* ('pull') and political demoralisation are rife in the outer corridors. Stavisky was not even a good crook. But he had 'pull'. This was not corruption; it was ordinary parliamentary 'manners'. When the story broke, Chautemps tried to cover up, which made it look much worse than it was. And the Right opposition, the *Action Française*, the Fascist leagues, the Comité des Forges, the oligarchy, seized on it and exploited it as a perfectly priceless opportunity to wreck the 'Freemasons', the radicals, the Leftists, the government.

Serge Alexandre (Sacha) Stavisky, was born in Kiev, Russia, in 1886. His family seems to have been of decent *petite bourgeoise* Jewish stock; his aged father, overcome with shame when Sacha's first defalcation was discovered, killed himself. . . . Stavisky's career in the underworld of Paris was quite typical. He was a pimp, a gigolo, a cocaine pedlar, a petty forger, a confidence man, finally a swindler of some proportion. He was successful, bought a theatre. gambled at Deauville, financed a newspaper. . . .

In 1926 he was arrested for the first and only time, on complaint of two brokers who asserted he had swindled them out of £70,000. He was soon 'provisionally' released, and he never saw the inside of a jail again; his trial was postponed by the Paris Parquet (public prosecutor) no fewer than nineteen times. The head of the Parquet, M. Pressard, was Chautemps's brother-in-law. The Paris police, who also 'knew' Stavisky, 'dealt' with his case forty-five times—without re-arresting him.

The years of 'provisional freedom' were the great years of Sacha Stavisky. He controlled two daily papers (both miserable rags, it is true), the *Volonté* on the Left, the *Rempart* on the Right. One of his lawyers, Renoult, was an ex-minister of justice. He knew countless public officials, and corrupted dozens of minor functionaries—pitiable creatures on minuscule salaries, who were dazzled by Stavisky's glory and joined his payroll; their careers were ruined afterwards, and at least two committed suicide. He had his own bodyguard, led by the remarkable Jo-la-Terreur. His friend Dubarry—a *soidisant* journalist who knew everyone in France, including Tardieu[1]—introduced him to Chiappe, the chief of police. Above all, a complicated fellow, he was employed as a sort of stool-pigeon by the Sûreté-Générale, the national police force—distinct from the Paris prefecture—of the ministry of the interior.

In 1933 Stavisky was frustrated in two coups, despite his eminence. So he contrived a new scheme, the flotation of fraudulent bonds issued presumably by the municipal pawnshop of Bayonne. Minister Dalimier in the Chautemps cabinet signed a letter recommending these bonds. Someone got suspicious. About Christmas 1933 the truth began to leak out. Secrecy pent up in a hundred mouths for seven years burst forth in an angry scandalous torrent. Stavisky's connection with the bonds became known, and then his police record. He fled—having received a false passport from the police. He rested in Chamonix for a fortnight, hoping the storm would pass. Instead it blew to tornado violence. On January 8, 1934, he knew that he was ruined, and the official story

---

[1] 'Dubarry got the Sûreté Générale to restore Stavisky's gambling licence; and when an inspector of the Sûreté was going to arrest an illegal bookie at the races one day, Dubarry pounced on him and said: "Don't you dare do that, or I'll report you to André." "André"—so Inspector Colombani said telling the story to the committee of inquiry—"*André, c'était M. Tardieu.*" ' *New Statesman*, April 14, 1935.

is that he shot himself. But the allegation that he was murdered was made almost everywhere in France.

The scandal was perfectly tremendous. It hissed and boiled during all of January, and came to climax in the bloodshed of February 6. The affair had the wildest ramifications. Daladier fired Chiappe; Thomé, the chief of the secret police, was kicked upstairs to become, of all things, director of the Comédie Française; the Right shrieked that Daladier did this to get rid of the former director, Emile Fabre, because he had put on Shakespeare's *Coriolanus*, which the Left had denounced as an 'authoritarian' play! The *Action Française* whooped and howled that the Sûreté and the Freemasons had murdered Stavisky to save their necks. Right deputies screamed execration on the government, for allegedly having accepted contributions by Stavisky to the party funds. The Fascist bands began to gather on the streets.

Some weeks later occurred the Prince affair. It is a shame to have to foreshorten drastically this perfect Arsène Lupin-Gaboriau-Lecocq case. Dr. Prince, a magistrate in the Parquet, was drawing up a report on the Stavisky case. A telephone-call, the origin of which is to this day unknown, decoyed him to Dijon, on the pretext that his wife's mother was ill. The next day his body was discovered, badly mangled, on the Paris-Dijon railway track. The official story was that Prince had been guilty of negligence in the Stavisky business, and had committed suicide in remorse. To accept this theory, Janet Flanner wrote, meant that 'the judge sent himself a bogus message, went to Dijon, anaesthetised himself in a strange automobile, and while unconscious tied himself on a lonely railway line and allowed a train to run over him.' So it seemed at first. Later researches proved fairly conclusively—incredible as it may seem—that Prince *was* a suicide: because of some connection with the Stavisky case. The Prince affair let loose new storms of denunciation and scandal. The *Action Française* insisted grimly that the Sûreté Générale murdered Prince to shut him up.

February Sixth

But let us turn back to the tragic events of February 6. The story of the riots may be briefly told. A riot in France is one of the most remarkable things in the world. The frenzied combatants maintain perfect discipline. Seventeen people were barbarously killed, and several thousand injured, but there was no fighting at all between about seven-thirty p.m. and nine, when everyone took time for dinner. When it started, no one thought of revolution; it was just a nice big riot. Communists, royalists, Fascists, socialists, fought shoulder to shoulder under both red flag and tricolour against the police and *Garde Mobile*. The fighting stopped on the stroke of twelve, because the Paris Métro stops running at twelve-thirty, and no one wanted to walk all the way home. Bloody, bandaged, fighters and police jostled their way into the trains together. Promptly at seven-thirty next morning the fighting started again.

All during January the Right gangs had been making demonstrations. Chautemps had been forced out of office on January 27, and Daladier succeeded him. Daladier announced that his government would be *'vite* and *fort'*; he genuinely feared a Fascist coup. The forces of Left and Right were nearly at the contact point. Daladier thought that Chiappe was deliberately encouraging the demonstrators to make trouble and might even deliver the city to Right insurrectionaries; certainly the police, all through January, treated the demonstrators very leniently, permitting them each time almost—not quite—to reach the chamber.

Daladier, spurred by Frot, determined to get rid of Chiappe. The circumstances were remarkable. He made the fatal error of not kicking him straight out, but offering him, as a sop to his wounded pride, the governorship of Morocco. Chiappe refused. Each man told a different story of the circumstances at the parliamentary inquiry. Chiappe, dismissed, said into the telephone—it was all done over the telephone—'All right, I will be on the street to-night.' His words, he claimed, were *'à la rue'*—out on the street, jobless. Daladier says that he said *'dans la rue,'* which means 'on the street, a rioter'. So the prime minister set about to defend himself from what he thought was impending revolution. (The *Canard Enchaîné*, the wittiest of French papers, has an alternative version: Chiappe really said *'chez Larue,'* a famous restaurant in Paris. cf. Werth, p. 132.) This was on February 3.

Daladier's first appearance in the chamber as prime minister was set for February 6. The various street groups, Camelots du Roi, Jeunesses Patriotes, Solidarité Française, the Croix de Feu, and, more pacific but most important of all, the National Union of Ex-Service Men, prepared fierce demonstrations against him. Daladier was in a bad position, because Chiappe had the confidence of a large part of the Paris police, who were consequently listless. He had to call in the tough countrymen of the Garde Mobile, a very hard-boiled body.

P

Daladier should never have allowed the thirty thousand demonstrators to get into the Place de la Concorde that night. He and Frot bungled the preliminary arrangements badly. They might have forbidden the demonstrations, but, not trusting the police, they didn't dare do so. It was unwise in the first place to use the Garde Mobile; the decision being taken, many more Garde Mobile should have been on hand, not just a few. No one will agree as to who fired the first shots. Once shooting began, the crowd was uncontrollable—crazy enough to storm the chamber and massacre every deputy inside. So seventeen Frenchmen, including war veterans who had fought for France, died.

The Would-be Hitler

French Fascist No. 1, the chief potential French March-on-Romer, is Lieut.-Col. Casimir de la Rocque, former Président-General of the Croix de Feu, the Volontaires Nationaux, and the Fils de Croix de Feu. He was born in the Auvergne in 1885, of a distinguished military family; his father, a count, was a general of artillery.

De la Rocque is spare, handsome, with thinning hair, a good organiser; not a demagogue; a man of considerable intelligence but little warmth or magnetism; plenty of poise and courage; no charm. His name is against him, because the French think that 'Casimir' is a comical name; it is as if an aspirant for high office in Britain or America were named Alphonse—or Casimir.

De la Rocque had an interesting military career; he left St. Cyr with high honours, and began active service in 1907 in Morocco, spending nine years in North Africa as one of the brightest lads around the great Marshal Lyautey. He learned to speak Arabic almost perfectly and he was several times wounded and decorated. He was on Foch's staff from 1921 to 1923, when he went to Poland with Weygand. In 1925 he returned to Morocco in the war against Abdel Krim, and became head of the celebrated 'deuxième Bureau' —military secret service. In 1928 he retired from the army to organise the Croix de Feu.

His milieu is upper middle class, Roman Catholic, illiberal. His brother, Count Pierre de la Rocque, is aide-de-camp to the Comte de Paris, who is heir to the Duc de Guise, the pretender to the French throne. But Pierre and Casimir are not on cordial terms; Casimir, who pretends that he is 'non-political' and who dissociates himself with most political groups, doesn't want overt royalist support.

He talks often of his 'mystique', which is a combination of patriotic fervour, military virtues, and churchly faith. Though he has a very considerable force behind him, he denies ambitions to be dictator; he says he wants 'order' in France, nothing more. He has never run a candidate in an election, but his followers perpetually threaten a *coup d'état*. He will, he says, support any 'useful' government, attack any 'dangerous' government. But he cannot be pinned down to defining exactly what he considers dangerous or useful. 'He is not Christ, he is merely John the Baptist,' one of his followers said—not explaining exactly what he meant—or who Christ was to be. His social programme is a sort of upper-class, Lady Bountiful charity-paternalism; his organisation runs soup kitchens in poor neighbourhoods, builds kindergartens and sanatoria.

De la Rocque seems a rather pallid Fascist; people, however, fear him. He founded a private army like Hitler, but on a more restricted scale; at first, membership was confined to front-line veterans who had won decorations under fire. Its aim was— vaguely—to 'restore the "mystique" of sacrifice for the fatherland, consecrate itself to duty to France.' His followers in the beginning were strongly Leftist, and part of the unofficial programme was to wipe out the regents of the Banque de France; but De la Rocque himself is allied to big industry. François de Wendel is believed to hold card of membership No. 13 in the group. And De Wendel and other industrialists, so it is said, had ambitions to be the Thyssens of the movement.

Like Hitler De la Rocque has tended to shed his early socialist supporters. These wanted what they called 'socialism for the middle classes', an obvious imitation of the Nazi programme. De la Rocque's leading supporter, Bertrand de Maud'huy, son of a general who commanded the Blue Devils in the War, left him because he wanted more socialism in the movement, just as Otto Strasser left Hitler.

De la Rocque not only has disappointed his Left followers; those on the Right think that he is too slow, too cautious. In April 1935, two or three of his men invaded and sacked the headquarters of the socialist federation on the Rue Feydeau in Paris, searching for arms; they found none. De la Rocque, embarrassed, quibbled and hesitated, and finally excommunicated the bold burglars. Later came the Rightist conspiracy of the *Cagoulards* (hooded men), which was promptly suppressed.

Three times he has had a chance to seize power; each time he missed it. On February 6 his cohorts could easily have captured the chamber. But he held his men back. 'France wasn't ready,' he explained. Perhaps, like Hitler, he hopes to gain power by legal means. Like Hitler in 1932, he reached the stage of one consultation with the head of government—after the resignation of Doumergue—but he was not asked to form a cabinet.

At its height the Croix de Feu comprised, so its leaders claimed, a membership of over half a million. All were ex-service men or sons of ex-service men. The discipline was strict, and the methods of organisation secret. De la Rocque insisted on fairly complete application of the Leader Principle, much as this would seem to affront French individualist character. The organisation commanded not only men and money, but automobiles and lorries for transport, and some sixty aeroplanes. 'Croix de Feu' does not, incidentally, mean Fiery Cross in the Ku Klux Klan sense of Fiery Cross; 'Croix' signifies decoration for war service, and 'Feu' means the fire of the front-line trenches.

All of which made it the more remarkable that, when the Blum cabinet dissolved the Croix de Feu and the other Leagues, Colonel de la Rocque submitted like a lamb. He tried to organise his followers into a legal political group, the P.S.F. (*Parti Social Français*), but it was a failure. He was severely discredited in 1937 after the Clichy riots, and then it was disclosed that for some time he, this pure and mystical character, had been secretly subsidised by André Tardieu.

Other Flowers of Fascism

The Croix de Feu, the most 'respectable' of the lot, overshadowed the other street groups, because the French, a respectable people, like their Fascism to be as mannerly as possible. (Incidentally, none of these organisations will admit to being 'Fascist'.) The only group which is openly pro-Hitler—commonly it is said to be subsidised by the Germans—is that of the 'Francistes'; they are of absolutely no importance.

The Jeunesses Patriotes, considerably backed by heavy industry, are led by a deputy, Pierre Taittinger. They are nationalist, anticommunist, and on the extreme Right. The organisation claims two hundred and forty thousand men, and among the leaders are some personages of consequence, like Deputy Ybarnégary. Marshal Lyautey was an honorary member of this group; General Weygand is said to be.

The Solidarité Française was founded by Coty, the Corsican perfume manufacturer. It is more to the Right than the Croix de Feu, not so Right as the Jeunesses Patriotes. Coty was never a member of the financial oligarchy, and thus the Solidarité affects to despise the Banque and the oligarchy. It is supposed to number one hundred and eighty thousand men.

The Union Nationale des Combattants, with nine hundred thousand adherents, is less inclined to street violence than the others; it is the Right offshoot of the far bigger and more important organisation the Federation des Anciens Combattants, with four million members, which is the *Left* veterans' association. All these Rightist groups were suppressed in 1936 by the Blum government, one of the most worthwhile things Blum did.

The royalists—were there enough space—should have a section to themselves. Their newspaper is, of course, the *Action Française*; their street gangs are the Camelots du Roi, organised in slugger squads, equipped with knuckle-dusters. The leaders are the sculptor Real del Sarte, the organiser Maurice Pujo, and the pamphleteers Charles Maurras and Léon Daudet. The royalists— supported largely by wealthy dowagers in the 'Association of Royalist Ladies'—are less important than the fantastic noise they make. The *Action Française* makes France a marvellously amusing country, journalistically; but its influence does not go much beyond that. The royal family itself has repudiated it.

Chiappe

The most dangerous man in France is probably not Weygand or De la Rocque, but little white-gloved Jean Chiappe, the ex-chief of police.

Chiappe (pronounced Kee-ahp) is, like Napoleon and François Coty, a Corsican. He got his start, strangely, through a radical cabinet; now he is on the extreme Right. His stepson-in-law Horace de Carbuccia, another Corsican, is owner of a newspaper, *Gringoire*, violently reactionary. One of Chiappe's friends is Zographos, the manager of the Greek syndicate which specialises in gambling at Deauville, Biarritz, and Monte Carlo. Chiappe was very popular with his police during his term of office.

Bald, swarthy, squat, athletic—he is a notable duellist—Chiappe is a remarkably melodramatic character. A creature of cabals and vendettas, he seems to represent the romance of the Corsican bush in Paris. He looks like a vaudeville villain; a confidence man; a jolly but undersized professor of medicine; an animal trainer; a hirsute attendant at a Turkish bath.

Chiappe's come-back in politics after his temporary eclipse on February 6 was startling at first. He was elected to the post of municipal councillor—alderman—in the Paris district of St. Germain des Près, part of the fashionable Faubourg St. Germain. Then he became president of the *conseil municipal* of Paris—mayor. If some day he should get ministerial post in a Right cabinet, fur—the fur of MM. Daladier, Frot and all the socialists and communists—will fly. For the white-gloved Corsican is a notorious Red-hunter.

Chiappe had to admit to having 'met' Stavisky, the indirect but effective author of his downfall. But that he had anything to 'do' with him he violently denies.

The Neo-Socialists

These are they who rebelled against Blum too early. Adrien Marquet, the Mayor of Bordeaux and a dentist by profession, seceded from the orthodox Second Internationale socialist party in 1933 to form a sub-group of his own, the Neo-Socialists. A bold and engagingly cynical politician, with a local machine which rivalled that of Herriot in Lyons, he carried about fifty deputies with him. Marquet is comparatively young, forceful, a great ladies' man, and what the French called *débrouillard*. One story is that an old time socialist, visiting him in the mayoralty in Bordeaux, incessantly called him 'Comrade'. 'Stop that "comrade",' Marquet said. 'Outside the office, I'm "comrade". In here, I'm the mayor!'

Marquet broke with Blum because he was convinced that orthodox socialism no longer met the urgent needs of post-War Europe. 'Order, Authority, Nation' were his watchwords. He professed himself an admirer of some qualities of Nazi Germany and said that the world—and France—needed renovation, revivifaction, and 'benevolent authoritarianism'. Then he made the mistake of joining the Doumergue 'National' government. His colleagues thought this represented a shift in principles—and threw him out of his own new-born party.

His successor as leader of the Neo-Socialists was Marcel Déat, an Auvergnat like Laval. He took a strong defeatist line in the Munich crisis, and led the 'Don't Die for Danzig' movement.

Turncoat Doriot

The dissident communist Jacques Doriot is an interesting character in French politics, because he personifies what remains of Trotskyism. His new 'Popular' party, formed in the spring of 1936, with its newspaper *Émancipation Nationale*, seemed at outset merely one of those maddening 'splinter' groups that obstruct effective co-operation by the Left; but Doriot has some significance as an anti-Stalin communist, opposing the trend of modern Soviet policy. Doriot, who wants his revolution right away, says that Stalin, a Russian 'imperialist', has sacrificed the needs of France to those of Russia and has betrayed the 'true' communists. He is not the only one to say so.

Doriot has a brilliant revolutionary career behind him. An orthodox communist for many years, he spent much time in Russia. Twice he went to jail, once for agitation in French Indo-China. For a time he shared the regular communist leadership with Thorez. He has been a deputy for many years, and until recently was mayor of the Parisian suburb of St. Denis.

Farmer Fascist

Henri Dorgères, whose real name is Henri d'Halluin, who at one time promised to be a remarkable phenomenon in French politics, is a peasant leader who organised a militant agrarian movement, a modern Jacquerie, which briefly swept the countryside as the 'Front Paysan'. He is not in the chamber, though he missed succeeding to Chautemps's seat by only a few hundred votes. Dorgères, one of the best natural orators in France, is, according to his enemies, a fraud; he is no true son of the soil, no peasant, but an aristocrat in disguise, the Viscomte d'Halluin. These stories are untrue. His name is Halluin, but he is no fraud. His father was a cattle merchant in Lille. His policy is drastically counter-revolutionary; clean up the chamber of deputies by 'shooting the whole damned lot', 'liberate' the farmers, build a peasant-corporative state.

Janet Flanner has described him thus: 'An odd-looking butcher's boy with a small, beautiful, aristocratic face; neat, intense manual gestures; and a sensitive, sensible eloquence that recently brought eight thousand wheat- and sugar-beet-farmers through miles of mud to hear him speak in the town's Grain Hall.'

Origins of the Popular Front

The *Front Populaire* really began back in July 1934, when after much psychological preparation and a year of negotiation, the national council of the French Socialist party approved, by a vote of 3,471 to 366, the proposal of the communists for a programme of common action against war and Fascism. The draft agreement had been hammered out by a joint committee of ten socialists and ten communists. Thus the way to the Popular Front was open. It was made possible by three things (1) fear of Hitler, (2) fear of Fascism in France, (3) the new policy of the Communist Internationale in Moscow which decided to play down the idea of world revolution, and permit the French communist party to go to the polls on a patriotic, non-revolutionary basis.

At first it seemed odd the socialists, to save democracy, should unite with communists, who heretofore had been enemies of democracy. But the events of February stimulated desire for fusion. Then Laval visited Stalin in 1935. Stalin announced that the comrades in France should call off the revolution, unite with other enemies of Fascism, and support the French Government and even the French army so long as was necessary, in opposition to Fascist forces. Thus, temporarily—only too temporarily!—the communists became 'respectable'. The years of Popular Frontism and Collective Security began. In 1939, of course, after the Russo-German pact, Popular Fronts everywhere collapsed.

In the early days of negotiation in France the communist leader, Marcel Thorez, announced that he did not regard the *Front Populaire* as an instrument of socialisation, much less of communism. He added his hope for the eventual arrival of a communist system in France, but he said that it must take an essentially French form —not something dictated from abroad. Thorez's motive was quite logical. No sensible communist wanted to weaken France with threats of civil war, when it seemed that a strong France was Russia's best ally against Hitler.

The socialists accepted the communist initiative. The two parties, which had fought each other bitterly, each claiming the exclusive right of representing the proletariat, began to work together. Later, as we know, Daladier and the radicals came in. The communists, however, never entered the French *Government*. They took much the same position that Blum's socialists took in relation to previous administrations—that of a Left group support-

ing the government so long as it behaved.   But there was a difference in that the communists were definitely committed to Blum's
programme—their joint programme—whereas Blum had never
been committed to the programmes of radical governments that
preceded him.   In the early days Blum said, 'I can do what I want
to do, unless my friends on the Left push me too hard.'

A subsidiary father of the Popular Front was a remarkable young
political idealist, Gaston Bergery, who began his career as a radical,
turned independent, and finally gave up a comfortable seat in the
chamber in protest at the formation and conduct of Doumergue's
national government.   He was the only deputy to do so.   He fought
a gallant by-election at his constituency, Mantes, and was beaten
after a tremendous fight by only a few hundred out of sixteen thousand odd votes.

Bergery is an acute and sophisticated young man, married to an
American girl, Bettina Shaw Jones, an assistant at Schiaparelli's.
She fought the election at his side, complete with dashing white
toque—and pet marmoset!   Mantes is an industrial, proletarian
constituency, and opinion is divided whether the 'wheat trust', the
instrument of Bergery's Right opponents, beat him—or his wife's
monkey.

Bergery founded an early group of his own, called at first the
Front Commun, then the Front Social, finally the Front Populaire.
It embodied the same aims as the United Front—coalescence of all
Left forces in a fight to the last trench against Fascism and the
military leagues.   This young man, not in the least doctrinaire,
an exciting combination of idealist and practical politician, had
the idea; the others worked it out.   Then the name *Front Populaire* was taken over to describe the entire movement.

As a result, Bergery came to be called the 'Lenin of France', the
'Nero of the French Republic' and a 'Marat and Robespierre' in
one.   Actually, he is neither a communist nor even a socialist.   His
movement, he says, is merely 'anti-capitalist'.   He wants a merger
of all the farmers, peasants, workmen, white-collar *bourgeoisie*,
middle-men, who form ninety-five per cent of the population of
France, against the five per cent of capitalists who exploit them.   A
cultivated aristocrat, he is no proletarian.   He believes the role of
the proletariat to be much exaggerated in the mechanics of socialism.   And in France, he points out, only seven million out of
forty-two million people are workers in the Marxist sense of the
term.

Two personages on whom a great deal in the *Front Populaire* depended were Léon Jouhaux and Maurice Thorez. The veteran Jouhaux, born in 1879, is the leader of the C.G.T. (Confédérations Générale du Travail, The Socialist Union) and the boss of French trade-unionism. His father took part in the commune; his grandfather fought in the revolution of 1848. Jouhaux went to work in a match factory at sixteen; since 1909 he has been the C.G.T.'s somewhat old-fashioned and benevolent dictator. Blum appointed him a Regent of the Banque; which is as if John L. Lewis should become a Morgan partner. Maurice Thorez, the communist leader, much younger and stronger meat, born in 1896, was a farm labourer as a boy, then a coal miner. Militant, persuasive, he worked himself up the secretary-generalship of the communist party in 1932. In 1939 he was arrested when, on the outbreak of war and after the Russo-German pact, the communist party was dissolved.

The *Front Populaire*, we have seen, collapsed for various reasons. The great thing to its credit was that it effectively abolished the threat of Fascism in France; it showed that French democracy was capable of protecting itself, and that Fascism can come to France only at the cost of civil war.

CHAPTER XIV

THE SPANISH CIVIL WAR

'There is no country in Europe which is so easy to overrun as Spain; there is no country which it is more difficult to conquer.'

—LORD MACAULAY.

O N Saturday, July 18, 1936, civil war broke out in Spain. A clique of predatory and 'nationalist'-minded military chieftains rose against the legally and democratically elected government of Spain, and turned the peninsula into a shambles. What began as a military *coup d'état* developed into a conflict of ideologies. The Germans and Italians helped the Spanish Fascists; the Russians— later and much less intensively—helped the democratic loyalists. The war cost almost a million lives. Bloodshed of such savagery had scarcely been seen in modern times. Following German and Italian intervention, possibility that the struggle might become a veritable World War became acute. For a time 'pirate' submarines were openly torpedoing neutral merchantmen in the Mediterranean. For month after haggard month, Europe watched the Spanish cauldron.

The cleavages, both horizontal and vertical, represented by the Spanish conflict were enormous. Poor against rich; workers against troops, the laity against the upper hierarchy of the church; volunteers against mercenaries; the peasantry against the aristocrats; the landless against the feudal landlords; democracy against Fascism; all these confrontations played their part in Spain. And these confrontations are not peculiar to Spaniards. It is not difficult to see why the struggle in Spain found developing repercussions all over the world. Emotionally the struggle became a world struggle. And it was waged with fierce partisanship, because it was represented as cutting across two of the most precious shibboleths of the average man, his feelings about class, and his feelings about religion.

Let us first underline a few primary and incontrovertible facts that have been obscured or misrepresented by propaganda. It is grossly and wantonly untruthful to speak of a 'Red' revolt in Spain. There never was any 'Red' revolt. This is simple fact. The revolt

213

was made by General Franco and his friends. There were no communists—not even any socialists—in the republican government which he sought to overthrow, though they supported it. The socialists and communists came in later, but when Franco moved on July 18 the Spanish Government was devoid of them. It was certainly a Left government—a moderate and not very efficient Left— but there were no Marxists in it.

Another point is the chronology of foreign intervention. It is now established beyond any doubt that German and Italian intervention occurred months before Russian help reached Spain. Indeed German and Italian aeroplanes were active at the very outset, months before the International Brigade was organised by foreign volunteers to aid the loyalists. And Russia at no time sent *troops* to Spain, as did Italy.

The forces on both sides can be summarised in a paragraph or two. On the rebel or insurgent side (called the 'Nationalists' in pro-Franco newspapers) were, speaking broadly, the officer class, the feudal aristocracy, the bulk of the politically-minded Roman Catholics, the monarchists, the Carlists from Navarre, the *Falangistas* or Fascists, the army officers, some of the industrialists, and part of the national police force or Civil Guard. Their rank-and-file fighting force contained Germans, Italians, Moorish troops from Spanish Morocco and the Rif, and the Spanish Foreign Legion—in a word, comparatively few authentic Spaniards except the Carlists and *Falangistas*.

On the government side was—the government. It came to include as time went on all the forces of the Left—republicans, liberals, democrats, socialists, communists, anarchists, syndicalists. It included also the Catalans centring on Barcelona, and such Roman Catholics as the Basque autonomists. The Basque clergy was solidly pro-government. It included the bulk of the peasants, the bulk of the landless, and all but a small fraction of the workers. It included most of the Freemasons, most of the middle class, most of the intelligentsia. Its army, since ninety-five per cent of the officers struck with Franco, was at first an extremely makeshift affair; the hardest kind of fighting and help from foreign volunteers turned it into a first-class fighting force. A militia of the *people* became a people's army, with an extraordinary discipline exercised not by officers but from below.

The essence of the Spanish struggle can be compressed into a single sentence. The people of Spain, the common people, groping towards progress after centuries of feudalism, fought desperately to overcome a reactionary revolt. The struggle was four-square between the Left and Right—and the Right was in the wrong. The people of Spain, after five years of a weak republic, rose to defend it —because, for good or ill, it was theirs.

Good-bye Monarchy

Under the monarchy Spain was almost as backward a country as Czarist Russia. The illiteracy rate was the highest in Europe (Portugal excepted), namely forty-five per cent. The national history had been a study in disintegration for three hundred years. The country, potentially rich, was stagnating with corruption and decay. The landless workers were little better than serfs, and some of them lived almost like animals. And the ruling classes—to quote the American magazine *Life*—'were probably the world's worst bosses —irresponsible, arrogant, vain, ignorant, shiftless, and incompetent'.

The monarchy, represented in the twentieth century by Alfonso XIII, was supported by three pillars, the landed aristocracy, the army, and the church.

Concerning the land—the central problem of Spain—a few figures are relevant. One per cent of the population owned no less than fifty-one per cent of the land. In all Spain, not more than fifteen to twenty thousand people owned as much as 250 hectares of land. The vast majority of the people on the land—and Spain is seventy-two per cent agricultural—were landless or owned nothing more than tiny strips. Forty per cent had no land at all. By contrast, one grandee, the Duke of Alba, held a territory almost as big as Belgium; on it were fifty-five villages. The landowners seldom put money back in the land; much fertile ground was turned over to grazing; only one crop was harvested each year; in some parts of Spain irrigation was unknown and modern machinery forbidden. Many of the landowners were absentees.

Spain had the most top-heavy army in the world. There were 365 *active* generals (700 in all)—one for every day in the year—and 21,000 officers, a proportion of one officer to every six enlisted men. Not even the German army in 1914 had 21,000 officers. The army, which had done little to distinguish itself since about 1640, consumed at least a quarter of the national budget. The military had feudal privileges. The Civil Guard was sacrosanct, and until 1931 civilians could be tried by military courts.

The church held an overwhelmingly dominant position in Spanish life. There were 40,000 priests and clergy, a fantastic number, all paid by the state, all part of the state, almost all associated in spirit and politics with the feudal landowners and the army. The church and the Jesuit order, through ownership of mines, industries, shipping, public utilities, banks, transportation, orange groves, expressed itself in business and industry as well as politics and religion. The church dominated education, through the state of which it was a part, and yet Spain was forty-five per cent illiterate. The church was rich and decadent; all the abuses of clericalism piled up. The church hierarchy and the religious orders exercised almost unbelievable powers. Blasphemy for instance was a crime. The Inquisition was not formally abolished until 1931.

The monarchy fell in 1931 of its own weight. There was no revolution. Only an election. Not a drop of blood was shed or a shot fired. Alfonso paid the penalty of years of misrule by driving to Cartagena from Madrid in perfect safety. No one molested him, and no one in the aristocracy, the army, or the church lifted a forefinger on his behalf. The dynasty which had ruled Spain for five centuries disappeared into the dust of history like a plum dropping from a tree. But—the forces behind Alfonso were still there.

Republic and Reaction

The quality of the republican government formed in April 1931 gave hope to liberals the world over. It was composed of middle-class intellectuals mostly—professors, civil servants, literary men. The spiritual fathers of the republic were not politicians or army generals, but physicians like Dr. Gregario Marañon, a specialist in ductless glands, in whose home the revolutionary committee met, and philosophers like Miguel de Unamuno and José Ortega y Gasset, whose *Revolt of the Masses* expressed the ideals behind the movement. Among members of the government were *littérateurs* like Manuel Azaña, who soon became prime minister, professors like Fernando de los Rios, and labour leaders like Largo Caballero, who had been a mason by trade.

You can judge a country pretty well by its ambassadors. Suppose the British Government should give its best embassies to H. G. Wells, Aldous Huxley, and Bertrand Russell. Well, look at the Spaniards. To Geneva went Salvador de Madariaga, a professor and journalist. To London went the distinguished novelist

Ramón Pérez de Ayala. The Germans got a Left-wing socialist intellectual, Luis Araquistáin; Julio Alvarez del Vayo, formerly the *Manchester Guardian* correspondent in Madrid, went to Mexico; Rome got a poet and Chili got the translator of H. G. Wells's *Outline of History*.

The first thing the republican government did was write a constitution. It was a remarkable document. It exuded the pure cool aroma of Jean Jacques Rousseau and Thomas Jefferson—and alas of Weimar. It disestablished religion and—tremendous item— separated church and state; it declared Spain 'a worker's republic of all classes'; it abolished illegitimacy, made free primary education compulsory, and—in Spain!—gave women the vote. It made divorce easy. It promised labour participation in the rewards of industry. It was the first constitution of any national state to concede authority to the League of Nations; Spain was, for instance, forbidden to declare war except under conditions authorised by the League covenant. Ironic that seems now!

What happened was that the constitution did not, of course, work. The youthful republic paid far too much attention to theory and wasted far too much energy in determining its aspirations—on paper—without attempting to put the aspirations into concrete effect. It concerned itself with fine phrases and neglected concrete policy. Its leaders, like Manuel Azaña, were such profound liberals that they believed in free speech even for those who would destroy free speech. Azaña and his men thought that they could profoundly change the organisation of society without a revolution. They were wrong.

The republican leaders knew well enough who their enemies were, and they did set about moving against them—but not drastically enough. They went just far enough to provoke a fury of reaction. They were unskilled politicians, and in the new *Cortes* (parliament) they were presently sabotaged and out-manoeuvred. Their job should have been to destroy feudal Spain. They might have been merciless to their enemies, as they knew their enemies would be merciless to them. They might have learned the lesson of Russia, that no revolution can succeed until the privileges of the propertied classes are not curtailed, but extirpated. Instead they dabbled, they temporised, they made half-hearted and inefficient reforms.

As to the nobility—the republic sought to emasculate it by taking its pretty titles away. The Duke of Alba, from twenty-six lines of fine type in the old official gazette, was reduced to plain señor; but the Duke of Alba himself was not eliminated. A land reform scheme was worked out—in theory—but very little land actually got to the peasants. In 1932 General Sanjurjo revolted against the new republic in the best Spanish manner; the revolt was quickly put down and as punishment all the land of all the grandees of Spain was confiscated—but only on paper.

As to the church, Azaña attacked it without destroying it; he deprived it of just enough privilege to make it stronger through anger. His Religious Orders bill of June 1933, 'nationalised' church property, valued at £100,000,000 but left it in the hands of the church; he theoretically dissolved the Jesuit order but the Jesuits were not expelled; he forbade the Jesuits to teach but the ban did not become effective. Within two years, like a black, solid, powerful mushroom, the church protruded itself again into power and prominence. Even during the Republic, it had more influence in Spain than in any country in Europe, Austria perhaps excepted.

As to the army, the republic thought it could solve the perennial problem of military treason by the simple expedient of pensioning off some ten thousand officers—at full pay for life.

On the other side were great and positive achievements of the new government. First, Azaña and his men gave Spain some political sense, they pulled Spain forward to contact with the modern world, they gave it hope. Second, they embarked on a tremendous educational programme; the education minister, Fernando de los Rios, spread schools—ten thousand of them—through the land with mighty fingers. Third, they abolished many of the minor survivals of feudalism. Fourth, they solved the Catalan problem, which had been a bugaboo to Spanish politics for four hundred years, by giving the Catalans provincial autonomy. They promised the Basques autonomy too.

In the autumn of 1933 Azaña was forced out of office. Thus the first period of the Left republic lasted two and a half years. A coalition of Rightish parties—loyal to the republic if it should be theirs—assumed power. The Rightists made what was tantamount to a counter-revolution. In October 1934 the socialists revolted against this counter-revolution, and were put down by force and with ghastly bloodshed. The Rightists (still loyal to the republic in theory) crushed the miners and workers in Asturias with Moorish troops. The Moors in Spain again! Some 1,400 men were killed, all but a few of them civilians. The Rightists wiped Asturias bloody.   And terror spread all over Spain.   By the end of 1935, some thirty *thousand* socialists and republicans were in jail.

The Rightists stayed in power, through a series of shambling governments, from the autumn of 1933 to the spring of 1936.   It seemed that the Rousseau-Jefferson revolution was ended.   But the brief flicker of daylight from 1931 to 1933 still lit the minds of the people.   Following a series of violent scandals, and forced into holding an election, the Right went to the polls in February 1936. The parties of the republic banded together in a Popular Front and won a narrow victory.   The Popular Front, plus the Basques, polled 4,838,449 votes; the Right got 3,996,931.   A Popular Front government was formed—not, however, including socialists or communists —and set out to revive the 1931 republic.

It did not have much time to do so.   On July 18, 1936, reaction rose in the person of General Franco.   The Left—elected to office in an incontestably free and legal manner—resisted.   So civil war —real civil war of the kind that Europe had not seen since Russia in 1919—came to Spain.

People

A word at this juncture on personalities.   Don Manuel Azaña became prime minister again after the February election—the second chance he had at the same big job—but soon he was elevated to the less active position of the presidency of the republic.   Azaña was born January 10, 1880, at Alcalá de Henares, the birth-place of Cervantes.   He is a student, a philosopher, and had he never been prime minister and president of Spain he would be well known wherever Spanish is read by intellectuals.   He has written essays, plays, novels, and at least one of his works is a minor classic, *The Garden of the Monks.*

Azaña spent many years as a civil servant.   But always he had politics in mind, and he made a special hobby of army organisation and military affairs.   Once a friend asked him, 'Why do you pore over these dull army books?'   'Because,' Azaña answered, 'in twenty years I am going to be minister of war.'   He was.   This would seem to show passionate forward-looking interest to his career.   But when Louis Fischer interviewed him in 1936 and said he hoped he would still be in office the next year, Azaña replied, 'Of course—unless I get bored with politics.'

He is unequivocal about his politico-philosophical stand.   When I interviewed him in 1932 and asked him where he belonged he

Q

replied almost defiantly, 'I am an intellectual, a democrat, and a *bourgeois*.'

Like no fewer than six other members of the first republican government, Azaña was a Freemason. This contributed somewhat to his collapse in 1933. Masonry, as in France, has played a powerful role in Spanish politics, though one dislikes to simplify the issue too much, to talk too glibly of the dividing line between Masonry and Catholicism as a major factor in the revolution. Indeed the line is illogically awry. Lerroux, the Freemason, and Gil Robles, the Jesuit, are—or were—ardent allies.

The two most interesting figures in the Rightist camp before the civil war were Don Alejandro Lerroux and Don José Maria Gil Robles. Lerroux, comparatively little known outside Spain, one of the most bizarre personages in modern Europe, had a long career as an agitator and a revolutionary, became rich and powerful, took office in the first republican government, and quickly then shifted to the Right. His whole career was a series of shifts. Marcelino Domingo, one of the founders of the radical-socialist party and an early comrade, formally charged him with betraying the other republican leaders in an uprising in 1917. Miguel de Unamuno, the great Basque philosopher, sardonically suggested that Lerroux claimed to be a republican so that everyone else would stop being a republican.

One of his friends was Juan March, the tobacco millionaire who helped finance Franco's revolt. Years before, during the Great War, Lerroux and March did a thriving business supplying war materials to German submarines off the Iberian coast. On a trip to Paris, Lerroux gave an interview to *Le Journal* nobly stating his and Spanish aims. 'When copies of *Le Journal* reached Madrid,' wrote one of Lerroux's former friends, 'people vomited in the Puerto del Sol.' And another of his early friends said of Lerroux, 'In this man's paunch are established the seven deadly sins.' The story went in the early days of the republic that a citizen filing an application wrote after 'Antecedents', 'Neither criminal nor *Lerrouxista*.'

More dangerous than Lerroux, however, younger and more vigorous—he was born in 1901—was José Maria Gil Robles. He was the son of a university professor; he studied with the Jesuits and his scholastic record was exceptional; he went into teaching first, then journalism, then politics. He organised the C.E.D.A. (Federation of Autonomous Parties of the Right), forced the

Lerroux government to take him into the cabinet, and openly proclaimed hostility to the republic he was serving. 'The republic is like a case of measles; we will live through it,' he said. A militant Catholic and reactionary, Gil Robles has an unusual trait for a Spaniard—energy. A formidable enough speaker, he lacks what the Spaniards call *elevación*; he has vehemence rather than emotion, anger rather than indignation. Gil Robles is clever, ambitious, sybilline. He fled to Portugal when the civil war broke out. Franco had no use for him.

The Outbreak and the Course of the War

From February 1936, when it was elected to power, until July, the Popular Front government maintained uneasy rule. But the country was throbbing with disorder. All the years of pent-up hate were rushing to explosive outlet. The people, as *Life* put it, had fired the bosses; the bosses refused to stay fired; violence was inevitable. There were several hundred political assassinations in six months. The Fascists deliberately provoked disorder as an excuse to invoke order later. The Left retaliated. A Leftist officer, Lieutenant Castillo of the Assault Police, was murdered by Rightist gunmen. Then Señor Calvo Sotelo, who had been finance minister under Primo de Rivera and who hoped to be leader of the United Right, was killed by comrades of Castillo.

The detailed course of the war can be sketched only briefly here. Following a careful plan—but speeded up because of the assassination of Calvo Sotelo—the garrisons in most of Spain rose on July 18th. The revolts were successful in some towns, like Salamanca, Seville, Toledo; but in the more important cities—Madrid, Barcelona, Valencia, Malaga, Bilbao—they either misfired or were crushed by the enraged people, who (in Madrid for instance) stormed the barracks almost literally with their bare hands. The *coup d'état* as a *coup d'état*, was a failure. It aimed to seize power in all Spain overnight. It did not. No one anticipated the capacity of the government and the people to resist.

But General Francisco Franco, the governor of the Canary Islands, flew to Morocco and with the aid of German and Italian aeroplanes succeeded in breaking the blockade at Gibraltar and flying Foreign Legion and Moorish troops to the mainland, whence they were dispatched to Seville and the front.[1] Moorish troops

[1] Also his planes drove off the loyalist fleet and he was soon able to get material across.

began to flood Spain. So Spain, which had so often invaded Morocco, was being invaded by Moroccans. The use of these Moors, excellent soldiers, in later campaigns—for instance against the Roman Catholics of the Basque country—by a junta steeped in political Catholicism, and with the aid of a government, that of Germany, at the moment engaged in a fierce religious struggle with the Vatican, provides one of the most interesting of modern historical ironies.

Of the fact of Italian intervention at this early stage there can be doubt no longer. As early as July 31 twenty Italian aeroplanes flew to Spanish Morocco to assist others already there; two came down in French territory. The French Government found them to be Italian air force bombers, with their marks painted over. The pilots carried military papers. Other Italian planes, it is believed, reached Morocco *before* the war began. German planes were active as early as mid-August. And soon German 'technicians' began to pour into the country.

The war started out as a series of disjointed offensives which became stalemates. The rebels held the coast around Gibraltar, Seville, and much territory in the north; the government held the central plain of Castille and most of the southern coast, as well as all of Catalonia. In August the rebels took Irun and San Sebastian and began to form their lines around Madrid. Then came the astonishing adventure of Toledo, where rebels had been trapped in the Alcazar since the war began. Franco's stubbornly advancing troops raised the seventy-day siege on September 28. The government, trying to blast the rebels out, seemed pitifully incompetent. The Moors, entering Toledo, found 600 government wounded in the hospital and assassinated them by hand-grenades. Previously, at Badajoz on the Portuguese border, 4,000 loyalist civilians and militiamen were captured by Franco's men and machine-gunned in the bull-ring.

Nothing, it appeared, could keep Franco from winning at this time. His lines drew closer to Madrid and early in October its siege began. But the loyalists miraculously stiffened. Franco's army reached the suburbs of the capital on November 7 and the government fled to Valencia. Apparently during one twenty-four hour interval Franco could have taken Madrid by walking in. But he waited. What really saved Madrid was the capture of Toledo; if Franco had not made that long detour Madrid might have fallen in September. After mid-November Madrid was safe, in a manner of speaking, though the enemy was still entrenched in the outskirts of the town. The siege lasted many months. Madrid was attacked incessantly from the air and by artillery fire, and in five different infantry offensives; they all collapsed. One third of the city was destroyed by bombs and shell-fire; the life of the capital was dislocated and transformed; thousands of civilians, women and children were killed.

At this point the story of the war becomes inextricably involved with the major fact of intervention. As early as mid-August a German warship appeared off Ceuta, and soon German destroyers and submarines dotted Spanish waters. German and Italian aeroplanes began to take active part in the land warfare, with German and Italian pilots. A Junker bomber was captured by the government as early as August 8. Soon the Italians were in virtual occupation of the island of Majorca. German and Italian tanks, munitions, anti-aircraft guns, and *materiel* of all kinds flooded Franco territory. Entry was easy either by the sea or through Portugal, which made little pretence of neutrality.

The reason for all this, from Franco's side, was very simple. He had to have foreign troops, the 'Aryan Moors' and the totalitarian 'volunteers', because not enough Spaniards were fighting for him. From the side of the interventionists it was simple too. The war was interpreted as a struggle between Fascism and Communism; Hitler and Mussolini would not brook a 'Bolshevist' régime in Western Europe. Spain was a perfect playground for them both politically and strategically. They knew too that a Fascist Spain would drastically weaken France. They delighted in the prospect of spheres of influence in Morocco and the western Mediterranean. They had been watching Spain a long time; General Sanjurjo visited Berlin just before the outbreak and the man whom the Germans sent to General Franco as ambassador, General Faupel, was head of an 'Iberian Bureau' in Berlin. Ties with Rome were also close. Italy to some extent and especially Germany had hungry eyes on Spanish ore and minerals, and before the war had proceeded six months cargoes of copper and iron were going to Hamburg to pay for German intervention. Both Germany and Italy recognised the Franco government by November.

Franco, interestingly enough, scoffed at Fascism at the beginning. Jay Allen of the *Chicago Tribune* and the *News Chronicle*, one of the most experienced of American correspondents in Spain, saw him on July 28—when the war was only ten days old—for an historic interview and Franco told him, 'This movement is not Fascist, it is Spanish and nationalist. . . . Fascism is ridiculous in Spain, ridiculous. The liberal middle class in Spain is all republican, masonic, and things like that. Fascism in Germany and Italy is a middle-class movement. Here these boys of Primo de Rivera's say they are Fascists because it is the thing to say, but they are ridiculous.'

Before long General Franco saw his need of German and Italian aid, and when he had to pay for this aid he began to pipe a very different tune.

Such emphatic intervention by Germany and Italy—by the spring of 1937 the Germans had eight to ten thousand technicians in Spain, the famous Condor Legion, and the Italians almost 100,000 troops—was bound to provoke retaliation. Counter-intervention took two forms. First, volunteers from all over the world, liberals, anti-Fascists, communists, socialists, flocked to Spain and formed the International Brigade, motivated by common hatred of Fascist aggression. Such an army had never been seen before. It included Poles, Belgians, Czechs, Americans (some 2,700 from the U.S.A.), English, French, and anti-Fascist Italians and anti-Nazi Germans. The Brigade, which reached a maximum force of perhaps 20,000 men, went into action November 8th and 9th in the defence of Madrid, and it saved the capital. Second, beginning in October, the government of the U.S.S.R. sent tanks, aeroplanes, food, and diplomatic counsel. No Russian troops arrived in Spain, but Russian aeroplanes did, and their help was of great value; their fast pursuit ships built on the American model, called Chatos, gave the loyalists temporary command of the air by early spring.

The war dragged on. Terrible tales of atrocities disfigured the world's news. The rebels won several important offensives, for instance they took Málaga in February 1937, and Bilbao in June, but they could not smash either the morale or the material defence of Madrid, and they got nowhere near Barcelona or Valencia. The government won a great victory on the Guadalajara front in March, when an Italian army was cut to pieces at Brihuega; the Italians lost more dead in this single engagement than in the whole Abyssinian war. Italian prisoners testified that they had 'enlisted' for service in Ethiopia, and were in effect shanghaied to Spain.

Horrors heaped on horrors dulled the palate of the world, but

Franco's march into the Basque country in June 1937 gave it a new sensation. German aviators bombed and destroyed Guernica, the holy city of the Basques, the first instance in history of the complete and wilful obliteration of a whole city, non-combatants as well as fighters, by bombing and machine-gunning from the air. Franco apologists have stated that the Basques blew up their holy city and its inhabitants themselves. The testimony of G. L. Steer, the correspondent of *The Times* on the spot, gives a somewhat different story:

'The whole town of 7,000 inhabitants, plus 3,000 refugees, was slowly and systematically pounded to pieces. Over a radius of five miles round a detail of the raider's technique was to bomb separate farm-houses. . . . All the villages around were bombed. Guernica was not a military objective. A factory producing war material lay outside the town and was untouched. . . . The town lay far behind the lines.

'The rhythm of this bombing of an open town was . . . a logical one; first hand grenades and heavy bombs to stampede the population, then machine-gunning to drive them below, next heavy and incendiary bombs to wreck the houses and burn them on top of the victims.

'I have seen and measured the enormous bomb-holes which, since I passed through the town the day before, I can testify were not there then. Unexploded German aluminium incendiary bombs found in Guernica were marked "Rheindorf factory, 1936".'

In January 1938 the loyalists, using their newly trained man power, took Teruel, but Franco's troops recaptured it the next month. The rebels then pushed through to the sea, splitting loyalist Spain and separating Barcelona from Valencia. The government withstood this grave loss at first, and the loyalist troops not only held ground, but made a great counter-offensive on the Ebro. During 1938 the non-intervention committee—of which more presently—continued its deliberations, trying to evolve a formula for the withdrawal of foreign troops. When this was finally hammered out, it was promptly accepted by the loyalists, but rejected by Franco. In September the new loyalist prime minister, Dr. Juan Negrín, announced at Geneva that the loyalist government would remove all the foreigners on its side. The International Brigade was thereupon demobilised. Then came a 'token withdrawal' of 10,000 Italian troops. Meantime, the rebels sought to enforce a rigid blockade of loyalist ports, and thus starve the government out. Franco's aeroplanes bombed neutral and especially British shipping persistently, even British ships carrying

officers of the non-intervention patrol.   Dozens of British ships
were attacked.

The war persisted all through 1938, and came finally to an end
early in 1939.   The government simply could not hold out against
the preponderance of German and Italian intervention.   After
pitiless air bombardments of Barcelona Franco opened a great
offensive by land which captured Tarragona on January 14.
Barcelona fell twelve days later; the loyalist government withdrew
first to Figueras, near the French frontier, then to the frontier
itself.   But Madrid was still holding out.[1]   With desperate courage
and persistence, Negrín and Del Vayo shuttled to Madrid and back.
Then, however, came an angry series of intrigues and fissures.   A
coup d'état by General Casado—instigated in part by foreign
influence—unseated Negrín, and his short-lived Council of
National Defence sued for peace.   Franco occupied Madrid without resistance on March 28.

Presently the terrible machine of a new law, the 'Law of Political
Responsibilities' went into action.   Thousands upon thousands of
loyalist Spaniards were executed.   In August Franco set up his new
régime under the dominating influence of the Falange, or Fascist,
element in his coalition.   He himself undertook supreme authority,
with 'responsibility only to God and history'.

Meantime the Germans finally admitted publicly the activity of
its Condor Legion, which marched down the streets of Berlin, and
was reviewed by Hitler and Goering.   The German U-boat
commanders—who got good practice for 1939—were publicly
honoured.   The Italians revealed that, during the war, Italian
aviators made 86,420 flights over Spanish territory, and dropped
more than eleven million kilograms of explosives in 5,318
bombardments.[2]   Italy lost 3,327 dead, 11,227 wounded, during
the course of the war, according to Italian figures.

General Franco

It would be naïve in the extreme to dismiss General Francisco
Franco as a villain or a butcher.   He is a creature of his caste, a
product of his moral environment, and a fairly typical example of
it.   He has been commended for intelligence and courage, and

[1] The loyalist garrison in Minorca surrendered to a *British* cruiser, the *Devon-
shire*, which had Franco officers aboard.
[2] cf. Bulletin of International News, published by the Royal Institute of International Affairs, Vol. XVI, No. 12, p. 627.

he doubtless possesses social grace and charm. Beyond doubt, as he sees patriotism, he is a patriot. But let it be remembered that he started the war, and that his war destroyed half of Spain.

Franco is a first-rate example of an historical accident. He was not scheduled to be the supreme leader of the rebels. The leader was Calvo Sotelo, assassinated in July; General Sanjurjo, who was killed in an aeroplane accident three days after the war began, was theoretically the military chieftain. Franco stepped into his shoes. He was abler than the rest, he was in a better strategic position, he had the Moors and Legionnaires, and before the war was two months old he was indisputably in command. On October 1, 1936, he was invested as head of the Spanish 'state'.

General Franco, a small man, only a little over five feet, graceful, paunchy, with tiny well-formed hands and feet, called the 'Baby General', was born in Galicia in 1892. He came of a family which had sent its sons into the army or navy for generations. His brother Ramon was Spain's most distinguished aviator. Young Franco had an exceptionally good military career. He saw service in Morocco, which taught him much, and at thirty-four he became the youngest general in the Spanish army. Under the republic he served in the Balearics and then again in Morocco. When the Lerroux-Gil Robles combination took power he was appointed chief of staff. This made the republicans suspicious, and when the Popular Front assumed office he was shelved and packed off to the Canary Islands.

Consider Jay Allen's interview with this 'graceful' and 'idealistic' little man:

Q. How long, now that your coup has failed in your objectives, is the massacre to go on?

A. There can be no compromise, no truce.

Q. That means you will have to shoot half Spain?

A. I repeat, at whatever cost.

Q. What would your government do if you won?

A. I would establish a military dictatorship.

Q. What would happen to the politicians of the republic?

A. Nothing, except that they would have to go to work.

Q. Why were you able to collaborate with the republic in apparent loyalty for so long?

A. I collaborated loyally as long as I thought the republic represented the national will.

Q. What about the February elections? Didn't they represent the national will?

A. Elections never do.

Franco tries to embrace as wide a Rightist front as possible. When, on April 20, he proclaimed himself dictator and leader of a one-party totalitarian state, he chose a comprehensive name for it: The Spanish Phalanx of Traditionalist and Offensive National Syndicalist Juntas.

Franco's admirers are lyrical in their praise. For instance this item translated from the *Paris Candide*, by one René Benjamin:

> 'Franco is not tall, he is a little heavy, his body is timid. Ah! His glance is unforgettable, like that of all rare beings. A troubled and trembling glance, full of sweetness; the man is delicious and mysterious; he is a miracle of tenderness and energy. . . . The ravishing thing about Franco is his purity.'
>
> —(New York *Sun*, July 27, 1937.)

And Mr. J. L. Garvin, in a pitiful article in the *Observer*, once called him 'a great gentleman'. To which one might fairly reply that he has broken his oath twice; first to the King, when he took service with the republic; then to the republic, when he rose against it.

The other general on the Rightist side most worth notice is that fabulous creature General Don Gonzalo Queipo de Llano, who fought mostly with his tongue. He was the broadcaster for the insurgent forces, and over the radio from Seville gushed nightly on the exploits of his faction. On August 27, he ordered the execution of five members of a communist family for every person murdered by a communist. 'Colonel Yague followed my instructions in Badajoz, and the result was admirable' (when four thousand people were massacred in the bull-ring!), he roared one night. He boasted that 'Red' women would be turned over to the Moors—one girl for each twenty Moors.

Terror

In the early days of the war a sporadic terror existed in both Madrid and Barcelona. The fact is unpleasant, but there is no use denying it. Churches were pillaged and wrecked, priests were murdered, and assassination of known Fascists occurred wholesale. The anarchists especially ran wild. But let it be remembered that these events occurred *after* Franco's revolt, when the population as a whole was exasperated to frenzy. The normal regulations of society broke down. Much of the killing occurred after a stupid boast by General Mola that a 'Fifth Column' of Fascists, the rebel sympathisers living in the city, would rise within the gates and help to capture it.   Naturally they were hunted out and shot.   Every responsible person in the loyalist government deplored the terror and sought to control it from the earliest days: soon it was stamped out.

The terror on the rebel side was infinitely more severe; killings took place on definite orders of the generals and as a part of policy. When a town was captured, known loyalists were shot out of hand. I have mentioned the horror of Badajoz.   But Badajoz was only one of several examples.   In the early days of the war, anyone who held a trade union card, anyone who was a Freemason, anyone who was known to have voted for the Popular Front, anyone who scorned going to mass, was liable to be executed.

The Times has stated that in Navarre 'in practically every village the three or four leading republicans are shot'.   In Cordoba 2,000 people were executed and 1,800 in Saragossa.   In Seville nine *thousand* people were shot, in Granada 6,000, in Pamplona 3,000. Leaflets were dropped by the rebels on Madrid reading as follows:

> 'The capture of Madrid by the National Army being imminent, you are warned that for every murder committed, ten of yours will be shot.   Do not forget that we hold over 1,000 of the Red Militia as prisoners in the provinces, while in Madrid the 25,000 wounded will be held responsible for your excesses.'

When Franco's forces captured Málaga the town knew what might be coming.   And, in an extraordinary mass exodus, almost one-third of the inhabitants left the city before the Fascists entered, walking with what possessions they could carry along the road to Almería.   They were willing to suffer any privation, to desert their home, to risk death on the road—which was incessantly bombed— rather than live in a Franco city.   The terrible scenes which accompanied this flight of 150,000 men, women, and children have been described by American doctors who witnessed them.   Almost the same thing happened after the capture of Bilbao.   But there were no neutral witnesses.

Left

The proletarian situation in Spain was, before the war, the most complicated in the world.   The Left comprised several camps.

First, there were several groups of *bourgeois* republicans, represented by men like Azaña and his allies.

Second, there were the autonomists in Catalonia and the Basque country, who knew that the republic insured their freedom, which centralists like General Franco would take away.

Third, one must always keep in mind that syndicalism in Spain, alone among European countries, is a very powerful force. The Spanish labour movement for several generations was almost equally divided between socialist and syndicalist unions. The socialists, with their U.G.T. (Union General de Trabajadores), allied with the Second Internationale, were strongest in Madrid and the north; the syndicalists, with their rival C.N.T. (Confederación Nacional de Trabajo), flourished especially in Catalonia and Andalusia, with headquarters in Barcelona. Ever since the days of Bakhunin, syndicalism has proliferated in these districts. It first took root when Marx and Bakhunin split on the anarchist issue in 1872.

The syndicalists, queer fish, have traditionally stood aloof from politics. Until recently they refused to vote. They were 'a-political'. Their anarchist friends were a potent source of mischief, because the anarchists do not believe in government at all, and therefore stood to gain from any sort of chaos. In the old days it was a frequent manœuvre of the Right to bribe anarcho-syndicalists to make trouble, so that it could use the pretext for severe measures against more orderly opponents, like the socialists. Lerroux was a past master at this. Theoretically the syndicalists believe in a state founded on vertical trade unions. They began to take a more normal interest in politics when they saw that Fascism was rising in Spain, and would give them no mercy. They became willing to co-operate with the more moderate Left. And almost for the first time in history, they went to the polls and voted in February 1936 —with the Popular Front. Syndicalist votes helped make the Left victory possible.

Fourth, the anarchists. They have their own organisation in Spain, the F.A.I. (Federación Anarquista Ibera), which comprised only about 8,000 members but which 'muscled into' the syndicalist C.N.T., and for a time partially controlled it. The more responsible syndicalist leaders then walked out of the C.N.T. to demonstrate solidarity with the government.

Fifth, the socialists. These traditionally were moderate Marxists, but one wing, led by Largo Caballero, jumped very much to the Left just before the war and demanded an active revolutionary policy, partly as a manœuvre to gain syndicalist support. The Caballero group went to the Left of the communists; the joke in Spain during the February elections was 'Vote communist to save

Spain from Marxism.' The other wing of the socialist party, led by Indelacio Prieto, was more moderate. A very rich newspaper owner and industrialist from the Basque country, Prieto wanted to co-operate with Azaña and the government. Later he was forced out.

Sixth, the communists. These were a minor factor in Spain until the war broke out. There were only sixteen communist deputies in a *Cortes* of 473. The socialists and syndicalists had skimmed the cream of radical Spain.

Seventh, the P.O.U.M. (Party of Marxist Unification), which began as a dissident communist group, led by Andrés Nin and Joaquín Maurín. Its strength was mostly in Barcelona. In 1936 it became frankly defeatist and Trotskyist and was presently suppressed.

. . . .

When the war came Madrid had three cabinets in twenty-four hours. The Left Republicans carried on, but in September they collapsed; the government was not prosecuting the war efficiently. On September 6, Largo Caballero formed a government in which five men beside himself were socialists. Del Vayo became minister of foreign affairs, and Prieto minister of marine and air. Two communists were included, to reflect the realities of the situation, one Basque nationalist, one Catalan, and two republicans. Later, the government was further enlarged and the syndicalists came in.

Francisco Largo Caballero held office until the spring of 1937. His integrity was beyond question, his prestige was great, his patience was tenacious. But he was a failure. He wasn't winning the war. Nor was he making the social revolution he had promised. For one thing he was too old for the job—sixty-seven—and not in the best of health; the story is that he went to bed at nine p.m. every night, and nothing could happen in loyalist Spain thereafter. Caballero was the perfect type of trade union boss. A worthy character, who had devoted his whole life to the Spanish proletariat; he was a manual worker as a youth and until twenty he could not read nor write; he went to jail seven times, and once was sentenced to death.

He was succeeded by Dr. Juan Negrín on May 15, 1937. Not a communist but a Left-wing socialist, Negrín worked well with the communists—who were rising steeply in influence—as well as the republicans, and his administration began on a note of competence and vigour. He dropped the anarchists, after a serious anarchist rising was suppressed in Barcelona. He muzzled Caballero and the

P.O.U.M. and he strove to devote the whole energy of loyalist Spain to the one supreme task—winning the war. Negrín, only forty-eight, widely travelled, a brilliant linguist, versatile, solid, urbane, was a doctor of medicine by profession. He began to be interested in politics, and became a financial expert. He had enormous integrity and courage. He performed almost super-human feats; he fought the bitter struggle to the bitter end.

Non-Intervention

According to the normal canons of international law, any government is entitled to purchase arms and munitions for suppression of a rebellion. Loyalist Spain was unable to do this. For one thing, General Franco's navy—though the rebels had no belligerent rights—set up a quite illegal but nevertheless efficacious blockade. For another, the great powers initiated the monstrous fiction known as the 'Non-Intervention Agreement' which established an embargo on the shipment of both munitions and volunteers to both Spanish sides. This was an almost fatal handicap to the loyalists. They could get nothing in from France and not much from the U.S.S.R. But Italy and Germany sent great quantities of arms and men to Spain before the pact was signed, and after its signature it seemed that they violated it almost at will.[1]

The Non-Intervention Pact was suggested by France and Britain in the early days in order to keep the war from spreading. They thought that a rigid system of non-intervention would prevent wholesale conflagration. The Pact was laboriously hammered out from August till February, against the incessant objections of Germany, Italy, and especially Portugal—which hindered the negotiations at every opportunity—and finally twenty-seven nations signed it; in April 1937 an international naval control was set up in Spanish waters.

The French point of view may be easily summarised. Most Frenchmen did not want Franco to win. A glance at the map will show why. A Fascist victory in Spain might mean that France would have a third frontier to defend in the event of war with Germany or Italy. Italian or German naval bases in the Balearics or Morocco would drastically shift the balance of power in the Mediterranean, and might cut France's 'life-line' of communication to her African reservoir of native troops. Yet a powerful section of

---

[1] The very day after the 'gentleman's agreement' was signed between England and Italy, 5,000 Italian troops landed at Cadiz.

French opinion favoured General Franco for class reasons. And the French were willing to make almost any concession, even if the loyalists should be defeated, in order to stave off the peril of *immediate* general war. The Fascists held their trump card again. They committed acts of aggression knowing that the French and British would not call the bluff because calling the bluff might mean war.

The British attitude was similar. From the nationalist and imperialist point of view a Franco victory would be an embarrassment to the British, even if they bought Franco up later. It would imperil Gibraltar—mysterious guns dominating the harbour were set in place by Franco or his allies early in the war—and give Italy and Germany a foothold in the western Mediterranean. The Mediterranean is an essential link in imperial communications. But from the point of view of property, privilege, and class, the British wanted Franco to win; they may like nationalism, but they like capitalism better. They quailed before the bogy of a Bolshevist Spain, of communism on the Pyrenees. Thus the British were divided by conflicting aims, stalemated by a dichotomy in policy. As a result they gave way to muddle, drift, and what almost seemed cowardice before repeated acts of aggression by the Fascists. They wanted peace at almost any price—until their own gigantic armament programme was ready.

The Non-Intervention Pact endured an agitated life. On May 29, a loyalist aviator bombed the German pocket-battleship *Deutschland* as she was lying in Ibiza harbour. Apparently the pilot mistook it for the rebel cruiser *Baleares*. The Germans, in a rage, bombarded Almería two days later, a formal naval action by the German fleet against a Spanish town. The hypocrisy of the Non-Intervention agreement passed belief. Italy and Germany were theoretically part of an international scheme to prevent foreign troops fighting in Spain while thousands of their own troops were fighting there! But little by little the pretence of Non-Intervention was given up. When Franco's troops, largely Italian, captured Santander, the battle was openly and flamboyantly celebrated in Italy as an Italian victory.

The *Leipzig* incident came on June 19. Three torpedoes, it was alleged, were fired by an unknown submarine at the German cruiser *Leipzig* off Oran. No one ever saw the submarine. Comment was free to the effect that the attack might have been invented. It sent Hitler into a violent tantrum; Europe tottered on the brink of war.

In September 1937, came another first-rate crisis. Submarines

presumed to be Italian, enforcing Franco's blockade, set about torpedoing neutral merchantmen in the Mediterranean. A dozen
British, Greek, Danish and other neutral ships were sunk in circumstances recalling the unrestricted U-boat warfare of 1917. The
'pirate' submarines, never showing themselves, crept marauding not
only in Spanish waters, but as far away as the Aegean. The British
and the small neutrals at first took this affront without rebuttal,
but when two Russian ships were torpedoed and sunk, the Soviet
Government angrily demanded reprisals and formally accused Italy
of being the pirate power. A conference was called at Nyon, Switzerland. Germany and Italy refused to attend, and it seems that
the categorical nature of the Russian note was designed to keep them
away. The British and French, their backs up at last, took decisive
action. The Italians, absent, were out-manœuvred, and the British
and French fleets set up a powerful 'piracy control' in Mediterranean
waters. The sinkings stopped. But aerial bombardment of neutral
shipping was resumed later on.

Portugal

This small country, with a population less than that of London or
New York City, undeveloped, backward, pleasantly remote, lives
by export of cork, fish, wine. Until the Spanish war it played a respectable and peaceable role in international affairs. The country
was a monarchy for some seven hundred years; in 1910 a revolution
overthrew the Braganzas and a republic came to power. Distrac-
tions and vicissitudes were many, and in 1933, Professor Dr. Antonio
de Oliveira Salazar, born in 1894, established a military dictatorship.

Professor Salazar, almost uniquely among dictators, was—and is
—a recluse. He was an economist by profession, and from 1926 to
1933 he served as minister of finance. Dictatorship was forced on
him, he says. A Jesuit, ascetic and devout, with hatred of pomp, he
gained great respect abroad for balancing the budget and funding
the national debt. Then the usual machinery of dictatorship came
into action. A corporative state of totalitarian character, called
the *Estado Novo*; an efficient secret police and a private army in
green shirts; a militant youth movement; close association with the
other Fascist powers; a single political party with Salazar at its head
—the paraphernalia is familiar.

Professor Salazar once disguised himself as a customs official,
worked on incoming baggage himself—because he heard tales of

lelay and inefficiency in customs inspection. Once his tourist
)ureau offered a £1 prize for the corpse of any flea or bug found in a
'ortuguese hotel—because a healthy tourist business is important
o the country.

Portugal for many years was regarded as a satrapate of England.
The country is Britain's most venerable ally—the treaty of alliance
lates from A.D. 1373—and Britain virtually controls its finance and
oreign policy. Portugal has an important colonial empire, a left-
over from its ancient Imperial days. It cannot possibly protect this
empire itself; thus it plays close to Britain, and hopes for British
help.

R

CHAPTER XV

MUSSOLINI

'I shall make my own life a masterpiece.'
—BENITO MUSSOLINI

'I am desperately Italian. I believe in the function of Latinity.'
—BENITO MUSSOLINI

BENITO MUSSOLINI, tempestuous and ornate, a blacksmith's son the creator of modern Italy and the author of the Abyssinian war, was born July 29, 1883, at Dovia di Predappio, a village in the Romagna. His career is that of the most formidable combination of turncoat, ruffian, and man of genius in modern history.

The obvious motivations, except poverty, are lacking. His father, a revolutionary socialist, was the anarchist of the village square, yes; but no tragedy occurred in Mussolini's life to compare with the execution of Lenin's elder brother, or Pilsudski's. His mother, a school-teacher, like the mothers of most great men, was an exceptional woman, but her influence on Mussolini was, it seems, slight; adoration of her never made him, like Hitler, a prisoner of infantile fixations. Kamal Ataturk's mother was ill-treated by the Greeks, and years later the Turkish dictator drove the Greeks into the sea; in Mussolini's life there is no such dramatic and direct impulse to redemption.

Nor can one easily discover any extraordinary personal accidents without which the Duce might have lived and died a blacksmith's boy in Forli. It is quite possible, as Bertrand Russell has pointed out, that the revolution in Russia might never have occurred had not a German general permitted Lenin to travel across Germany in a sealed train. It is quite probable that Soviet Russia would have never had a Five-Year Plan, had not Trotsky succumbed to a fit of pique and refused to attend Lenin's funeral. The Dollfuss dictatorship in Austria was, as we shall see, made possible because a socialist deputy went to the bathroom during a crucial parliamentary vote. Such personal accidents, which play a large part in history, are not prominent in Mussolini's life. He made his own

236

uck. His career has been a growth, steady and luxuriant, like that
f some monstrous weed.

The chief personal influence on Mussolini as a young man was
probably that of a Russian exile in Switzerland, Madame Angelica
Balabanov. She took care of him in his early revolutionary days,
mended his health, gave him food of both the body and the spirit.
Mussolini, a bricklayer, apparently met Lenin through Balabanov.
Years later Lenin rebuked the Italian socialists for having 'lost'
Mussolini, their best man.

Every man is an arena, a pool, of forces. Those in Mussolini's
early life were mostly literary and intellectual. Voraciously intel-
igent, he read Marx, Hegel, Machiavelli, La Salle, Nietzsche,
Pareto, Sorel. He absorbed them like a blotter. From Nietzsche
he learned to hate the mob, from Marx to love it. He records that
in his early days he kept a medallion of Marx in his pocket.

Bombastes Furioso

The son of Alessandro Mussolini (who named him after Benito
Jaurez, the Mexican revolutionist who ordered the execution of
the Emperor Maximilian) and of Rosa Maltoni who was the school-
teacher of the village, he grew up in the most crushing poverty. He
never tasted coffee until he was twenty. He slept on a bundle of
hay instead of a mattress, and the bedroom in his birth-place, which
has been made a museum, preserves this symbol of extreme in-
digence. Mussolini often returns to his native village, and has
built a model farm in the vicinity. Unlike Hitler, he takes some
interest in the lives of his surviving relatives.

Though his father was a blacksmith, the family for generations
had tilled the soil. Speaking to an assembly of peasants in October
1935, he said: 'The sort of people who like to rummage among old
papers thought they would please me by discovering that my
ancestors were of noble birth. So I said to them "Stop it." All my
grandfathers, all my great-grandfathers were tillers of the soil, and
to remove all doubts of it I stuck a tablet on the wall of the old farm
which says that generations of Mussolinis before me have always
tilled the soil with their own hands.'

Mussolini, at his mother's insistence, went to a religious school
(like Stalin and Kamal Ataturk), though his father was an extreme
anticlerical. Then he taught school himself, at a wage of 56 lire
(then £2 5s.) per month, until he fled to Switzerland when he was
nineteen. He earned a living as a mason and a labourer in a

chocolate factory; he was hungry often, and Balabanov describes
how on one occasion he snatched at food from two Englishwomen
picnicking in a park. At night he studied socialism. Becoming
an agitator, he got into trouble with the police, and was jailed and
expelled from one Swiss canton after another. Altogether, in Italy
as well as Switzerland, Mussolini was arrested eleven times.

He hated jail; he despised the moral obloquy and physical dis-
comforts of confinement. Once he was finger-printed by the
Geneva police; he has loathed Switzerland ever since, and it is not
fanciful to assume that his dislike of the League of Nations was
partly conditioned by this early Genevan insult. Certainly Mussolini's prison experiences caused his present pronounced claustrophobia. Once he refused to enter the Blue Grotto in Capri. And
it is obvious that his famous predilection for enormous rooms, like
his office in the Palazzo Venezia, which is sixty feet by forty by forty,
is over-compensation for early confinement in small prison cells.

Mussolini returned to Italy in 1904 at the age of twenty-one and
spent ten years as a red-hot socialist.

He earned a living the while by teaching school and by incessant
journalism. Not as great a pamphleteer as Shaw or Trotsky, he is
nevertheless one of the best journalists alive. An early venture into
creative writing, a novel called *The Cardinal's Mistress*, was not
successful; it was, however (I quote Francis Hackett), 'hard, violent,
cynical, proud, strong, and troubled'. He also wrote a biography of
John Huss. At Forli in 1909 he founded his own paper, *La Lotta
di Classi* (The Class Struggle), and it made him known among
socialists and revolutionaries all over Italy. In 1912 he became
editor of the *Avanti*, the official socialist daily, and he trebled its
circulation in three months. Previously he had spent some time
in Trento, then in Austria, and this experience in irredentism
awakened something cardinal in his character—nationalism.[1] In
1924 he was one of the organisers of 'Red Week', an attempt a
socialist uprising in the Romagna.

The immense catastrophe of the Great War amputated his socialist career. The orthodox socialists wanted Italian neutrality.
Mussolini stood for intervention on the side of the allies. 'To
know why he became a warrior,' says Dr. Finer in his penetrating

---

[1] He was arrested by the Austrian police and deported. The man who got him
out of jail was the Viennese socialist Ellenbogen, who, twenty-five years later, was
himself arrested following the February 'revolt' in Austria, which was the result of
Mussolini's Austrian policy.

and exhaustive *Mussolini's Italy*, 'it is hardly necessary to do more than observe his physique.' On political nationalist grounds and purely personally through love of adventure, Mussolini wanted war. He gave up the editorship of *Avanti* and was expelled from the socialist party. When his former comrades howled him down, he shouted, with rare psychological discernment, 'You hate me because you still love me.' A few months later, he founded the newspaper he still directs, *Popolo d'Italia*. French money—since France was eager to drag Italy into the War—helped him.

Mussolini, so recently an anti-militarist, sounded a violent call to arms. 'We must distinguish between war and war,' he said, 'as we distinguish between crime and crime, between blood and blood. . . . We are not, and we do not wish to be, mummies, everlastingly immovable. We are men, and live men, who wish to give our contribution, however modest, to historical creation' (Finer, p. 101). He did not, however, go to the Front himself until December 1916, and he had only thirty-eight days in the trenches when he was severely wounded by the explosion of a trench mortar. He was in hospital for seven months. This, at least, is the official version of the incident.

After the War, on March 23, 1919, Mussolini formed the first *Fasci di Combattimento*, mostly from men who had joined him early in the War demanding intervention. He was still a socialist, though not a member of the party; his first programme asked for an eighty-five per cent tax on War profits. He disliked and distrusted the *bourgeoisie* and capitalist aristocracy. 'Fascio' is simply the Italian word for group or bundle; to Mussolini it conveniently symbolised the 'Fasces' of Imperial Rome. The original Fascists were augmented by local correspondents of the *Popolo d'Italia* in Lombardy, who organised the movement. It was not a party at first, but a militia. Its chief strength was among ex-soldiers, especially the *arditi*, front-line volunteers. 'We, the survivors, who have returned,' Mussolini wrote, 'demand the right of governing Italy.'

The movement developed speedily. Its roots were those which grew analogously in Germany and produced Hitler later: unemployment among the ex-soldiers, the weakness of democratic cabinets, parliamentary corruption, powerful nationalist feeling, restlessness on the Left coupled with dissatisfaction at orthodox international socialism. As Mussolini became stronger, the army backed him, exactly as the Reichswehr backed Hitler. The politicians, watching him warily, tried to buy his movement;

Giolitti was the Italian Papen. The industrialists, precisely as in Germany, prepared to give his machine support.

Labour troubles shook Italy in 1920 and 1921. The workmen rose against intolerable wages and living conditions. Mussolini appears to have first supported the 'Occupation of the Factories', when six hundred thousand workers in the industrial north attempted to take over the means of production. The Occupation was a failure, partly because socialist leadership was weak. This made it easier for Mussolini to appeal to the mob. But the legend that he 'saved' Italy from Bolshevism was nonsense. Even Italians do not believe this any more.

By 1921 and 1922 Mussolini steadily expanded his influence, and by a weapon which later dictators were to imitate—violence. He became a sort of gang chieftain. (He was still an active journalist, however; he reported the Cannes Conference in 1922 and sought interviews with Briand and Lloyd George. This trip taught him, he records, his first lesson in the mysteries of foreign exchange, when he discovered to his shame that an Italian lira was not worth as much as a French franc.) Mussolini's gangs slugged their way to power in half a dozen districts. Balbo in Ferrara and Faranacci in Cremona attacked the 'reds'. Virtual civil war, of a minor guerilla type, terrorised Italy. Mussolini still claimed, theoretically, to be a socialist, but to gain powers he had to have an enemy; thus he fought the working classes, under the pretence that he was 'liberating' them.

The full reaction—and more violence—came after the March on Rome, in October 1922. As prime minister he was simply a gang leader who had become big enough to bluff the government into submission. He did not demand full power until he was quite certain that the army would not oppose him and when he was sure that the King would make him prime minister. The March on Rome was not, of course, a March on Rome at all; the Fascists took possession of a number of cities, with the army, 'neutral', standing aside. Mussolini travelled to Rome by sleeping-car, and the fifty thousand Fascists who had assembled in Rome quietly dispersed the next day.

After 1922 Mussolini's history is familiar. He formed a coalition government, then, like Hitler ten years later, kicked the non-Fascists out. He was supported by Morgan loans. His only severe crisis till the Abyssinian war in 1935 was the Matteotti affair. Most critics nowadays do not think that the Duce directly ordered the assassination of Matteotti, the socialist leader, but his moral responsibility is indisputable. What happened, good informants think, is not only that Mussolini threatened Matteotti in the chamber, but angrily denounced him in private, spurting irritably at mention of his name. One can easily imagine him exploding to his underlings, 'That Matteotti—!' (Similarly, by a chance remark, Henry II caused the murder of Thomas a'Beckett.) The underlings, taking the hint, and thinking to gain favour with the Duce, went ahead on their own initiative and kidnapped and murdered the young socialist. Such a sequence of events is convenient for a dictator; if the business turns out 'well', the result is simple gain, if it turns out badly, viz., makes a scandal, the dictator can disclaim complicity. Mussolini, however, was bold enough to admit his responsibility; and he had to concede that the murderers were Fascists of 'high station'. Indeed some of his closest associates were involved. In a famous speech to the chamber he blustered his way out as follows:

> 'But after all, gentlemen, what butterflies are we looking for under the arch of Titus? Well, I declare here before this assembly, before all the Italian people, that I assume, I alone, the political, moral, historical responsibility for everything that has happened. If sentences, more or less maimed, are enough to hang a man, out with the noose! If Fascism has only been castor oil or a club and not a proud passion of the best Italian youth, the blame is on me!'
> —(Mussolini's *Autobiography*, p. 231.)

This, be it noted, is almost the same technique that Hitler followed after the June 30 murders. He too assumed all responsibility; and in Italy and Germany both, this removed the burden of bad conscience from large quarters of the nation. The Matteotti affair, however, shook the Duce deeply. But on the whole it was of great value to him, because following it he was able to isolate and thus the more conveniently destroy the opposition.[1]

'And Changes Fill the Cup of Alteration'

It is interesting in the light of the Abyssinian campaign to think back to the Italo-Turkish war of 1911–12 and recollect that Mussolini vigorously opposed it. This war, also fought in Africa, seemed to Mussolini, then a socialist, an imperialist crime. He organised an anti-war strike in Forli, and spent five months in prison as a

---

[1] The actual assassins of Matteotti got very light sentences. One was an American gangster from St. Louis.

result. He wrote that the newspaper articles evoked by the Lybian war were 'manifestations, typical, qualified, and cynical, of nationalist delirium tremens'.

In one editorial in the *Avanti* he wrote a passage which read strangely at the time of the Abyssinian war in 1935:

> 'We are in the presence of a nationalist, clerical, conservative Italy which proposes to make of the sword its law, of the army the nation's school. We foresaw this moral perversion; it does not surprise us. But those who think that preponderance of militarism is a sign of strength are wrong. Strong nations do not have to descend to the sort of insane carnival in which the Italians are indulging to-day; strong nations have a sense of proportion. Nationalist, militarist Italy shows that it lacks this sense. *So it happens that a miserable war of conquest is celebrated as a Roman triumph.*' (Italics mine.)
> —(*Daily Express*, October 19, 1935.)

Dr. Finer has unearthed a precious quotation of similar vintage. 'Imagine an Italy,' wrote Mussolini indignantly in 1912, 'in which thirty-six millions should all think the same, as though their brains were made in an identical mould, and you would have a madhouse, or rather, a kingdom of utter boredom or imbecility.'

To which the detached observer might reply, Even so!

Man Mussolini

Most people meeting Mussolini are surprised at his shortness of stature. He is, like Napoleon, only five feet six. His shoulders are powerful and his hands finely formed and almost delicate. His smile is gritty. Usually he wears the uniform of a corporal of the Fascist Militia.[1] He works in the Palazzo Venezia, in the centre of Rome, and lives about ten minutes away by car, in the Villa Torlonia, a comfortable house with a luxuriant garden on the Via Nomentana, near the Porta Pia. A Roman aristocrat, Prince Torlonia, offered the villa to Mussolini because he couldn't afford its upkeep; now he would like to have it back but Mussolini has fallen in love with the place, especially the garden.

For some years his wife, Donna Rachele Guidi, resided in Milan, but lately she moved to Rome and now lives in the Villa Torlonia. Donna Rachele, whose origins are obscure, was, according to one story, a waitress in a Forli pub, according to another the servant of Mussolini's father after he retired from blacksmithing. She has borne Mussolini five children.

[1] Note the Napoleonic significance.

Indeed Mussolini is the only contemporary dictator conspicuously fecund; he is also the only dictator with a very strong regard for family life. Like Napoleon (and Hindenburg) he trusts members of his immediate family, and not many other people. For years his only real friend was his brother Arnaldo, who succeeded him as editor of the *Popolo d'Italia*: Mussolini telephoned him from Rome to Milan almost every evening. Arnaldo's sudden death was a serious blow to the Duce. His daughter Edda, who is his living image, is the only person who dares to twit or heckle him; he adores her. Her husband, Count Galeazzo Ciano, became Mussolini's Press-director, then the leader of the *Desperata* squadron of bombing and pursuit planes in Ethiopia, and finally his foreign minister. Mussolini's two elder sons, Vittorio, then nineteen, and Bruno, seventeen, also went to the war as aviators. As if to give the two younger children, Romano and Anna-Maria, a touch of the air, Mussolini himself piloted the plane which gave them their first experience off the ground.

Young Vittorio was so indiscreet as to publish an account of his adventures in Ethiopia. Listen:

> 'I still remember the effect I produced on a small group of Galla tribesmen massed around a man in black clothes. I dropped an aerial torpedo right in the centre, and the group opened up like a flowering rose. It was most entertaining.'

During his great years of power Mussolini's health was robustly excellent, partly as a result of attention to a severe regimen. But in 1939 reports were widely credited that he was ill with heart trouble. Shortly after he became prime minister he was desperately ill with a stomach ailment; he eats very little nowadays but milk and fruit. He told a recent American interviewer, pointing to a basket of fruit on the table, 'That is the secret of my continued health—fruit, fruit, fruit. In the morning I have a cup of coffee and fruit; at noon I have soup or broth and fruit, and at night I have fruit. I never touch meat, but sometimes I have a little fish.' He loves exercise, and takes a lot of it: riding in the Torlonia gardens, fencing, swimming, hiking. He neither drinks nor smokes. He was fond of women in his younger days, but for the last few years he has paid little attention to them.[1]

Mussolini is built like a steel spring. (Stalin is a rock of sleepy

[1] But early in 1937 a French lady, Madame de Fontages, told a dramatic story of his tempestuous attentions.

granite by comparison, and Hitler a blob of ectoplasm.) Mussolini's ascetic frugality is that of a strong man who scorns indulgence because he has tasted it often and knows that it may weaken him; Hitler's that of a weak man fearful of temptation. Stalin, on the other hand, is as normal in appetites as a buffalo.

The Duce has no social life. When, as foreign minister, it was incumbent on him to entertain, he greeted his guests not at the Palazzo Venezia or the Villa Torlonia but in a hotel he hired for the occasion. No friend of the rich, he despises the decadent and profligate Roman aristocracy. He gave up the theatre, of which he was very fond, because he could not spare the time; he sometimes has private cinema shows at home. In his autobiography, written in 1928, he says that in his first six years of power he never once passed the threshold of an aristocrat's salon or even of a coffee-house.

As a rule, Mussolini works very hard for five or six hours a day—except when a crisis makes more time necessary—and spends the rest of the day in reading, meditation, or exercise. He is neat, precise, orderly; as Ludwig[1] records, he hates the *à peu près*. His work is systematised to the ultimate detail; he is a perfect executive, considering the floriferousness of other aspects of his character; he never leaves the Palazzo Venezia till the day's work is done.

He cares very little for money, though his large family makes him less impervious to financial considerations than other dictators. His official salary is 8,000 lire per month (about £135), but he has a drawing account, 'small, unspecified, and variable', at the treasury. For his autobiography he received £5,000 in America; he gave some of it to the Rome poor. For a long period his chief source of income was reputed to come from the Hearst press; early in 1935, however, he gave up writing regular articles because international politics were so delicate that he could not express himself frankly. He gave a share of his Hearst income to Margherita Sarfatti, his biographer, who helped him prepare the articles. Mussolini's brother Arnaldo was rich, because the *Popolo d'Italia* was—and is—a prosperous newspaper; its director now is Mussolini's nephew.

The Duce is the only modern dictator who has come to terms with religion. In 1929 the Lateran Treaty adjusted the relations of church and state in Italy. Shortly thereafter Mussolini and the then Pope, strong characters both, clashed over the education of Fascist youth; in 1932 the Duce went to the Vatican, knelt in prayer,

[1] cf. *Talks With Mussolini*, by Emil Ludwig, a fascinating record.

and, it is believed, took holy communion. He was an avowed atheist, like his father, in youth; latterly he has become very religious. He prays daily. His wedding-gift to Edda was a golden rosary; his youngest child, Anna-Maria, was his first to be given a religious name.

The most accessible of Europe's statesmen for a long time, Mussolini saw an enormous number of people. Nowadays, however, he cuts down on appointments, partly because of his reported ill-health. His first visitor every day is the chief of police; (Alexander of Jugoslavia likewise saw a security official the first thing every morning.) The Duce, pervasively curious, interested in human nature, and an accomplished brain-tapper, like Franklin Roosevelt, enjoys his visitors. Finer quotes him as saying that he has given over sixty thousand audiences; he has interested himself in 1,887,112 individual 'affairs of citizens'.

Mussolini listens to people—but he seldom takes advice. He alone makes decisions. When he wishes, he can make himself as inaccessible as a Tibetan Lama. During the Geneva crises in 1935, when he was in a roaring temper, no one could get near him. Baron Aloisi and others made reports; he listened or not, as he chose. Mussolini is proud of having thousands of acquaintances, and—with Arnaldo dead—no friends; he told Ludwig that he trusted 'no one'. This remark was expurgated from the Italian translation of Ludwig's book, since many Italians have served the Duce well and think that they deserve his trust.

A very good journalist himself, he likes newspaper men. But he is very much a prima donna, and needs careful handling. He is never 'charming'; he is contemptuous of all but the most skilful flattery; he may be brutal, gruff, cheerful, or stentorian, depending on his mood, which he seldom bothers to gloss over or conceal. He pays intelligent interlocutors the compliment of interviewing them; sometimes he asks many more questions than he answers. Boldness is the best avenue to his favour. I remember seeing Francis Hackett after his interview for the *Survey Graphic*, a little breathless because he had dared to ask a supremely audacious question: 'Where, your excellency, would you have been in *your* career, if you had applied to yourself the Fascist virtues of discipline, loyalty, and obedience?'[1]

Interviews, Mussolini knows, are the best of all possible forms of propaganda; thus he is so lavish with them. Most newspaper men

---

[1] Rather weakly Mussolini replied that 'the War' had changed things.

—and their editors—cannot resist the flattery of conversation with a dictator or head of a state; once they have been received by Mussolini or Hitler, they feel a sense of obligation which warps their objectivity. It is very difficult for the average correspondent to write unfavourably about a busy and important man who has just donated him a friendly hour of conversation.

A British interviewer saw Mussolini recently and, rare phenomenon, Mussolini laughed at one of his remarks. Preparing a draft of the interview, the correspondent wrote, 'The Duce's laughter encouraged me to make one criticism of the Fascist régime, that it permitted very little expression of humour.' Reading the draft for approval before publication (as he does with most interviews) Mussolini sternly elided the reference to the fact that he had laughed. Dictators never laugh!

Two newspaper men were the source of the only recorded instance of public embarrassment of the Duce. He was in Locarno to initial the security pact of 1925. (Incidentally, from that day until he visited Germany in 1936, he never stepped off Italian soil; before that, he had as prime minister been abroad only twice; he attended the Lausanne conference in 1922, and in 1923 fleetingly visited London.) His régime had just taken over the great liberal newspapers of Italy; the corps of international correspondents resented this, and boycotted his Press conference. Annoyed, pouting, Mussolini found himself surrounded in the hotel lobby by the journalists who had slighted him. He addressed George Slocombe of the *Daily Herald*, a conspicuous red-bearded figure, whom he had met covering the conference of Cannes. 'Ha!' exclaimed Mussolini surlily. 'How are your communist friends getting on!' Slocombe replied with perfect good temper, 'I am not a communist, *Monsieur le Président*, but a socialist.' 'Ha!' Mussolini snorted again; 'then I am mistaken.' Whereupon a Dutch correspondent, George Nypels, piped out, 'And it is not the first time.'

Mussolini reads all the time; no modern statesman—except, perhaps, Masaryk—is so well acquainted with current literature. He keeps a systematic note-book of his reading. He astounded Ludwig by the range and accuracy of his historical knowledge. Like most people who like to read, he likes to write, and he writes extremely well. He compressed in the dozen pages of his pamphlet on Fascism what it analogously took Hitler six hundred pages to express in *Mein Kampf*. He is easily the best educated as well as the most sophisticated of the dictators—he is the only modern ruler who can genuinely be termed an intellectual—and he taught himself both French and German, which he speaks expertly. In about 1925 he began to learn English, so that he might read the political leaders in *The Times*. He chose an English newspaper woman, Miss Gibson, as his teacher. He writes often—anonymously—for the *Popolo d'Italia*; he is part author of one play, *Campo di Maggio,* dealing with Napoleon during the Hundred Days, and the author of another, not yet produced, about the chief of his heroes, Julius Cæsar.

The things that Mussolini hates most are Hitler, aristocrats, money, cats, and old age. He detests old people, especially old women. He dislikes references to the fact that he is a grandfather; and when, on July 29, 1933, he reached the age of fifty, the Italian Press was not allowed to mention it. The things that Mussolini loves most are the city of Rome (he has assiduously fostered the 'cult of Rome'), his daughter Edda, peasants, books, aeroplanes, and speed.

He is apt to straddle a motor-cycle, and like the late Colonel Lawrence hurl himself across country at night. He learned to pilot an aeroplane shortly after the War, and recounts in his auto-biography a number of crashes and forced landings, from which he escaped miraculously, and which intensely exhilarated him.

'The Race by Vigour not by Vaunts is Won'

From the complex strands of Mussolini's character one may draw bright and brittle threads indicating the sources of his power.

He has, first of all, spine and starch, in a country sometimes lacking both.

For all his bombast and braggadocio,[1] his intelligence is cold, analytical, deductive, and intensely realistic.

His flaming egoism, his *sacro egoismo*, is cherished by Italians. His vanity is, as is obvious, extreme; for instance he stabilised the lira at nineteen to the dollar, far too high a rate, mostly to better the figure chosen by the French. He was called a paranoiac as far back as 1910.

Overwhelmingly he is a man of action. The single episode that amazed him most about the 30th of June in Germany was that Hitler consumed five hours *talking* to a man (Roehm) who was potentially a traitor.

His intuition, personal and political, is sensitive. He says, 'I

---

[1] My colleague F. A. Voigt has noted that only the countries where grand opera flourishes have produced Fascism.

cannot change myself. I am like the beasts. I smell the weather before it changes. If I submit to my instincts, I never err.'

He is an orator of the pen. He *wrote* his way to power.

Like all dictators, he is implacable. No Hitler, no Stalin, no Mussolini, has ever forgiven an enemy.

He is no hypocrite. He never made any secret of his ambition, which he said frankly, was to seize power and stay in power as long as possible. On the other hand, he insists that he is no mere 'profiteer in patriotism'. *Duty* to Italy is his passion. 'Is it lust for power that possesses me?' he once said. 'No, I believe, in all conscience, no Italian thinks this. Not even my worst adversary. It is duty. A precise duty towards the revolution and towards Italy.' (Finer, p. 295.)

His histrionic ability is extreme. No modern politician except possibly Trotsky is so good an actor.

He distinctly has a 'world sense' of politics. Hitler thinks of Germany as an isolated entity; Mussolini knows well that the world contains much aside from Italy.

Above all, he possesses a passionate physical magnetism. His vitality expresses itself in every gesture; when he salutes, for instance, he shoots out his arm with such intensity you think the hand may fall off. This vitality is readily absorbed by others. When he arrives before troops ready for review, his presence has almost the effect of an electric shock.

Among more negative qualities in Mussolini the following might be mentioned.

He is intensely touchy. A journalist well known to him, whom he admired, visited Italy in August 1935 and wrote a quite objective story saying that the Abyssinian campaign was not universally popular. Mussolini saw it (he reads most of his Press cuttings) and cancelled an appointment for an interview, a few hours before it was to take place. Again, a minor instance, he caused the Italian number of *Fortune*, which was very fair to him, to be suppressed in Italy, largely it is believed because of one remark quoting him (in his early days) as follows: 'What do I do first when I wake up? Jump straight out of bed! No matter how beautiful the head beside me on the pillow.'

He is superstitious. Early in his career he had accepted among the thousands of gifts which poured in on him, an Egyptian mummy. Then Lord Carnarvon, excavator of the Tomb of Tutankhamen, died. Mussolini ordered the mummy to be removed. He woke up the staff of the Palazzo Chigi (where he then worked) to have it instantly taken away, his fright of it having descended on him late at night.

His claustrophobia I have mentioned. It is possible also that his reckless addiction to speed and violent movement is compensation for the days when prison cells bound his steps to six feet by four.

He is, like many Italians, inclined to be suspicious. For instance when the King telephoned him from Rome to Milan offering him the premiership, he did not disbelieve the message, but refused to act on it until it should be confirmed by an official telegram.

He is not strikingly original. Most of his ideas are derivative. Ideologically Fascism is the distorted creation of Marx, Nietzsche, and Sorel. Mussolini did not invent the Fascist salute, which was a suggestion of D'Annunzio's; he did not devise the symbol of the Black Shirt, which he copied from the uniform of the *arditi*.

He is occasionally capable of humility. 'A man in my position,' he told Ludwig, 'must be stupid at least once a week.'

Mussolini, who is quite aware of the complexities of his character, read with interest a serial discussion of it in a Fascist newspaper. Then he telegraphed the local prefect: 'Be so good as to send for the editor and ask him to close his series of articles with the following statement! "Inasmuch as Mussolini himself says that he does not know exactly what he is, it is somewhat difficult for others to find out." '

After his visit to Rome in 1926, Francis Hackett wrote, 'Mussolini is an Italian masterpiece, all shade and all sun, concrete, bold, and tangible. . . . He is the hero of one of those terrific dramas of upstart genius which in England lead to Parliament Hill and in Italy to Vesuvius. Mussolini is Vesuvian. He is capable of a rush of blood to the head, a tower of rage, a surge of demoniac wilfulness, that may end in smoke, lava, destruction.' Hackett wrote with Corfu in mind. Nine years later came Abyssinia.

He is nothing if not frank. In October 1937 he said in a speech in Bologna, 'I hold out a great olive branch to the world. This olive branch springs from an immense forest of eight million bayonets, well-sharpened and thrust from intrepid young hearts.' (*Bulletin of International News*, Vol. XIII, No. 10.)

In an interview with a German journalist he exclaimed, 'We have made a big step forward. We have forged the Rome-Berlin axis. This is the beginning of a European consolidation process. Understand—I do not believe in the United States of Europe. That

is a Utopia, an impossibility with historical and geo-political limitations. . . . We are experiencing a change of epoch, a total break-up
of political and social ideologies. The democracies are done for.
They are—centres of infection. The future turns away from collec-
tivism, from the uncertain reaction of the masses. Democracies are
like sand, like shifting sand. Our State-political ideal is rock-
granite peaks.'

Soon the Duce began to back up his words—in Spain.

Violence

'There are those who have to be crushed by truth before they can understand
it.'
                                                              —MUSSOLINI.
'Not believing in force is the same as not believing in gravitation.'
                                                              —TROTSKY.

Mussolini's first published work, written when he was twenty-
one under the strong influence of Nietzsche, was an essay on the
philosophy of force. The concept of force has always fascinated
him. Yet, as he says, violence should be 'surgical', not 'sporting';
defining the terror in Italy as 'national prophylactics', he wrote that
certain 'individuals should be removed from circulation as the
doctor removes an infected person from circulation.' At one point
in his career, early in 1921, he resigned—extremely temporarily—
the leadership of the Fascist movement, in protest at violence which
he considered excessive by *squadristi* bands. He did not, however,
abolish the *squadristi* till 1927, when their work with castor oil and
clubs was safely done.

Mussolini's considered opinion on the subject of violence is the
following:

> 'Was there ever a government in history that was based exclusively
> on the consent of the people and renounced any and every use of
> force? A government so constituted there never was and there
> never will be. Consent is as changeable as the formations in the
> sands of the seashore. We cannot have it always. Nor can it ever
> be total. No government has ever existed which made all its sub-
> jects happy. Whatever solution you happen to give to any problem
> whatsoever, even though you share the Divine wisdom, you in-
> evitably create a class of malcontents. . . . How are you going to
> avoid that this discontent spread and constitute a danger for the
> solidarity of the state? You avoid it with force—by employing force
> inexorably whenever it is rendered necessary. Rob any government
> of force and leave it only with its immortal principles, and that govern-
> ment will be at the mercy of the first group that is organised and
> intent on overthrowing it.'

There have been five or six attempts to assassinate Mussolini; he is a profound fatalist, but not so much so that severe precautions to guard him are not taken. The story is that only one man in Rome, the chief of police, can or cannot tell Mussolini what to do; the Duce obeys him in regard to routes he takes. There are some streets in Rome he never travels on. On the other hand, he travels daily from home to office without special guard.

Hitler, the story goes, keeps a small revolver in his desk drawer. Suicide would be understandable with Hitler if his régime collapsed. Not so the Duce. Mussolini, a compact gorilla, will not perish by such facile means.

Psychograph

Dr. Wilhelm Stekel, the Viennese psycho-analyst, has made a fascinating study of Mussolini. His will to power, his intense sense of great historical mission, may, according to Stekel, derive from bipolar tendencies of love and hatred of his father. Mussolini père was the first man of the native village. So young Mussolini became the first man of Italy. The boy, as a socialist, identified himself with his father; then differentiating himself, he kicked socialism overboard. The turning-point of Mussolini's life was, Stekel believes, his flight from Italy to Switzerland, which may well have been a flight from paternal influence. His father was sent to prison by the local police; now Mussolini sends father substitutes to prison.

Mussolini must always lead. As a schoolboy he sat at the third table, the one reserved for the poorest boys; he has never forgotten this humiliation. Climbing mountains, he records that his only pleasure is getting on top and resting there, the victor of the heights. As a bricklayer, he wanted always to put the very topmost brick in place. The fact that he was a mason is of psychological significance, Stekel believes. He was a builder first of houses, then of the house of Italy.

Throughout his whole life there has been conflict between the journalist in him and the artist. Like all newspaper men, he wanted to write novels and dramas. He learned to play the violin.[1] The men he chiefly admires, aside from Caesar and Napoleon, are imaginative writers—Shakespeare, Goethe, Balzac, Petrarch, Pascal. He himself was a failure as a poet; therefore he set out to make his

---

[1] In a vivid interview with George Seldes he explained what music—especially Italian music—meant to him.

like a work of art.   He became a dictator partly because great creative art was denied him.

His life, Stekel says, has been to some extent a regression to childhood; he wants to be a stoic, to compensate for juvenile humiliations and defeats; he is fascinated by the history of Rome, which was the youth of his own country.   Julius Caesar he thinks was the greatest man who ever lived.   He has identified himself with Caesar closely. (Like Caesar, a minor but interesting point, he is sensitive to bad weather.)   The only rival to Caesar in his political affections is Napoleon, whom he always thinks of as an Italian.   It is of some significance that his Napoleonic play described the Hundred Days: the period when Napoleon, returning from Elba, flung himself finally against destiny.

Mussolini hates Hitler because he can tolerate no rival dictator. There must be no second Duce.   He has striven not only to check and defeat Hitler (as in Austria after the Dollfuss murder) but to outdo him.   Hitler left the League of Nations; but Mussolini, in effect, made war on it.   Hitler asked for colonies, and got none; Mussolini carved one from Ethiopia.

In Caesar's time, as Mussolini showed Rome in the gigantic new historical tablets he has conspicuously set up near the Forum, Britain was merely an outpost of the Roman empire.   In the eighteenth century Britain beat Napoleon, humiliating him at Elba and St. Helena.   And in modern times Britain has sought to transform the Mediterranean, the Roman sea, *Mare Nostrum*, into a British lake.   It is not entirely fanciful to think that Mussolini has visions of vindicating Caesar and avenging Napoleon.

What Fascism Is

When Mussolini took power he had no programme except to retain his job.   He admits this candidly.   But he quickly found a programme, which derived from a desire to replace the class struggle, which—certainly—he had done more than most men to intensify, by some sort of class collaboration.   This was the origin of Fascism in practice.   The contrast to Hitler is striking.   Hitler came to power with a very definite programme, and soon lost it; Mussolini, devoid of programme, quickly invented one.

The outlines of Fascist economy are known to everyone.   Private property, private profits, are preserved, but under strict state control.   The entire productive capacity of the country, theoretically

represented by employers and employees both, is organised into a
series of twenty-two 'corporations', from which deputies to the lower
chamber of parliament are chosen. Representation will be on a
basis of occupation instead of geography; a deputy will represent,
say, the hotel business instead of the province of Turin.

The scheme was put forward cautiously, and expanded very
slowly; in 1939 it was still an embryo structure. Every corporation
contains three supervising delegates of the Fascist party; each corporation is headed by a member of the cabinet or an under-secretary,
appointed by Mussolini. The deputies, moreover, are 'voted' into
the chamber from an approved list chosen by the Grand Fascist
Council; electors are privileged simply to say Yes or No to the whole
list. Mussolini's two general 'elections' have been grossly dull
affairs.

The state, being supreme, regulates economy for its exclusive
benefit. Fascism may be, spiritually, 'an attempt to make Romans
out of Italians', but physically it made Italy a prison. 'Fascism is a
series of ideas turned into a person,' according to Gentile; and the
peculiar person and character of Mussolini determined the repressive shape it took.

Mussolini told an English publicist late in 1935 that he would
find no orthodox capitalism surviving in Fascist Italy. And in a
famous speech to the National Council of Corporations he announced that the world economic crisis of 1931-34 had bored so
deeply into the capitalist system that it had become an organic crisis
of the system itself. 'To-day,' he said, 'I declare to you that the
capitalist method of production is finished.'

Indeed one may assemble a seemingly impressive list of anti-
capitalist forces in the corporative state. No employer may discharge labour without government consent. No capitalist may
undertake such comparatively minor independent activity, as, say,
enlarging his factory, without state approval. Wages are determined by the government; the employer may hire labour only at
government labour exchanges. A factory owner may not liquidate
his business without state permission; the government controls his
sources of credit; and it takes a large share of his income in
Draconian taxation.

On the other hand, the disadvantages to labour under Fascism
are more severe. Liberty, in a Fascist system, ceases; the question
for the individual is whether the merits of the régime compensate
its loss. Workers have lost their right to bargain; their trade unions

have been dissolved; they are the weaker party vis-à-vis the employers in the syndicates; they are still subject to the crises of capitalist economy; their wages may be (and have been) mercilessly deflated by decree; above all, they have lost the right to strike. The capitalist on the other hand, even if he has suffered inconvenience, maintains his fundamental privilege, that of earning private profits. Fascism as Mussolini introduced it was not, probably, a *deliberate* artifice for propping up the capitalist structure, but it had that effect. The restriction on the mobility of capitalism was in effect 'a premium which the capitalists were willing to pay in order to get full security against the demands of labour'.

Mussolini, in his essay on Fascism in the *Enciclopedia Italiana*, begins by saying how a series of 'aphorisms, anticipations and aspirations' were welded by time into 'an ordered expression of doctrine'. He sketches the history of Fascism by describing the things it combated: (1) Pacifism, (2) Marxian Socialism, (3) Liberal Democracy. He attacks the materialist conception of history; 'Fascism, now and always, believes in holiness and heroism.' And as to democracy: 'Fascism denies that the majority, by the simple fact that it is a majority, can direct human society; it denies that numbers alone can govern by means of a periodical consultation, and it affirms the immutable, beneficial, and fruitful inequality of mankind. War,' he concludes, 'alone brings up to its highest tension all human energy and puts the stamp of nobility upon the peoples who have the courage to meet it.'

His best passage is devoted to Fascism as the totalitarian expression of the state:

> 'No doctrine has ever been born completely new, completely defined, and owing nothing to the past. . . . The foundation of Fascism is its conception of the state, its character, its duty, and its aim. Fascism conceives of the state as an absolute, in comparison with which all individuals or groups are relative, only to be conceived of in their relation to the state. . . . The state, as conceived of and as created by Fascism, is a spiritual and moral fact in itself, since its political, juridical, and economic organisation of the nation is a concrete thing; and such an organisation must be in its origins and development a manifestation of the spirit. . . .
>
> 'The Fascist state is unique, and an original creation. It is not reactionary, but revolutionary, in that it anticipates the solution of the universal political problems which elsewhere have to be settled in the political field by the rivalry of parties, the excessive power of the parliamentary régime and the irresponsibility of political assemblies; while it meets the problems of the economic field by a system of

syndicalism which is continually increasing in importance, as much in the sphere of labour as of industry; and in the moral field enforces order, discipline, and obedience to that which is the determined moral code of the country.'

And he ends the essay by an urgent appeal to imperialism: 'For Fascism, the growth of empire, that is to say the expansion of the nation, is an essential manifestation of vitality.'

CHAPTER XVI

WHO ELSE IN ITALY?

'If I advance, follow me; if I retreat, kill me; if I die, avenge me.'

—MUSSOLINI.

'There is no revolution that can change the nature of man.'

—MUSSOLINI.

MUSSOLINI is three things: the *Duce* (leader) of the Fascist party, the *Capo del Governo*, or prime minister, and the head of the Grand Fascist Council, the highest organ of government in Italy. The three posts, quite distinct, merge in his person. As *Capo del Governo*, he is theoretically responsible to the King; as Duce of the party, he appoints the Grand Fascist Council and presides over it. The Grand Fascist Council controls parliament. Hitler, in Germany, has united party and state; he is *Reichsführer*. Not so Mussolini, though the effect is the same. In the U.S.S.R., Stalin, in contrast to Mussolini, is—in theory—appointed by and is responsible to the other members of the central committee of the communist party, whereas in Italy the members of the Grand Fascist Council are Mussolini's underlings. Stalin, however, like Mussolini, keeps party and state theoretically separate.

The Duce is the only dictator who, so far as is known, has made arrangements for his succession.[1] The Grand Fascist Council numbers about twenty-five men; its membership, except for ex-officio and life members, shifts continually and is secret, and it meets in secret. (The secretary of the party and certain other dignitaries are members so long as they hold their party or cabinet jobs; the three surviving quadrumvirs of the March on Rome— Balbo, De Bono, and De Vecchi—are life members.) If Mussolini dies, the Grand Council has the duty of submitting a list of men from which the King will choose a successor. Three names are, at present, understood to be on the list, selected in advance—of course —by Mussolini.

[1] But in September 1939 in the emergency of the Polish war, Hitler said that if anything 'happened' to him Goering would take over, and after that Hess.

Mussolini told Ludwig that there will never be a second Duce; he meant obviously that there will never be a second Duce like himself. The men around him are, indeed, small fish. There is no Goering in Italy, no Kaganovitch. Whenever a subordinate like Grandi or Balbo becomes too prominent, Mussolini who doesn't like the luxury of seconds in command, contrives to get rid of him. De Bono was removed from Abyssinia as soon as he had captured Adowa and Makale. The last secretary of the party, Achille Starace, held on to his job for a long time, but late in 1939 he was sacked.

The Duce *is* the Fascist system; if he dies, can it survive him? The temptation is to answer in the negative, but one should not forget the precedent of other countries. Five post-War dictators have died: Lenin, Ataturk, Dollfuss, Alexander of Jugoslavia, and Pilsudski. In each case the systems they established—they differed enormously, of course, in scope and spirit—survived.

Dux and Rex

The King provides assurance of some sort of continuity—if he wants it—because he still has the right to name the new prime minister. Mussolini differs from all other dictators in that he preserved a symbol of permanence above him.

Vittorio Emanuele III, born in 1869, is the doyen of European kings, having reigned almost forty years. He acceded to the throne on the assassination of his father. His formative years were spent in the army. He married a Montenegrin princess, Elena. The two great decisions of his life were the dismissal of Giliotti in 1915, which brought Italy into the War, and his acquiescence to Mussolini's March on Rome. He is an enthusiastic numismatist. He is mild, well educated, and, like almost all Italians, intelligent. His salary is 11,250,000 lire per year, or roughly £200,000. His relations with Mussolini are, contrary to gossip, quite good.

Nevertheless the little story is told that Vittorio Emanuele greeted the Abyssinian war with satisfaction.

'If we win,' he is reported to have said, 'I shall be King of Abyssinia. If we lose, I shall be King of Italy.'

The Crown Prince, Umberto Nicola Tomaso Giovanni Maria, Prince of Piedmont and Heir Apparent, is potentially a character of great importance. This is because the King's influence, under the constitution, may be decisive in determining the successor to Mussolini. And presumably old Victor Emmanuel will not be king for ever. Umberto may be on the throne when the crisis that would be entailed by Mussolini's death finally comes. For a long time Umberto, an attractive and amiable young man, was somewhat cool to the Fascist régime; lately, however, he is believed to have become more friendly.

Umberto was born in 1904. He married Princess Maria José of Belgium in 1930. They have two children.

Ciano and Underlings

Count Galeazzo Ciano, born in Leghorn in 1904, has two jobs. First, he is Mussolini's son-in-law. Second, he is foreign minister of Italy. Young Ciano has had a meteoric career to date. He went to law school, wrote two plays, and dabbled in journalism; then he entered the diplomatic service and served first in South America and then China. He became consul-general in Shanghai, and minister to China. Meantime, he fell in love with the strong-minded Edda Mussolini, and married her. On returning to Italy, Ciano became chief of the Italian Press department—where he was extremely popular with the foreign newspaper men in Rome—and then Minister of Press and Propaganda. Came the Ethiopian war. Ciano entered the air service, and had six months of fighting. His was the first aeroplane to land in Addis Ababa after the Emperor fled. Returning to Rome again, Ciano was promoted to be foreign minister. Already, it seemed, Mussolini was grooming him for the succession. He was only thirty-three.

Ciano owed something of his position to his father, Count Constanza Ciano, who died in 1939. Father Ciano was a distinguished naval officer during the Great War, and for ten years, 1924 to 1934, was Mussolini's minister of communications. It was part of his responsibility to see that Italian trains—early Fascist feat!—ran on time. Mussolini later promoted him to be President of the Chamber of Deputies. Until the startling rise of his son, the elder Ciano was supposed to have been a possible successor of the Duce.

It goes without saying that Edda Mussolini has had great influence on young Ciano's career and character. An ambitious and colourful person herself, she had—and has—colourful ambitions for her husband also. Edda is Mussolini's darling of darlings. Naturally Ciano entered closely not merely into the family circle, but into the heart of politics. Mussolini likes him better than any man in Italy.

Edda had a great deal to do—more than had Ciano himself possibly—with the evolution of the Rome-Berlin axis. She liked Germany, and was liked there, especially by the Goerings, who named their daughter after her. When Ciano signed the first German accord in 1936, which created the axis, he was quoted in a remarkable interview with the New York *Times* as follows: 'My pet plan— a close tie-up with Germany, has become a reality.' But when the 1939 crisis came Ciano was bitterly disillusioned. Both Hitler and Ribbentrop treated him badly. The axis began to creak.

Mussolini did not want to fight over Danzig. He—and Ciano— knew that neutrality was the only possible policy for Italy. They disguised 'neutrality' with the phrase 'non-belligerence'.

Ciano's friends on one occasion were somewhat shocked at his light-hearted description of the modern technique of massacre. Interviewed after one of his bombing exploits in Ethiopia, young Ciano was reported to have said:

> 'When you see a concentration of Ethiopian troops, you give them a few rounds with a machine-gun and they scatter and hide in the long grass. Then, when you fire a few more rounds at random, each of them thinks the bullets are falling near him, and they promptly emerge and run in all directions, when you can pop them off in real earnest.'
>
> —(*Evening News*, October 17, 1935.)

Young Ciano did not have an easy time as foreign minister. Spain was exploding, the Mediterranean crisis intervened, and his relations with Britain continued to be troublesome. It seemed that Neville Chamberlain, following an Anglo-Italian 'Gentleman's Agreement', did everything possible to conciliate Mussolini, but without much success. But when war came he still held his job and late in 1939 a cabinet reshuffle strengthened his position.

.   .   .   .

The job of the secretary of the Fascist party is to make the mistakes. Mussolini gives the party secretary all the inside work to do; when he has made himself sufficiently unpopular by exerting discipline, refusing promotions, picking out men for jobs, and so on, he is dismissed and replaced by someone else. Since 1919, when the party was organised, there have been seven secretaries; in other words it takes an average of three years for one to outlive his usefulness. Bianchi, one of the quadrumvirs, the first secretary, was involved in the Matteotti business, and Mussolini dropped him. His successor, Giunta, was one of D'Annunzio's legionnaires in the attack on Fiume. The next was Roberto Faranacci, boss of Cremona; he was too violent even for the Duce and to-day he is an almost forgotten figure. Next came Augusto Turati, a more capable and respectable man, who managed to hold the job for four years; he is now, however, interned on the island of Rhodes. Following him was Giurati; he was the author of the Fascist Ten Commandments. Then came Achille Starace, who was followed in turn by Ettore Muti.

It happens that Starace has exophthalmic eyes, somewhat like Mussolini's, and he was accused of slavish physical imitation of his master when his eyes popped and rolled. A minor victim of megalomania, within safe bounds, he maintained an imposing office, and was supposed to exercise his fingers with a mechanical device in order to strengthen his handshake. Starace is still head of the *Dopolavoro* movement which is an effort to supervise Fascist leisure as well as working hours. His job made him unpopular; his honesty was however admitted. Starace made one amusing blunder once, his announcement that letter writers should say *Evviva Il Duce* in their correspondence. The next day one of Mussolini's typical anonymous and scornful editorials in the *Popolo d'Italia* repudiated the idea; he didn't want to copy the *Heil Hitler* of Nazi Germany.

Another comparatively powerful subordinate was Edmondo Rossoni, under-secretary to the Duce in his capacity of *Capo del Governo*, who spent many years in America as a labour organiser. Rossoni was the man who built up Mussolini's labour syndicates. He lost his job, however, in the 1939 shake-up.

Balbo

Italo Balbo, reputedly the inventor of the castor-oil treatment for recalcitrant non-Fascists, 'a Fascist from the first hour' and Mussolini's whilom 'right hand', was still in 1939 exiled in Lybia, of which province he was governor. He was given no part in the Abyssinian campaign, of which, it is believed, he (like the general staff) at first strongly disapproved. Balbo was packed off to Lybia in June 1933, after his dramatic and successful flight to Chicago from Rome. His name may not be mentioned in an Italian paper more than once a month.

The story was that Mussolini exiled Balbo first because his spectacular success in aviation had made him too popular. But another reason was apparently Balbo's close friendship with Umberto, the

Crown Prince. In 1932 and 1933 Umberto had anti-Fascist leanings; grimly Mussolini changed the army oath of allegiance, cutting out the reference to the King's 'royal successor'. The report
was heard that the Duke of Aosta, a great favourite with the régime,
and now Viceroy in Abyssinia, might displace Umberto as heir-
apparent. Balbo at the time was Umberto's 'man'. Now, most of
those well-informed think, the King has prevailed upon Umberto
to see the foolishness of his ways. But Balbo still is very close to
Umberto; every once in a while he flies from Lybia to Naples, where
the Crown Prince lives, and conspicuously stays in the palace for a
day or two.

Balbo is the only man in Fascist Italy who even now, within
limitations, does what he pleases. Once, when he was air minister,
the Duce disapproved of his aviation budget; Balbo, arriving in the
Palazzo Venezia, saw that the usual chair next to Mussolini's desk
was missing, while his master remained seated. This meant that
Balbo was being disciplined like a schoolboy; he would have to talk
standing up. So promptly he sat down—*on* Mussolini's desk.

Tall, copper-bearded, a picturesque as well as arrogant figure,
Balbo was born in Ferrara, near Bologna, in 1897. He enlisted in
the army as a boy, and won decorations in his 'teens; he founded
a newspaper at twenty; he took part in the D'Annunzio adventure
and was among the first to join Mussolini in 1919. In the braggadocio days, he was conspicuous among the bludgeoners; he captured Ravenna from the socialists, besieged Parma, and for a time
was expelled from the party. At the age of twenty-six he was first
commander of the Fascist militia; then he became under-secretary
of national economy, finally secretary for air. Before his flight to
Chicago he had organised and led similar formation flights to
Odessa, around the Mediterranean, and to Brazil.

Balbo is quoted in Finer with a passage which strikingly shows
the similarity between the early Fascists and their subsequent
analogues in Germany:

> 'When I returned from the war—just like so many others—I
> hated politics and the politicians, who in my opinion had betrayed
> the hopes of the soldiers, reducing Italy to a shameful peace and
> the cult of heroes. To struggle, to fight in order to return to the
> land of Giolitti, who made a merchandise of every ideal? No.
> Rather deny everything, destroy everything, in order to renew every-
> thing from the foundations.'

Marshal Emilio de Bono, another of the quadrumvirs, was the

first commander-in-chief of the Italian forces in Abyssinia. Born in 1866, a generation older than Balbo, he had a long career as a regular army officer; he was the commander of Mussolini's regiment in the War. Disgusted at the 'collapse' of Italy in 1919 and 1920, he resigned his command of the army corps at Verona and joined the Fascist movement. An amateur musician, he wrote the first marching song of the Black Shirts. He was governor of Tripoli for a time, then minister of colonies.

The Other Warriors

In November 1935, Mussolini replaced De Bono in Abyssinia by Marshal Pietro Badoglio, Italy's most distinguished soldier. The reasons for the shift were several. For one thing, De Bono had done his job, even though the campaign was going slowly. For another, appointment of Badoglio made the business an affair squarely of the regular army, not merely of the Black Shirts. Cleverly the Duce saddled Badoglio with responsibility for making the war succeed. It certainly succeeded, and Badoglio became first Viceroy of Ethiopia and Duke of Addis Ababa.

Marshal Badoglio had a brilliant military career. He was born in 1875, and joined the artillery in 1890; he has fought in every Italian war since, and was one of the survivors of Adowa in 1896; he has been decorated for bravery seven times. After the Great War he was variously a senator, ambassador to Brazil, chief of the general staff, and president of the army council. He could have crushed the March on Rome had the King given assent. It is generally believed that at the beginning he opposed the Abyssinian war; the general staff prepared a report on the possibilities of the campaign which Mussolini, it is said, tore up in rage. But Mussolini was right; they were wrong.

General Rudolfo Graziani, at first the leader of the Somaliland forces, knows Africa well; he spent seven years as junior officer in Eritrea, and from 1926 to 1930 he was the 'pacifier' of Cyrenaica. Military experts call him Italy's best officer. He succeeded Badoglio in the supreme Abyssinian command. In 1937 came an attempt on his life in Addis Ababa; a massacre of Ethiopians followed. He is now the Italian chief of staff, and a highly able one. . . .

Diplomats

For a time the Duce's favourite for work in foreign affairs was

Dino Grandi, but at the Lausanne reparations conference the French and British composed an agreement excluding Italy, and Grandi was punished by being sent to London as ambassador— there, presumably, to learn better the manners of the subtle British. Mussolini was supposed to have been furious at him in the summer of 1935, because Grandi had not warned him that the British would take the lead in imposing sanctions against Italy. But many besides Grandi were deceived. Grandi, once a *squadristi* leader, has long since lived down his salad days. He is connected with the Sorima company at Genoa, which recovered the gold from the submerged liner *Egypt*, one of the most remarkable of modern marine exploits. A man of great personal charm, he was probably the most popular of the ambassadors at the Court of St. James's. He left London in 1938, and is now Minister of Justice.

Grandi may still have a great career, because he represents moderation, and he is extremely well-liked abroad. Both Grandi and Balbo are believed to have disliked the axis policy invented and followed by Ciano; both, moreover, disliked heartily the new—and totally un-Italian—policy of anti-Semitism which Mussolini and Ciano, slavishly imitating the Germans,[1] adopted in 1938. Italy took more and more drastic action against the Jews. They were excluded from state schools, they were barred from the stock exchange and government jobs, they were forbidden to marry 'pure' Italians. Grandi, it is believed, opposed all this. A Fascist (an *Italian* Fascist) from the earliest days, he was born in 1895.

. . . .

Baron Pompeo Aloisi, the man who represents Mussolini at Geneva, did well with a stiff and ticklish job; he had to maintain a modicum of self-respect and persuade others of the independence of his judgment while he was, in the strenuous days of October 1935, merely the Duce's mouthpiece. His ferocious master raged in the Palazzo Venezia; at the Council table in Geneva Aloisi had to give the impression of steadiness and poise. Mussolini gave him impossible orders like the injunction to accuse the Abyssinians of 'aggression', which he had to present plausibly and with a straight face.

Born of a noble Roman family in 1875, Aloisi began life as a naval officer, then turned to the diplomatic service. He had wide experience; in 1919, far from the *squadristi* in Tuscany and the

[1] For instance the Italian army adopted the goose-step, conveniently renamed the *passo Romano*.

Emilia, he was Press officer of the Italian delegation at the Paris peace conference. He was a *diplomate de carrière*, one of the few whom Mussolini retained, and he served as minister or ambassador in Copenhagen, Tirana, Bucharest, Ankara, and Tokio. He was the agent of Mussolini's penetration of Albania; in Japan, a cultivated man, he found time to write a book on Japanese art. The Duce sent him to the League in 1932. He worked well as chairman of the League committee organising the Saar plebiscite.

The former under-secretary for foreign affairs, Fulvio Suvitch, well known for his foppish clothes, was born in Trieste, then part of Austria. During the War he crossed the lines from the Austrian to the Italian army. He is of no consequence nowadays in execution of policy; in 1936 he was named ambassador to the United States.

'Jesters do oft Prove Prophets'

'There is a widespread belief,' wrote the *Manchester Guardian* recently, 'that dictators are iron-souled and thick-skinned; the truth is that they are the most sensitive creatures in the world. . . . It is the leaders of the democracies who are tough and wiry. They can stand criticism, and either bear it in good part or put up with it. Not so the dictator; an unfriendly remark or even good-humoured banter is so intolerable that the very sinews of the state are felt to shake dangerously in response to the jangled nerves of the dictator.'

Jokes in the U.S.S.R., as we shall see, mostly deal with the rigours of the Five-Year Plan; German jokes are based most often on the Terror, jokes in Italy perhaps significantly—aside from those international jokes which are applied indiscriminately to all the dictators —deal mostly with corruption. Mussolini himself is above any whisper of financial irregularity, but if the current of suppressed laughter in Italy is any indication, the rank and file Fascists think poorly of the integrity of petty bosses and sub-leaders. The party, of course, controls all the best jobs; on this fact the wits flourish.

Most Italian jokes hinge on the word *mangiare*, which means two things, 'to eat' and 'to graft'.

Little Romano Mussolini, for instance, says to the Duce at the dinner-table. 'Father, what must I do to become a great man like yourself?' Mussolini answers, *'Mangi e taci'* (Eat and be quiet).

The most Fascist of animals is the elephant; because it first makes the Fascist salute—and then eats. The Fascist insignia have been placed on all locomotives—because they 'eat up' the road. Mount Vesuvius was recently given an honorary degree, because it opened its mouth—to eat. A traveller stops a policeman, 'Where can I eat well in this town?' Reply: 'At the party headquarters.'

Another type of story goes like this. At a congress of veteran Fascists someone calls out, 'To whom does Italy belong?' Chorus: '*A NOI!*' (to us). 'To whom belongs victory?' Chorus: '*A NOI!*' 'To whom the Duce?' Chorus: '*A NOI!*' Then a voice interrupts: 'To whom belongs work?' (*A chi il lavoro?*) The chorus stops in embarrassment, then begins to sing the Fascist anthem, *Giovinezza.*

No street has ever been named for Mussolini. This is because the word *via* means not only street, but 'away'.

The New Pope

On March 2, 1939, Eugenio Cardinal Pacelli, the Papal Secretary of State, succeeded the venerable Pius XI as Pope. Thus a distinguished son of the Church reached its supreme office. The new Pope—to emphasise the association of his ideas with those of his predecessor—assumed the name Pius XII. As such, he instantly became a dominant force in world affairs.

From many points of view the election of Pius XII on that day, March 2, was striking. For one thing—an odd and attractive detail —the day was the new Pope's birthday. The conclave was the shortest in history, lasting only one day, and Pacelli was chosen after only three ballots. On the first he got thirty votes from the sixty-two cardinals present, on the second forty. The third ballot was sixty-one to one. Everyone voted for Pacelli except himself. He, it is believed, cast his vote for Cardinal Granato di Belmonte, the Dean of the Sacred College. When the vote was taken, the new Pope buried his face. He muttered, 'I accept because in this I see the will of God. I commend myself to the mercy of God.'

The elevation of Cardinal Pacelli was notable for other reasons. He was the first Papal Secretary of State to become Pope in 271 years, and the first Camerlengo (Papal Chamberlain) ever to attain this eminence. Not for generations had a man reached the Papacy who never, in his career, had any purely pastoral duties. He was the first Roman nobleman to become Supreme Pontiff for more than a century. He was a man of the modern world—one who sometimes typewrote his own letters, who used an electric razor, who had travelled widely. Above all, he was representative of a profession— diplomacy. His life for forty years had been consecrated to statecraft as well as religion. The pressure of events plus his superb brain and character *trained* him for his papacy.

The gaunt, lean-jawed Pacelli, with his extraordinarily beautiful eyes and hands, is scholar, linguist, traveller, diplomat, statesman. He is beyond doubt the best educated Pope of modern times. Among other things he speaks nine languages.

The new Pope was born in Rome in 1876, of a distinguished Roman aristocratic family. His father was Dean of the College of Consistorial Advocates. Sons of the family had traditionally been lawyers closely associated with religious affairs; Francesco Pacelli, the Pope's brother, is in fact one of the Vatican's lawyers, who played an important role in drawing up the Lateran treaty. The Pope has two sisters, Elisabetta and Giuseppina. On his elevation to the Holy Seat, almost the first thing he did was to telephone them. He has a very strong sense of duty and devotion in personal as well as ecclesiastical life.

Young Pacelli decided to become a priest instead of going into the law, and in 1899, at the age of twenty-three, he was ordained. He was a sensitive and accomplished lad, with a fine scholastic record. Entering the Vatican service, he was appointed to the Congregation of Extraordinary Ecclesiastical Affairs, which is a division of the Papal Secretariat of State, or foreign office. Here his chief was Cardinal Gasparri, under whose benevolent influence he worked for many years. Gasparri saw that this young Father would go far; he taught and trained him well. In 1917 came a turning point in his life. Heretofore he had been, as it were, a brilliant civil servant within the Vatican walls. Now he entered the world outside, as a diplomat, a negotiator. He had been an assistant secretary of state; he became now an ambassador abroad.

This was the first result of his appointment, in 1917, as Apostolic Nuncio to Munich. He was elevated at the same time to the rank of Archbishop. It was he who presented the peace plan of Benedict XV to the Kaiser, but the Kaiser would not listen. The Archbishop Nuncio remained in Germany for twelve years, first in Munich, then in Berlin. This experience of Germany is, it goes without saying, of inestimable importance to him now. He saw the breakdown of Germany after the War; he saw the struggling Weimar republic at first hand; he watched the rise of Hitler. Once, in Munich, some communist desperadoes entered his house, intending to murder him; he persuaded them calmly, without lifting his voice, to go away. During his twelve years in Germany he negotiated two concordats, one with Bavaria, one with the Reich as a whole.

Archbishop Pacelli was recalled to Rome in 1929, promoted to be a Cardinal, and soon appointed to the Secretaryship of State in succession to Gasparri. So he became the foreign minister of the Vatican, watching the interests of 330,000,000 Catholics in every country of the globe. The political experience which the Cardinal accrued in those years was tremendous. During all the turbulent 30's, he directed Vatican foreign policy. He travelled often: to France, to South America, and in 1936 to the United States. During his American visit he flew 8,000 miles across the country and back, saw the natural and political wonders, inspected Boulder Dam and lunched with President Roosevelt.

The new Pope's dominant characteristics—grace, dignity, and saintliness aside—are an acute sense of political realities and great skill and subtlety in negotiation. In Berlin, in the old days when he was Nuncio, he was universally admired and liked. But his fellow cardinals chose him as Supreme Father not merely because he is one of the most attractive of contemporary historical figures. They chose him for his experience and ability. He was their answer to the disastrous political situation in the world, to the upheavals that were bound to come in the uncharted future, and above all to the threat to Catholicism that war would bring. They wanted a man who *knew*.

The new Pontiff lives, it goes without saying, a life of extreme simplicity. He rises at six, works hard all morning, and for his only relaxation walks after luncheon in the Vatican gardens. He receives a great many people, working into the night, and makes decisions himself on an infinity of matters. He is dependent on no one to the extent that Pius XI—who ardently wished him to be his successor—was dependent on him. Yet his austerity, his simplicity, do not deprive him of human qualities. The Pope can smile; the Pope can weep too.

Immediately war broke out, six short months after he became Pontiff, the responsibilities of Pope Pius XII naturally became more onerous. Germany had already seized one Roman Catholic country—Austria. Promptly it proceeded to seize another—Poland. And the Germans were uneasy at his elevation to the papacy; they called him a 'political' pope. From the beginning he took a strong line against totalitarianism. He felt that both Naziism and Bolshevism were enemies of Christianity, and he deplored the

T

doctrine of racism as it became interjected into Italian Fascism. In one of his early speeches, he talked of 'the defence of the Christian heritage against the enemies of God'.

The new Pope's first Encyclical, of date October 28, 1939, was a powerful condemnation of racism, treaty breaking and totalitarian aggression.

CHAPTER XVII

WAR IN ABYSSINIA

'Our future lies to the east and south, in Asia and Africa.'

—MUSSOLINI.

'Statesmen only talk of fate when they have blundered.'

—MUSSOLINI.

'If it wasn't for myopia,
We could see to Ethiopia.'

IN October 1935 the campaign against Abyssinia began. Mussolini, cold-blooded as only an Italian can be, set out, 'in violation
of covenants he was pledged to support, to rob and conquer a
country he had promised to defend'.

For years he had threatened a push to the east. The campaign
should have surprised nobody. He had cast hungry eyes at Tunis;
an arrangement between Soviet Russia and Turkey prevented an
adventure some years ago in Anatolia. He needed room—colonies
—for Italy to expand in. But his habit of bluster, had, lamentably
enough, persuaded folk in Western Europe that he was bluffing.
Why did he choose 1935 as the time for the adventure he had long
foretold? And why, as proof that his bite was worse than his bark,
did he pick Abyssinia?

One must pause a moment to describe Italy's fundamental realities, Mussolini or no Mussolini, in economics.

Italy has forty-two million people, as many as France, crowded
into one-third the arable land of France. The population increases
by the astounding total of four hundred and fifty thousand births
per year. 'We are hungry for land,' Mussolini himself put it,
'because we are prolific, and intend to remain so.' Of the forty-two
million Italians, overwhelmingly the largest proportion are engaged
in agriculture; the country is only ten per cent industrial. No less
than twenty-one per cent of the population is illiterate. The country cardinally lacks raw materials; it has no rubber, tin, nickel,
tungsten, mica, or chromium; it is dependent on imports from
abroad for ninety-nine per cent of its cotton, eighty per cent of its
wool, ninety-five per cent of its coal, ninety-nine per cent of its

mineral oil, eighty per cent of its iron and steel, ninety-nine per cent of its copper. Despite Mussolini's 'battle of the grain', it does not produce enough food for its own requirements; it must import fifteen per cent of its meat, and twenty per cent of its grain. Finally, Japan excepted, Italy has the most exposed coastline of any important country in the world.

Mussolini's job in the first years of Fascism was, in general terms, an attempt to transform a country so meagrely favoured by nature into a great power. He succeeded, but at a frightful cost. Taxation increased till it ate up no less than thirty-eight per cent of the total national income. The trade balance remained monstrously adverse. The budget deficit increased from a modest £11,000,000 in 1930-31 to £60,000,000 in 1932-33, and £107,000,000 in 1933-34, which was twenty-five per cent of the total national revenue. The preparations for the Abyssinian campaign, before the war began, cost two thousand million lire, or roughly £33,000,000. The Italian gold reserve was halved; Mussolini, who had sworn to defend the lira to the 'last drop' of his blood, was forced in effect to leave the gold standard. The war itself cost an incalculable sum.

Now it is quite true, as H. R. Knickerbocker and Dorothy Thompson have pointed out, that under dictatorships the economic laws which apply in democratic countries may be simply suspended. Hitler or Mussolini can do tricks with money that are impossible under orthodox *laisser-faire* capitalism. Economics under Hitler and Mussolini became purely a political question; the only issue was how long the people would bear the merciless strain of dictatorial manipulation. Even so, the internal situation of Italy, towards the end of 1934 and the beginning of 1935, contributed to make an 'external diversion', so popular among dictators, necessary. The very reasons why he should not have made war were those why Mussolini did. 'It was not a question of whether he could afford to fight, but whether he could afford not to.'

I do not think, however, that Mussolini (who like Hitler is not much interested in economics) was prompted to war exclusively by economic factors. They were immensely buttressed by politico-nationalist considerations.[1] Mussolini is not the man who thinks of countries or frontiers predominantly as functions of economic stresses. His mind much more directly seized on territory as a symbol of political prestige. One should never forget the secret treaty of London, which tempted Italy to break the Triple Alliance

[1] Nationalism is, of course, partly an economic phenomenon.

and enter the War on the side of the allies. By that treaty Italy was promised more spoils of victory than it got; Italy was shockingly let down.

Mussolini's foreign policy was, on the whole, a failure. He stood in a contradictory position; Italy, one of the victor powers, wanted treaty revision just the same. The French blocked him off from Tunis; his penetration of Albania was a costly and not very lucrative experiment; his Four-Power Pact, an attempt to form a sort of twentieth century Holy Alliance on quasi-revisionist grounds, was still-born; he played the wrong side in the Arabian wars; he tried to keep the Balkan pot boiling, and was defeated by a Balkan Pact virtually uniting Jugoslavia, Rumania, Turkey, and Greece against him; finally, Hitler took Austria, which seriously compromised his prestige in Central Europe.

But politics alone might not have sufficed to cause the Abyssinian war. The climate of Fascism is strenuous. Like all dictators, Mussolini was 'a prisoner of prestige'. He had to keep on doing something. Hitler was stealing far too much space from him in world headlines. He was *personally* a warrior and imperialist; he talked of 'imperialism' as the eternal and immutable law of life. Every rational or objective consideration told Mussolini, a strikingly intelligent man, that the Abyssinian war was a difficult and dangerous business. It had long been a truism in European politics that Italy was permanently condemned to dependence on Great Britain, because of its exposed coastline and the control of the Mediterranean by the British fleet. Mussolini flouted this truism. An interesting example of the importance of personality, perhaps of megalomania, in politics. The Duce was not alarmed by the pessimistic reports of the geologists in Abyssinia. He knew what its chief crop was—glory.

'Upon What Meat Has This Our Cæsar Fed?'

Mussolini himself would lift an eyebrow at it, but parenthetically one should quote the following manifesto by the well-known Italian futurist, F. T. Marinetti, called 'War Has a Beauty of Its Own':

1. Because it fuses strength and kindness. Strength alone tends to cruelty and kindness to debility, but the two together 'generate solidarity and generosity'.
2. Because it assures the supremacy of mechanised man, equipped with gas-masks, megaphones, flame-throwers, and tanks, over his machines.
3. Because it begins the long-dreamed-of 'metalisation' of man.

4. Because it completes the beauty of a flowery meadow with its machine-guns, 'passionate orchids'.

5. Because when the symphony of rifle fire and artillery bombardment stops, the songs of soldiers can be heard and the perfumes and odours of putrefaction can be perceived.

6. Because it 'genially remoulds terrestrial scenery' with its inspired artillery.

7. Because it creates new architecture, such as the heavy tank.

8. Because it exceeds in violence the battles of the angels and the devils.

9. Because it definitely cures man of individual fear and collective panic with a refined and stylised heroism.

10. Because it rejuvenates the male body and renders the female one more desirable.

11. War has a beauty of its own because it 'serves towards the aggrandisement of the great Fascist Italy'.

(—*Manchester Guardian*, November 15, 1935.)

Another factor was that intangible and elastic concept known as national 'honour'. The same factor, we have seen, helped bring Hitler power in Germany. Italians, despite Mussolini, still smarted under the humiliation of Adowa where the Abyssinians had massacred them in 1896, and of Caporetto, where the Austro-German army had broken through in the worst defeat suffered by a western power in the Great War. Mussolini, like Hitler, was avenging an earlier degradation, returning to Italy, as on a bloody salver, its self-respect.

The Dogs of War

Why did Mussolini choose Abyssinia? For the simplest of reasons, that Italy grew up too late to join the other imperialist powers picking colonial fruit, and Abyssinia was the only territory left. Why had Abyssinia been spared the colonial 'attentions' of Great Britain and France? Because it was a country where settlement by Europeans was costly, where the wealth of natural resources was dubious, and where, above all, peculiarly impregnable warrior tribes made military conquest difficult. Dislike of the Italian campaign should not make anyone think that the Abyssinians are a gentle or charming people.

As to difficulties of settlement, the following excerpts from an article in the *New Republic* (August 7, 1935), are illuminating:

'An Italian settler going to Ethiopia to engage in farming would need to take with him complete supplies, including building materials for his home. Ethiopia could not serve as an outlet for Italy's surplus population unless the government heavily subsidised each emigrant. For about forty years Italy has made sporadic attempts to colonise Eritrea, which, in the uplands, resembles much of Ethiopia. The present European population of Eritrea is 4,565, most of whom are government officials. . . .

'There is another drawback to mass emigration to Ethiopia—with an estimated native population of ten million. Many natives develop into highly skilful workmen, as has been demonstrated on two Belgian coffee plantations already established there. . . . Throughout Africa, the individual white farmer, depending on his own labour, has never succeeded in competing with the native worker under white management. An Italian peasant farmer in Ethiopia would either drop to the native standard of living or starve to death.

'In attempting to use Ethiopia as a source of raw materials, Italy will be confronted with its obdurate geography. . . . For years adventurous white men have prospected in Ethiopia and tried to interest European capital in their supposed discoveries. None of them[1] has yet told a story convincing enough to obtain backing. . . .'

But Abyssinia's 'obdurate' geography did not prevent the great powers from the usual imperialist aggressions. As far back as 1891 and 1894, Britain and Italy set up 'spheres of influence' in Abyssinia; that of Italy was not very valuable, but the British sphere included the Lake Tsana region, from which flow the headwaters of the Blue Nile, which irrigates the Sudan and Egypt. In 1906, although Abyssinia's independence was recognised by Italy, a Tripartite agreement formally partitioned the country into French, British and Italian spheres; this was a typical pre-War imperialist treaty. Abyssinia protested against it, but no one paid attention.

In 1915 the secret treaty of London mentioned above, provided that 'in the event of France and Great Britain increasing their colonial territories in Africa at the expense of Germany, those two powers agree in principle that Italy may claim some equitable compensation, particularly as regards the settlement in her favour of the questions relating to the frontiers of the Italian colonies of Eritrea, Somaliland, and Lybia'.

Abyssinia entered the League of Nations in 1923, with France and Italy as her godmothers. Italy was particularly eager to press Abyssinian membership, in order to forestall suspected encroachments in Ethiopia by Great Britain. This was a mistake of Mussolini's. Anyone who tries to hoodwink the British suffers for it—in the long run. Had not Abyssinia been a member of the League, the

[1] Except Francis W. Rickett, whose Standard Oil concession of August 31, 1935, was shelved.

British could not have mobilised world opinion to harass Italy in the 1935-36 war.

In 1925 Sir Austen Chamberlain and Mussolini negotiated an agreement confirming their respective spheres of influence in Abyssinia. Referring to this document, Mussolini angrily stated in September 1935, that 'it divided—you understand me—virtually *cut up* Abyssinia'. The British wanted to build a dam near Lake Tsana. In return for Italian approval and support, they promised 'to recognise an exclusive Italian economic influence in the west of Abyssinia' and to support an Italian project for a railway through Abyssinia connecting Eritrea and Somaliland. But Abyssinia was a member of the League in 1925 and the Emperor Hailé Selassié (then the Regent) protested so vigorously at Geneva that the agreement lapsed.

In 1928 Italy signed a treaty of 'friendship, conciliation, and arbitration' with Abyssinia. In Article Two, each government pledged itself 'not to take any action detrimental to the independence of the other'. Then seven years passed, until Mussolini struck.

The initial incident, that of Walwal on December 5, 1934, was called a 'frontier' squabble, but in reality, as even Italian maps showed at the time (they have been hurriedly changed), Walwal is about a hundred miles from the Somaliland border, well inside Abyssinian territory. The fight began when a joint Anglo-Abyssinian frontier commission discovered an Italian military detachment camped at Walwal. The British retired; the Abyssinians fought. Thirty-two Italians, one hundred and ten Abyssinians were killed. This was probably the pretext Mussolini was waiting for; at any rate a flaming ultimatum in the Corfu manner, descended on Addis Ababa; the Duce demanded that the Abyssinians apologise, salute the Italian flag, and pay £20,000 indemnity.

What happened thereafter is well known. The British Empire began to move.

Albion Perfide?

Mussolini must have assumed that Great Britain would not object to his adventure. Otherwise it is doubtful if even the Duce would have launched it. At any rate he accuses the British of having seriously misled him. On January 29, 1935, he sent Signor Grandi to the Foreign Office, 'inviting the British Government to consider specific agreements for a harmonious development of the Italian and British interests in Ethiopia'. He was, he said, willing

to 'table his case'. The British answered 'evasively'. The Foreign
Office did not, apparently, look with favour on the Duce's proposal;
on the other hand it seems to have given no very definite warning
of opposition.

When it became clear that Britain was opposing him and lending
the immense weight of its influence to the League, Mussolini began
to storm and bluster. He snarled at one interviewer that he was
'not a collector of deserts',[1] when the Committee of Five proposed
minor territorial adjustments. He threatened to leave the League
'at once' if sanctions against Italy were applied; and subsequently
did so. While Eden, Laval, and Aloisi put their heads together in
Paris, he mounted a howitzer shouting encouragement to his Black
Shirts, saying that he would go forward 'with Geneva, without
Geneva, or against Geneva'. Sir Samuel Hoare made an historic
speech to the League assembly, pledging Britain to 'collective main-
tenance of the Covenant in its entirety, and particularly for steady
and collective resistance to all acts of unprovoked aggression'.

Mussolini's reply to this was twofold. First, he proceeded with
the war, and on October 3 invaded Abyssinia. One of his rare
hypocrisies, he claimed that Hailé Selassié was the aggressor, who,
as Vernon Bartlett ironically put it, 'by ordering withdrawal of his
own troops in his own territory, had committed a provocative act'.
Second, he issued a series of tumultuous statements and interviews
which were perhaps justifiably plaintive in tone.

'We are on the march,' he told the *Morning Post*. 'It is too late
now to tell us to stop. . . . Look at Portugal, and Belgium, and
Holland. They all have fruitful colonies. Surely Italy must have
fruitful colonies too. As soon as we get such colonies, Italy
will become conservative, like all colonial powers. . . .' To
the New York *Sun* he complained: 'Why are we condemned for
what you yourselves do whenever the need arises? You never
hesitated about war when your interests were involved. Think
about Mexico and Cuba and your own civil war between North
and South. How did the United States end slavery?' He said in
one speech, 'The wheel of destiny moves towards a goal—the
rhythm has become faster and cannot now be stopped. An attempt
is being made to commit the blackest injustice against Italians,
that of refusing them a little place in the sun. Until it is proved to

[1] He told Ward Price of the *Daily Mail*, 'I got 110,000 square miles of Sahara
desert from the French a little while ago. Do you know how many inhabitants
there are in that desolate area? Sixty-two!'

the contrary, I refuse to believe that the people of Great Britain wish to shed their blood and to drive Europe towards catastrophe to defend a barbarous country unworthy of ranking among civilised peoples.'

He foamed with rage at England. Britain, he did not need to point out, while sitting on roughly one-quarter of the world, while dominating an empire of 450,000,000 people (384,000,000 of whom represent coloured races), was frustrating his tiny adventure, a colonial adventure of the kind that Britain had herself so many times indulged in. It was no use trying to explain to him that the British Empire was built up before the War, that the Covenant of the League of Nations put a different face on the piracy of new territory. Britain had fought the Boer War. Britain suppressed the 350,000,000 people of India. Britain had not stopped Japan in Manchuria. Mussolini raged.

And indeed others than Mussolini were able to assemble a list of British imperialist adventures.

From 1788 till 1925 Great Britain fought, it was calculated, approximately twenty campaigns or wars to keep the route to India open.[1] The British fought Napoleon on the Nile, at Trafalgar, at Aboukir, and indirectly in Copenhagen, which they wantonly bombarded. The British intrigued in Egypt, annexed Aden, invaded Abyssinia, penetrated Persia, and joined the Turks against Russia in the Crimean War. The British acquired Cyprus, extended their control of Egypt, advanced into the Sudan, and fought the Great War to prevent the German *Drang Nach Osten*.

In October the French newspaper *Gringoire*, an organ of the Right, published an article entitled 'Should England be Reduced to Slavery?' Its unamiable strictures caused a minor diplomatic incident, and M. Laval apologised to the British Ambassador. 'England's policy,' murmured the *Gringoire*,[2] 'consists of troubling the earth so that she can rule the seas. . . . I think English friendship the most cruel present the gods can give a people. When I see England, the Bible in one hand, the League of Nations Covenant in the other, upholding the cause of the weak or righteous, I can't but believe she has her own reasons. . . . I have seen His Majesty's

---

[1] Britain was not, of course, the only country with an imperial policy. The United States of America in the same period acquired Texas, the Panama Canal, the Philippines, etc.

[2] Janet Flanner's translation in the *New Yorker*.

police slashing Egyptian students in the streets of Cairo. I saw the
Lord Mayor of Cork dying in London in a criminal's cell. I saw
convicts, disguised by Lloyd George, as soldiers, shooting down the
Balbriggan martyrs at their cottage doors. . . . Is it indispensable
or human happiness that the route to India be British?'

Recently the *New Leader* printed a list of 'independent terri-
tories' which the British Government has annexed since 1870.
Baluchistan. Burma. Cyprus. Wei-hai-Wei. Hong-kong. Koweit.
Sinai. North Guinea. South Guinea. East Guinea. Solomon
Islands. Tonga Islands. Sudan. Uganda. British East Africa.
British Somaliland. Zanzibar. Transvaal. Orange Free State.
Rhodesia. British Central Africa. Nigeria. In addition the British Empire was in effect enlarged by mandated territories acquired
by the peace settlements of 1919. Palestine. Transjordan. Tanganyika. Togo. Cameroons. South-West Africa. Apparently the
British themselves began to think this was a little too much. And
the Italians greeted with interested scepticism Sir Samuel Hoare's
careful hints in his Assembly speech of September 11, 1935, that
colonial raw materials were inequitably distributed.

Sanctions

British policy in regard to sanctions that might be applied to
Italy for violation of the Covenant of the League of Nations[1] did
not become clear till late in the teeming summer of 1935. At the
beginning the government took no strong line to *prevent* war. 'It
was,' wrote the anonymous author of *Inquest on Peace,* 'passionately
sincere in its desire that the lion and the lamb should lie down
together. But it was hazy whether the lamb ought to be outside
or inside the lion.' Once Mussolini had committed himself too far
to go back, with a hundred thousand troops in Abyssinia, British
policy sharpened. The Admiralty filled the Mediterranean with
warships, and Eden pushed economic sanctions at Geneva. Thus
it was commonly bruited about that the British were 'out to bust'
the Duce. This was far too blunt a way to put it. What happened
was that Britain was perplexed by the difficulty of the decision it
had to make. Its policy, founded on a double negative, was equi-
vocal. It did not want a war; at the same time it did not want
permanently to affront Mussolini. On the one hand, the British
disliked the rupture of peace entailed by the Abyssinian campaign;
on the other they did not want to rupture the collective security

[1] For the League itself see Chapter XXXVI below.

system by forcing Mussolini out of the League, and into the hand
of Hitler.

Germany, as always, remained the chief preoccupation of British
foreign policy in Europe. A perfectly good case for or against
sanctions against Italy could be made with only the German impera
tive in view. One might have favoured sanctions, on the ground
that vindication of the League system and a sound setback to Mus
solini in Abyssinia would discourage Hitler from breaking the
peace later. Or one might have opposed sanctions, on the ground
that they would weaken Italy, shake up Central Europe, and give
Hitler an excellent chance to expand and profit.

There was also the question whether Britain could stop Musso
lini without risking a much bigger war than the Abyssinian one
The British cabinet was divided on this issue. Mussolini himsel
provoked a preliminary decision against Italy, by rashly filling
Lybia with Italian troops and giving the impression of Italian
designs on Malta and Egypt. The British fleet did not concentrate
in the Mediterranean until after at least several Italian divisions
for no purpose connected with the actual campaign in Ethiopia
had been sent to Lybia and Cyrenaica.

The reasons for the sanctions policy provisionally adopted were
roughly, the following:

First, as indicated above, the Abyssinian crisis was interpreted
as a 'final' test of the League system. The issue was quite clear
whether the League would go into the discard for good, or be made
to work. The very fact that Japan in Manchuria had successfully
defied the League made it the more necessary for the League powers
to assert themselves against Mussolini. Defiance of the Covenant had
occurred, without penalties, in distant Asia. Ethiopia—in Africa—
was nearer home. Let the Italians succeed in Ethiopia, and aggres
sion would break out in Europe next. Sanctions against Italy were
in effect sanctions against Germany later.

Second, the British Dominions, which since the Statute of West
minster have the right to secede from the British Empire, and
which are bound together only by the symbol of the crown, were
vigorous in support of sanctions policy. There was plenty of idealism at Geneva in September and October in 1935, and Canada and
South Africa supplied a fair share of it. It became clear to the
seasoned and wary brains of Whitehall that the League of Nations
might turn out to be an inestimably valuable agency for keeping
the Empire solid.

Third, liberal opinion in England, which hated Fascism, was eager to down Mussolini on moral-political grounds.[1]

Fourth, an extraordinary informal plebiscite, the 'Peace Ballot', was taken in June in England by the League of Nations Union, under the powerful leadership of Lord Cecil. 11,500,000 people voted, and no fewer than 10,088,000 of them favoured economic and non-military sanctions against an aggressor, and actually 6,748,000 were willing to support, 'if necessary', military sanctions. Now the average total vote in a British general election is only about 20,000,000; obviously the government could not afford to dismiss this registry of opinion by one half of the electorate. The Peace Ballot greatly strengthened the hands of the pro-sanction members of the cabinet, like Anthony Eden, and confounded those who disliked the League.

Fifth, the labour party, the official opposition, overwhelmingly approved a sanctions policy.

Sixth, British imperial interests, as outlined above, became involved. Idealism and what is called 'character' play a certain role in British policy, but idealism alone would not have prompted the first vigour of British response to Italian aggression. Idealism plus Egypt, the Red Sea and India turned England against Italy. The conflict was between an old and surfeited and a new and untried imperialism. As soon as Mussolini began to mass troops near Egypt, the British jumped.[2] Sir Samuel Hoare—till he lost his job—was the luckiest foreign minister in modern times; he was able to write a policy in which idealism and imperialism exactly coincided. Not only God, but the British route to India, was on his side.

Hoare-Laval Plan

But sanctions started slowly and half-heartedly in actual practice. Oil was not included in the embargo, and British companies actually furnished some of the petrol feeding Count Ciano's planes. And at no time were *military* sanctions—or closure of the Suez Canal—

---

[1] Dean Inge, writing to *The Times*, expressed his fear of this. 'I think all friends of the League,' he wrote, 'should beware of their involuntary association with socialists who care nothing for Abyssinia or the League, but who wish to embroil us with Italy because they hate and fear Fascism. If Russia were attacking Afghanistan they would sing a very different tune.'

[2] At Geneva the story went that 'S. d. N.' (*Société des Nations*) really stood for 'Source du Nile'.

contemplated by Britain or the League. Even so, a General Election was fought in November in England largely on the peace-and-sanctions issue, and the government, going to the country on a firm League platform, was overwhelmingly successful. Thus it was an acute shock to public opinion when, in December, news of the celebrated Hoare-Laval plan leaked out.

The 'inside' story of this plan seems to be the following. For some weeks experts of the Foreign Office and the Quai d'Orsay were at work trying to hammer out a formula to end the war. On Sunday, December 8th, Hoare went to Paris, had a few hours with M. Laval, and proceeded to a badly-needed rest and ice-skating holiday in Switzerland. A joint Anglo-French statement was issued guardedly noting the progress made towards a settlement. 'There could be no question at present of publishing these formulas,' the statement said. Then—what often happens—someone in Paris leaked. The Monday papers in England were full of more or less authoritative statements of the deal whereby Italy was to be given a good share of Abyssinia as a bribe to call off the war.

The original statement had made it clear that the arrangement had not yet been sanctioned by the British cabinet. Therefore the cabinet had to do something in a hurry. It happened that the inaugural session of the London Naval conference was held in London this morning—Monday, December 9th. I remember how everyone was surprised at the extreme briefness of Mr. Baldwin's opening address, and his apology that he must depart at once to attend to urgent business. It certainly was urgent, though few people knew then what was going on. The cabinet, its hand forced by the leakage in Paris and the growing agitation of public opinion, had to decide whether to accept the Hoare-Laval plan, or repudiate Sir Samuel Hoare. It decided to accept the plan. Everything happened in a hurry. One story is that there were no maps in the cabinet-room, and ministers had to approve the plan without any idea of how much Abyssinian territory Italy was to get.

The next day Baldwin made an amazing speech in the House, as more and more details of the plan became known. Baldwin said that his 'lips were sealed', but that if the trouble were over he could make such a case that 'not a man would go into the Lobby against us'. This piquant observation aroused, naturally, much curiosity. Hoare himself was still away. On the 13th the Anglo-French proposals were at last published. They were even worse than had been anticipated in sanctionist circles. And on the 14th it was revealed hat Hoare had sent the British minister in Abyssinia a telegram urging him to use 'his utmost influence' on the Emperor to give careful and favourable consideration' to the proposals.

The storm in the country grew. Britain rose in bewilderment, indignation, and alarm. Eden had the unpleasant job of explaining o his friends how the British and French Governments—after all— were selling the Abyssinians down the river. *The Times* and *Daily Telegraph*, usually staunch supporters of the government, began o waver. Personage after personage descended on Baldwin at 10 Downing Street and told him that the business simply would not do. Even the Tories revolted. Hoare came back from Switzerland. Somebody had to be the culprit, someone had to suffer or the government itself might have been overthrown. Pitched overboard like a blood sacrifice, Hoare resigned. And the plan was buried.

In his speech to the House of Commons on December 19th Hoare could not tell the whole story. But he made a dignified defence of his policy. There were many who thought that it was Baldwin who should have resigned, not his foreign minister. After all, the cabinet as a whole had presumably sanctioned Hoare's dealings with Laval and certainly had approved the plan. Baldwin, incidentally, has never 'unsealed' his lips. No word of explanation ever came from him as to what, precisely, he meant. Ever since the cartoonist David Low has portrayed him with sticking-plaster across his mouth. One famous caricature shows Baldwin with the corpse of the League behind him, muttering through the plaster, 'You know you can trust me.'

Six months later, in cooler days, it was easier to make an explanation. Baldwin almost certainly was alluding to the possibility that sanctions, especially if they were implemented by an oil embargo, might make Mussolini angry enough to perish in a cloud of glory by attacking the British fleet. What the British were doing was an attempt to stave off a general European war. There were subsidiary considerations also. One was the feeling in some British circles that Mussolini was losing the Abyssinian war, and that if he lost he might collapse in Italy, which would shake the whole European structure. Another—quite contrary—was the conviction of some well-informed people that Mussolini was not losing, but *winning*, the war, and that it was best to buy him off with a slice of Abyssinia before he took it all.

If Mussolini had accepted the Hoare-Laval proposals, *before* they were dropped by the British, what an odd irony it would have been!

Finis

Early in 1936, still worried by sanctions, Mussolini decided to transform a colonial campaign into a major engagement, a real war, and with almost half a million troops in Africa, using poison gas, the result could not long be in doubt. Even so, the speed and vigour of the Italian advance confounded all experts. They did not realise how badly armed and led were the Abyssinians, nor the immense advantage of mechanisation even in guerilla fighting on such difficult terrain. Badoglio's campaign was a military and engineering masterpiece. By April 15th the Italians had captured Dessie, having advanced the 120 miles from Quoram in the incredible time of nine days, and on May 5th they were in Addis Ababa. The Emperor fled.

Hitler's various victories, the Abyssinian campaign, the war in Spain, are branches of the same poisonous tree. Qualified as the victories may prove to be, they indubitably represent the temporary triumph of swift, hard-hitting Fascism against the slow motion and diffusion of power of the democracies. Mussolini's victory was followed by Fascist forwardness everywhere in Europe, as those who had hoped to check him with sanctions had foreseen: Greiser in Danzig, Franco in Spain, put on their several performances. Hitler and Mussolini came to represent almost identical dynamic forces. What went on in Europe was a struggle between law and right on the one hand, and the big fist and the machine-gun on the other. The struggle was between respect for international obligations and the most forthright kind of adventurous and predatory nationalism. The adventurers have won several highly important skirmishes. But democracy may have the final word.

.   .   .   .

Mussolini, a discerning and powerful gambler, set the Italian people on new paths. But the future of Italy, like that of Germany, depends on the British Empire. The cruel and youthful obstreperousness of the Fascist states must sooner or later come into conflict with the mature vitality of England. So now we pause in this counter-clockwise tour of Europe and turn to Britain.

CHAPTER XVIII

ENGLAND: THE RULING CLASSES

'England is not to be saved by any single man.'
—WILLIAM PITT.

'This royal throne of kings, this sceptred isle,
This earth of majesty, this seat of Mars,
This other Eden, demi-paradise. . . .'

A T one and the same time, England, a puzzling nation, is the
world's firmest monarchy, strongest oligarchy, and freest democracy, and its empire is the only one that survived the War. It is
also an island of country houses, built on a foundation of coal,
which, in spite of the strenuous difficulties of the age, remains
prosperous. Two per cent of the property owners of England own
sixty-four per cent of the national wealth. These persons comprise
a fluid and impregnable ruling class, or caste, which is one of the
most remarkable phenomena of the world to-day.

It was produced partly by geography; it supports itself by ownership of land or by trade in all the markets of the world; it pays
service to conscience and religion; the House of Commons and the
House of Lords are its clubs; it believes in freedom of speech and
the democratic process; it responds very sensitively to public
opinion; among its bastions are the Navy, the Bank of England,
and the civil service; it was educated in public schools and week-end
houses; its empire is its greatest pride.

The ruling classes absorb an acutely disproportionate share of
the national income and of economic power. Take, for instance,
the land of London. One peer owns no less than two hundred and
seventy acres in the West End. Only about forty thousand of the
eight million inhabitants of London own any land at all, and the
really valuable slices are in the hands of about twenty men.[1] There
are about one hundred thousand men and women in England with
incomes over £2,000 per year, who take sixteen per cent of the
national income; there are eighteen millions whose wages, under
£250 per year, are only fifty-six per cent of the national income. Of

[1] See Hugh Dalton, *Practical Socialism for Britain*, p. 151.

those who die in England, 'only one in four leaves as much as a hundred pounds' worth of property'.

The House of Commons represents a considerable concentration of wealth; a writer in the *Sunday Express* has found, for instance, that 170 members of the House of Commons held 650 company directorships. One M.P. had 34. A recent book, *Tory M.P.*, is packed with suggestive details of this kind. The *New Statesman* once published an analysis of the occupation of the 729 peers who comprise the House of Lords. 246 owned land. 112 were directors in insurance companies, 74 in financial or investment houses, 67 in banks, 64 in railway companies, 49 in shipbuilding or engineering companies, and so on. Interestingly enough, of the 729 peers, 371 or more than half, never once spoke in any debate in the House of Lords from 1919 to 1931; 111 of them never voted in a single division; the average number taking part in a division was 83.

The most important basic fact in British public and political life is geographical. The British Isles are islands. And, as the school-boy put it in a famous definition, 'an island is a piece of land entirely surrounded by the British navy'. The English, a mixed race—composed of Angles, Saxons, Jutes, Romans, Normans, Teutons, Celts—grew up and coalesced in comparative isolation. Since Elizabeth they have been free from intrusion by others and were free to intrude themselves upon others. And their island heritage gave them a long view, because for generations they looked out to the sea. Geography has produced, in this imperial race, some magnificent provincialism. Two or three winters ago a heavy storm completely blocked traffic across the Channel. 'CONTINENT ISOLATED', the newspaper posters couldn't help saying.

The weather has in fact—the same thing is true of many countries—been an important political factor. In Austria, for instance, as I shall try to show when we reach Central Europe, the enervating *Föhn* is responsible for many of the eccentricities of Austrian behaviour. So in England, fog and damp have chilled the national bones. I know that from one point of view the English climate is the finest in the world, because, as it has proudly been pointed out, you can play golf almost every day in the year; you may get wet, but you *can* play. The Englishman has his umbrella within reach almost from birth; growing up, he is conditioned in preparation for any emergency, not merely those in the realm of climate. The British Empire was the inevitable result of geographical and meteorological factors; anyone who has survived a few London winters knows why the Empire Builders sought the sun.[1]

England produces only about three-fifths of the food it needs and only about twenty per cent of the raw materials which it transforms into manufactured goods for all the markets of the world. But it is a country rich in the right things—coal and iron and steel. It is, of course, the most highly industrialised state in Europe. It produces so much wealth that roughly forty per cent of its trade is export trade. And it gives the world not only steel and shoes, cotton shirts and locomotive engines, razor blades and cantilever bridges, but ships, insurance, and financial services. I have mentioned the disproportion in individual British incomes. But the national income as a whole is much greater than that of any other European country; according to G. D. H. Cole, it is £87 per capita in England, as against, for instance, £46 for Germany, £43 for France, and only £28 for Mussolini's Italy.

The ruling classes make most of their money by trade. Some members live on the land, but trade is the predominant national occupation. 'The British,' it has been written, 'are serious about their trade. It is the one thing in life they are serious about. In England's case, uniquely, God and Mammon *are* one. Mammon's appetite is tempered by the knowledge that honesty is the best (paying) policy. God is goodness, justice, love, mercy, and five per cent on a sound investment.' Factors of many sorts contribute to make a trade respectable and profitable; as Douglas Jerrold wrote referring to older days, 'No consideration of social justice must interfere with the right to buy cheap and sell dear.' Britain is one of the few countries in the world where the use of the Union Jack, the national flag, is permitted in the advertising of commercial products. Even the Crown Jewels pay interest; to see them in the Tower, you pay sixpence.

For six days a week the Englishman worships at the Bank of England, and on the seventh day at the Church of England. For religion is a powerful force on the side of the ruling classes. Uniquely among modern nations, the country has a national church, 'an island religion', serving this one people. Associated with it, drawing strength from its cool and privileged ritual, is the factor of morality. The standard of public life in England is the

---

[1] And a psychologist might say that the national instinct for the accumulation of wealth is associated with the concept of the *rainy* day.

highest in the world; honour and idealism play a part in politics that the suspicious foreigner finds it difficult to understand. Honour and idealism do, of course, correspond as a rule with practical interests. The Germans not only broke a treaty by invading Belgium; they shot an arrow towards the channel ports. But the fact remains, as a diplomat of consequence remarked to a friend of mine, 'England is the most dangerous country in the world, because it is the only one capable of going to war on behalf of another country.'[1]

The ruling classes believe in freedom, in democracy, partly because, as Trevelyan says, freedom and democracy are so much more *efficient* than despotism. The English people, like the French, have paid a high price for freedom; to gain freedom they had to shed the blood of kings. The execution of Charles I made great inroads on the English conscience, and the constitutional privileges and prerogatives of parliament are, to this day, zealously guarded. One is astounded in reading English history to note the great number of men who had their heads chopped off for freedom. English democracy is conservative, and the Englishman defines the word 'conservatism' quite literally; it means to conserve things. Nothing but a great fire can destroy anything in England.

The parliamentary tradition of Westminster is the envy of the world; and with reason. In a dictatorship, the individual exists as a servant of the state; in democracies, the state is theoretically the servant of the individual. No Englishman forgets this. And, as Stanley Baldwin said in one of his most famous speeches, England has had only ten years of dictatorship in the past three hundred years. The English parliamentarians play the game in the grand manner. After an election the opposing candidates shake hands, exactly as if it had been a game of tennis. When Baldwin became prime minister for the first time, one of the first things he did was to call on Lord Oxford, his most eminent adversary, to ask advice.

Most Englishmen, of course, prize England above party: which is one reason for British capacity for self-government. When a prominent Tory, like Lord Curzon, dies, the labour members eulogise him in the House of Commons. During the General Strike

[1] One may point out, on the other hand, that few of the many Britons who were profoundly shocked morally by the Abyssinian war noted that at the same time 30,000 British and Indian troops were 'cleaning up' the Afridis on the North-West frontier of India. Not that the two cases were analogous.

of 1926, as everyone knows, Welsh strikers and police took Sunday off to play football.

Even the poorest of the poor are loyal. Visitors from abroad to the Tyneside and Durham are incredulous that poverty of such miserable proportions does not produce revolution. There are almost two millions of unemployed in England, and of them perhaps a million can never hope to get jobs again; but not only is the thought of revolution an absurdity, but a good proportion of the unemployed vote conservative instead of labour. One reason is the fear of the middle classes that labour is not 'experienced' enough to form a successful government. Another is the social insurance and paternalistic legislation of modern England; the country buys off unrest by paying £2,000,000 per week to support the unemployed.[1]

The instruments of domination by the ruling classes are several. There is, for instance, the Admiralty, which is a law unto itself. There is, for instance, the Bank, 'a most peculiar institution'. The elasticity of the nobility, which constantly enriches itself by vulgar blood, is another factor. So is the public school—the fetish of the 'old school tie'. Of the fifty-five members of the British cabinet and junior ministers, no fewer than sixteen went to Eton, six to Harrow, and seventeen to other public schools of recognised quality.'[2]

'When the call came to me to form a government,' Mr. Baldwin has written in *On England*, 'one of my first thoughts was that it should be a government of which Harrow should not be ashamed. I remembered how in previous governments there had been four or, perhaps, five Harrovians, and I determined to have six. To make a cabinet is like making a jig-saw puzzle fit, and I managed to make my six fit by keeping the post of chancellor of the exchequer for myself. . . . I will, with God's help, do nothing in the course of an arduous and difficult career which shall cause any Harrovian to say of me that I have failed to do my best to live up to the highest ideals of the school.'

Another instrument of rule is the country house. No one should

---

[1] The British grumble a great deal at such charges, but they remain, on the whole, impregnably good-humoured. What is one to say about a House of Commons that greets the new 1939 income tax—basic rate 37½ per cent!—with laughter and cheers?

[2] Of the ninety-seven ministers who have been in the cabinet since the War, forty went to either Oxford or Cambridge. But a university career is not quite so important ritualistically as education in a great public school.

think that a group of aristocratic plotters spend the week-end putting their heads together for conspiracy or mischief. It is ever so much more casual and less sinister than that. But suppose that the editor of a great newspaper wants to meet a promising labour politician. The country house, like that of the Lady Astor at Cliveden, is the perfect place. Wealthy and influential people, often bored with their formal duties, go to the country in order to get out of London, the ugliest and most uncomfortable city in the world; they invented the long week-end to stay away as long as possible. Their *métier* is politics; they talk politics; and they make politics, quite spontaneously.

The Tories, it was explained to me when I arrived in London, make a practice of lassoing the best brains in England. When someone arises with brains who is not a Tory, the Tories promptly attempt to appropriate him. Social flattery is an excellent weapon. It was the country-house system that helped to divert Ramsay MacDonald from nationalisation of the mines to nationalisation merely of the cabinet. One must be to the country house born. Otherwise, it goes to one's head, feet, and tongue. Let any really intelligent and vigorous champion of the Left arise, and presently he will find his way thorny with the invitations of the rich.

Newspapers are also a powerful instrument of rule. The ruling classes pay little attention to Lord Rothermere of the *Daily Mail* or Lord Beaverbrook of the *Daily Express,* the 'Press lords' of the nineteen-twenties, who, for all their shouting—and despite Beaverbrook's impishly attractive personality—are nowadays without much influence. Their ill-advised campaign to wreck Baldwin proved to be a boomerang. But Geoffrey Dawson, the editor of *The Times,* is certainly one of the ten most important people in England. And J. L. Garvin of the *Observer* is a potent influence, even though he took the unpopular side in the Abyssinian war, and lost all contact with reality in regard to Spain and Czechoslovakia.

Then consider the civil service, which is the incorruptible spinal column of England. My office boy, if he were reasonably presentable and adaptable, could conceivably fill the office of chancellor of the exchequer or minister of war; the permanent staff would carry on. Men like Sir Robert Vansittart, formerly the head of the Foreign Office, and Sir Warren Fisher, who for years ran the treasury, are among the characters who really rule England. About most of these all-but-anonymous men—Vansittart, who has published belles lettres and poetry, is an exception—little is known.

They avoid the limelight. They flourish in the shadows. And their power is immense. Consider, for instance, the indispensable quality of a man like Sir Maurice Hankey, whose very name is unknown to millions, but who combined in his person the posts of secretary to the cabinet, secretary to the privy council, and secretary to the committee of imperial defence.[1] What is more, other Vansittarts, other Fishers, even other Hankeys, shadows behind shadows, are continually in course of training, to take over their masters' jobs after retirement. No man is indispensable. The mechanism is self-perpetuating.

England is a thicket of stylistic difficulties, and the ruling classes are able to entrench themselves behind a massive hedge not only of privilege but of tradition. In no country may a man be so easily penalised for *gaucherie*; and a young M.P. told me the other day that it had taken him about two years to master the intricacies of parliamentary procedure. What is one to say about a country where the 'Lord' Privy Seal may be a commoner, where the King's youngest son only became a peer after his marriage, where the monarch may not even enter the House of Commons? The English constitution is not a document. No British M.P. may resign (he must make application for the 'Chiltern Hundreds'). And the prime minister gets no salary as prime minister!

The ruling classes employ propaganda far more artful than any ever dreamed of by Dr. Goebbels. They often stoop to censorship, but always in the quietest possible way; it is usually censorship not by ukase but by voluntary conspiracy. Every editor in Fleet Street knew, for instance, of British fleet movements during the sanctions crisis; but no one printed anything, not even the opposition papers. The conspiracy of silence in regard to Mrs. Simpson before the abdication is another case in point. The method of persuasion is the only one employed. 'Look, my dear fellow,' an official of the Foreign Office may say, 'I can't ask you to do this for me, but it would be awfully decent if you would.'

The ruling classes, by virtue of the single-member constituency system, gerrymander elections in a manner which, if it happened in Bulgaria or Turkey, would make liberal editors explode in indignation. In the 1931 'National Government' election for instance, the Baldwin-Simon-MacDonald coalition got 556 seats for 14,500,000 votes, whereas the opposition, with the quite respectable total of

[1] In 1939, on the outbreak of war, Hankey became a cabinet minister without portfolio.

7,200,000 votes, got only 59 seats.   In the election of November 14,
1935, the government polled only fifty-four per cent of the votes cast,
but got 428 seats out of 615.   If the voting had been by proportional
representation, the government's majority would have been 48
instead of 250.   But as it happened, the opposition got no less than
forty-six per cent of the total poll—and was condemned to impo-
tence for another four or five years.

The ruling classes, finally, despite the misery of the 'Special'
Areas, have produced not only complete political stability but a
striking measure of industrial recovery.   There were Cassandras in
the middle twenties who said that Britain was 'done'; they were
wrong.   Together with domestic strength came a renewal of
predominance in international affairs.   Britain, which had been
tempted towards isolation by imperial preoccupations, joined once
more, in full voice, the concert of European powers.   Then—necessarily in the turbulent period that was impending—the British
inaugurated a tremendous programme of rearmament, called
'national defence', to cost *at least* £1,500,000,000.

Miscellany

Among many other forces and counter-forces, players and counter-
players, in the broad arena of English political life:

Cricket and the ritualistic attitude to fair play that it has produced.

The nonconformist conscience.

The decline in the birth-rate, which, according to competent
estimates, will reduce the population to thirty-three million by
1985.

Personalities like the Very Rev. W. R. Inge, the former Dean of
St. Paul's, the Countess of Oxford and Asquith, and Professor
Harold J. Laski.

The bold and irreverent cartoons of David Low, the greatest cari-
caturist in the world.

The open forum in Hyde Park, something unique and cardinal.

The father-to-son tradition in politics; not only does Randolph
Churchill seek to follow Winston, but labour politicians pass on
their hopes and aspirations: the son of Arthur Henderson is in the
House of Commons.   So are Lloyd George's children.

The publishing house of Victor Gollancz, Ltd.

The fact that politics are the first profession of the land.

Letters to *The Times*.

Willingness of party or personality to admit defeat, and play the game loyally thereafter. Winston Churchill fought his own party's India Bill with magnetic persistence for a number of years; when it became law he re-entered the party fold.

The rule of thumb.

Economists of various breeds: J. M. Keynes, Sir Arthur Salter, Lord Stamp, Sir Walter Layton.

The formidable severity of English law.

An ingrained pacifism in the younger men, who dislike their former military titles. Captain Duff Cooper, former first lord of the Admiralty, is Mr. Duff Cooper; Captain Anthony Eden is Mr. Anthony Eden; Captain Ormsby-Gore, the former colonial secretary, is Mr. Ormsby-Gore. Some years ago Major Walter Elliot went so far as to issue an announcement saying that he was to be known thereafter as Mr. Walter Elliot.

The intelligence service of the Admiralty.

The investigations of Royal Commissions.

The death duties.

The radicalism of many Oxford and Cambridge undergraduates.

The tradition of venerableness. A politician may be still a promising young man at fifty-five. Mr. Baldwin once referred to the 'tender age' of one of his parliamentary secretaries, a stripling of forty-two. Baldwin himself did not enter the House of Commons until he was forty-one.

The habit of the Archbishop of Canterbury occasionally to write to *The Times* appealing for public prayer in regard to a political issue, e.g. in February 1935 when the India Bill was nearing completion.

The fantastic number of humanitarian societies.

The cathedral close.

Clubs.

The Federation of British Industries.

The pacifism of the late Canon 'Dick' Sheppard and the Oxford group.

The apparent disposition of women to have an Oedipus Complex on their fathers. The British is a masculine civilisation. Women wear mannish clothes; they hunt foxes; they are fierce parliamentarians.

The village pub.

The tradition of what is 'done', and the fact that everybody who is 'in' has known everybody else since childhood.

Imperialism, which extends beyond Empire bounds. Portugal for instance is almost as much in the British sphere of influence as Malta. So—following the return of George II of the Hellenes—may be Greece.

Punch.

The high salaries paid judges, members of the cabinet, and ambassadors.

Inner Circle?

One should not be tempted to think that the ruling classes comprise a body which could meet in a room, elect a chairman, and perform the organic functions of domination. England possesses no close, tight oligarchy like that once represented by the regents of the Banque de France. One might say that a certain number of persons comprise an 'inner-ring', for instance Lord Baldwin, Lord Tyrrell (former ambassador to Paris), Lord Salisbury, the great economist, Lord Stamp, Geoffrey Dawson of *The Times*, Neville Chamberlain, Lord Derby, Montagu Norman, and Sir Maurice Hankey. But no two observers would agree on the names to be included, Baldwin and Chamberlain aside. The 'ring' is not a ring in other words: at least not a fixed immutable ring. Indeed the great strength of the ruling classes is fluidity. One may be a member of one of the oldest aristocratic houses in the British Isles, and yet not be 'in'; mere wealth has very little to do with privilege; brains alone are not enough; character may be.

Royal

King George V, who died in January 1936, was one of those rare kings, it is realised now, who made history. First, he supported Mr. Asquith in the great struggle with the House of Lords in 1910, by agreeing to create enough new peers to inundate the old aristocracy, if the Lords persisted in their refusal to accept the 'People's Budget' of the Commons. Second, he 'sent for' Baldwin instead of Lord Curzon in 1923 to succeed Bonar Law as prime minister, and thus paved the way for the long Baldwin premiership later. The next year, though labour could form only a minority government, he named Ramsay MacDonald prime minister, making possible the first Socialist Government in British history. Finally, on his own initiative he travelled from Balmoral to London on August 22, 1931, in the middle of the financial crisis, and persuaded MacDonald to form a National Government.

King George—considerable tribute to the stability of British politics—had only five prime ministers in the twenty-five years of his reign which were celebrated by the Silver Jubilee of May 1935. The Jubilee, silver in name, was worth its weight in gold. Not only did it symbolise the return of comparative prosperity to Britain (and incidentally bring millions of pounds in trade to London), but it expressed with great brilliance the affection with which the nation regarded the Royal Family. The King was intensely touched, and, since he was a modest man, astounded at the colossal mass emotion his presence evoked. The origins of the Jubilee were obscure. There was no precedent for the celebration of the twenty-fifth anniversary of the accession of a monarch. No one, when the matter was first discussed in the House of Commons, anticipated the depth and range of celebration that occurred.

The King of England, no matter who he happens to be, is a personage of great political consequence. First of all, the Palace is the ultimate citadel of the ruling classes; the men who rule England live in widening concentric circles around the throne. Second, since the Statute of Westminster the King is the chief link between England and the self-governing dominions. Third, the King is a sort of gyroscope stabilising the machinery of government. The King is—and must be—outside party politics (as was demonstrated in no uncertain way by Edward VIII's abdication), but he exerts serious influence through his choice of advisers and he has the right to appraise and consult in all matters of foreign and domestic policy.

Foreign Policy

British foreign policy, which is extraordinarily constant, changing little (as Sir Samuel recently said) from generation to generation, is based, broadly speaking, on the concept of the balance of power with Britain holding the balance. 'All our greatest wars,' Sir Austen Chamberlain put it, 'have been fought to prevent one great military power dominating Europe, and at the same time dominating the coasts of the channel and the ports of the Low Countries.' Trevelyan has said, 'From Tudor times onwards, England treated European politics simply as a means of ensuring her own security from invasion and furthering her designs beyond the ocean.' In modern times, following this policy, Britain has tended, when France was stronger than Germany, to support Germany; when Germany was stronger than France, to support France. For a time the League of Nations was a convenient mechanism to this end; thus

came the period of Collective Security. Since, with great shrewdness in 1919, Britain obtained the entrance of the Dominions (and
India) into the League as separate states, she is always able to
dominate its deliberations. Before the War it was a cardinal principle of British politics not to commit the nation to any action on
the continent in regard to hypothetical future contingencies.
Locarno, the apex of the balance of power policy, changed this. All
these considerations are, of course, dominated by the principle of
Pax Britannica; Britain, a great trading nation, wants peace.

Another and very curious minor factor should be mentioned. It
causes much puzzlement to observers on the continent. The British
think even of foreign policy as a sort of game. Unlike the Germans
or the French to whom politics is a matter of life or death, the
British are capable of extreme detachment in the direction of their
complex foreign affairs. Europe is a sort of stage; the play that is
going on *is* a play. And if someone misses his cue, or blunders with
his lines, the average Briton always assumes that the drama is merely
in rehearsal, and can be played over again—better.

Roughly there were two groups in the Foreign Office before 1939.
The first comprised pro-leaguers who are idealists. They hoped
through a system of collective security to bring Germany into the
amicable concert of great powers. They thought of war as a literal
horror; the Abyssinian crisis meant to them the collapse of moral
law in Europe. The second group, mostly represented by older
men, were willing enough to give the League a bit of rope, but
they distrusted the efficacy of the collective security principle, and
put their hopes in (1) a powerful navy, and (2) isolationism. The
opinions of this group served to encourage Germany, because isolation—non-interference in Europe—was for a time tantamount to
taking the German side.

Strong pro-German influences existed in England, even after the
dictatorship of Hitler. The war of 1939, of course, blotted them
out. Here is a summary of them:

(*a*) Many Tories feared Bolshevism, and stupid ones thought of
Hitler as a sort of guarantee against future encroachments westward
on the part of Russia. England and Germany should be allies
against Russia, the great communist enemy. Moreover, Russia has
always been a 'traditional' foe; communism serves to make it doubly
dangerous.

(*b*) The City of London, with enormous investments in Germany, allowed itself to be dazzled by the brilliance of Dr. Schacht.

(*c*) A great many powerful persons in Britain hated France and the French, and therefore tended to be pro-German.

(*d*) A group of personalities around Lord Lothian (formerly Philip Kerr, Lloyd George's *alter ego* at the Peace Conference, and now British Ambassador to the United States), for a considerable time thought that a stable Germany, under Hitler, would ensure peace. Lothian is a Christian Scientist, and Christian Scientists, who do not believe in death or evil, found it easier than members of other religions to accept at face value Hitler's promises.

(*e*) *The Times* (Lothian and Geoffrey Dawson, its editor, are close friends), is of course, irrefragably independent; its Berlin correspondence has performed noble service in revealing Nazi brutality and prejudice; but it dislikes the communists more than the Nazis, and sometimes it gave Hitler more than the benefit of the doubt in matters of foreign policy.

(*f*) A tendency existed in England to be sorry for Germany in its role of conquered but honourable foe. (By contrast, the French will never forgive *Germany* for the injustices of the Treaty of Versailles.)

(*g*) Oddly enough, some forces in the labour party were pro-German. It is obvious that British socialists and trade unionists under Naziism would suffer even as their German colleagues, but labour foreign policy in Great Britain was erected on dislike of the Versailles Treaty and plea for fair play to Germany, and even outrages performed upon labour by Hitler did not much modify pro-Germanism in some circles of the British Left.[1]

The British reply to Hitler's programme of aggression was a typical compromise; first, the British bought off competition at sea by the Anglo-German naval pact of June 1935; second, the cabinet announced measures to triple the British Air Force, and the great rearmament programme got—slowly—under way.

The former sympathy for Germany in England produced a certain paradox. Among personalities it was that they were pro-German and (many of them) anti-Fascist at the same time, which was tantamount to eating an orange, say, with one half of the mouth, and spitting it out at the same time with the other half. In policy it was that Britain was rearming might and main against Germany, the

[1] Harold Laski mentioned once that Woodrow Wilson was responsible for this, because he invented the demarcation between the ruler of Germany and the German 'people'. To many labourites and liberals Hitler was Wilson's Kaiser Wilhelm.

only conceivable enemy, while a powerful share of opinion did what it could to strengthen the putative enemy's hand.

Britain was, of course, waiting, playing for time, until its own tremendous rearmament plans should be complete.

CHAPTER XIX

THE ABDICATION CRISIS

L ong ago in February 1936, I started to write a character sketch of Edward of Wales. I didn't finish it but in rummaging to-day through my notes for that old article I found one of the lines I had contemplated using. I had completely forgotten it. It was, 'Perhaps Edward is one of those kings who will have to make history some day—even if he doesn't want to.'

Edward, the most famous young man in the world, began his brief and startling reign on a note of sensible modernity. He turned the clocks in Sandringham to the right time (they had been set half an hour fast since the time of Edward VII, to give more daylight for hunting). He broke all precedent by flying to London immediately his father died. He addressed Parliament in the first person. On March 1st, he spoke to millions of listeners throughout the Empire on the radio. At once it was apparent that a new freshness, a note of informality and daring, was blowing through royal affairs.

Nervous, headstrong, inclined to be very stubborn, extraordinarily likeable, with great private and public charm, Edward was always supposed to have been somewhat 'pink'. He had strong humanitarian feelings about poverty, slums, and the under-dog. When he visited Austria in 1935 he embarrassed the clerical authorities by insisting on visiting the Karl Marx Hof, the socialist tenement which the year before they had attacked and partially destroyed by shell fire. Though a crown was on his head, Edward was emphatically a people's man. Early in his reign he went to Glasgow to inspect the *Queen Mary* and stayed to sympathise with the people in its slums. This note in his character caused some political alarm when, in the autumn of 1936, he visited the distressed mining districts in South Wales, saw the unutterably grisly conditions of blight and suffering there, and said—perhaps rashly—that 'something would be done'.

Rather illogically, some whisperers had it that Edward had Fascist or even Nazi sympathies. Incipient Fascists and Nazis are 'pink', too, in that they try to cash in on the sympathies of the labouring class. The Royal Family in England has had a long reputation of being privately pro-German. Edward was rather conspicuously cordial to Von Neurath when the German foreign minister came to London, and some of his friends were good friends of Von Ribbentrop. On the other hand, Edward was cordial to Litvinov, too. And seemingly Edward blasted for ever any talk of Naziness by choosing, of all persons in the world, to seek refuge after his abdication with someone who was not only Jewish, but an Austrian Jew of a great international banking family—the kind of Jew that the Nazis particularly detest.

Edward's first months as king rolled along smoothly and easily. He was enormously popular. He swallowed the ritual and stuffiness of monarchy, which he didn't very much care for, with dignity and good grace. He was unconventional, yes; he got rid of some of the oldsters around the Palace and found new friends, yes; but as far as most good informants could judge the way was clear for a long and perhaps uneventful reign, cheerier and more vivid than that of his father, but sound and in the Georgian tradition nevertheless. The good informants were wrong. Everybody was wrong. A storm gathered around the Palace such as had not been seen in England for a thousand years. The storm was personified by an American, Mrs. Wallis Simpson.

Enter Mrs. Simpson

Such a blazing tornado of words was spilled on the whole incredible case that it is necessary now to foreshorten it drastically. Bessie Wallis Warfield was born in Blue Ridge Summit, Pennsylvania, in 1896, of an old Southern family that had come on hard times. Genealogists even tried to trace her descent to William the Conqueror. She grew up in Baltimore, a Southern belle who was chic and amiable but not particularly distinguished—just one of dozens of pretty, bright, modern young girls—and she caused the most severe constitutional crisis in modern British history and became the central figure of what H. L. Mencken called 'the greatest news story since the Resurrection' because—in 1916—she met and married a young American naval officer, Lieutenant Earl W. Spencer, Jr.

Eleven years later, in 1927, she divorced him. That divorce doomed everything. In those days Mrs. Spencer could not possibly have imagined, in her most vivid dreams, that the legal dissolution of this marriage would prevent her later from being a queen, and cost the throne of a king who loved her. One divorce would have been enough.   The implacable fury of the bishops, the Puritans, the parliamentarians, was directed against Mrs. Simpson not because she was a commoner (the present Queen was a commoner until her marriage to the Duke of York), not even because she was an American by birth, but because she was a divorcee.   It was intolerable to their minds that anyone living could have known the person of the Queen.

One divorce, it is clear, would have been enough to cause catastrophe.   Re-marriage after divorce simply filled the cup to angry overflowing.   In 1928, freed from Lieutenant Spencer, she married a young New Yorker, Ernest Aldrich Simpson, who had served in the Coldstream Guards, entered a London shipping business, and become a British subject.   The Simpsons moved to London (by marrying Mr. Simpson she herself automatically became a British subject) and entered the smart life of young Mayfair people.   In 1931 she was presented at court, and a year or so later she and the then Prince of Wales became friends.

There was nothing in the least abnormal or vicious about this. The Simpsons and their circle did nothing that millions of people in the world don't do.   They danced; they flirted; they drank cocktails (for some reason the word 'cocktail' always connotes ominous scandal to an archbishop); they had good conversation.   Mrs. Simpson was not—and is not—in any sense a vulgar, pretentious, or grasping person.   She had—and has—great social grace, modesty, tact, and a very fair wit.   She was a great deal more intelligent than many in the Palace circle.   She was a comfortable person to be with. She was an excellent influence on the Prince.   She treated him like a man and a human being, not as an Heir Apparent and a puppet, and he became deeply devoted to her.   Seemingly for the first time in his life, he was happily in love.

While he was still Prince their attachment went forward without embarrassing publicity.   Mrs. Simpson was first mentioned in American newspapers in the summer of 1934 during a holiday at Cannes.   Later she was a member of a party that accompanied the Prince to Budapest and Vienna early in 1935.   When King George V died in January 1936, it became more difficult for the Prince, as King, to keep his personal affairs purely personal.   A man can be so public, G. K. Chesterton once wrote, that he can have no private life.   The new King determined, thereupon, to bring matters gradually to light.   He had always detested sham and humbug.   In the summer of 1936 Mrs. Simpson and a party accompanied him on

x

a yachting cruise in the Mediterranean and Ægean. They were widely photographed together on the Dalmatian coast and in Turkey, but few of these photographs were published in England, and none of them identified Mrs. Simpson. The more the King tried to get the matter aboveboard, the more conspiratorial became the British Press to bury any hint of 'scandal'. Twice, as if trying to give a lead to the people, the King saw to it that Mrs. Simpson's name was included in the court circular. Once the occasion was a dinner party at which Mr. and Mrs. Baldwin were present, the other the arrival of Mrs. Simpson and several of her friends at Balmoral.

What happened then was that the King, irritated, decided to settle matters once for all by marriage. The friendship might have gone on gaining slow ground and sympathy. But torrents of gossip were loose. In exclusive circles in England—and everywhere in America—people talked of nothing else. It became known in mid-August that Mrs. Simpson was about to bring divorce proceedings against her husband. The King wanted marriage. He was dissatisfied with the *status quo,* and perhaps he realised that it was untenable. Mrs. Simpson got her decree *nisi* on October 27th at Ipswich Assizes. By this time the whole world—Britain excepted, where a voluntary censorship remained in force—was standing in line to see what would come next. In six months, on April 27th, Mrs. Simpson would be free to marry the King and perhaps become Queen, provided the Proctor did not intervene and make a final divorce decree impossible.

But some other things intervened—the Church of England, the House of Commons, and Mr. Stanley Baldwin.

'When I Give I Give Myself'

The storm is bound to break. *The Times* on November 30th uttered a curious covert warning in an otherwise meaningless editorial; 'The Commons may well prove itself what the country has often required in similar times . . . a Council of State [to govern] in any crisis, foreign or domestic.' The next day, as if by prearranged signal, the Bishop of Bradford struck against the King with the words, 'The King's personal views are his own, but it is still an essential part of the idea of kingship . . . that the King needs the grace of God for his office. We hope he is aware of his need. Some of us wish he gave more positive signs of his awareness.'

Some observers believe that a Palace clique, together with high and stodgy members of the Conservative Party, manœuvred to make the Bishop speak as he did. The clique was offended, so the stories went, not so much at Mrs. Simpson (whom they might have swallowed), but at the King's disregard of ancient norms and traditions, his political 'capriciousness', his alleged determination to be an active ruler, not a mere symbol.

The Bishop himself soon explained that he had not referred to any aspect of the King's private life, only to the fact that the Coronation (mostly a religious ceremony) was coming on and that Edward didn't go to church. He said categorically that when he wrote his address he had absolutely never heard of 'these [Simpson] rumours'. This may quite possibly be true. It may also be true that the Bishop was the innocent victim of subtler powers behind the scenes who put him up to making his address.

At any rate, the British public, that vast mass which was not 'inside' on all the gossip, heard with utter surprise and bewilderment that a Bishop of the Church of England had rebuked the monarch in terms unknown in England for hundreds of years. Why? And for what? What had the King done? The country held its collective head in amazement and alarm. Their curiosity was soon satisfied. By December 3rd the papers had broken the censorship self-imposed through the Newspaper Proprietors Association, and the whole terrific story surged out.

Not just the story of Edward's attachment to an American woman with two husbands living. The story of a major struggle over the future of the King himself.

Mr. Baldwin—the account of him in the next chapter may illuminate some of the factors in his complex character—went to the King on October 20th, on his own initiative, for what was in effect a secret meeting at Fort Belvedere. Baldwin reported to the Monarch his alarm at the growing wave of stories about Mrs. Simpson, his fear that publicity was imminent and would damage the Crown, and his concern at the changed situation which might follow the Ipswich divorce.

(No one knew of this meeting between Baldwin and the King until Baldwin spoke in Parliament on December 10th. Nor of the subsequent secret meetings. The country was almost entirely in the dark. Yet one cannot fairly complain to Mr. Baldwin for not having shouted the details from the chimneypots.)

A second meeting took place, at the King's command, on November 16th.

By that date [Mr. Baldwin told Parliament] the decree *nisi* was pronounced in the divorce case and I felt it my duty . . . to begin the conversation, and I spoke to His Majesty for a quarter of an hour on the question of marriage.

Again you must remember my Cabinet hadn't been in this at all. I reported to about four of my senior colleagues the conversation at Belvedere.

I told him [His Majesty] that I did not think that the particular marriage was one that would receive the approbation of the country.

That marriage would have involved a lady becoming Queen, and I did tell His Majesty once that I might be a remnant of the old Victorians but my worst enemy could not say this of me—that I did not know what the reaction of the English people would be to any particular course of action.

I cannot go further into the details, but that was the substance, and I pointed out to him that the position of the King's wife was different from the position of the wife of any citizen of the country. It was part of the price the King has to pay. His wife becomes the Queen. The Queen becomes the Queen of the country, and, therefore, in the choice of the Queen the voice of the people must be heard.

And then His Majesty said to me, and I had his permission to tell you this, that he wanted to tell me something that he had long wanted to tell me. He said: 'I am going to marry Mrs. Simpson and I am prepared to go.'

I said: 'Sir, that is most grievous news and it is impossible for me to make any comment on it to-day.'

So Mr. Baldwin, on his own personal responsibility, told the King on November 16th that the marriage was an impossibility. At this point only four members of the Cabinet had been informed, and apparently there had been no contact at all with the Dominions. Baldwin himself—and only Baldwin—decided that Mrs. Simpson could not be Queen.

The third meeting was on November 20th. Here the possibility of a compromise in the form of a morganatic marriage was first brought up. The King might marry Mrs. Simpson and Parliament might pass a bill—since morganatic marriage does not legally exist in England—specifying that she should not be Queen. Mr. Baldwin does not say who precisely suggested this compromise. His words are simply, 'The suggestion had been made to me.' He does not say specifically that the King suggested it. The King, in his words, merely 'asked me if that proposition had been put up to me'. Baldwin replied 'Yes' and the King asked him what he thought of it. Baldwin goes on:

I told him that I had given it no considered opinion, but if he asked me my first reaction, it was that Parliament would never pass it.

I said that if he desired I would examine it formally. He said he did so desire. Then I said it will mean my putting it formally before the whole Cabinet and communicating with all the Prime Ministers of the Dominions, and asked if that was his wish. He told me that it was, and I said I would do it.

(Meanwhile, among the 45,000,000 people of Britain, not a dozen knew that these tremendous colloquies were going on. Baldwin consulted—he was 'ashamed to confess'—none of his colleagues ....)

On December 2nd Baldwin saw the King again for the fourth decisive meeting. And Baldwin told him that although his inquiries were not complete, they had proceeded far enough to indicate that neither Britain nor the Dominions would tolerate a morganatic marriage.

In this statement is the crux of the whole story, so far as Baldwin's conduct is concerned. Were his inquiries correctly performed and did he derive the correct conclusions therefrom? If so, he was right in being the agent whereby Edward was chucked off the throne. If not, Baldwin cost the Empire its King unjustly.

The Prime Minister's speech proceeds:

His Majesty asked me if I could answer his question [if a morganatic marriage was possible]. . . . I gave him the reply. . . . His Majesty said he was not surprised at that answer. He took my answer without question, and he never referred to it again.

December 2nd was the dawn of the storm. For eight tremendous days the King fought out the decision he had to make. The whole business took place in a Turneresque sunset of burning publicity. Tension reached an almost intolerable pitch. The King could decide three ways: (1) he could give up Mrs. Simpson and keep the throne; (2) he could refuse to accept Baldwin's advice, ask his resignation, try to govern with a new Cabinet, and perhaps be forced into the position of ruling with a 'King's party', (3) he could abdicate.

Baldwin says:

In the last days from that date until now, that has been the struggle in which His Majesty has been engaged. We had many talks discussing the aspects of this limited problem, the House must realise—and it is difficult to realise—that His Majesty is not a boy. He looks so young that we all thought of him as our Prince, but he is a mature man with a wide and great experience of life and the world.

He always had before him three motives which he repeated in the course of conversation at all hours and again and again; that if he went he would go with dignity; that he would not allow a situation

to arise in which he could not do that; and that he wanted to go
with as little disturbance to his Ministers and his people as possible.

He wished to go in such circumstances that the succession of his
brother would be made with as little difficulty as possible, and I may
say that any idea to him of what might be called a King's party was
adhorrent.

He stayed down at Belvedere because he said he was not coming
to London while these things were in dispute because of the cheering
crowds.   I honour and respect him for the manner in which he
behaved at that time.

It is a little difficult for an American to realise with what power
Constitutionalism is intrenched in England, and with what horror
the possibility of a King's party was greeted by a great majority of
the House of Commons.   Parliament is supreme over the King.
That principle has been clear since the Magna Charta, and
Charles I paid with his head for defying it.   Many members—for
instance Winston Churchill—thought when everything was still
hush-hush that the King was being shabbily treated and presented
with an unfair ultimatum, but very few indeed would have been
willing to envisage a royal dictatorship.   The King's party idea was,
moreover, discredited by the type of people who tried to benefit by
it, like Mosley, Lady Houston, and Lord Rothermere.

Mrs. Simpson meantime had fled the torrent.   No Dido, no
Helen of Troy, has ever been heroine of a more remarkable adventure.   Stealthily, accompanied by one of the King's trusted friends,
she crossed France by motor-car, and took refuge in the villa of
Mr. and Mrs. Rogers in Cannes.   Her behaviour during the crisis
was impeccable; it remained so.   She tried, a supreme feat, to
appear perfectly natural; she bought flowers, went out shopping.   A
doctor and a lawyer flew to visit her in a fog that grounded regular
passenger aeroplanes.   Finally she issued a statement that for dignity and decency matched any words of any of the parliamentarians:
'I have throughout the last few weeks—wished to avoid any action
or proposal which would have hurt or damaged His Majesty or the
throne.   To-day . . . I am willing . . . to withdraw from a situation both unhappy and untenable.'

On December 10th the climax came.   The lawyers, the officials,
and the comptrollers had got all the unprecedented details straight.
Baldwin and the King were in incessant communication, and the
Royal Family gathered for a last painful farewell dinner.   Queen
Mary issued a poignant statement.   Edward signed the deed of
abdication, which was witnessed by his three brothers, and the Duke

of York prepared to take the throne. In the afternoon Parliament assembled, the Speaker read out Edward's message, and Baldwin spoke. The crowds, numb with shock and the conflict of emotions, which had booed the Cabinet a day or so before, set about somewhat glumly cheering the new King.

On December 11th Edward read over the radio his farewell, and the whole world listened. It was a masterpiece to which a quarter-century of frustration gave perfect form:

> At long last I am able to say a few words of my own. I have never wanted to withhold anything, but until now it has not been constitutionally possible for me to speak.
>
> A few hours ago I discharged my last duty as King and Emperor. And now that I have been succeeded by my brother, the Duke of York, my first words must be to declare my allegiance to him. This I do with all my heart.
>
> You know the reasons which have impelled me to renounce the throne, but I want you to understand that in making up my mind I did not forget the country or the empire which, as Prince of Wales and lately as King, I have for twenty-five years tried to serve.
>
> But you must believe me when I tell you that I have found it impossible to carry the heavy burden of responsibility and to discharge my duties as King as I would wish to do without the help and support of the woman I love.
>
> And I want you to know that the decision I have made has been mine and mine alone.
>
> This was a thing I had to judge entirely for myself. The other person most nearly concerned has tried up to the last to persuade me to take a different course.
>
> I have made this the most serious decision of my life, only upon the single thought of what would, in the end, be best for all.
>
> This decision has been made less difficult for me by the sure knowledge that my brother, with his long training in the public affairs of this country and with his fine qualities, will be able to take my place forthwith without interruption or injury to the life and progress of the empire, and he has one matchless blessing, enjoyed by so many of you and not bestowed upon me, a happy home with his wife and children.
>
> During these hard days, I have been comforted by Her Majesty, my mother, and by my family. The Ministers of the Crown and in particular Mr. Baldwin, the Prime Minister, have always treated me with full consideration.
>
> There has never been any constitutional difference between me and them and between me and Parliament. Bred in the constitutional traditions by my father, I should never have allowed any such issue to arise.
>
> Ever since I was Prince of Wales, and later on, when I occupied the throne, I have been treated with the greatest kindness by all classes of the people wherever I have lived or journeyed throughout

the empire. For that I am very grateful. I now quit altogether
public affairs and I lay down my burden.

It may be some time before I return to my native land, but I shall
always follow the fortunes of the British race and empire with profound interest and if, at any time in the future, I can be found of
service to His Majesty in a private station I shall not fail.

And now we all have a new King. I wish him and you, his people,
happiness and prosperity with all my heart.

God bless you all! God save the King!

It is somewhat shocking incidentally that a country which traditionally prides itself on free speech and fair play should submit
to the stupid censorship which prevented gramophone records of
this speech being bought anywhere in England. (Of course, the
ruling classes, trying desperately to 'build up' the Duke of York,
did everything possible to bury Edward and his memory at once.)

That night, lonely, Edward left England on a destroyer for France
and exile in the shadows of the Austrian Wienerwald.

Afterthoughts

The whole stupendous business is full of puzzles, paradoxes, and
contradictions. Contradiction Number One: The person of the
King is so unimportant that the transition from Edward to York
proceeds on the surface with the utmost smoothness; yet the person
of the Queen is so critically important that it cost Edward the
throne.

Another is that the Church of England, which forbade this marriage on the issue of divorce, was itself founded by Henry VIII, in a
manner of speaking, to make divorce possible to a monarch.

Another is that England, above all things, is a 'free' country; yet
ruthless censorship of the greatest story of a generation helped
Edward to lose the crown. Incidentally the American Press was
not so wild as many people uncritically imagine. No breath of
scandal about Mrs. Simpson was ever unearthed. She was simply
a lady who had had two husbands. The papers merely went in for
informality and abbreviation, a form of fondness.

Why did it all have to happen? Old Family Doctor Baldwin
said that growing publicity made him go to the King. But everyone
who counted in England had known for at least six months that
Mrs. Simpson's special position greatly improved the character and
happiness of the Monarch and made him a better King. The issue
of censorship is of great importance. If public opinion had been
allowed gradually to form a favourable opinion of Mrs. Simpson

and her excellent influence on the King, there might have been very little scandal. If Mrs. Baldwin had asked her to tea or if Queen Mary had taken her out shopping, the results might have been very different.

It is quite possible that Mrs. Baldwin had a considerable amount to do with shaping her husband's mind.

Of course Edward must have made up his mind very early that he would absolutely marry Mrs. Simpson. Otherwise the story doesn't make sense. He gave up the throne not just for a woman, but for a wife, which is something quite different.

This brings up another terrific contradiction. Edward did not want to live a loose life. He could have had plenty of mistresses. But he wanted marriage and a family. Mr. Baldwin, the moralist, denied him this. He used a moral position to deny the King a moral solution to the problem. It was not immorality, but just the opposite, which provoked the Church of England's wrath.

The case seemingly attaches a stigma to all divorced persons in England. Mrs. Simpson's divorces were strictly conventional and proper. Her ex-husbands 'now living' admire her greatly. Supposing she had been twice widowed. Would that have made a difference? Suppose both her ex-husbands had died the next week. Would the whole crisis have been in vain?

Mr. Baldwin said that no precedent existed for a morganatic marriage. But none existed for an abdication—infinitely more iconoclastic—of this kind.

The quotation from Laertes in the prime minister's speech was striking. Had Mr. Baldwin forgotten how Hamlet ends?

Many people wished the Labour Party had not been so glacially 'constitutional'. The English constitution permits new precedents. If Mr. Attlee and his advisers had had more push and sting and farsightedness they might, from January to October, have got much closer to the King than they did get; the King was not unsympathetic. If, thoroughly warm relations having been established, the Labour leaders had not been quite so stick-in-the-muddish over divorce, they might have been in a position to tell Baldwin that they were willing to go to the country on the issue. Perhaps the Labour Party is too hopelessly bankrupt for revival. But plenty of observers thought they missed a grand chance for resuscitation. Again the business of censorship comes up. The *people*, the bulk of them, knew nothing of the crisis until it was splashed into their faces on December 3rd, and Baldwin certainly never gave them a chance of expressing an opinion.

I do not think that Baldwin, the Archbishop, *The Times*, and so on formed a cabal to squeeze Edward off the throne. Things don't happen that way in England. Nor was Edward's visit to Wales more than a minor embarrassment to the Cabinet. No one important in the ruling classes wanted an abdication, by choice, even though they might have been willing to see Edward put in his place rather sharply, perhaps, and even though they have taken the whole business with almost unseemly grace.

Baldwin's speech was an authentic masterpiece. Its strength derived from the curious Puritan mysticism in his character. Perhaps, though, he left some things out. Edward's speech was a masterpiece, too, and also with great emotional quality.

If Parliament is going to interfere with the private life of a king— even a king cursed with inability to love anyone except a woman who belongs or belonged to someone else—then Parliament should be responsible for his education and upbringing.

The whole thing was a great imperial as well as personal tragedy. Edward's position may be tinged with a certain neuroticism, but surely his abdication represents a tremendous wastage of human material. And the political consequences must be considerable. At once Mr. de Valera squeezed out from under with the governor-general's head. What are the people in India and Africa and the South Seas going to think—if they get a chance—about the value of the Crown as a symbol of imperial unity, when a king in the full spring of his reign tosses it into the junkpile like a can of soup. The political value of monarchy is the assurance it gives—or should give—of fixity, dignity, stability, permanence. This crisis proves that a king, after all, is just a man.

When I was in England there was a good deal of talk about Edward's alleged pro-Germanism. I do not think that this could have become a very important political force. It was based not only on heredity but upon a sort of good-fellowship feeling that the Germans had been treated badly after the War and deserved some sporting aid. The new King probably had much of the same basic impulse and ideas. So one might conclude that the shift from Edward to York will not mean much difference on this important issue. York, however, is much less vivid a character than Edward and will doubtless be more under the influence of his advisers.

Finally, I am curious to hear the Marxist interpretation of all this. What do the economic determinists say of Mrs. Simpson?

George VI

Of the Duke of York, who chose the title George VI, there is very little to be said. He is quite unambitious and dutiful and apparently he did not want the throne; the story is that he suggested a regency for his daughter Elizabeth, but the Cabinet overruled him. So he began what everyone hopes will be a long and very colourless reign. George VI was born in York Cottage in 1895 and served manfully but without brilliance in the familiar Royal curriculum; he fought in the Navy, went to Cambridge, and toured the Empire. In 1923 he married Elizabeth Bowes-Lyon, the daughter of the Earl of Strathmore; thus a Scotswoman is Queen of England. In 1939 he and the Queen visited the United States.

No one with normal standards ever mentioned it in print, but the Archbishop of Canterbury saw fit to give it prominence in a radio broadcast, and so there is no harm now in noting that George VI is afflicted with a stammer. The Archbishop said, 'When his people listen to him, they will note an occasional momentary hesitation in his speech. But he brought it into full control, and to those who hear him it need cause no sort of embarrassment, for it causes none to him who speaks.'

This was the radio sermon in which Canterbury severely rebuked Edward—after his abdication and departure—'for having sought his happiness in a manner inconsistent with Christian principles of marriage and within a social circle whose standards and ways of life are alien to all the best instincts of his people.' Subsequently the Archbishop of York spoke similarly if not quite with such vengeful point. The two speeches provoked bitter reaction. The archbishops, it seemed, after perfect propriety by everyone in the most difficult circumstances, had added a vulgar note when it was all over.

In the spring of 1937 Edward and Mrs. Simpson were quietly married in France. The tumult died, and people of good heart wished them well.

CHAPTER XX

CHAMBERLAIN, BALDWIN, CHURCHILL

THE British prime minister, Arthur Neville Chamberlain, is a business man. He personifies something very striking in the politics of England—the emergence of the middle trading class to a dominant note in government. Baldwin, who preceded him, was an iron manufacturer from the Midlands; Chamberlain spent all his early years in business. He is one of the comparatively few British statesmen of eminence who went neither to Eton nor Harrow, Cambridge nor Oxford. His public school was Rugby, and he never went to University at all.

Shortly after he assumed the prime ministership Chamberlain said, 'Although I cannot boast of the blueness in my veins or of the fame of my forbears, I am yet prouder of being descended from those respectable tradesmen than if my ancestors had worn shining armour and carried great swords.' The prime minister, unlike so many of his predecessors, is not an aristocrat; he is not wealthy or socially ostentatious; he is no student or scholar; he is not a philosopher like Balfour, or a great classicist like Asquith.

Yet Chamberlain is as British as beef. Back in 1730 the Chamberlains were malsters in Wiltshire; the next generation turned to cordwaining (shoemaking and leather work) and five successive Chamberlains were cordwainers. No fewer than eleven members of the family have been at one time or other members of the honourable Cordwainers company. In the past fifty years the family developed high political importance, as everyone knows. Neville is the son of the great Joseph, Gladstone's most formidable opponent, and half-brother of Austen, who died in 1937 after a distinguished life in politics.

Neville was born in Birmingham, which had become the bailiwick of the Chamberlains, in 1869. Thus he is only two years younger than Lord Baldwin, who gave up the premiership because, at his age, the strain of office was too onerous. It is a striking historical curiosity that Neville should finally reach the highest office in the state, which his father just missed, rather than Austen, whom Joseph had trained from boyhood for a political career. Austen

twice gave up his chances to be prime minister. Now Neville, who
was destined for a purely business life, takes on the job.

The dynamic, rugged, almost brutal figure of father Joseph profoundly influenced Neville's character. Joseph was one of the
great radicals of British history, and Neville's preoccupation with
housing and social problems, during his term as minister of health,
was certainly an inherited characteristic. Joseph was the first
modern imperialist, and Neville seemed to be standing in his shoes
at the Imperial Conference in Ottawa which opened the way to
Imperial Preference. Joseph, above all, fought for a tariff programme, and Neville, as chancellor of the exchequer, reversed
British free trade policy after a hundred years and gave Britain a
protective tariff.

Neville began his business career with seven years in the British
West Indies, to take care of his father's sisal plantations there, sisal
being a sort of hemp. He returned to Birmingham, and in 1911
married Miss Annie Cole, who has been his inseparable and devoted
companion ever since. She turned him to politics, he says. In 1915,
a prosperous business man, he was chosen Lord Mayor of Birmingham (his father had been Lord Mayor forty years before); he became
a national figure for the first time when the liberal War prime
minister, Mr. Lloyd George, created a post for him as Director of
the National Services. Lloyd George says that he was a failure at
it; apparently other ministries cut across his unmarked sphere of
authority, and soon he returned to Birmingham.

He first entered parliament in 1918; he was almost fifty before
becoming an M.P. His rise was rapid, because like Bonar Law and
Baldwin he deserted the Lloyd George coalition, and the conservatives, in the wilderness, had few competent men. (Austen stayed
faithful to Lloyd George, and thus missed his chance to become
leader of the conservative party.) Neville was chancellor of the
exchequer for a brief interval in the first Baldwin government—
he had no time to introduce a budget—and then minister of health.
When Baldwin became prime minister for the second time in 1924
he offered Chamberlain the exchequer again. 'What a day!' Chamberlain wrote to Baldwin from Scotland. 'Two salmon this morning, and the offer of the exchequer in the afternoon!' (For Neville
is a notable and enthusiastic fly-fisherman.)

He turned down the exchequer, preferring the more modest post
of health minister. He held this job with one interruption till
1929. His ministry helped build some 900,000 houses, and his

Rating and Valuation Act (1928) and Local Government Act (1929) were widely praised—by Tories. When the National Government was formed he took the exchequer. His budgets were orthodox and parsimonious; he commanded the complete confidence of the plutocracy in the City. His outstanding performance was the introduction of Protection. He was accused of starving the social services; his defenders applauded his 'refusal to be rattled into prodigality'.

His power in cabinet grew and also his reputation in the country; when it became clear that Baldwin would retire his succession to the prime ministry was inevitable; for considerable periods in 1935 and 1936 he was, in fact, prime minister in all but name.

Chamberlain is shy rather than stiff, upright and austere, unimaginative, a convinced democrat, without a particle of the 'personality' distinguishing men like Lloyd George, without a trace of Baldwin's mysticism or Churchill's rhetoric, one who abhors the grandiose, a hard and conscientious worker, sound in health (except for occasional twinges of gout), orderly as a blue-print, he seemed to many to be an efficient—perhaps—but completely uninspired war prime minister, when war broke out in 1939.

He loves gardening, fishing, and nature study; these are his only relaxations. He is a profound bird lover. He installed a bird-bath in the garden between No. 10 and No. 11 Downing Street, and Mrs. Chamberlain recounts that each morning at breakfast they watch the blackbirds bathing. The 1936 report of the Committee of Bird Sanctuaries in Royal Parks contains three observations by the new prime minister. Walking through St. James's Park or the Green Park he saw, on February 13 and 14, 'large flocks of redwings'; on January 16 and February 17, 'pied wagtails, the bird on the latter date being an unusual dark specimen'; on August 1, 'a swift crossing the Horse Guards Parade'.

During one serious financial crisis he found time to write a letter to *The Times* as follows:

'Sir: It may be of interest to record that in walking through St. James's Park to-day I noticed a grey wagtail running about on the now temporarily dry bed of the lake near the dam below the bridge, and occasionally picking small insects out of the cracks in the dam. Probably the occurrence of this bird in the heart of London has been recorded before, but I have not previously noted it in the park.

'P.S. For the purpose of removing doubts, as we say in the House of Commons, I should perhaps add that I mean a grey wagtail not a pied.'

He is exceptionally shy, and his intimate friends are few. Photographs exist showing him masking his face from news cameras. An odd point is that reputedly he enjoys singing negro spirituals, which he learned many years ago in the West Indies. His stepmother, by the way, Mrs. W. H. Carnegie, is American.

He talks no more than is necessary. In his last budget he gave exactly forty-five words to the £350,000,000 Exchange Equalisation Fund, saying that the fund showed a profit, but that its operation 'must continue to be wrapped in mystery'.

During the *Leipzig* crisis during the Spanish war, when hostilities were nearly at the point of spreading, Chamberlain appealed to the House for coolness and caution. Lloyd George jibed at him, 'Any fish can keep a cool head.'

Someone said of him casually once: 'Neville? Town-clerk of Birmingham in a lean year!'

And once it was reported: 'The trouble with Neville is that he has a retail mind for wholesale problems.'

Taking Over

Mr. Chamberlain's cabinet, formed on May 28, 1937, contained few surprises. Ramsay MacDonald stepped out of politics, and Lord Halifax took his post as Lord President of the Council. Sir John Simon, leader of the Liberal Nationals, succeeded Chamberlain as chancellor of the exchequer, and Earl de la Warr, representing National Labour, became Lord Privy Seal. Ministers like Mr. Eden at the Foreign Office, the Marquess of Zetland as secretary for India, W. S. Morrison (a rising star in the Tory party) as minister for agriculture, Malcolm MacDonald (Ramsay's high able and attractive thirty-six-year-old son) as minister for dominions, stayed in their posts. Sir Samuel Hoare took the Home Office, Mr. Duff Cooper was transferred to the Admiralty, and Leslie Hore-Belisha became secretary for war.

Almost at once the new prime minister was confronted with a serious crisis. His budget included a heavy tax on profits, amounting to roughly thirty per cent on increase of profits as compared with the averages for 1933-35. The motives behind this tax, known as the 'National Defence Contribution', were twofold, to check profiteering and to help pay for Britain's gigantic rearmament programme. It aroused a violent storm. The stockmarket collapsed, and in a week prices fell almost £500,000,000. Counsellors from all sides, including even the labour party, begged Chamberlain to withdraw the bill; Mr. Churchill brilliantly made it easy for him to retreat (Churchill quoted an ironic Disraeli to the effect that 'in a democratically governed country, it is sometimes necessary to defer to the opinions of the people'); and, with more grace and suppleness than his opponents believed possible, the new prime minister acquiesced and introduced a new measure.

Overwhelmingly Chamberlain's job was to superintend British rearmament. The armament programme was initiated before he became prime minister, but it became his baby. And a baby of some weight. The cost of rearmament was estimated at no less than £1,500,000,000 for three years. Obviously Britain would not lend itself to such a major operation without good reason. Anyone who chose to look across the channel or in the Mediterranean saw it. The rearmament programme, stirring the country to its vitals, affecting almost every industry, providing for the revitalisation and re-equipment of every branch of the service, including especially the air, became by all odds the most important event in recent British history. But Britain did not rearm—enough.

The new prime minister faced an angry and disordered world in his first months of office. The Spanish war, as we have seen, led to a severe Mediterranean crisis; British merchantmen were torpedoed by pirate submarines, and a British destroyer was attacked. Chamberlain wanted good relations and conciliation with both Germany and Italy. He exchanged cordial notes with Mussolini. Nevertheless he had to join France in patrolling the Mediterranean. Concurrently the Germans continued to kick about, and the Japanese made almost perpetual trouble following the war in China. Hitler was, of course, the biggest and most dangerous problem. The ugly year 1938 brought the seizure of Austria, the Sudeten crisis, and the Munich settlement.

Lord Baldwin

'Is Stanley Baldwin the luckiest of incompetent politicians or the subtlest of competent statesmen?' —Wickham Steed.

'Mr. Baldwin has the Englishman's genius for appearing an amateur in a game in which, in fact, he is a superb professional.' —Harold J. Laski.

'Dictatorship is like a giant beech-tree—very magnificent to look at in its prime, but nothing grows underneath it.' —Stanley Baldwin.

Mr. Baldwin retired from office in 1937 after the coronation of George VI, became a knight of the garter, and accepted an earldom, amid universal praise. He had, as we know, surmounted the terrific crisis of Edward's abdication; he then left public life.   Baldwin's career is one of the most astonishing of modern times.   This man was so obscure twenty years ago that a prominent leader of the Conservative party confessed that he didn't know him by sight when he became prime minister.   Baldwin himself records that a 'well-known lady of society' asked one of his friends, 'Is the new prime minister what you would call an educated man?'

Baldwin was—and is—two things: a sort of John Bull, the embodiment of British solidity and substance; and a sort of Scandinavian mystic, a profound Puritan whose strength of character comes partly from 'spiritual' values.   He was not an 'intellectual'; he was not strikingly clever or energetic; he groped towards solutions of problems instead of thinking them out rationally; he responded to emotion easily, and he could evoke strong emotion in even British listeners.   No one could shake him from his convictions.   'The spiritual home of Stanley Baldwin,' it has been written, 'is the last ditch.'

Baldwin was born at Bewdley in Worcestershire—the constituency he represented for many years—in 1867.   His father, Alfred Baldwin, was chairman of the Great Western Railway and head of Baldwins Ltd., one of the great iron works of England; the Baldwins founded the company and had operated it for four generations, since the middle eighteenth century.   Baldwin is a typical Englishman: that is to say, his mother was of Scotch descent, his father Welsh.   His maternal grandfather, a Wesleyan minister, G. B. Macdonald, was an ardent prohibitionist, who wrote tracts against alcohol.   Of his mother's sisters, one married the painter Burne-Jones, another Sir Edward Poynter, and a third was the mother of Rudyard Kipling.   Baldwin and Kipling are first cousins.

Baldwin has described[1] how he failed in the entrance examinations for the Fourth Form Room at Harrow.   He was disappointed, but, he says, 'I got over it in subsequent years when I learnt that two of the most distinguished men in public life to-day had shared my fate.'   One was F. E. Smith, who later became Lord Birkenhead. Baldwin, reminiscing, said that it was the first time he had ever been classed with first-class brains.   This was, of course, an effective retort to the brilliant but unstable Birkenhead, who had scoffed at Baldwin once, saying his brains were 'second-class'.   After Harrow Baldwin proceeded to Trinity College, Cambridge, where

---

[1] Perhaps not altogether seriously, he wrote once that one of his early ambitions was to be a blacksmith.

Y

he was thoroughly inconspicuous. 'I did nothing at the university,' he records. And in one of his speeches he said, 'I attribute such faculties as I have to the fact that I did not overstrain them in youth.' Far cry from Trotsky or Mussolini!

He entered his father's iron foundry and no record exists of any public speech or activity for almost twenty years. 'I lived in a backwater,' he says. His father died in 1908, vacating the parliamentary seat he had held since 1892; the younger Baldwin, at the age of forty-one, succeeded to it in a by-election. He waited for four months to make his maiden speech in the House of Commons; it was in opposition to the eight-hour day for miners. He was so little noticed that Hansard, as if detecting no difference between father and son, called him 'A. Baldwin' by mistake. In his first nine years in the House he made only *five* speeches.

When the Canadian-born statesman Bonar Law became chancellor of the exchequer in 1916 he made Baldwin his parliamentary private secretary. This, the legend said, was because Bonar Law knew that Baldwin was too honest to intrigue against him, and not clever enough to get into trouble. In reality he was suggested to Bonar Law by a Scottish conservative M.P., J. C. C. Davidson, an old friend of Baldwin's. In 1917 Baldwin was promoted to be financial secretary of the treasury—the threshold to the cabinet—on Davidson's recommendation. Bonar Law, according to Wickham Steed,[1] at first demurred. 'He doubted whether Baldwin deserved ministerial rank or "carried enough guns" for the job.'

After the War occurred the famous incident of the letter to *The Times*, wherein Baldwin announced his intention of anonymously donating one-fifth of his fortune to the state. The letter was signed with the initials 'F.S.T.', and Steed records that Baldwin's card was enclosed; but no one for some time guessed that 'F.S.T.' stood for Financial Secretary of the Treasury, and the editor of *The Times* kept the secret well. The letter is of such importance to an understanding of Baldwin's character that it should be given in full:

> SIR,—It is now a truism to say that in August 1914, the nation was face to face with the greatest crisis in her history. She was saved by the free-will offerings of her people. The best of her men rushed to the colours; the best of her women left their homes to spend and be spent; the best of her older men worked as they had never worked before, to a common end, and with a unity and fellowship as new as it was exhilarating. It may be that in four and a half

[1] In *The Real Stanley Baldwin*, an acute and dispassionate study.

years the ideals of many became dim, but the spiritual impetus of those early days carried the country through to the end.

To-day, on the eve of peace, we are faced with another crisis, less obvious, but none the less searching. The whole country is exhausted. By a natural reaction, not unlike that which led to the excesses of the Restoration after the reign of the Puritans, all classes are in danger of being submerged by a wave of extravagance and materialism. It is so easy to live on borrowed money; so difficult to realise that you are doing so.

It is so easy to play; so hard to learn that you cannot play for long without work. A fool's paradise is only the ante-room to a fool's hell.

How can the nation be made to understand the gravity of the financial situation; that love of country is better than love of money?

This can only be done by example, and the wealthy classes have to-day an opportunity for service which can never recur.

They know the danger of the present debt; they know the weight of it in the years to come. They know the practical difficulties of a universal statutory capital levy. Let them impose upon themselves, each as he is able, a voluntary levy. It should be possible to pay to the Exchequer within twelve months such a sum as would save the taxpayer fifty millions a year.

I have been considering this matter for nearly two years, but my mind moves slowly; I dislike publicity, and I hoped that someone else might lead the way. I have made as accurate an estimate as I am able of the value of my own estate, and have arrived at a total of about £580,000. I have decided to realise twenty per cent of that amount or, say £120,000 which will purchase £150,000 of the new War Loan, and present it to the Government for cancellation.

I give this portion of my estate as a thank offering in the firm conviction that never again shall we have such a chance of giving our country that form of help which is so vital at the present time.

Yours, etc.,   F.S.T.

An unfriendly critic would have to decide for himself what other considerations, if any, beside patriotism, prompted Baldwin to this extraordinary letter. Did he know that the secret of his identity was bound to be revealed, with resultant publicity *wie noch nie*? Had he not, possibly, a pang of conscience that Baldwins Ltd., like all similar firms, had boomed during the War, and was he not protecting himself from a possible charge by his inner self of profiteering?[1]

In 1921 Baldwin reached cabinet rank as president of the Board of Trade; he was as mute in cabinet as in the Commons. Then in the next year the turning-point of his life occurred. The Lloyd

[1] Very few people followed Baldwin's lead in surrendering part of their fortunes to the treasury. The total realised was less than half a million pounds.

George coalition was breaking up; the conservative party split on whether or not to continue support of the prime minister, and Bonar Law and Baldwin led the dissidents who chose revolt. A meeting was called at the Carlton Club to consider the position. In an astonishing speech Baldwin helped to turn the tide against Lloyd George; the Tories withdrew their support from the government, and Lloyd George has been out of office ever since.

Thus one of the most obscure public men in England brought down its most celebrated figure through a largely moral and emotional appeal. The lumbering tortoise tripped the bright sharp fox —and the era of Versailles was over.

Baldwin became chancellor of the exchequer in the conservative Bonar Law cabinet that replaced Lloyd George, largely because in the attenuated Tory ranks (Austen Chamberlain, Churchill, Birkenhead, Sir Robert Horne, stayed out with Lloyd George) no one else was available for the job. He went to America and, faithful to the conviction that the Briton pays his bills, negotiated a debt settlement on what in England were considered extremely onerous terms.[1] Bonar Law, horrified, said that the agreement would depress the standard of living in England for a generation.

Bonar Law was too ill to work and early in 1923 resigned. He recommended no one to be his successor, and the King had to decide between Lord Curzon, the foreign minister, and Baldwin. He chose Baldwin, both on personal grounds and because labour had become the largest opposition party, which made it almost impossible for the prime minister to be in the Lords. Curzon was stunned. 'Not even a public figure,' he wailed, referring to Baldwin. 'A man of no experience. And of the utmost insignificance!' Baldwin received journalists after he had visited the palace. 'I don't need your congratulations,' he said, 'but your prayers.'

'The Methodist Machiavelli'

Baldwin sees few people nowadays; Worcestershire and his new house in Eaton Square circumscribe his life. The chief personal influence on him is undoubtedly his wife, Lucy. Even if he should want to do so, he would have small chance of straying from the strict line of nonconformist probity while his wife was at his side. Once at least it was her firm character which kept him from resigning the leadership of the party, when the attacks of the Press lords

---

[1] And which Neville Chamberlain ten years later repudiated.

had depressed him. The Baldwins' son, Oliver, a vigorous socialist, has been a political grief to them.

Baldwin writes all his own speeches; he is supposed never to read the newspapers; his favourite reading is Thucydides; he takes no exercise; he smokes a pipe. The pipe has become, of course, the symbol of his 'personality', but ten years ago, before the Baldwin legend grew, caricatures usually portrayed him pipeless. He always has enjoyed a pipe; now he *has* to smoke one, on all occasions.

'The pose of simplicity,' Professor Laski wrote, 'which Mr. Baldwin affects ought to deceive no one; a simple man has never been prime minister of England. His pigs and his pipe are simply the technique of propaganda. Like the orchid of Mr. Chamberlain or the ringlets of Disraeli, they create an image which the multitude can remember, and they give a satisfaction to innumerable followers who believe that a common interest in pigs and pipes is a permanent basis of political adequacy.'

Most of his life Baldwin has seemed to show bad conscience about the responsibilities of wealth. He opposed the eight-hour day; but he paid out of his own pocket the wages of workmen at Baldwins Ltd., during a post-War stoppage. He is apt to think of industrial management as a personal responsibility of employer to labour, as a manorial business within family walls. His government passed the Trade Union Law of 1927, 'the first legislation hostile to trade unions in over a century of British history'; but his extreme Tory opponents have called him a socialist. Steed records as characteristic 'both of his generosity and his love of doing good by stealth' a remarkable incident when Baldwin, tramping in Gloucestershire, overheard two old ladies discussing how they could scrape enough money together to maintain an asylum for feeble-minded girls. He collected two hundred dirty one-pound notes, wrapped them in a bit of old newspaper, and sent them to the ladies with a purposely badly-written letter as a gift of 'a passing vagabond'.

While he was prime minister he had his salary as first lord of the treasury, £5,000 per year; but he had to live, he announced, on capital and borrowings. In May 1928, he said: 'For every shilling I had when I took office I now have something less than a penny,' and his remark that he exists 'on an overdraft' has been widely quoted. Yet, according to the *Sunday Express*, in 1935 he held 181,526 ordinary shares in Baldwins Ltd., and 37,591 preference shares, which at the market price at the time were worth roughly £100,000. No one, of course, knows what his obligations may be. He has no expensive hobbies.

A familiar criticism of Baldwin is that he is lazy. Another is that he is sly. Another is that he is too supine, too 'passive'. When really roused, however, he can make mincemeat of his enemies. It takes a great deal of unpleasantness to stir him to protect himself; when he does so, he is irresistible. Twice he has surmounted major crises within the party, once when the Press lords sought by every possible means to deprive him of the leadership; second, a less overtly dramatic but inwardly more serious struggle, when Churchill and some of the greatest dignitaries of the party sought to oust him because of his liberal attitude to India—liberal, at least, compared to theirs.

He moves slowly; but he *can* move. Consider, for instance, his activity in the abdication crisis, described above. Another item: In November 1935 he dropped Lord Londonderry from the cabinet; and the great reception in Londonderry House traditionally given on the eve of the opening of Parliament did not occur. Londonderry had been severely heckled during the election campaign for a remark he had made as air minister and which pursued him with ghoulish zest. Referring to the disarmament conference, he told the House of Lords, 'I had the utmost difficulty at that time, amid the public outcry, in preserving the use of the bombing aeroplane even on the frontier of the Middle East and India.'

Baldwin disappointed the hopes of that rare adventurer Winston Churchill of inclusion in the cabinet reconstruction of 1935. Churchill's speeches in the campaign were in his best flamboyant style, and he pointed vigorously to the peril of German rearmament. But Baldwin, cautious, knew that however valuable Churchill would be in vitalising matters of defence, his presence in the government might be a diplomatic liability. Baldwin did not want, at that time, to confess to a full-blast arms policy. Also his majority was so great that he didn't need the support of Churchill's wing of diehards, and he was probably jealous of Churchill's superior ability.

Baldwin is no backslapper; he has described his discomfort at the electioneering expected from him in his first contest and which he erased from his soul by reading Horace or the Odyssey every evening. He dislikes rhetoric; but he is capable of a good deal of it. He confesses that he is of a 'somewhat flabby nature', who always 'prefers agreement to disagreement'; but the Quaker strain in his blood would make him go to the stake, he says, rather than give up a principle. Rather enviously he quotes Seneca to the effect that 'a strong man matched with fortune is a sight for the gods to witness'. And he says, 'Success is not necessarily a matter to which you should devote your whole life.'

Baldwin seldom promises anything unless he is sure he can make the promise good. This was one source of his power. He is almost quixotically generous, and his loyalty is staunch; never did he intrude on Ramsay MacDonald's prerogatives as prime minister during the first phase of the National Government, although he, Baldwin, held the real power. His political discernment is vivid; he was one of the first to seize on and dramatise the new phase of international relations which accompanied Hitler's rise to power, by his speech stating that Britain's frontier had become the Rhine. Finally, he stays put.

One of his early speeches, delivered to the Classical Association in 1926, gives insight to his character:

> 'I remember many years ago standing on the terrace of a beautiful villa near Florence. It was a September evening, and the valley below was transfigured in the long, horizontal rays of the declining sun. And then I heard a bell, such a bell as never was on land or sea, a bell whose every vibration found an echo in my innermost heart. I said to my hostess, "That is the most beautiful bell I have ever heard." "Yes," she replied, "it is an English bell." And so it was. For generations its sounds had gone out over English fields, giving the hours of work and prayer to English folk from the tower of an English abbey, and then came the Reformation, and some wise Italian bought the bell . . . and sent it to the Valley of the Arno, where after four centuries it stirred the heart of a wandering Englishman and made him sick for home.'

Three Times Prime Minister

His first premiership, in 1923, lasted less than a year; he was feeling his way, with only a slim majority, and decided to go to the country—to the horror of most of his colleagues—on the issue of protection. The country was not ready for tariffs; he was turned out of office. It was during this administration that he made the remarkable statement, 'Well, having been prime minister will have been an interesting experience to have had.'

Ramsay MacDonald formed the first Labour Government and lasted only a year; the Zinoviev letter crushed him and Baldwin returned to the premiership with a tremendous majority; his first act was to forgive his enemies in the party, and bring Churchill, Birkenhead, Austen Chamberlain back from the wilderness and give them his best portfolios. He was in office from 1924 to 1929, by which time his majority had dwindled away; he went to the country on a 'Safety First' slogan—which was strange politics—and was roundly beaten.

The 1924-29 administration has lessons for the student. The prime minister, who hardly seemed interested enough in his job to keep a grip on things, succumbed to inertia, to muddle, to bad advice. He mishandled the coal situation, which is insoluble except on the basis of nationalisation of royalties, and reaped the harvest of the General Strike. He flirted with the project to 'reform' the House of Lords, viz., make it stronger, so that J. L. Garvin covered acres of space in the *Observer* calling his government 'Doomed!' His foreign policy was a glowing list of blunders. His government threw over the Geneva protocol, encouraged Mussolini in Albania and Abyssinia, signed the Kellogg Pact only after weakening it, annoyed the United States by the Anglo-French naval compromise, and botched the Geneva naval conference so badly that Lord Cecil resigned in protest.

But when Baldwin became prime minister again in 1935 he had an immense majority once more. His manœuvre in calling an election on November 14, in the very middle of a grave international crisis when the people were inevitably bound to support a strong, 'safe', government, was called vulgar; but it was, of course, shrewd politics. And the results were a great tribute to Baldwin personally. The people were not voting so much for the Tory party or for the National Government; they were voting for a man. Then in 1937 after the abdication and the coronation he resigned. He has lived in strict political retirement—save for occasional speeches in the Lords—ever since.

England, he said once, has never sought a second Cromwell. But it may yearn for other Baldwins.

The Incomparable Winston

'There is not much collective security in a flock of sheep on the way to the butcher.'   —WINSTON CHURCHILL.

I have mentioned Mr. Churchill often in these pages, and I shall mention him often again. This is inevitable, since he is the most vital, pungent, and potentially powerful figure in British public life to-day. Chamberlain is prime minister. But warfare is a dynamic process, and just as Lloyd George replaced Asquith in 1916, so the ineluctable force of events may eventually push Churchill into Chamberlain's seat. When war came in 1939, the nation demanded that Churchill—who had been in the wilderness for ten years—be included in the government. And he became First Lord of the Admiralty, the same position he had held in 1914.

Churchill's squat figure has Renaissance quality. He is omniverous for experience; he has a swashbuckling love of life and experiment; he is basically an artist and at the same time a builder; he is incredibly versatile. Like the giants of seventeenth-century Italy he can turn his pliable and powerful fingers to almost anything. He has been a war correspondent, soldier, historian, sportsman, water-colour painter, politician, lecturer, administrator, journalist, and bricklayer. His oratory has stimulated thousands; his politics have maddened, perplexed, or encouraged millions. He has scarcely been idle five minutes in his life. Two supreme attributes—energy and abstract *talent*—merge to make his character and career the restless dramatic success they have been.

He is an artist, yes—few men write better English prose—but also he is a man of action. Consider the following passage:

> 'Once again I was on the hard, crisp desert, my horse at a trot. I had the impression of scattered Dervishes running to and fro in all directions. Straight before me a man threw himself on the ground. The reader must remember that I had been trained as a cavalry soldier to believe that if ever cavalry broke into a mass of infantry, the latter would be at their mercy. My first idea therefore was that the man was terrified. But simultaneously I saw the gleam of his curved sword as he drew it back for a ham-stringing cut. I had room and time enough to turn my pony out of his reach, and leaning over on the off side I fired two shots into him at about three yards. As I straightened myself in the saddle, I saw before me another figure with uplifted sword, I raised my pistol and fired. So close were we that the pistol itself actually struck him. Man and sword disappeared below and behind me. . . . I pulled my horse into a walk and looked around again.'

No, this is not a paragraph from an old-time thriller by Henty or even part of the script of a Hollywood Beau Geste. It is by the Rt. Hon. Winston Leonard Spencer Churchill, M.P., P.C., His Britannic Majesty's First Lord of the Admiralty. It describes the youthful author's experiences in the cavalry charge at Omdurman (in 1898), when Kitchener destroyed the forces of the Khalifa, and is taken from *My Early Life*, Churchill's fascinating autobiography.[1] Proceed:

'In one respect a cavalry charge is very like ordinary life. So long as you are all right, firmly in your saddle, your horse in hand, and well armed, lots of enemies will give you a wide berth. But as soon as you have lost a stirrup, have a rein cut, have dropped your weapon, are wounded, or your horse is wounded, then is the moment when from all quarters enemies rush upon you. I pulled my horse up and looked about me. There was a mass of Dervishes about forty or fifty yards away on my left. . . . They seemed wild with excitement, dancing about on their feet, shaking their spears up and down. The whole scene seemed to flicker. . . . Where was my troop? Where were the other troops of the squadron? Within a hundred yards of me I could not see a single officer or man. What a fool I was to loiter like this in the midst of the enemy! . . .

'The other three troops of the squadron were reforming close by. Suddenly in the midst of the troop up sprang a Dervish. How he got there I do not know. He must have leaped out of some scrub or hole. All the troopers turned upon him thrusting with their lances; but he darted to and fro causing for the moment a frantic commotion. Wounded several times, he staggered towards me raising his spear. I shot him at less than a yard. He fell on the sand, and lay there dead. How easy to kill a man! But I did not worry about it. I found I had fired the whole magazine of my Mauser pistol, so I put in a new clip of ten cartridges before thinking of anything else.'

Churchill's blood is not merely blue, but practically purple. He was born, on November 30, 1874, in Blenheim Castle, the son of Lord Randolph Churchill and grandson of the seventh Duke of Marlborough. His mother was, as everyone knows, American; Winston—though on many occasions he has seemed to dislike things American—is half-American by birth. His mother, an extraordinarily beautiful and magnetic woman, was the daughter of Leonard W. Jerome, a famous New Yorker of the 60's and 70's, a part owner of the *New York Times* and other newspapers and one of the fathers of American sport and horse-racing.

So far as I know, no good biography of Winston Churchill exists. His own books—from *My Early Life* straight through the six massive volumes of *The World Crisis* and *The Aftermath*—are of course tantamount to a biography, though we have no detailed

[1] This book is my source for much of this account of Churchill's youth. The extracts are made by kind permission of Messrs. Thornton Butterworth, Ltd.

ecord from roughly 1902 to 1911. They are indispensable to the
tudent, and marvellous reading besides. But I wish that some
ntelligent modern biographer with a gift for psychological insight
nd the patience to read a million words of documents—also one
vho has not succumbed too deeply to the post-War disillusion that
»rings the 'debunking' spirit to everything, including science, the-
logy, and politics—would tackle the formidable job of writing a
ull critical biography of Winston. Treasure in limitless profusion
waits him.

The pattern of a man's career, to an extraordinary degree, is
vritten in infancy and childhood. No man ever escapes himself, it
eems; no man ever changes himself completely. At birth, or before,
haracteristics are implanted which are like the metal divisions in
·loisonné. Later, the colour, the enamel, is filled in, and the
urface texture acquires refinement. Every man is born with a
nental and psychological as well as a physical skeleton. The bony
tructure of the mind, the character, is there along with ribs and
aw-bone.

Churchill's childhood is a forecast of his whole career. He lived
dangerously from the earliest time. Who but Winston would have
nad concussion of the brain at four and a half, as a result of being
:hrown from a donkey? Who but Winston would recall with
extreme vividness—as his very first memories, memories of events
:hat took place before he was five—such things as a Viceroy, 'a great
black crowd', processions of terrorists and revolutionaries, and
'scarlet soldiers on horseback'. At five, he sees a white stone tower
in Dublin, and is told that Oliver Cromwell blew it up. Winston
writes:[1] 'I understood definitely that he (Cromwell) had blown up
all sorts of things, and was therefore a very great man.' From the
beginning, he loved conversation, audacity, experiment, and soldiers.

He adored his mother, one of the most brilliant women of the
time; she was his 'fairy princess, a radiant being possessed of limitless riches and power'. With his father he was never close, though
he admired him passionately. He records that he never had more
than 'three or four' really intimate conversations with him. His
father died when Winston was twenty-one, wrecking the son's
hopes that they would work and fight together in the House of
Commons. Winston found his mother an 'ardent ally' when Randolph died. 'She was still at forty young, beautiful, and fascinating.

[1] *My Early Life.*

We worked together on even terms, more like brother and siste
than mother and son.'[1]

Young Churchill's scholastic records and achievements shoul
be a considerable spiritual solace to those young men who, eve
nowadays, dislike school and do badly at it. He loathed—and t
this day loathes—the Classics; he found Latin a bore and Greek
useless luxury; he detested—and still detests—mathematics. H
was the bottom boy in his class at Harrow, where he was acutel
unhappy; he failed three times in the entrance examinations fo
Sandhurst (the officers training school) before passing finally afte
merciless cramming. His father once saw him, when he was a
schoolboy, playing with his 1,500 toy soldiers, arrayed with th
utmost flowery precision and exactitude. Lord Randolph asked
him if he would like to go into the army. Winston said, 'Yes.
The boy thought that his father really appreciated his talent fo
military things. But, he records, Lord Randolph suggested mili
tary life because he didn't think he was clever enough for any othe
career.

(But during his school years Winston showed other qualities. H
learned to like English prose. He learned to stay on horses. H
learned to speak. It is of considerable interest that, even as a boy
he dictated essays, walking up and down the room, pacing, dictating
exactly as he paces and dictates now.)

At twenty-three Winston wrote a novel, called *Savrola*. It wa
published and still exists, but copies are very rare. Its theme wa
that of a liberal politician who, in an imaginary Balkan state, attack
and overthrows a conservative dictatorship—to be overthrown in
turn by a socialist revolution! It is extraordinary that Winston, in
1897, was thinking in such terms. The climax of the book—an
other highly revealing psychological detail—is an attempt by a fleet
of battleships to force 'a sort of Dardanelles' in order to win final
victory over the opponent revolutionaries. Exactly eighteen years
later Winston Churchill conceived the real Dardanelles campaign,
and sent the British fleet to attack the real Dardanelles.

After Sandhurst young Churchill was commissioned in a fashionable cavalry regiment (much to the distress of his father who had
an infantry regiment picked out), and his life as a soldier began.
At once—typically—he managed to get leave, and went to Cuba
to inspect the rebellion which led to the Spanish-American war.
His sympathies were with the Cubans; he fought however with the

[1] *My Early Life.*

Spaniards. On his twenty-first birthday—again typically!—he for the first time in his life heard gunfire. He returned to England, having won a decoration for bravery, and went to India with his regiment. Here he spent two exciting years. He played expert polo, fought in the Mamund valley, learned to like whisky, wrote a book about the Malakand Field Force, contrived to get work as a newspaper correspondent at the same time that he was an officer —something quite unprecedented—and by the exercise of every possible artifice succeeded in joining the Tirah Expeditionary Force that went into action on the North-West frontier.

But at the same time, during those Indian years, Winston—no one ever dreamed of calling him anything but Winston—was learning, not merely to act, but something more important—to think. He became suddenly aware that he had had a very bad education indeed. So, while his fellow officers napped in the hot afternoons, he began to read. He thirsted for books and knowledge as a sponge thirsts for water. His mother sent him cargoes of books: for the first time in his life, he read serious books seriously—everything from Plato to Gibbons and back again. Having learned to read, he set himself to learn to write. He studied the art of the English sentence, and found that 'paragraphs must fit on to one another like the automatic couplings of railway carriages'. When, subsequently he returned to England, he determined to go to school all over again, and sought to enter Oxford; but he was too old, and Oxford wouldn't take him.

Then came two experiences in Africa. He joined Kitchener's expedition down the Nile and fought at Omdurman. He wrote a book on this campaign, *The River War*, which is still its standard history, and then quit the army. But in 1899 he was back in Africa again, this time as a war correspondent for the London *Morning Post*, at a very large salary indeed for those days. He participated in the great adventure of the armoured train (November 15, 1899), and was captured by the Boers. The man who captured him, by remarkable coincidence, happened to be a Boer officer named Botha, who in later years rose in South African politics exactly as did Churchill in British politics; the two, captor and prisoner, became the warmest friends. Churchill escaped from confinement at Pretoria by a combination of luck, ingenuity, daring, and intuition. Once more he returned to England. This time he found himself a national hero.

Already he had stood for parliament once, and had been defeated.

He ran again. And in 1901—he was now twenty-seven years old—
he became Conservative M.P. for Oldham. Churchill determined
to settle down, and devote his whole life to politics. And he has
devoted his whole life to politics ever since, except for interstices
filled with bricklaying, the study of military science, half a dozen
lecture tours, plenty of travel, water-colour painting, and the
writing of nineteen big books. When his political career began he
needed something that had not bothered him before—money. He
was by no means rich, as wealth goes in aristocratic England. But
money had never been an urgent preoccupation. Now he wanted
money. So in five months he proceeded to make £10,000 on a lecture tour!

Churchill's career as a politician after 1901 is so well-known that
it scarcely needs repeating. He changed party three times. This
is as if, say, Mr. Roosevelt had begun life as a democrat, spent long
years in office as a republican, and then turned democrat again—
again to receive high office. Winston was a conservative from 1899
to 1906. Then, disagreeing with his party on Free Trade, he crossed
the floor of the House—amidst a blast of objurgation—and became
a liberal. It was as a liberal that he participated in the 1914 war
cabinet. In 1924 he became a conservative again, and crossed the
floor again. Winston's great reputation for 'unreliability', the deep-
seated antipathy with which both diehard Tories and surviving pure
liberals held him for years, was not caused so much by his audacity,
or even his reputation for 'cleverness', but because he had so signally
changed his party spots, deserted his party line.

Churchill's first cabinet post came early. He was president of
the Board of Trade in 1908, when he was only thirty-four. He
became Home Secretary in 1910, and First Lord of the Admiralty
in 1911, which post he held till 1915. Asquith chose him for the
Admiralty because, in the growing international storm, his energy
and fruitfulness were necessary to revitalise the Fleet. Churchill
developed battleships of the *Queen Elizabeth* class, and had the
Fleet mobilised for instant action when war came. It is hopelessly
unsatisfactory to attempt even to mention the drama, the excitement, the spectacular crowded activity, of Churchill's Great War
years. One must read his own *World Crisis*. Even to summarise
briefly such episodes as the Antwerp and the Dardanelles expedi-
tions would take pages.

When the Dardanelles campaign failed he resigned from the
government almost in disgrace—though the failure was not his

fault—and went to France as an active infantry officer. Lloyd George brought him back in 1917 as minister of munitions. Then he served in turn as war minister, air minister, and secretary for the colonies. Again, these years, crammed and packed with events, bursting with decisive action, cannot be part of my story here. They are in the history books. Churchill was a major force in settling the Irish question; humanely, he sought to lift the blockade of Germany; he promoted allied intervention in Russia; he 'invented' the country of Transjordan. In 1924 he became chancellor of the exchequer—the boy who could not understand mathematics! —under Baldwin in calmer days, and held this post until 1929. He went out when Labour came in, and the ensuing National Government would not have him. For ten years he retired into the wilderness. But it was a wilderness which he tidied and cultivated neatly. He wrote his books, worked over his ideas, learned to relax—a little —and improved his mind.

During the ten years 1929-39 Churchill—who was becoming greyer, stouter, solider—remained, of course, a Member of Parliament. He became the leader of a small dissident band of last ditch imperialists who bitterly, for long years, fought Baldwin's quasi-liberal India Bill. Then in about 1933, from his lonely and isolated corner seat, Churchill turned into the great Cassandra. He—almost alone among British politicians—sensed the peril to Britain in the rise of Hitler. For six years, day in, day out, he spoke, wrote, argued, exhorted, about Hitler's dangerousness, exploring especially every phase of German rearmament. Few paid him much attention. But gradually his hammering voice became heard. His two compilations of speeches in the middle 30's, *Arms and the Covenant* and *Step by Step*, are outstanding examples of political realism and prescience.

Then when war came, in September 1939, Prime Minister Chamberlain accepted the inevitable, and Churchill re-entered the cabinet.

.   .   .   .

To-day, at sixty-five, Churchill looks at least ten years younger than he is. And, of course, considering the tradition of venerableness in British politics—and considering his great vitality—sixty-five is mere babyhood. His cheeks are a clear child's pink, his sparse reddish hair is curly at the edges. He has extremely pale but very bright blue eyes. His manner, receiving someone, is at first deliberate. Those very bright eyes survey the visitor with a curious

mixture of patience, reserved amusement, and curiosity.   When
Churchill begins to talk, with an odd clucking intonation, the words
roll and bounce.   He chooses words, even in conversation, as a
lapidary sets gems.   He loves rhetoric, and is a formidable phrase
maker.   In a forty-minute talk I had with him, he used at least one
word I had never heard aloud before, 'marplot', and invented one
phrase—'a mystery inside a mystery inside a mystery'—that he later
elaborated in a radio address.   His talk is so good, so full of balance
and antithesis, and so incredibly fluent, that one longs for a secret
dictaphone to take it down.

But Mr. Churchill can listen too.   And good listening is, in a
way, the basis of good conversation.   He asks more questions than
he answers.

As to his inveterate habit of rhetoric—in writing as well as speech
—consider the famous and perhaps too purple passage about Lenin
from *The Aftermath*:

> 'Implacable vengeance, rising from a frozen pity in a tranquil,
> sensible, matter-of-fact, good-humoured integument!   His weapon
> logic; his mood opportunist.   His sympathies cold and wide as the
> Arctic Ocean; his hatreds tight as the hangman's noose.   His purpose
> to save the world: his method to blow it up . . . but a good husband;
> a gentle guest; happy, his biographers assure us, to wash up the
> dishes or dandle the baby; as mildly amused to stalk a capercailzie
> as to butcher an Emperor. . . .   Confronted with the need of
> killing any particular person he showed reluctance—even distress.
> But to blot out a million, to proscribe entire classes—these were
> sublime abstractions. . . .
>
> 'Lenin was the Grand Repudiator.   He repudiated everything.
> He repudiated God, King, Country, morals, treaties, debts, rents,
> interest, the laws and customs of centuries, all contracts written or
> implied, the whole structure—such as it is—of human society.   In
> the end he repudiated himself. . . .   He alone could have led
> Russia into the enchanted quagmire; he alone could have found the
> way back to the causeway.   He saw; he turned; he perished.   The
> strong illuminant that guided him was cut off at the moment when
> he had turned resolutely for home.   The Russian people were left
> floundering in the bog.   Their worst misfortune was his birth;
> their next worse—his death.'

His wit and irony, rather heavy sometimes, are famous.   Once
he called Chamberlain 'that undertaker from Birmingham'.   Once
he wrote a letter to *The Times* in answer to Lord Hugh Cecil, who
had been denouncing Italy, France, Japan, Soviet Russia, and Germany with equal firmness.   Winston wrote, 'It must be very painful

to a man of Lord Hugh Cecil's natural benevolence and human charity to find so many of God's children wandering simultaneously so far astray. . . .' Then he points out that the French don't deserve as much censure as the others. He concludes, 'In these circumstances I would venture to suggest to my noble friend, whose gifts and virtues I have all my life admired, that some further refinement is needed in the catholicity of his condemnations.'[1]

In December 1937, during a debate on non-intervention in Spain, Mr. Churchill had good fun with Mussolini. The British and French had recently managed to check activity by pirate (Italian) submarines in the Mediterranean. The Italians then decided to join the piracy control. Mr. Churchill said, as reported by *The Times* (December 22, 1937):

> 'In this connection he (Mr. Churchill) must pay his tribute to Signor Mussolini, who joined the common exertions of the Mediterranean powers—(laughter) and whose prestige and authority by the mere terror of his name quelled the wicked depradations of these pirates. (Loud laughter.) Since the days of Caesar himself there had been no more salutary clearance of pirates from the Mediterranean. (Laughter.)'

One of the most delightful of Mr. Churchill's ironical sallies came many years ago, when he discovered—just as he himself was becoming a well-known author—that an American novelist, the author of *Richard Carvel, Coniston,* and so on, also bore the name Winston Churchill. He wrote to his namesake as follows:

London, June 7, 1899.
> 'Mr. Winston Churchill presents his compliments to Mr. Winston Churchill, and begs to draw his attention to a matter which concerns them both. He has learnt from the Press notices that Mr. Winston Churchill proposes to bring out another novel, entitled *Richard Carvel,* . . . Mr. Winston Churchill is also the author of a novel now being published in serial form. . . . He has no doubt that Mr. Winston Churchill will recognise from this letter—if indeed by no other means—that there is grave danger of his works being mistaken for those of Mr. Winston Churchill. He feels sure that Mr. Winston Churchill desires this as little as he does himself. In future to avoid mistakes as far as possible, Mr. Winston Churchill has decided to sign all published articles, stories, or other works, "Winston Spencer Churchill," and not "Winston Churchill" as formerly. He trusts that this arrangement will commend itself to Mr. Winston Churchill, and he ventures to suggest . . . that both Mr. Winston Churchill and Mr. Winston Churchill should insert a

[1] London *Times,* May 12, 1936.

z

short note in their respective publications explaining to the public which are the works of Mr. Winston Churchill and which those of Mr. Winston Churchill. . . .'

Mr. Winston Churchill, the American, replied in kind, with equal grace and charm.

Sir Edward Marsh, who was for many years Churchill's private secretary, tells in his engaging memoirs, *A Number of People*, a good many Churchill anecdotes. Once Wedgwood Benn, a small man, rose in the Commons and spluttered with indignation at something Winston had said. Churchill replied, 'My Right Honourable Friend should not develop more indignation than he can contain.' Once he almost missed a train. Mrs. Churchill was alarmed. But Marsh simply remarked, 'Winston is such a sportsman, he always gives the train a chance to get away.' Once Marsh accompanied him on an election campaign in the Midlands. Winston walked out in the slums. ' "Fancy," he said, "living in one of these streets —never seeing anything beautiful—never eating anything savoury —*never saying anything clever!*" '

Churchill's attitudes are, indeed, sometimes juvenile. He has once or twice been somewhat ridiculous, for instance when he summoned artillery—way back in 1911—to blast some miserable anarchists out of a house in Whitechapel. For years—not now—it seemed that he stood always on the wrong side of great social issues. He was against the suffragists. He was against a liberal constitution for India. He was against every shade and aspect of even the very mild brand of socialism advocated by the British Labour Party. He was against the working classes. During the General Strike, when he edited the official government newspaper, he behaved like a schoolboy. In 1919—as if the world were not sufficiently exhausted by war—he was the moving spirit behind the utterly useless and disastrous intervention of the allies in Russia.

Sometimes, when one inspects his leading political ideas, one feels that they are the ideas of an incredibly talented, wilful, badly educated child. He seems planted in the nineteenth century, while the world has moved on. For years, he adored warfare. He blamed 'democracy' for taking the fun, the style, the glamour out of war. He writes of the Mamund campaign, 'Sir Bindon sent orders that we were to stay in the Mamund valley and lay it waste with fire and sword in vengeance. This accordingly we did.' He is a convinced constitutionalist and democrat, but elections have at times bored him. He wrote in *My Early Life*: 'I have fought up to the present fourteen contested elections, which take about a month of one's life apiece. It is melancholy, when one reflects upon our brief span, to think that no less than fourteen months of life have been passed in this wearing clatter.'

Winston has an estate, Chartwell, in Kent, twenty miles from London where he likes to spend most of his time. He has built pools, gardens, brick walls, fences, and several small structures with his own hands. For years his favourite exercise was bricklaying; for a time he belonged to the bricklayers trade union, though his hatred of socialists was ferocious. He wears blue overalls, smokes his inevitable long dark cigar, hunches himself before the wall, mixes the mortar, slaps the bricks into place. For relaxation he paints. There have been several exhibitions of his work, for which he uses the name Charles Morin.

Churchill's health is good—though for years he suffered from a dislocated shoulder incurred in an accident in India—and his stamina is sufficient for his task. He records that by taking a short nap every afternoon, he can increase his working day by two hours. He is something of a sybarite in food and drink; he loves the good things of life. Lord Birkenhead once said of him, 'It is simple to satisfy Winston; he demands only the best.' The best things cost money, and thus he works so hard. His income as journalist and lecturer probably averages £20,000 per year. Of this he spends plenty.

He has a very warm family sense; years ago he married Miss Clementine Ogilvy Hozier, and their life has been very happy. She was—and is—an exceptionally beautiful and talented woman. They have one son and three daughters. The son, Randolph, has already had a stormy career in politics—he fought several by-elections unsuccessfully—and journalism. Until war broke out, he wrote for the 'Londoners Diary' in the *Evening Standard*; when war came, he joined up. One of the Churchill daughters, Sarah, an actress, married an American actor, Vic Oliver. Another married a rising young M.P., Duncan Sandys.

When one attempts to list Churchill's qualities and the sources of his power, the first item to come to mind is, perhaps, imagination. For instance, he was largely responsible for the evolution of the tank, which revolutionised modern warfare and helped enable the allies to break the deadlock in the west in 1918. Associated with his brilliantly fertile imagination is the quality of foresight. He was not only the first British politician to appraise correctly

Hitler's power; he was the first to see that this made big-scale British rearmament inevitable, and from the earliest days he appealed for it.

Another source of power is his pertinacity. His powerful, stocky body with the very big head bears a not unreasonable resemblance to that of a bulldog. His escapades seeking permission to join Kitchener's force in Africa, when every obstacle—including Kitchener's own acute personal distaste—confronted him, when he was repeatedly checked and rebuffed, are an early case in point. Nothing could stop him in his almost comically stubborn and dogged determination to get what he wanted. As to his courage, it has never been questioned. Once, when a boy, he spent three months in bed, as a result of injuries suffered when he jumped thirty feet off a bridge, in order to avoid capture in a game of hide-and-seek.

His energy, too, is prodigious. On finishing his huge Life of Marlborough, he plunged at once into a long history of the Anglo-Saxon peoples, though he was continuing his ordinary work in parliament and politics. He is willing to do any kind of spade work. For years, because he was afraid he did not speak fluently, he committed to memory every speech he delivered. Hard work—as well as a natural genius for language—contributed to his present almost excessively accomplished oratory.

Again, his political realism has always been acute. He could see fundamentals, even if they were distasteful. After the occupation of Prague, for instance, in 1939, he would instantly have made a pact with Russia, on almost any terms, despite his hatred of the Bolsheviks. His first radio speech to the people of America, in October 1939, was a masterpiece of political acumen, though he did inadvertently offend some Americans in the south by his innocent enough peroration about the Civil War.

Finally, he is a supreme and sagacious individualist. He wrote once that he always had a tendency 'to swim against the stream'.

. . .   .

When I saw Mr. Churchill shortly after the outbreak of war in September 1939 it was understood that I would not, of course, quote him. But there can be no harm in saying that I asked him two main questions. First, How does the war of 1939 differ from that of 1914? Second, How strong are the allies vis-à-vis the Germans? Mr. Churchill's answers were vivid, perspicacious, and confident in the extreme.

Behind his desk in the great Admiralty room is a large chart inside a folding wooden frame. Mr. Churchill explained that he had ordered this chart to be constructed in 1911, when he first took charge of the Admiralty, so that he could see every day the position of every German battleship. When he returned to office in 1939, the first thing he did was to see if that old chart was still there. It was. And no one had looked at it in twenty years.

One thing about Churchill is unique. He is the only top rank cabinet officer or leader on either side during the last war who survives to hold important office to-day.

CHAPTER XXI

MEN OF WHITEHALL

The Débâcle of MacDonald

'What we have to do is to pile up and pile up and pile up the income of the industry in this way and that way and the other way.'
—MR. MACDONALD, quoted in the *Manchester Guardian*.

'Because thou art neither cold nor hot will I spew thee out of my mouth.'
—Quoted at Seaham Harbour by LADY HOUSTON.

JAMES RAMSAY MACDONALD, the creator and the despoiler of the labour party, despicable or heroic as you choose, a man of Olympian or Stygian loneliness, was born in Scotland in 1866 of obscure parentage. The fact of his humble origin has been of profound psychological importance in his career. All his life he sought compensation for the miserable poverty of his boyhood. When, according to Philip Snowden, he became prime minister of the National Government and chuckled, 'To-morrow every duchess in London will be wanting to kiss me,' he was no more than finally squaring the accounts of his arduous and unhappy youth.

The record of his career until and during the War was conspicuously honourable. He left school in Scotland when he was fourteen to earn a living; penniless in London, he found a job in a warehouse, working as a clerk for 12s. 6d. a week; he studied science and economics at night. On August 3, 1914, he had courage enough to stand up against the whole House of Commons and denounce the War. He seemingly ruined his political career; some extreme Tories continued for years to print the socialist manifesto, which he prominently signed, urging support of the Russian revolution in 1917. During the War a ship's company threatened to strike rather than carry MacDonald, a militant pacifist, to the Stockholm peace congress. He was forced to resign from his golf club at Lossiemouth; his meetings had to be protected by the police. And, be it noted, in those days the bulk of the socialist party deserted *him*.

336

Twice MacDonald owed great good fortune to chance. In 1900, the story goes, 'Mr. James R. MacDonald' was elected secretary of the newly-formed labour representative committee, which later became the labour party. But many of the delegates, according to the *Daily Herald*, were under the impression that they were voting for a *different* MacDonald—one Jimmie MacDonald, a prominent member of the London trades union council. The name proposed was J. MacDonald. Two J. MacDonalds were present. Mr. J. Ramsay MacDonald won.

More than half a generation later, in 1922, he was elected leader of the party in parliament by a majority of two over J. R. Clynes, and thus, as leader of the opposition, he automatically became prime minister the next year. The Clydesiders, radicals from Glasgow, supported him because they thought he would undertake a genuinely Left policy. He was, indeed, when he first reached the premiership, a picturesque and challenging personality. His rich Scottish eloquence, his instructive air of leadership, his poise and parliamentary skill, his undoubted courage and facility in negotiation, made him—the first labour prime minister in British history—a world figure. And at the Foreign Office he joined Herriot to inaugurate a new era in post-War affairs by a peaceful policy towards Germany.

But even within his own party, even in the early days, MacDonald was not popular. 'He was never,' Robert Bernays wrote,[1] 'at ease in the world he had conquered.' Inordinately proud and vain, he walled himself off from his subordinates; the story is told that he never spoke even to Arthur Henderson, his worthy second in command, except in cabinet. Like Woodrow Wilson he could not bear criticism. And his followers began to complain of his 'insufferable superiority'.

MacDonald, born without much sense of humour, a creature of angular and obstinate desires, with a highly oblique vision of his fellow men, full of Scotch mists and tempests, required, above all, adoration. And adoration was hardly the emotion he could inspire in his hard-headed and individualist colleagues. His wife, whom he had worshipped, died in 1911; he was an extremely lonely man. It was inevitable that he should turn to 'society'. He was 'taken up' by people like the Londonderrys, and few things mattered to him more than lionisation.

He became capable of profound ridiculousness. In 1929, *en*

[1] *In Great Contemporaries.*

route to visit the United States, he is said to have wirelessed London for advice as to what he, the first socialist prime minister, should wear at the reception. The Foreign Office, terrified that he might step off the boat in a deerstalker hat or leather stockings or something else he would consider appropriate, wirelessed back that a top hat and morning coat would see him through.

In 1935, after the Stresa conference and when he was prime minister in the National Government, he warmly shocked a group of quite friendly journalists by asking them to leave the public restaurant-car until he had concluded his dinner. Everybody was hungry, but Ramsay, rolling towards Geneva, wanted to be alone.

A 'National' Government is a convenient device by which the leading party exploits a crisis by giving other parties representation in the cabinet, but on disadvantageous terms. Its result is permanently to split and weaken the opposition; it rubs down party lines, but maintains the pretence of comprehensive party support. MacDonald became prime minister in the first National Government in 1931. Possibly he thought that his labour colleagues would follow him in *toto*. Probably he didn't care much if they did or not. They didn't.

The financial crisis of 1931 was caused, basically, by the shrinkage of British exports and the decline of British shipping and oversea investments. The City of London had borrowed money on short-term; and lent it on long-term; it made money by paying three per cent on loans from France, and receiving six per cent from Germany. This process was a happy one until Germany, caught by the crisis, could not repay; London found itself with only £55 millions in gold, and with £250 millions in immediate outstanding liabilities. The London bankers might, they thought, save themselves by a loan from New York, but Wall Street refused to advance credit until the British budget, swollen by perfectly legitimate expenses of the social services and the famous but misnamed 'Dole', should be balanced. MacDonald went to the country on a promise to stick to gold and clean house. Campaigning, he descended to un-British demagoguery by exhibiting German banknotes of the inflation period, and threatening that presently a million British pounds would not suffice to buy a postage stamp. The country, frightened, gave him immense support. And then the cabinet was forced to do just what MacDonald had sworn it never would do. Britain devaluated her currency.

The National Government, of which Baldwin and not Mac-
Donald soon became the leading power, helped to kill the disarmament conference, and it repudiated the American debt; the
World Economic Conference held under its auspices in London in
1933 was a grisly failure. On the other hand, it revolutionised
British tariff policy by introducing protection, which stimulated
industrial recovery; it inaugurated a sort of empire customs union
by the Ottawa agreements; it converted £2,000 millions of War
Loan bonds from five to three and a half per cent.

Midway in his administration MacDonald's health began to fail.
His eyesight troubled him, and he became seriously ill.

At about this time an incredible and frightful woolliness became
noticeable in his public utterances.

Regarding unemployment, he described the problem to the
House of Commons as follows:

> 'Schemes must be devised, policies must be devised if it is humanly
> possible to take that section (i.e., those unemployed who are un-
> likely shortly to be reabsorbed into industry) and to regard them
> not as wastrels, not as hopeless people, but as people for whom
> occupation must be provided somehow or other, and that occupation,
> although it may not be in the regular factory or in organised large-
> scale industrial groups, nevertheless will be quite as effective for them-
> selves mentally, morally, spiritually and physically than, perhaps if
> they were included in this enormous mechanism of humanity which
> is not always producing the best results, and which, to a very large
> extent, fails in producing the good results that so many of us expect
> to see from a higher civilisation based upon national wealth.
> 'That is a problem that has got to be faced.'

Regarding disarmament, he told the general committee of the
disarmament conference the following:

> 'You are faced with the problem of what to do in respect to this
> question, to that question, and to the other question, but perfectly
> obviously, after you have faced the more superficial aspects of the
> separate questions, you want to know in relation to a complete plan
> what you are actually giving and what you are actually getting.
> Therefore, when the departmental, or compartmental, exploration
> has gone on to a certain extent it cannot be finished until somebody,
> co-ordinating all your problems, sets out in one statement and
> declaration the complete scheme that this Conference can pass in
> order to give security, to give disarmament, to give hope for the
> future—until that scheme has been placed before you, you cannot
> complete your examination of compartmental problems and questions
> . . .'

Lady Astor asked him in the House if he would consider appointing a woman to the front bench. He replied:

> 'I should be very glad not only to have one in the administration
> but half a dozen, and if my Noble Friend will find that there are not
> quite so many, or even perhaps worse than that, I having made
> that statement to her and given her that assurance, am perfectly
> certain she will not blame me for the result.'

Mr. Churchill once called MacDonald 'the boneless wonder'; the
prime minister, he said, possessed the 'gift of compressing the maximum of words into the minimum of thought'.

MacDonald had seemingly lost all traces of socialism. He was
howled down by his former colleagues, during the Means Test
debate, as a 'mountebank' and 'a swine', 'a low, dirty cur who ought
to be whipped out of public life'. He spent his time alone, brooding, or in the parlours of the rich. At a public dinner he once
excused himself with the remark, 'I am sorry to leave this con-
genial company, but I must preside at a Coal committee.' And the
wits said, 'Ramsay has finally succeeded in nationalising something
—the government.'

One sentiment is to his credit; in the spring of 1935 he took a
strong line against Hitler; he realised how dangerous Germany was
becoming. But apparently it was not only the persecution of
pacifists or socialists like (theoretically) himself in Germany which
turned him against the Nazis, but—a more or less emotional consideration—his horror that the German Government had executed
two handsome and aristocratic women spies.

In November 1935 MacDonald was beaten for re-election at
Seaham—to the relief of some millions of his countrymen. He had
already given way to Baldwin as prime minister. A lonely and
almost forgotten figure, he died suddenly in 1937.

Hoare

Rather arch, rather delicate, bookish, fond of sports like ice-
skating, Sir Samuel Hoare, the Lord Privy Seal in the 1939 War
Cabinet, gives an impression of primness which his inner character
belies. He was an active air minister; he flew twice to India and
back. As secretary of state for India he wrote the India bill, the
longest in the history of the British parliament; with supernal
industry he answered 15,000 questions about it, made 600 speeches,
read 25,000 pages of reports and participated in a debate which

asted seven and a half years and comprised 15,500,000 words in
Hansard, which is equivalent to twenty books the size of the English
Bible.

Moreover, during most of this labour, his chief antagonist was
Winston Churchill, the most accomplished and tenacious debater
in the House of Commons.

Hoare became foreign minister in June 1935, partly because
Baldwin knew his abilities, partly as reward for his prodigious
Indian labours.   The bill itself, a typically Baldwin measure, was
a middle-of-the-road affair.   It outraged Indian nationalist and
diehard Tories, both, by extending a measure of self-government
to India while retaining the essentials of British control.

Mr. Gandhi liked Hoare, because, as he said, Hoare said No
when he meant No, instead of evading direct statement with pious
platitudes, as MacDonald did.   The great Indian leader once told
Lord Halifax, then viceroy, as Lord Irwin, whom he deeply admired despite their political antagonism, 'You know, I trust that
man Hoare as I do you'—which was as high a compliment as
existed in Gandhi's vocabulary.

Hoare comes from an old banking family.   He learned rudimentary Russian (his teachers were the translators to the then
Imperial Russian Embassy in London and the cantor of the Orthodox Church), and went to Russia during the War, as a member of
the British Intelligence Service.   He was so expert at his job that—
as he himself revealed in a speech in 1933—the Czar accused him
of foreknowledge of the murder of Rasputin.   Hoare left Russia
in February 1917, and went to Italy with Lord Milner, as a general
staff officer.   After the War he spent some time in Czechoslovakia
and he has been president of the Anglo-Czech Society in London.
Meantime, he has uninterruptedly been a conservative M.P. for
Chelsea since 1910.

Hoare's literary affiliations with France are close.   I read in the
Evening Standard recently that his wife's grand-aunt, Aimée de
Coigny, inspired André Chenier's *La Jeune Captive*.   Like the
former permanent under-secretary, Sir Robert Vansittart, he is
widely read in French literature, and he speaks French well.   He
mildly startled the House of Commons in October 1935, by being
the first foreign minister ever to quote Marcel Proust there.
Emotionally, Hoare is very much closer to the French than to the
Germans; and considerations like these are apt to play a certain role
in policy.

We have noted Hoare's part in the Abyssinian negotiations, and how the Hoare-Laval plan—only temporarily—ruined him. Obviously he had been made a scapegoat, and within six months after retiring as foreign minister he was back in the government in charge of the admiralty, an equally important job. One footnote to the affair caused titters. Explaining the Abyssinian business to his constituents in Chelsea in February, he defended himself for having gone to Paris to meet the wily Laval. He didn't want to go, he said but the British Ambassador in Paris pressed him to break his journey to Switzerland for the visit. 'I could not refuse,' Sir Samuel' letter read, 'though it meant separating myself from Lady Maud and the luggage.'

Hoare is often spoken of as the next prime minister when Neville Chamberlain some day retires.

Eden for One

No one need go far in seeking the sources of Anthony Eden's sincerity in the cause of peace. Two of his brothers were killed in the War, Edward, the eldest son of the family, in France, and the youngest, William Nicholas, who, a midshipman at Jutland perished at sixteen.

Eden, one of the most attractive figures in world politics to-day, who succeeded Hoare as foreign minister, was born in 1897. His mother was a famous society beauty, his father, Sir William Eden, a terrifyingly 'county' baronet who, interested also in art, once quarrelled famously with Whistler. His family connections are typical of the gentry. His wife is the daughter of Sir Gervase Beckett; once he fought an election against Frances Countess of Warwick, who (only a genealogist could get the details clear) was both his sister's mother-in-law and his wife's stepmother's sister. Eden went to war at seventeen and was gassed at Ypres; at twenty-one he was captain. Then he went to Christ Church, Oxford. He was not faintly interested in politics; he did not even join the Union. He studied (and got first-class honours in) Oriental languages; his only conspicuous undergraduate activity seems to have been an essay he wrote on—Cézanne.

But presently he found himself in politics, and his rise was extraordinarily rapid. It seemed at first that he was a typical specimen of the young man-about-politics: good family; Eton and Oxford; war service; handsome wife; two sturdy boys; comfort-

ıble private means; impeccable clothes; conventional good looks.
But by 1926 he had become parliamentary private secretary to
Sir Austen Chamberlain, then the foreign secretary. This was
partly because the shrewd Baldwin had an eye on him, partly
because the conservative back-benchers were demanding jobs for
the young men. By 1931 he was parliamentary under-secretary to
the Foreign Office, and as Sir John Simon's popularity in Geneva
and Whitehall waned, Eden's rose. He did most of the hard work
at Geneva. In 1934, as Lord Privy Seal, he was practically the sub-
foreign minister; in 1935 he entered the cabinet as minister without
portfolio for League of Nations affairs.

It was not merely his sincerity for peace and his extreme charm
and likeableness that brought him this post. What counted were,
first, the picturesque unorthodoxies in his character, which were
especially notable because his outward stamp appeared to conform
so closely to the common mould. He had studied Persian; this was
odd. Once in Sweden, guest of honour at a hunt, he refused to shoot
a stag, because it was 'too beautiful'. Second, he was Baldwin's
'man' in the Foreign Office, and thus a check on Simon, who was
detested by the Tories. Third, the permanent staff of the Foreign
Office swore by him.

Eden is a skilful and patient negotiator; he made the Jugoslavs
and Hungarians agree after the murder of King Alexander, which
is as if he had made Goering and Dimitrov kiss. He was the first
British cabinet minister to enter Russia since the revolution in
1917; the job called for the maximum of tact, resilience, candour,
and common sense. The Soviets had been deeply suspicious of
British policy, and the British Tories thought that Stalin and his
men were poison. Then came Abyssinia, and Eden's importance
in British politics steeply rose; he was the darling of the peace-
balloters and the pacifists, so much so that his departure from the
government might have wrecked it. To millions in the country,
Eden personified peace.

Why didn't Eden resign after the Hoare-Laval fiasco? Probably
because the 'old-school-tie' tradition demanded that he stay loyal
to his chief. Three years later, in 1938, he did resign, as I have
noted in Chapter VIII above. He stood by his principles, against
Chamberlain's policy of 'appeasing' the dictators. When the War
Cabinet was formed in 1939, Eden became Dominions Secretary
with access to it.

Pious Halifax

We have several times mentioned Lord Cecil, England's foremost apostle of disarmament. There should also be a word about Lord Halifax, called the 'saintliest' character in British public life, the present foreign minister. Like many Englishmen of the upper class his name has changed with bewildering frequency; as minister of agriculture he was known as Edward Wood; as the most notable Viceroy of India of modern times he was Lord Irwin. He was born in 1881, and went to Eton and Christ Church. Now called Lord Halifax since his father's death, he is a member of the War Cabinet and one of the three or four most important men in England. Halifax, like Simon and several other British intellectuals who are also politicians, was a Fellow of All Souls at Oxford, a great distinction; since 1933 he has been Chancellor of Oxford University. He is a devout churchman. A 'liberal' among the conservatives, the modesty, detachment, unworldliness and extreme moral dignity of his character have brought him fame.

The War Cabinet and Military Leaders

Chamberlain, Churchill, Halifax, Hoare, and Simon are perhaps the most conspicuous members of the British War Cabinet. But there should be mention at least of the others, especially Leslie Hore-Belisha, the former war minister,[1] and Sir Kingsley Wood, the minister for air.

Mr. Hore-Belisha is one of those fabulous creatures who intrudes on the dull uniformity of British official life like an orchid among primroses. For a considerable time, despite his intelligence and likeableness, his career was frustrated; first he was a liberal during a period of predominant conservative drift in public affairs, second he was considered just a shade too clever, too flamboyant, to be 'safe'. The Colonel Blimps and dilapidated lordships were afraid of him, as they were afraid of Churchill.

Hore-Belisha was born near London of an old and distinguished Jewish family that came originally from Portugal. The year was 1893. He went to Oxford, became president of the celebrated debating society known as the Oxford Union—as have so many British politicians before him—and during the War rose to the rank of major. He entered politics, becoming an M.P. in 1923, and since the formation of the National Government, has been, like Simon,

[1] Who resigned from the Government in January 1940.

a 'Liberal National'. He got his first big post as Minister of Transport in 1934. Promptly, with great vigour and capacity to attract attention, he became a national institution through his 'Belisha beacons', the orange bulbs telling pedestrians where to cross streets in presumptive safety. In 1937 he became Secretary of State for War. He has been the most enterprising British war minister in a generation.

Bustling, industrious, unconventional, Hore-Belisha did his best to revivify the army. He cut out dead wood at the top; he tried to make openings at the bottom. He advocated mechanisation; he listened—attentively—to Captain Liddell Hart, the foremost British authority on military affairs. Blasts of ventilation swept through the War Office. He organised a new retirement scheme, so that good young men could rise quickly. Hereafter a British major retires at forty-seven—if he isn't any good. Seniority is abolished above the rank of major, with promotion on the basis of ability. One recalls the old sarcastic maxim: 'No damned nonsense about merit.' Hore-Belisha tried to make merit—youthful merit—count.

Hore-Belisha's job was probably the most difficult in England. In March 1939, he announced that in the event of war the British intended to send roughly 300,000 men to France. In April—to meet the exigencies of a fast-changing and dangerous world—Britain adopted conscription. Hore-Belisha had to put conscription into active operation, no mean feat. Meantime he reorganised the Territorials.

Sir Kingsley Wood, the minister for air and as such automatically a member of the War Cabinet, is a cherubic-looking small man, born in 1881, a lawyer by profession. His chief interest has always been in the realm of public health, social insurance, and the like, and he was minister of health from 1935 to 1938. Before that he was a highly successful Postmaster-General; he believed in such 'innovations' as bright and effective publicity, and he used unique promotion methods to 'sell' the British postal and telegraph services to the people. When the Air Ministry, under Lord Swinton, had reached a shocking stage of muddle, stalemate, and ineptitude, Kingsley Wood was called in to take charge and renovate it; he became air minister in 1938. Britain needed a tremendous air fleet; Britain wasn't getting a tremendous air fleet; Wood had the task of making one. When war came in 1939, he hadn't quite caught up to General Goering, but he was moving fast.

The Minister for Co-ordination of Defence, also a member of

the War Cabinet, is Admiral Lord Chatfield. He is sixty-six; he retired from active service last year, when he was Admiral of the Fleet, on reaching the age limit. Immediately he was put to work in administrative fields. Chatfield was Beatty's flag captain on the *Lion* in the 1914 war, and he fought at Jutland. For five years, from 1933 to 1938, he was First Sea Lord, that is, the professional director of British naval forces. Chatfield is quiet, shrewd, un-assuming, and of vast experience. His job is to correlate activity of the three defence ministries, and link them to the prime minister.

. . . .

Not in the War Cabinet, but hovering just outside, is Sir John Anderson, the Home Secretary and Minister of Home Security. Anderson, a lean, flint-like, tight-lipped Scotsman, has had an astonishing career. He was a civil servant—one of the men, like Vansittart and Hankey, who form the concrete matrix of the British governmental structure. He worked in the Colonial Office, in the field of social insurance, in the ministry of shipping, in Ireland, and in the ministry of health; for ten years, 1922-32, he was Permanent Under-Secretary of the Home Office, the same job that Vansittart had in foreign affairs. Then Anderson was pushed upwards into the limelight. He became Governor of Bengal, though it was most unusual for a civil servant to get such a post, during the most active period of Bengal terrorism; his régime was hard-handed in the extreme. His term concluded, Anderson returned to England, ran for parliament, and almost at once was given cabinet rank. He is one of the few civil servants ever to become a minister. When war broke out he was in charge of Air Raid Precautions.

Also outside the War Cabinet—but of great consequence in prosecution of the war—are W. S. Morrison, the Food Minister, Leslie Burgin, the Minister of Supply, and especially Ronald H. Cross, the youthful head of the newly-created Ministry of Economic Warfare, i.e., minister of blockade.

. . . .

General Sir Edmund Ironside, Chief of the Imperial General Staff, and as such the first soldier in Great Britain, is fifty-nine. Two distinctions may be mentioned at once: he is six feet four, a tremendous blunt pillar of a man (and thus, of course, he is nick-named 'Tiny'); and, an extraordinary linguist, he knows not less than ten languages. Ironside at various times has been an artillery subaltern, a military historian, the commander of British forces at Archangel and in Persia (where he 'discovered' the present Shah,

Reza Pahlevi), commander of the staff college, and governor-general of Gibraltar. It was he, in the summer of 1939, who led a mission to Poland, seeking to find out how—if at all—Britain could defend the Poles, and the Poles defend themselves. Ironside is a sturdy campaigner—and one as much at home with maps as guns.

General John Standish Surtees Prendergast Vereker, Viscount Gort, V.C., is commander of the British field forces in France. He is only fifty-four; the ebullient Hore-Belisha chose him three years ago as an officer destined for supreme command, and picked him as Chief of the Imperial General Staff—which job Ironside has now assumed—over the heads of *ninety* officers. Lord Gort is a gallant and picturesque figure. He won his Victoria Cross in 1918 when, a battalion commander, he continued to lead his men to their objective on the Canal du Nord although he was twice severely wounded. He has also won the D.S.O. (with three citations) and the Military Cross. In the Great War he never commanded a larger unit than a battalion. He became a colonel in 1926, and a general in 1935. He was commandant of the staff college for a time, and then became Hore-Belisha's military secretary.

Tories

Alfred Duff Cooper, husband of Lady Diana, is the best and ablest of the younger Tories: intelligent-plus, combative, thoroughly sound on foreign policy, liberal, tenacious. He and Eden were the 'young Turks' in the Baldwin cabinet, opposed to the ossified conservatism of the elder statesmen. When he became minister of war late in 1935, after years of impatient second-stringing, Duff Cooper made things hum. He doesn't mind being indiscreet when necessary. Early in his tenure of office he tilted a lance at the pacifist bishops, and in Paris he raised a minor storm by a sensible speech (in French) which was interpreted as a bid for an Anglo-French alliance. In September 1938, after Munich, he was the only cabinet minister—he was First Lord of the Admiralty at the time— to resign. This showed sharp foresight, and took great courage. Chamberlain was bitterly hurt, and has never given him office since. Duff Cooper is only forty-eight. The social grace and beauty of his wife have been of considerable importance to his career. Their young son, like his father, will go to Eton. Duff Cooper is the author of an admirable book on Talleyrand, and a long biography of Field-Marshal Lord Haig.

Major (now Mr.) Walter Elliot, formerly the food dictator, now

2 A

minister for health and the man responsible for the highly successful
evacuation of children from the great cities in 1939, began political
life as a fabian socialist; he is a Tory to-day but the Tory who is
most susceptible to the contemporary shibboleth of 'planning'. His
abstruse experiments in reorganising British agriculture, his complex net of subsidies and quotas and marketing acts are necessary because a *complete* policy of agrarian protection would starve England.
He was educated to be a doctor; he wants to be a scientist in politics.
Even Mr. Wells is not enough a planner for his taste. Commenting
on a speech by Wells, 'Whither Britain?' Elliot said, 'He consigned
himself to the nineteenth century with his opening remarks.'

Like many Britons, Elliot has a rhyming sense of the ridiculous.
The philosophy of determinism, he remarked in his presidential
address to Aberdeen university, might be expressed by the following ditty:

> 'Oh, damn! At last I perceive what I am,
> Just a creature that moves in predestinate grooves,
> I'm not even a bus, but a tram!'

Then, describing the astronomer Sir James Jeans, Elliot said:

> 'Oh cuss! Though his picture grows steadily wuss,
> I shall go on my way whatever they say,
> For I won't be a tram, I'm a bus!'

And when he was a student at Glasgow university he wrote an
Ode to the Pig, two lines of which were:

> 'Alive it is a loathsome beast,
> But dead provides a toothsome feast.'

His visions of economic reconstruction follow quite orthodox
lines; the 'leisure state', he thinks, can be produced by *laisser-faire*
capitalism. He is a relentless empiricist; the saying was that he
remained minister of agriculture because no one else could possibly
understand the complicated structure of his regulations. Their
result has been, of course, to make much friction with the dominions, who quarrelled about how much meat they might export to
Britain, and to raise the prices of foodstuffs for the British con-
sumer, in order that the producers might survive.

Oliver Stanley, formerly President of the Board of Trade, now
war minister, is the son of the Earl of Derby, and he married
Lady Maureen Stewart, daughter of Lord Londonderry. He has,
like most Tory politicians, a good War record; unlike most of them,
he is a wit: once he said that Sidney Webb had 'blue books in his

veins'. During the General Strike he served as a clerk in the Westminster tube station. With the willingness to admit mistakes that is an excellent tradition in British politics, he offered to resign as minister of labour when the Means Test regulations broke down. 'That the responsibility for the error was mine is a thing,' he said, 'that I have never attempted to evade.' He didn't explain why he had made the error in the first place. Ramsay MacDonald, the 'socialist', refused to accept his resignation.

Sir Thomas Inskip is the sixty-three-year-old man of mystery who, to general astonishment, was promoted early in 1936 to be minister for the co-ordination of defence. Inskip, a devout churchman, is above all 'safe'; therefore he was sometimes spoken of as a future prime minister. One cruel story accounts for his defence appointment on the ground that Baldwin, with great difficulty, had to find someone for the job 'even less brilliant than himself'. In 1939 he became Lord Chancellor.

Not So Simple Simon

Sir John Simon, the Chancellor of the Exchequer in the 1939 War Cabinet, just squeezed home in the 1935 general election, with his group of 'Liberal National' supporters of the coalition government reduced in number. No matter how unpopular Simon may be, his position in the cabinet is secure, because inclusion of his liberal supporters is necessary to retain the pretence of 'National' government. This, of course, causes dissatisfaction in Tory ranks; the MacDonald 'National Labourites' who possess exactly seven seats in the House of Commons, have three cabinet posts[1]; the Simonites have no fewer than four jobs in the cabinet for their meagre thirty-three seats in the House; the Tories, with a colossal block of three hundred and eighty-four seats, have to be satisfied with the rest of the cabinet posts, twenty-two in all.

Simon, the greatest lawyer in modern England and the least successful foreign minister, has always wanted to be liked more than people liked him. This is the tragedy of his life. About no other man in English public life, except MacDonald, is there such a miscellany of cruel legends.

One story has it that he won so many cases against others that he lost his own.

Mr. Lloyd George is reported to have said of him that 'John

[1] Reduced to two when J. H. ('Jimmy') Thomas resigned in June 1936, after the budget leakage scandal.

Simon had sat on the fence so long that the iron entered his soul!'

One apocryphal story is that Simon, finding an acquaintance of long standing to be at last useful, came up to him, put his arm around his shoulders—and called him by the wrong Christian name.

Mr. Garvin, referring to the 'half-headedness and half-heartedness' of the foreign policy of the first National Government, said that Simon created the impression of a man marking time with an agility intended to resemble walking.

The story is told that when Sir John Simon plays golf, he putts around bunkers.

He understands things, it was said, 'only through his mind'.

In one of his really bad-tempered moments, Mr. Lloyd George said, 'Many a better man than he has crossed the floor of this house before him, but none has left such a slimy trail of hypocrisy behind him.' (*Inquest on Peace*, p. 356.)

Philip Snowden said, 'Sir John Simon is the chief advertising agent of the government and of himself; but if he had any sense of the pitiable failure he made of the high and responsible office he held, but of which he was happily deprived for his country's good, instead of appearing so much on the public platforms he would hide his head in some place of suitable obscurity in the hope that his miserable record would be forgotten.'

Simon is, of course, not nearly so forbidding a creature as these stories make out. An exceptionally shy man, lonely and anxious to be popular, he was afraid to offend people. That he was an able and devoted public servant for almost a generation was never doubted.

His unpopularity as foreign minister was largely the result of his virtual advocacy of the Japanese case in the Manchurian crisis at Geneva. Matsoaka, the Japanese delegate, told friends that Simon had said in fifteen minutes what he had been trying to express for weeks. Simon offended the United States during the Manchurian crisis; he disastrously weakened the League; he was accused of responsibility for the failure of the disarmament conference.

It was Simon who, in an historic speech during the General Strike, declared the strike illegal, which more than any other thing broke the spirit of the workers. This has not endeared him to labour.

It was Simon who, as chairman of the Indian Statutory Commission, produced a report hundreds of pages long (which was a dead letter before it was published); he gave Mr. Gandhi only a few paragraphs.

Liberals

The opposition liberals were practically wiped out in the 1935 election. Sir Herbert Samuel, the brilliantly cultivated Jewish philosopher who had been leader of the party, lost his seat; his successor was Sir Archibald Sinclair, a young Scot who is half-American and who began politics as Winston Churchill's secretary. Sinclair was honest and bold enough to sacrifice his career—temporarily— by sticking to free-trade and the remnants of the historic liberal party, when after the Ottawa agreements he crossed the floor of the House and resigned his membership in the first National Government.

David Lloyd George and his family group survived in the 1935 elections. They are 'independent' liberals. Lloyd George himself has sat in the Commons uninterruptedly for forty-seven years, a dazzling record. But at the end of his career the great Welshman was fighting a more serious enemy than any political adversary: he was fighting—time. His last speeches, however illuminating they may have been on domestic affairs, have acutely disappointed his friends when they touched on the situation abroad. Lloyd George has turned into a defeatist and something of a pro-German; doubtless this is conscience money for the Treaty of Versailles.

Sir John Reith

Sir John Reith, for years director-general of the British Broadcasting Corporation, is not a resident of Whitehall, but his modernist citadel on Portland Place was more important in the life of Britain than most government offices. Reith, 'a fanatical Puritan, in awe of hell, yet suspecting Heaven', is a complex character; he ruled the B.B.C. with a hand of granite. 'A great black tower of a man, one eye burning fiercely, one a little scared, mouth moulded in a cynical No.' (I am quoting an anonymous commentator in the *New Statesman*.) 'His smile is so rare and so lovely that the humanity it discovers seems a mirage. . . .'

Reith is a Scotsman, the son of a Glasgow clergyman. He had long experience as an engineer, first in the civil engineering department of the Admiralty, then as general manager of Wm. Beardmore and Sons, the steel firm. He made the B.B.C. an expression of his nonconformist conscience, also what is probably the finest broad-casting organisation in the world. Even socialists like it, because it is a public body ruled by charter, and its relation to the state is semi-socialistic. Reith left the B.B.C. just before the war to re-organise British civil aviation. He is almost certain to have a big political job some day.[1]

Norman and the Bank of England

'Unless drastic measures are taken to save it, the capitalist system throughout the world will be wrecked within a year.'

—Montagu Norman in 1931.

Montagu Collet Norman, since 1920 governor of the Bank of England, is to banking born. Both his grandfathers were directors of the Bank of England, one of them for more than fifty years. He went to Eton, King's College, Cambridge and served in the South African war. For some years he worked in commercial banking (he was connected with the house of Brown-Shipley); like many important bankers, he is not much interested in money personally, and he is by no means a very rich man; money and its mechanism is rather a fascinating problem to him as a diplomat, a mathema-tician, almost a creative artist.

His *farouche* air of international intrigue-cum-artistic worldli-ness is famous. Everything is permitted him, because he has been governor of the Bank of England longer than any man in history. He wears flowing capes, black slouch hats, and a waggish beard; his house on Campden Hill is decorated with extraordinarily silken elegance. Yet he takes the tube to work every morning, and likes to be the last man on the escalator. He enjoys appearing to be mysterious, and he has made only three public speeches in his life.

Norman's experience alone would make him indispensable. But he has more than mere experience. His technical capacity to handle banking problems and his skill and boldness in negotiation are considerable. Like many Englishmen, he knows how to make a virtue of humility; in October 1932 he said 'the difficulties are so great, the forces are so unlimited, precedents are so lacking, that I approach the whole subject in ignorance. . . . It is too great for me —I will admit that for the moment the way, to me, is not clear.'

Once, amiably chatting with a banker friend, he listened imper-viously to the argument that the gold standard would impoverish Britain in the long run. 'Tell me,' Norman is reported to have

[1] Now (January 1940) Minister of Information.

asked, 'do you think it better to be rich than to be poor?' His friend replied, 'Well, I have been poor, and now I am fairly rich, and I hope to be richer.' Norman replied that he was not sure but that countries which were too rich went to pieces; he pointed to the example of Periclean Athens and Imperial Rome. His friend did not reveal the substance of the conversation; the intimation that the governor of the Bank of England might consider it his duty to impoverish his country for its eventual benefit would not have been too popular.

He was, of course, the main spirit forcing England back to the gold standard in 1925. This severely punished British industry, but, like most central bankers, Norman worshipped gold. By insisting that Snowden (who didn't need much persuasion), should stick to gold, he was the spiritual author of the 1931 financial crisis. He has admitted, too, that various foreign (mostly German) concerns had been able 'to borrow on short credit sums which, had the various lenders all been aware of it, would have been quite out of the question'. Apparently there was little co-operation between the lending agencies in London; competitively they threw their money away.

Norman has, as is well known, great regard for Dr. Schacht; the governors of all the central banks play together closely. . His high opinion of Schacht's shrewdness dates, it is believed, from 1927, when both attended a conference in New York. Schacht opposed, speaking broadly, a world easy money policy; Norman favoured it. Events ultimately proved Schacht to be right, because the unstable Wall Street boom, when it collapsed, provoked the world crisis; and Norman ever after has respected Schacht for his prescience, and for having proved that he, Norman, was wrong.

Hugh Dalton, who was under-secretary for foreign affairs in the second Labour Government, records how he became aware that Norman pursued a foreign policy quite his own. There was a 'dyarchy'. No matter what the real Foreign Office might be doing. Norman's policy proceeded on the basis that 'unless Germany is economically strong and prosperous, it is impossible to balance the one-sided political strength of France on the continent'. When the Credit Anstalt, the great Rothschild bank, crashed in Vienna in 1931, Norman on his own responsibility advanced to Austria enough credit, it was hoped, to tide the crisis over. Two years later the loan was transferred from the books of the bank to the treasury, i.e. the British taxpayer.

But it should not be assumed too glibly that Norman always rules the treasury. Snowden fed out of his hand; but not Neville Chamberlain. Indeed the treasury, ever since the devaluation of sterling, has been more important than the Bank, because the treasury, by controlling the exchanges through the £300,000,000 Equalisation Fund, has usurped one of the Bank's primary functions. Norman would like to see the pound high and stable, and perhaps even a return to gold. The treasury wants to keep the pound fairly low and, within limits, variable, in order to reduce the debt charge on the budget and to encourage industry. So far the treasury has been the winner.

Lord Beaverbrook

The circulation of his chief newspaper, the *Daily Express*, is the largest in the world, some two and a half million daily, and soon it may be three million. The quality of his ambition is inconstant: business, politics, journalism, have taken him by turn. The bitterness of his feud with Baldwin is partially forgotten; his influence in crusading for empire free trade, friendship with the United States, and isolation from the Continent, is still considerable. His reputation as a host is fabulous; all over the world friends testify to the magnitude of his charm. William Maxwell Aitken, Lord Beaverbrook, the chief of the 'Press Lords', is one of the most provocative and original public men in England.

Beaverbrook, the son of a Presbyterian minister, was born in Ontario, Canada, in 1879. A poor boy, he amassed an astounding fortune, at least a million pounds, by the time he was thirty. Electric power and cement were his magic lamps. He dropped business, went to England, ran for parliament, and became the close friend, the *eminence grise* of Bonar Law. For ten years, mostly behind the scenes (though he was a cabinet minister for a time) Beaverbrook —a new 'incomparable Max'—shifted other cabinet ministers like puppets. He made the alliance between Bonar Law and Lloyd George; he played a prominent part in overthrowing Asquith. Then apparently politics began to bore him. His health, too, was uneven. He took over the *Daily Express*, founded the *Sunday Express*, obtained control of the *Evening Standard*, and ever since has been the restless Puck of British journalism.

CHAPTER XXII

LEFT AND RIGHT IN ENGLAND

'When a revolutionary party has not the support of a majority either among the vanguard of the revolutionary class or among the rural population, there can be no question of a rising. A rising must have not only the majority, but must have the incoming revolutionary tide over the whole country, the complete moral and political bankruptcy of the old régime—and a deep-seated sense of insecurity among all these irresolute elements.'

—Lenin.

Socialism in England, as is notorious, is not revolutionary, and not even the grisly condition of the depressed areas, the suffering of two million unemployed, and the eloquence of Sir Stafford Cripps can make it so. It is difficult to organise effective solidarity among the poor in a country where, as Mirsky puts it, 'the smallest white collar clerk thinks of himself as the opposite of a workman'. The measure of British recovery that has occurred has occurred partly at the expense of the working class; but this does not much increase the labour party, the I.L.P., or the exiguous communist vote.

The labour party itself, a product of the Fabian doctrine of the 'inevitability of gradualness', made no official declaration of socialist principles until 1918. The influence of Marx among British socialists was always comparatively small; and when the first Labour Government was formed, it took office not only on sufferance but on the understanding that, even if it could, it would introduce no socialist measures. The trade unions (who represent eight million British workmen) only became formally committed to socialism in 1924. Trotsky quotes MacDonald to the effect that revolution is 'a ruin and a calamity, and nothing more'.

When labour was called upon to form a government, Hugh Dalton says, it had the choice of three alternatives. It could have refused office, since there was no clear labour majority in parliament. It could have accepted office, introduced 'some bold socialist measures', and gone down to defeat, then appealing to the country in a new election. Or it could have co-operated freely and frankly with the liberals who held the balance of power. Instead, the MacDonald cabinet did none of the three; it only muddled.

Labour had won two hundred and sixty-one seats in 1929, a very respectable total (caused partly because so many fights at that time were three-cornered). It sank to fifty-seven after the financial crisis of 1931 and the formation of the National Government. In 1935 it rose only to 154, though the total opposition vote was forty-six per cent of the electorate. There were several reasons why the showing was not better. First, the National Government boasted of the prosperity it had produced. Second, labour was in an impossible position as regards foreign policy, since on the one hand it supported the government in sanctions, while on the other, illogically, it opposed rearmament.

Armament has been a disastrous issue for Leftists everywhere for several years. If they took a genuinely long view, they had to concede the necessity of eventual defence against Germany. Yet if they supported armament and a strong government they would assist to make capitalism stronger and thus write the doom of socialist reform in their own countries. The first duty of genuine Leftists was to support the U.S.S.R. But since Germany was the chief potential enemy of the U.S.S.R., they could do this only by strengthening the capitalist states which were anti-German, and which would then be in a stronger position to destroy revolution at home.

Besides labour in England suffered from divided leadership. The death of Arthur Henderson removed the one personage in the party both vital and venerable. Henderson, a doughty figure, whose heart and health were broken by the sabotage of the disarmament conference, spoke in a language few of his subordinates had the courage or capacity to copy. When he was foreign minister in the second Labour Government, the *New Statesman* relates, one of his officials suggested that he send telegrams to Mussolini and the Pope congratulating them on the Lateran Treaty. 'No,' replied Uncle Arthur. 'I shall send no telegram to the Pope; I am a Wesleyan. I shall send no telegram to Mussolini; I have denounced him in a public speech as the murderer of Matteotti.'

Of the contemporary labour chieftains, the most interesting are probably Morrison and Cripps.

The Boss of London

'The socialist minister of the future must try to be as good a man at business for public ends as the ablest of the capitalists or managing directors are for private ends. . . . It is essential that socialism should be sound public business as well as being healthy in its social morality.'

—HERBERT MORRISON.

Morrison is a born Cockney. He is the son of a policeman. He has lost an eye. He had only board school education. He has been an errand boy, a shop assistant, and a telephone operator. The curl in his hair, his unquenchable good humour, his gift for pungent repartee, his realistic optimism, make him resemble early characters by H. G. Wells, for instance Kipps. He has been secretary of the London labour party since 1914, and he is an efficient and indeed almost a ruthlessly good organiser. Since 1932 he has been not only party chief in London but majority leader of the London County Council. As minister of transport in the second Labour Government, he put through its most praiseworthy legislation, the bill reorganising London transport. He is plausible, lively, and inquisitive.

'Mr. Morrison,' wrote A. J. Cummings in the *News Chronicle,* 'is the rising hope of the labour party—one might say its only hope.' He is a comparatively young man with a political future that holds out the dazzling promise of the premiership as its crown and climax. He is an astute politician with sincere convictions whose party loyalty has never been questioned.

But in 1935 Morrison was not chosen as the leader of the parliamentary labour party, but instead a man somewhat his inferior in personality and push, Major Clement Attlee; which was a bitter disappointment to those who had thought of Morrison as the inevitable leader. Reasons: Morrison was too much on the Right for the Leftists in the party. Moreover, the trade unionists suspected he was too strong a character to be easily manageable. He was a London product, and the trade unions dislike the London labour party, in which their influence is comparatively small. Finally, Morrison was the victim of inertia. Attlee had succeeded to the temporary leadership of the party when old George Lansbury resigned, and he led the party in the election fight; it seemed discourteous to remove him.

Morrison is not an expert on foreign affairs, but his intuition is quick and his instincts good. At the 1935 party congress, for instance, he 'urged that the labour movement (which had just adopted sanctions by a twenty to one vote) should not make the mistake of assuming that it could destroy Fascism by upsetting Mussolini as it once hoped to destroy militarism by getting rid of the Kaiser.'

He is distinctly on the Right wing of the labour movement; but even so the Leftists thoroughly respect him.

Cripps

'You have only got to look at the pages of British imperial history to hide your
head in shame that you are British.'

—SIR STAFFORD CRIPPS.

The best intellect among labour M.P.s is probably that of Sir
Stafford Cripps, son of Lord Parmoor and nephew of the Sidney
Webbs, socialist by conviction, one of the best parliamentarians in
England, and, like Simon, a great lawyer and advocate. He founded
the socialist league (within the parliamentary labour party); he is
very far to the Left. He shocked a good many people by saying
once that eventually 'we shall have to overcome opposition from
Buckingham Palace'. Tories—a significant point—are afraid of
Cripps, whereas few of them fear Morrison. They think that
Cripps might, if he got the chance, inaugurate a real socialism-in-
our-time policy, and even try to abolish the House of Lords, and
rule by an Enabling Act. This has frightened conservative labourites too; after a good start towards the party leadership, he underwent comparative eclipse.

England is a country of superb surprises, for which reason one
should not be surprised to learn that Cripps, the last possible remove from the workman-agitator, is a man of considerable wealth;
he fights entrenched privilege from the inside. His fees as a K.C.
are estimated at £30,000 per year. Once he told a political audience that as a lawyer he met the people of the ruling classes: 'They
pay me fabulous and fantastic sums to get them out of their
difficulties. I have no hesitation in saying that the working class
of this country are more capable of ruling than they are.' And the
passionate radical sincerity of his convictions is beyond doubt. He
was expelled from the party in 1939 largely because he wanted a
United Front with the communists.

Cripps has pointed out that during the first term of the National
Government the number of people on Poor Law Relief increased
by four hundred thousand and he is convinced that Fascism
has already protruded ugly fingers in the life of Britain. The
Manchester Guardian quoted him recently saying that the first
definite and conscious step towards Fascism was the Trades Dispute
Act of 1927. The 1931 elections were 'essentially Fascist in nature';
the forces of capitalism had such a triumph at the polls that 'there
was no need for any formal personal dictatorship'. He notes the
contrast of subsidies to capitalists—for instance those of Elliot's

agricultural schemes—with 'the discipline imposed on the workers through the Means Test'.

His definition of the corporate state is interesting: 'A method by which complete power is given to the capitalist to produce that scarcity which will ensure him a share of the national wealth out of all proportion to his efforts, and which will enable him to enslave the workers by substituting for their freedom and right to combine a nominal and ineffective minority voice in the government of industry.'

Cripps and Morrison might be quite capable of working well together, despite their ideological differences. The former could supply theory and strategy; the latter organising power and sense of political tactics. But against them both is the great conservative force of the trade unions.

The T.U.C.

'For my part I would rather rely on Sir Walter Citrine, arch-priest of British trade unionism, than on Mr. Baldwin, the conservative prime minister, to keep the present system intact. There is to-day no Toryism more fearful and immovable than that which is enshrined in the ideals and practice of trade union leadership.'
—A. J. CUMMINGS.

Among labour M.P.s in 1939 there were seventy-two nominees of the labour party itself, and seventy-four representatives of the trade unions. These were sub-divided as follows: thirty-seven men of the miners' federation, seven municipal workers, six railway clerks, six transport workers, five distributive workers, three from the national union of railway men, two compositors, and one each from eight other unions. The last thing that most of them want would be socialism in our time.

The most prominent trade unionist, like the general secretary Sir Walter Citrine, whom the National Government shrewdly knighted, and Ernest Bevin, the boss of the comparatively new and powerful Transport and General Workers' Union, are not M.P.s. The general rule is that the T.U.C. chieftains stay outside active politics. But they control the labour party, because they control the funds.

The triumph of Sir Walter Citrine is that of method. He was a member of an electrical union and then became assistant-secretary of the Trades Union Congress; his extreme organisational skill made him indispensable; and he succeeded to the leadership. He lives, it has been said, on his files; he is a filing Robot. When, once, he was invited to an informal discussion among labour intellectuals, to thrash out some party business, he brought the files—and a secretary—along; the secretary took down everything that *he* said, presumably so that later he could not be incorrectly quoted.

Citrine visited Moscow in the autumn of 1935 and wrote a book about Russia which sought to be impartial. He has opposed all efforts for a communist-socialist united front, and since 1928 has been president of the International Federation of Trade Unions.

Attlee and Others

The leader of the labour party and head of his Majesty's most loyal Opposition, Major Clement Attlee, would not have been leader had not the whole labour front bench been wiped out in the 1931 elections. But since 1935 when he has had a chance to show himself, his capabilities have vastly improved. Attlee was of middle-class parentage and background, and became a socialist through intellectual conviction rather than through the hard school of poverty and direct awareness of social injustice. He has considerable grace and pertinacity and a very fair wit. He is only fifty-six, but recently he has been severely ill. Unlike most Labour leaders, he is a public school and Oxford man. What he lacks most is colour, personality. For two years he laboured with Sir John Simon as labour representative on the Indian Statutory Commission.

Among the younger socialists the most interesting is perhaps Aneurin Bevan, the member for Ebbw Vale. His wife is Jennie Lee, the youthful member of Scottish I.L.P. Bevan is a Welshman, a miner's son, who worked underground as a child and then educated himself despite formidable obstacles of poverty. Vital, ambitious, magnetic, with an impetuous Welsh laugh, he is one of the most attractive characters in the Commons. His comment on sanctions gives a clue to his pungent quality: 'Britain's policy is that of the successful burglar turned householder who wants a strong police force. If I am going to ask any worker to shed his blood, it will not be for medieval Abyssinia or for Fascist Italy, but for the making of a better social system in this country.'

Arthur Greenwood, a veteran Labourite, born in 1880, became acting leader of the party during Attlee's illness in 1939. He rose to the occasion. His speeches during the war crisis were the best of his career, and among the best the House heard from anybody.

Greenwood was minister of health in the second labour government. His great interest is workers' education.

The Red Fringe

One communist M.P. was elected to the House of Commons in November 1935, Willie Gallacher, a veteran Scottish revolutionary. A typical enough Clydeside crusader, he began as a liberal, turned socialist, finally became a communist; he led the first strike against the War—in 1915—that took place in England; Lenin admired him greatly. But Gallacher is not as important to the communist movement as Harry Pollitt, the secretary of the party and a member of the executive committee of the Communist International. Pollitt is a Marxian theorist, who, a boiler-maker by trade, is also a practical journalist and politician. One of the most acute journalists in London told me that he considered Pollitt's 'news-sense' to be better than his own. Pollitt worked hard for a United Front in Britain, but unsuccessfully. As an organiser of the party, he receives its maximum salary, £4 per week.[1]

From several points of view the I.L.P. (Independent Labour Party) is to the Left of the communists, as was the late P.O.U.M. in Spain. It opposed sanctions, which the communists approved; it refused any compact with labour, and the labour machine fought it even on the Clydeside, where it was impregnable. Four I.L.P. men sit in the present House; it is a small group, but noisy. The I.L.P. was founded as far back as 1893, and in early days it had great influence on labour policy. In 1932, devoted to genuinely revolutionary tactics, it broke with labour.

The leader of the I.L.P., James Maxton, was once, like Litvinov, a soldier; he belonged to the territorials. His first instincts were conservative; the story is told in Glasgow that while Elliot was a Fabian, Maxton was a Tory. Lean, with a famous mane of black-white hair, a 'cadaverous British Danton', Maxton sardonically denounces the government for planning to spend one hundred million pounds on road development—to make them safer for the next hunger marchers. Maxton, a unique personality, provides yet another British paradox; he is an overt revolutionary, yet is probably the most popular man in the House of Commons. He was one of the few M.P.s to oppose the war in 1939.

[1] After the Russo-German pacts of 1939 Pollitt retired from secretaryship of the British Communist party.

'This Rock Shall Fly from its Extreme Base as Soon as I'

On the extreme Right, far beyond even the Hailshams and Londonderrys, are two last-ditch imperialists, L. S. Amery, former minister of colonies, and Lord Lloyd, once governor-general of Bombay and high commissioner of Egypt. Amery has lately been conspicuous as the leader of those M.P.s most resolutely determined to block the possible return of colonies to Germany. 'If I were asked to name the most convinced diehard among the great politicians of to-day,' wrote Robert Bernays, 'I should pass over the claims of Mr. Churchill and plump for Mr. Amery. . . .' And thus he is out of office. Amery is diminutive, pugnacious, a formidable debater, and, like most top-flight English politicians, a man of great intelligence and culture.

Lord Lloyd, whose tradition is that of Empire administration rather than Westminster debate, traces his ancestry back to the princes who ruled Dyfed (South Wales) nine hundred years ago. He was one of Colonel Lawrence's early companions in the Arabian adventure. It was he who first caused Gandhi to be arrested; he lost his job in Egypt when the conciliatory Arthur Henderson became labour's foreign minister. Like Amery, he is an isolationist and an imperialist. As a proconsul, he was a famous martinet; he believed in pomp. Once when the Prince of Wales visited him in Bombay, His Royal Highness is reported to have murmured, 'I never knew how royalty lived until I stayed with George Lloyd.'

Mosley

'Over the whole of this Abyssinian dispute rises the stink of oil, and stronger than even the stink of oil is the stink of the Jews.'

—MOSLEY.

With Sir Oswald Mosley, Fascism became a thrice-told tale; it became a watery English stew that compared to Italian Fascism as a soggy British cabbage compares to the fiery authority of Italian wine. If the other dictators of the age, Hitler and Mussolini, are boils and pimples, as H. G. Wells expressed it, Oswald Mosley is a blackhead.

Mosley is ambitious. He is (he rather resembles Starhemberg) strikingly handsome. He is probably the best orator in England. His personal magnetism is very great. He was competent enough intellectually to draw into his camp, before he turned Fascist, some of the best young minds in England, like John Strachey. Nevertheless his movement petered out. In the 1935 elections he did not run a single candidate. By 1939 he had become a half-forgotten combination of joke and menace.

In *The Town Labourer* J. L. and Barbara Hammond wrote, 'In 1596 a Mr. Oswald Mosley . . . bought the land on which Manchester now stands for £3,500. In 1846 the town of Manchester bought the manor and all the rights and incidents from Sir Oswald Mosley for £200,000. . . .'

The present Sir Oswald, the sixth baronet to bear the name, inherited a fortune of £247,000 from the late baroness; from his grandfather, who died in 1915, he received £60,000 more. In 1920 he married Lady Cynthia Curzon, the daughter of the late Lord Curzon and the granddaughter of Levi Leiter, the Chicago million-aire; she too was wealthy. At the wedding two kings and two queens were present.

Mosley entered politics as conservative M.P. for Harrow, but presently became 'independent'. There were several reasons for this. As a rich young conservative, he was only one among many rich young conservatives. As an independent who was rich, other parties would be interested in him. Finally, the labour party was rising in influence, and Mosley had strong ideas about economic reform. In 1924 he became a labourite. 'When my wife and I joined the labour movement,' he wrote, 'it meant a complete break with family and former associations.' This plunge into proletarian existence had however its compensations. He bought one of the most beautiful and ancient manor-houses in England (price £9,000) and spent £10,000 rebuilding and furnishing it. Meantime, the toiling masses heard with interest that his wife wanted to be called 'plain Mrs. Mosley'. But when his father died, he assumed the parental title.

In 1929, at the age of thirty-three, he went into the labour minis-try as chancellor of the Duchy of Lancaster. This job is a minis-terial sinecure; Mosley was in effect a minister without portfolio to deal with unemployment. Of his intelligence, his magnetism, there was no doubt. He advocated a vigorous policy of public works; but J. H. Thomas and the stand-pat labour leaders rejected his 'Mosley Memorandum'. He resigned his post, and set about organising a party of his own. Several labour people were tempted to join him, but when he formed his 'New Party' it had only five members in the House, and as his ideas became more and more Fascist, his Left supporters dropped him. The New Party had only one year of life, and in September 1932 Mosley emerged as leader of the B.U.F., British Union of Fascists.

The movement is compact of all the familiar Fascist nostrums. Mosley attacks the City of London and the Jews; he demands a strong policy for India; he appeals for support of the working classes by demagoguery very much like Hitler's; he does not go so far as to threaten revolution, but he hints that the 'Gordian knot' must be cut; he brings little fresh salt to the Fascist pie. Arrogant, super-cilious, dressed in black like a skating champion, he puts on a superb show; but what he talks is mostly nonsense. Spectacular, he organised his Black Shirts on more or less the German model; but at a great meeting at Olympia in 1934, rough-house by his body-guards seriously discredited the movement.

On May 11, 1935, Mosley sent the following communication to Julius Streicher, the SA boss of Nuremberg:

> DEAR HERR STREICHER,—I thank you very much for your telegram regarding my speech at Leicester, which arrived in London during my absence.
> I value this message of yours, in the midst of our hard fight, greatly. The might of Jewish corruption must be overcome in all great countries before the future of Europe can be assured in justice and in peace.
> Our fight is a difficult one. Our victory certain. I thank you. Yours very faithfully, MOSLEY.
>
> —(*Daily Herald*, May 11, 1935.)

Sometimes, in view of his attack on the Jews, Mosley was heckled by people who alluded to his first wife's Jewish blood. Arms akimbo, shoulders arched back, he replied (on one occasion), 'My wife is of Dutch extraction.'

In 1939, as was inevitable, Mosley opposed the war. No one paid much attention.

CHAPTER XXIII

DE VALERA

IKE many modern chieftains, Eamon de Valera was not born a citizen of the country he rules. Hitler, as we have seen, was an Austrian; Pilsudski was Lithuanian in origin, as well as Polish; Josef Stalin still speaks with his native Georgian accent; the late Kamal Ataturk was born in Salonika, Greece, and Dr. Kurt von Schuschnigg, the former Austrian chancellor, in Riva, Italy.

This is a demonstration, among other things, of the way frontiers have danced about since the War. Salonika was still part of Turkey when Kamal Ataturk was an infant; Riva was part of Austria when Schuschnigg went to school. Eamon de Valera's birth-place is separated from his capital by 3,000 miles of ocean. He was born, in 1882, in New York, his father was a Spanish immigrant from Cuba, his mother an Irishwoman lately an arrival in America. De Valera's American birth—and citizenship—saved his life.

Whereas Austrianism has been something of an encumbrance to Hitler, the fact that the Irish leader was American made him President of Ireland. For he was saved from execution after the Easter rebellion in 1916 purely because the British military tribunal had no wish to alienate American opinion by shooting an American citizen. Almost every other commandant in the rebellion was shot. Had he been born elsewhere than in America, the history of the Irish Free State would have been very different. Perhaps— it is quite possible—there would have been no Free State at all.

Eamon de Valera is one of those rare statesmen, like Disraeli and Theodore Roosevelt, who are blessed by a universally known nickname. To everyone in Ireland de Valera is simply 'Dev'. This at once gives some indication of his quality. The Irish are not particularly prone to giving nicknames; Mr. Cosgrave never had one. A nationally-used nickname indicates intimacy and affection; it is a tribute worth thousands in votes; it is the ultimate in honours conferred upon a statesman by the lay public. Mere demagoguery cannot win a nickname, nor can mere success, no matter how great. Hitler has never been nicknamed, and neither was Woodrow

Wilson. But Theodore Roosevelt became 'Teddy' or 'T. R.' and Mr. Lloyd George became 'L. G.' No one in his own country has ever dared to nickname Mussolini or Kamal Ataturk. But everywhere in Ireland Eamon de Valera is just 'Dev'.

Not many people, however, call him 'Dev' to his face. His wife does, and those who are intimate enough to address him by his Christian name, if it were commonly used. Some of his mother's relatives in County Limerick, where he was reared, still call him Eddie. His friends and colleagues usually say Chief, or if addressing him in Irish, Uachtaran (President). He himself addresses most of his staff by their first names, in their Irish form. But 'Dev' is what people call him when he is not in the room.

Ten years or so ago, when he was in opposition, known as 'the President of the Republic' to his followers, the Cosgrave government introduced a Bill in the Dáil Eireann (National Assembly) making it a serious offence to use the title 'President' to describe anybody but Mr. Cosgrave, who was then president of the Executive Council. At a public meeting in Dublin, one of the de Valerists, Countess Markievitz, rose and said that she had never called the President of the Republic anything but Dev, but that henceforth she would call Dev nothing but the President of the Republic. Whereupon the Bill was dropped.

Like most men with a single-track mind, de Valera gets a lot of work done. He puts in a gruelling day. Usually he arrives at his office in Government Buildings between 9.30 and 10. He receives, as a rule, the heads of all departments under his direct administration; he scrupulously pays attention to the smallest details. He returns home for luncheon and is in the office again shortly afterwards. He works till six, goes home to tea, and frequently returns to the office again at night. Often, passing Government Buildings, one may see lights in the President's quarters till after midnight. He has bread and butter for supper. He has never, except for reasons of illness, taken a holiday.

He has the spare but rugged frame that fanatics need. He was a first-class rugger player in his youth, and is still an excellent horseman, very fond of riding. He likes to hike and climb. Almost every Sunday he may be seen walking across a pass in the hills about ten miles from Dublin. His car, empty except for the chauffeur and detectives, drives slowly along; Dev walks behind it, very rapidly, hatless, his hair on end. His clothes, even on this occasion, are usually black. Members of his family have a hard time keeping up with him, so rapid is his pace. Behind are other detectives—members of a group of eight chosen men—who are never far from his person.

He never touches a drop of any kind of alcohol in Ireland or England. He believes drink—hard drink—to be the curse of his country. But, an odd point, he drinks wine or beer when he is on the Continent. He likes nothing better than to sit in a café in Zurich or Geneva sipping a glass of beer and watching people. He does not smoke. But until 1916 he was a heavy smoker. The story is told that he filled his pipe and was about to light it when, after the Easter Rebellion, he was on his way to penal servitude. He stopped suddenly and said, 'I will not let them deprive me of this pleasure in jail!' He threw away the pipe, and has never smoked since.

His hobbies, apart from exercise, are chess, listening to the radio, and above all, mathematics. He was an omnivorous reader until his eye complaint grew serious. He especially read Shakespeare and the Gaelic writers. He speaks Irish fluently and correctly, but with a strong guttural accent. The intellectual pleasure that matters most to him is mathematics. One day going to Rome he asked his secretary what he thought of the quaternary theorem. 'Nothing,' the secretary replied, who knew only elementary mathematics. It was a boiling hot day, and the rest of the staff dozed, but Dev spent twelve solid hours teaching the secretary the quaternary theorem. The secretary said that Dev's twelve-hour lecture was the most brilliant intellectual performance he had ever known. When in jail in 1918, incidentally, de Valera spent all his time mastering the Einstein theory.

His wife was a school-teacher, Sinéad Ní Fhlannagáin (Jennie O'Flanagan), whom he met at the Gaelic League when he was learning Irish. The legend is that de Valera was unable to enter the Civil Service because he failed in his examinations in Gaelic; the story may be apocryphal, and, anyway, Dev married his teacher. That was in 1910. They had seven children. One boy, Brian, was killed riding in Phœnix Park, Dublin, in February 1936. The eldest boy, Vivian, has his Master of Science degree from the National University of Ireland and is now a demonstrator in University College, Dublin; he has also been gazetted lieutenant in the National Volunteers. The eldest girl is also a Graduate of the National University. The younger children are still in secondary school or college.

Mrs. de Valera was a beautiful fair girl. Her golden hair is now turning grey. She is reserved in character, like her husband. The family has almost no social life, except the minimum necessary for official functions. When de Valera became President his wife said that she wished the government would give him an official wife to tend to the official entertaining. The de Valeras live in a simple house on Cross Avenue, Blackrock. They have only one servant, a maid. Before 1932 they had no servants at all, and lived in a much smaller house; Mrs. de Valera did all the work. They entertained guests in the dining-room. Like all the Irish, Mrs. de Valera has a long memory. The younger children are clever and very popular in Blackrock. They have been invited to parties by families who were desperate political opponents of de Valera in the early days. Mrs. de Valera refuses the invitations on the ground that the children are 'too busy'.

President de Valera is extremely accessible as a statesman and he receives a great number of people. (He is very particular about newspaper interviews, however; everything must be checked and okayed by him.) He has many friends. One is a rich farmer doctor, by the name of Farnan. De Valera often visits him late at night and they take long walks together. Another is his secretary Kathleen O'Connell. She has been with the Chief for almost twenty years, and knows his work and the method of his mind inside out. De Valera is very attractive to women, but pays no attention to them. They follow him about at functions; he is smiling but reserved, and, without ever being rude or pompous, manages to create a sense of distance between himself and them.

He has utterly no interest in money. He reduced his salary from £2,500 to £1,500 on taking office. He has no private means, no expensive hobbies, and no taste for luxury. He is very fond of music. His views on art are unknown; he does not appear to be much interested in graphic art. He is, of course, extremely religious, but his Catholicism is neither ostentatious nor bigoted; several of his friends are Protestant. Whenever possible, de Valera is a daily communicant at Mass. As one of his staff expressed it to me, 'His whole life is a prayer.'

His sense of humour is hardly robust; but it exists. It is on the ironic side. He rarely makes jokes, but he appreciates comic situations, and when he laughs, he laughs very heartily. Once he was arrested, at Ennis, in the middle of a speech. A year later he was released. He went forthwith to Ennis, and began to speak again with the words, 'As I was saying when I was interrupted——'

His personal traits are clearly marked: rigid self-control; fanatic faith in his duty to Ireland; extreme seriousness of mind; complete unworldliness; a certain didacticism; stubbornness and humanity. People say that he has lost his temper publicly only once in his life; it occurred during a debate on the Irish Press bonds. Similarly his friends can recall only very rare and isolated cases where he gave way to emotion. Once in 1921, when the Treaty had been ratified by seven votes, he got up and said, 'During these last four years we have worked together like brothers—'; then his voice broke and he sat down and cloaked his face with his hands. He was intensely fond of his son Brian; but immediately after his tragic death he appeared at a party meeting quite calm. When he enters a public place—for instance, the stands at a football match—he does not smile or nod to the crowd. He walks straight ahead, very reserved, and seems to pretend that the crowd is not there.

. . . .

Eamon de Valera discovered Ireland at the age of two. His father (in New York) died and he was dispatched to Ireland in the care of his mother's brother. He lived in his grandmother's home near Bruree, in County Limerick. His mother, who stayed in America, married again; no one seems to know accurately how much contact there was between mother and son during his early years. He went to the local school, living meanwhile on a farm, and won a scholarship, owing to his skill at mathematics, in a religious school near Cork. For a time he thought of entering a Jesuit college. Instead he went to Blackrock College, near Dublin, where his own children were subsequently educated. He got his degree at the Royal University, learned Irish, became a teacher, and opened his career as a nationalist and a revolutionary.

In many European countries to-day many young men follow roughly the same pattern. In Jugoslavia, in Bulgaria, in Turkey, in Syria and Egypt and Palestine, I have met young de Valeras of various breeds. They may also—who knows?—become fathers of countries. Not many have the great intellectual equipment de Valera possessed, and very few can be his equals in force of character; but the general type is the same. Poverty in youth; the struggle for an education combined inextricably with nationalism; deep religious faith in many cases; dedication of the totality of life to a passionate desire for freedom. Many of the nationalisms represented by these young men seem feeble and petty. The hatreds they engender—that of a young Syrian for the French, for instance, or a Croat for the Serb government in Belgrade—seem deplorable. But they are living factors in the Europe of to-day.

De Valera, from the beginning, was an extremist of extremists. It was inevitable that he should join Pearce, MacDonough, Mac-Dermott, and the others in the proclamation of the Irish Republic at Easter 1916. It was a mad adventure. It could not possibly succeed. It was sheer suicide. So the level-headed ones said at the time. They were wrong. The rebellion was put down by force of arms, true, after a week's fighting; all the leaders except de Valera, true, were sentenced to death and shot. But the Easter rebellion was not a failure. It was a success. So at least de Valera would look at it. For out of its fire and bloodshed came—after terribly tragic years—the Irish Free State, with himself on top of it.

De Valera was one of the 'commandants' who were charged with the actual military operations, and his handful of men were in occupation of a place outside Dublin called Boland's Mills. This was a key spot, because the British had to pass it to reach Dublin from the sea. De Valera's men were the best trained, the best led, in the Irish Army. The British themselves conceded this. One of de Valera's tricks was to station a very few men, with a couple of machine-guns, in an outhouse from which the Irish flag was flying. This deceived the British into thinking that it housed his main force. De Valera did not want to surrender when the revolt—inside Dublin—was crushed, but he obeyed his superior officers. He came out of Boland's Mills to surrender, saying, 'Shoot me if you like. Let my men alone.'

He was sentenced to death by military tribunal, but the sentence was commuted to life imprisonment when it became known that the leader was an American. The British at the time were very anxious that America should come into the war on the side of the Allies; the Irish-American vote and sentiment were important. He spent only a year in Dartmoor, because in 1917 there was a general amnesty. Promptly—since most of the other republican leaders had been shot—he was elected president of Sinn Fein. He was also Sinn Fein M.P. for Clare. He never got a chance to sit at West-minster—of course he was an abstentionist and he would not have gone to London even if permitted—because early in 1918 he was again arrested, and this time sent to jail in Lincoln.

About his escape from Lincoln there are many legends. The true story appears to be this. He drew a grotesque picture on a postcard! it showed a drunken man fitting an enormous key into a lock. The card passed the censor, but its Irish recipient, dull-witted, put it away in a drawer thinking that Dev was off his head. The picture, in reality, was an accurate drawing of the key to the prison yard. Later the friend got another similarly grotesque post-card, this time depicting a smaller key. The friend now saw what Dev meant. A key was made and smuggled into de Valera. It did not fit. Then Dev managed to make a wax cast of a key from a bit of candle. This was smuggled out; later a key blank and a file, concealed in a cake, were smuggled in. And one fine evening Dev walked out of jail.

There was a tremendous man-hunt for him. De Valera got to Manchester and hid in the house of a priest. As he walked in, the priest had been reading in the Bible the words, 'Knock, and it shall be opened unto you.' De Valera got to Liverpool, and made his way —with some difficulty—to Ireland. One story is that he disguised himself as an ordinary seaman, and was scrubbing the decks under the very feet of the detectives who searched every boat for him; another is that he was hidden by a friend in the potato stores, was literally buried in potatoes till the search was over. Then he went to America, disguised as a stoker. His arrival in New York was a nine days' wonder. The police were still scouring England and Ireland for him. He spoke all over the United States, raised money for the Irish cause, and established himself as the undisputed spokesman of free Ireland.

He returned to Ireland to the tune of more narrow escapes and adventures. He landed first in Liverpool, aboard the *Celtic*. He bribed an officer of a tramp steamer to smuggle him into Ireland; the fee was £100. Whereupon the officer went ashore and had a drink or two. De Valera was hidden in his cabin. The officer did not return as the ship was due to sail. The captain, furious, came to his cabin to investigate. Thinking quickly, de Valera pretended to be very drunk himself. After a tense few moments, the captain dismissed him as a harmless if exhilarated friend of his absent officer. And the ship sailed. Once in Ireland again—this was in 1919—history began.

It was history of a most disorderly, cruel, factional and bloody kind. The story has been told too often, and at too great length, to bear detailed repetition here. De Valera was elected President of the Dáil Eireann comprising the Sinn Fein deputies from Southern Ireland. The de Valerists constituted themselves a national assembly, refused to take the oath to the King, and proclaimed their independence. Civil war began: the Black and Tans and Irish nationalists slaughtered one another. The war ended in a truce in July 1921, and negotiations went on for five months until the Irish Treaty was signed. This gave Ireland dominion status, but separated the Free State from Ulster. The de Valerists split. De Valera, though the delegates who went to London were his plenipotentiaries, disowned them and refused to accept the treaty. He wanted more. He went into opposition; which meant that civil war started once again.

It ended with mutual exhaustion, and in the spring of 1923 a Cease Fire order stopped the bloodshed. De Valera and his group of followers, now a minority, insisted that the Treaty had been imposed on the Free State by Lloyd George's threat of war, and refused to sit in the Dáil so long as members took the oath to the King. In June 1927 the Cosgrave government passed a bill requiring that candidates for the Dáil, must, if elected, promise to take their seats. This brought de Valera and his forty-three men into the Dáil. A new election increased his strength to fifty-seven. Finally, in 1932, he won a majority, by coalition with the Labour Party, and displaced Cosgrave as President. He went to the country in 1933 and got a clear majority—but a slight one—and has been in power ever since.

When I saw de Valera a few years ago it was with the understanding that I would not quote him directly on Irish affairs. It was not an interview; merely a brief chat. His office is a simple small room, with 'President' printed in black on the frosted window. It resembled the kind of room which a modest executive of a modest business might use. No particular decoration; no covey of secretaries; no swank. Just a big desk next to a small window and a tall, gaunt man behind it.

De Valera looks less severe than his pictures. The long nose and the deep lines to the mouth are his most characteristic features. He seemed younger, I thought, than his fifty-four years. He was alert, interested, and extremely courteous. He speaks with a perceptible brogue, words like 'that' or 'this' come out with the 'th's' thickened.

I explained that I had recently been appointed London correspondent of my newspaper and that this was my first visit to Ireland. I said that I was very happy, after many years on the Continent, to be exploring these new realms, and that life in the

British Isles was most exciting. My use of the term 'British Isles' was an unconscious little slip. Mr. de Valera did not allow it to go uncorrected. Quite soberly he smiled and said that if I had meant to include Ireland in the British Isles, he trusted that I did so only as a 'geographical expression'. I explained that my chief duty to my newspaper was to gain knowledge, background, education. 'Very well,' Mr. de Valera said, 'let your instruction begin at once.' And he set out to explain the difference between Ireland and the 'British Isles'. Some moments later, having again necessity to describe my field of operations, I sought a phrase and said, after a slight pause, 'a group of islands in the northern part of Europe.' Mr. de Valera sat back and laughed heartily. I hope he will not mind my telling this little story.

The President thought that the most disconcerting thing about Europe as a whole was the way people—good and intelligent people —had been forced by the pressure of events to think of war as an inevitability. Five years ago that was not true, he was inclined to think. War was something that people feared, and which they hoped would not come. But nowadays it seemed that people considered war as the normal thing to expect. He shook his head gravely, and said that if he had been born a German or a Frenchman he would have devoted his whole life to trying to make permanent peace between France and Germany.

Then Mr. de Valera turned to Ireland, and my 'instruction' began. He was patient, explicit, and formidably, sombrely reasonable. But in that gaunt face I saw the eyes of a fanatic. When I left him, deeply impressed by his terrific Irishness, I recalled the little story about his first talk with Lloyd George. 'How did you get along with de Valera?' the Welshman was asked. 'We have talked for two days,' Lloyd George sighed, 'and he has got up to Brian Boru.'

.   .   .   .

Beyond the obvious things—tenacity, intelligence, and so on—it would seem that a main source of de Valera's power is his community with people. His position—especially since the abolition of the Senate—is virtually that of a dictator, but he is an unchallengeably firm democrat. He believes in the people; his people believe in him. He said recently that he did not think he would ever again have to take arms in his hands and fight for Ireland, but that he would gladly fight—and die—for democracy. His faith in the fundamental goodness and rightness of people is profound. In

1933, however, he was quick to smash the Blueshirt (Fascist) movement, because he was well aware that even the best of people may
be misled, and that the first duty of democracy is to protect itself.
Almost immediately on reaching power, it will be recalled, he
submitted himself to an election which he did not, technically,
have to hold. The instant his majority is lost, he will resign. In
1934 an organised campaign against local rates and taxes began.
Some of his friends appealed for more vigorous action against
saboteurs who were felling trees across roads and cutting telegraph
wires. 'No,' de Valera said. 'Leave them to the people. The
people themselves will check them.'

The faith of the average Free Stater in de Valera is little short of
idolatrous. Way back in 1921, when it seemed that civil war was
imminent again, de Valera organised his volunteers. During a test
mobilisation near Dublin a road mine was found to be defective.
De Valera examined it, discovered what was wrong, and put it right.
'He's a greater soldier than Napoleon,' one of the men exclaimed.
Now, however fine a military amateur de Valera may be, the comparison is, of course, ridiculous. 'But it is a great thing,' the Irishman who told me this story commented, 'that a leader should have
followers who really think of comparing him to Napoleon.'

He is utterly without personal ambition. His only ambition is
the unity and self-determination of the Irish people. 'It is not a
question of what I want,' he told an interviewer once, 'but what the
people of Ireland want.'

Since reaching power de Valera has, as was inevitable, tweaked
the British lion's tail. The Dáil has abolished the oath of allegiance
to the King, greatly reduced the power and privileges of the
governor-general, denied the right of appeal from the Irish Supreme
Court to the Privy Council, and withheld the land annuities. These
were payments of roughly £5,000,000 per year by Ireland to Britain
on account of loans during the last century by which Irish tenant
farmers purchased land. The British retaliated by a prohibitive
tariff on Irish goods, chiefly the agricultural produce—cattle and
milk and butter—which was the bulk of Ireland's export business.
An economic war began, and still continues. As a result de Valera
has had profoundly to change the texture of Irish economic life.
He has cut down imports, built sugar factories, sown the land
with wheat, and killed off his surplus cattle by trying to encourage
leather and meatmeal industries; in a word, he has been forced
by Britain to an experiment in self-sufficiency. How successful it

will be none can tell. The effort has been great, and the cost tremendous.

De Valera's whole life has been dominated by one idea and ideal: a united and independent Ireland. This he has not achieved. What he has achieved is the creation of a Free State which, as it was aptly expressed, is *in* the British Commonwealth, but not *of* it. The Free State is a compromise between republican aspirations and the blunt realities of British power. De Valera's feeling is, perhaps, that a generation is very short in the life of mankind, and that the creation of the Free State is a beginning that will develop to its proper end. He wants and needs only two things, one of his friends told me—peace and time.

.   .   .   .

In April 1937 the new constitution of the Irish Free State was published, and in 1938 the Free State—having adopted the good old Irish name of Eire—separated itself from the British Commonwealth, though the sovereignty of the crown was recognised in matters of defence. Dr. Douglas Hyde, the veteran man of letters, became first president of Eire, with Mr. de Valera—who won an easy general election in June—as his prime minister.

During 1939 severe outrages by members of the Irish Republican Army took place throughout England. These Irish extremists go further even that Mr. de Valera in their desire to see the British out of Ireland. . . . When war came in 1939 de Valera announced that Eire would remain strictly neutral. This produced a certain paradox. The British Empire went to war with Germany, but not Eire.

CHAPTER XXIV

DANUBE BLUES

'The situation in Germany is serious but not hopeless; the situation in Austria is hopeless but not serious.'

—VIENNESE SAYING.

'AUSTRIA is ruled,' said old Viktor Adler, the founder of Viennese social democracy, 'by Absolutism modified by *Schlamperei*.' I do not know exactly how to translate this lovely Viennese word, *Schlamperei*, but roughly it means slovenliness plus a certain charm, provided you do not lose your temper. Adler made his little joke many years ago; despite the terrible trials Austria underwent after 1919, including the two civil wars of 1934 and the *Anschluss* in 1938, it still holds good to-day.

But Austria and its entrancing capital Vienna no longer represent the undiluted joy of life of other days. The *Föhn*, that seductive and enervating breeze from the Austrian Alps, the source of much of Vienna's pervasive, exasperating charm, still blows—yes. The Viennese, a profoundly civilised people, still drink gallons of beer and the best coffee in the world, discussing placidly the really important things of life, like Mozart and whipped cream—yes.

We who lived in Vienna through the early and middle 30's had to alter our comfortable view that the Viennese were invariably shiftless, easy-going, sophisticated, gentle. We found that some things, in the last analysis, were more important to the Viennese than the first act of the newest Jaray comedy, or the latest subtle embroidery on the theories of Freud or Stekel. We learned that the Balkans *do*, as Metternich said, begin at Landstrasse Hauptstrasse. And so does Germany.

.   .   .   .

Austria before the union with Germany in 1938—which event I have already described in Chapter VIII above—was a country roughly three-fifths the size of England, with a population of six and a half million, a good deal less than that of London. Before the War of 1914 Austria-Hungary, with fifty million people, stretched

376

from the Carpathians to the Adriatic; the chief psychological problem of the country in post-War years was adjustment to this shrinkage from imperial greatness to meagre exiguity. The story of the
two Tyroleans was well known. 'Let's take a walk,' one said,
'around Austria.' 'No,' replied the other, 'I don't want to get back
before lunch.'

The capital, Vienna, like a swollen head atop a dwarfed and
shrunken body, contained more than one-third of the country's inhabitants, and this acute disproportion was its chief economic problem after 1918. The country had to import more than it exported;
it did not raise enough to feed itself; therefore it was very poor.
Vienna, a gaping maw, swallowed more than the mountainously
beautiful but economically almost useless hinterland could produce.
The chief crop of provincial Austria is—scenery.

The weakness of Austria was for a time its greatest strength.
Until 1934 at least its foreign policy was largely one of gentle blackmail; it demanded and got financial or political help from the
other powers because it was a buffer state in a key position, and if
it collapsed the whole Danube equilibrium would go to pot. A
joke from Germany was relevant. Hitler, Goering, Goebbels, discuss what they will do if the Nazi régime crashes. Goering says:
'I will wear civilian clothes, and no one will recognise me.' Goebbels
says, 'I will keep my mouth shut, and people will not know who I
am.' But Hitler says he need do nothing: 'I am an Austrian, and
therefore the powers will have to protect me.' Strangely ironic this
seems now!

Austria is not only the pivot of the Danube, but the key to great
events far afield. In March 1931, the German foreign minister
Curtius and the Austrian chancellor, an honest but dull-witted
policeman Dr. Schober, suggested a Customs Union between their
respective countries. This, of course, aroused French rage, because
the Quai d'Orsay saw it as the first step to *Anschluss*. So the French
withdrew credits from Austrian banks and helped to provoke the
collapse of Credit Anstalt, the chief financial institution in Central
Europe. Results: the German banking crisis, the reparations moratorium, the flight from sterling. Banks crashed through Europe like
tin pans down a concrete alley. A politico-economic quarrel in
remote Vienna, it was proved, could—and did—shake Great Britain
off gold. Confidence, betrayed by the pound sterling, left the earth;
and it has not yet returned.

The disequilibrium between Marxist Vienna and the clerical

countryside was the dominating *Motiv* of Austrian politics until
the rise of Hitler. Vienna was socialist, anti-clerical, and, as a
municipality, fairly rich. The hinterland was poor, backward,
conservative, Roman Catholic, and jealous of Vienna's higher
standard of living. The socialists, to defend themselves in what
they thought was their impregnable citadel, founded a private
army of young workmen and intellectuals, the Schutzbund. The
countryside promptly countered with a similar army—but recruited
from primitive and hungry peasant lads, in leather breeches and
green hats—the Heimwehr. The struggle between these two forces
resulted in the civil war of February 1934.

In Vienna the socialists produced a remarkable administration,
making it probably the most successful municipality in the world.
By means of an ingenious taxation system they financed paternalistic
reforms of unparalleled quantity and quality; they built health
clinics, baths, gymnasia, sanatoria, schools, kindergartens, and the
imposing sunshine dwellings which, in decency and cleanliness if
not luxury, housed sixty thousand families—socialist families.
They eliminated slums; they cut down drastically the tuberculosis
rate; they took money from the rich, who could spare it, and used
it for the benefit of the worthy poor. The achievements of the
Vienna socialists were the most exhilarating social monument of the
post-War period in any European country. Result: the clericals
bombed them out of existence.

Through the terrible years of poverty and deflation in the early
30's tension between the socialists and their opponents grew.
The Credit Anstalt crash cost the country one thousand million
schillings, about £28,000,000. The fall of agricultural prices in
the Danube basin ruined Austria's attenuated trade. The political structure of the country creaked with strain. The socialists,
with a cool forty-two per cent of the electorate, were the largest
political party, but they shut themselves up in Vienna and turned
their back on the country at large; had they tried to form a
minority government—because a coalition of all the other parties
could outvote them—there might have been civil war. Little
Putsches, instigated by the Heimwehr, did occur. Angrily tension
increased.

The man in the street, sipping his coffee, dreaming of the great
days before the War, seemingly paid little attention to the crisis.
Vienna's familiar lassitude, product of the warm, sirocco-like *Föhn*,
enveloped politics in a fog of languor. When the Customs Union

and Credit Anstalt stories raged across the front pages of the world,
the Vienna papers carried scare headlines—about the deficit in the
Burg theatre. Man, said Aristotle, is a political animal; but Vienna
is a woman. She had no practical head for politics, especially her
own politics. The plan for a Danubian confederation got scarcely
a yawn out of the Viennese—but when Jeritza missed a high C in
Tannhäuser, the whole town rocked with shame. The country was
poor, but it still managed to subsidise the Opera to the tune of
£200,000 per year—so all was well.

Then two things happened to jerk Vienna from its pensive
lethargy. One was Dollfuss. The other Hitler.

Duodecimo Dictator

Dr. Engelbert Dollfuss, who had a vivid couple of years as the
political darling of western Europe, the 'Millimetternich'—so
called because he was only four feet eleven inches high—the
youngest and littlest of the post-War dictators, was born in Texing,
a village in Lower Austria, on October 4, 1892. His origins were
humble. He worked his way through school, studied law at the
University of Vienna, and when the War came served three years
at the Front. He went in a private—in the famous *Kaiserchützen*
regiment—and came out a first lieutenant, no small feat in the old
imperial army.

Dollfuss was born a peasant and with belief in God. These
were the two paramount facts in his character. Much of his personal
charm and force came from his extreme simplicity of character; his
modesty and directness amounted almost to naïveté. A foreigner
approaching him with a compliment would hear a broad farmer's
accent in reply, '*Ach—abr gehen Sie*' ('Oh, go on. . . .') His
speeches were extraordinarily unsophisticated; he listened to
speeches of members of his cabinet who were experts in their field
with the respectful attention of a child in school. Speaking himself, he was tense, awkward, overworked. A devout Catholic, his
religious faith gave him something of the curious innocence of old,
wise priests, an innocence as impregnable to the wiles of adversaries
as the most glittering sophistication.

Of course his stature—or rather lack of it—helped him inordinately. He became David to the Goliath of the Nazis. His diminu-
tiveness dramatised him into the heart of Austrian politics. He
was a sort of mascot. One could be angry with a six-footer, but a
prime minister barely five feet in his stocking-feet was irresistible.

2 C

(These feelings were, of course, blasted by the events of February 1934, when he wrong-headedly moved against the socialists.) Tiny physically, Dollfuss was not however a dwarf. His smallness was shapely; all the features, diminutive, were well-formed.

The jokes about his size were famous. He broke his leg one day falling off a ladder; he had been picking a dandelion. The police discovered an *attentat* against his life; a mouse-trap had been secreted in his bedroom. Postage stamps were to be issued commemorating his victories, adorned with his portrait—life size. An Austrian physicist won the Nobel prize for his experiments splitting the atom, with Dollfuss as his subject. When agitated at night, he either paced up and down under the bed or went skating on the frozen surface of his *pot*. He did not take the train to Rome when he visited Mussolini; he was dispatched air mail. When the chief of the staff of the Austrian army, reviewing troops, was startled to see a turtle at the head of the formations, his shock was quickly dispelled; the turtle was the *Herr Bundeskanzler*—in a steel helmet.

Dollfuss entered politics as a member of the Christian Social (conservative) party, led by that astute cleric, Monsignor Ignaz Seipel. The little man was interested in agriculture; he organised a peasants' league in Lower Austria and presently became a deputy in the Austrian parliament. The federal railways needed an agrarian expert and he joined its administrative council; in October 1930 he became president of the railways. In March 1931 he got a cabinet post as minister of agriculture. A year later an exasperating crisis provoked the resignation of the Christian Social government of Dr. Buresch. Dollfuss was asked to form a new government. No one else would take the ticklish job, because the party had a majority of only one in the chamber. Dollfuss prayed all night before accepting. This was on May 20, 1932. He remained prime minister until the Nazis murdered him in little over two years later.

No one, when he assumed the chancellorship, thought that he would last long; no one, indeed, thought that he was of any consequence at all. With a group of newspaper men I had lunch with him during the first week of his rule. Earnest, shy, tired, excited, Dollfuss sat, smoked and talked till dusk. And we became aware that here might be a person of original quality. The two main factors in his career became manifest soon after: (1) his capacity to take immediate advantage of a situation, (2) his sense of drama.

Ratification of the Lausanne Loan[1] which was to bring 300,000,000
chillings to the country was up before parliament. The socialists
and pan-Germans opposed ratification. Early that morning Dr.
Seipel died. Dollfuss' majority of one had gone to heaven. So the
miniature chancellor promptly swore in a successor and dragooned
every member of his party, sick or well, to the chamber: one man
was carried in by three comrades, another man came from a hospital swathed in bandages. Dollfuss won—by one vote. And by
such unconventional, even tyrannical behaviour!—exclaimed the
Austrians, shocked and impressed. A few weeks later another
crucial vote impended. Dollfuss won again, and again by a single
vote. The missing adversary was the former chancellor Dr. Schober
—who had died the night before.

On March 4, 1933, the Austrian parliament committed suicide.
It was a marvellously, typically Viennese occasion. A socialist
deputy, just before an important vote, went out, as the phrase goes,
to wash his hands. A colleague voted for him, but carelessly inserted
into the box an incorrect ballot, one marked with his own name
instead of that of the missing deputy. The vote was eighty-one to
eighty against the government. The high-minded socialist speaker,
Dr. Renner, announced however that an irregularity in the voting
had occurred.[2] Long did he regret it. Because the chamber got
excited and in the confusion Dr. Renner so far lost his head as to
resign and walk out of the meeting. The two deputy speakers likewise resigned; the session ended in pandemonium.

Then clever Dr. Dollfuss discovered that legally the parliament
could not reconstitute itself, since by law only the speaker or deputy
speakers could call a session, and all three, having resigned, were
powerless to do so. It was a ridiculous little *contretemps*, but the
Austrians are extremely legal-minded, and it ended parliamentarism in the country. Dollfuss, like a bulldog, pounced on his
opportunity. He resigned office—having learned the good political
lesson never to offer resignation until you are indispensable—and

[1] Austria was nearing default on the 1923 League of Nations Reconstruction
Loan, which was guaranteed by the Powers. The Powers thereupon lent Austria
more money because they themselves would have had to pay the original investors
if default persisted. This was known as 'saving' Austria.

[2] The issue was a motion asking lenience for railway workers who a few days
before had gone on strike. The railway administration was hopelessly in debt
and could not pay the men their full wages. The workmen protested. For want
of a few thousand schillings in the railway cash box, parliamentarism in Austria
expired.

was reappointed with emergency powers. On March 7 a flood of decrees splashed on Vienna. People read them—and discovered that Dollfuss was their dictator.

His luck, until the end, was always of phenomenal quality, but at two-fifteen p.m. on October 3, 1933, the luckiest thing of all happened: he was shot. At two-fourteen he was only a chancellor; at two-sixteen, he became a martyr, and a living martyr at that. Only good luck stood between his heart and the two bullets fired at less than a yard's range. It was his great sense of occasion that made him deliver a radio speech from his bedside which turned him into the world's favourite convalescent. The would-be assassin was discovered to be a slightly Van-der-loony Nazi. How Hitler must have wanted to choke him for having made a hero of his own worst enemy! For the enormous and foreboding shadow of the Nazis had begun to fall on Austria.

Marauders from the North

Hitler, who had become chancellor that year, wanted Austria for a variety of reasons; he mentions the union of Austria and Germany in the very first paragraph of *Mein Kampf*.

(1) Himself an Austrian, he viewed the little country's 'misbehaviour' as direct repudiation by his own people and thus an unforgivable assault on his personal prestige.

(2) The pan-Germanism of the Nazis was bound to look ridiculous as long as 6,500,000 Austrian Germans, directly contiguous to the Third Reich, sniggered at the Swastika instead of worshipping it.

(3) Germany badly needed a triumph in foreign policy, and a successful assault on Austria would have cloaked possible discontent at home.

(4) Austria possessed valuable reserves of iron ore, the Eisenerz deposit in Styria, which would compensate for Germany's mineral starvation.

(5) If Austria became part of Germany, the *Mittel-Europa* dream would begin to be realised: the dream of an encircled Czechoslovakia, of a Nazi push into the broad plains of Hungary and beyond.

At the beginning Nazis within Austria represented only a very small force. In the general election of November 1930—the last free election held in Austria—they didn't get a single seat, though Hitler at that time in Germany commanded six million votes. But when Hitler became chancellor, Naziism among Austrians, who are, after all, German, steeply grew. Had the Nazis behaved less stupidly Austria might very well have fallen into their lap without a struggle. Dollfuss, quarrelling with the socialists, was in a ticklish position; his Heimwehr support was unreliable; jealous clerical politicians were undercutting him. And the biggest Nazi card was Austrian defeatism; the Austrians hated fighting and their attitude was more or less, 'Oh, well, if the Germans want to take us in and support us, why not?' But instead of waiting the Nazis began an extraordinary campaign of terrorism and violence. This served to challenge Austria to stand on its own feet; it backed the country against the wall of its own dormant patriotism. Then Hitlerism inside Germany alienated large numbers of Austrian clericals, socialists, and Jews.

Even so, as the full-dress campaign of the Nazis got under way, Dollfuss faced formidable difficulties. Nazi violence in the form of shootings, intimidations, assaults, bombings, slanders, libels, occurred almost daily. The small but tough chancellor fought back. On May Day he forbade the usual social democrat demonstrations and to the amazement of the populace filled the Ringstrasse in Vienna with troops and barbed wire—as a show of force. Then he expelled the Bavarian minister of justice, Dr. Frank, who was visiting the country on a speaking tour. The Germans retaliated by imposing a 1,000 mark fine on German tourists to Austria, a serious blow to the tourist traffic; Dollfuss retaliated by outlawing the Nazi party. In Berlin, the Austrian Press attaché was arrested and expelled. This happened the night before Dollfuss was to address the London Economic Conference. The incident dramatised his appearance and he got a great ovation. The Nazis countered with more violence.

And then began a war, one of the queerest wars ever known anywhere, a war fought bloodlessly (except for casualties in minor border frays) but a war nevertheless. The Nazis invaded Austria. They crossed the frontier—through the air. Their planes dropped propaganda leaflets; their radio station in Munich, through the mouth of Herr Habicht, Hitler's 'inspector-general' for Austria, hurled speeches across the ether. As Austrian Nazis fled Austria, they were organised on German soil into an 'Austrian Legion', the avowed aim of which was reconquest of the homeland. Tension increased till the Great Powers found it intolerable; France, Italy and

Great Britain joined to present a vigorous *démarche* in Berlin, and
for a time the Nazis quieted down.

Even so, at the end of 1933, things looked very dark for Dollfuss.

Protector from the South

Three developments of great importance then occurred. First,
Mussolini took Dollfuss in his pocket and became to all intents and
purposes the Lord High Protector of Austria. This was because
Italy could not endure the thought of strong Prussians instead of
weak Austrians on the Brenner Pass, the frontier between Italy and
Austria. If Austria went Nazi, it would in effect mean that Germany was in the backyard of Trieste and overlooking the fields of
Lombardy, whereas it was then a cardinal point in Italian policy to
keep independent Austria as a buffer state between the Fascist
giants. Moreover, there were two hundred thousand German speaking people in the South Tyrol—and the further Germany was away
from them the better Mussolini liked it. Dollfuss visited Mussolini
three times. Their interests coincided.

Second, Dollfuss was forced to concede more and more authority
to the Heimwehr, led by a young aristocrat and freebooter, Prince
Ernst Rudiger von Starhemberg, and a tough Viennese ex-army
officer Major Emil Fey. The Heimwehr, malignantly anti-socialist,
became in effect the private army of the Dollfuss régime. As price
for its support, it demanded more and more strenuous action against
the social democrats. Dollfuss dissolved the socialist Schutzbund;
he pinpricked and heckled the socialist leaders; he curtailed the
financial privileges of the Vienna municipality; he gave way steadily
to Heimwehr provocation. Moreover, the Heimwehr was financed
partly by Italy, with the result that Dollfuss was doubly in Italian
hands.

Third, Dollfuss, who had assumed five of the nine portfolios in
the Austrian cabinet, becoming a dictator in name as well as fact,
announced his intention to promulgate a new constitution reforming the state on an authoritarian *Staendische* (guild) basis. He
borrowed the idea from a papal encyclical, the *Quadragesimo Anno*
of 1931, wherein Pope Pius XI pleaded for the end of social strife
and urged the adoption of a corporate organisation of society as a
'cure' for class war. This meant, if introduced full force, the end of
trade unionism under socialist control; so the socialists fought it
tooth and hammer. As an adjunct to the new constitution, Dollfuss
created the *Vaterlaendische Front* (Fatherland Front), a national

movement above the parties, grounded on a patriotic basis. Musso-
ini approved both measures.

But the crisis with Germany got hot again. The equilibrium of
Austrian affairs was permanently shattered. Instead of the former
ug of war between two more or less equal opponents, socialists and
clericals, Dollfuss had to survive an angry triple struggle; the
country became divided into three groups, roughly approximate in
power—socialists, Nazis, and government-plus-Heimwehr. The
dynamics of this struggle were unpredictable. Dollfuss was in the
Centre, fighting both Left and Right. If the Nazis and socialists had
joined forces, he would have been crushed. But hatred of Hitler by
the socialists made a socialist-Nazi coalition impossible. Another
danger then cropped up: the Nazis and the Heimwehr—bad actors
—started secret negotiations.

To ease himself from these predicaments, Dollfuss himself began
a flirtation with the Nazis. His policy had been consistently defensive; he was willing to negotiate peace on the basis of independent Austria. Hitler agreed to negotiation. The details were to be
settled between Dollfuss and Habicht, and on January 8, 1934,
Habicht by terms of the arrangement, stepped into a plane at
Munich and headed for Vienna. At the very last moment, Dollfuss
—the explanation is that more Nazi terrorism, contrary to the truce,
occurred the night before—called off the plan. Habicht was
stopped in mid-air by radio.

The next week Signor Suvitch, Mussolini's under-secretary of
state for foreign affairs, arrived on an official visit to Vienna. He
suggested a new way out. The Austrian régime, attacked on both
flanks, could not possibly survive as it stood; Dollfuss had to
eliminate one of his enemies in order to free himself to fight the
other. Mussolini detested the Austrian social democrats. They
had exposed his smuggling of weapons to Hungary in the Hirtenberg arms affair the year before. So the Italians told Dollfuss to
'solve' the problem by getting rid of the socialists. 'Liquidate the
socialists somehow,' they said. This is the true explanation of the
terrible event that then took place—the February civil war.

CHAPTER XXV

THE FEBRUARY TRAGEDY

THE civil war, which echoed ominously in every chancellery in
Europe, was called a socialist 'revolution' by the Dollfuss
government. Just as the Nazis in Germany tried to foist on the
world the legend that they saved the Reich from Marxism, so did
the Dollfuss-Heimwehr-clerical apologists explain that they used
field artillery to kill women and children in residential buildings
in order to crush a 'Bolshevik insurrection'. This was, of course,
not true. The tragic bloodshed of February 12 was the result of a
cold-blooded Fascist (Heimwehr) *coup d'état*. The socialists resisted, certainly; so did the Belgians when Germany crossed the
frontier in 1914. The Belgians may have fired the first shots, but
they didn't start the War.

The government charged Dr. Otto Bauer and Col. Julius
Deutsch, the two leading socialists, with being Bolsheviks. The
fact was that their brand of social democracy saved Austria from
Bolshevism in 1919 when both Bavaria and Hungary succumbed
to communist régimes. The government alleged that members of
the Socialist Schutzbund possessed illegal arms. They did indeed
—arms which the government itself gave them. It was conveniently
forgotten that the Schutzbund was armed as a defensive measure
against Jugoslavia during a frontier crisis in 1920, and that for
some years the Schutzbund and federal army held the arms in
common. The socialist tenements, the government said, were
'fortresses'. Of course. Any modern building is a fortress as soon
as artillery starts to fire on it and if defenders with guns are within.

The Heimwehr, under Starhemberg and Major Fey, who was
vice-chancellor in the government, had violently threatened extirpation of the socialists since 1927. A Heimwehr *Putsch* was
averted in 1929 only by the narrowest of margins, and in 1931
a Heimwehr rising in Styria was put down by military action:
Starhemberg was arrested and jailed.[1] Then in 1932 Monsignor

---

[1] And fined £5 10s. See G. E. R. Gedye's admirable book, *Heirs to the Habsburgs*, p. 105.

Seipel took the Heimwehr into his government, and under Dollfuss the movement was blessed officially as an auxiliary armed force. The socialists wrote their doom, not by aggression, but by temporising, by seeking compromise. This was seized on by the Heimwehr as a sign of weakness. The socialists wanted peace; but the Heimwehr wanted war.

After the Habicht fiasco and the Suvitch visit the Heimwehr got beyond control. Its leaders decided to force Dollfuss' hands, because the little chancellor, afraid of bloodshed, seemed to be wavering. Conveniently, he went to Hungary on a state visit, it is unknown exactly to what extent he encouraged what happened in his absence. The Heimwehr throughout Austria progressively ran wild through the provinces. Let extracts from the chronology of the *Bulletin of International News*, published by the Royal Institute of International Affairs, tell the story:

Jan. 31. The Heimwehr leaders presented the Governor of the Tyrol with six demands which, if carried out, amounted to the establishment of semi-military rule in the Province.... This followed the mobilisation of 8,000 Heimwehr on Jan. 30 to avert disorders threatened by the Nazis.

Feb. 6. The leaders of the Upper Austrian Heimwehr, supported by the Patriotic Front, were understood to be making the same demands as those in the Tyrol, and detachments of them occupied some of the public buildings at Linz, the provincial capital.

Feb. 7. The Heimwehr leaders in Styria and the Burgenland submitted to the Provincial Governors at Graz and Eisenstadt demands for a more authoritative government and a semi-military administration.

Feb. 8. The police raided the offices of the *Arbeiter Zeitung*. ... This was a sequel to the seizure a few days previously of arms and explosives in buildings to which the socialists had access at Schwechat. ...

Feb. 9. The Heimwehr leaders in Salzburg presented authoritarian demands to the Provincial Governor. The Governor of Lower Austria was understood to have refused to see the local Heimwehr leaders, on the ground that their demands were unconstitutional. Following on reports that the Heimwehr were demanding of the Government the banning of the socialist party and the occupation of the Vienna City Hall, the socialist headquarters, intimated that any such action would be the signal for a general strike. Herr Dollfuss returned from Budapest and received the Heimwehr leaders.

Feb. 10. The vice-chancellor deprived the Mayor of Vienna (a Social Democrat) and other City Officials of the authority to supervise matters of public safety.

Feb. 11. Speaking at a Heimwehr parade, attended by the

minister of war, Major Fey (the vice-chancellor) said, 'In the last
two days I have made certain that Herr Dollfuss is with us. *To-
morrow we are going to clean up Austria.*' (Italics mine.)

Major Fey was as good as his word. On February 12 the fighting
began.

Gemütlichkeit Gone Wrong

At about eight-thirty that morning one of the local Press
agencies telephoned me that fighting had broken out at Linz. He
had few details. Apparently socialist workers resisted when Heimwehr guardsmen invaded their premises. As early as February 7
I had concluded a dispatch to my newspaper with the words 'civil
war is possible'. But even on the morning of the twelfth I thought
that there was still some hope that Dollfuss would keep his head
and avert a crisis. Otto Bauer had told me not long before that he
and Dollfuss would 'negotiate'. I phoned the *Arbeiter Zeitung*, the
socialist newspaper, and got no reply. I rushed out to pick up what
information I could find, and returned home at about eleven-thirty
to write my story. At eleven-forty-five my wife said, 'Try to turn on
the electric light.' I twiddled the button; no light. General strike!

So we thought, but as we learned later, the strike of the electrical
workers was not, alas, general. They had downed tools spontaneously as word of fighting came from Linz. I noted the strangely
quiet streets, because the tramcars had stopped; most of the motor-
men and conductors didn't know why the current had snapped off;
small, curious crowds surrounded the stranded trams. (Later that
day, we saw innumerable horse-drawn and motor-tractors pulling
them along the dead rails to the barns. . . .) At the *Arbeiter
Zeitung* I learned that the police, wearing steel helmets and armed
with carbines, had evacuated the building. My wife and I with two
friends drove hurriedly through the working-class Ottakring and
Hernals districts. We were nearing one of the great municipal
tenements when I heard for the first time in years that unpleasantly
brittle and discordant music—rifle fire.

The battle in Vienna lasted four days, and in the provinces five
or six. Almost a thousand men, women, and children were killed.
Nine socialist leaders, including one man seriously wounded, and
dragged to the gallows from a stretcher, were hanged. The Karl
Marx Hof and the Goethe Hof were badly smashed by shell fire—
two of the finest blocks of workers' dwellings in the world. I
remember a scene in the Goethe Hof a few hours after the bombard-

ment. Mournful women and frightened children stared miserably at the police. The simple, clean little flats were blasted to bits by shells. I walked through the kindergarten. Desks, black-boards, school-books, paint-boxes, shattered toys, were smashed together with broken beams and fallen plaster. On one wall stood a coloured-paper design proudly inscribed with the name of its author, aged six. A bullet had crashed through it. On the other wall, in this Marxist, 'atheist' cathedral, was a lithograph of the crucifixion. The glass was shattered—by a Christian Social shell.

I did not see Dollfuss to talk to until the twenty-second. When I mentioned that Bauer and Deutsch, who, when the fight was hopeless, fled to Czechoslovakia, had told me in Bratislava that they tried vainly to get in touch with him on the morning of the twelfth, in order to avert bloodshed by some last minute compromise, the chancellor looked puzzled and said, earnestly, blandly, that he had been at mass in St. Stephen's when the lights went out!—a signal that he could only interpret as the call for a general strike. On the afternoon of the thirteenth, incidentally, when fighting was at its hottest, Dollfuss spent a quiet hour having tea with the Papal Nuncio.

The spoils of victory for Dollfuss and the Heimwehr were enormous. Literally not since the Turks had there been such loot. The socialist municipality owned about thirty-five per cent of the land of Vienna; it employed fifty-four thousand people and was by far the largest enterprise in Central Europe; from 1923 to 1929 it spent about £22,000,000 on housing and similar projects, and its funds in the municipal savings banks alone were about £14,000,000. It collected about £5,000,000 in taxes per year, and it owned the municipal gas works, the electrical plant, the street-cars and sub-ways and omnibuses, the slaughter-houses and the public baths, a cemetery, a brewery, a bakery, and a big department store. All this went into government hands. Thousands of people were arrested, and thousands lost their jobs; the social disorganisation resulting from the outbreak was tremendous.

Socialist Side

The secret history of the socialist end of the 'revolt' has never been fully told. One vitally important factor of the conflict was the bitter personal enmity between Bauer, the socialist leader, and Dollfuss.

Otto Bauer, a brilliantly cultivated Jew of fifty-five, was the brains of the social democratic party. A gentleman-politician, Bauer acted as he thought British gentlemen-politicians acted; and he idealised them slightly. He was honest, he was scrupulous, he was fair. An intellectual in the best and worst senses of the word, he composed sound theories, but was utterly inadequate to meet an unforeseen situation, the importance or even the existence of which he would proceed to belittle or deny. Dollfuss, on the other hand, was about as theoretical as a flea; he hopped from place to place by instinct.

Bauer, in judgments of people, was far from sound. He had had an exaggerated admiration for the intellect of Monsignor Seipel, whom he called an enemy worthy of his pen; the politics he liked were polemical debates between himself on the front page of the *Arbeiter Zeitung* and Seipel in the *Reichspost*. And Bauer underestimated Dollfuss seriously. He called him a fool. And Dollfuss, cunning as a peasant, charming as a child, was very far from being a fool. Openly in the chamber Bauer denounced the chancellor as a liar and '*Schuft*' (scoundrel). Dollfuss never forgave him. A simpler man might have eliminated Bauer by manœuvring him from the leadership of the party, but the chancellor was too subtle for that; he knew the party was more important to Bauer than his own position and that he would not greatly care what happened to him so long as the party went on; therefore Dollfuss decided that the party had to go, and Bauer with it.

Behind this first-rate personal quarrel was, of course, the critically difficult position of the socialists both ideologically and politically. Orthodox Second Internationale socialism was, in 1934, as old-fashioned as horse-cars. Flattened between the opposites of Fascism and communism, the socialists became, instead of a revolutionary party, a party of the middle. They represented workers *in work*; and after some years of comfortable, almost *bourgeois* living in the Engels Hof or the Goethe Hof they lost a good deal of revolutionary fervour; they were not so anxious as before to man the barricades.

Socialism lost out in Austria because of its own decency. The socialists hated bloodshed and violence; they could not believe that their enemies were capable of ruthlessness and treachery; innocently they believed the lies of their opponents, because their own characters were grounded on probity and truth.

'Tactically, the socialists were in a hopeless position,' Frances Gunther wrote at the time 'As socialists they believed in the dictatorship of the proletariat. As democrats, they believed in the tolerant rule of the majority. Through the gap between these two stools, they crashed. They socialised some of the luxuries of life, but none of the necessities. Back in 1919 they had a chance to acquire the Alpine Montangesellschaft, the pivot of Austrian industry; they let it go, and instead built lovely swimming-pools and gardens for Vienna kiddies, by means of taxes which were just and therefore doubly intolerable to the former upper classes. Militarily, they succeeded in arming themselves—as socialists. But as democrats, they failed to disarm their enemies.'

From 1932 on Bauer and his men were pressed closer and closer against the wall. The Dollfuss technique was to whittle away their advantages, but never give them a square issue to fight on. Unemployment and the growth of the economic crisis had made use of the supreme socialist weapon, the general strike, more and more dangerous. The quintessence of unrealism and decency, Bauer—who, after all, commanded the largest party in the country, with sixty per cent of the Vienna electorate—offered to let Dollfuss rule dictatorially for two years, provided only the steering committee of parliament kept in operation. Dollfuss refused. 'The socialists *seventeen different times* offered to disarm the Schutzbund if the government would disarm the Heimwehr. Dollfuss made no categorical answer, but simply kept Bauer dangling. Finally the socialists announced the four things which *would* cause a general strike: (1) imposition on Austria of a Fascist constitution, (2) installation of a government commissar in Vienna, (3) dissolution of the social democratic party, (4) dissolution of the trade unions. Dollfuss simply pasted these four items in his hat, gleeful; he knew that he must merely avoid these major provocations and the fight was won.

Bauer himself generously—too generously—admitted his error. Writing (*Austrian Democracy Under Fire*, p. 42) of the death of parliament, he says:

'We could have responded on March 15 (1933), by calling a general strike. Never were the conditions for a successful strike so favourable as on that day. The counter revolution which was just then reaching its full development in Germany had aroused the Austrian masses. The masses of the workers were awaiting the signal for battle. The railwaymen were not yet so crushed as they were eleven months later. The government's military organisation was far weaker than in February 1934. At that time we might have won.

'But we shrank back dismayed from the battle. We still believed that we should be able to reach a peaceable settlement by negotiation.

Dollfuss had promised to negotiate with us at an early date . . . and we were still fools enough to trust a promise of Dollfuss. We postponed the fight, because we wanted to spare the country the disaster of a bloody civil war. The civil war, nevertheless, broke out eleven months later, but under conditions that were considerably less favourable to ourselves. It was a mistake—the most fatal of all our mistakes.'

Confusion Worse Confounded

On the night of February 11—the day before the outbreak—Bauer and his wife and two friends went, of all places, to the movies where they saw Greta Garbo in *Grand Hotel*. Thus was the 'Bolshevist plotter' making ready for the 'revolution'! Returning home, he found a message from the leader of the Schutzbund in Linz, a man named Bernacek, announcing that he, Bernacek, would resist by force the Heimwehr attack expected for the morrow. Bauer, agitated, sent Bernacek the following telegram, appealing to him not to provoke action: AUNTIE'S ALL RIGHT BOTH THE DOCTORS AND UNCLE OTTO THINK THAT NOTHING SHOULD BE DONE AT THIS MOMENT. Bernacek, a hothead, contemptuous of Bauer's caution, disregarded this message, and next day, defending himself, he took to arms.

What happened then was one of the ghastliest muddles in revolutionary history.

Bauer got news at about eight-thirty of the bloodshed in Linz. He summoned a meeting of the *Aktions-Ausschuss* (executive committee) of the trade unions and the party. A vote to call a general strike was carried by a majority of only one. Meantime, the workers in the powerful electrical union, inflamed, infuriated, preferring death fighting to death by slow suffocation, had—without orders—already struck. Then a terrible thing occurred. The general strike manifesto was rushed to the *Arbeiter Zeitung* presses for publication. But no contact had been established between the electrical workers and the *Arbeiter Zeitung* building, where the committee met. At the very moment that printing of the manifesto was to begin, the presses stopped. The electrical workers had shut off the power! So the call for a general strike was never promulgated, because of an unofficial strike of men who should have been an essential part of the general strike.

It appears that the general strike was set for five p.m. The idea was to bluff the government. What it did was give the government seven precious hours of warning. Bauer and Deutsch went to

Schutzbund headquarters to direct operations in the field, but other prominent socialists waited upon the government to appeal once more for conciliation.   General Koerner, a Schutzbund executive, went to see President Miklas; a group of Right-wing socialists, led by Dr. Renner, called on the Governor of Lower Austria to ask him to intervene with Dollfuss for them.   (They did not go to Dollfuss direct; they hated him too much, and they knew he wouldn't see them.)   The government did what any hard-boiled government would do.   Conveniently the whole leadership of the party, Bauer and Deutsch excepted, were in the lions' den and the authorities simply arrested the lot.   Koerner was apprehended actually in Miklas's anteroom, and the others—including the socialist journalist Braunthal who was simply reporting the event—were bagged wholesale.   The only socialist who behaved with sense and dignity was the veteran mayor of Vienna, Karl Seitz, who stuck to his desk in the town hall like a captain on the bridge of a battleship, and was finally dragged off by force.

The strike was a terrible failure.   Everything that could possibly go wrong went wrong.   Of course no one counted on the relentless acumen and energy of Dollfuss and Fey.   By mid-afternoon, every important socialist leader was in jail.   Anticipating this the party had appointed second and third men for each post; they were all arrested too.   As a result no one remained to give orders.   The signal for the strike was to be the stoppage of the trains.   But the railwaymen did not stop the trains, because they never knew a strike had been officially declared.   Couriers were sent out—too late—to rouse the countryside.   Most of them were caught.   A liaison committee had been set up in advance for communication between fighters and staff.   It never met, because of a childish inaccuracy in the location of the rendezvous.

The fighting that followed was heartbreaking.   I saw most of it. The lack of organisation was pitiful.   Bauer, a stern disciplinarian, had ossified the party, so that young men eager to go on the streets obediently waited all day Monday and even till Tuesday expecting *orders* to fight.   The orders never came; the young men then began shooting and were slaughtered.   As early as February 3, the government—assisted by turncoat Schutzbunders, who sold secrets of the organisation—had arrested a group of key Schutzbund leaders. Most of the workers did not know where their arms were hidden. Only a few men in each district were cognisant of the location of the secret depots.   The consequence was that young Schutzbunders

I know dug with their hands all Monday and Tuesday nights in
the courtyards of their tenements, searching wildly for the arms
that they knew were there. They never found them.

One band of three hundred Schutzbunders never received arms
because the second-in-command refused to disclose their location
without orders from above, even though he must have known that
his superior had been arrested. Another man I know could have
machine-gunned a whole detachment of police, but the rule was
that no socialist should fire until fired upon; so my machine-gunner
had to wait till the police were nicely in position and ready for
attack. The government cut key telephones so that no communication was possible between one besieged tenement and the others.
Workers in one house fought with no idea whether their comrades
were keeping up the battle or not. And the government maintained over the radio a stream of lies and slander—for instance,
that Bauer and Deutsch had walked off with the trade union
funds.

One can say what one likes about the leadership of the party.
But about the valiant courage of the men there can be no doubt.
It took a modern army of nineteen thousand men, equipped with
machine-guns, armoured-cars, and field artillery, four whole days
to crush the resistance of perhaps five thousand forlorn and desperate Schutzbunders, their backs to the wall or their necks in the
noose. It was a hopeless fight, but it was magnificent. The workers
of the world will never forget the February heroism of the Vienna
proletariat.

'Down Thou Climbing Sorrow!'

After February Dollfuss promulgated the new corporative constitution. The old parliament, comatose, was revived so that it
could commit legal suicide. An extraordinary document, the constitution made one think that Austria was going to be in the twentieth
century what it had been in the nineteenth—the heart and soul of
European reaction. The last vestiges of free popular suffrage disappeared. Way was opened for a Habsburg restoration. A chamber
chosen on a guild basis replaced the old parliament. And the pre-
amble to the constitution announced that all the 'rights' of the
Austrian people derived from God.

But more mundane affairs preoccupied the little chancellor. A
confusing period of inner rivalries and shifts of power began,
concurrently between Dollfuss and Starhemberg for control of the

country and between Starhemberg and Fey for control of the Heimwehr. Fearful that the Heimwehr was too powerful, Dollfuss encouraged the growth of another private army, the extreme clerical and monarchist *Sturmscharen* of the minister of justice Dr. Schuschnigg. The Heimwehr,[1] angry, flirted with the Nazis. And on the honey of these confusions the Nazis fed like bees.

From February to midsummer Dollfuss, desperately needing all energy for settlement, was unexpectedly tender to the Nazis, his worst enemies. A new campaign of violence began. Time and time again he threatened to hang a Nazi terrorist; he never did. Reasons: (1) he feared retaliation; (2) he was sabotaged by his own civil service; (3) he didn't want to make martyrs of Nazi criminals; (4) he wanted—still—to leave the way open for negotiations with Germany.

Events promptly showed that the Nazis were the chief beneficiaries of February. The Mussolini-Suvitch plan turned out all wrong. Instead of strengthening himself by the murder of the socialists, Dollfuss was disastrously weakened, because he had destroyed the political morale of the country. The Nazis were delighted that he had done their own job for them in removing the working-class movement which was the best defence of democracy. Socialists down! Nazis up! Nevertheless, Mussolini's support kept Dollfuss in.

For five months there was an uneasy lull, punctuated steadily by Nazi bombs. Then, on July 25, 1934, civil war again struck Austria. A socialist lad wounded a policeman in a scuffle and the authorities chose to make an example of him; it was a splendid chance to make good the threats of the death penalty and at the same time avoid the danger of Nazi vengeance. The boy, Josef Gerl, was hanged on July 24. This event did not directly precipitate the Nazi revolt. But within twenty hours Dollfuss himself was dead. He hanged a socialist, and, illogical as it seems, the Nazis killed him.

[1] One of the most popular anecdotes of the period described two Heimwehr men who met two others. The first two said after they separated, 'I wonder if those two Nazis know that we are socialists.'

CHAPTER XXVI

DEATH OF DOLLFUSS

THE murder of Dollfuss in 1934 marked the entrance of gang-sterism into European politics on an international basis. On June 30, inside Germany, the Nazis imitated Al Capone, and on July 25 these methods crossed into a neighbouring land. The assassination was a deliberate exercise in policy; the Nazis had to murder Dollfuss because every other method to defeat him failed. The story of the Dollfuss killing is that of an organised conspiracy to murder.

All the Putschists seem to have been members of the eighty-ninth SS regiment, one of four SS (Hitlerite guard) detachments which secretly existed on Austrian soil. The rank and file of the plotters were former non-commissioned officers or privates of the regular Austrian army who had been dismissed from the service for their Nazi sympathies. Also among them were active officers of the Vienna police whose surreptitious Nazi activities had escaped detection—an extremely important point.

The plotters looked for support in three directions. (1) In Germany there were Frauenfeld and Habicht, the exiled leaders of the Austrian section of the Nazi party. (2) In Vienna there was a group of high police executives and officials, who were later arrested or fled the country. (3) In Rome there was 'King Anton' Rintelen. There was another leader, a mysterious civilian whose *nom-de-complot* was Kunze, of whom more later.

Dr. Anton Rintelen, a white-cropped man of fifty-eight, who looked less like a conspirator than almost anyone I ever met, was promoted by Dollfuss to be Austrian minister in Rome in order to get him out of the country. He was too powerful to be overtly sacked. For ten years Rintelen had been Governor of Styria, the turbulent province south of Vienna. He was clever and cold and ambitious and, though named by the Nazis to be their chancellor, he was not a Nazi. He was Rintelen. Years before he flirted with the socialists hoping to reach power by a socialist coalition. When the socialists faded and the Nazis rose he intrigued with the Nazis.

It is not the least of the ironies of July 25th that this chief actor should have been motivated by aims so crass. He ran with the Nazis not because he loved Hitler but because he wanted a job and loved power. The Nazis, on their side, needed him. He was 'respectable' and they knew they could most easily gain Austria through the medium of a transitory coalition government. Rintelen was to be the Austrian Papen.

Various Styrian industrialists were friends of Rintelen. In their factories, like the Alpine Montangesellschaft, the largest industrial concern in Austria, the workmen were secretly organised on an SA basis. Here the Styrian rebels hid their arms.

Germany fed the springs of dissatisfaction and treachery with a powerful stream of gold; for instance it spent 75,000,000 marks in Austria for propaganda in the seventeen months between January 1933 and July 1934. Of German moral responsibility for the Dollfuss murder there was no doubt. Munich day in, day out, preached violence. And plenty of indication of German foreknowledge of the actual plot may be cited. As witness:

(1) The Munich headquarters of the Nazi party, according to the official *Wiener Zeitung*, had a special aeroplane ready at nine a.m. on the 25th for the victorious flight of Habicht and Frauenfeld to Vienna.

(2) As early as July 21st, a Berlin photograph agency sent out pictures of Rintelen marked 'New Austrian Chancellor—Hold for Release'.

(3) A Nazi named Abereger, arrested in Innsbruck and later sentenced to life imprisonment for bomb smuggling, testified that on July 22nd, three days before the murder, he was informed by courier from Munich that an armed rising was scheduled in Austria for the 25th.

(4) Italian secret agents reported movements of the Austrian Legion (Austrian Nazis on German soil) to the frontier on the evening of the 24th. The legion was to take posts two miles behind the border.

The Nazis were in a hurry because Dollfuss planned to visit Mussolini in Riccioni, an Italian seaside resort, later that week, and they feared that some new agreement between Mussolini and Dollfuss would finally beat them. One story is that the *Putsch* was first planned for July 24th, but was postponed a day when secret information came to the plotters that Dollfuss' last cabinet session in Austria would take place on the 25th, not on the 24th

as first believed.   It was the intention of the conspirators to capture
the whole cabinet.   Rintelen had arrived in Vienna from Rome
on July 23rd, ostensibly on a holiday.

So much for the setting.   The actual events of July 25th began
as follows:

At about eleven a.m. the conspirators assembled at various
points in the streets of Vienna.   Their organisation was excellent
and they acted with the utmost smoothness and precision.   One
group gathered, man by man, on the pavement of the Kolowrat
Ring.   They had received weapons from their leaders the night
before, and some had found cards in their letter-boxes notifying
them of the rendezvous.   Not all the plotters knew who the higher-
ups were; the password was the number '89'.   Fourteen started from
Kolowrat Ring for Ravag, the radio headquarters, where the signal
for the *Putsch* was given.   They were not disguised and they went
on foot.   Loitering on the Johannesgasse, where Ravag is situated,
were two uniformed policemen, members of the gang, who 'covered'
them and led them to the door.

A larger group meantime assembled at the gymnasium of the
German Athletic Club on Siebensterngasse.   This building, it is
interesting to note, directly adjoins an army barracks.   The plot
had been organised with such sureness that one of the conspirators
confessed later to have been informed by open telegram where to
come and what to do.   The group numbered one hundred and forty-
four, of whom no fewer than one hundred and six were former
army non-coms or privates, and ten were *active* police.   The hour
of attack was chosen with beautiful precision so that the plotters
would reach the chancellery at the moment of the changing of the
guard, when it was most vulnerable.

At about ten a.m. a police office named Dobler who was also a
prominent (secret) Nazi turned traitor to the Nazis and in a very
befuddled and Viennese way betrayed the plot to the authorities.[1]
Had they acted promptly, Dollfuss would never have been shot.
But the police who were loyal had been fatigued by a plethora of
false alarms, and the disloyal police sabotaged attempts to take precautions.

Dobler's movements that morning form a fascinating record.
Trying to notify the authorities without giving himself away, he

---

[1] Dobler later committed suicide or was murdered by either loyal or Nazi police.
The full story is in the official Austrian version of the events, translated into
English as *The Death of Dollfuss.*

nd intermediaries of the most astoundingly fortuitous variety
ucceeded, between ten and eleven-thirty, in holding meetings
vith public officials in at least three different—of course—coffee-
ouses. By about eleven-fifteen Major Wrabel, the aide-de-camp
o Major Fey, minister of public security, had heard the gist of the
natter. He sent a trusted detective, Marek, to Siebensterngasse to
nvestigate. Fey seems to have been informed, 'rather vaguely', at
leven-forty-five. He acted promptly and at once informed the
abinet, but it was too late.

The detective, Marek, arrived at the Siebensterngasse barracks
nd saw the plotters but the presence of uniformed police threw
im off the track. The whole plot was made possible by the factor
f disguise. Nevertheless his suspicions grew and three times he
elephoned to Wrabel between twelve-ten and twelve-thirty, once
rom a public phone-booth, once from a coffee-house, once from a
urniture shop. Wrabel transmitted the alarm to the public
ecurity officials, but police headquarters were only informed later.
Meantime loyal police had been misled by clever and daring spies
vho reported that an attack on Dollfuss was being prepared in a
lifferent part of town.

After his third call Marek was seized by the conspirators. He was
lragged into the hall, where he saw the men changing into army
iniform, the uniform of the crack Vienna *Deutschmeister* regiment.
The rebels clambered into three private trucks, which they had
lired, one marked BUTTER AND EGGS, and started for the chan-
ellery. They did not know what to do with Marek and so (amaz-
ng cheek) they took him with them. When they were close to the
hancellery Marek jumped out, and none of the Nazis, for fear of
aising the alarm, dared shoot him. The reader may well ask how
hree trucks full of 'soldiers' could traverse a dozen streets of a
rowded city at noon without attracting attention; but troop move-
nents were not uncommon in Vienna at this time, and the uni-
ormed police on the running-boards allayed suspicion.

The plotters reached the chancellery at twelve-fifty-three p.m.
The scene was set for dramatic and terrible events. But first there
s the Ravag episode to tell.

Revolt on the Ether

July 25th was a hot day, though not sunny, and I wanted to go
.wimming. I had finished my morning's work and put on my hat
o leave for lunch when at seven minutes past one the telephone

rang. One of my tipsters said in a low voice, 'Have you heard th
radio? The Vienna radio has just made this announcement: *"Th
government of Dr. Dollfuss has resigned. Dr. Rintelen has assume
power."* It may be a joke. I don't know. I'll check it up and cal
in a minute.'

I put in a call for Paris at once (we sent our stories by telephone
and while waiting for it I telephoned (*a*) the American legatior
(*b*) a friend, M. W. Fodor of the *Manchester Guardian,* with whor
I worked closely, (*c*) the Bundeskanzleramt or chancellery. Th
legation had heard the radio announcement and was investigating
Fodor rushed to meet me down-town. The Bundeskanzleramt—
interesting! did not answer. Then Telegrafen-Compagnie, a loca
news service, called with the radio announcement, and said that
Nazi *Putsch* was in progress. I wrote a brief story and finishe
it just when the Paris call came through. It was one-nineteen.
still had my hat on.

I lost about ten minutes because a police officer stopped me an
made me drive him to his headquarters. A general alarm ha
been sounded, he said, but he didn't know about what. I got t
the Bundeskanzleramt at about one-thirty-five. The tawny oa
doors were shut and a few policemen were outside, but otherwis
nothing seemed wrong. I assumed that the government ha
locked itself in, preparing defence.

An armoured car passed by and with a couple of other new
paper men I followed in pursuit. It turned away from th
Bundeskanzleramt and lurched round the Ring to the Johar
nesgasse, the Ravag headquarters. The locale is comparable t
Regent Street or Piccadilly in London. The car got into positio
and the police on the turret ducked inside the steel shell. The
I heard revolver shooting and machine-gun fire. The police wer
storming Ravag to blast out the Nazi Putschists there. I had
feeling that it was all monstrously unreal. The police pushed u
back, but we were eager to see: it isn't often you get a pitche
battle in the heart of Vienna. Then PRPRPRFFBUM we hear
exploding hand-grenades. A waiter in a white-duck jacket sli
through the crowd with a platter of beers.

What had happened at Ravag was this. At two minutes to on
the fourteen plotters from Kolowrat Ring entered the building
They shot the loyal policeman on guard and the chauffeur of th
Ravag director who were lounging in the doorway. Four Nazi
reached the studio, where a broadcast of gramophone records wa

going on. They grabbed the announcer, put a gun in his ribs, and made him give their message. This was the signal for the *Putsch.* All over Austria it throbbed.

But a courageous telephone girl had had time to sound an alarm, although all the lines to police headquarters—an interesting point—were 'busy'. And an official with great presence of mind cut the wires to Bisamberg, the sending station, so that the Nazis were unable to give a second message. Their plan had been to repeat 'Dollfuss has resigned; Rintelen is chancellor' every ten minutes, interspersing this aerial tattoo with instructions to the country, false news, and so on, which would have paralysed any defence action of the government. I remember that a British radio expert told me years before how marvellously a revolution might be organised by radio.

An unfortunate actor rehearsing a broadcast skit became hysterical with excitement, started to scream, and was shot. The police broke into the building and another policeman was killed, also the Nazi leader. Of the five who died, three bled to death because no doctor was available. Outside we waited till the police, victorious, began to drag out their captives at about three-twenty. I proceeded home and wrote my story, longer this time, and put in my telephone call to Paris.

I went to the Bundeskanzleramt again at about three-fifty. On the way I ran into G. E. R. Gedye of the *New York Times*, who was returning from Ravag, and we stopped a second, both saying, 'Well, it seems to be all over.' We certainly were wrong, but very few people knew then that anything was amiss except at Ravag. I had passed the Bundeskanzleramt myself before, and it looked entirely normal except for the closed doors. Feeling a flicker of doubt, I said to Gedye, 'You know, a government doesn't usually lock itself in at a moment of great crisis.' He agreed. 'Funny.' And we remembered that the phone had not answered. I walked towards the building. A patrol had been flung round the area and I couldn't get in. Then the story burst.

Policy by Murder

The Bundeskanzleramt, or Federal Chancellery, is the old Metternich palace where the Congress of Vienna met in 1815. Certainly from that day to this it can have witnessed no more dramatic and agitated situation. A stately baroque building, its cream-coloured façade opens on the Ballhausplatz. Grilled balconies of

graceful iron project twenty feet over the pavement. Directl[
opposite is a post office built into the heavy walls of the Hofburg
the former imperial palace, and on the west side a high gate lead
to the green meadow of the Burg garden.

The hundred and forty-four Nazis from Siebensterngasse, swee[
ing into the courtyard, had seized those members of the goverr
ment within, Dollfuss, Fey, and Fey's assistant Karwinsky, an
about one hundred and fifty members of the staff, civil servant:
clerks, and so on. The guards in the building, sixty of them, su[
pected nothing or at least put up no resistance and were disarme
and arrested. The police plotters knew well the corridors an
rooms of the complicated building (some of them, indeed, ha
previously been posted there on duty), and the occupation wa
quick and thorough. The analogy for England would be th
seizure of 10 Downing Street, since the Bundeskanzleramt was th
central ganglion of government in Austria.

Nothing whatever of these events was known to the small grou[
outside the building. Among the newspaper men who, havin
heard the radio signal, had arrived by one-fifteen and stayed til
nightfall were Nypels of the Amsterdam *Algemeen Handelsbla*[
Diez of the New York *Herald Tribune*, Werner of the A.P., tw
Hungarians, one Albanian, and one Czech. They did not succum[
to the temptation to follow the armoured-car which led me away t
Ravag. They saw the whole story, and from a correlation of thei
records I made the following chronology.

The very first arrival on Ballhausplatz after Nypels was a tal
blond youthful German photographer, who had arrived in Vienn
from Berlin the day before. Calmly he set up his tripod. At on[
twenty-five some plain-clothes detectives and four uniforme
police wearing steel helmets and carrying rifles arrived. A shou[
pierced the basement window, 'Go away, or we shoot.' At one-fifty
five a Heimwehr lieutenant arrived, unarmed and alone, an
smashed his fists against the door, shouting with quixotic magn
ficence, 'I give you five minutes to open the door, or I will blow i[
up.' This gesture accomplished, he went away and was not see[
again.

(Dollfuss was already bleeding to death by this time, the bloo[
pumping from the hole in his throat, but no one knew. . . .)

Several other officers arrived, looked about, decided that nothin[
was wrong, and went away again. Traffic was still entirely norma
Then, at five minutes past two, came Dr. Funder, the venerabl[

editor of the government organ *Reichspost*. A voice from inside was heard, '*Machen Sie sich keine Sorgen.*' (Don't be alarmed) 'Rintelen is chancellor and a new police chief is coming from Berlin.' Funder hurried away. Many Heimwehr men and police had now arrived. At about two-thirty began a series of ultimatums that lasted the whole day. A Heimwehr officer knocked on the door at two-thirty-five and said, 'We give you twenty minutes and then we blow up the building.' 'Go away or we shoot,' a voice, distorted and hollow, answered through the door. The impression was now general that the whole government had been taken prisoner.

At three o'clock Major Baar, a Heimwehr officer and vice-governor of Lower Austria, arrived. A police officer told him, 'I don't know what to do. I am awaiting reinforcements and orders.' The Heimwehr were now massed along the road to the Burg Theatre, but the police pushed them back. 'Who is inside?' Baar was asked. He answered, 'Dollfuss, Fey, and Karwinsky are inside, prisoners of the Putschists. A new government has been formed and is meeting at the war ministry on Stubenring.' Police reinforcements came and a courteous officer said, 'Look here, gentlemen, this is not a good place to stand because here you are in the direct line of fire.' At three-forty-five traffic was finally stopped and the little group of onlookers were a compact island in the broad empty pond of the square.

At three-fifty-seven Major Fey, who has a face like a battle-axe, appeared for the first time on the balcony. He was pale as paper. He wrung his hands as if to free them from dust on the door-handle. With him was Holzweber, the leader of the rebels, a bespectacled little man who looked like a clerk on a stool despite his captain's uniform, blazing with decorations. The crowd started to shout, and Fey called in a low voice, '*Ruhe!*' (Quiet.)

Everyone thought at once. 'It is a *Putsch* made by Fey and the regular army.'

Fey called, 'Where is the commandant?' He could not be found, but a policeman walked up and saluted respectfully. 'Who are you?' Fey asked. 'I am Captain Eibel, awaiting orders,' the policeman said. Holzweber whispered to Fey and Fey said, 'Come without weapons to the back door.' Eibel nodded and Holzweber called after him, 'Be sure you are without arms and come alone.'

Heimwehr men in the square had recognised Fey and they began to shout 'Fey! Our Fey!'

At eight minutes past four Eibel returned from the back door on Metastasiogasse. He was running hard, his helmet was off, and his hair was damp and disorderly. He grabbed an open alarm phone. Everyone heard what he said, talking to headquarters:

'I've been inside, I've spoken with Fey. The Bundeskanzler (Dollfuss) is apparently badly wounded. He has resigned. There is a new government, and Fey remains vice-chancellor.' Headquarters asked something and Eibel replied, 'They are disciplined and look like the military. The staff of the chancellery, one hundred and fifty men and women, are under guard in the courtyard.'

By this time the commandant, Hofrat Humpel, had turned up and he said to Eibel, 'If the chancellor is wounded he should have a physician. Run to the back door and offer to bring a doctor.' Eibel came back: 'I knocked and the sentry said, "No need for a physician any more." ' So it was known to this limited group that the chancellor was dead.

At four-twenty Fey appeared on the balcony again, Holzweber at his elbow. The idea that it was a *Putsch* with Fey in charge was exploded because obviously Holzweber was in command and giving Fey orders. Fey called '*Ruhe!*' (Quiet.) Then, bending over the balcony, he called, 'Where is Rintelen?' The Heimwehr started to shout to the Nazis inside:

'Woe to you if you harm our Fey. Touch our Fey, and we will hang every one of you on these trees.'

Fey shouted: '*Nichts unternehmen!* (Take no action.) Nothing may be done until I give the order. I am in command here.' He beckoned to Humpel and ordered him round to the back door. A big Heimwehr man, just under the balcony, crossed his hands like a seat and gestured to Fey to jump. Humpel came back in about twenty minutes and shouted, 'Rintelen is chancellor, Fey is vice-chancellor. They are waiting for Rintelen, who will come in a few minutes.'

On the Balcony

But it was not Rintelen who came: it was quite another person. Neustädter-Stürmer, a member of Dollfuss' cabinet. He waited a few moments and then Fey appeared on the balcony again and called, 'Where is Rintelen?'

Neustädter-Stürmer shouted, standing in the street, '*Rintelen kommt nicht!*' (Rintelen is not coming.)

Astonished, Fey turned to Holzweber at his elbow and a Heimwehr man called, 'Shall we storm the building?'

Fey shouted down: 'No, nothing is to be done. Take no action
without my orders.'

Neustädter-Stürmer answered, 'A new government has been
formed and I represent it. In the name of the government I
promise a safe conduct to the rebels. They will be conducted to
the German frontier. If you do not surrender in twenty minutes
we storm the building.'

Fey called: 'No. You will not storm the building. I am state
secretary of public security and you are to take no action without
my authority.'

Neustädter-Stürmer, looking up (sharply): '*Sie irren Sich*, Herr
Fey! (You are mistaken!) The members of the government who
are prisoners are under duress and are not competent to give orders.
It is now five-twenty-eight. At five-forty-eight the building will be
stormed.'

When the ultimatum expired everyone took cover but there was
no shooting. Neustädter-Stürmer kept pacing up and down and
Fey had disappeared. 'It was just an Austrian ultimatum,' someone joked. But the tension was terrific. At four minutes past six
Fey came out again and said that the rebels agreed to surrender
but asked what guaranty there was of safe conduct. They wanted
military protection to the border. 'That can be arranged,'
Neustädter-Stürmer replied, and Fey, speaking for Hudl (another rebel on the balcony) called, 'Can we have fifteen minutes
more?' A civilian shouted, 'They mustn't harm anyone in the
building.'

At six-thirty Fey came out once more. He tried to talk to General
Zehner, the under-secretary of state for war, who had taken charge.
There was such a tumult that no one could hear. Police, journalists, Heimwehr, lookers-on were all under the balcony shouting.
So Zehner and Neustädter-Stürmer went round to meet Fey at the
back door. Then Dr. Rieth, the German minister arrived. At
about five-fifty Zehner reappeared and announced, 'They will get
military protection to the frontier under the command of a staff
officer.'

At about seven-thirty Fey came out of the back door. He walked
up to Neustädter-Stürmer and said, 'Give me a cigarette.' A journalist called, '*Pfui* on their safe-conduct!' Fey, lifting his voice
with effort, said, 'Quiet!' Neustädter-Stürmer asked him. 'Is it

true that Dollfuss is dead?' Fey said, 'Yes, I spoke to him just before he died. When I came in he was lying on a divan wounded and bleeding.' He crushed the cigarette in his hand and said, 'Give me another cigarette.'

At seven-forty Rieth and Karwinsky came out. Schuschnigg, the new prime minister, arrived and led Fey, Zehner, and Neustädter-Stürmer into the Burg garden. The police closed the gates behind them and, standing there on the grass, in the dusk, they held a cabinet meeting. By now twenty military trucks were lined up along the Ballhaus, and police streamed into the building to disarm the rebels and conduct them to the frontier. The rebels came out cocky and confident. Everyone thought their free passage to Germany was assured. They thought so too. But they were wrong.

Death

Dollfuss had opened his last cabinet meeting at eleven. Among the items on the agenda were—of all things—regulations governing a famous Vienna theatre devoted to comic opera. The warning did not reach the cabinet till after eleven. Vienna *Schlamperei*, as well as treason, is probably responsible for the fact that the chancellery doors were not shut in time. Once he got the alarm, Dollfuss acted with great energy and coolness. He dismissed the cabinet and ordered the ministers to scatter to their separate offices, only Fey and Karwinsky remaining. This saved Austria, because if Schuschnigg and Neustädter-Stürmer had not been outside the building the *Putsch* would probably have succeeded.

By twelve-fifty-five the rebels were inside the gates, one hundred and forty-four of them. 'We arrest you in the name of President Miklas,' they falsely shouted.

Officials at the chancellery told me the next day that they first thought a surprise military drill was in progress. The uniforms seemed genuine and the men were disciplined. Then, along each tier of offices, rude voices shouted, 'Come out! Hands up!' Doors were battered down and the staff herded into the courtyard. The more prominent officials were imprisoned in a small room and told that they were the first batch of hostages who would be shot if the plot miscarried. A second batch was then chosen to be shot after the first batch. It became clear that the men were Nazis when the first thing they did was to open the telephone switchboard to get in touch with the German legation. And one rebel told a riend of mine, 'Curious, are you? In half an hour you'll hear all about it on the Munich radio.'

Immediately on disarming the guard one detachment of rebels went up the main staircase, ignoring other objectives, to search the state departments, find Dollfuss, and murder him. There is little doubt but that this group was specifically charged with this duty. It was led by an ex-corporal in the army, Otta Planetta, with a chin like a boxing glove. Dollfuss was given no chance to escape. He might easily, like Fey and the others, have been captured alive. But the rebels had one predominant aim, to kill him. They entered the building at twelve-fifty-five and by two minutes past one at latest he was shot.

Having dismissed the cabinet, Dollfuss retired to his private study, a small room papered in yellow silk. His valet, Hedvicek, looked out of the window and saw the rebel trucks unloading in the courtyard. He told Dollfuss to try to escape through a passage that led through the complicated web of archive rooms upstairs. Briskly the chancellor left the yellow room and started across an oyster-white room towards the famous congress hall. The oyster-white room has three doors. One gives on the main staircase, and here the rebels entered. The door to the congress hall was locked and Hedvicek fumbled with the key. Dollfuss, a small man, reached for the knob and at a range of about twenty inches Planetta shot him in the exposed arm-pit. The chancellor reeled and Planetta fired again, this time in the throat, at about a distance of eight inches. The chancellor fell. ('How his head cracked on the floor!' Hedvicek said.)

'*Hilfe, Hilfe!*' Dollfuss muttered ('Help, help.')

Planetta said, 'Stand up.'

'I cannot,' Dollfuss whispered.

They picked him up and laid him on the rose-and-cream Louis XV divan. Servants were still sucking up the dust and blood with vacuum cleaners when I saw the room next morning. On the embroidery of the divan were three large blood spots, almost exactly the shape and colour of large oak leaves.

Fey, who was detained near by, had heard the shots but did not know their meaning. At about two-thirty a group of Nazis summoned him and led him to the room where Dollfuss was still dying. The chancellor recognised him and whispered weakly:

'I charge you to take care of my family if I die.'

The rebels had a revolver in Fey's ribs and permitted him to say
nothing. Dollfuss went on, very faintly:

'Where is Schuschnigg?'

Fey shook his head and, mustering strength, Dollfuss whispered,
'Try to settle this without bloodshed. Tell Rintelen to make
peace.'

Fey was hustled out of the room. He appealed to the rebels to
get a doctor or at least a priest. They refused, although they asked
the prisoners if a doctor were among them, and one of them gave the
dying chancellor a glass of water. Dollfuss must have thought he
had been betrayed by his own army; not only that the *Putsch* had
succeeded but that his own men had killed him. Later he apparently believed that loyal troops, not rebels, were surrounding him
staring at his shrunken face, because he whispered, '*Kinder* (children) you are so good to me. Why are the others not as you are?
I wanted only peace. May God forgive the others.' The last blood
was now streaming from his small body. A basin to catch it was
put under the divan. At three-forty-five he died.

The rebels thought they had won, until about five p.m. At four-
thirty Hudl, the second in command, told the prisoners in the
courtyard, that a new government had been formed and that
Rintelen, the new chancellor, would arrive at once. Thereupon
about twenty officials gave him the Hitler salute and others called
out '*Heil* Hitler'. Hudl testified at his trial that Wrabel, who was
caught inside the building, gave him his card and said, 'Call me
du.' (The familiar form of the second person.)

After five, when Neustädter-Stürmer was outside, the morale of
the rebels began to break. Holzweber went to Fey and said frankly,
'There has been some hitch. I do not know what to do.' Fey
shrugged. Then, a characteristically Viennese touch, Holzweber
proceeded, 'Ah! I shall telephone the Café Eiles and ask if Herr
Kunze is there.' So with the chancellor dead, the government
disrupted, Austria convulsed, and Europe at the ragged edge of
war, the leader of the rebels rang up a coffee-house, to ask if a man
who *might* be there could tell him what to do.

Kunze was a civilian who had been at Siebensterngasse. Holzweber led the first truck and Hudl the second and Kunze was to
have been in the third. But he never arrived. No one knows certainly what happened to him or how he disappeared. The Viennese police think he was a Nazi lawyer who ratted at the extreme
moment and fled to Germany.

At about six the rebels decided to surrender, following the promise of safe conduct. All the one hundred and fifty hostages would be shot, Holzweber declared, if free passage was not given. Fey said to the government negotiator, 'Do not allow considerations of my safety to influence you one way or another.' Then Hudl suggested telephoning to Dr. Rieth, the German minister, as witness for the safe conduct. Fey explained the business over the telephone, and Rieth asked him whether or not to come. Fey said, 'It is not my business to give you orders or dissuade you. I have only to pass on these men's demand.' Rieth came, the negotiations were completed, and the exodus began.

Still the mass of the imprisoned hostages did not know the chancellor was dead. Leaving the building, one of the rebels called out, 'We've left a dead one in the corner room upstairs.' An official rushed up and found Dollfuss there. The body had completely shrivelled like a raisin and was clammy blue. The face was uncovered and wore an expression of extremist agony. A piece of canvas covered part of the body. There was a terrible wound in the throat. Underneath the divan, spilled beyond the basin, was a lake of blood.

The Missing Chief

And now about Rintelen. Why did Rintelen not come? Why did the *Putsch* fail?

He did not come because he was arrested. He was arrested not by the police or government, but by his old friend Dr. Funder, the editor of the *Reichspost*, who, leaving the chancellery at ten minutes past two, went straight to the Hotel Imperial where Rintelen was staying and on his own responsibility persuaded him to give himself up at the war ministry, in order to avert scandal. Owing to his position as a minister he was not searched. It is said that the Ravag got through to Rintelen at about one-fifty and asked him to deny the radio report naming him chancellor. 'I have no authority to do that,' Rintelen answered, and rang off. At midnight that night he shot himself. The wound was not mortal, though so dangerous that the actual heart had to be stitched up.

About the position of Fey there will probably be dispute as long as the story is told. I do not think he knew anything about this particular plot. No one knows exactly what passed between Fey and the rebels when they first arrested him; but the evidence of both police officers who entered the building is that they understood that Fey, with Dollfuss dead hardly a minute, was vice-chancellor in the new Rintelen régime. On the other hand, Fey can hardly be blamed for telling the loyalist forces not to bombard the building. He had not only his own life to save but he was responsible for the safety of the one hundred and fifty other prisoners. If Fey had shouted early in the afternoon, 'They have murdered the chancellor; storm the building even if we die,' it would have been a magnificent gesture but it would have cost much bloodshed. One must remember that Fey knew nothing of what was going on outside. He thought Rintelen *was* chancellor. Even so, if he had greeted Neustädter-Stürmer's appearance with a whisper of pleasure instead of a reiterated demand for Rintelen his reputation for loyalty and courage would not have suffered such a severe setback.

There was much bad feeling about the withdrawal of the safe-conduct. The rebels were shipped, not to the German frontier, but to the Marokanner police barracks hardly a mile away. The government defended what was certainly bad faith by saying (*a*) Fey was not authorised to give a safe-conduct, and (*b*) Neustädter-Stürmer gave it unaware that the rump cabinet at five o'clock made it conditional on no casualties. I imagine the final decision not to free the Nazis was taken at the cabinet meeting outside the chancellery at seven-thirty. Here Schuschnigg was informed for the first time of the circumstances of Dollfuss' death and he decided simply not to let the murderers go. Neustädter-Stürmer said at Holzweber's trial, 'Yes, I gave my soldier's word of honour. But a soldier's word of honour is given to other soldiers, not to men who deny medical aid and priestly services to a mortally wounded man.'

Another reason for the failure of the *Putsch* was that the country as a whole did not rise. In Styria and Carinthia, where the Nazis had arms, there was severe but brief fighting, but nowhere else. For a year all of us were deluded into believing that the Nazis were fifty or sixty per cent of the country. Possibly this was true, but at the critical moment the Nazis did not take action. The rebel signal had reverberated through the land; for four hours there was no regular government; but nothing happened. The Nazis had not bothered to arm their adherents, feeling sure that the army would mutiny and provide weapons; but the army remained loyal. Thus they lost their supreme chance.

Above all, the *Putsch* failed because Hitler welshed. The one hundred and forty-four conspirators were betrayed three times on July 25th; by their own higher-ups, chiefly Kunze; by the promise of safe-conduct; above all, by Germany. For a year and a half the Germans had incited their Austrian cousins to violence and rebellion and then, at the crisis, they let them down. The Austrian Legion did not march; instead, as soon as the *Putsch* was seen to have failed, it was disbanded. Habicht was dismissed from his post as Hitler's 'Inspector' for Austria, and Frauenfeld disappeared. Dr. Rieth was summarily fired, to give way to Franz von Papen. Instantly it was known that Mussolini had mobilised and would march into Austria if the *Putsch* succeeded, and this was clear by six p.m. of the 25th, the Germans wretchedly crawled and washed their hands of the whole business and ever since have sought to evade responsibility.

Thirteen of the Putschists were hanged, including four of the traitorous policemen, and, of course, Holzweber and Planetta. I have seldom seen a court-room more stirred than when Holzweber just before his sentence, rose and said:

'I was assured that there would be no bloodshed. I was told that I should find Rintelen at the chancellery and that the new government was already formed. Not meeting the leader of the operation at the chancellery I disclosed myself at once to Major Fey. I told him, "Here I stand, and I do not know what to do." '

Three hours later he and Planetta were hanged. Both died bravely, and both with the words '*Heil* Hitler' on their lips. But Hitler did not hear them. In East Prussia President von Hindenburg was dying. And Hitler was busy becoming President of Germany.

. . . .

Rintelen, seven months later, went on trial and was sentenced to life imprisonment on a charge of high treason. After serving a brief time in the penitentiary he was transferred to a sanatorium, under police surveillance. The evidence against him at the trial was not particularly concrete. As a result rumours rose that Rintelen had come to Vienna expecting to take part in a *different* revolt against Dollfuss, in which others too were involved. The July 25 *Putsch* was, it was said, made by Habicht, to forestall a Rintelen *Putsch* scheduled for about the same time. Habicht in Munich distrusted the Rintelen group, even though—according to this story—it was to pave the way for a Nazi régime; therefore Habicht jumped the gun on July 25 and therefore Rintelen and his friends, not knowing whether the *Putsch* going on was their *Putsch* or not, behaved with such confusion.

2 E

Rintelen might have been acquitted except for the evidence of his Italian servant Ripoldi, who testified that his master in Rome had frequently consorted with alleged Nazi emissaries. This contributed an obscure, bizarre footnote to the whole affair. Ripoldi had previously been the valet of a friend of Rintelen's, the financier Camillio Castiglione. He admitted in court that Castiglione had persuaded him to telegraph the court from Milan about his knowledge of Rintelen's doings, and had paid for the telegram. Apparently Rintelen and Castiglione, old friends, had fallen out.

CHAPTER XXVII

AUSTRIA INFELIX

'I am young.   I am not yet ready for supreme power.'
— PRINCE STARHEMBERG.

Dr. KURT VON SCHUSCHNIGG, the Austrian chancellor who succeeded Dollfuss, and who since the *Anschluss* has been a Nazi
prisoner in the Hotel Metropole in Vienna, was born in 1897 in
the Lake Garda region of Italy, which was then Austrian territory.
He volunteered for war service when he was eighteen and was captured in 1917 by Italian troops.   The rest of the War he spent in
an Italian prison camp.

After Schuschnigg had been chancellor a short time two Viennese met in Stephensplatz.

'I have a job,' said one.

'What?   A job!   Impossible,' replied the other.

'Yes, I sit in the bell-tower of St. Stephen's Church and wait for
the first joke about Schuschnigg to be born.   Then I toll the bells.'

'Hmmff.   That's not much of a job.   How much do you get?'

'Fifty *groschen* (five-pence) a day.   But it's a job for life.'

Dr. Schuschnigg, rather dull a personality indeed, was the son of
a general.   His family belonged to the minor aristocracy, devoutly
Catholic, devoutly monarchist.   He was educated in law at the
University of Innsbruck, and entered politics as a protégé of the
Christian social chancellor, Monsignor Seipel.   He became first
minister of education, then minister of justice, and finally Dollfuss'
most reliable aide and confidant.

He had very little of Dollfuss' magnetic nimbleness; he was cold,
severe, logical, dutiful, dry.   But absolutely honest and conscientious, he was valuable as an offset to the erratic and unpredictable
Starhemberg.   Schuschnigg had no demagoguery.   But demagoguery was the last thing Dollfuss wanted—except his own.   He
wanted a man who knew his business, who kept his mouth shut,
and whom he could trust implicitly.

It was Schuschnigg's ambition to be, not a politician, but a

413

professor—a scholar in the history of law. But events seized him. As an attempt to wean the youth of the Tyrol from Hitlerism and turn it to patriotic Austrian nationalism, he founded his militant Catholic youth organisation, the Sturmscharen. As we have seen, Dollfuss promptly utilised the Sturmscharen as an offset to Starhemberg's Heimwehr, when the Heimwehr momentarily became too powerful.

Dr. Schuschnigg began to show his quality in a struggle with the Heimwehr in 1936. For a long time it was supposed that Prince Starhemberg, the vice-chancellor and Heimwehr leader, was the real force behind the Austrian Government; Schuschnigg was thought—by the ill-informed—to be no more than his 'front'. But gradually Schuschnigg manœuvred the young Prince into a difficult position and finally got rid of him.

The immediate reason for Starhemberg's dismissal was, it is said, a hotheaded and somewhat indiscreet telegram he sent to Mussolini congratulating him on the downfall of Ethiopia. 'I congratulate you,' Starhemberg wired, 'on the famous and magnificent . . . victory of the Fascist spirit over democratic dishonesty and hypocrisy.' This was too much for Schuschnigg, who was trying at the time to make his régime appear as democratic as possible. The underlying reason for the split was Schuschnigg's intention to make some sort of accord with Germany. This Starhemberg, who was on the Italian side, would not countenance.

Schuschnigg knew that Starhemberg was famous for his delight in pretty girls and fashionable female company. As if in ironic acceptance of this, the dry semi-dictator—after throwing Starhemberg out—made him honorary president of the Austrian Mothers Aid Society.

Methodically Schuschnigg went on to clean up the Heimwehr. He reconstructed the cabinet in November, eliminating Heimwehr members again in March 1937, he whittled his government down, concentrating authority to himself and his own friends. Finally the Heimwehr was dissolved as an independent armed force and incorporated into the government militia.

But then—a year later—the Nazis took Austria. And to Schuschnigg came a fate almost worse than that of Dollfuss.

Prince Out of Politics

Prince Starhemberg, born in 1899, owed much of his career to his family, especially his mother. A direct descendant of one of the

twelve original families of the Holy Roman Empire, he is a lineal
scion of Ottakar I, Count of Steyr a thousand years ago. The name,
corrupted from Storchenberg, means 'Stork's Mount'. One of his
great-great-grandfathers saved Vienna from the Turks in 1683. A
proud and ancient family, the Starhembergs are apt to consider
mere Habsburgs as distinctly parvenu. His mother, Countess
Franziska Starhemberg, a profound influence on his life, was a
considerable force in the inner workings of the Christian Social
party.

Young Ernst Rüdiger joined the Austrian army at seventeen.
After the War he became a soldier of fortune, a freebooter, fighting
with the Bavarian Oberland organisation in frontier squabbles
in Silesia. He met Hitler, joined him, and took part in the Munich
beer-hall *Putsch*. His mother, horrified that her blue-blooded son
should come too much under Hitler's *Lumpen-Proletariat* and anti-
Catholic influence, brought him back to Austria. She intervened
with Monsignor Seipel to keep an eye on her boy, start him on a
'respectable' political career.

Young Starhemberg decided to found a private army of his own.
He owned fourteen castles throughout Austria. In one of them,
Waxenberg, he organised eight hundred of his retainers—practically serfs—into the *Starhemberjaeger* (hunter) detachment. This
group merged with the Heimwehr. For some years Starhemberg
financed the movement himself. His fortune disappeared; he borrowed money right and left. At one time his liabilities were
reported to be about £120,000. When he was on the verge of
bankruptcy some rich industrialist friends—and Mussolini—rescued him.

Opinions differed about Starhemberg's ability in the days of his
power. Myself I thought he was an exceptionally intelligent young
man; liberals, I feared, underestimated him just as they underestimated Dollfuss. I heard Starhemberg speak at Dollfuss' funeral;
he addressed the dead leader with passionate thee-and-thou intimacy
in one of the most moving orations I ever heard. At lunch a few
weeks later Starhemberg talked off-the-record to a group of newspaper men; his answers were deliberate and a little long, but brilliantly phrased and apposite.

Opinions did not differ about Starhemberg's good looks. He was
—and is—an exceedingly handsome fellow. Nor did they differ
about the basic aims of his character and intelligence. He was a
perfectly definite clerical reactionary. Also he was ambitious—if

temperamental. One of his dreams was to become Regent of Austria, like Horthy in Hungary. Since the *Anschluss* he has been in exile in Switzerland and Paris—perhaps waiting for his new day.

Dictatorship on Crutches

After the Dollfuss murder the Austrian Government proceeded like a man with one foot on the street, one in the gutter; it wobbled, it tottered, it managed to span unnatural extremes of distance—but it stood. A dictatorship it was, and one of the most complete—if sloppy—in the world. Hitler 'makes' elections; but at least he holds them; Mussolini is head of a political party which contributes some vitality to the state; Stalin is part of an organism to which he admits responsibility. But in Austria there was nothing but Schuschnigg, the Fatherland Front, and the Almighty.

The combination ruled by police power and the support of Italy. It evaded elections, because it feared that elections would let the Nazis in. It assaulted the rights of citizens in a fantastic manner. In the year 1934, for instance, 106,000 dwellings in Vienna alone were raided by the police. No fewer than 38,141 persons were arrested, of whom 19,090 were Nazis, 12,276 social democrats, and 6,775 communists. But—and it was an important 'but'—the terror never reached anything like the repressive force of the Nazi terror. Most of those arrested promptly got out of jail again. Even at its most extreme phase, it was difficult to take the Schuschnigg dictatorship completely seriously, although Schutzbunders tried in 1935 got mercilessly severe sentences. This was because of Austrian gentleness, Austrian genius for compromise, Austrian love for cloudy legal abstractions, and Austrian *Schlamperei*.

The social democrats, smarting from the February wounds, and the communists, forgetting their usual propaganda which was restricted exclusively to those who were already communists, formed, early in 1935, a United Front. A new Schutzbund arose from the ashes of the old; the social democrats, taught a lesson in realism, changed their name to 'The Revolutionary Socialists of Austria.' They assaulted the country—with literature. The dissemination of illicit propaganda in Austria, although severely punishable, reached a point where scarcely a day passed without a shower of leaflets or handbills somewhere in Vienna. Miniature newspapers were passed around from hand to hand; some thirty thousand copies of the new-born miniature *Arbeiter Zeitung* crossed the frontier secretly every fortnight. In my mail-box I would find

luscious specimens daily of almost every kind of subversive literature. The government did its best to check the flow. But it was
like trying to mop up the Danube with a sponge.

Agreement with Germany

In July 1936 Schuschnigg and Franz von Papen, the German
minister to Austria, came to an agreement normalising the relations between the two countries. The event was hailed by Dr. Goebbels as a masterpiece of the new German diplomacy; the Austrians,
on their side, seemed reasonably satisfied. Germany agreed to
recognise the sovereignty of Austria; Austria agreed to release Nazi
political prisoners and allow the Nazis, as individuals, to join the
Fatherland Front. The long period of tension between Austria
and Germany was, it was announced, ended—obviously a development of great importance.

Papen's tactics had, it was proved, been very sensible. He had
seen that the iron fist would fail and so he tried the suède glove.
His plan was to take prominent Austrians aside, whisper to them
that he himself found distasteful things—indeed!—in the Nazi
régime, and try to persuade them that both should work together
for good old pan-German ideals. Papen worked very slowly—and
confidently. His policy was based on the fact that there is no use
ravishing a girl whom you are to marry next week. But his campaign was made difficult by two things. First, he was not trusted.
Second, as Frances Gunther put it, no Austrian could be a Nazi
twenty-four hours a day. It took too much energy.

Nevertheless Schuschnigg had to come to some sort of *modus
vivendi* with Germany. The German boycott was killing Austria.
For a time Mussolini prevented any compromise, because the Duce
was still boiling with rage at the death of Dollfuss—Frau Dollfuss
was a guest in his house at Riccioni, it will be remembered, when
the murder took place. But apparently in the summer of 1936
Schuschnigg told Mussolini that he could not hold out much longer,
and that some sort of Austro-German pact was essential, no matter
on what terms. Thus the gate was opened.

The Austrians were, after all, not Italians; they are of German
stock and eighty per cent of them were pro-*Anschluss* before
Hitler. The oft-laboured scheme of a Danube confederation as a
solution of the Austrian problem cannot work while nationality
remains a spiritual as well as economic barrier between the Central
European countries. Austria's fate was indissolubly connected with

that of Germany; the only eventual path of Austria was in the German orbit. And it seemed possible that Austria, long an obstacle separating the two Fascist states, might become a bridge connecting them.[1]

[1] For the last days of Austria—Hitler's final attack, the incorporation of the Austrian State into the Reich, and the Italian reaction—see Chapter VIII above, *The Fascist Offensive.*

CHAPTER XXVIII

HUNGARY AND DR. HABSBURG

'I believe in God, I believe in the unity of my country.
I believe in the eternal divine justice,
I believe in the resurrection of Hungary.
Amen!'
                                        —HUNGARIAN NATIONAL CREED.

BEHIND Otto Habsburg are some seven hundred years of madness, murder, melancholia. At least five of his cousins and forbears, in the last couple of generations, have met violent deaths, and several died insane. Crown Prince Rudolf shot himself at Mayerling in the greatest of modern royal mysteries and Archduke Franz Ferdinand was killed at Sarajevo.

Archduke Franz - Josef - Otto - Robert - Marie - Antoine - Karl - Maximilian - Heinrich - Sixtus - Xavier - Felix - Renatus - Ludwig - Gaetan-Pius-Ignaz, Prince of Habsburg-Lorraine, the exiled pretender to the Austrian and Hungarian thrones, comes of fertile blood. He is one of eight children of the late Emperor, Karl, and his widow, Zita of Bourbon-Parme, who was herself the tenth child of a litter of seventeen. Royalty produces at least an insurance of complex continuity. Otto was born near Vienna—in a chalet that is now a pension—on November 20, 1912.

The Habsburgs are more than a family, they are a sort of organism—a resplendent fungus long attached to the body politic of Europe. They are as prolific as white mice and as international as counterfeiters. The Archduke Franz Ferdinand had 2,047 ancestors, including 1,486 Germans, 124 Frenchmen, 196 Italians, 89 Spaniards, 20 Englishmen, 52 Poles, and 47 Danes. The Habsburgs ruled in Europe for some sixteen generations. Their polyglot and bulbous holdings included at one time or other twenty countries, but never, one might say, a single country. The family was always superior to the state. Family laws in old Austro-Hungary had precedence over state laws, and the provisions of the Family Charter, drawn up in 1839, are still unpublished and secret. When he heard of Franz Ferdinand's death in 1914 (which removed the possibility of uncertainty in the succession), old Franz Josef, who had been emperor for sixty-six years, exclaimed, 'Ah! A higher power has restored the order that I was unhappily unable to maintain.'

The Habsburg power toppled at the end of the War in 1918, but not the Habsburg dynasty. When the last Emperor, Karl, a weak man, was asked to abdicate the Empress replied fiercely: 'Rather will I die with you here. Then Otto will come, and when all our own family has gone there will still be Habsburgs enough.' Karl, indeed, never abdicated, although he renounced all participation in the governments of Austria and Hungary. He and Zita fled to exile. Twice Karl made abortive *Putsches* in Hungary, in March 1921, and October 1921; the Hungarian Government of Admiral Horthy beat him. He died in Madeira in 1922. Ever since Zita trained her eldest son, Prince Otto, for kingship.

Otto grew up grave, intelligent, sensitive, and extraordinarily good-looking. Through some pleasant chance he missed the traditional pouched eyes of the Habsburgs, the pendulous under-lip. 'Let that boy loose in Austria and give people a chance to look at him and he'll capture the country like a Valentino,' a friend of mine said after a recent visit to Stenockerzeel, the ramshackle castle in Belgium where after vicissitudes all over Europe the royal family now lives.

Otto is a modest boy and extremely well-mannered, but seven hundred years of Habsburgs have driven into his brain complete appreciation of the privileges and prerogatives of kingship. Already, in his occasional public pronouncements, he refers to Austrians as 'My People'. An English friend asked Otto—before *Anschluss*—what he thought of Hitler and the prince regally replied, 'Unfortunately not having had an opportunity as yet to receive Mr. Hitler, I cannot say.'

The young prince has had to pay for his choice and dangerous lineage by performing the inevitable chore of royalty, learning languages; he speaks German, French, Italian, Spanish, English, and Hungarian quite fluently. Zita had never been able to learn Hungarian, a staggeringly difficult tongue; the chauvinist Hungarians never forgave her for this and she saw to it that her son did not make the same mistake. He was brought up, of course, a Roman Catholic, and he prays thrice daily.

After years of tutoring Otto went to the University of Louvain, graduating with a Ph. D. degree in the spring of 1935. He is, I imagine, the first royal pretender in history with a legitimate doctorate. His oral examinations included questions on the closer economic co-operation of the Danube states, the reconcilability of the corporative Austrian constitution with democratic development, and the reafforestation of parts of the Hungarian plain. The written thesis, which ran to three hundred and sixty-eight pages in its French text, concerned 'the right, born of usage and of the peasant law of inheritance, of the indivisibility of rural land ownership in Austria.' He wrote it first in German and then translated it into French. The published brochure was signed 'Dr. Otto von Habsburg'.

He travelled a good deal in his early years, visiting Scandinavia, Germany, Italy. Each trip done, he returned dutifully to Stenockerzeel, his books, and Mother Zita. So far the old Empress has not found him a bride. A good match would be with Princess Maria, the youngest daughter of the King and Queen of Italy. But Mussolini, contrary to general opinion, does not like the idea of a Habsburg restoration—which would tend to recreate an empire on his Adriatic flank—and largely for this political reason the engagement didn't occur.

Otto was popular in Austria; of that no doubt. His mother Zita was not so popular. It is a private idea of mine that restoration would have been a good deal more possible if Otto's return would not have meant the return also of his mother—to say nothing of hundreds of assorted and impoverished Habsburg cousins and aunts, who would have flocked to Vienna like ants to a keg of syrup. The ex-Empress, a woman of enormous strength of character and some old-fashioned ideas, is a good mother, so good a mother that she might have found it difficult to let Otto be king alone. And many Austrians had no fancy to see Otto swaddled to the throne with Zita's apron strings.

The only excuse for kingship in the modern world is the symbol it provides of permanence. It gives a country an anchor into the dark furrows of the future. Otto, if Austria or Hungary had taken him back, might have given them the security of a fixed headship of the state and a fixed succession. It is unfortunate that to make such provision for the future one must dredge so deep into the shadows of the past. A restoration seems a very backward gesture. 'We did not wage the war,' Dr. Beneš once said, 'in order to go back to former times.'

Otto's chances in Austria, even though the Schuschnigg-Starhem-

berg régime cancelled the Habsburg exclusion laws, of cours
automatically disintegrated and disappeared when Hitler took th
country. Hitler and Habsburgs don't mix. But the possibilit
that Otto may some day be King of Hungary cannot be excluded
One obstacle—Czechoslovakia—has disappeared; another, the per
sonal opposition of Admiral Horthy, may some day wane.

Noblesse Oblige?

The chief internal problem of Hungary, which has been an in
dependent kingdom since A.D. 1001, is that of the land. The coun
try is almost exclusively a pool of wheat. Agrarian prices fel
drastically after 1930; the nation was terribly overborrowed, witl
the largest *per capita* foreign debt in Europe. The urgencies of th
resultant crisis were not improved by the maldistribution o
economic power in the country. The feudal aristocracy rule th
land almost absolutely. One-third of the total arable land of Hun
gary is owned by nine hundred and eighty men.

Another sixth of the land—the figures remind one of Spain—i
owned by some 1,112 magnates of the landed gentry class. Ther
come about 250,000 small-holders who have up to 150 acres each
Following are about 600,000 owners who are restricted to a plot s
small that they have to sell their labour power as agricultura
workers elsewhere. Finally there are about 1,130,000 peasants
quite without land—out of Hungary's total population of roughly
8,600,000—proportionately the largest group of landless agrarian
proletariat in the world.

The aristocrats, though many of them lost much power and
wealth by the amputation of Hungary after the War, are still a lush
and fantastic lot. The Esterhazys, the Karolyis, the Czekonitchs,
the Hunyadis and Telekis and Szaparys, maintain a shadow-
glamour like nothing else in Europe, now that similar remnants of
colossal feudal power have disappeared from Poland. Once an
Esterhazy used a Titian painting as lining for his cloak. A Karolyi
once sent a precious bottle of tokay to a sweetheart by special train.

These noblemen and their families intermarried to an unusual
extent. The wife of Count Windischgraetz is a Szechenyi.
Their daughter married a son of the Karolyis. One Countess
Karolyi is an Apponyi. The wife of Michael Karolyi, president
of the extremely temporary Hungarian republic, was an Andrassy.
Admiral Horthy's daughter Paulette married a son of Count
Emmerich Karolyi, relative of Michael and his son married a

daughter of the same Karolyi. The daughter of Count Julius Karolyi, who may be Horthy's successor as Regent—if he has a successor—married one of the Esterhazys.

These noblemen, practically without exception, favour the return of Otto to the throne. But Horthy and his late prime minister Goemboes heartily opposed restoration. Their motives were not exclusively personal, although Otto's return would lose Horthy his pleasant job; Zita would never forgive him for having crushed the Karlist *Putsches*. Horthy and Goemboes thought that a restoration would weaken Hungary, not strengthen it; they felt that the house of Habsburg has brought more harm to Hungary than good; the choice, in their minds, was quite flat between dynasticism and patriotism.

Hungary is not, as is usually said, a dictatorship; the Hungarian Parliament, founded in A.D. 1222, is one of the oldest in the world, and theoretically, just as in England, it can overturn any prime minister by an adverse vote. Horthy, the Regent, though reactionary as far as social or economic ideas are concerned, is in effect the guardian of constitutionalism and what vestigial democracy remains in the country, because it is largely his influence that prevents any ambitious prime minister from abolishing parliament and setting up dictatorial rule.

As long as Horthy and Count Julius Karolyi live, the squabbles of domestic politics in Hungary do not mean much, because the inside leaders are all members of a secret society, heritage of the civil wars and White Terror, called the 'Double Cross', in reference to the Holy Apostolic Cross of Hungary. It was founded by Horthy and his cohorts when they organised a provisional government in Szeged in 1919 to fight the communists then ruling in Budapest. Every Hungarian prime minister since the counter-revolution has been a member of the Double Cross. There are about thirty-five surviving members; most of them dine together informally every month in a beer-hall, the Matthias Keller, near the Elizabeth bridge in Budapest. Bethlen and Karolyi may quarrel but their brotherhood in this secret organisation outrides personal feuds, and they combine against outsiders. The Double Cross is mostly landed gentry and Protestant. The great legitimist aristocrats are not members.

Choleric Admiral

Nicholas Horthy de Nagybánya, born in 1868 of a Transylvanian

family, was for a generation a naval officer. Hardly brilliant, h
nevertheless had qualities of candour and courage, and in thirty-si
years of service he rose without much influence of wealth or famil
to be first, naval aide-de-camp to the old emperor Franz Josef, an
second, admiral commanding the Austro-Hungarian fleet. As sucl
he was partly responsible for the suppression of the mutiny whic
some time ago was celebrated by the New York Theatre Union i
Sailors of Cattaro.

The most unpleasant thing about Horthy is his White Terro
history. He was minister of war in the counter-revolutionar
government that followed the crash of the communist régime Bel
Kun. On August 10, 1919, his detachments were stationed a
Siofok, in trans-Danubia. Some officers, drunk and cheerful, talke
blood-thirstily about Bolshevik atrocities. Horthy remarked
'Words, always words! And never any action!' So the officers, in
cluding men who later became infamous as wholesale sadists, wen
out and that night murdered sixty Jews and communists. Thi
was the beginning of the White Terror. When members of .
British labour delegation investigating the atrocities complained t
Horthy that the officers responsible had not been punished, th
admiral replied in naïve indignation, 'Why, they are my best men!

Horthy is one of the most indiscreet men in Europe. A bluff an
friendly fellow nowadays, he likes to see visiting notables and jour
nalists, but his aides try to isolate him on account of his enormous
full-blooded disposition to air his views—frankly. What he says ir
private conversation about the Serbs and Czechs and Germans and
anyone you mention will make your hair dance and quiver. He i
seventy, but aflame with a sort of humorous-choleric vitality. H
positively explodes with passion and pathos. At one moment h
may burst a collar discussing Hungarian revisionism; at the next
pick up a paper-knife and go through the gestures of murder t
illustrate a point; at the next, mention with tears in his eyes how
good a human being old Franz Josef was, but how that 'poor boy'—
Otto—cannot hope to rule in his (Horthy's) stead.

His many years of Regency have mellowed him a good deal;
whatever the defects of his character he has been a loyal and
courageous patriot; when he dies it may be an evil day for Hungary

Goemboes and His Successors

General Julius Goemboes de Jákfa, was an adventurer, a nationalist, a desperado politician, all his life. He was born in 1886 in a

strict of Hungary populated mostly by Germans. The family
me from the Rhineland, and the name was originally Gelb. His
ther, who was a school-teacher, Magyarised it to Goemboes some
ears before the future prime minister was born. His mother never
arned to speak correct Hungarian. Goemboes died in October
936.

A rebellious Magyar chauvinist, he went to cadet school and then
ae war college in Vienna. He was almost expelled when a pro-
:ssor asked him if he would be faithful to the Habsburg régime
a the event of a revolution. Goemboes answered vigorously No.
le would, he said, as a Magyar officer, fight for nationalist Hungary,
ot for the dynasty. As with Hitler and Pilsudski, the dominant
ote in his character from childhood was a fanatic nationalism.

Goemboes was wounded in the War on the Rumanian front and
nen served on the staff in Vienna. A man of plot and counter-plot,
ighly ambitious, he organised the 'M.O.V.E.' (Magyar Orszagos
edo Egylet), a sort of officers trade union; for Goemboes had like
is idol Mussolini a strong early socialist streak. The Hungarian
:volution occurred and Goemboes offered to reorganise the social-
.t Michael Karolyi's army. Karolyi, distrusting him, refused, and
e fled to Vienna where—meeting in secret—he and Count Stephen
ethlen, another *émigré*, plotted the downfall of the Karolyi
égime. When Bela Kun came to power, Goemboes went to
zeged and joined Horthy in organising the counter-revolutionary
orces, and his great days began.

Beyond doubt, much more than Horthy, he was responsible for
he White Terror in which at least several thousand innocent Jews
nd communists were tortured and murdered. Beyond doubt, too,
e was the force behind Horthy repelling the two adventures of
he Emperor Karl to regain his throne. On March 21, 1921, it was
e who intervened between Horthy and Karl saying, 'Majesty, I
rder you to leave this country by eight o'clock to-night.' On the
ccasion of the second *Putsch*, in October of the same year, Goem-
oes, distrusting the regular army, called out and armed the secret
ocieties and students corps.

The Hungary of that time was the worst dictatorship in Europe.
n it were Magyar traces of all the Fascist tendencies we know to-
lay: violent economic nationalism, hatred of Jews, and vigorous sup-
•ression of liberals, pacifists, socialists alike. Goemboes was indeed
n active touch with Hitler in 1922 and 1923, but he disavowed him
fter the Munich beer-hall *Putsch*. The murderers of the German

foreign minister Rathenau were hidden for some years on his esta
at Nagy-Teteny, disguised as gardeners.

Goemboes originally was a member of Bethlen's Union part
which ruled Hungary for a decade. In 1923 he seceded to form
sort of Hungarian Fascist party, and stayed in the political wilde
ness for five years. He rejoined Bethlen in 1928, and becam
minister of war. When the complex and enigmatic Bethlen resigne
in the middle of the Hungarian financial crisis of 1931, after te
years as prime minister, Goemboes succeeded him. He was neve
Bethlen's equal in cultivation or intelligence.

Goemboes attracted much attention in 1935 by attempting t
broaden Hungary's sphere of foreign political action. From th
time that Bethlen had contrived the tie-up with Italy, Hungary ha
been Mussolini's puppet. Goemboes glanced northward to th
Nazis. He was active, moreover, in negotiating what promised the
to become a Central European *bloc* of dissatisfied states, Germany
Hungary and Poland, and he joined one of General Goering'
famous hunting parties in East Prussia to this end.

One successor to Goemboes as prime minister was the remarkabl
—and unfortunate—Dr. Bela Imredy, one of Hungary's leadin;
economists. He sponsored severe anti-Semitic legislation, partly a
a result of Nazi pressure; he was accused then of being partly Jewisl
himself by indignant liberals and Jews. He denied this, and se
out to prove it. But research made it clear that he was, in fact, o
remote Jewish descent. There was nothing for Imredy to do bu
resign; which he did. The little story then went around that h
had to eat standing up, because he wouldn't sit down with a Jew
Imredy is still a considerable power behind the scenes. He repre
sents the strongest Nazi influence in Hungary.

His successor, appointed in February 1939, was the veteran aris
tocrat Count Paul Teleki, a moderate. Teleki is anti-Nazi (like hi
old friend and sponsor Count Bethlen), but pro-German in genera
sympathy. He was born in 1879, and, a geographer by profession
is one of the most learned men in Central Europe. His foreigr
minister, who embraced an extreme pro-Axis policy, but who wa
more pro-Italian than pro-German, is Count Stephen Czaky. Ir
the great crisis of 1939 Czaky desperately rushed between Berchtes
gaden, Salzburg, and Rome, seeking protection from one partner
Italy, in case his country was attacked by the other, Germany. Czaky
was for years head of the news department of the Hungarian Foreigr

Office. Like almost everyone who counts in Hungary, he, too, was —and is—a Bethlen protégé.

Nem Nem Soha

In Hungary is the strongest, the most pervasive nationalism in all Europe. In the chauvinism sweepstakes the Hungarians beat even the Poles. A little story is relevant. The proud father of an eight-year-old schoolgirl entering a geography class bought her a globe. She surveyed it and broke into tears. 'Papa,' she wailed, 'I want a globe with only Hungary on it.'

Hungarian nationalism has fed ever since 1919 on the open wounds made by the peace treaties which, in their comparative iniquitousness, reached in the Treaty of Trianon the most iniquitous point. Hungary lost, after the War, no less than 68.5 per cent of its territory—191,756 square kilometres out of a former total area of 282,870 square kilometres. Hungary lost no less than 58.2 per cent of its population—10,782,560 people out of 18,264,500. Hungary lost all its gold, silver, copper, salt, and mercury; it lost its best collieries, eighty-five per cent of its forests, sixty-five per cent of its vineyards. It lost fifty-six per cent of its horses, sixty-nine per cent of its cattle, fifty-two per cent of its factories, fifty-seven per cent of its arable land, and fifty-two per cent of its total wheat production. Amputated from Hungary was its outlet to the sea. The economic unity of the old Danube basin, an almost perfectly balanced area, was destroyed.

On the other hand, one should point out that these terrible losses included districts not populated by Hungarians. A full forty-five per cent of the old population were minorities—Slovaks, Rumanians, Serbs, Croats, Ruthenians, Italians, Slovenes. The ostensible justification of the Trianon Treaty was liberation of these minorities. Of the 10,782,560 people lost, 6,345,500 were not Hungarians. But here is precisely where the trouble lies. Had the victor powers been content to draw really accurate minority and frontier lines, Hungarian revisionism would have had little pretext. But some three million people who *were* pure Magyars were grabbed along with the others, and made to live, a new minority, within the new borders of Rumania, Jugoslavia, and Czechoslovakia.

The sole basis of Hungarian foreign policy since the War has been revisionism—to change the treaties in order to get its lost territory back. To frustrate Hungarian aims, the Little Entente —Czechoslovakia, Rumania, Jugoslavia—was originally formed.

2 F

What has happened to it we shall explore in the chapters that follow.

After Munich, in 1938, the Hungarians—by grace of German help—regained their lost Slovak territory. And in March 1939, after the German seizure of Bohemia-Moravia, the Hungarians—this time without German help—reacquired their former territory in Ruthenia, and thus established a common frontier with Poland. In September Poland disappeared. Now Hungary has Soviet Russia on its new Ruthenian frontier, and probably wishes it had not taken Ruthenia after all.

Hungarians still look longingly on the 'unredeemed' minorities in Jugoslavia and Rumania. But Germany, it seems, looks longingly—and hungrily—at them.

CHAPTER XXIX

MASARYK AND BENEŠ

'The master of Bohemia is the master of Europe.'
—BISMARCK.

'We shall always be a small minority in the world, but, when a small nation
accomplishes something with its limited means, what it achieves has an immense
and exceptional value, like the widow's mite. . . . It is a deliberate and discerning
love of a nation that appeals to me, not the indiscriminate love that assumes
everything to be right because it bears a national label. . . . Love of one's own
nation should not entail non-love of other nations. . . . Institutions by themselves
are not enough.'

—MASARYK.

MASARYK—what grandeur the name connotes![1] The son of a
serf who created a nation; the blacksmith boy who grew to
have 'the finest intellect of the century'; the pacifist who organised
an army that performed a feat unparalleled in military annals—the
Czechoslovak legions who marched across Siberia to the Pacific; the
philosopher who became a statesman in spite of himself; the living
father of a state who is also its simplest citizen; an unchallengeably
firm democrat who, in the *débâcle* of the modern world, still believes
in rule by tolerance; the man who more than any other smashed the
old Austro-Hungarian empire, so that Czechoslovakia, a free republic, rose from its ruins—the stablest, strongest, and most prosperous
of the succession states.

In his autobiography Masaryk says that his life has been 'shot
through with paradox'. He is, for instance, the son of a coachman
—and he lives to-day in the castle of the old Bohemian kings. His
father was, moreover, a servant on an imperial estate, so that in
throwing the Habsburgs out of Czechoslovakia Masaryk also sym-
bolically threw them from the front yard where he grew up in the
most crushing poverty.

He was, for instance, both a locksmith's apprentice and a helper
in a blacksmith's shop, because in early youth he disliked school.
During the War he was a first-class practical conspirator, a specialist

[1] I print this section on Masaryk exactly as I originally wrote it in 1935.

in decoys, codes, and stratagems. Yet the whole basis of his career
was moral-intellectual. He was one of the most formidably learned
men of his time, a philosopher and prophet of almost Judaic
stature.

The greatest of living Czechoslovaks, the first act in his life to
bring him prominence was an investigation which proved a set of
documents hallowed and revered by the Czech and Slovak peoples
to be forgeries. A Roman Catholic who turned Protestant, he
gained early distinction by defending a Jew wrongfully accused of
an obscure ritual murder. He exposed as fabrications of the Austrian Foreign Office the documents in the Friedjung case, which
ruined what was then his official career; but this occasion made him
a hero of the oppressed Slavic peoples. Dominating his life have
been two factors, faith in Czechoslovakia and the pursuit of truth.

It was not idly that Masaryk called his philosophy 'Realism'.
Once he all but decided to return to Austria during the War so
that he might be hanged—he knew that his martyrisation would
help the Czech national cause. There were several attempts on his
life which he shrugged off—he was psychologically incapable of fear
—but he took the precaution of drawing up his own obituary so that
it would be the best possible propaganda for the liberation of his
people.

He founded the most central of central European states in Pitts-
burg, Pa., where he negotiated a Czech-Slovak unity pact, and in
Washington, D.C., where he issued the Czechoslovakian declaration of independence. He was proclaimed president of Czechoslovakia after he had not set foot in it for four years, and when he
was 4,500 miles away.

His autobiography is warm and rigid with insistence on the most
complete intellectual, moral, and emotional probity. He records
how a simple lie might have saved his life when he was in acute
danger in Moscow—to gain cover in a hotel he would have had to
say incorrectly that he was registered there; he refused although
the bullets were splattering about him—and his life was saved anyway. Yet in his career he was a splendid opportunist.

In Washington, before attempting to make any appointment at
the White House, Masaryk spent weeks in a detailed and penetrating study of Wilson's writings. The old professor was knee-deep
in books about and by Wilson. Then he drew up his manifesto on
Czech aspirations for independence and presented it to Wilson.
Half a dozen times in the document Masaryk had cleverly used cita-

tions from Wilson's own works as legal and political authority for the Czech claims.

Two quotations from his great book *The Making of a State* give fleeting illustrations of his quality:

'Hardly had I settled in Geneva when news of my son Herbert's illness came unexpectedly from my family in Prague; and, on March 15 (1915), a telegram announcing his death. Thus, like thousands of families at home, we were stricken. He was clean and honourable in rare degree, a poet-painter whose ideal of beauty was simplicity. Healthy he was, too, and strong through physical exercise. He had done all he could to avoid fighting for Austria and yet found death through the War. Typhus, caught from some Galician refugees whom he was helping, killed him—a case for fatalists! My old Clerical opponents did not fail to send me from Prague their coarse and malicious anonymous letters. "The finger of God!" they said. To me it seemed rather an injunction not to abate or to grow weary in my efforts.'

And discussing one of his visits to Tolstoy,

'Neither morally nor, I think, psychologically, did Tolstoy recognise the distinction between aggressive violence and self-defence. Here he was wrong; for the motives are different in the two cases and it is the motive which is ethically decisive. Two men may shoot, but it makes a difference whether they shoot in attack or defence. The mechanical acts are identical but the two acts are dissimilar in intention, in object, in morality. Tolstoy once argued arithmetically that fewer people would be killed if attack were not resisted; that, in fighting, both sides get wilder and more are killed; whereas if the aggressor meets with no opposition he ceases to slay. But the practical standpoint is that, if anybody is to be killed, let it be the aggressor. Why should a peace-loving man, void of evil intent, be slain and not the man of evil purpose who kills? . . . I know, too, that it is hard sometimes to say precisely who the aggressor is, yet it is not impossible. Thoughtful men of honest mind can distinguish impartially the quarter whence attack proceeds.'

Thomas Garrigue Masaryk was born on March 7, 1850, in the Moravian town of Hodonin. His mother, a cook, seems to have been a remarkable woman; Masaryk pays touching tribute to her strength, her ideals, her clamour to give her son an education. Apparently he had little sympathy with his father. He went to school in Vienna, became a professor at Prague, wrote exhaustively (of some psychological interest is the fact that his first book was on suicide), entered politics. His wife was an American woman, Miss Charlotte Garrigue, whom he met in student days at Leipzig and

whose name he added to his own. He writes of her: 'She was beautiful to look at; she had a magnificent intellect, better than mine.'[1]
Their son, Jan, a turbulent and candid character, became Czechoslovak minister in London.

Masaryk's real career did not begin until he was well over sixty.
He records a testimonial dinner given him at the time, a sort of
climax to his work as a distinguished savant; he tells wryly of his
inner feeling that he was being buried before he was dead. Then
came the high years, between sixty-five and seventy, when he fled
from Prague to organise the Czech movement abroad. His final
work, nurture of the new Czechoslovak state, began at an age when
the lives as well as careers of most men are long since over.

He is a very old man now, but still alert, and the range of his
interests is extraordinary. His conversation is a bit diffuse; he is
inclined to get lost in the flow of his own sentences. In one half-
hour's talk I had with him, he mentioned, aside from domestic
politics, such things as birth control, Irish nationalism and the
Catholic Church, Senator Borah, biology, modern American literature (of which he has an amazing knowledge), the Polish corridor,
the amount of pocket-money of American soldiers in France, the
Habsburgs, Dostoevesky (he is, at eighty-five, just finishing a book
on Dostoevesky), Bill Hard, the world economic crisis, the Jugoslav
sculptor Mestrovic, and a new English novel he had just been reading and the title of which he couldn't for the life of him remember.

I had expected to meet a man excessively stern, even self-
righteous. But Masaryk has a strong sense of humour. He cackled
vigorously. His interest in human nature, immense, neglects no
comic facet. He told Čapek that academic psychology was of no
help to him in learning about human nature—'only life and novels'.
For seventy years, he said, he has been reading novels every day.
'Man is a damned complicated and puzzling machine. And each
man different.' During the whole period of the War, he has related,
he slept only half a dozen nights; presumably he read novels instead.

After seeing him I made a few rough notes as follows: 'Warm,
strong handshake; no glasses; old man's eyes, hard to tell the colour
of them, probably deep grey; still a fuzz of white hair on the scalp;
all his own teeth, plus a bit of gold shining when he laughs; plenty
of moustache, small beard; glazed hard, shiny, cheeks; prominent
nose; a typical *peasant's* face; distinctly not patrician or "intellectual"; a boulder, shrunken, hard-bitten, out of the soil.'

[1] Čapek, *President Masaryk Tells His Story*, p. 121.

Masaryk is old. But his work is done. He has built a nation. The story, in its perfection of sequence in cause and effect, is like a Greek tragedy—except that it ended happily. He will die soon. There is no man of our time who will leave a better memory, for others to remember.[1]

Beneš

'I can tell you that without Beneš we should not have had our revolution,' Masaryk told Čapek. The two men worked together from the time of the War, though Beneš was thirty-five years younger. The old philosopher roamed the world, seeking sympathy for the Czech cause: Beneš, likewise a refugee, stayed in Paris —he was the organiser, the filing clerk, the skilful and adhesive practical politician. Masaryk wrote Czech aspirations amid the stars; the pertinacious Beneš wrote them into treaties which redrew the map of Europe.

Dr. Eduard Beneš, sharp-nosed, sharp-eyed, an intelligent and responsible world statesman, one of the soundest of European public men, has been uninterruptedly Czechoslovak minister of foreign affairs since 1919; thus he was the doyen of the foreign ministers of Europe. He was the son of a peasant, and was born in 1884 in Kozlany, Bohemia. As poor a boy as Masaryk, like his master he was self-educated; but whereas Masaryk's Ph. D. thesis was on suicide, that of Beneš in 1908 was on a more practical issue, 'The Austrian Problem and the Czechoslovak Question.'

Beneš is as efficient as a dynamo. I have never seen him laugh. He is small and slight. He wears a flat-brimmed hat cocked high on the head. He works about fifteen hours a day, and like Mussolini (whom he doesn't otherwise resemble) he delights to see people if they can tell him things; he is one of the most accessible statesmen in Europe. He has no cant or side. He talks facts. Listening to you, he forms your ideas into an orderly progression, One—Two— Three—and then discusses them in series. Expressing his own viewpoint he again uses numerals, but with alphabetical subheads 1A, 2B, and so on. He is a wiry negotiator, but the basis of his success is method. No one ever put anything over on Eduard Beneš.

It gives one a queer oblique glimpse through the years to remember that Beneš was not always Beneš. His names, at one time or other, have been 'Spolný', 'Bělský', 'Berger', 'Novotný', 'König',

---

[1] Thomas Garrigue Masaryk died at the age of eighty-seven in September 1937. His countrymen united as one man to mourn him.

'Šícha', and 'Leblanc'. Fifteen years ago the Czechoslovak foreign minister was busy, like Masaryk, forging passports, crawling across frontiers, in momentary danger of being shot as a spy—which he was. Once he was arrested in England for travelling with a false passport. Within six months he was officially signing passports of the nation he helped to create.

Like Masaryk, Beneš has tried to be a good European. He performed the complex miracle of adjusting complete national patriotism to a deep and conscientious regard to his duties, as he saw them, to Europe as a whole. He helped to found the League of Nations, and for years he helped to run it. One of the greatest living authorities on security and disarmament, he was almost as active in Geneva for a long time as Prague. Whenever an important European issue arose, Beneš wrote an 'exposé', usually a pamphlet eighty or ninety pages long, which he read to the Czech parliament; and it was always a complete and authoritative statement of the problem. Beneš was president of the Sanctions Assembly in September 1935. His dearest ambition was to organise an effective United States of Europe.

When Masaryk retired in December 1935, Beneš, as was expected, succeeded him to the presidency of Czechoslovakia.

I have already described the harrowing crisis Beneš went through at Munich, when his country was destroyed. He behaved like a good European to the end. After Munich, he fled to London, and subsequently accepted a teaching appointment in the United States, at the University of Chicago.

Then war came again in 1939. Dr. Beneš scurried back to London, and once more, after twenty weary years, began exactly the same sort of work for the resurrection of his country he had performed in 1919.

Czech Complex

The good wife is the one you don't hear about. So it is with countries. Almost everyone who visited Czechoslovakia in the old days returned to quote the old saying, 'Happy is the country that has no history.' Czechoslovakia had, of course, plenty of history, but it was certainly true that local Czech politics, under the inspiration of Masaryk, pursued a very smooth and inconspicuous course. Tragically ironic this seems now!

One of the first persons I met on the first of many visits to Prague was the dramatist Karel Čapek, author of the robot play R.U.R. He said at once, 'Why do you come here? We have no Hitlers, no royal pretenders, no *Putsches*, no communist riots, no palace scandals. I warn you immediately—we are terribly uninteresting.' And the dour Czechs were, indeed, a great contrast to the flamboyance of Hungary, the paralysis of Vienna, the hysterics of Berlin.

I met a Press officer in the foreign office—then one of the best Press offices in Europe, incidentally. Czechoslovakia having been a civilised country, there was no need for a newspaper man to waste his first three days convincing the authorities that he was not a burglar or spy. The Press bureau in Prague was so well run that it was often accused of 'propaganda'. Of course. Propaganda was what it existed for. What enemies of Czechoslovakia objected to was that Czechoslovak propaganda was so friendly, efficient, and, in general, honest and accurate that rival countries were outrun.

Czechoslovakia was, of course, more fortunate to begin with than its partners or opponents. Its people were, for one thing, a closely-knit cultural unit, deriving from the tradition of Bohemian kings older than Habsburgs or Hohenzollerns. The Czechs were steadier than their volatile southern Slav cousins, more industrious than the Poles and Rumanians, and with a better background of administrative experience—the Czechs were the civil servants of the old empire—than Slovenes or Serbs.

They inherited, moreover, about three-quarters of the industry of the old empire and most of its mineral and other resources. Thus the great streams of toys, ceramics, glassware, textiles, steelware, munitions, beer, paper, yarn, hams, buttons, that poured from Czechoslovakia in the post-War days. Again, Czechoslovakia, unlike Jugoslavia or Poland, had been untouched by actual battle; physical reparation was not a problem. Finally, Czechoslovakia had a solid and unbeaten army, comprised of the Russian legions, in contrast to the wrecked fugitives that had to restore order in the other succession states.

On this lucky basis the young country, wedged like a downward-pointing long-nosed dachshund in the very centre of Europe, built, and built well. It eschewed foreign loans and foreign short-term credits, and so was not caught frenziedly short like Germany and the other Danubian countries in the 1931 financial crisis; it strictly limited imports ('Any Czech citizen who buys an orange,' said the first finance minister, 'is a traitor to the state') in an effort to maintain its favourable trade balance; it kept its budget in good order; it made a fairly successful land reform; it built schools for free education; it permitted inner politics to evolve on a very wide coalition basis including the social democrats; and it adopted a fairly reasonable policy towards its numerous minorities.

Even so, after a decade of almost uninterruptedly calm development, Czechoslovakia in the middle thirties began to encounter serious troubles. Two events of great importance occurred. One was the sudden and powerful rise of a disguised Nazi party under the former gymnasium instructor Konrad Henlein. In the 1935 elections this party, representing the bulk of Czechoslovakia's minority of 3,300,000 Germans, polled 1,247,000 votes and became overnight the second largest party in the country, rising from zero seats in the chamber to forty-four. Henlein protested loyalty to Masaryk and the Czechoslovak state—at first.

Intelligent Dr. Beneš recognised the Nazi danger. Therefore the second event. He went through Europe mending fences with assiduous alacrity. The first plank in his policy was the alliance with France, the second, the presumptive solidarity of the Little Entente—Czechoslovakia, Rumania, Jugoslavia. But as the German menace mounted and Czech relations with Poland grew steadily worse, Dr. Beneš saw that he needed something else, and so he went to Moscow and signed a mutual assistance pact—not merely a 'non-aggression' pact which is the form such treaties usually take —with the U.S.S.R. Czechoslovakia became the military link between France and the Soviet Union as defence against Germany and the other revisionist states.

But neither Beneš nor anyone else counted on the savage efficiency of Hitler, and the weakness of the democracies.

Dr. Hodza and Other Leaders

Dr. Milan Hodza, a Slovak agrarian, became prime minister after the elevation of Dr. Beneš to the presidency. His appointment was shrewd politics, a gesture to the large Slovak component of the republic. Ambitious and hard-boiled, Hodza took office after many years of opposition and started off well. He was born in Sucany (then a town in Hungary) in 1878, a protestant. He took his Ph. D. at the University of Vienna, became a journalist, and sat in the old Hungarian parliament as a representative of the Slovak minority.

After Munich, in November 1938, Dr. Emil Hacha became president of what was left of the Czechoslovak republic, as we have seen. The unfortunate Hacha, a Nazi puppet—nothing more, nothing less—was a distinguished lawyer, who had been chief justice of the

Czechoslovak Supreme Court, and also a justice in the World Court
at the Hague. He is sixty-six, and a devout Catholic. He once—
of all things!—translated Kipling's jungle books into Czech.
Hacha's first 'prime minister' was Rudolf Beran, an anti-Beneš
man and a reactionary agrarian.

More interesting as a human being—and of a good deal more
potential importance—than Hacha or Beran is the Slovak priest,
Dr. Joseph Tiso, who became first president of the Slovak 'republic'
in October 1939. Tiso, as we know, was the man who opened the
way to Hitler's seizure of Bohemia and Moravia in March. Theoretically his Slovakia is 'independent', while Bohemia-Moravia,
under Hacha, became merely a 'protectorate'. Tiso is of course
completely under the German thumb. Behind him is a well-
known Slovak secessionist, by name Bela Tuka.

Danube Pact

It is in the Danube region that those two doughty warriors, politics and economics, fight some of their grimmest battles. Nothing,
on the face of it, would seem to be more sensible a solution of the
difficulties of the area than an economic recreation of empire unity.
Abolish the tariffs that deface the territory; cut out mushroom
nationalist industries; exchange agrarian goods for industrial products on a basis of efficiency. Simple? Far from it! The Danube
countries far preferred to sink alone than swim together. The
nationalist hatreds of these regions cannot be expressed in graphs
and charts. They defy belief. I remember a young Hungarian's
response to a proposal for a mutual ten per cent cut on Czech-
Hungarian tariffs.

'What!' he exclaimed. 'Do you imagine we rate our hatred of
the Czechs at only ten per cent!'

The pre-Munich political cleavage of the Danube powers did
not, of course, correspond to the natural economic realities of the
region. The six states were stratified into two groups, the winners,
Czechoslovakia, Rumania, Jugoslavia, against the losers, Austria,
Hungary, Bulgaria. This political groupment was bad business, as
business. Economically, Czechoslovakia and Austria should have
formed one *bloc*, an industrial *bloc*, vis-à-vis an agrarian block of
the predominantly grain producing countries, Hungary, Rumania,
Jugoslavia, Bulgaria. All attempts at Danube salvage broke on this
issue, the fundamental and inescapable dichotomy between the
political and economic interests of the region.

There were other political difficulties. Austro-Czechoslovakia (if it had existed) would not have been big enough a market for all the grain of Hungaro-Rumano-Bulgoslavia. Germany, the best natural purchaser, would have had to join the industrial brethren. Then politics protruded its ugly face again: because France objected to this. So did Italy. The Little Entente itself was far from being a happy economic unit. Czechoslovakia bought comparatively little grain from its allies Rumania and Jugoslavia, because the strong Czech agrarian party, defending its internal interests, demanded high tariffs on grain from the Entente partners.

Balkans

'The war between Hungary and Jugoslavia has been averted, and the League of Nations will try to find a way to settle the controversy. Perhaps the best solution would be to plough under every third Balkan.'   —HOWARD BRUBAKER.

Beyond and below what was once Czechoslovakia lie the deep Balkans. They are, it has been said, a sort of hell paved with the bad intentions of the powers. The Great War was fought, remarked the Greek statesman, Venizelos, to Europeanise the Balkans; what the War of 1914 did, more or less, was Balkanise Europe. The Balkan peninsula is an unstable pyramid of nationalist hatreds, and of minority hatreds within nations.

One can make a pretty list of them. What is the worst hatred in southern and eastern Europe. Does a Bulgar hate a Serb more than a Croat hates a Serb? Do the hatreds of both combined equal the hatred of either for, say, an Italian or a Greek? Does a Hungarian hate a Rumanian more than a Rumanian hates a Bulgarian? Does a Galician hate a Pole more than a Ukrainian hates a Russian?

It is an intolerable affront to human and political nature that these wretched and unhappy little countries in the Balkan peninsula can, and do, have quarrels that cause world wars. A million young Englishmen died because of an event in 1914 in a mud-caked primitive village Sarajevo. Loathsome and almost obscene snarls in Balkan politics, hardly intelligible to a western reader, are still vital to the peace of Europe, and perhaps the world.

CHAPTER XXX

CAROL, RUMANIA, AND LUPESCU

RUMANIA, a rich country, with 18,800,000 people, is ruled by King Carol, who in turn is ruled by Magda Lupescu. The land swims in oil, smothers in grain and timber, though much wealth has been lost by the depredations of corrupt politicians. The capital, Bucharest, is a tinselly sort of little Paris where the main street, the Calea Victoria, flutters with silken skirts and the leather trappings of gay carriages transporting perfumed, corseted officers. Here wealth produced by the sweating and starving peasants is spent on *tsuica* (plum spirit), on caviare from Danube sturgeons, on huge red strawberries from the Transylvanian hills.

For three generations Rumania was ruled by a family of hereditary semi-dictators, the Bratianus; it was a Bratianu who peddled the Rumanian crown around the courts of Europe and brought back Carol's grand-uncle as the country's first king. The policy of the Bratianus was that of the Turk suzerains and Phanariot Greek concessionaires who had preceded them—despoil the land with artful greed. No country in Europe has been so corruptly manipulated and exploited. Baksheesh was the national watchword. After the War came a land reform. The peasants, to buy seed and tools, borrowed money at interest rates of thirty, forty, even fifty per cent. But they could not sell the glut of grain the land produced. As a result agrarian bankruptcy ruined them in thousands and the agricultural debt became, *per capita*, the highest in the world. The finances were paralysed, the budget deficit mounted out of sight— and in the ornate streets of Bucharest money flowed like silk in the hands of a corrupt and chosen few.

There is a cruel little joke about Rumania. 'Mania' means madness. 'Kleptomania' means madness to steal. 'Rumania' means madness to steal applied to a nation.

Rumanians are good-natured and fatalistic folk, colourful and easy-going; they don't like trouble or bloodshed. They are not like Serbs, who have high qualities of heroism and a predisposition to patriotic murder. There has never been a revolution in Rumania.

The Rumanians are oddly mixed in blood, being originally Latin
the descendants of Roman legions sent to the province of Dacia by
the emperor Trajan; atop this were superimposed centuries of Slavic
blood.   And there are traces of Gipsy, Tartar, Greek, and Turk in
most Rumanians.

   To this country and its primitive and illiterate people came a
young British princess about forty years ago. She was Marie,
daughter of the Duke of Edinburgh and grand-daughter of both
Queen Victoria of England and the Czar of Russia, representing a
unique concentration of royalty rare in the modern world.   Marie
married Ferdinand, the Rumanian heir apparent, and gave birth
to six children, the eldest of whom was Carol.   She and Ferdinand
ruled from 1914 till Ferdinand died in 1927.   Meanwhile all manner of scandalous things had happened.   And kept on happening.

. . . .

   Carol was a complicated, truculent, and strongwilled youngster.
Even as a boy he was hard to manage.   He disliked his father, the
arid, flinty Ferdinand, and adored his mother—at the beginning.
He bitterly resented, however, the power in the court of one of the
great Rumanian nobles, Prince Stirbey, and of Jon Bratianu, the
dictator, who was Stirbey's brother-in-law.   Carol grew up to follow
the example of the court, and himself began to lead an emotional
life of considerable complexity.

   In 1918 he met Mlle Zizi Lambrino in Jassy, the provincial town
where the Rumanian court had taken refuge during the German
invasion.   Marie tried to frustrate his affair with Lambrino with
the result, of course, that she strengthened it.   As if going out of his
way to annoy his family, Carol actually married Lambrino.   It was
not a clandestine or morganatic marriage, but took place in the
cathedral of Odessa, fully solemnised.   The Rumanian supreme
court annulled the marriage and Carol was angry enough to abdicate.   But after a year or so he tired of Lambrino, and in the crush of
war both marriage and abdication were allowed to be forgotten.
Lambrino bore Carol a son, by name Mircea.

   Carol, still more or less a boy in the hands of Marie and the
Bratianu bosses, was told to take a trip around the world to re-
cuperate and forget.   He got as far from Rumania as Switzerland,
where he met Princess Helene, the daughter of King Constantine
of Greece, whose son George, by the efficient management of Marie,
was to marry Carol's sister Elizabeth.   Carol decided to settle
down.   He married Helene.   This was in March 1921.   The royal

couple returned to Bucharest and prepared to live happily ever after.

But subsequently Carol met Magda Lupescu, and a new phase of Rumanian history began.

Carol had come by this time to open conflict with Jon Bratianu, the dictator. He resented Bratianu's influence, and had served formal notice that when he became king he would wipe out the Bratianu-Stirbey clique. Bratianu was no person to take a threat like this lying down. Carol's affair with Lupescu was becoming a bit of a scandal, and it gave Bratianu a chance to strike. Carol was sent off to represent Rumania at the funeral in London of Queen Alexandra. This duty performed, he met Lupescu in Milan. They were going to Venice together, but he found a message telling him to return to Bucharest at once, without his mistress, or forfeit the succession. Bratianu had prevailed on Ferdinand and Marie thus to 'discipline' their son. Carol flashed into temper, refused to return. Thereupon, with extreme haste, Bratianu wangled a crown council into accepting Carol's 'abdication'.

Carol thus began his five years' exile. During this time Lupescu never once left his side.

Ferdinand died in 1927, and Carol's six-year-old son Michael—by Helene—became king. Then, more important, Jon Bratianu died, and the clique lost power when a peasant chieftain, Juliu Maniu, took advantage of the troubled situation to assert leadership; he became prime minister. The remnants of the Bratianu gang wanted Carol out. Maniu, patriotically eager to preserve the dynasty, wanted him back. Maniu's idea was that the divorce between Carol and Helene made during the exile should be annulled, and that Carol might then really settle down. So he arranged for Carol to return—by means of the celebrated coup of June 1930, when the exiled prince flew back to Bucharest. Carol proclaimed himself king, unseating his boy Michael, and thus taking a throne that had already been held by both his father and his son.

Maniu, as we shall see, reckoned without Lupescu. He had assumed Carol would desert her. He was wrong.

The Lady

Magda Lupescu is, beyond doubt, one of the most remarkable women of the time. She is fortyish now, and getting fat; nevertheless Carol is still devoted to her, and life without her is unthinkable

for him. She is a King's Favourite in the grand line of Du Barry
and de Pompadour. Her personal influence on him is probably, on
the whole, good, but the fact that she is Jewish, and has come to
head a sort of secret government within a government, has had
serious political consequences.

Lupescu is in fact only half-Jewish. She was born in Jassy, the
daughter of the keeper of an apothecary shop named Wolff. He
changed his name to Lupescu, the Rumanian equivalent, in order
to get permission to practise as a chemist, since only a certain proportion of Jews were allowed to enter the professions. On a trip
to Vienna he met a Roman Catholic girl and married her. Lupescu
was the child of his marriage. She was actually baptised a Roman
Catholic.

She met Carol in 1923 in Sinaia, the summer capital, where his
coterie of bucks and bloods went to hunt and play roulette. Previously she had married an army officer; when Carol became attentive she quietly divorced him. A woman of great intelligence and
commanding personality, with flaming red hair, her charms were
such that Carol gave up a throne for her.

Until recently she lived at No. 2 Alea Vulpache, in a two-story
red brick villa at the left of the Polish legation, near the corner of
the Alea Alexandria, in the residential outskirts of Bucharest.
There is a big garden, and the visitor is impressed by a row of
chicken coops along one wall. Leghorns and Plymouth Rocks, also
a couple of turkeys, scamper and strut behind the wire. The story
is that not only does Lupescu tend these domestic creatures, but
with her own hands helped the carpenters build the sheds and coops.

She and Carol cannot live together openly. This would not be
too great a shock for Rumanian morals but it would be politically
imprudent. Everyone in the kingdom knows that she is his mistress, and she is openly attacked as such in speeches and pamphlets
by the opposition, but a certain discretion is necessary in Carol's
personal routine. Sometimes she motors into town at night and
enters the palace grounds by a garden gate. In the garden,
separate from the palace but connected with it by a passage, is a
small cottage. The palace, be it understood, is situated on the main
street of Bucharest, in a location comparable to that of Piccadilly in
London. So privacy is difficult. Therefore, Carol and Lupescu
live as much as possible in the mountain village where they first
met, Sinaia.

People resent Lupescu for a variety of reasons. Some of the princely families which had ruled and pillaged Rumania for so long cannot endure it that Carol lives such an irregular personal life. Many other Rumanians, both patrician and of common stock, would not mind if the king had twenty mistresses, but they dislike Lupescu's Jewishness. Above all, she has come to typify and concentrate the opposition of the politicians, for the special reason that she has become a politician in her own right, and the most important one in the kingdom—head of the palace *camarilla*.

This *camarilla* grew up partly because Carol, in his unwedded state, could not have a queen and a regular court, partly because he was naturally attached to a few old cronies. These were friends of Lupescu also. The *camarilla*, as it originally existed, was led by a man named Poui Dimitrescu, for many years the King's private secretary. The first *camarilla* was broken up early in 1934, following the assassination of the prime minister, Jon Duca, by fanatical adherents of the Iron Guard, a Fascist organisation pledged to extirpate Lupescu and all her friends. But a new *camarilla* took its place.

Lupescu has friends in all the key positions of the realm. She has her own secret service. She puts people in the big jobs. She has, in fact, almost usurped the functions of the prime minister; no prime minister can rule independently of her, yet she is not responsible to anyone. She isn't, even her enemies admit, interfering with things *badly*, but nothing important can be done without her consent; and this infuriates the politicians. Her activity of course enhances her value to the King, because she is the convenient instrument whereby he exercises extra-curricular functions—so necessary to the fun of kingship, especially in Rumania, where almost everything is 'fixed'.

Two people have dared come out in the open against Lupescu. One is Maniu. He is able to do so because, to date, the King can touch him only at the risk of a revolution. But Maniu lost his job as prime minister on Lupescu's account. The other was Colonel Vladimir Precup. This officer was the agent chiefly responsible for the outside arrangements of Carol's *coup d'état* when he flew back to Rumania. For years he was one of Carol's best friends, along with the all-powerful private secretary, Dimitrescu. Later Precup thought that Lupescu's influence on Carol was ruining the country and he concocted a fantastic plot to get rid of her. He was arrested, dismissed from the army, and sentenced to ten years in jail.

One person dared to combat her—to a point. He was, and is,

2 G

Nicolai Titulescu, for years Rumania's voluble and eccentric foreign minister. After the Duca killing, Titulescu declined to enter the cabinet until there was a house-cleaning. He refused to serve in any government so long as the King was surrounded by a gang which aroused the Iron Guard to murder. Titulescu was indispensable to Carol, as the only Rumanian with a European prestige in international matters. As price for his entry in the government, he demanded the break-up of the old *camarilla*. For a week, the struggle went on between Lupescu, the King's mistress, and Titulescu, who is uninterested in mistresses. Titulescu won— provisionally. But he was far too shrewd to threaten the position of Lupescu herself.

Lupescu is practically an ideal mistress, were it not for politics. She is not frivolous; on the contrary her discretion is notorious. Not forty people in Bucharest, outside her own circle, have ever seen her. She is not avaricious; indeed she learned the value of cold cash during the years of exile, and she persuades Carol to save his money. She is, according to all gossip, faithful to him, and this in a country monstrously licentious. She has no desire to marry Carol. She knows it would be the end of the dynasty. Nor has she encumbered him with illegitimate children. And Madame de Montespan, be it remembered, inflicted on Louis XIV seven.[1]

Magda Lupescu is a striking anachronism. Kings are dull folk these days; and royal favourites, like court jesters, have practically fled the field. Louise de la Vallière was the daughter of an officer; Lupescu of a small town chemist. Nell Gwynn sold oranges at Drury Lane; Lupescu frequented the Athena Palace hotel in Bucharest. Her mileage is good. Du Barry lasted five years a king's mistress; Lupescu has been with Carol over ten.

They tell a little story in Bucharest to the effect that her father scolded her severely at the time that Carol's brother, Nicholas, was indulging in amorous and scandalous affairs. Carol had settled, as it were, down. But Nicholas was acting up. Against his brother's orders he had committed marriage with a certain Madame Saveanu. Carol had done something exactly similar in his youth but there was no puritan like a reformed rake and he was wild with fury; Nicholas, he said, was bringing a bad name to the crown. Bucharest rocked, especially at the report that Nicholas blacked his royal brother's eye. And old Lupescu came to Magda saying,

---

[1] Occasionally rumours crop up that Lupescu is to be married off to someone. Also reports of Carol's 'engagement' to a German princess were recently heard.

'Daughter, daughter, what kind of a family are you getting mixed up with!'

Royal Rapscallion

Carol to-day is rather portly, with something of a midriff; he is no youngster. He is vain, stubborn, wilful, and by no means unintelligent. He has very little sense of humour. He speaks letter-perfect English with a hint of German accent, letter-perfect French with a hint of English accent, and letter-perfect German with a hint of French accent. Even his Rumanian is not quite perfect—familiar symptom of the polyglot training of Balkan kings.

He is pretty well off. His personal salary is £72,727 per year (at present exchange) and, contrary to general opinion, he lives fairly modestly and must be able to save a third of it. One Bucharest estimate gives him savings, deposited mostly in banks or securities abroad, of 20,000,000 French francs, or something over £200,000. The official civil list is the following:

King Carol	40,000,000 lei	(£72,727)
Ex-Queen Helene	7,000,000 ,,	(£12,726)
Crown Prince Michael	7,000,000 ,,	(£12,726)
Travelling Expenses	6,000,000 ,,	(£10,909)

Carol's relations with his whole family are indifferent, except with his son Michael, the only lad in history who has been king of a country once and may with reasonable expectation be king of the same country again. His system for Michael's education is eminently sensible, Carol having realised how bad his own education was. But Carol persistently avoided his mother; he has exiled his ex-wife, Helene; he and Nicholas are far from friendly; and he is said to dislike his sister Ileana, now wife of the Archduke Anton Habsburg, who is the nicest of all the royal Rumanians.

Carol has very few friends; few kings, indeed, can afford the luxury of friendship. He is apt to be rude, and overbearing, and on his dignity; people find it hard to talk to him. There is an ugly, jagged streak of maladjustment in his character, caused possibly by jealousy of his mother. His closest friend is probably Titianu, the man who is under-secretary of the interior in all cabinets; another intimate is Professor Nicolas Jorga, the fantastic pundit who was his tutor in his youth, who became professor of universal history at the University of Bucharest at the age of twenty-two, and who has written two hundred and fifty-seven different books and pamphlets.

Until very recently Carol was not a dictator. The plain truth was that he had no need to be. He was willing to practise almost any compromise to save him from the danger of *overt* dictatorial rule, because he took good note of the fate of his royal cousins Alfonso of Spain and Alexander of Jugoslavia. He did not need to exert dictatorial power largely because of the Rumanian electoral law, by which the party getting forty per cent of the votes takes a thirty per cent bonus of the seats in the chamber. And Rumanian politics are such that a government in office is never voted out; the king determines the time for a change, superintends the appointment of a new ministry, and then this ministry makes new elections and always wins them.

After Duca was killed the King suddenly developed an extremely diplomatic illness, which prevented him from attending the funeral of the murdered prime minister. He feared the Iron Guard might bomb the cathedral where the services were being held. The decision to stay away was made at the last moment. Charts prepared in advance had shown where he would be. He wasn't there. Whispers surged through Bucharest that Carol was hiding in his palace, paralysed with fear. Possibly he was only being prudent. But he lost a fine chance to prove that bullets which could kill a prime minister could not scare a king.

Mother Marie

There should be another word about Marie. She was a gorgeous woman until the end. There are large sections of purest nonsense in her autobiography, a book she never should have written; but from childhood she sought to express herself. She was born with no sense of envy, no jealousy; she had not the faintest shadow of inferiority complex; she might have been a superb actress; for her dramatic ability was extreme.

The tragedy of her life was the failure of her personal relations with Carol. She spoiled him as a youngster, and she always loved him deeply, but she could not take him seriously as a king. He remained a boy to her. It was almost impossible for her to resist thinking that he was being absurd when he was acting like a monarch. And that he detested. In contrast, Lupescu's hold on Carol came partly because she does see him for what he after all is, King of Rumania.

Marie was fond of young Michael and hoped desperately that he would grow up with her character in his bones, that he would skip the generation of his father. She wanted him to get a good education, marry a princess, be a good king. She did everything possible to salve the unhappiness of his situation vis-à-vis his parents. Lupescu, incidentally, sees Michael casually but regularly, and is fond of him.

One is apt to forget what a first-class political queen Marie was. In the modern world royalty should earn its keep. Marie not only gave Rumania six children; she more than doubled its population and territory. An Englishwoman, she influenced Ferdinand, a German and a Hohenzollern, to side with the Allies instead of the Central Powers during the War; and thus at a stroke converted Rumania from a somewhat ridiculous semi-principality to the seventh largest country in continental Europe.

Marie was out of the political picture for some years, until her sudden death in 1938.

More Fascist Scurvy

Only two streets away from the town palace where Carol lives is a hotel which, to put it mildly, expresses much of the spirit of Bucharest, amorously and politically. In this hotel, almost every afternoon, two or three young men, well-dressed and multi-lingual, sit and sip Turkish coffee and talk about revolution. They are members of the Iron Guard.

This organisation was founded in 1927 by a young zealot, Corneliu Codreanu, who was of Polish not Rumanian origin; his real name was Zelinski. At first he called it the 'Legion of the Archangel Michael'. Its programme was a fanatic, obstreperous sub-Fascism on a strong nationalist and anti-Semitic basis. Its members trooped through the countryside, wore white costumes, carried burning crosses, impressed the ignorant peasantry, aroused the students in the towns. Presently its enrolled strength was two hundred thousand men.

Codreanu believed in *overt* violence; in fact he once shot and wounded the Mayor of Jassy, whom he accused of being pro-Semite. But his movement was only a sort of unpleasant eczema on the face of the land until Hitlerism came to power in the Reich. Then it straightway reached considerable political importance, because if the Iron Guard came to power, it might transfer Rumania's traditional allegiance from France to Germany. Meanwhile, the person of Magda Lupescu was a perpetual red flag in the faces of Iron Guardsmen. Finally Duca, the prime minister, was murdered by Iron Guard desperadoes.

After the murder the Iron Guard split up, and the leadership passed to another man, Nicolai Stelescu. Officially, he separated from Codreanu because he did not believe in terrorism. He sought to make the Iron Guard respectable. It was forbidden as a legal party, but he tried to fight by legal means. He was a youngster of thirty, a fanatic, an idealist, with a council of advisers who worshipped him. In July 1936, he was murdered by rival Iron Guardists, as he lay in a hospital bed.

After Stelescu's death his formidable rival Codreanu became important again. Rumania had an agitated time. For a time a violent anti-Semite named Goga was prime minister; he was followed by the aged patriarch of the orthodox church, Miron Cristea. More and more, the King was having to govern the country himself—under martial law. In 1938 Codreanu was arrested, and then murdered in sensational circumstances with thirteen Iron Guard comrades. They were all shot while being moved from one prison to another, on the pretext that they sought to 'escape'. A fantastic creature named Armand Calinescu was minister of the interior at the time. He accepted full responsibility—and then became prime minister. Calinescu was a Maniu man. He was only a bit over five feet tall, but tough. He always wore a black patch over one eye. He bade fair to create a real dictatorial government for Carol, but he was himself murdered by Iron Guardists late in 1939—as reprisal for the murder of Codreanu.

Men of the Iron Guard say that they expect to come to power through country-wide agitation centralised in local clubs called 'Culte de Patrie'. They intend to eliminate political parties when they reach power, but to leave the King alone, if he gives Lupescu up. They talk of the King quite respectfully. They deny that the organisation is any longer financed by Hitler. They say, in fact, that when their men visited Rosenberg in Berlin, he was astonished that they did not want money and complimented them on being the only Balkan sub-Hitler group which had ever come to Berlin without begging.

The Iron Guard recently became allied to the great National Peasant party of Juliu Maniu. This is an important development. Maniu thinks he is using the Iron Guard; they are his shock-troops. The Iron Guard assumes it is using Maniu; he is their political tactician. Other leaders, other parties, joined for a time this informal common-front, like the dissident liberals of George Bratianu, and the adherents of General Averescu, Rumania's chief War hero. All are linked by common hatred of Lupescu.

Maniu Tells his Story

One of the finest characters in all the Balkans, in fact in all Europe, and certainly the most distinguished citizen of Rumania, is Juliu Maniu. Ascetic, incorruptible, stately, devout, Maniu is a Transylvanian, the son of a peasant. He is a bachelor. Like Matchek in Croatia, whom his career resembles, he is a Roman Catholic; he was educated as a Jesuit. He has no interest in women, in money, or in personal power; he is that rare thing, a Rumanian patriot for Rumania's sake.

Maniu was born in 1873. Before the War he was a deputy in the Hungarian parliament, representing the (then) Rumanian minority. His health is not good. His faults as a politician are an unyielding stubbornness and inability to compromise; and his mind, tenacious enough, is slow-moving. He is capable of immense disinterestedness. He resigned the premiership because he was convinced Carol had treated Helene unjustly. He resigned his presidency of the National Peasant party because he felt that Carol's dislike of him prejudiced the party's chances of political success.

Maniu's first great achievement was binding together two wings of the submerged opposition, just after the War, and making a united force of it. From the old kingdom came the 'peasant' (Tsaranist) half of the party; from Transylvania and the other districts acquired by the peace treaties came the 'national' half. Rumania had a decent government for the first time in history when Maniu became prime minister. He tried to promote essential governmental economics and reforms; he set about re-organising agriculture and the railways; above all—a negative but valuable accomplishment—he ended the vicious Bratianu tyranny.

What is more, Maniu did something for which he got small thanks later—he brought King Carol back.

The world has heard a great deal of that dazzling aeroplane coup in June 1930, whereby Carol regained his throne. The true story of that coup has never been written. It is assumed that Carol, with the aid of a couple of gallant desperadoes, did the job himself.

He was described as a hard-flying prince, a modern Allen Quarter-maine, a hero. Nothing could be further from the truth. Carol did nothing whatever to bring himself back except get in the aeroplane. The whole business was engineered, *inside* Rumania, by Maniu.

His motives were clear. He knew that Carol, outside the country, was a perpetual focus of unrest and intrigue. He was aware that the regency was weak and he believed strongly in the three essential conditions of monarchist institutions: stability, continuity, authority. Moreover, he knew that inasmuch as the 'Liberal' (Bratianu) party was against Carol, his own National Peasant party, on realistic grounds, should favour him. Logic compelled him to try to bring the errant prince home. But he wanted him home without Lupescu.

Deeply disillusioned years after, Maniu himself wrote the whole story, as a speech which he was refused permission to deliver in the Rumanian parliament on December 12, 1934. It recounts in full detail his incessant manœuvres on behalf of Carol even while Ferdinand was still alive. When Ferdinand died Maniu's activities redoubled. He committed the National Peasant party to the idea of Carol's restoration, sounded out the regency, and carefully tested public opinion. Following is part of the speech, which has never before been published:

> 'The impatience of H.R.H. Prince Carol (to return to Rumania) was growing, but he showed not the least sign of an intention to separate from Madame Lupescu. . . . In all conversations which I had with H.R.H. the Princess Mother Helene, I tried to remove her explicable bitterness towards H.R.H. Prince Carol, with the aim that should Prince Carol return the ground would be spiritually prepared for a reconciliation. . . . H.R.H. Prince Carol judged my foresight as indecision.
>
> 'My attitude, which was confirmed by messages I received, was not caused by hesitation but by the fact that for me two things were important: first, I needed assurance from H.R.H. Prince Carol that . . . he intended to reign in constitutional manner and not through personal friends; and secondly, that he would separate from Madame Lupescu whose fatal influence on Prince Carol enshadows him. . . .'

Maniu proceeds to relate how he sent an emissary to Paris to sound out Carol; the emissary saw not only the prince but Lupescu herself, who said that she would not upset plans by returning to Rumania with him. She is quoted as having said, '*The day that H.R.H. is restored to the throne for the happiness of the country,*

I shall disappear for ever, and my only wish is that thereafter no one shall speak of me.' Maniu, cautious, wanted this declaration implemented by a statement from Carol. He determined to send Nicholas to see him. He proceeds:

'In this situation, one day at the end of May 1930, Major Precup, well known to me, a devoted supporter of H.R.H. Prince Carol, presented himself and informed that he had been to see H.R.H. Prince Carol who begged him to ascertain what my final attitude would be were H.R.H. Prince Carol one day to decide to return home. I charged Major Precup to say to H.R.H. Prince Carol that there was no need for such a step because Prince Nicholas on July 18th would leave for Paris and meet H.R.H. Prince Carol and discuss matters until I could come myself.

'I asked Major Precup about Madame Lupescu. He replied: "She is not returning to the country." I then told him that in that event if . . . H.R.H. Prince Carol should decide independently to return, he would not find an enemy but a good friend in me.'

Maniu then details the astounding labours he went through preparing for the event. He tended to every detail. He called Colonel Manolescu, the adjutant of Prince Nicholas, and communicated with Nicholas. He arranged that the minister of war, General Condescu, should prepare troops at Cluj and Jassy to receive Carol, and that the garrison in Bucharest should be on duty at the aeroplane field. He informed the cabinet and the regents, and arranged that one of the regents, Sarateanu, should resign his place so that Carol could take it. He even arranged for a room for Carol to sleep in at the palace.

Carol arrived; and at five the next morning Maniu was informed that he wished to be proclaimed King at once. Maniu had had the different idea that Carol should first enter the regency, until his marital affairs were adjusted and the country got used to the new régime. Carol was insistent. Maniu dutifully and with some difficulty procured the consent of the regency and then held a cabinet meeting:

'Five ministers voted for the entry of H.R.H. Prince Carol into the regency, while six were in favour of his being proclaimed King. My view was the minority, but several ministers said they were prepared to submit to my decision, whatever it might be. . . . During the cabinet meeting a large delegation of members of parliament of our party had come to see me. I received them. They were of the opinion that H.R.H. Prince Carol should be proclaimed King immediately and begged me not to obstruct their desires. I saw at once the problem had taken a turning from which no efforts of mine could divert it, even though it was obvious what evil results would follow if H.R.H. Prince Carol were proclaimed King without first having arranged the question of Princess Helene and Madame Lupescu. . . . But I could not force my views in the face of public opinion . . . and it was too late to obtain the results at which I had aimed. I therefore took recourse to the only logical and honourable solution; I . . . resigned.'

Carol, after a few days, was compelled to reaccept Maniu as prime minister. Maniu proceeds:

'Immediately after the formation of the government, in accord with the wishes of H.M. the King, I proposed that the coronation be held without delay. I fixed the date between September 15 and 20, 1930, and established that H.M. the King should be crowned together with Princess Mother Helene. I presented the programme of the coronation and took the preliminary measures at Alba Julia. Tired but glad at the result obtained, I left for a two weeks' holiday.

'Upon my return I found the situation entirely changed. H.M. the King no longer wanted to hear of the coronation. The situation which, to my great joy, had been improving, tending to become more normal, had been aggravated. I did not know how this change had come about. . . .

'Then, accidentally, I learned that Madame Lupescu had returned to the country. I refused to believe it. I made inquiry of the directors of the Security Service, Messrs. Cadere and Bianu. They denied it. I asked M. Vaida; he knew nothing. I was again informed that Madame Lupescu had returned. I again asked M. Bianu, who replied that it was another Madame Lupescu. I learned, however, that she had returned on August 4, 1930, and that she was stopping at Foisor Palace.'

Shortly thereafter Maniu resigned again. He was 'extremely tired' and saw that 'under these conditions government with results was not possible'. The King, he records, received his resignation with 'evident pleasure'. Maniu learned the lesson that royalty does not like to be too much indebted to its subjects. What had happened was that Carol tried to give Lupescu up. He stuck it out alone for just two months. Then he found life unbearable without her.

Diplomat De Luxe

Another Rumanian politician worth note is the fabulous exforeign minister Nicolai Titulescu. He looks like a mongoloid monkey; he is the best conversationalist in the Balkans; he controls most of the journalists in Bucharest; he is the one man in Rumania trusted by the French general staff; he is torrentially voluble in half a dozen languages; his wit and unquenchable vivacity are famous all over Europe: he wears an overcoat indoors, even on the hottest day; he is No. 2 on the death list of the Iron Guard; he has twice been president of the League of Nations Assembly and in 1935 was president of both the Little Entente and the Balkan Entente, comprising populations of almost seventy million people.

Carol, jealous of Titulescu, booted him from office while he was ill and in France on a holiday.

George Tatarescu, Carol's premier off and on since 1935, a young 'liberal', took his job.

Germany or U.S.S.R.?

Rumania was the second country in the former ring of the Little Entente. Its army is not very good but its resources in oil (one-third owned by British companies), are enormous and it is of great strategic importance in the French system of alliances throughout Europe. And as we know, the British guaranteed Rumania in the spring of 1939. Neither the British nor French would like to lose Rumania. And they have no intention of doing so.

Yet Rumania has been tempted on occasion to German leanings. There are several reasons:

(1) Rumania's chief crop is grain and Germany is potentially its best market. France and Rumania's partners in the Little Entente and Balkan Entente (Jugoslavia, Turkey, and Greece) are able to buy very little Rumanian grain. Germany could buy it all—for a political price. Thus a Rumanian-German trade agreement—all but forced on Rumania by Germany—came in 1939.

(2) Not only is anti-Semitism very acute in Rumania, but there exists a German minority of eight hundred thousand Saxons; these naturally feel the swastika itch. Besides the Iron Guard there are at least three Fascist parties in Rumania.

(3) Rumania's chief enemy is Hungary. France is not near enough to help Rumania in the event of war with Hungary, even if it were willing to. When war broke out in 1939, it became increasingly possible that Germany might egg Hungary on in an attempt to seize its lost Transylvanian provinces from Rumania.

(4) Carol is half a Hohenzollern. And like many men with power who would like more power, he probably has a surreptitious admiration for Hitler.

The Franco-Soviet arrangement, on the other hand, tended to keep Rumania in line while it lasted. For years Rumania feared a

Russian attempt to regain Bessarabia, the rich province along the Dniester which Rumania seized from the U.S.S.R. after the War. In 1934 the Bolsheviks renounced aggressive intentions towards Rumania. But after the Russo-German pact of 1939 and the Russian invasion of Poland, Rumania began again to fear that it might lose Bessarabia some day.

CHAPTER XXXI

JUGOSLAVIA AFTER ALEXANDER

Peter II, Europe's youngest monarch, seventeen years old, King of Jugoslavia in succession to his murdered father Alexander, is titular ruler of some 13,500,000 powerful Serbs, Croats, Slovenes, Slavones, Macedonians, Montenegrins, Bosnians, Dalmatians, united in the Kingdom of Jugoslavia. He was a shy and awkward boy. The trouble seems to have been a considerably mangled education. Through carelessness or ignorance, or both, his father and mother brought him up badly. His only teacher until he was ten was an English governess. She was a worthy character and devoted to the backward, lonely child, but her share in his training should have ended when he reached school age.

The King, Alexander, only realised this shortly before his death, and it was Queen Marie of Rumania, the boy's grandmother, who stepped in and insisted on some proper education for the prince. So he was sent to England to school. Then his father was murdered and Peter, succeeding him, returned to Jugoslavia and was unable to resume school abroad, because the provisions of the Jugoslav constitution forbid the monarch from leaving the country for any extended stay. It was a pity Peter could not finish school in England. The next best thing was done: an English tutor, Parrott, was put in charge of him.

Peter learned the news of his father's death from Queen Marie. She didn't know how to break the terrible news to him. Finally she said, 'Peter, you know people will call you Majesty now.' The boy burst into tears, crying, 'Grandmamma, I am too young to be a king.'

In strict contrast to Peter's mismanaged education is the example of his cousin Michael of Rumania. Father Carol has been very sensible about Michael. He goes to school with twelve other boys picked from all over the kingdom, and on terms of almost complete democracy with them. The boys are chosen from different parts of Rumania—Transylvania, Bessarabia, and so on—so that Michael will absorb different Rumanian characteristics, and they come from

various walks of life: the father of one, for instance, is a railwa
switchman, another is the son of a minor government official.   The
school, which sits in the palace, is completely staffed, and Carol ha
the boys to lunch once a week or so. As a result, Michael is a poised
and confident youngster, and when he and Peter are together, the
contrast between his bright ebullience and Peter's shy timidity i
striking.

Peter is one of the richest boys of his age in Europe, perhaps the
richest. The financial section of his father's will has never been
published, but so far as is known, Peter is sole heir, and Alexander'
fortune was estimated at £2,000,000. Much of it—not a patriotic
detail from the viewpoint of orthodox nationalism—was held in
bank accounts abroad, not in Jugoslavia, and in foreign (not Jugo
slav) securities. Alexander differed from other dictators, Hitler or
Mussolini, in having a passionate acquisitiveness to money.

The Jugoslav civil list is paid as a whole to the King and the
King determines how it shall be apportioned in the family. Ob
viously a boy of seventeen cannot do this and his cousin, the Regent
Prince Paul and his mother have charge of the income, though
purely as trustees. The civil list is enormous, amounting to
55,000,000 dinars a year, or about £250,000 at present exchange:
half of it is paid in dinars in Jugoslavia, half deposited in Swiss
francs abroad. Regent Paul's allowance is 720,000 dinars a year,
and in addition he gets a salary as Regent of 540,000 dinars, a total
roughly equal to £5,760—a pittance compared to the money at
theoretical disposal of the boy.

Peter is a boy with a throne—and few playmates. He has
£2,000,000—and very little to spend it on. His income is somewhere around £600 a day and he earns it by being afflicted with
kingship in the most obstreperous of Balkan countries. All the
glamour of royalty, if there is any, is hardly recompense for the formidable strain which accompanied this unlucky lad's adolescence.
He should be playing football; instead he has a court chamberlain
behind the curtains. He has, moreover, the most terrible prospect
in the world; he can never change his job, he is King for life, he can
never escape the steep walls of his own future.

Martyred Monarch

Alexander is dead, and his bullet-torn body lies in the Karageorgeovitch crypt in Oblenetz, near Belgrade, a highly decorated
structure that will look well in a century or two, when time has

dimmed the colour of its burning mosaics. But to understand Jugoslavia, to chart even an approximate projection of events, we must pause a moment and study the dead king's life and works.

In pictures, as the American magazine *Time* unvaryingly pointed out, he resembled a small-town dentist. In reality he looked like what he was—a King. He was industrious, charming, capable of almost inexplicable sudden flights of worry, temperament, and fury, yet disciplined and shrewd—a complex character. He was both implacable and bright-hearted. He died at forty-six, and he is stronger dead than alive, because his murder served to unify his country.

First and last Alexander was a soldier. He fought all through the War. He walked with common soldiers in the terrible retreat across Serbia in 1915. Moral in his personal life to the point of austerity, he despised his brother-in-law Carol as a wastrel and profligate. He liked Boris of Bulgaria but was suspicious of his timidity and lackadaisical qualities. It would have been unthinkable for Alexander, like Boris, to walk the streets of his capital unguarded. He was brought up at the court of the Czar in Petrograd, where he was a page; the glitter and absolutism of this resplendency dazzled him, permanently influenced his life. He did not love pomp but he did uncompromisingly love the display of authority. He spent his large salary with extreme frugality; his only extravagances were books and motor-cars. In the Dedinje library he had twenty thousand books. He owned twenty-three motor-cars, all Packards; he was one of the largest individual owners of Packards in the world.

Like all dictators except Hitler, he was a tremendous worker. Alexander rose early and was at his desk by eight; his secretaries had to have the whole of his day's correspondence, papers, etc., ready for him at this hour. At ten every day the audiences began. Every Monday he received first the chief of the general staff, the town commandant of Belgrade, and the chief of police. He worked till late in the evening, when, stupefied with fatigue, he either played bridge with the Queen and a few close friends, or, like Hitler, listened to music. He played the piano himself quite often, and fairly well. He never wore civilian dress; always uniform. In his reception-room the only ornaments were showcases filled with models of field artillery and cross-sections of shells, burnished till they glowed like jewels.

Behind Alexander, behind young Peter, are a couple of genera
tions of the most turbulent Balkan genealogy imaginable. The
family, the Karageorgeovitch dynasty, is pure Serb; unlike almos
all other dynasties, it intermarried with other royalty only with
extreme reluctance, and then only with next-door Balkan neigh
bours. Alexander's father, Peter I, married the daughter of the
King of Montenegro; he himself went as far as Bucharest to espouse
Marie, daughter of Rumania's Marie.

The Karageorgeovitch family (the name means 'Black George'
was descended from a *haiduk*, bandit chieftain, who freed Serbia
from the Turks in 1810. This original Black George was a person
of some character. Aside from his patriotic exploits he is said to
have murdered both his own father, to keep him from capture by
the Turks, and his own brother, and he was himself assassinated
Through the nineteenth century the family wound through Serbian
history like a crimson rope. Sometimes it was in power, sometimes
out.

In 1903, when modern Jugoslav history began, the rulers of
Serbia were King Alexander Obrenovitch, who belonged to a rival
dynasty, and his Queen a disreputable commoner named Draga.
They were murdered by officers owing allegiance to the Kara
georgeovitch group, temporarily in exile. The Karageorgeovitch
who then ascended the throne, Peter I, was the late Alexander's
father. He ruled till 1914, when Alexander became Regent. Peter
was afflicted with the family temperament. A story, never proved
and probably without foundation, says that he murdered his wife,
Zorka of Montenegro. At any rate he was a violently unstable
character. When his mind began to deteriorate, the clique of
officers who really ruled Serbia removed him from the throne.

The Regent should have been, not Alexander, but the eldest
son, George. But George, the Crown Prince, was unbalanced. He
thrashed his servants in violent fits of rage, and following a series of
exciting scandals, he was quietly certified as insane and removed
to confinement in a fortress at Nisch.[1] There, in 1939, he still
was.

Alexander, be it hastily said, inherited none of these Kara
georgeovitch qualities. He was neither a murderer nor a madman.
He was a King conscientious to the point of stuffiness, and, a com
plete patriot, he did what he thought was best for the country. A

[1] Gedye, *Op. cit.*, quotes an Italian journalist who describes how George prac
tised with a revolver by shooting cigarettes out of the mouth of his unhappy valet.

large section of the country, as we shall see below, wanted something different, and Alexander's abrasiveness did not make negotiations easy; but the monarch, even though his egoism may have been
distorted by the family history, was incorruptibly sincere. The
tragedy was that he drove the country to the verge of chaos, through
his method of trying to unite it.

So much for Peter's family and Peter's father. It is not a whole-
some heritage.

. . . .

Prince Paul, the first Regent, was a cousin of Alexander's, and
his nearest competent adult relative. Therefore the King had to
choose him, simply to preserve the dynasty, although it is said
that they were not close friends. Paul was educated at Oxford, the
worst possible training ground for a man of action. His wife,
Princess Olga, is the sister of the Duchess of Kent. He loves books,
music, pictures, the life of a country gentleman. He would like to
die, when he must, in bed, a feat only one Karageorgeovitch ruler
has accomplished (and that one, Peter I, was insane). He is, the
Serbs say, 'too English', and indeed he is more at ease with foreigners than his own people.

Paul never had much desire to be Regent. The panoply of
royalty may induct him into appreciation of its glamour, but certainly he would prefer less glamour if he could get it with less
responsibility. It is no joke, being the ruler of a country like
Jugoslavia. Paul was unable to sleep during the first few months
of his regency except with the aid of sedatives, so the gossips
said.

Paul has a pleasant personality, and people are not afraid of him,
afraid to tell him the truth, as they were afraid of Alexander.
Although at first he was quite approachable, now his appointments
are carefully watched. One of the curses of Balkan politics has
descended on him—army intrigue. When Paul takes a walk—for
exercise—the affair is almost tragi-comedy. One motor-car filled
with troops immediately precedes him through the wooded road,
another immediately follows him; the route is lined with soldiers
and Paul and his consort amble along, suffocated by petrol fumes,
unable to admire a bird or tree without a sentry jumping.

Paul has given the country good administration during a trying
period. He fought the old Serbs when they tried to hush up the
King's testament. His influence has been on the conciliatory side,
and it was he who sensibly persuaded his first prime minister,

2 H

Bogolub Yevtitch, to release Matchek, the chief of the Croat opposition from jail. His next prime minister, Milan Stoyadinovitch, held office for several years, but lost it when Paul thought that he was too Fascist-minded and sympathetic to the Rome-Berlin axis. The prime minister in 1939 was a comparative unknown named Tsvetkovitch, of Gipsy descent. He is very close to Paul and to the important Slovene leader, Father Koroshetz.

The other two regents are Radekno Stankovitch, who was Alexander's personal physician, and Ivan Perovitch, former governor of Croatia. Neither Stankovitch nor Perovitch are orthodox Serbs, and the appointments caused alarm in Belgrade. Apparently the King chose them for reasons which were Balkan-typical. They were personally honest men, a rare distinction and neither colourful nor likely to become big popular heroes. Moreover Stankovitch and Perovitch don't like each other; the King was aware of this and knew that they would quarrel and that, therefore, *one* of them would always be on Paul's side, thus giving Paul the majority in any decision.

Stankovitch, a good doctor, cured Alexander of a troublesome stomach ailment after half a dozen foreign specialists had failed. Stankovitch simply said: 'Your Majesty, nothing is wrong with you except nerves. There is no organic ailment. Forget it, and you will be well.' The King discovered himself cured through this simple process, and asked Stankovitch what he could do to reward him. Stankovitch replied with Oriental parable. Once, he said, the Sultan of Turkey had greatly benefited from the advice of an obscure courtier; asked what reward he wanted the courtier replied, 'Talk to me conspicuously at your next reception.' The Sultan did so. The court watched in envy and excitement. The courtier's name was soon on everybody's lips. This man, it seemed, was the King's favourite. So the Grand Vizier offered him a job. And then another job. And finally the inconspicuous courtier became Grand Vizier.

The story may be apocryphal, but it is a fact that Stankovitch, completely unknown politically, became minister of education after the King's recovery. Then his rise was rapid. And now he is a regent. He is generally unpopular. People say that he has never forgotten or forgiven any person who slighted him in the long years when he was obscure.

Perovitch, the third regent, has more quality. Louis Adamic writes of him respectfully, and I know no higher tribute for a politician in Jugoslavia. He is not a Croat, as usually reported, but a Dalmatian. His rule as governor of Croatia was better-minded than that of his predecessors, though pressure from Belgrade prevented him from being really moderate. He is, of course, an ardent centralist, believing in the 'essential, natural homogeneity of the Serbs, Croats, and Slovenes'.

Psychology of Assassination

Another name should be mentioned at this point, the name of Vlada Georgiev, the King's assassin. By what mysterious sequence of casualty did Alexander, the monarch, and Georgiev, the killer, meet at that precise moment on the cobbled streets of Marseilles? Almost everyone saw the remarkable film of the assassination. Its great quality of emotion came from the fact that the audience knew, from the time the King stepped off the boat, that he would be dead in ninety seconds. And the King did not know this.

Georgiev was a Macedonian terrorist. This means in Balkan terminology that he was a 'patriot' and an 'idealist'. He believed in a free Macedonia; the object of his group, in other words, was to wrest the Serb part of Macedonia from the Jugoslav Government, and unite it with the Bulgarian segments of that forlorn, invisible province. A Macedonian movement to this end has existed for forty years. The eventual hope is the erection of an independent or autonomous Macedonia; failing this, which is a political impossibility, to unite Macedonia with Bulgaria.

The Macedonian organisation, the I.M.R.O., was led by a redoubtable chieftain, Ivan Mihailov. He was a sort of Robin Hood murderer, never attacking the virtuous, but only the Serbs. Mihailov and his men perfected a government within a government that had its own army and police, its own courier service, its own taxation and standards of law and justice. The arm of the organisation was long and relentless. A traitor never escaped. Mihailov's wife, for instance, followed an enemy all the way to the Burg Theatre in Vienna and there shot him. Georgiev was Mihailov's chauffeur.

The Macedonians split into factions, and Georgiev first distinguished himself by patriotic slaughter of members of the anti-Mihailov group. He killed two notable figures, the communist Hadzidimov and the moderate Tomalevsky. Then, although the Bulgarian Government of the day protected the Macedonians, he was forced to flee. He devoted himself to two projects. These

dominated his able and distorted intelligence. He became a
fanatic, and the most dangerous kind of fanatic, one with a cold
heart. One of his projects, on which he laboured for years, was to
blow up the League of Nations building at Geneva. The other
was to kill Alexander. Georgiev never got around to blowing up
the League. . . .

.   .   .   .

The year 1934 produced a veritable carnival of political assassinations: Dollfuss, Roehm, Schleicher, Duca, Alexander, Louis
Barthou, the Polish minister of the interior Pieracki, and Serge
Kirov, the second man in Soviet Russia. There was a precise
common denominator to several of them, which were performed
by fanatics with the purpose of overthrowing or weakening the
régime in power and opening the way for a government more
representative of the common people. Constantinescu, the murderer of Duca; Planetta, the Dollfuss killer; Georgiev, the assassin
of Alexander, and the Ukrainian who killed Pieracki were all good
democrats, though they called themselves Iron Guardists, Nazis,
and the like.

What is the psychological basis of the desire to kill? In Vienna
Dr. Wilhelm Stekel, discussing this problem, told me that most
political murderers are offshoots of a distorted father fixation.
Cranks and anarchists, who seek out and kill statesmen to satisfy
some mysterious personal grievance, are usually psychic invalids as
a result of some unhappy experience in childhood; often—like the
anarchist who killed the Empress Elizabeth of Austria-Hungary—
they are illegitimate. The assassins are living out some infantile
conflict. The assassinations they perform are supreme efforts at
self-justification, to make up for the miseries of thwarted youth.

No one commits suicide, says Dr. Stekel in a famous essay, unless
he has a tendency to kill some other person. Conversely, no one
commits murder unless he has a tendency to suicide also. Most
assassins are desperate enough to perform the act of murder because
they are disappointed in life; they are candidates for suicide and
thus do not mind risking their own lives to kill someone else. In
fact, their tendency to murder may arise from a desire to make a
spectacular exit from life; they say: 'I shall die, but before doing so
I will take another with me.'

Behind most political assassinations, according to this theory, is
a history of conspiracy. Secret terrorist groups always deal in the
attentat. The psychological basis of conspiracy is dislike of being

an average man; the conspirator and potential murderer is contemptuous of the organised majority; he takes fascinated delight in
being the member of a repressed minority with a political grievance, real or imaginary. Most men are born with a sense of a great
historical mission. All assassins are motivated by a compelling
desire to become prominent.[1]

Very often the assassin kills a statesman as a father-image. He
blames his father for his precarious and ill-nurtured position in
life (almost all assassins are poor); the prominent person he slays
is, psychically, his father, whom he holds responsible for his fate;
the prominent person may be first admired as a father-substitute,
then hated, finally killed. Or, Dr. Stekel proceeds, the assassin may
love his father-substitute enough to kill him; the bipolar nature of
love and hate is obvious. Brutus, for instance, may have killed
Caesar because, his spiritual son, he wanted to be closest to Caesar's
heart, and saw himself displaced by Mark Antony. He murdered
Caesar not because he hated him but out of jealousy.

A psychic injury such as doubt of the facts of paternity or any one
of the innumerable trauma that may occur in childhood are permanent in a neurotic personality. They form a suppressed nucleus
of eternal discontent with life. In extreme cases, says Dr. Stekel,
they may cause murder. 'The murdered king is in reality atoning
for something in the hidden life of the assassin.' An *attentat* is a
displacement of a small personal conflict into the life of nations;
the assassin is transposing the source of his unhappiness into the
horizon of world affairs. Perhaps Booth was beaten by a drunken
father. So—possibly—Lincoln died. Perhaps Princep had an
unhappy childhood. So the World War came.

Jugoslavia—Hot on the Griddle

The Kingdom of Serbs, Croats, and Slovenes was, J. Hampden
Jackson points out[2] the product of 'an unnatural union of motives'.
President Wilson, applying the doctrine of self-determination,
wished to liberate and unite the South Slav peoples, excluding Bulgaria. Clemenceau and his realistic associates wished to set up a
buffer state which would serve two purposes: (1) remove territory
from the old Austro-Hungary, and thus weaken the new Austria
and the new Hungary, and (2) keep Italy off the Dalmatian coast,

[1] And note Mussolini's remark to Ludwig: 'Every anarchist is a dictator who
missed fire.'
[2] In his admirable *The Post-War World*, p. 59.

which as we know, had been promised her by the secret treaty by which she was bribed to enter the War.

The word Jugoslavia ('Jugo' means 'south') may connote to many Englishmen a vague Balkan something-or-other of no particular beam or bulk. But in fact Jugoslavia is one of the most important and powerful countries in Europe; it stretches from the plains of Hungary almost to the Aegean, and from the gateway to Austria to the bottle-neck of the Adriatic. Its population is 13,500,000, and it covers an area as big as England; the people are mostly peasants or mountain folk, raw-boned, poor, hard-lipped, superb fighters, primitive.

Jugoslavia's chief domestic issue should have been to consolidate itself politically and sell its grain; like Rumania, it lives largely on the land. But almost from the beginning it was torn by domestic quarrels and split by internal fissures. The dominant political note since the War has been the angry quarrel between Serbs and Croats. Alexander's dictatorship was made necessary, fundamentally, by the absolute failure of Serb-Croat relations during the ten years 1919–1929 of the parliamentary régime.

The Serbs are Balkan folk centring in Belgrade, Greek Orthodox in religion, semi-Turkish in culture, and militant in spirit. The Croats, centring in Zagreb, lived for centuries in the orbit of Vienna, and represented a more European culture and tradition: they are Roman Catholic. The Serbs fought with the Allies during the War, the Croats (against their will, it is true) with the Central Powers. The Croats number three million three hundred thousand people, almost thirty per cent of the realm. Allied to them have been their cousins to the north, the Slovenes. The Croats use the Latin alphabet, the Serbs the old Cyrillic script.

After the War the country was given a handsome new democratic constitution and the discordant parts of the kingdom were expected to live happily ever after. Of course they didn't. The ruling Serbs, led by Alexander, made some tactical mistakes; for instance so convinced was the King of the intractability of the Croats that for a period of ten years he never set foot in Zagreb, although it was the second capital of his realm; which is as if the King of England refused ever to visit Scotland. The Croats, convinced that they were being treated like second-class citizens, grew more and more intransigent; passion finally exploded in the massacre in the *Skuptchina* (parliament) when the Croat leader, Raditch, was killed.

The psychological core of the quarrel was probably resentment by the Serbs at their inferiority to Zagreb; therefore they punished Zagreb. The Serbs had a subconscious hatred of 'European' civilisation, which had been personified to them by German and Austrian invaders. And the Croats, though Slav by race and language, were thoroughly Teutonised. They were richer than the Serbs, with most of the industry of the kingdom. No wonder the Serbs, who had stood the whole brunt of the War, and whose country had been terribly devastated, were jealous.

The Croats called the Serbs 'Mexicans' and 'bandits'. The Serbs called the Croats lazy trouble-makers. The Croats said they would prefer even the old monarchy to the tyranny of Alexander's dictatorship in Belgrade. The Serbs scoffingly quoted the old proverb that if there were only three Croats left alive, there would be four Croat political parties. The Croats martyrised Raditch, their murdered leader. The Serbs replied that the Croats had done everything for independence for a thousand years—except fight for it. And the Serbs dragooned the Croats into submission.

All of this, for which both sides were at fault, was a pity. What Jugoslavia needed was forty years of peace. It needed time to develop its mines and farms and magnificent natural resources. The country is sketched out; it needs to be built up. Take Belgrade, for instance. The majority of its shops, in the main streets, are still devoted to the sale of the most primitive necessities of life, the simplest kind of manufactured goods, like pins, buttons, cotton cloth. Belgrade is blessed as few cities are with natural beauty, lying high on the confluence of two great rivers, Danube and Save; but it is like a pretty peasant girl with the carriage of a queen and the raiment of a dirty beggar.

When Alexander died the Croats did not make the revolution that many people expected. Reasons: the dissidents were, as the Serbs charged, soft folk, not given to bloodshed or revolution; they had no arms; Croat detachments of the army had been carefully scattered in remote parts of the kingdom; the Serb police, veritable myrmidons, were watchful; above all no help came from Italy. And in homage to Alexander a political truce began.

Revolution in the Balkans—Why Not?

The question is often asked why the miserable Danube and Balkan folk do not rise from their poverty and squalor and make a thorough-going social revolution. There are several reasons, aside from the obvious difficulty of proletarian revolt in a country ruled by police power.

1. The basic passion of most Balkan folk is nationalism. Their primitive and turbulent energies are directed to the preservation of their own political minority or country, rather than social revolution; nationalism is the pipe through which their energies are discharged.

2. Danubia is at least three-fifths agrarian, and the majority of peasants, though poor, own their own land. The industrial proletariat is scanty. A middle class has grown up only in the last two generations, and is still very new and shaky; in Jugoslavia, for instance, as in Hungary, there is scarcely any middle class at all. The extreme primitiveness of Balkan social structures makes revolutionary propaganda difficult.

3. Social democracy, long a considerable force, has produced in most of these countries a considerable paternalism; there is a proverb in Hungary, for instance, that the state takes care of you from birth till you are fifteen, and then from sixty until you die. As long as the people get assistance from the state, in however rudimentary a form, revolt is unlikely.

4. A White Terror of terrible ferocity followed the only two attempts to introduce communism to the Danube, those of Bela Kun in Hungary and Stambolisky in Bulgaria. To justify their mass murders, the Whites kept alive the legend of communist barbarity and secret strength. Having tasted blood, the Whites would not mind tasting more. Therefore any outcropping of communism is mercilessly crushed.

5. Hunger. Prolonged misery and distress, such as have afflicted the people of Danubia, are likely, it seems, to produce not revolt but apathy and inertia, and a torpor of almost pathological quality. People do not make revolutions when hungry—at first—simply because hunger makes them weak.

Black Hand and White

General Peter Zivkovitch was a young man in 1903, a junior lieutenant in the royal guard. Mark that date. 1903 was the year in which, as mentioned above, King Alexander Obrenovitch and his wife Draga were murdered by officers who subsequently put Peter Karageorgeovitch on the throne. The officer whose special job it was to force open the palace gates was ever after nicknamed by his intimates 'Peter the Door'. His name was, and is, Peter Zivkovitch.

Zivkovitch, the son of a blacksmith, was for many years a dominant factor in Jugoslav military life. For a long time he received only normal promotions, but his influence behind the scenes, as a survivor of the original murder gang, was great. In 1921, King Alexander Karageorgeovitch appointed him commander of the palace guard, a sort of army within an army, eighteen thousand strong, which garrisons Belgrade. It seemed strange to some that a witness to the murder of one king should be charged with the security of another. In 1929, when the King abolished democracy, he appointed Zivkovitch prime minister, which job the general held till 1932. Subsequently he was minister of war.

After the 1903 murder the leading conspirator-officers formed the nucleus of a secret society, the Black Hand, officially called *Ujedinjenje ili Smrt*, which means Society of Union or Death. Its adventures in patriotic murder and terrorism caused, among other things, the Great War, since Princep, the Sarajevo assassin, was schooled by Black Hand men. In Sarajevo to-day there is, incidentally, a public monument to Princep, who is a national hero to the Serbs, even though he indirectly cost the loss of twenty million lives.

Zivkovitch was a prominent Black Hander for sound political reasons. The Black Hand stood for greater Serbia; it sought to keep Serb chauvinism, no cool thing anyway, at fever heat; it was the military clique behind the throne. The Black Hand society was truly secret. Members knew each other only by number, and no one was sure who was not a member. The leader was a general staff officer of marvellous ruthlessness and fervour, Colonel Dragutin Dimitrijevitch. Had not Dimitrijevitch founded the Black Hand, it is quite possible that the World War would have come—in a different way.

The Black Hand was broken up during the War. This was because some of the members were believed to have turned republican. They did not trust the young Alexander. Zivkovitch, however, gambled on Alexander, and formed, so far as is known, a sort of counter-movement to the Black Hand, called—without startling originality—the White Hand. The White Hand men were those who depended for their careers on the young King.

Dimitrijevitch and the out-and-out Black Handers were eliminated by a conspiracy in which Zivkovitch, possibly with the knowledge of Alexander, played at least the role of winner. In 1917 Serbia seemed doomed. Wanting as good terms as possible, the

Serbs destroyed the archives linking the Black Hand with the Sarajevo murder. It remained to put Dimitrijevitch out of the way, and direct witness to the preparations of the assassination of Franz Ferdinand would be silenced. With four fellows Dimitrijevitch was tried at Salonika, charged with an attempt on Alexander's life. The evidence was flimsy, but after a sensational trial the Black Handers were convicted, and Dimitrijevitch was put to death.

This cleared the field for Zivkovitch. The White Hand took over from the Black.

He forgot all about political terrorism and conspiracy, and devoted himself to the interests of Alexander.

Zivkovitch's influence notably waned after the assassination of Alexander. In 1937 he left politics and was pensioned out of the army.

Croat Crusader

The opposition leader most worth noting is Vladimir Matchek. His resemblances to Maniu in Rumania are very strong: an idealist, stubborn, Roman Catholic, a lover of the peasants, incorruptibly honest, narrow, old-fashioned in his belief in the natural goodness of people and that right will prevail in politics, because it is right. He is a lawyer by profession. He did not, like so many leaders in the Balkans, go into politics because politics was the only way for the educated to earn a living. As with most Croats, oppositionism, particularism, is ingrained in his character.

Matchek in Croatia, like Maniu in Transylvania, is revered by his people almost like a messiah. He has suffered imprisonment on trumped-up charges; his best friends have been murdered by police spies; his lieutenants beaten and tortured in a manner unknown in modern Europe until Hitler took power in Germany. He is a messiah; but a messiah without much prospect of power. He is defeated by the central illogicality of his position; he does not want complete separatism for Croatia, and indeed separatism is a political impossibility; therefore, since he won't go the whole way, his opposition is permanent—and sterile.

Foreign Affairs—and Affaires

The position taken by Jugoslavia in regard to the present war is of the greatest possible importance. The army is the sixth largest in Europe, numbering 187,000 men with 1,200,000 trained reserves;

it is competently advised by the French general staff and armed by French and formerly by Czechoslovak munition companies, particularly the Skoda works at Pilsen; moreover, the fighting quality of the men is superb. The Jugoslav army is probably, man for man, the most formidable in Europe.

The chief enemies of Jugoslavia, the third country in the Little Entente, are Hungary and Italy, though relations with Hungary have considerably improved lately. Jugoslavia took part in sanctions against Mussolini even though Italy was her best customer: which goes to show that bad blood counts more in the Balkans than an export surplus.

For a long time Italy had aggressive intentions towards Jugoslavia. Mussolini coveted Jugoslav territory because the seizure of Dalmatia would make the Adriatic an Italian lake. Italian interests encouraged, and probably subsidised the less respectable elements of Croat, Slovene, and Macedonian opposition to the Belgrade Government. Italy made alliances with Austria and Hungary and sought to make one with Bulgaria, thus encircling Jugoslavia. But after 1935 Mussolini with his energies occupied in Spain, tended to let Jugoslavia alone. In March 1935 the new Italian minister to Jugoslavia outdid himself in conciliatory messages from his government. (In contrast, think of 1927, when a Jugoslav minister to Rome had to wait seven months before being received by Mussolini.) Meantime Jugoslav relations with Bulgaria have been improving, because the new Bulgarian Government made a genuine attempt to suppress the Macedonian movement, the chief source of Bulgar-Jugoslav friction.

Jugoslavia, though a French ally, has had considerable pro-German feelings. Reasons: (1) Germany is the best potential customer for Jugoslav—like Rumanian—grain; (2) Good armies tend, as a rule, to admire each other, and the Jugoslav general staff deeply respects the Reichswehr; (3) French loans, for many years the prop of Jugoslav finance, don't flow as freely as heretofore; (4) German seizure of Austria has excluded the possibility of a Habsburg restoration, which had been Jugoslavia's chief foreign bugaboo, and also weakened Italy vis-à-vis the Germans. It put the mighty Reichswehr instead of the weak Austrian battalions on the Brenner Pass and thus helped solve Jugoslavia's most pressing military problem. 'Make friends with the enemy of your enemy,' is a cardinal principle of Balkan politics. Despite the recent nibblings towards cordiality, Jugoslavia's 'permanent' enemy is Italy.

The Germans have courted Jugoslavia hotly for years. Early in 1934 I met an amiable servant of the Wilhelmstrasse in a Belgrade *wagon-lit*, who made no bones about the fact that his job was passing out money to German language newspapers in the Balkans. General Goering swooped into Jugoslavia for several visits, and pleased the boy King with a tremendous toy railway train as a birthday gift. Dr. Stoyadinovitch, until recently the Jugoslav premier, was invited to one of the Goering-Goemboes-Polish hunting parties, and later he saw Hitler in Berlin.

CHAPTER XXXII

BALKAN KINGS

'Must every little language have a country all its own?'
—JEROME FRANK.

Zog—Once of Albania

THIS picturesque former monarch, who was ruler of the smallest
country in Europe, Albania, from 1928 to 1939, is now an exile.
The Italians invaded and occupied his unhappy country during the
Good Friday weekend, thus providing Mussolini with his chief
foreign adventure since Spain, and his only conquest since Ethiopia.
King Zog and his queen were forced to flee after a three-day 'war'
together with their infant child who had just been born. They
escaped, after arduous trials, to Greece.

'Zog' is the indefinite, Zogu the definite form of his name, which
in Albanian, a chaotically difficult language of Illyrian origin,
means BIRD. Zog is often called 'The Bird' or 'The Big Bird'.
He is a Moslem by religion, and he was born of distinguished
parents, his father having been hereditary chieftain of the powerful Mati tribe, in upper Albania. He was educated in Constantinople and speaks Turkish and a little dilapidated German as well
as Albanian. In Zog's homeland, remote and barbarous, law is
informally administered by what is known as the blood feud. If
you kill a man, his relatives kill you, and so on for a couple of
generations. There are supposed to be about six hundred blood
feuds out against King Zog.

He was destined to a political life. His uncle was Essad Pasha,
who created Albanian independence. Zog returned to Albania
after his Turkish education in 1912 and took part in the guerilla
fighting of the Balkan wars. Many pleasant legends grew up about
him: they tell you in Albania how at first he was so inexperienced
that he could not properly tie the straps of his *opanji*, native shoes;
that once he killed seven horses riding to his men; that he took over
command of the district by blunt force of character and courage;
that he led a sortie into Montenegro and cut his way in and out of

471

two whole armies; and so on.   There are always such stories abou
Balkan princelings.   Not impossibly these are true.

The bloodshed among Albanian politicians in this period, im
mediately after the War, was immense.   Essad Pasha, Zog's uncle
was assassinated in Paris by a compatriot, Aveni Roustemi.   Thi
Roustemi was himself later assassinated in Tirana, Albania's vil
lage capital.   Tzena Bey, Zog's brother-in-law, was killed in Pragu
by a student, Alcibiades Bedi.   Bedi was shot and killed in th
court-room where he stood trial by colleagues who thought he migh
inform on them.   There have been two attempts on Zog's life, bu
he escaped each time.

The way to play politics in Albania was to make a revolution
Zog made several.   He was minister of interior in an Albania
government that was forced out of office and into exile by th
Putsch of a radical priest, Monsignor Fan Noli.   Zog lived in Bel
grade, Jugoslavia, for a year, and then made another revolutio
whereby he ousted Fan Noli and became president of Albania
This was in 1925.   Three years later Zog promoted himself, witl
Italian help, to be King.

Zog did very well out of kingship financially.   His acknowledge
civil list for the year 1934-5 was the following:

Compensation to H.M. the King	300,000	gold francs
Rent allowance	20,000	,, ,,
Compensation to H.M. the Queen Mother	88,000	,, ,,
Salary to Master of Ceremonies	4,752	,, ,,
Salaries, royal household	14,900	,, ,,
Travelling expenses	2,000	,, ,,
Office supplies, etc.	2,500	,, ,,
Salaries of the Inspectorate	22,282	,, ,,
Travelling expenses and supplies	9,000	,, ,,

463,434 gold francs.

which was 2.63 per cent of the total revenue of his realm.

The cardinal fact of the Albanian situation before Italy took th
little country in 1939 was this: Zog started out as Jugoslavia's man
and then sold out to Mussolini.

Both Jugoslavia and Italy were interested in Albania, because i
lies at the bottleneck of the Adriatic.   When Zog was a refugee ir
Belgrade the Jugoslavs decided to support him, because they dis
liked Fan Noli.   From Jugoslavia Zog got not merely moral anc
political assistance, but actually troops.   Imagine, then, the horro

and anger of Belgrade when, having put Zog back into power, it saw him immediately turn his country over to the Italians. Zog's excuse is that he had to have money to build up the country and strengthen his position, and that Jugoslavia could give him none. So he became an Italian puppet.

Very promptly—this was in the middle 20's—the Italians implemented their advantage. First came a series of loans whereby an Italian company, the Society for the Economic Development of Albania, received exclusive rights to build roads, dredge harbours, and undertake other public works. An oil concession was given Italy. Italian officers reorganised the Albanian army. In November 1926 Mussolini and Zog signed the first Treaty of Tirana, which virtually made Albania an Italian protectorate. A year later—just in time to stave off a revengeful Jugoslav *Putsch* this treaty was strengthened by an outright military alliance.

Italy then poured millions of lire into Albania. The country became, in fact, a sort of bottomless marsh swallowing Italian gold. The pace of this financial debauch had to be retarded when the world economic crisis hit Italy, but even in 1931 Italy agreed to lend Albania 10,000,000 gold francs (£400,000 gold) per year for ten years, free of interest 'in order to make the financial position of Albania sound and to facilitate development of its national economy'. In 1934 and later there came still other loans.

Then, however, developments in Albania began to discourage Italian enterprise. The Italians threatened to cut off the stream of gold. This was because Zog, a flirtatious fellow, commenced to be friendly again with Jugoslavia. Italians—the doctors, soldiers, engineers, topographers, road builders—became increasingly unpopular in Albania. Zog quarrelled with his Italian advisers. He resented his dependence on Italy; he lamented the bargain he had made. For a time the Italians had to continue to pay him, because their position in the country rested on his person. Then Mussolini decided to terminate the comedy. Italy invaded the country, Zog fled, and Albania ceased to exist.

Zog is not at all an unpleasant character, despite his former tendency to flirt. He betrayed Jugoslavia and sought to double-cross Italy, and he suffered for it, but his motives were good, viz., thoroughly consistent with Balkan nationalist ideals. By playing Italy and Jugoslavia against one another, he thought he was ensuring the one thing that mattered to him—his country's independence. He was wrong. A patriot, he stood for free Albania. The nationalism of Albania does not whisper even if the country is small—and now extinct.

Boris of Bulgaria

Boris III of Bulgaria, gentle and retiring, now forty-five, is a doubter, not a man of action. Groping, honest, theoretical rather than realistic, he likes to believe the best of people. His personal charm is considerable. He is extremely obliging. The little story is told in Sofia that he was found in the palace gardens one morning, engaged in netting butterflies—because he was receiving an entomologist for lunch that day.

He and his queen, the Italian princess Giovanna of Savoy, lead a quiet life. During the first years of their marriage, October 1930, they went out not at all, because Boris wanted his bride to feel at home in Bulgaria and learn a little Bulgarian before exposing herself to the rigours of Sofia society. Even now they seldom entertain or go to diplomatic functions, first because the frugality of Bulgarian character tends to discourage such displays, second because the King—incredible as this may seem—feels that he might not be able to repay the hospitality in kind. He is not so indigent that he cannot afford a few dozen cases of champagne, but the country is so threadbare-poor that he thinks any ostentatious display of luxury to be bad taste.

Boris knows an astounding number of his subjects by name and face, literally thousands, from peasant farmers in the valley of roses near Plovdiv to civil servants in government ministries. He is fond of mechanics, and his only hobby is locomotive driving. Once he jumped into the sea off Varna and rescued a villager from drowning. Frequently he himself pushes the perambulator containing his baby daughter through the modest palace gardens. After his marriage, the story goes, he would meet old friends on the streets and introduce the Queen by saying simply, 'Meet my wife.'

Boris is the worst-dressed king in Europe. He insists on wearing Sofia-made clothes. And Sofia is not exactly Savile Row. He drinks little alcohol. He knows five European languages, and in bed each morning he reads newspapers in them all: French, German, Bulgarian, Italian, English. His study is lined with photographs of his multitudinous cousins, uncles, aunts, and other relatives scattered through the reigning houses of Europe. All his instincts, his associations, are with the past.

Boris gets about £12,000 per year. This is not much for a

king, but the Bulgarian Government pays most of his expenses. He has little of Zog's interest in money and nothing of the financial capacity of the late Alexander of Jugoslavia. Queen Giovanna received a dowry of 25,000,000 lire from her father, the King of Italy, on the occasion of her marriage, and the income from it should make her as rich as Boris. In addition she gets an allowance of 950,000 leva, about £2,200, a year from the Bulgarian state. Boris should become very rich when his father, ex-King Ferdinand, 'the Old Fox', dies.

King Carol of Rumania got the fright of his life when he and Boris met at the Danube town of Roustchuk in 1934. Boris greeted him, persuaded him to descend from his car, and walked with him arm in arm down the streets. Carol would never have dreamed of so exposing himself in any Rumanian town. He was alarmed at first by his unwonted proximity to the common herd, then impressed at the friendly way the crowd greeted Boris. Exactly the same thing happened when the late King Alexander of Jugoslavia visited the Bulgarian monarch. Boris drove him to Plovdiv to see the roses; they went alone, without even informing the Mayor of Plovdiv that they were coming. There were plenty of Macedonians in the crowd, and Alexander didn't like it at all, but Boris insisted on walking with him through the streets. The fact that he was in Boris's company kept him safe.

.   .   .   .

In Bulgaria when villagers go on a journey they often carry their shoes in their hands to save wear and tear on the leather. Thus one knows that Bulgaria is a frugal country. Among the six million inhabitants of Bulgaria, fewer than six thousand have been divorced; thus one knows its folk are morally conventional. The Bulgars, poor, clean, intensely honest, are probably the best people in the Balkans.

Look at some Bulgarian salaries. A cabinet minister gets £40 per month, a tremendous sum for the country. The Rector of Sofia University gets £17, and an ordinary professor £16. Judges range from £6 to £10 a month; generals get £15, policemen £2 15s.; archbishops £20, high school teachers £7, a locomotive driver £3. And there is no baksheesh—bribery—in Bulgaria.

To Bulgaria, during the worst of the economic crisis in the early 30's, went the distressing honour of owning the most tragically extreme statistics in Europe. For instance, the weight of Bulgarian exports in 1930, increased by eighty per cent over the previous year

—but their value decreased by three per cent. In 1931, again, the volume of exports went up by forty per cent—and the value fell again—by four per cent.

The depression, by emphasising economic discontent, aggravated political unrest. Boris is a pleasant man, but he is in a dangerous predicament. His timidity, his lack of decision, got him in a pretty mess, and for one extensive period during 1934, he did not dare to leave his palace. The people may have liked him—but certain powerful officers in the army didn't. Three men who are real forces in the political life of Bulgaria, Professor Tzankov, Colonel Kimon Gheorgiev, and Colonel Damien Veltchev, are his enemies.

Tzankov is the reactionary who crushed the peasant government of Stambolisky in 1923. He was prime minister then till 1926. During the first part of his rule a White Terror, for which he was partly responsible, ruled the land. Tzankov built up a powerful Fascist movement, and is bidding for power again.

Gheorgiev is the blunt, one-eyed colonel of reserve who performed the *coup d'état* of May 19, 1934, when the King was forced to abolish parliament and consent to the establishment of a dictatorial régime. The Gheorgiev government performed a useful service, however, in bettering Bulgaria's relations with Jugoslavia. This it did by outlawing one faction of the Macedonian movement and expelling Ivan Mihailov, the chief of the Macedonians, from the country.

Gheorgiev was forced from office on January 22, 1935, when officers of the Military League, royalist in sympathy, accused him of republicanism and a plot to dethrone the King. The government that succeeded Gheorgiev was the King's government, made by his authority; this was dangerous, because Boris could be accused of taking an active partisan role in politics.

The third man of importance is an overt republican, Colonel Damien Veltchev. He was the man behind Gheorgiev, who did little but take his orders. Veltchev was for many years the commandant of the cadet school in Sofia, and thus most of the younger officers of the army are 'his' men. He is a typical Balkan adventurer: able, unscrupulous, a fanatic nationalist. Veltchev, whose insurrectionary activity goes back a long way, organised the 1923 *Putsch* which murdered Stambolisky and put Tzankov into power.

Both Gheorgiev and Veltchev were arrested late in 1935.

Veltchev was sentenced to death, but in March 1936 the sentence was commuted to life imprisonment.

.   .   .   .

Bulgaria, a loser in the War—the unfortunate little country always picks the wrong side in wars—was mercilessly chopped asunder, like Hungary, by the peace treaties. Rumania got the Dobrudja; Turkey got Thrace; Greece got part of Thrace and part of Macedonia; Jugoslavia got the rest of Macedonia.

The Bulgarians, decent folk, and too small and too far away to create much international noise, have not been as umbrageous as the Hungarians in demanding their territory back. But the country is officially one of the 'revisionist' powers, and, as such, has tended to associate itself with Italy and Germany.

Early in 1934 the countries surrounding Bulgaria decided to check this tendency, and so formed the Balkan Entente. The participants were Rumania, Jugoslavia, Greece, Turkey; and the diplomat who did most of the negotiating was the Rumanian foreign minister, Titulescu. Just as Hungary was encircled by the Little Entente, Bulgaria is encircled by the Balkan Entente.

It is hard luck for small and sinned-against Bulgaria; the only way out seems to be individual *rapprochement* with Jugoslavia.

.   .   .   .

Can a king be a dictator? Alexander of Jugoslavia is the only one who tried it: and look what happened. Indeed, with Boris in mind, it seems a safe generalisation that royalty and dictatorship do not lie well together. There are many reasons. This is an age of *bourgeois* or proletarian adventurers, Hitlers and Mussolinis, the age of the strong man with a fist. Kings have not enough freedom of education to be good dictators. They are inveterately international, and thus cut across the deep exclusive nationality of men like Pilsudski or Kamal Ataturk. They have no real contact with the common man. And modern science, modern economics, have destroyed the will of the masses to believe in kings as kings.

Greece and Metaxas

In November 1935, George, King of the Hellenes, regained the throne of Greece. This amiable and complex young man, long an exile in Brown's Hotel, Dover Street, London, had reigned for a brief period in 1922, in succession to his father Constantine. Greek politics for twenty years has been an angry quarrel between royalists and republicans. Venizelos, the great republican leader, an old and tired man, was forced to flee the country when his final attempt at a rising was crushed in March 1935, and shortly afterwards he died in Paris. Subsequently a royalist general, Kondylis, long a bad actor in Greek politics, prepared the way for a monarchial *coup d'état*.

George, a cautious monarch, who well remembers the chequered history of his family on the throne—his father for instance had to flee the country twice—was not passionately eager to return. Very different from his ex-brother-in-law Carol (George and his Rumanian wife Elizabeth have been divorced), he did not yearn to regain the crown, for the simple reason that he didn't want subsequently to be pushed out again. George told his adherents that he would not return until an honest—well, fairly honest—plebiscite demanded him. It did.

In August 1936 Greece became a military dictatorship, with George's consent, under a royalist general with a long record of mischief-making, General Metaxas. A general election was held, according to the newly returned King's pledges; it resulted in a virtual draw between the monarchists and republicans, with a communist *bloc* of fifteen deputies holding the balance of power. Thereafter parliamentary government became even more difficult than it had ordinarily been. On the pretext that the communists were planning a general strike, General Metaxas suddenly declared martial law and set out to rule the country by decree.

Metaxas was born on Ithaca, the island of Ulysses, in 1871. He is thus the oldest of the dictators. He was educated in Berlin—note well—and from 1890 was an army officer. During the Balkan wars he was director of operations on the general staff. At about this time his loyalty to the Constantine dynasty began to assert itself; from 1917 he became an inveterate enemy of the Venizelists. Once he was condemned to death; several times he was exiled; he always came back. People called him the 'Little Moltke'. In 1934 he started a party of his own, Fascist-monarchists, which was severely defeated in the polls. Then came the unsuccessful Venizelist *Putsch* of 1935 which he helped to put down.

He is quite frank about his aims. 'Parliamentary democracy is ended in Greece for ever,' he said in September 1936. His régime is seemingly an overt despotism, and King George has acted like a puppet in his hands.

Greece lies outside the *grande ligne* of European politics, despite the Balkan Entente, and although the British pledged themselves to guarantee Greek independence early in 1939. Roughly speaking, the Greek royalists are pro-ally and pro-status quo; the republicans like Venizelos, are revisionist and pro-Italian. Because George might be supposed to be anti-Mussolini, the British foreign office looked with cautious favour on his return, provided it was managed without a civil war. George is, of course, a cousin of Princess Marina, the wife of the Duke of Kent, and is thus associated with the House of Windsor. Britain would find Greek naval bases convenient in the event of war with Italy. For some time there was talk that the Duke of Kent, instead of George, might become Greek king.

George's restoration was popular among the other royalties of the region. There is a fourth internationale in the world, as my friend M. W. Fodor has pointed out. Kings like more kings.

CHAPTER XXXIII

THE TURKISH COLOSSUS[1]

THE blond, blue-eyed combination of patriot and psychopath who is dictator of Turkey has changed his name seven times. First he was simply MUSTAFA, so called by his parents in Salonika. At school he was given the name MUSTAFA KEMAL to distinguish him from other little Mustafas, and because a teacher admired his skill in mathematics; 'Kemal' in Turkish means 'perfection'. After the Dardanelles campaign, he became MUSTAFA KEMAL PASHA, 'pasha' being a military title equivalent to general. After he crushed the Greeks in 1921 he assumed the name GHAZI MUSTAFA KEMAL PASHA; 'ghazi' means 'destroyer of infidels', an odd sobriquet for Kemal, inasmuch as he was the greatest infidel in Turkish history. Ten years later he became GHAZI MUSTAFA KEMAL when he abolished military titles. In 1934 he ordered every Turk to assume a patronymic in the western fashion and chose for himself 'Ataturk', which means 'Father of Turks'. So he was simply KEMAL ATATURK.

Finally he modified this to the Turkish form of the Arabic, to become KAMAL ATATURK.

His own is by no means the only name he changed. When I went to Constantinople recently after an absence of several years I was astounded at the metamorphosis in names placarded on the streets. Kamal westernised the Turkish alphabet—quite completely. Modern Turkish is strictly a phonetic tongue. These were some of the compulsory renderings of names which greeted me:

Kahve	*instead of*	Coffee
Tabldot	,,	Table d'Hote
Amerikan Ekspres Ko. Ink.	,,	American Express Co. Inc.
Jorj	,,	George
Moris Sovaliye	,,	Maurice Chevalier
La Jones	,,	La Jeunesse (a shop)
Dizl Enjn	,,	Diesel Engine

[1] Mustafa Kamal Ataturk died after a long illness in November 1938. I am printing this sketch of his career and character as I wrote it in 1935, without alteration.

Star Su Sop	*instead of*	Star Shoe Shop
Vagonli-Kook	,,	Wagon-Lit-Cook
Enstitu do Boté	,,	Institute de Beauté
Or Duvr	,,	Hors-d'Œuvres
Foxs Film Korporeysen	,,	Fox Film Corporation
Waytaus	,,	White House (a shop)
Lozan Palas Otel	,,	Lausanne Palace Hotel

Kamal Ataturk, who strides the Turkish landscape like a colossus —significantly a bronze statue of him in a dinner-jacket (with the trousers cuffed) commands the Golden Horn—is in a position of a man with no more worlds to conquer. His reforms have been so drastic and so comprehensive that in cultural and social fields at least there is very little left to do. He abolished the fez, turned the mosques into granaries, Latinised the language. He ended polygamy, installed new legal codes, and experimented with a (paying) casino in the sultan's palace. He compulsorily disinfected all the buildings in Istanbul, adopted the Gregorian calendar and metric system, and took the first census in Turkish history. He cut political holidays down to three, demanded physical examination of those about to marry, and built a new capital, Ankara, in the Anatolian highlands, replacing proud Constantinople. He limited most business activity to Turkish nationals and Turkish firms, abolished books of magic, and gave every Turk a new last name. He emancipated the women (more or less), tossed the priests into the discard, and superintended the writing of a new history of the world proving that Turkey is the source of all civilisation.

Kamal Ataturk, a somewhat Bacchic character, the full record of whose personal life makes you blink, is the dictator-type carried to its ultimate extreme, the embodiment of totalitarian rule by character. This man, in personality and accomplishments, resembles no one so much as Peter the Great, who also westernised his country at frightful cost. Kamal Ataturk is the roughneck of dictators. Beside him, Hitler is a milksop, Mussolini a perfumed dandy, and Goemboes a creature of the drawing-room. At one of his own receptions Kamal, slightly exhilarated, publicly slapped the Egyptian minister, when he observed the hapless diplomat wearing the forbidden fez.

No man has ever betrayed more masters, and always from motives of his own view of patriotism. In 1918, a staff officer, he was chosen to accompany Vahydu'd-Din, the Crown Prince, to Berlin, and there assist him in consultations with Hindenburg, Ludendorff and the German high command.   Three years later Kamal booted him, as Sultan Mehmed VI, out of Turkey.

After the armistice Kamal was sent by the authorities as inspector-general of the eastern vilayets to investigate a nationalist insurrection in Kurdistan. He was ordered to find and quell these rebels. He found them all right.   But instead of crushing the movement he took charge of it.   Within two years he brought victory in all of Turkey to the very organisation his superiors had sent him to suppress.

In 1926, following a not very professional attempt on his life, he hanged what amounted to the entire leadership of the opposition.   Among those he allowed to be sentenced to death and executed were Colonel Arif, who had been his comrade-at-arms in the Greek campaign, and Djavid Bey, the best financial mind in Turkey. Kamal had a champagne party in his lonely farm-house at Chankaya, near Ankara, to celebrate the occasion, and invited all the diplomats. Returning home at dawn, they saw the corpses hanging in the town square.

(In 1930 Kamal decided that totalitarian rule to the extremity which he carried it was a bore, and, uniquely among dictators, he proceeded to *create* an opposition, naming various men to be its leaders. Somewhat timidly, they accepted. Kamal wanted to see if western democratic methods would work; he wanted an opposition bench to argue with in parliament. The system didn't work. The Turks, with the memory of 1926 in mind, didn't quite seem to understand. . . .)

His psychological history is of surpassing interest. Two things have dominated the secret springs of his life, his mother and illness. For his mother he had a typical love-hate obsession. During the early years he was continually fetching her to live with him, then flinging off alone again. Finally he brought her to the Chankaya farm-house and she died there. It is possible that his merciless campaign against the Greeks was subconsciously motivated by his mother's experiences in a refugee camp in Salonika during the Balkan wars. Kamal rushed across the Aegean (he had been fighting in Tripoli against the Italians) to see her, and found her a prisoner of the Greeks in indescribable circumstances of suffering.

In 1917 Kamal took time off from the War to visit Carlsbad for a cure. A famous Viennese professor, Dr. Zuckerkandl, looked him over and told him that if he did not stop drinking he would

die in a year. The illness was troublesome. Kamal returned to the
Front (he had just been the most important Turkish officer in beating back the British at the Dardanelles) for service in Syria and to
his well-known habits. His health remained, and has remained,
about the same. The dear old Viennese professor, however, died
two years after prophesying Kamal's collapse and demise.

A favourite theory is that Kamal's extraordinary bursts of
reformist energy are due to chronic pain. The familiar and excru-
ciating twinges return, and lo! the dictator abolishes the Turkish
alphabet or decrees the formation of a dozen new investigating
commissions; if true, this is an interesting example of what the
psychiatrists call 'displacement'. Kamal punishes someone else for
his own early sins, purifies a nation as a surrogate for purification
of his own painful blood.

Kamal was born in 1881, the son (like Hitler) of a minor customs
official. The father, Ali Rasa, was nothing more than a petty and
narrow bureaucrat, but the mother, named Zubeida, was, like the
mothers of Pilsudski, Mussolini, and Masaryk, a woman far above
the normal of her station. She wanted her son to get an education
and become a priest—exactly like Stalin's mother who sent the
future dictator of all the Russians to theological school in Tiflis.
It is clear to the point of triteness that most of the great men of
the world had remarkable mothers, and that the development of
their sons' Oedipus complex was of paramount importance in
their characters and careers. Kamal's mother, not an unimportant point, married again after her first husband's death, and
young Mustafa bitterly hated his stepfather, an interloper in the
home.

Ali Rasa, Kamal's father, was apparently of Albanian origin.
Zubeida, the mother, was the daughter of a Turkish peasant whose
wife was Macedonian. Kamal is thus far from being purely
Turkish. As great an authority as Toynbee (*Great Contemporaries*,
p. 291) suggests that Jewish blood may have been in the family.
Salonika has, of course, been a citadel of Jews since the Diaspora;
many, called 'Dönme', were converts to Islam. But Kamal's
irrefragable blondness and his cold blue eyes would seem to pre-
clude more than a hint of Jewish—or for that matter Turkish—
ancestry.

Kamal's early life was that of a rebel and above all of a hater.
He wrote revolutionary pamphlets and even poems. He was sentenced to jail in Constantinople but his skill as an officer made him

valuable, and he was released. Although a 'Young Turk', his position was that of a suppressed oppositionist; he detested the Young Turk triumvirs, Talaat, Enver, and Djemal, a feeling which they reciprocated. But his reputation as a soldier was invincible, after service on the most remote, dangerous and hopeless fronts, and the way to his career was open.

That career is without parallel in modern times. Kamal engineered the congresses of Erzerum and Sivas and organised the nationalist movement, leading it to victory. Other people have created nations. Kamal's job was harder. He took a nation that was centuries deep in rot, pulled it to its feet, wiped its face, reclothed it, transformed it, made it work. In 1919 Turkey was so crushed and broken that it would have welcomed renunciation of sovereignty and a British mandate. In 1922 Turkey was the one enemy state so strong that it practically dictated its own peace terms.

In those three years Kamal (1) drove out the Sultan, (2) abolished the caliphate, (3) fought and won the war against the Greeks and drove them into the sea, (4) bluffed Great Britain to a standstill at Chanak, (5) negotiated, through Ismet Pasha, the Treaty of Lausanne, which ended the régime of capitulations (foreign judicial rights) in Turkey and established the new frontiers on a basis that the wildest Turkish nationalist could not have dreamed possible, (6) wrote a republican constitution and created a parliament in his new impregnable capital, (7) became Turkey's first—and only—president.

Kamal, alone, it may be said, does not deserve credit for all this. The general programme of westernisation was planned by the Young Turks and he simply appropriated it. The Greeks were destroyed by the defection of the allies, also by their own incapacity, not by Kamal's armies. Sultan and caliph were doomed in any case, and it is no tribute to Kamal that he ejected them. The Treaty of Lausanne was won not by Ismet Pasha but because of jealous squabbles between the western powers. And so on.

Kamal lives nowadays in Chankaya, a complete recluse. His model farm is his avocation; a true megalomaniac, he designed the water reservoir in the shape of the Sea of Marmora! He married a woman named Latifé Hanum in 1923, but divorced her a few years later; now he lives alone. He is the most inaccessible public character in Europe. King George V himself would not have been more difficult to interview. Unlike all other dictators, he keeps

from the foreground; the Turkish papers do not mention his name
half a dozen times a month. He has a group of soldier underlings
and cronies with whom he plays poker. Rarely, he gambles at
cards with foreign diplomats; he usually wins, then insists on returning his winnings. He still likes to drink.

The Turkish dictator differs from almost all others in that he
had no socialist period in youth and even in maturity betrays not
the faintest interest in socio-economic stresses. His only policy was
Turkey for the Turks. He is certainly a revolutionary, but as far as
economics is concerned he might be President of Switzerland. The
theory that all nationalist dictators must bear to extreme Right or
extreme Left breaks down on Kamal Ataturk, as it did on Pilsudski.

The two foreign powers that Kamal is most interested in are
(except Great Britain, which he hates), the U.S.S.R. and Italy. In
the bleak year 1932 he set a new peak in picturesque achievement
by procuring loans from both these countries, which are states not
given to the export of credit in the best of years. Kamal plays
them, of course, against each other. Italy wants Turkish support
in the eastern Mediterranean, and Turkey is bound always to be an
important factor in Soviet foreign policy because the Dardanelles
comprise Russia's only outlet to warm seas. Kamal disliked the
Abyssinian adventure. Therefore his policy took on a stronger
Russian tinge. For some years the Soviet Union and Turkey were
close allies at Geneva, and Dr. Twefik Aras, the Turk foreign
minister (who, incidentally, was Kamal's personal physician in
Salonika many years ago), was generally recognised to be Litvinov's
hand inside a Turkish glove. Meantime, Kamal began to fortify
the Dardanelles. In June 1936, a conference of the European
powers at Montreux gave him what he didn't particularly need—
permission.

General Ismet Inönü

This fifty-nine-year-old general, for years known as Ismet Pasha,
was for more than a decade Kamal's prime minister, and when the
great Kamal died in 1938 he succeeded him, as was fitting, in the
presidency of the republic. Ismet had to change his name to Inönü
some years ago when his master decreed that all Turks must have
last names. He took his from the town in Asia Minor where, in
1921, his hard-bitten army crushed the Greeks and drove them into
the sea.

Ismet, about whom comparatively little is known, holds a key position in world affairs.   He is short, graceful, dark-eyed, and very deaf; he looks less a soldier than a diplomat.   And he is, indeed, one of the best diplomats of modern times.   It was he who negotiated the Lausanne settlement.   Ismet was born in Smyrna in 1880. His father was an official.   As Kamal's right hand man for many years, he has had a comprehensive training in the hardest kind of political work.   Kamal taught him to play poker.   But he did not acquire Kamal's other vices.

In the autumn of 1939 Ismet had to make a tremendous decision —whether to sign up with the British or the Russians.   He chose the British, but he very carefully left himself loopholes and reservations.   Turkey is not obliged to fight *against* Russia.

CHAPTER XXXIV

POLAND AND THE BALTIC STATES

T HE theory that nationalism is the most powerful of politico-economic forces and that nationalism is best represented politically by the power of personality is well expressed by the case of Poland. The Polish nation—destroyed and partitioned by the Germans and Russians in 1939—was created by two factors, nationalism and Pilsudski. The dictator, Pilsudski, died in 1935, but the fabric of Polish Government, as long as it survived, was based on his living character and idiosyncrasies.

On August 6, 1914, Josef Pilsudski, a Polish patriot and revolutionary, went to war against Russia with an army of—three hundred men. This was the celebrated *Kadrówka* (literally 'cadre'), and with it Pilsudski crossed the frontier and invaded the giant body of Russia. The three hundred men grew into a brigade and the brigade into three brigades. Eventually the *Kadrówka* became the Polish Legion, fourteen thousand strong, a revolutionary army for the deliverance of Poland from the enemies who were ruling it. But until well into the middle of the War, most people—even Poles—thought that Pilsudski was a quixotic lunatic.

In 1916 the Germans captured Warsaw. They offered to permit the Polish Legion to continue operations against the Russians as an auxiliary force, but Pilsudski held out unqualifiedly for Polish independence, and he was incarcerated in prison at Magdeburg. But first he had time to transform the Legion into a secret underground organisation, the P.O.W. (*Polska Organizacja Wojskowa*), to carry on its work. In 1918 the Central Powers were defeated; Pilsudski returned in triumph to Warsaw to become head of the Polish state; and the Legions and the P.O.W. were its first armed force.

Now the points to be made are that the Legions were absolutely the single-handed creation of Pilsudski and that until collapse came in 1939, twenty-five years later, Poland was still the instrument of his creation. The Legionnaires ruled Poland. A clique of the marshal's officers, fanatically devoted to him in life, reverent of his memory after the gruff old walrus died, dominated comprehen sively almost every aspect of Polish life.

Let us list the names that counted. They are difficult names, but each man was important.

General Thaddeus Kasprzycki was the minister of war. What had he been in the old days? Field chief of Pilsudski's first three hundred men.

General Jan Soznkowski, commander of an army division, was the No. 2 military man in the country. What had he been to Pil sudski? Chief of staff of the Legion.

General Eduard Rydz-Smigly, immediately on Pilsudski's death, succeeded him as inspector-general of the army. He had been com mander of the first brigade of the Legionnaires.

The late Colonel Valerian Slawek, the prime minister when Pil sudski died, and for years one of the three or four most important men in Poland, was an intelligence officer in the first three hundred.

Colonel Blazej Prystor, several times prime minister, one of the famous little circle of 'colonels', was special adjutant for political affairs in the Legion.

Colonel Joseph Beck, who was Polish foreign minister during the years leading to the tragic events of 1939—and who made plenty of mistakes—was Pilsudski's chief adjutant in the latter period of the Legion and P.O.W.

Among others, Colonel Adam Koc, leader of the former Polish government party, the 'Camp of National Unity', was chief assistant to Pilsudski in organising the P.O.W. Boguslav Miedzin ski, now the editor of the semi-official newspaper, *Gazetta Polska*, was an intelligence officer both in the Legion and P.O.W. Henri Floyar-Rajchmann, also an intelligence man in the Legion, was minister of commerce and industry. General Roman Gorecki, president of the Polish state bank, was commander of the second brigade of the *Kadrówka*. Waclaw Jedrejewicz, chief of intelli gence for Lithuania in the P.O.W., became minister of education and religion. Finally, General Sikorski, who is now the prime minister of the Polish government in exile (and who resisted the 1926 Pilsudski *Putsch*), was a Legionnaire.

These men were the essence of the ruling power in Poland. Pilsudski was Alpha and Omega to them. Only those officers who were in the original three hundred or who entered *Kadrówka* ranks immediately thereafter, who were trained by Pilsudski him self in this strange Polish equivalent of Eton and Oxford, counted in Poland. Thus Pilsudski's colossal power. Like a father, he brought Poland up. And his children ran it. Thus too, an inherent narrowness and weakness in the Polish state structure—as 1939 proved.

Grandpa

As a rule Pilsudski was called not father—he was getting too old towards the end—but *Dziadek*, grandfather. He called all his men 'Du' or 'toi'; respectful, they did not respond with such intimacy, but addressed him as *Komendant*, chief. That the old dictator was a turncoat, a ruffian, a lover of scatological language, a brigand, a befuddled and idiosyncratic martinet (in his old days) was undeniable; undeniably also he was honest, capable of arousing great affection, and an implacable patriot for Poland.

The career of the *Dziadek* was one of the most extraordinary of modern times. He was what the biologists might call a 'sport' among post-War revolutionary dictators. He was not, for instance, a man of the people like Mussolini or Dollfuss or Kamal Ataturk; he was born (in 1867 on an estate near Vilna) of an aristocratic Lithuanian family. But passion for Poland drove him to revolutionary activity. Hatred of Czarist Russia, on nationalist grounds, dominated his life.

His mother a tremendous Polish patriot and Russia-hater, allowed him to desert the family tradition and become a Marxist, because at that time the only effective revolutionary organisation was socialist. As a student of medicine (Pilsudski just failed to get an M.D. degree at the University of Kharkov) he began insurrectionary activity. He was arrested in 1887 and sentenced to exile in the Siberian lead mines for participation in the plot to kill Czar Alexander III for which Lenin's older brother was hanged. One of Pilsudski's brothers was likewise executed. Motivation for a revolutionary!

In 1893 he returned from Siberia and became editor of the socialist newspaper *Robotnik* (Workman). He flitted from place to place publishing it; the police did not find him and his secret peripatetic printing-press for seven years. In 1900 he went to jail again in the terrible 'Pavilion No. 10' of the Warsaw citadel, a dungeon reserved for the worst political offenders. He escaped—by feigning insanity! Fooled, the prison doctors sent him to an asylum in St. Petersburg. With the connivance of a Polish medical man he got away and returned to Poland.

He spent some years as a patriotic bandit, and in one coup in 1908 he robbed a mail train and got away with two million roubles. Almost at the same time another socialist revolutionary, Josef Stalin, performed almost an identical feat in Tiflis, Georgia. (When, years later, Polish-Soviet relations were straightened out, Stalin sent Pilsudski his Czarist police dossier as a memento of their comradeship.) When the War came Pilsudski dropped socialism, because he felt that the best way to resurrect Poland would be to work first with the Austrian armies against the Russians, then with a Polish army against the field. So he created the Legions; witless, the Austrians permitted their organisation.[1]

Pilsudski had by the time of the War become a potent and baffling romantic legend. One story about him, widely believed, was that he disguised himself as a Russian cavalry officer, rode up to the Warsaw jail, and ordered the release of all the Polish political prisoners! On the pretext that he had orders to lead them to a new jail he secured the freedom of the lot.

He left his first wife in 1912. His second wife was a socialist comrade. She went to work in a factory at Grochow, just outside Warsaw, when Pilsudski was imprisoned by the Germans. When he returned to Poland in 1918 his first act as head of the state was to fetch the President's carriage, and, with a tremendous retinue behind silver horses, drive to Grochow, find her, and return with her to the palace. By her he had two children; Wanda, now twenty-two, and Jadwiga, eighteen, of whom he was passionately fond.

Pilsudski was the author of the *coup d'état* by which Poland seized Vilna from Lithuania in 1920. Questioned by the allied ministers in Warsaw, he staunchly denied his responsibility. Several days later he resigned office as head of state. He called the ministers together. 'Gentlemen,' he said, 'the other day I lied to you. I was a public character and I had to lie. Now I am a private individual and I can tell you the truth. I *did* engineer the Vilna coup. Gentlemen, good morning.'

Blunt, gruff, he loved mystification. As he grew older his facial resemblance to Friedrich Nietzsche was very close; there were plenty who said that he was unbalanced, who hinted that when he feigned lunacy to escape the Russians the feat was not purely his-

---

[1] Pilsudski in later years told a former comrade, 'My friend, you and I caught the socialist train together. I got off at "Polish Independence" station. I wish you good luck on your journey to . . . Utopia.' (*Spectator*, May 17, 1935.)

trionic. He continually perplexed his subordinates by trapping them with misleading statements; he sent Beck and Prystor to the verge of nervous breakdowns by never communicating to them the policies he held them responsible for executing.

After the War the old marshal retired from politics; he returned to power in 1926 to 'restore order' (incidentally killing six hundred men on the streets of Warsaw); thereafter he governed from the back seat, as minister of war. He was contemptuous of the deputies; the grizzled vigour of his language to them became famous. Few speeches by Pilsudski could be printed verbatim in a western newspaper. He died thinking of his birth-land, Lithuania, and whispering messages to his daughters. His last gesture was characteristic, he ordered his brain to be given to the University of Warsaw for research; his heart to be preserved in the crypt in Vilna which held his mother's ashes; and his body to be sent to a third place, Cracow, where lie the tombs of Poland's ancient kings.

The 'Colonels'[1]

Marshal Eduard Rydz-Smigly, the country's dominant figure after the death of Pilsudski and until the invasion of Poland in 1939, was not a professional soldier, but a Legionnaire. It was he, however, who captured Kiev in the wild Polish assault on the U.S.S.R. in 1921. Rydz-Smigly studied to be a portrait painter in his youth, and several Polish museums contain—or contained— examples of his work. He was born in 1886. The army became devoted to him—apparently—and therefore Pilsudski arranged that he should become its chief, so that he could bring it loyally to support whatever new civil régime took power. Cultivated, quiet, he was the student type of officer. In June 1936, he was formally named 'First Citizen' of Poland. He was—perhaps unfairly— accused of negligence in the 1939 war, and is now in exile in Rumania.

Of all the Legionnaires, the man Pilsudski loved best was General Soznkowski, the comrade who shared his imprisonment at Magdeburg. This officer, ten years later, performed a feat of deeply quixotic and Polish devotion; he was a general in command of the

[1] Most of the 'colonels', incidentally, are not colonels. Either they got beyond that and became generals (like the former minister of war Gen. Kasprzycki, who began adult life as a mathematics teacher in Paris), or (like Kasprzycki again) they were not soldiers by profession, but men who followed Pilsudski into the Legion from various occupations.

2 K

division at Posnan when he heard that Pilsudski, his old chief, was marching on Warsaw. Soznkowski joined neither Pilsudski nor the forces of the government. Instead—he shot himself. In shame that Poland was undergoing civil war, which might split the army, he fired a bullet in his breast, committed *hara kiri*—and recovered! By some miracle, the hole next to his heart was stitched up. Pilsudski rewarded this dramatic expression of divided loyalty by intimating that Soznkowski should be the next President of Poland.

Colonel Slawek, a companion of Pilsudski's from the earliest revolutionary days, was a socialist conspirator; making bombs for Pilsudski in 1903, he lost one side of his face in an explosion. His origins are mysterious; no one but Pilsudski, so the story went, knew where he was born, or his real name. The report is that he was really a Count Czetwertynski, a scion of one of the greatest Polish noble families, who hid these connections without trace when he joined the marshal thirty-five years ago. Slawek became a pet of the Polish aristocrats, the Radziwills and Potockis, who look to him as their own; and it was Slawek who was the bridge between Pilsudski and the aristocracy in the early days of the re-born state. He killed himself in 1939.

Colonel Joseph Beck, born in 1894, somewhat less amiable a character than his colleagues, was a special favourite of Pilsudski in the latter days; the old man had great affection for him. Complicated, ingrown, moody, elegant, Beck came from the low nobility in the Austrian part of Poland, and began his career as a student of economics in Vienna. He joined the Legion; after the War Pilsudski gave him regular officer's training in the new military academy he set up in Warsaw. For a time he was Polish military attaché in Paris. As foreign minister Beck, as we know, pursued a pro-German policy for a considerable time; it did him no good—as we also know. Beck went into exile in 1939.

The President of Poland until the present war was Ignacy Moscicki, known as 'Ignace the Obedient'. He was, of all things, a distinguished electro-physicist, called to politics from a professorship of the University of Lwow. He was also head of the Chemical Research Institute in Warsaw. He has something like five hundred inventions in the field of electro-physics and chemistry to his credit, and holds fifty-three patents. Like the pianist Paderewski, he was valuable to Poland's politics largely because his life was utterly unpolitical.

Rzeczpospolita Polska

The nationalism of Poland, like that of Hungary, was—and still is—flamboyant and tenacious. This is partly because the country, as everyone knows, has four times suffered the unique and terrible experience of partition. Yet when Poland disappeared from the map in the eighteenth century there were only eight million Poles; when Woodrow Wilson put it on the map again in 1919 there were twenty million. Despite the supreme ordeal of concrete geographical dissolution, the country lived—and grew. Poland's resurrection gave it a sort of crucifix complex. This was the source of many of its troubles. It rose from the dead and thus there was something holy about its survival. It began a career of proselytising. It suffered from the delusion that it was not merely a succession state, but a great power.

Polish nationalism was nicely illustrated in the old days by the elephant story, which, if legend is correct, was invented in an objective moment by Paderewski.

Five men of different nationalities each write a book about an elephant. The Englishman goes to India, organises a hunt, and composes a thick illustrated travelogue, 'How I Shot my First Elephant'. The Frenchman casually visits the Zoo and promptly produces a yellow-back '*L'Eléphant et Ses Amours*'. The German plunges into research and emerges some years later with a five-volume work, 'Introduction to a Monograph to the Study of the Elephant'. The Russian gets drunk on vodka, retires to his garret, and issues a slim philosophical treatise, 'The Elephant—Does it Exist?' The Pole sits down in the national library and turns out a flaming pamphlet, 'The Elephant and the Polish Question'.

Poland may not have been a great power, but it was a country the physical bulk of which could not be ignored. Its population was thirty-two million, which increased at the tremendous rate of five hundred thousand per year; in area it was the fifth state in Europe, Russia excluded. Its first tremendous job was to amalgamate the Russian, German and Austrian divisions of the country into a homogeneous and viable whole. After that the chief internal problems were two: settlement of the minorities issue, because the hungry Poles took more than their share of territory; of the thirty-two million people, between eight and ten million were not Poles at all, but Ukrainians, Germans, White Russians, Galicians,

Ruthenes, Lithuanians.   Second, to persuade God to raise agricultural prices.

As is the case with most Central European and Balkan countries,
between thirty-five and forty per cent of the budget went to armament.   A peasant country, not rich in industrial resources, it bore
the burden of one of the most formidable military machines in the
world.   This was necessary for reasons which now, alas, are only too
obvious.   Poland lay exposed, without natural geographic borders,
between two greater powers, Germany and the U.S.S.R.

The foreign policy of Poland after 1919 was that of the nut in
the nutcracker.   At first the orientation, as we know, was the
alliance with France and the Little Entente.   Beck changed this;
aware of the growing strength of Germany, and Germany's desire
to recover the Polish Corridor, he took advantage of Hitler's offer
for a ten-year peace pact; Germany temporarily gave up claims on
the Corridor in return for Polish friendship.   Germany and Poland
united in what was potentially an anti-Soviet *bloc*; nevertheless
Beck went to Moscow as well as Berlin, and a Polish Soviet non-
aggression treaty was duly signed.   Russia nevertheless invaded
Poland in September 1939 a few weeks after the German invasion
had begun.[1]

General Sikorski

The leader of the refugee Polish government in France is one
of the best of Poles, General Ladislas Sikorski.   He was born in
1881 near Lvov, and became one of Pilsudski's indispensable
assistants when war came in 1914.   He was an engineer by education, a soldier—and later a politician—through circumstance.
In the early days of Polish independence, say from 1919 to 1926,
he was the most powerful figure in the republic after Pilsudski,
being at various times chief of staff, minister of war, and prime
minister.   After 1926 he fell from favour, and lived mostly in Paris.
Here he came into close touch with the French general staff; he
had been one of Weygand's best friends for years.   A convinced
democrat and very pro-French, he strongly disapproved of the Beck
policy which brought disaster to Poland.   In 1938 he returned to
Poland, and was virtually interned.   After the 1939 war, with
Rydz-Smigly and Beck disgraced, he inevitably came back to

[1] I have already described the Polish crisis before September in Chapter IX
above.   Events of the war itself are discussed briefly in the introduction to this
edition.

power. He is now prime minister of the Polish government in exile, with a man who shares his democratic views, the veteran August Zaleski, as his foreign minister.

Eyes North

To the north of Poland are the four Baltic states, each with individual problems, but united by the same overwhelming geographical consideration: former provinces of Russia, they were from 1919 to 1939 buffer states between Germany, Poland and the Soviet Union. For a long time they represented a descending order of anti-Russianism and pro-Germanism from north to south. Finland hated the Russians most; Lithuania, at the bottom, disliked them least. Lithuanian policy was grounded on fear of Germany and Poland. In 1939, as everyone knows, Russia established naval and military bases in Lithuania, Latvia, and Esthonia, and invaded Finland.

Finland resembled a good deal the states we shall discuss in the next chapter—the neutrals, like the Scandinavian countries, with their sensible social ideals, advanced democratic methods, and comparatively high standard of living. A sturdy and highly attractive country, Finland lived on cellulose and timber and paid its debts; alone among European countries it did not default on its war debt to America. It was part of Sweden from A.D. 1154 to Napoleonic times, when the Russians grabbed it; its affiliations to Sweden are close but it has tenaciously held to its own language and national tradition. The Finns do not consider themselves either 'Baltic' or 'Scandinavian', and a local political issue has always been rivalry between 'authentic' Finns and those of Swedish blood.

The president of Finland, in December 1939 when the Russian attack got under way, was still Kyosti Kallio, the country's first peasant-born prime minister. He is an agrarian; the basis of his support is social democratic. He succeeded seventy-five-year-old Pehr Evind Svinhufvud, who had been something of a reactionary. Under Kallio the most interesting of contemporary Finns is the youthful foreign minister Juho Erkko, who, the son of an exiled Finnish patriot, came to America at the age of three and lived many years in Brooklyn, New York. Erkko is a staunch and convinced democrat. His wife is British. He had a vivid career in journalism and diplomacy before becoming foreign minister. The veteran of Finnish military and political life is General

Mannerheim, who commanded the White Forces in the Finnish civil wars. He was merciless to the Bolsheviks in 1919.

By contrast the next state to the south, Estonia, has been—until 1939—more in the German orbit, and pro-German influences are strong. Estonia is a republic about the size of New Hampshire and Vermont together; its strategic position to the mouth of the gulf of Finland is important, and the harbour of Tallinn, its charming capital, one of the pleasantest cities in Europe, is an excellent naval base. The chief political personality is General Laidoner, the commander-in-chief. Estonia was under martial law for a considerable period, all political parties were suppressed, and, although a plebiscite in 1936 favoured a return to representative government, a new corporative constitution was created. But the dictatorship was on the whole mild and benevolent.

The next country, Latvia, is an overt but sensibly run dictatorship under an astute and picturesque peasant leader, Dr. Karlis Ulmanis. For years he was a professor at the University of Nebraska; he still subscribes to American farm journals. In 1934 Ulmanis dismissed the diet—at the same time shrewdly buying off discontent by pensioning the deputies for life! He dissolved the political parties, and assumed office as both president and prime minister. He is a doughty character; and his foreign secretary, Wilhelm Munters, is one of the youngest and most attractive foreign ministers in Europe. The Latvians are tough folk, the toughest—man for man—in all Europe probably. Latvia has always sought to be the leader of the Baltic states; Finland excepted, it is the largest, the strongest, and the most advanced. Most Letts have a strong pro-German streak; they hate the U.S.S.R. intensely.

Lithuania, the fourth Baltic state, has the liveliest history of them all. It is a wretchedly poor country, but picturesque; the primitive capital, Kaunas, was for years a Russian garrison town—which it seemed, in 1939, to be becoming again. From 1920, when Pilsudski seized Vilna, until 1938, when Colonel Beck forcibly readjusted the situation, Lithuania was technically in state of war with Poland, with the Polish-Lithuanian border closed. Those who recall the middle twenties may still remember the first prominent Lithuanian leader, a bouncing character named Valdermaras. In 1934 he attempted to make a *coup d'état*. The strongest man in the country to-day is the commander-in-chief, General Rastikas, who began life as a veterinarian. The president of the republic, Professor Smetona, is best known for his remarkable wife, who is a

powerful personage in the affairs of the little state. Her sister is
—or was—the wife of the prime minister. The two sisters ran the
country. Lithuania for years feared and hated the Germans even
more than the Poles, and for a long time sought to be friendly with
the U.S.S.R. When the Russians entered Lithuania in 1939, after
the Polish war, they promptly gave Vilna back to Lithuania.

All the Balts are sturdy and—the Esthonians possibly excepted
—somewhat insensitive folk. The story is, 'Stick a pin in a Balt's
hand; it will be half a minute before he jumps.'

None of the Baltic states quite grew up. They would have
reached their twenty-first birthdays in 1940. But, as we know, in
1939, the Soviet Union established virtual protectorates over all
three.

Two Danger Spots

Two specific danger spots in the northern area were formerly
Danzig and Memel. Both were predominantly German cities
separated from the Reich by the Treaty of Versailles; both grew up
under the tutelage of the League of Nations; in 1939 Germany
took both back. Danzig was technically a free city, however,
whereas Memel was on Lithuanian territory.

The Polish Corridor, a wedge of land which outraged the
Germans by giving Poland an outlet to the sea at the cost of
separating East Prussia from the rest of Germany, was for years the
most perilous territorial issue in Europe. The Polish-German
pact shelved it, and by so doing temporarily reduced much of the
dangerousness of Danzig, which is the Corridor's natural port. The
Nazi party in Danzig, however, began to stir up trouble; when
Hitler started his 1939 campaign against Poland, Danzig became
its inevitable focal point. The Poles, at tremendous expense, had
built a rival port to Danzig—Gdynia. Germany, of course, took it
over in 1939 as spoils of war. It now seems inevitable that Danzig
and the Corridor—Gdynia also—will remain part of Germany.

Memel was detached from Germany in 1919 presumably to give
Lithuania an outlet to the sea; it was to be the Lithuanian equivalent of Danzig. While the allies were still deliberating how
exactly to draw the frontiers, Poland under Pilsudski unconscion-
ably seized the Lithuanian territory of Vilna; tit for tat, Lithuania
then grabbed Memel. The German Nazis violently agitated for
the return of Memel to Germany; in retaliation, the Lithuanians
treated the German minority none too gently. The Memel issue

became the kind of villainous nationalist snarl for which there seemed no reasonable territorial solution. Then Hitler took Memel, in March 1939, when it became clear that neither the Lithuanians nor anyone else could possibly resist.

The Aaland Islands

This group of islands in the Gulf of Bothnia between Finland and Sweden may become a geographical and political issue of the first importance. Both Finland and Sweden claimed them in the 1919 settlements; the Aalanders themselves wanted autonomy. The dispute was brought to the League of Nations, early in the 20's, and the League did one of its first big jobs—ironic this seems now! —in settling it amicably and fairly. The Finns retained sovereignty over the islands, it was provided that they should be demilitarised, and the population was given wide autonomous rights. So, for almost twenty years, the Aaland Island issue was forgotten.

In 1939 the Finns, seeing how the eastern winds were blowing, opened negotiations with Sweden for permission to refortify the islands. The Finns feared Russia; the Swedes feared Germany. The Aaland group is the key to the Baltic. A great power entrenched there could control almost impregnably any shipping between Swedish, Finnish, Russian, German, and Baltic ports; such shipping might include Swedish iron ore, of inestimable value to a belligerent. The Swedes and Finns agreed to refortify the islands jointly. Then the U.S.S.R. protested, on the ground that the plan was a unilateral violation of the 1919 treaties. So—in the angry summer of 1939—the question of the islands was still a potential danger.

CHAPTER XXXV

THE NOTABLE NEUTRALS

ABOUT Sweden there is a fine and honourable thing to say; it has had no war since 1814. This is a unique record, which no country in the world can match. Likewise Sweden is notable in that it has no foreign alliances of any kind; the Swedes live alone and like it. Yet their policy of strict neutrality, of comfortable self-assurance, does not isolate them from the rest of Europe; with a great history and healthy nationalism, they are intensely European in the best sense of that term; from the beginning they have been sturdy advocates of the League of Nations and international co-operation.

The Swedes have no empire to worry about, no big army to main-tain, no foreign entanglements to unwrinkle or smooth over; partly for this reason—also of course because of something inherently solid and decent in their character—they have made their own country, like Denmark, peaceable and prosperous. Sweden and Denmark to-day are the two healthiest countries in Europe. It is vastly refreshing to pause in this swing around tortured Europe and inspect the Scandinavian states, islands of tranquillity, rational behaviour, and good government.

Sweden, together with Denmark, may be said to represent the highest type of state paternalism yet seen in the world. When a Swede—or a Dane—is born he becomes state property in a sense then and there. In every town and village there is a child welfare board. Children go to schools and universities maintained by the state; they grow up to join an exceedingly elaborate social insurance scheme; their old age is taken care of by the most advanced old age and disablement insurance in Europe. The Swede travels on rail-ways operated by the state; he uses state telephones; the mines which produce the bulk of his exports are state controlled; even the alcohol he drinks is managed by an ingenious system of state regu-lation.

There are the co-operatives too; they deserve a chapter to them-selves. 'Approximately one third of all retail trade and more than ten per cent of wholesale trade and manufacture for domestic consumption are carried on by co-operatives without profit,' writes Marquis Childs in *Sweden: The Middle Way*. The co-operatives have opened the way to cheap housing (there are no slums in Sweden—or Denmark—any more than there are any aged poor) and a comprehensive raising of living standards. Denmark and Sweden have the highest standards of living in Europe. Yet the essential privileges of capitalism are not abrogated. People may possess private property, they may trade at a profit, they may own production. Sweden, as Mr. Childs says, is the country where capitalism is controlled, but where the individual remains free.

. . . .

The three Scandinavian countries are brothers, but, as is often the case with brothers, they are rather dissimilar in character. Denmark, a country of islands, swept always by a fresh swift breeze, is developed to the last square inch. Of the tiny farms more than ninety per cent are cultivated by their owners. The Danes are, speaking broadly, more 'continental' than Swedes and Norwegians; they are closer to Europe and the pressure of Germany. Sweden is a much more spacious country—if you turn it around at the southernmost tip it would nearly reach Africa—less intensively developed, bursting with water-power, living on export of ore and manufactured goods as well as agriculture, and, in its northern emptiness, reminiscent of Russia perhaps and even Asia. The Swedes, by and large, are more formal than the Danes, more rugged perhaps, with less cosmopolitan a capital—but one equally beautiful—and with a shade more conscious nationalism. The Norwegians, again speaking broadly, are more like the Danes than the Swedes. Their independence is so comparatively recent that they take their nationalism very seriously and sometimes fear that their neighbours don't take it seriously enough; they changed the name of their capital from Kristiania to Oslo and revived the indigenous Norwegian language, although for generations Dano-Norwegian was almost a common tongue. 'The Norwegians,' one of my Scandinavian friends once put it, 'are, like their landscape, rather vertical.' Their country is less rich than Sweden or Denmark, the people are mostly of peasant stock, their chief exports are timber, paper, pulp.

The resemblances are closer. The three countries have tightly inter-related royal families; indeed the Danish and Norwegian kings are brothers. Internal politics have followed the same general courses in all three countries, and all three have social democratic governments. Postal rates are the same, the currency until recently was interchangeable, and the languages are very similar. The three are friends, and work together very closely; the prime ministers meet regularly. All three represent the same ideals socially—child welfare, social reform, a high standard of living, curtailment of the privileges of capitalism, education and cultural development, evolutionary progress. There is no illiteracy in Scandinavia. Infant mortality rates are the lowest in the world. None of the three, in international affairs, has ambition beyond its frontiers; there is no instinct for aggression and no delusion of national grandeur.

Peace among the three, interestingly enough, is a comparatively recent development. Denmark and Sweden fought each other more than once before the nineteenth century. Both had designs on Norway. Norway got loose from Denmark, rushed into the arms of Sweden, got tired of Sweden, and set up a kingdom for itself—with a Danish prince as king. The only recent international issue occurred in 1931 when Norway made claims on the east coast of Greenland, Denmark's property. Instead of fighting they turned to the Hague court; Norway lost, and like a gentleman has never mentioned the matter since.

The royal families in each country are deliberate and successful democrats. For the last two or three generations they have been born in captivity, and any inkling towards despotism long since left the blood. They are pleasant human beings, considerably popular, and much less expensive politically than presidents. Nowadays they work in close harmony with socialist prime ministers.

The three kings make a handsome picture. All are spare and lean, more than six feet tall; Christian of Denmark is the tallest king in the world, and the tallest man (reputedly) in his kingdom—six foot six. All have reigned a long time, Haakon of Norway since 1905, Gustave of Sweden since 1907, Christian of Denmark (Haakon's brother) since 1912. Gustav, at eighty-one, is still an active tennis player; he enters the Riviera tournaments disguised as 'Mr. G.'. Possibly the ablest of the three is Christian; his silver jubilee, celebrated in 1937 was an impressive testimonial. Christian rides alone, through the streets of Copenhagen, every morning at seven a.m., he stops at traffic-lights and the passers-by salute him without ostentation. He likes to sail among the Danish islands, dropping in without warning at the villages; he knows an extraordinary number of his subjects by name and face.

The families have intermarried regularly. The Danish crown prince, Frederick (the Danes have alternated Christians with Fredericks for 400 years), married Ingrid, the daughter of the crown prince of Sweden; the crown prince of Norway, Olaf, married another Swedish princess. They had a son, amid rejoicing, in 1936 —the first royal prince to be born in Norway since 1370. The oldest of the three families is the Danish. The Swedish dynasty began in Napoleonic times with Marshal Bernadotte, and the Norwegians have less history than the others, having started from scratch in 1905.

All three families have distinguished themselves outside the royal province. For instance the Danish crown prince is an accomplished musician and orchestra conductor. The King's uncle, Prince Waldemar, has four sons: one is in the French Foreign Legion, one in business. Prince Eugene, brother of the King of Sweden, is a painter of distinction; Prince William, second son of King Gustav, is a widely travelled lecturer and poet; the Swedish crown prince is a professional archaeologist.

The dominant issue in Scandinavian foreign affairs is fear of Nazi Germany—and since September 1939—of Soviet Russia. When I was in Denmark and Sweden some years ago I wandered through their foreign offices for days, looking for an issue. I would find it promptly enough to-day. The Germans have designs on Scandinavia, particularly Denmark, for obvious reasons. The Scandinavians are first-class Aryans. Denmark might be a larder in case of war; Sweden might provide precious raw material for arms. The Germans would like diplomatic support at least from their northern cousins. Sweden has a tradition of pro-Germanism, and there are prominent Danes, like the foreign minister Dr. Munch, who have seemed to favour the German side.

More than anywhere except Austria the Nazis turned the full weight of their propaganda machine to Scandinavia. Emissaries flooded Denmark and Sweden; the indigenous Germans were organised into Nazi or quasi-Nazi groups; parties closely analogous to the Nazis entered Swedish, Danish, and Norwegian politics. For a time[1] there were three Nazi factions in Sweden, four in Norway, in Denmark two. A local group of the *German* Nazi party exists in most important Scandinavian towns.

The fervour of German attempts at penetration defeated its own ends; it might fairly be said that Nazi agitation served to decrease

[1] See *The Nazis in Scandinavia*, by Joachim Joesten, *Foreign Affairs*, July 1937.

rather than increase normal pro-German sentiment.   As Germany became more powerful, more restless, in international affairs, the Danes and the Swedes became more alarmed.   The Anglo-German naval pact seemed to give the German navy domination in the Baltic.   German naval vessels were continually experiencing 'engine trouble' in obscure Norwegian fiords (where Swedish ore might be shipped to German ports); German leaders developed the habit of cruising in Scandinavian waters outside the tourist season. The Germans made no secret of their fortification of the island of Sylt, off the Danish coast.

When Finland was invaded by Russia, alarm throughout Scandinavia became pressing.   The Soviet Union replaced Germany as the chief potential foe.   As a result came (a) an increased socialist and labour vote in all three Scandinavian countries and (b) Scandinavian rearmament.   The three countries, reluctantly, regretfully, after so many years outside the sphere of continental politics and competitive armament, were forced to mend their military programmes.   Denmark, which only a few years before had contemplated abolishing its army altogether, introduced a defence bill of 20,000,000 kroner; Norway lifted its military budget from about nine to more than thirteen million dollars; Sweden raised its defence appropriation twenty-two per cent.

.   .   .   .

Per Albin Hansson, born near Malmo in 1885, is the Swedish prime minister.   His father was a mason; he was once an errand boy in a country store.   At twelve he worked in a grocery at four shillings per week, with hours from six a.m. to nine p.m.; through a co-operative he entered the trade union movement and labour politics; at nineteen he was editor of a socialist newspaper.   He has always liked journalism.   In his first cabinet there were five journalists besides himself.

Hansson, the story goes, tried to evade military service by drinking a lot of black coffee, smoking a dozen cigars, and racing to the medical examination.   He was accepted just the same—and became the strictest corporal in the regiment.   He was an early prohibitionist, and thundered against alcohol with a quotation from Aristotle: 'Those who go to bed drunk beget only daughters.'

Mr. Hansson, universally known in Sweden as Per Albin, succeeded to the leadership of the social democratic party on the death of the grand old man of Swedish socialism, Hjalmar Branting. (Incidentally Branting and King Gustav were classmates at the

University of Upsala and close friends.) Hansson formed his first cabinet in 1932, the first labour prime minister in Swedish history, when the liberals then in power were discredited by repercussions of the Kreuger crash; he took office again in 1936. The agrarians are represented in his coalition.

The leader of the agrarian party is Axel Pehrsson, Bramstorp. (There are so many Pehrssons in Sweden that often they add their village to their names.) He is a wealthy farmer, born near Hansson's birth-place in the fat lands of Skaane, fifty-eight now, powerful, ambitious. He likes to tackle any variety of job. The story goes that a friend of Pehrsson's looking through the local paper, said, 'A position as midwife is vacant; it's strange Pehrsson hasn't yet applied.'

Denmark, the oldest kingdom in the world, is a slender little country—though it lives on butter, bacon, and eggs. It is small, less than twice the size of Vermont—but its sinuous coastline is as long as that of European Russia. The unmelancholy Danes number only 3,550,000 people—but they provide thirty per cent of the world's export butter, more than sixty per cent of its bacon. Their co-operatives are even more advanced than those of Sweden; they handle ninety per cent of Danish milk and they send to England alone no fewer than 56,000,000 neatly stamped and dated eggs per year.

The dominant Dane, one of the most remarkable of present-day European figures, is Thorvald Stauning, the prime minister.

Stauning is a modern Viking—in a workman's cap. He is six foot three; he weighs 250 pounds; he has a luxuriant red beard, now turning grey. His features are massive, his voice is like a foghorn, he has, even notably among Danes, who like life, an inordinate capacity to enjoy existence. Yet this decisive and dramatic character, exuding vigour and masculinity was weakly and poor as a boy; he started work in a tobacco factory when still a child; his struggles were crushingly long and difficult.

Stauning is sixty-six. He was born in Copenhagen, the son of a cartwright. He worked as a cigar-roller and led his trade-union. He entered journalism on a social democrat newspaper and in 1906 was elected to the Rigsdag. His rise was quick. Very early he showed the chief reasons for his success—vigour plus great common sense and practical faith in his ideals. As long ago as 1916 he was a cabinet minister, the first labour cabinet minister in Scandinavia;

in 1924 he became prime minister. He resigned in 1927 when he was defeated on a proposal to introduce a capital levy (to augment the social services); he returned to power in 1929 and has been in power, the leader of a labour coalition, ever since.

In 1930 he proposed what amounted to the abolition of Denmark's armed forces. A step so sensible (at the time) and sensational shocked Europe. Stauning said that Denmark was bound to be defeated if it were invaded by a great power; therefore it was nonsense to resist and that the business of policy should be to avert war, not prepare for it. He suggested the reduction of the army to a nominal police force of 13,000 men, severe restriction of the navy, and diminution of the defence budget from 56,000,000 kronen a year to 18,000,000. The bill was defeated. Presently the Nazis came to power in Germany, and it is doubtful if Stauning to-day would reintroduce his bill.

In 1934 he presented a bill to abolish the Landsting or Upper Chamber of Parliament, because it was impeding socialist reforms. Yet, like most of the Scandinavian socialists, Stauning is a moderate, with a strictly pragmatic view of progress.

Stauning vigorously opposed a suggestion by the Swedish foreign minister Dr. Sandler for a Scandinavian defensive entente. 'Denmark will not be Scandinavia's watchdog,' he announced. Denmark, as he well knows, the nearest state to Germany, is the one most in danger of aggression; he fears that Denmark might have to pull Swedish or Norwegian chestnuts from the fire if all were united in a common policy.

Literate, literary, Stauning has written plays. One, *The Lies of Life*, was a great success in Copenhagen.

. . . .

The Norwegian prime minister is Johan Nygaardsvold. He was the son of a poor farmer, and worked in a sawmill from his twelfth year. For six years, emigrating to the U.S.A., he did pick and shovel work on the western railways. He was a member of the I.W.W. for a time. He returned to Norway, got a trade-union job, and entered politics. He has been in the Storting (parliament) since 1915 and has led the labour party since 1932, a socialist to the bone. When he gets into difficulties he says, 'It's because I couldn't shut up.'

Nygaardsvold, with the help of the farmer's party, became Norway's first labour prime minister in 1935.

Paul van Zeeland and the State of Belgium

Belgium, the most densely populated state in Europe, has been an independent kingdom since 1830, when it broke away from the Netherlands. The country is a compact triangular bridge between France and Holland, and its people partake of the nature of both neighbours. Powerfully industrial, the factories of Belgium ship manufactured goods all over the world. The chief problem of internal politics—seldom reaching an acute stage however—has been the fight of the Flemish provinces, where Flemish (instead of French) is spoken, for what might be called linguistic autonomy. The constitution, under which Belgium is 'a constitutional and representative' monarchy, has one unique provision—that the king, if he has no male heirs, may with the consent of parliament nominate his successor.

The most prominent Belgian politician at the present time, since Emile Vandervelde, the socialist leader, became inactive, is a brilliant new star in the constellation of European statesmen, Paul van Zeeland. This young man—he is only forty-six—has rare quality.

One thing making him attractive to Americans is his close connection with Princeton University. He did post-graduate work at Princeton after the War, and in 1937 returned to accept an honorary degree. He told Frederick Birchall of the *New York Times* recently that he always thinks of himself as a Princeton man, that his brother followed him there, that his nephew is a Princeton student now, and that assuredly his son will go to Princeton too.

Once in 1934—according to the American magazine *Time*—Van Zeeland and a Yale graduate worked together at a banking conference; the friend scribbled him a note to the effect that Yale footballers had just beaten Princeton 7-0. Van Zeeland sent a note back. 'Belgian cabinet: Princeton 2; Yale 0.' For one of his cabinet ministers, Vicomte de Warnaffe, was also a Princetonian.

Van Zeeland was born in Soignies, the seventh of eight children, in 1893. The family were Dutch burghers—but profound Roman Catholics—who emigrated to French-speaking Belgium generations ago. Van Zeeland is a strict Catholic. He went to the University of Louvain, and was taken prisoner when the War came. He spent the next years in prison camps in Germany and then, after the War, joined a mission of the Belgian Relief Commission in the United States.

A wide traveller, an earnest student, he has visited the United States several times, the U.S.S.R. once, the Near East once. His thesis at Princeton dealt with the federal reserve system; he wrote a book on Soviet Russia; in 1933 he delivered a series of lectures at Johns Hopkins for the Walter Hines Page school of international relations.

Van Zeeland, one of the most valuable of European politicians, was drafted into politics almost despite himself. From 1922 to 1935 he was quite busy at two other careers: in the Belgian National Bank, of which he became vice-governor in 1926 at the age of thirty-three; and at the University of Louvain, where he was professor of economic science from 1928. He entered the cabinet inconspicuously as minister without portfolio, to watch economic matters; in 1935 he became prime minister for the first time and as his first major job devalued the Belgian currency. His general policy followed with some similarity the New Deal of Franklin Roosevelt.

Two notable events have distinguished the history of Belgium— and of Paul van Zeeland—during the past few years. One was the rise and fall of a Fascist party, the 'Rexists' led by a young sub-Hitler, Leon Degrelle. He was a good-looking young man, stuffed with personality as well as Fascist doctrine; he got votes, so they said, by 'Rex-Appeal'. The movement was a serious menace to Belgian democracy until Van Zeeland, who had never run for office, accepted Degrelle's challenge to run against him in a bye-election. Van Zeeland won crushingly.

The other event, of great international importance, was the announcement made directly by King Leopold III in October 1936, that Belgium would give up the French alliance and revert to its pre-War status of neutrality. This caused some months of worry and uneasiness for French and British statesmen. The Belgian case was simple: the Belgians didn't want to be the cockpit of the next war, yet both the Locarno Treaty and the temporary post-Locarno agreement between Britain, France, and Belgium provided that Belgium go to the defence of France if France were attacked by Germany. In April 1937 a joint Anglo-French declaration released Belgium from its Locarno obligations and at the same time renewed French and British guaranty of Belgian independence.

In other words Belgium is no longer obliged to help its big friends, but the big friends continue their pledge to help her.

2 L

Dutch and Swiss

Dr. Hendrikus Colijn is the most important of modern statesmen of the Netherlands. He has been prime minister off and on since 1925. Dr. Colijn, like his friend Van Zeeland, only entered politics after successful years in several other professions. He was born of Calvinist stock in 1869, destined by his parents to become a farmer. But he wanted to be a soldier; he enlisted in the Dutch army as a private, and went for service to the Dutch East Indies, where he spent almost twenty years.

In 1909 he returned to the Netherlands and entered business. For some years he was a director of Royal Dutch Shell and other oil companies. Concurrently politics gained his attention, and Colonel Colijn, the soldier-administrator (for a time he had been deputy governor of Sumatra) became Dr. Colijn, the leader of the 'Anti-revolutionary' party. He edited a newspaper, reflecting his strong Calvinist views, served as war minister, minister of finance, and minister of colonies, and finally reached the premiership.

Colijn's chief characteristic—omitting such personal details as that he smokes twenty-five cigars a day—is a middle-of-the-road shrewdness. He is the 'no-nonsense' type of hard-headed Dutchman, and his canny intelligence was such as to command the intense respect of his sovereign, the massive Wilhelmina, one of the shrewdest persons alive herself. Colijn always headed a minority party, and led coalitions chiefly through the favour of the Queen. His colonial experience gave him perspective and a world view of politics, as well as intimate knowledge of the precious life blood of Holland—the Indies.

By all odds the chief political preoccupation of the Netherlands, from both domestic and external points of view, is fear of Germany. Holland for a time had an obstreperous Nazi party, led by A. A. Mussert; Dr. Colijn squashed him in the 1937 elections. Dutch conceptions of national defence had to be radically revised when Hitler came to power. For one thing, the traditional Dutch method of defence—opening the dykes—had to be augmented. For another, both France and Belgium have their lines of concrete fortifications; Holland has none, and therefore feared that Germany might be tempted to attack through the exposed Dutch flank. Holland raised her defence budget by £7,200,000 in 1937.

Dr. Colijn is one of the fathers of the so-called 'Oslo group' of powers, the states named in this chapter plus Finland, Luxembourg, and Iceland. They are parties to a convention pledging members not to raise tariff barriers without mutual consent, and to work otherwise for economic unity and betterment.

On January 7, 1937, the heiress to the Dutch throne, Princess Juliana of Orange-Nassau, married young Prince Bernhard of the house of Lippe-Biesterfeld. So far they have two daughters.

. . . .

Switzerland, the oldest republic in the world, trilingual, irrefragably neutral, tough and independent, is governed by a federal council of seven men. One of them each year becomes president of the confederation; the others are the equivalent of cabinet ministers. The president cannot succeed himself except after an interval. In practice, the presidency rotates among the seven counsellors; the president to-day, Dr. Giuseppe Motta, was also president in 1915, 1920, 1927, and 1931.

Dr. Motta, a strong Catholic, was born in Ticino in the Italian part of Switzerland, the son of a hotelkeeper. He studied law at Fribourg, Munich, Heidelberg, and entered politics as a young man; for twenty years he has been a member of the federal council. He is the father of a large family, reputedly he knows Dante by heart, he gets a salary of £1,400 per year, he has a blameless record in private life, and in external politics he seems very decidedly to follow a pro-Vatican, pro-Mussolini course.

Switzerland too feels the Nazi menace, and fears possible attack by Germany. A local Nazi party, the Grey Shirts, rose in prominence after 1933; all the countries on the periphery of Germany, without exception, have seen these sub-Hitler movements rise and fall. Switzerland, like the Netherlands, is mending her defences. In 1936 a bill was introduced providing for a professional army— after 650 years of reliance on a national militia. In 1938 the Defence Bill was a cool £50,000,000—a staggering sum for the small republic.

CHAPTER XXXVI

HALF A LEAGUE ONWARD

'Breathes there a man with soul so dead
Who never to himself hath said
This is my own, my native land.'

Nothing is easier than to sneer at the poor old League of Nations, foisted on the allied powers by an American, Woodrow Wilson, because he happened to care more for the United States of the World than the United States of America. Like a virgin in a bawdy house, calling piteously for a glass of lemonade (as Ben Hecht put it), Wilson roamed the corridors of Versailles, emerging finally with the League as America's only spoils of war. It gives one a start to read the Covenant to-day and see that paragraph three of Article Five still says, 'The first meeting of the Assembly and the first meeting of the Council shall be summoned by the President of the United States.'

Nothing was easier in the old days than to list the charges commonly made against the League. Speaker after speaker mounts the Assembly tribune—and tells the world what everybody already knows. Nothing happens at the Council table until the powers that be have settled the business beforehand—and in secret. What the League mostly does is try to act long after the time for action. The League does nothing but spawn a plethora of feeble committees. The League provided a means for minorities to voice their grievances, therefore minorities have been doubly nuisance-makers. The League compelled the registration of treaties; so treaties now-adays have more secret clauses than before. The League is a junta of the Versailles powers. And so on. And so on.

Some of these charges are true. But the point to make is that the countries themselves, not the League, are responsible for most of the weaknesses of the Geneva system. The League as such has no sovereign rights. It has no authority to compel a state to follow its recommendations. The League is a pool of all the member powers, but it has no executive rights over any individual country. The League is not a super-state; it is merely a mouthpiece of member states when happily and rarely they reach agreement. The League itself decides nothing; the *individual states* bear all responsibility.

The Covenant, moreover, was written on the assumption that the United States of America would be a signatory. When Senator Lodge and his band of irreconcilable isolationists refused ratification of the Versailles Treaty, they torpedoed the Covenant almost beyond recovery. With the United States a League member, sanctions would have effectively outlawed an errant state. But American withdrawal from the League system made sanctions all but impossible, because America, by insisting on its neutral right of trading with an aggressor, could frustrate any League blockade. The British Navy, necessarily the chief instrument of a blockade, would not risk conflict with the United States.

In assessing the value of the League one should first separate its non-political activities from those entangled in nationalist politics. That the League has done sturdy service in extra-political fields is, of course, undeniable. In collating statistics on a wide international basis, in forming the nucleus of a reasonable world approach to matters of health, agriculture, the drug traffic, transport, refugees, codification of law, its value is indisputable, and only a persimmon-minded Pharisee could minimise it. One should not forget, too, the able work of the League in finance and economics, particularly the attempt to stabilise the Danube countries after the War.

As to politics, the thing to keep in mind is that the League is an admirable mechanism for settling international disputes when—and only when—the great powers agree. It is silly to say that the League, even if it has no executive authority, cannot stop wars; it has stopped at least one war which might have been extremely dangerous—for instance the Bulgar-Greek conflict in 1925—and it can stop others *provided* Britain and the other great powers are united in wanting them stopped. When the British and Russians and Italians see eye to eye, the Geneva system works—swiftly and well. For instance the League prevented the Jugoslav-Hungarian outbreak in 1934 from developing into war. This averted a first-rate international crisis. But when the powers disagree, then the League is blocked.

The League's record as an administrator of doubtful territories is almost beyond reproach. Remember the Saar. The prime minister of Saarland was a tough and gallant Briton, Geoffrey Knox. In his 'cabinet' were a Frenchman, a Saarlander, a Jugoslav, a Finn.

They were neutral and impartial; they had no local axes to grind; they had no political ambitions; and they (their predecessors also) gave the Saar fifteen years of distinct prosperity and peace. Another case in point is Danzig, where, until the Nazis got completely out of hand, the Irishman Sean Lester, the League's man, made an excellent administration.

Suppose Lithuania, say, or Austria, should be internationalised and placed under a completely impartial and disinterested extra-national cabinet. Suppose that the minister of finance was a Swede, because he was the best man in the world available for the post, and the minister of communications a Greek or Swiss, chosen for efficiency. Suppose the police were commanded by a Dane and his men were Indian, Italian, Uruguayan, or what you will, picked like the Saar 'Expeditionary' Force. The idea is so sensible that it is, of course, fantastic. It won't work because it strikes at the most 'precious' boast of a people, its nationalism. The only thing against it is human and political nature. Which is what makes evolution of the League so heart-breakingly difficult.

The League is, as Edgar Ansel Mowrer put it, the product of thousands of years of slow ethical growth. Feeble as it may be, it 'speaks for a much larger proportion of the world than any other human institution'. It represents—I quote a recent letter in *The Times*—'man's first fumbling approach to national decency, conceived in the spiritual anguish of the War.' And it has been in operation less than a generation, which in the historical process, is a very brief interval indeed. I remember President Masaryk saying to me in Prague, 'It is only fifteen years since the War—an instant's flash. Give us time—time——'

The brief history of the League may be divided into four periods. Until the Treaty of Locarno in 1925 it was for the most part the instrument of the victorious powers, strengthening the peace against the upward writhings of the vanquished. Then till 1933, when Germany departed, it laboriously struggled with the problem of disarmament; viz., the allied powers refused to obey their pledges and to disarm, and the disarmament conference collapsed. From 1933 to 1937 the major issue was 'collective security', so called. This meant an attempt to bring Germany into a security system on the basis of more or less equal rights.

The Abyssinian dispute cut dramatically across this movement. The greatest day in the history of the League was October 6, 1935, when Article Sixteen was invoked and sanctions against Italy were

put into motion. For the first time, a major power was formally
condemned for violation of the Covenant, and by a unanimous
vote of the Council—despite the prophets who never dreamed that
Article Sixteen could be applied—Italy was declared an outlaw
state, deemed to have declared an act of war against all League
states. Shades of Wilson! The League was born!

Thereafter came the fourth period—which persisted until the
outbreak of war in 1939—of bitter disillusion. The League was
helpless and impotent before the immense pressure of Fascist
aggression. But the prestige of a person or an institution often ebbs
and flows. The League was at low-water after the Abyssinian
débâcle and during the successive Hitlerite coups. But this was
not the fault of the League, as the League, but of the great powers
comprising it.

Peace Palace

The League secretariat comprises six hundred and thirty-seven
men and women of forty-four nationalities, and there are some
queer fish among them. All take a solemn pledge to the League,
and the group represents the nearest approach to an international
civil service that the world has yet seen.

The secretary-general, Joseph Avenol, is a Frenchman; his
deputy is Irish. The under secretaries are British and Argentinian,
and the chiefs of section comprise two Britons, one Italian, one
Greek, one Swiss, one Norwegian, one Swede, one Pole, one Dutchman, one South African, and one American, the astute and amiable
Arthur Sweetser. These men are the 'cabinet' of the League. In
various sections the number of different nationalities is augmented.
In the information section, for instance, there are men and women
of seventeen countries.[1] This mêlée does not, however, produce
much discord. The former secretary-general, Sir Eric Drummond,
told a friend that quarrels in the staff, when they rarely occurred,
were usually between people of the same nationality.

Members of the secretariat represent a cross-section of equipment as well as nationality. There are former soldiers, professors,
engineers, diplomats, newspaper men, health officers, lawyers,

---

[1] Holland, the United States, Switzerland, France, Italy, Poland, Jugoslavia,
Belgium, England, Canada, Australia, Sweden, Spain, China, Hungary, India,
Chile. Several individuals are, moreover, multi-national; for instance, one
vigorous member of the secretariat, M. Zilliacus, was born in Japan of a Finnish
father and American mother; he was educated in Sweden, England, and the
U.S.A.; he married a Pole and is a naturalised Englishman.

economists. Most are strenuous idealists, and all are devoted to the League. A fair share of them entered League service, young men— in the original secretariat there were only two men over forty—fresh from the War and determined to give voice to their disillusion and idealism. Some were inveterate internationalists even then; Pierre Comert, for instance, for many years head of the information section, was a teacher of French in a German University.

The chief 'personalities' commonly associated with the League were conspicuous delegates from the powers, like the fabulous Titulescu of Rumania, Dr. Beneš of Czechoslovakia, and young Anthony Eden who was by all odds Geneva's star attraction. The head of the secretariat, M. Avenol, born in 1879, is French and yet has been called the Frenchman's conception of a typical Englishman. He is extremely shy, a little slow, tenacious; he never gets excited, he loves England, and has a passion for bulldogs and gardening. Avenol was a financial expert, an adviser to the French treasury who worked in England on inter-ally financial problems; he was once offered the governorship of the Banque de France but he preferred Geneva.

In 1939 the League went into forced temporary retirement. The great new building on Lake Geneva looked like an ivory mausoleum. Inside, ghosts walked.

Perish the Treaties?

The Treaty of Versailles, the alleged source of all our woes, is a sturdy document running to four hundred and fifty-three pages which weighs just under three pounds. You can buy it at H.M. Stationery Office for the very respectable sum of two shillings and sixpence, and it is an interesting lot of reading matter for the money.

Some of its clauses, written in passion in 1919, seem outrageous and indefensible now, like the 'Hang the Kaiser' and war-guilt paragraphs. Large parts, you discover with some amazement, are long since out of date; the cry to revise the treaty still resounds, but as a matter of fact the document has already been so whittled down that not much except the territorial clauses are left. Reparations, Rhineland, disarmament, the Polish corridor, are no more than waste paper now. Parts VI, VII, VIII, IX, X, XI, XII, of the treaty have disappeared.

This served to make more pressing the demand for territorial revision. The allies gave way to Germany, though with ill grace, first on the financial clauses of the treaty, then on German rearmament, then on the Rhineland. Territory was not so easy for the allies to give away. So the Germans simply took what they wanted. Then came deadlock on the question of returning the mandated territories, former German colonies, to Germany.

As a matter of blunt fact, the territorial provisions of the treaties, including even those dealing with the Danube and Baltic, were not so utterly indefensible—some minor instances excepted—as is generally assumed. The basis of the settlement was self-determination; frontiers were drawn with ethnic considerations predominant. As a result, whereas in pre-1914 Europe something like 45,000,000 people lived under foreign domination—including the whole of what was Poland till 1939, the whole of Czechoslovakia, the whole of the Baltic states and much of Jugoslavia—the situation before the outbreak of war in 1939 was that only 16,800,000 were genuine minorities. The fact cannot be denied that, as Hamilton Fish Armstrong put it, 'vastly more people on the continent of Europe live under their own national régimes than before'. The trouble was that the allied powers overstepped themselves, and created—as we have seen—new minorities by grabbing what didn't belong to them. But it should be pointed out that some frontier lines, like that between Hungary and Rumania, can never be drawn without leaving some miserable folk on the wrong side of the border. In much of Europe, no finally and completely national frontier can be written.

Another point should be kept in mind. If Germany had won the War, the Treaty of Versailles might not have been nearly so nice a one.

War and Peace

The forces making for war, the source and embodiment of all indecency and evil, were before 1939 the following:

First, rival nationalisms. We have noted *ad nauseam* the internecine hatreds of much of Europe. 'Patriotism is the last refuge of a scoundrel'; war is the last refuge of a patriot. And there were many 'profiteers in patriotism' in Europe during the 30's.

Second, economic stresses. The last war caused the last economic crisis; the last economic crisis helped cause the next war. The unity and confidence of capitalism were shaken; national poverty unloosed unpredictable international forces.

Third, the outward push of countries like Germany and Italy

that were starved for raw materials, which coincided with their political revisionism, their nationalist urge to destroy the treaties and thus expand. Five countries in the world possess about seventy-five per cent of the total of the world's key-products. Germany, Italy and Japan were not among them.

Fourth, the difficulty of localising civil disturbances; Europe was so interlocked that a revolution in Austria with 6,500,000 people, could set 100,000,000 marching; frontiers were multiplied by Versailles, Europe 'balkanised', and the whole continent enmeshed in rickety alliances.

Fifth, the incapacity of certain peoples to develop democratically.

Sixth, the growth of armament. Millions of armed men could not sit around with billions of dollars' worth of guns and ammunition and just twiddle their thumbs—indefinitely.

Seventh, the fact that the United States of America was not a member of the League, which would have been a thousand per cent more effective with American adherence.

Eighth, the spread of Fascism, and the explosive force of personalities like Hitler.[1]

The forces making for peace might—before 1939—have been outlined as follows by an optimist:

First, wars cost money, and everybody was poor. Nobody paid for the last war—except the dead. (On the other hand, of course, domestic poverty may tempt a country—Italy for instance—to break out, both as an effort to cloak discontent at home, and, more 'legitimately', to seek wealth abroad. Also one may note that the less wealth a country has, the less it stands to lose by war.)

Second, the general tempo of the economic crisis seemed to be an anodyne. The struggle of almost all nations to keep from drowning in the seas of their own poverty seemed for a time, to a certain extent, to minimise the danger of conflict. (On the other hand, note that in Austria, for instance, economic difficulties tended to increase the chance of *civil* war.)

Third, the peace treaties went a considerable way towards drawing a correct ethnic map of Europe, and thus removed many former sources of revolutionary and international friction. There should have been approximately thirty million fewer Europeans anxious to upset the status quo.

[1] The actual course of events leading to the outbreak of war in 1939 are sketched in Chapters VIII and IX above.

Fourth, in 1914 in Europe there were eighteen kingdoms or empires, four of them ruled by absolute or nearly absolute monarchs, and only two republics. In 1938 there were twelve kingdoms, none of them absolute, and fifteen republics. Absolutist wars in the fashion of former centuries, arranged between royal houses almost like their marriages, seemed out of fashion. (On the other hand, totalitarian Fascist dictators could with equal impunity throw their countries into war.)

Fifth, it could have been said that a general European war might, if it went on long enough, produce revolution and communism everywhere. The knowledge that the Kremlin would very likely be the beneficiary of a new world war might, conceivably, have tended to prevent one. But—lamentably!—it didn't turn out that way, even though the Kremlin may indeed turn out to be the beneficiary.

'In Vishnuland What Avatar?'

So now we come to the end of this long and crowded parade through Western Europe. War aside, what are the other tendencies made manifest? What chords, subordinate to the main diapason peace-or-war, are clear?

1. The status-quo group of powers, beneficiaries of the peace treaties, has begun to lose this overwhelming dominance.

2. Political nationalism, founded on poverty, hate, and economic jealousy, is still the biggest force determining the policy of every country.

3. Powerful personalities like Hitler, Goering, Mussolini, Horthy, Stalin, Franco, Inönü, Metaxas, dominate those countries where people are too feeble or immature politically for democracy.

4. The small democratic states are those which—until the outbreak of war in 1939 at least—survived the trying ardours of the 30's best. Scandinavia, Switzerland, Holland, have a higher living standard than their neighbours; they sought to stay outside the general stream of European madness.

5. The world economic crisis has lifted considerably. But the agricultural countries in Central Europe and the Baltic regions are still hard hit by the agrarian collapse and the industrial countries still find their markets shrivelled.

6. Liberal democracy was a handmaiden to private capitalism; the world economic crisis dealt private capitalism a staggering blow, and democracy innocently enough took the consequences. The

party system, in any number of countries, was discredited, and in most states it was replaced by authoritarian régimes.

7. Fascism covered two-thirds of Europe. And gradually it came to be realised that Fascism was more of a radical than a conservative economic force.

8. The Rome-Berlin axis, following the seizure of Austria by Hitler, broke down. Complete collaboration by the Fascist powers did not take place.

9. The British and French after the outbreak of war in 1939 came closer together than ever in their history.

10. The great broad mass of middle liberals and democrats were almost everywhere perplexed by the painful necessity to turn sharply to either right or left. The good old comfortable middle ground was disappearing.

11. Left groups, despite immense obstacles, sought to unite; in the Saar, underground in Austria, in Spain, in France, a United Left Front was organised against reaction. In almost all countries some sort of movement towards the *Front Populaire* idea began.

12. Czechoslovakia, Poland, and Albania disappeared. Finland was attacked, and the three Baltic states came under Russian domination. Everywhere, the small border states shivered.

13. In almost all responsible circles, the idea of a federation of Europe of some kind, a United States of Europe if possible, came to be a dominant preoccupation.

. . . .

And now let us turn to that other and more powerful and perhaps sinister and grasping League of Nations—the Soviet Union.

CHAPTER XXXVII

STALIN

'The art of leadership is a serious matter. One must not lag behind a movement, because to do so is to become isolated from the masses. But one must not rush ahead, for to rush ahead is to lose contact with the masses. He who wishes to lead a movement must conduct a fight on two fronts—against those who lag behind and those who rush ahead.'

—JOSEF STALIN.

'No revolution can be made with silk gloves.'

—JOSEF STALIN.

STALIN is probably the most powerful single human being in the world. Even dialectical materialism demands personality to assert itself, as the case of Stalin proves. He is different from other dictators because he is not only the undisputed leader of a national state but of a movement, the Communist International, which has roots in almost all countries. Also he differs from Hitler and Mussolini in that he is of the second generation of dictators, having taken over authority from a predecessor, Lenin.

He was not appointed by Lenin to the job. Indeed quite the contrary. Stalin was the man whom Lenin did *not* want to be his successor. Lenin was quite explicit on this point. Listen:

'Comrade Stalin is too rude. . . . I propose to the comrades to find a way of removing him from that position (secretary-general of the party) and appointing another man who in all respects differs from Stalin only in superiority—namely, more patient, more loyal, more polite, and more attentive to comrades, less capricious, etc. . . .'

This was in 1924. Fifteen years later Stalin was extolled by his subordinates in terms much more extravagant than those which Lenin himself evoked. In the Soviet Press you may find him fulsomely called 'Great', 'Beloved', 'Bold', 'Wise', 'Inspirer', 'Genius'. Half a dozen cities have been named for him, like Stalingrad, Stalinabad, Stalinogorsk, Stalinsk. In speeches he had been addressed by ordinarily uneffusive folk as, 'Our Best Collective Farmer Worker', 'Our Shock-worker, Our Best of Best', and 'Our Darling, Our Guiding Star'. Celebrations have concluded with the words, 'Long Live Our Dear Leader, Our Warmly Beloved Stalin, Our Comrade, Our Friend.' He has become practically an Oriental deity.

Sources of Power

First, one may mention his durability and physique. He suffers from a dilated heart, but otherwise his physical strength and endurance are enormous. He is no high-strung neurotic or somnambulist like Hitler, nor is his command of physical power closely associated with emotion, as is the case with other dictators. Stalin is about as emotional as a slab of basalt. If he has nerves, they are veins in rock.

Then consider his patience, his tenacity. His perseverance, as Walter Duranty says, is 'inhuman'. He is a slow builder of bricks, so slow that often his followers are impatient, because they do not see the outline of the finished structure he is building. His line is undeviating; he takes only 'the long view'.

Again, his shrewdness—cunning or craft are perhaps better words to express this quality—is obvious. He is, of course, an Oriental; moreover he admits it. 'Welcome,' he said to the first interviewer, a Japanese, whom he ever received, 'I too am an Asiatic.' Years ago he sought to suppress Lenin's testament denigrating him. He had not quite the power to do this. But presently the U.S.S.R. was flooded with five hundred thousand copies of a photograph showing Stalin and Lenin sitting on a bench together, conversing with earnest friendliness. Stalin's double campaign, first to rid himself of the left opposition of Trotsky, Zinoviev, and Kamenev, second the right opposition of Bukharin, Rykov, and Tomsky, was a triumph not only of extreme ruthlessness, but of great imaginative shrewdness and subtlety.

When candour suits his purpose, no man can be more candid. He has the courage to admit his errors, something few other dictators dare do. In his article 'Dizzy from Success' he was quite frank to admit that the collectivisation of the peasants had progressed too quickly. He wrote in *Leninism*:

> 'The main thing in this matter is to have the courage to admit one's errors and to have the strength to correct them in the shortest possible time. The fear of admitting one's errors after the recent intoxication by successes, the fear of self-criticism, unwillingness to correct one's errors rapidly and decisively—that is the main difficulty.'

This book, *Leninism*, is one of the frankest—if long-winded—

expositions of political philosophy ever written. In its eight hundred and twenty-five pages you may find record of things good, bad, and indifferent in the Soviet Union in illimitable profusion. Stalin emphasises the good, naturally, but he does not conceal the bad. The book has sold over two million copies in the Soviet Union.[1]

Again, there is his sense of detail, which is very great. His wary eye penetrates to the smallest elements in the national life, and in general he tends to detail in a way neither Hitler nor Mussolini would dream of doing. Hitler, for instance, refuses to read even glowing samples of his mail. Stalin reads everything, down to the last paragraph in the *Pravda*. His day begins with perusal of local reports, carefully sifted from all parts of the Soviet Union. W. H. Chamberlin (cf. *Russia's Iron Age*, p. 187), certainly no friendly critic, notes that Stalin, by personal intervention, remedied injustices in spheres far removed from his normal business.

In the summer of 1933 Stalin wanted to see the building of Magnitogorsk, the industrial city created in Siberia during the Five-Year Plan, dramatised and made colourful in the newspapers. He remembered a bright feature-reporter on the *Izvestia* named Garry and asked what had become of him. He was found in a concentration camp! Stalin had him released, sent him to write about Magnitogorsk.

During the February 1934 congress of the communist party Stalin was listening to a speech by his first assistant, Kaganovitch. He was talking about certain text-books which had been unsatisfactory. Stalin interrupted, 'Not those text-books, but the loose-leaf text-books.'

Still again one must mention his ability to handle men. He is a good political tactician, a party boss and organiser *par excellence*. Friends told me in Moscow in 1935 that Stalin possessed great magnetism, that you felt his antennae as soon as he entered a room. His personal as well as political intuition is very considerable. Plenty of communists would deny that he had any sense of human relationship—to put it mildly!—but he chooses men with great perspicacity.

He is no orator. His speeches are simple and businesslike but very long. His writing, when he tackles the dreary wastes of Marxist dialectics, particularly when he voices the ideological differences

[1] The complete works of Lenin, incidentally, in twenty-seven volumes, have sold four million *sets* in the U.S.S.R. since publication.

with the opposition, is dull and tedious; he sounds like an applicant for a Ph.D. in a minor university. When, as in his recent address to graduates of the Red Army college, he avoids philosophical issues, he is much more successful—direct, simple, full of sense of the concrete. Generally, he likes the question and answer method of exposition. His speeches are like catechisms. And in style he aims to hit the broad level of the masses.

His intelligence is wary, cautious, thorough, rather than acute or brilliant. Yet witness his talk with H. G. Wells, wherein he more than held his own, with that glib and eloquent interlocutor. And witness his remarkable interview in 1927 with an American workmen's delegation, when he answered questions for four solid hours, questions of great diversity and difficulty. He talked strictly extemporaneously, but with a perfect organisation of material, of a kind only possible to a man completely sure of himself. The verbatim report, about 11,800 words, comprises one of the most comprehensive and discerning statements of Soviet aims ever made; it was a *tour de force* quite beyond the capacity of any but an exceptionally intelligent man.

When the delegation, thoroughly exhausted, had concluded its queries, Stalin asked if *he* might ask questions about America—and he did so for two hours more. His questions were penetrating and showed considerable knowledge of American conditions; Stalin, single-handed, answered the delegation's questions much better than they replied to him. During this six solid hours of talk, the telephone did not ring once; no secretary was allowed to interrupt—another indication of Stalin's habit of utter concentration to the job in hand.

Another source of his power is, of course, zeal. Communism is strength to Stalin, and his belief in it is that of the Pope in Jesus Christ.

Again, there is the very important factor of ruthlessness. He is extravagantly ruthless. It is stupid or silly to deny this. The Russian terror was a wholesale punitive assault on a class. Soviet Russia differed from other dictatorships in that it assumed from the beginning the necessity of destruction of class enemies. Stalin did not, at the moment of crisis, flinch from obliterating several million peasants by literally starving them to death. All governments, in the last analysis, rule by force. In Soviet Russia force is applied directly, and with social aims in view which are intended—by the communists—to benefit not only one hundred and sixty-five million Russians, but the whole human race. The end justifies the means, in the Soviet view. Stalin is perfectly frank about this. Lady Astor asked him, 'How long are you going to go on killing people?' Stalin replied, 'As long as it is necessary.'

A Soviet worthy, absent from the U.S.S.R., was asked his opinion of Stalin. He replied, 'The man is just a little too bloody for me.' Rare burst of indiscretion!

Still another source of his power is his early career. Almost alone, Stalin[1] had the courage to stay and work inside Russia after the collapse of the revolution of 1905. The other revolutionaries scattered into exile, and lived, like Lenin, in libraries or coffee-houses till 1917. Stalin remained within Russia the whole time. He did the dirty work; he was 'the hall sweeper'. Thus he built up an immense acquaintance with submerged revolutionaries, and was able to transform an underground organisation into his own party structure when he needed it.

Then there is the party and his control of it. The communist party is no longer divided on questions of principle, as it was during the Trotsky episode; no discernible opposition remains; Stalin is absolutely its boss, its master. Discipline in the party is overwhelmingly severe; and Stalin controls discipline. Party and state are one, and Stalin, as Louis Fischer puts it, 'controls every wheel and screw of the party machine.'

Note well that Stalin created the importance of the post of party secretary, not vice versa. Several men were secretaries of the party before Stalin. One was Bogdanoff, now a nonentity; one was Krestinsky, later an official in the foreign ministry, who was recently executed. Stalin alone saw the advantages to be accrued from control of the party mechanism; thus, as he packed each office with his men, friends from underground days, his power grew.

Naturally Stalin's espionage within the party was—and is—of the best. The story is told that he turned to a comrade suffering from a disease of a peculiarly private and secret nature. 'Well,' Stalin greeted him, 'How's your ——— to-day?'

He is not a dictator of the first generation, I have noted, but the successor to Lenin. His tactics have always been to use Lenin as a stick to beat opponents with. In his long struggle with Trotsky, Stalin pretended never to put himself forward for his own sake, but only as the 'instrument of Lenin'; he persistently accused Trotsky

[1] cf. *Duranty Reports Russia*, p. 234.

2 M

of 'false Leninism', the most heinous sin in Russia, thus doubly confounding him. No man ever quoted scripture to better purpose than Stalin quoted Lenin. Mussolini and Hitler can plead only themselves for justification; Stalin always had the mighty shadow of Lenin for support.

This leads to another point. The basic strength of the Soviets is that all the outside world is the enemy. Thus the Soviet State, thrown back on itself, is close-knit and self-sufficient. It has its cohesive ideology, the Marx-Lenin dogma, without possibility of deviation. Stalin, representing himself as the authentic voice of dogma, is the mouthpiece not merely of the masses in Russia, but of Russians vis-à-vis the hostile world.

Job

Stalin holds no government post, except that since 1934 he has been one of the thirty-seven members of the Presidium of the All-Union Central Executive Committee. This is the keystone of what might be called the Soviet Parliament. The cabinet (council of people's commissars) is responsible to it—theoretically. But Stalin is not a cabinet member, not a commissar.

He is no longer 'secretary general' of the communist party incidentally—as is generally assumed—but is merely one of five theoretically equal party 'secretaries'; the others being Kaganovitch, Zhdanov, Ezhov, and Andreyev. He is, it goes without saying, one of the nine members of the Politburo, the highest party organ, which controls everything in Russia.

The Central Committee of the party, from which the secretaries and members of the Politburo are drawn, could—in principle—dismiss Stalin. He is theoretically subject to majority decisions of the Central Committee. In practice his dismissal is out of the question, since election of the committee members is absolutely in his hands.

Party and state in Soviet Russia are, I have said, one; but Stalin maintains rigid theoretical separation between party and governmental functions. Lenin was not only head of the party, but chairman of the council of people's commissars—prime minister. Stalin has rejected this coalescence. He prefers to remain in the background—the party boss.

Boy of Tiflis

His real name is Yosif (Josef) Visarionovitch Dzhugashvili, and he was born in the town of Gora, near Tiflis, Georgia, in 1879. The legend is that Lenin gave him his nickname, Stalin, which is the Russian word for 'steel', as tribute to his iron durability. In reality some anonymous comrade suggested it as an 'underground' name way back in 1910 or 1911, long before Lenin knew him well.

Stalin was the son of a cobbler who had been a peasant. The family was miserably poor, probably as poor as Mussolini's, but Josef nevertheless got an education. For four years, from the ages of 15 to 19, he attended the Orthodox Theological Seminary in Tiflis training, of all things, for the priesthood.

His father, like Hitler's, of blunt imagination, wanted him to follow the parental vocation. But Stalin's mother—apparently like Hitler's an exceptional woman—refused to have him become a cobbler. She insisted that Josef go to school. It is commonly thought that Stalin was expelled from the Seminary for Marxist activities. This may not be so. One story is that his mother withdrew him after four years because privation had hurt his health.

H. R. Knickerbocker has interviewed this old Georgian mother of Stalin's, Ekaterina Dzhugashvili, who speaks hardly a word of Russian. She said that 'Soso', as she called him, had been quite 'a good boy' and she seemed quite bewildered at his immense success. Stalin fetched her to Moscow some years ago. She spent an unhappy month in the Kremlin, puzzled, so the story went, at her boy's prominence, because she could not discover what it was he 'did' to earn a living! Then she retreated to the Tiflis hills, morose, content.

Georgians are not Russians. Even to-day Stalin speaks Russian with a hint of Georgian accent. The Georgian language not only differs from Russian as much, say, as English differs from Portuguese; even the alphabets are dissimilar. The Georgians are a southern race of complex Caucasian blood; they are mountaineers, with the primitive defensive instincts of the frontiersman; tenacity, temper, are ingrained in their physiognomy; like Armenians they have their own proud national history; they have purple-black hair, and eyes black as midnight.

Stalin's motivation to revolution came first from poverty, second from his experiences in the Seminary. He detested authority as it was voiced by the cunning, dogmatic priests, who combined parochial intolerance with the backwardness of the provincial

Orthodox Church. The years in the Seminary were crucially important in the formative period of Stalin's life. He left the Seminary, met Marxist friends—and his long revolutionary career began.

Those submerged nineteen years, from 1898 to 1917, were years of incessant, overwhelming labour, always to the same end—revolution; of patient, tenacious establishment of an organisation; of pain, cruelty, persecution, arrest. Both Hitler and Mussolini have seen the inside of jails. But Stalin was much more real a jailbird. Five times he was caught by the Czar's police, five times exiled. Four times, a veritable Houdini, he escaped; the 1917 revolution liberated him from the fifth imprisonment, when he was incarcerated above the Arctic circle.

Stalin was an actual terrorist, personally. The party needed money and undertook a policy of 'expropriations', raids on banks which were pure robberies, nothing more, nothing less. As member of the Tiflis party committee he was partly responsible for an outrage in 1907 wherein some twenty persons were killed: his men bombed a shipment of currency, got away with £15,000. The bloodshed was criticised by Stalin's superiors, and on Lenin's insistence he was expelled from the party for a short period.

He found time—between jail sentences and exile—for much activity of less tumultuous nature. At Baku, on the Caspian Sea, he edited a Bolshevik paper, *Vremia*, in the Georgian language. He went to Stockholm, Cracow, and Prague, to attend party congresses. He had managed to write a book, *Socialism and the National Question*, as early as 1912. He was leader at this time of the Bolshevik section of the social democratic party in the Duma, and an editor of *Pravda*, the party newspaper; then in 1913 he was arrested and sent to his last exile.

All this was preparation. In 1917 real life began. The revolution, overnight, transformed his function—and that of thousands of others—from conspiracy to organisation, from insurrection to administration. He was a member of the Politburo from the moment of its creation, on October 10, 1917; other members, besides Lenin, were Trotsky, Zinoviev, Kamenev, Sokolnikov, Bubnov. Also he held two cabinet portfolios when the government was organised: commissar for workers and peasants inspection, and commissar for nationalities.

He was not as active as Trotsky during the civil war period, though he was a member of the revolutionary military committee, and saw service both in the Ukraine and in Petrograd against Yudenitch. In 1921 Lenin, little dreaming what use Stalin would make of it, gave him the secretary-generalship of the party. His main work was then in the sphere of nationalities. As a non-Russian, he was peculiarly fitted for this task. Soviet Russia was a *mélange* of at least one hundred quite separate races and nationalities, and the job was to combine them into a stable unity while conceding some measure of provincial autonomy, at least in spirit. Stalin, under Lenin, invented the idea of the U.S.S.R.— the convenient device by which 'independent' and 'autonomous' republics became the Soviet 'Union', surrendering central authority to Moscow, retaining local administrative privileges.

Stalin was jealous of Trotsky from the beginning, and they came into conflict early. Duranty records that Stalin, mending a breach in the front, shot a group of officers for inefficiency, and that Trotsky, as supreme War Lord, telegraphed in protest. Stalin scrawled across the telegram, 'Pay no attention,' and left it to moulder in the archives.

Another anecdote of this period shows him in different mood. He was reviewing troops near Petrograd. A sullen soldier refused to salute. Stalin questioned him and the man pointed first to his own feet, wrapped in coarse burlap, soaked in snow and dirt, then at Stalin's substantial boots. Without a word Stalin took his boots off, tossed them to the soldier, insisted on donning the soldier's wet and stinking rags—and continued to wear them till Lenin himself made him resume normal footgear.

Stalin, says Duranty, was picked by Lenin as one of his successors because he knew the Georgian could *endure*. The proverb in those days said, 'Lenin trusts Stalin; Stalin trusts no one.' Some authorities, Paul Scheffer among them, assert that Lenin and Stalin broke about four months before Lenin's death, because Lenin distrusted his ambition, and thought that Stalin was already intriguing to supersede him. Certainly we have seen that Lenin, in his testament, showed his disapproval of some aspects of Stalin's character. 'This cook,' he wrote, 'will make too hot a stew.'

The Georgian began to act the moment that Lenin died. He and Zinoviev carried Lenin's coffin. This was in 1924. It took Stalin just five years to perfect his organisation, unmercifully weed out heretical opponents—whom he attacked by accusing them of deviation from the sacred 'party line', which he alone was competent to interpret—and establish himself as undisputed dictator of the U.S.S.R.

The Struggle with Trotsky

Stalin denies (cf. *Leninism*, I, p. 377) that his differences with Trotsky were personal. Nevertheless personal differences occurred. The two leaders cordially disliked each other. They came from different worlds, and not even the bridge of Marx could link them. Stalin called Trotsky an aristocrat and an actor. And Trotsky *was* an aristocrat, in all save the social sense, i.e., he had brains, he had courage, and he had style. Trotsky called Stalin a boor, treacherous, barbarous, cruel, corrupt.

It is an odd fact that such a *bourgeois* and 'trivial' conception as personal hatred, based on the irrationality of passion, should have been an important factor in the history of the Russian revolution. But it was so—though, of course, the personal considerations were buttressed by other factors. Trotsky detested Stalin so heartily that he studiously insulted him in public; for instance, in committee meetings he would ostentatiously pick up a newspaper and begin to read to himself whenever Stalin made a speech.

The difference in their characters was, of course, profound. Stalin, a passionate politician, above all a creature of committees; Trotsky, a lone-wolf, a violent individualist, who for twenty years could not bear to shackle himself with allegiance to either the Bolshevik or Menshevik divisions in the party. Stalin, patient as an icon; Trotsky, vivacious as a satyr. Stalin, immobile, silent, cautious; Trotsky, a lively, frank, and inveterate conversationalist, Stalin a bomb-thrower, literally; Trotsky horrified by sporadic violence. Stalin, a hard-headed practical wirepuller, unyieldingly jealous of his career; Trotsky, lover of the abstract, impulsive, vain. Stalin, a supreme organiser; Trotsky, a bad politician, incapable of compromise, very hard to work with. Observe their smiles. Stalin smiles like a tiger who has just swallowed the canary. Trotsky smiles brightly and spontaneously like a child. Observe their escapes from Siberia. Stalin went about it sombrely, efficiently, with methodical coldness; Trotsky—puff!—has disappeared into clear air; he escapes like Ariel.

Above and beyond their personal conflict was divergence in political views of extreme importance. The passion of each came to embody cardinally opposed theories of the operation of the Soviet Union. Trotsky's 'Left Opposition' arose out of the doctrine of 'permanent revolution'. He did not believe, as Stalin did, that socialism could succeed in a single state. He believed that the Marxist régime could maintain itself in Russia only if permanent, progressive revolution took place outside.

The Trotskyists were horrified at the way things went after Lenin's death. They thought that the socialisation of the U.S.S.R. was going on far too slowly. They feared that Lenin's tactical and temporary concession to capitalist forces, the N.E.P. (New Economic Policy) would continue indefinitely; they thought that communism in Russia itself, with such meagre spoils of victory, would perish without help from proletarian revolution in the external world.

Stalin took the opposite view. He said, in effect, 'You comrades outside cool your heels for a couple of decades, then we'll get around to you.' Trotsky said, 'Join your Russian comrades in revolution and free yourself from your chains at once.' Stalin said, 'Russia first. When we get our state in order, then comes your turn.' Trotsky said, 'Whatever country you live in comes first.' Russia, as Stalin saw it, was settling down to the prosaic ardours of married life. But Trotsky, an incorrigible romantic, wanted permanent revolution as a perpetual honeymoon.

Stalin broke Trotsky and his friends by the same method he subsequently employed to break the 'Right Opposition' (which thought that the socialisation of Russia was going at too *rapid* a pace). He (1) controlled the party machine, (2) his interpretation of Leninism made all his opponents heretics, and therefore punishable.

Stalin's detestation of Trotsky led him to exaggerated meanness in revenge. Yet his extirpation of Trotsky's name from the official records and school-books, so that unborn generations may hardly know his name, is not as complete as one is led to believe. In his *October Revolution*, which is purchasable anywhere in Russia, Stalin pays tribute, albeit grudgingly, to his enemy. 'Let us admit this, it is impossible to deny that Comrade Trotsky fought well at the time of October' (p. 72).

Stalin hated Trotsky partly, in the complicated way of human beings, because he, Stalin, owed him so much: he stole part of his programme. Trotsky advocated super-industrialisation in the manner of the Five-Year Plan as far back as 1921, and he wanted to expel the kulaks (rich farmers) in 1925, a task which Stalin did not set himself till almost five years later. But that was the trouble.

Trotsky, impulsive, demanded these things prematurely, at the wrong time; Stalin had the strength to wait.

And Trotsky never seemed to realise that when Stalin said he could build socialism in a single country, the country was Russia, which is not a country at all—but a continent. Nor did it occur to Trotsky apparently that far and away the best single advertisement for world communism, in the future, would be a Russia which was successful, stable, safe.

The Iron Will of Stalin

Of course there was a famine. None can deny this any longer. It occurred in the spring of 1933, in the great grain-producing areas of the U.S.S.R., the North Caucasus and Ukraine. Communists, after preliminary hesitancy, now admit the fact of the famine, though in circumlocutory jargon. For instance, Miss Anna Louise Strong writes (*New Republic*, August 7, 1935), 'There was a serious grain shortage in the 1932 harvest due chiefly to inefficiencies of the organisational period of the new large-scale mechanised farming among peasants unaccustomed to machines.' This is quite a mouthful—a mouthful that the peasants didn't get.

The chief point about the famine is not—it might be said—that several million people died. Chamberlin puts the mortality as high as five or six millions. This is too high, other authorities believe. The point is that the Soviet Government was engaged in a tremendous, epochal struggle to socialise the land, for what they claimed to be the eventual good of the peasants; the peasants, however, resisted and—terribly enough—suffered. To balk the government, they refused to harvest grain. Therefore they did not have enough to eat. And died.

The real story of the famine is briefly this. The Five-Year Plan included 'collectivisation' of the peasantry. Russia, overwhelmingly an agrarian country, contained in 1927 almost twenty-five million peasant holdings; Stalin's plan was to unite them into socialised collective farms. The peasants would turn over implements and livestock to a farm manager, and work in common on comparatively large rather than very small holdings, assisted by tractors furnished by the state. This was the idea. On it, the future of socialism in the U.S.S.R. depended.

What happened was that the peasants, bitterly indignant, staged two major resistances to the immense forcible process of collectivisation. First, they slaughtered their livestock, rather than turn it over to the collectives. It was an extraordinary and tragic event—though not so tragic as the human starvation later. There was no organisation among the peasants, no communication; yet in hundreds of villages, separated by hundreds of miles, a *simultaneous* destruction of animals began. Rather than turn over their precious pigs, sheep, cattle, to the collective authorities, the peasants murdered them.

The cost was terrible. Stalin—four years late—admitted it. The agrarian economy of the Soviet Union suffered a blow from which it cannot fully recover till about 1940; it will take till then to replenish the slaughtered stock. For, once the killing began, it progressed till about *fifty per cent* of the animals in the Soviet Union were killed. Official figures admit that the number of horses in the country diminished from 33,500,000 in 1928 to 19,600,000 in 1932; the number of cattle from 70,500,000 to 40,700,000; sheep and goats from 146,700,000 to 52,100,000; pigs from 25,900,000 to 11,600,000.[1]

The peasants, stunned by this catastrophe, sank into temporary stupor. The government—when the worst of the damage was done—retreated hastily. Probably Stalin had not realised the formidable extent of the slaughter until it was too late. . . . The tempo of collectivisation had been far too rapid. The plan called for full collectivisation only after ten years, but within two years, in 1930, sixty-five per cent of all the farms had been collectivised. So the pace was toned down.

Even so, in 1932, the peasants, stiffening into a final vain protest, rebelled again. As if by underground agreement, another psychic epidemic spread through the rich fields of the Caucasus and Ukraine. The farmers, those still outside the collectives, were paid miserable prices; either they could buy no manufactured goods at all, or goods only of indifferent quality. They hit on a plan. They had sowed the crop, which was abundant; but they decided not to harvest all of it. They harvested exactly what they calculated they would themselves need during the winter, and left the rest to rot. 'What was the use of slaving to produce a handsome crop, if the state simply seized it all?'

This was, of course, mutiny. It was not only defiance of Stalin; it was a threat to starve him into submission. The Soviet

[1] Premier Molotov's speech at the 1934 party congress. (cf. *Socialism Victorious*, p. 394).

Government needed the grain to distribute to the industrial regions, the great cities; it needed grain for export, to pay for the machinery it had to import for the Five-Year Plan.

Even the farmers already in the collectives let their grain rot. There were few communist overseers, few trained and loyal farm managers. Word got to Moscow that the harvest, which should have been handsome, was largely lost. Stalin saw that this was a major crisis. If the peasants were permitted to get away with this, the revolution was beaten. ('Obsolete classes don't voluntarily disappear,' he told Wells.) He had to act. And he acted.

Government grain collectors descended on the farms, tall with weeds, and seized that small share of the crop that the peasants had saved *for their own use!* One by one, they visited every holding, and took every bit of grain due the government in taxes. If a man's normal crop was, say, sixty bushels, the tax might be twenty bushels. So when the government took twenty, the farmer and his family had only five—instead of twenty-five—to live on the whole winter and spring.

Russian economy is still extremely primitive. The question of grain, of bread, is a matter of life and death. When there was no grain left, the people began to die. The government might have diverted some grain from the cities—though that was a pinched, hungry year everywhere—to feed the peasants. But the government did not do so. Stalin decided that the peasants must pay the penalty for their rebellion. They had refused, blindly, stupidly, to provide grain; very well, let them starve. And they starved.

Meantime, the kulaks had been liquidated by a more direct process. These were peasants of more than average industry or ability or wealth; the capitalist farmers, 'class enemies on the agrarian front'. In 1928 there were seven hundred and fifty thousand people officially classed as kulaks in the Soviet Union. To-day there are none. They were rooted out like trees, packed into prison trains, dispatched to labour camps in far parts of the country, put to forced labour on building railways, digging canals.

The famine broke the back of peasant resistance in the U.S.S.R. Since the famine collectivisation has proceeded slowly but steadily. From 1930 to 1935 another twenty-five per cent of the land was socialised. All but a small fraction of the best arable land in Russia is now organised into about two hundred and fifty thousand farms. The peasants tried to revolt. The revolt might have brought the

Soviet Union down. But it collapsed on the iron will of Stalin. The peasants killed their animals, then they killed themselves.

Stalin the Human Being

Let no one think that Stalin is a thug. It would be idle to pretend that he could take a chair in fine arts at Harvard; nevertheless his learning is both broad and deep, especially in philosophy and history. One is instinctively tempted to consider this reticent Georgian as a roughneck, a man of instincts and muscle, not of brains. But his speeches quote Plato and Don Quixote; he knew about the monkey trial at Dayton and the composition of Lloyd George's shadow-cabinet and the unionisation of workers in America; in his talk with Wells he showed as much knowledge of Cromwell and the Chartists as Wells himself.

In 1933 he shocked and horrified a deputation of Bolshevik writers by telling them their work was rubbish, because it had no broad basis in general culture. 'Read Shakespeare, Goethe, and the other classics, as I do,' he said.

Nor are his manners bad. He sees visitors only very rarely, but one and all they report his soberness, his respectful attention to their questions, his attempt to put them at their ease. His speeches are full of a curious sort of sardonic courtliness; for instance he refers to capitalists usually as 'Messieurs the *Bourgeoisie*'.[1] He restrains his personal appearances to the minimum; once, during the crucial period of the Five-Year Plan, he made no speech or public appearance for eighteen months.

He has a sense of humour, though it is heavy to western ears; that he has a sense of humour at all differentiates him from Hitler or Mussolini. Addressing the 1930 congress of the party, he ticked off the Right Opposition of Bukharin and Rykov by asserting that if Bukharin saw a cockroach he proceeded at once to smell catastrophe, foreseeing the end of the Soviet Union in one month. 'Rykov supported Bukharin's theses on the subject,' said Stalin, 'with the reservation, however, that he had a very serious difference with Bukharin, namely that the Soviet Government will perish in his opinion, not in one month, but in one month and two days.'

At the 1934 congress he took time out to deal with those who indulge in the great Russian habit of talkativeness:

[1] Incidentally, an odd point, he sometimes speaks of himself in the third person. cf. *Leninism*, I. 300, and II. 225.

I had a conversation with one such comrade, a very respected comrade, but an incorrigible chatterbox, who was capable of submerging any living cause in a flood of talk.   Well, here is the conversation:

I: How are you getting on with the sowing?
He: With the sowing, Comrade Stalin? We have mobilised ourselves.
I: Well, and what then?
He: We have put the question bluntly.
I: And what next?
He: There is a turn, Comrade Stalin; soon there will be a turn.
I: But still?
He: We can observe some progress.
I: But for all that, how are you getting on with the sowing?
He: Nothing has come of the sowing as yet, Comrade Stalin.

Stalin makes occasional pretences to humility. When Wells asked him what he was doing to change the world, he answered mildly, 'Not so very much.'   And he concluded the interview by saying, 'Much more could have been done had we Bolsheviks been cleverer.'[1]

Stalin, has, however, permitted and encouraged his own virtual deification. Pictures of him share the place of honour everywhere with Lenin. His photograph leaps at one from buildings in Moscow, illuminated at night like theatre advertisements. Worship of him is Byzantine. Obviously he could stop the public expression of adulation very easily. He does not do so. One reason may be his shrewd Orientalism; the flattery, the pictures, are a good political weapon; he knows the Russians understand a master. Or perhaps he likes them.

The blackest thing against Stalin—until the invasion of Finland —was of course the great purge that began in 1936, and ran like wildfire over the Soviet Union, killing thousands as it went.

Private Life

Stalin lives, as is well known, in the Kremlin when he is in Moscow. The Kremlin is not a building, but a compound, a walled fortress, containing forty or fifty buildings, churches, barracks, gardens. Stalin lives in three rooms. He does not, however, as is generally believed, *work* in the Kremlin. The legend that Stalin, a virtual prisoner, stays always within Kremlin walls, is without

[1] Duranty says that Stalin made him change a phrase in their interview 'inheritor of the mangle of Lenin', to 'faithful servant of Lenin'. A dictator Stalin certainly is, but not a flaming egoist.

much foundation. For a long time he worked daily outside the Kremlin, in the building of the central committee of the party, on Staraya Ploshad, in the busiest part of Moscow.

Also he spends much time in the country, at his *datcha*, or country villa. This is about an hour from Moscow, in the region of Usova-Arkangelskaya, near the Moskva river. The house belonged to a former millionaire, a gold miner and merchant, who had a persecution complex, and therefore surrounded the ten-acre estate with a heavy wall. Stalin has a good, healthy persecution complex himself. He has not torn down the wall.

The region of the *datcha* is, indeed, heavily guarded, and so is the Moscow road leading to it. Stalin usually drives there in three cars, Packards, going very fast; he sits as a rule with the chauffeur, and the position of his car in the procession is changed daily. Picknickers and sightseers in the vicinity are told politely to move on.

Yet Stalin is not, on the whole, so drastically guarded as Hitler or Mussolini. He exposes himself a good deal more than they do. He has several times been seen returning to the Kremlin from the Opera on foot, walking with friends through the crowded square. And at least twice a year, on May 1 and November 7, the two great Soviet holidays, Stalin stands on the tomb of Lenin and literally several million people pass him at a range of about thirty yards.

He cares nothing for pomp or ceremony. He does not wear a uniform, but a dark olive-green jacket buttoned at the neck, riding-breeches, and boots. When he goes out, he wears a cap with a visor. Not an official uniform, this costume has nevertheless been widely imitated throughout most of Russia; the high people in the party, all the sycophants and flatterers, have faithfully copied it, and wear it as a proof of devotion to the chief.

Stalin's usual routine is to work hard for about a week or longer, then go to the *datcha* for two or three days to rest. He has few relaxations, but he likes opera and ballet, and attends the Bolshoi Theatre often; sometimes a movie catches his fancy, and he saw *Chapayev*, a film of the civil wars, four times. He reads a great deal, and plays chess occasionally. He smokes incessantly, and always a pipe; the gossip in Moscow is that he likes Edgeworth tobacco, but is a little hesitant to smoke publicly this non-Soviet product. At dinner he keeps his pipe lit next to his plate, puffs between courses. He is fond of alcohol, especially brandy, and holds his liquor well.

His attitude to sex is quite normal and healthy. He has married twice. He is rather naïve, apparently. One evening, dropping in to see his friend Karl Radek, he noted on the table a German pseudo-scientific picture-book cloaking pornography as science. Stalin turned the pages idly, saw one of the more fantastic illustrations. He turned to his friend: 'Tell me, Radek: do people really do this sort of thing?'

Records of his first wife are lost in the mists of pre-revolutionary days. She died of pneumonia in 1917. In those days love was more or less an instrument of the class war; the old Bolsheviks paid little attention to the forms of marriage. By this first wife, Stalin had a son, now about twenty-nine. He has not turned out too well. He did badly at technical school—the rumour has it that he spent most of his time playing billiards with a classmate, the son of Menzhinsky, late head of the G.P.U.—and Stalin, annoyed, packed him off to work in a factory at Tiflis.

In 1919 Stalin dropped in to see an old revolutionary friend in Leningrad, Sergei Alliluiev (the name means Hallelujah), a locksmith. He met his daughter, a seventeen-year-old girl Nadyezhda (Nadya), and married her. By her he had two children, a boy Vassily, now eighteen, and a girl, Svetlana, thirteen. Mrs. Stalin entered the Promakademia, or school for industrial arts, in 1929, studying the manufacture of artificial silk. There was no publicity attached to this; she worked like anyone else, and even battled her way into the ordinary street-cars, instead of using a Kremlin Packard. Her ambition was to become head of the rayon trust.

On November 8, 1932, in sudden and seemingly mysterious circumstances, Nadyezhda Alliluiev Stalin died suddenly. She had been seen, apparently in normal health, at the Opera only a few days before. The news of her death was announced without elaboration, and she was buried (not, curiously enough, cremated) in the churchyard of the Convent of New Virgins.

Reports were quick to spread that she tasted all food prepared for Stalin and had been poisoned. But the facts seem to be that she had been having acute intestinal pains for several days, and had neglected them. She did not wish to trouble her husband with what she thought was a minor ailment. Probably she was somewhat afraid of him. . . . She sought to hide her pain, to keep the tough spirit of the Bolsheviks. The ailment was appendicitis, and by the time she admitted she was ill, it was too late, and she died of peritonitis.

Stalin's relation to his younger children is quite paternal, but he has taken pains that in school they are treated exactly as other children. He has never visited the school, which is one of three model schools in Russia; it is called School No. 25, and is on Pimenovsky Street, just off Tverskaya. The boy had seven fairs, five goods, on his last report-card; no very goods or excellents. His best subject was literature.

Money, Attitudes, Friends

Stalin's salary is about 1,000 roubles per month, the equivalent of which, in Russia in 1939, was about £40. He is completely uninterested in money. Like all the Soviet leaders he is a poor man, no breath of financial scandal has ever touched any of them. Salaries of communists are adjusted by category, this system having replaced the former rule whereby no man in the party could earn more than 225 roubles per month. There is no upward limit; the average is 600. No communist may accept a salary for more than one post, no matter how many he holds; and no member of the party is allowed in theory at least to retain royalties from books.

On the other hand, Stalin could, like the Czars, eat off gold plate if he so wished. There is no wealth in all of Russia that he could not have, if he wanted it. He lives modestly, but his *datcha* is the Soviet equivalent of the country home of an American millionaire. He has servants, motor-cars, books.

His attitude towards conventional religion is purely negative. His religion, like that of all the dictators, is his work; communism is enough faith for him. Stalin has said, 'The party cannot be neutral towards religion, because religion is something opposite to science.' Nevertheless, it is noteworthy that he permitted his wife an almost orthodox religious burial. He is the only dictator who may be said thoroughly to have read the Bible; he did so, of course, in his seminary days.

He has few friends. Voroshilov, Kaganovitch, and Zhdanov are the three closest. He is on thee-and-thou footing with old colleagues in the party, but it is hard to address him intimately because there is no ordinary diminutive for Yosif, his Christian name. People who know him well call him 'Yosif Visarionovitch'; others simply say *Tovarish* (Comrade) Stalin. He has no title.

He seldom sees outsiders. William C. Bullitt, the American Ambassador, dined with him once. Until Bullitt arrived in Moscow, Stalin had never received a foreign diplomat; even Lord

Chilston, the then British Ambassador, had not met him until Anthony Eden's visit in the spring of 1935. Retiring, uncommunicative, in twenty years he has seen only seven journalists—two Germans, two Japanese, three Americans—for formal interviews.

He 'received' Bullitt in typical and indirect fashion. Voroshilov had arranged a dinner-party, and Stalin simply dropped in. He was cheery and cordial, toasted everybody around the table, talked with great intelligence and knowledge of America, and relaxed, smoking his pipe, while the commissars sat at piano, singing songs almost like brothers in a fraternity.

Lately Stalin has given evidence that he may come out of his shell. He visited the new subway unannounced; he spoke over the radio recently for the first time; he has even kissed babies—final concession to popularity—in the Culture Park. When he received Eden, Laval, and Beneš in the spring and summer of 1935, he jointly signed the communiqués with Molotov, which was unprecedented.

Also, Stalin has taken a new tack lately, as the champion of men as men—even non-party men—provided they follow *his* line. In May 1935, he denounced the 'heartless bureaucracy' and said that 'first of all we must learn to value *people*, to value cadres, to value every worker capable of benefiting our common cause. It is time to realise that of all the valuable capital the world possesses, the most value and decisive is people.'

As a symbol of the former contempt for men, which he deplored, though his purges were to decimate the party, Stalin told this little story:

> 'I recall an incident in Siberia, where I was at one time in exile. It was in the spring, at the time of the spring floods. About thirty men went to the river to pull out timber which had been carried away by the vast, swollen river. Towards evening they returned to the village, but with one comrade missing. When asked where the thirtieth man was, they unconcernedly replied that the thirtieth man had "remained there". To my question, "How do you mean, remained there?" they replied with the same unconcern, "Why ask—drowned, of course." And thereupon one of them began to hurry away, saying, "I have got to go and water the mare." When I reproached them for having more concern for animals than for men, one of them, amid the general approval of the rest, said, "Why should we be concerned about men? We can always make men. But a mare—just try and make a mare." '

But this concession to humanity came very late, after terrible struggles, terrible sacrifices. If Stalin can relax now and search for human values, well and good. But his historical mission was quite different. Stalin is the man who took over the Russian revolution and made it work. Human values disappeared. He is the creator of the 'iron age', the director of the Five-Year Plan, the man who, by ruthlessly industrialising Russia, made the beginnings of socialism possible in a single state.

CHAPTER XXXVIII

MEN AROUND STALIN

'Among the masses of the people, we (the communists) are but drops in the ocean and we will be able to govern only when we properly express that which the people appreciate. Without this the communist party will not lead the proletariat, the proletariat will not take the lead of the masses, and the whole machine will fall to pieces.'

—LENIN.

'The mills of our revolution grind well.'

—STALIN.

You may not know the names of the men in this chapter, these men around Stalin. They are not morphiniacs, hysterics, thugs, adventurers for personal power, cynics, or neurotic misfits. But Kaganovitch is almost as important to Russia as Goering is to Germany; Molotov, Zhdanov, Voroshilov, are as noteworthy in their way as Goebbels, Himmler, or Hess. They have no genius for personal publicity. Their personalities hardly exist. They are servants of the all-powerful state; they exist only for their jobs, and they do their jobs extremely well.

Many of these men—who rule one-sixth the land surface of the globe—were workmen with their hands, manual labourers, fifteen or twenty years ago. Of the ten present members of the Politburo, four never went to school at all; not one has a university education. This may account, incidentally, for much of the subsidiary confusion in Russian business affairs—the red tape, bureaucracy, lack of technique, lack of facility. Even so, a neutral diplomat in Moscow, in a position to know, told me that he thought the members of the Politburo were personally as able as any governing body in the world.

The lives of most of Stalin's men follow a similar pattern. They were workmen who turned revolutionary, and all but the youngest of them have a history, like Stalin, of underground political activity.

The most important fact in their lives was the date when they entered the communist party; as a rule, their hierarchical position depends on this. Several have been in prison, and their prison sentences are proud badges of distinction.

540

'Their penal servitude is not a stigma,' wrote a well-informed anonymous commentator,[1] 'but a token of their new nobility. They are proud of their criminal record as the emblem of their new aristocracy. Yet the leaders of the Bolshevist régime are "good" men in the most ominous meaning of that word. They are fanatics with a single track mind. . . . The comparison with the early Church militant and the Jesuit order is irresistible. The Bolsheviks are latter-day saints and crusaders, but of a material not a spiritual world, and they are the most thorough-going reformers and moralists in history—in their own way. Some of them drink, some have mistresses, but their morality is of another kind. They are the first autocratic rulers in history who do not use their power for personal profit. They do not graft; those who do get shot. They have no castles, no titles, no purple robes; they live in a couple of rooms on a standard below that of an American bricklayer; they are pledged to personal poverty and service.'

Of course, careerism may become a career in itself; abolish property as a social motive, and a substitute immediately arises— power. And power is dear to all men, even Bolsheviks. Instead of wealth, communists are apt to measure ambition and accomplishment in terms of jobs, influence, power.

From the Central Committee of the party, numbering seventy-seven members and sixty-eight alternates, the Politburo is chosen, its supreme organ. There are nine regular members of the Politburo, two alternates. All are more or less friends; they have a common background, common aims; and they are the central directorate of the Soviet Union. Technically, Stalin has no more voice than other members.

Members of the Politburo put on a sort of show at every congress of the party. They take the stage and hold a public meeting before the audience of party members. Within the iron circumscription of 'the party line', argument, disagreement, discussion may be very lively. Members of the Politburo interrupt each other vigorously; the audience is entitled to heckle, and often does. The analogy would be for a British cabinet meeting to be held in the House of Commons, with backbenchers entitled to join free and vehement discussion.

The Politburo is not, however, the cabinet. A Politburo member may also be a cabinet member. But most cabinet ministers have not reached the dizzy height of Politburo membership.

[1] In *Not to be Repeated*, New York, 1932.

Cabinet ministers are *government* officials; Politburo members are *party* officials, though every Politburo man is a member of the Central Executive Committee of the U.S.S.R. too. Cabinet ministers in the Soviet Union have purely administrative functions, with no voice in the general sphere of political policy and management, unless they happen to be members of the Politburo also.

One Politburo member is Georgian (Stalin); one, Mikoyan, is an Armenian; one Kaganovitch, is a Jew; one alternate member (Beria) is a Georgian; the others are Russians of various breeds. It is frequently alleged that Russia is run by Jews. Nothing could be further from the truth. All the Jews except Kaganovitch (a comparative new-comer) are exiled or dead: Trotsky (whose real name was Bronstein), Zinoviev (Apfelbaum), Kamenev (Rosenfeld), and the old intellectuals of similar stamp. Litvinov is a Jew, but he was never a member of the Politburo.

The Politburo is assembled with great care and skill, so that its members form a sort of interlocking net over Soviet activity. No neater system of ramifying authority has ever been devised. This was part of Stalin's slow, laborious effort to get all the threads in his own hands. Suppose we go through the Politburo man by man, and see how it is 'packed'.

First there is Molotov. He is president of the council of people's commissars, in other words prime minister, and, since Litvinov was ousted, foreign minister also. Thus the functions of the cabinet and foreign office are focused in the Politburo. He is also president of STO, the Council of Labour and Defence, probably the most powerful official government organ in the U.S.S.R.

Next there is Kalinin. He is the president of the central executive committee of the R.S.F.S.R. (Russia proper) and senior president of the central executive committee of the U.S.S.R.—thus the top dignitary of the country, its nominal 'president'. He carries to the Politburo the outward symbol of governmental authority.

Next—my order is arbitrary—is Voroshilov, the minister of war. He brings the Red Army to the Politburo. Then comes Kaganovitch, who has held every sort of job, and who is now commissar for heavy industry, which likewise fits neatly into the Politburo fold. Mikoyan is fuel commissar, as well as being vice prime minister. Andreyev, predominantly a party man (though for a time he was commissar of railways), is, like Stalin, a secretary of the party, and— if necessary!—can bring the machine itself into line. L. P. Beria, an alternate, is the new head of the G.P.U.—the secret police. And a man of great potential importance, Andrey Alexandrovitch Zhdanov, who is nowadays spoken of as Stalin's eventual successor, is a member of the executive committee of the Communist Internationale, the Comintern; this brings the Politburo into external party affairs.

One point about the Politburo is the comparative youth of all the members except Kalinin, who is sixty-four. Kaganovitch is forty-six, Voroshilov fifty-eight, Molotov forty-nine, Andreyev and Mikoyan only forty-three, and Zhdanov only forty-two. The average is well under fifty. It is the youngest group of men of such illimitable power in the world.

White Hope of the Jews

At one time the greatest shortage in the Soviet Union was not of bread, or houses, or newsprint, or textile fabrics—but of railway tickets. A British diplomat I know was stranded in the Crimea and unable to return to Moscow for some days, simply because he could not buy transportation on the trains. The reason was that Lazar Moiseyvitch Kaganovitch had been appointed by Stalin to reform the Soviet railway system, expedite essential shipments of grain and freight. And Kaganovitch did the job with his accustomed thoroughness.

The railways were in such a mess because the rolling stock was antiquated, trackage—over such enormous distances—was insufficient, and the personnel slovenly. In 1934 there were sixty-two thousand 'mishaps', some of them serious wrecks, on the Soviet railway system. Engineers and switchmen convicted of carelessness were shot. This was no remedy—it simply made the survivors nervous and caused more wrecks—and Kaganovitch stopped it. During the great purges in 1936 and 1937, however, shooting began again.

It is quite a habit of Stalin to give Kaganovitch all the hardest jobs. He was appointed head of the Moscow Soviet and also chief of the party organisation in Moscow to clear this most important of Tammany Halls of Trotskyists: his Moscow machine became the strongest in the Soviet Union. He built the Moscow Subway, no mean feat. And it was he who was charged by Stalin with enforcing the grain collections in the tragic autumn of 1932; he took city workers and Red Army men out into the fields, seized every *pood* of wheat the government could claim.

Kaganovitch is black-haired, black-moustached, tall and powerful in physique, somewhat melodramatic in facial features. He is probably the best orator in the Soviet Union, and he inherits something of Trotsky's magnetism. He is the only member of the Politburo the report of whose speeches are punctuated with the remarks 'Laughter', or 'Loud Laughter'. He has, indeed, a considerable gift for pungent comedy. His speech to the last party congress was devoted largely to an attack on faulty management, bureaucracy, inefficiency. He mentioned that the People's Commissariat of Agriculture had twenty-nine boards and two hundred and two sectors. (A voice: 'Oh! Oh!') Kaganovitch went on, 'That's nothing. Each sector manages the whole of the U.S.S.R.' (Laughter.)

He made great play by describing two officials in a rope factory, one named Neoslabny (the word in Russian means 'indefatigable'), the other Prelestnikov (charming). 'One was in charge of the knot-tying department, the other of the knot-untying department. As one tied knots, the other untied them (laughter). . . .' And he mentioned a government department known as the Sector for the Supervision of Fulfilment of Decisions, which took five months to perform a job it should have done in five days. The initials of this department form the Russian equivalent of the word S.L.E.E.P. Kaganovitch mentioned this, and brought the house down.

'The plan for the Red Dawn Knitted Goods Mills,' said Kaganovitch, 'was examined in five different commissariats and boards, and also in forty-six sectors. The mills received nineteen different sets of instructions every one of which contradicted all the others. The plans were altered over and over again. The result was that the factory worked without any plan. The plan for 1933 was finally endorsed on January 4, 1934. The plan for 1933 was only one year and four days late.' (Laughter.)

He is merciless in flaying inefficiency. On one occasion he caustically described an order for 'haberdashery' which included dog-collars—and enough dog-collars 'to clothe all the dogs in the region in collars from head to foot'—and a shipment of tons of lamp burners without lamp glasses, lamp glasses without lamp burners.

Kaganovitch: 'And so the red tape is spun out.'

Stalin (interrupting): 'And then the document is put in the files.'

The details of Kaganovitch's life are interesting in that they so typically represent the careers of many younger communists. He was born in the Ukraine in 1893, and had only two years of elementary school, then went to work for a living, first as an ordinary factory labourer, then as an apprentice saddler. He entered the party in 1911, and fought through the civil wars. He held party posts in Samara, Nizhni-Novgorod, and Turkestan, and in 1922 attracted Stalin's attention, to become chief of the party organisation in the Ukraine. Stalin brought him to Moscow in 1928.

When he became commissar for ways of communication (the official name of the railways job) he had to give up his presidency of the Moscow Soviet. But he has plenty of other positions. He is a member of the Politburo of the party, of the organisation bureau, and of the central committee. He is on the presidium of the Central Executive Committee of the U.S.S.R. and of the R.S.F.S.R. And he is an executive of the Red Trade Unions, and of STO, the council for labour and defence. Lately he has been put in charge of heavy industry.

His sister is—or was—a close friend of Stalin's, not an unimportant point.

Boss of the Red Army

Kleminti Efremovich Voroshilov, the chief military man of the Soviet Union, is minister of war. He was born of a workman's family, like Kaganovitch, and he went to work in a mine at the age of *six*. He never went to school. Born in 1881, he joined the party as early as 1903, and thus ranks among the veterans. As a boy he was arrested for refusing to take off his hat to a Czarist officer. Then he began his career as an active revolutionary; in the revolution of 1905 he was chairman of the soviet of workers deputies in Lugansk.

He lived, like Stalin, half underground till 1917. Then he organised the first red detachments in the civil wars in the Ukraine. He became commander first of the fifth Ukrainian Army, then of the tenth, and in 1919 was appointed leader of cavalry for the whole Soviet Union. In 1924-1925 he was commander of the Moscow military district. He was on Stalin's side, not Trotsky's, and when the war commissarship became vacant, Stalin saw that Voroshilov got it. His country house is in the neighbourhood of Stalin's, and the two are very close friends.

Voroshilov is the most popular leader in the Soviet Union. He is not ambitious, not a politician, and his personality is pleasing. He is blond, short in the waist, and looks almost like a cherub. He is not an intriguer, not a wirepuller; neither a fanatic nor an arid intellectual, he is easily the most personable of the commissars.

When Trotsky, mounted in the Red Square, reviewed troops, the crowd cried 'What a man!' When Voroshilov does it, they cry, 'What a horse!' So the joke goes. But in fact Voroshilov is very popular in the army. He is not a very strict disciplinarian, but his men respect him because he allows no cliques or favouritism; he is the guardian of fair play. Also, he is a crack shot, and his sharpshooters like to think that their chief is as good as they are.

He is too easy-going to be very quick-witted. At the last party congress he rambled on, speaking of difficulties in transport. 'Which difficulties are greater,' he asked, 'the subjective or the objective? Undoubtedly the subjective ones are greater. In what do they consist? In disorganisation and in the absence of elementary discipline. I don't know if I am revealing secrets. . . .' (Laughter and applause.)

Quick as a bee, Kaganovitch, on the platform, caught this indiscretion. He interrupted: 'Even if you did reveal something, we would not have the right to forbid revelations at the party congress. . . .'

Voroshilov may be slow in speech, but he has all the jargon pat. He calls the kulaks working at forced labour the 'army of heroic canal diggers'.

His main difficulty as the man responsible for the defence of the Soviet Union is transport. Thus it is a good thing that he works on terms of the greatest cordiality with Kaganovitch, though they might easily be rivals. Backwardness in transportation is one of the reasons for the abnormal size of the Soviet army, which is by far the largest in the world. It is really two armies, one in the east, one in the west. Both are necessary, because in the event of war the immense distances in Russia and Siberia, plus inefficiency and inadequacy of the railway system, would make the transfer of even one division from front to front a long, laborious process.

The Red Army is an unknown quantity. It is strong in numbers and in mechanical equipment; as to its stamina and morale, no one knows. The great purge in 1937 killed off, it is believed, at least *fifty per cent* of its higher officers. The rank and file were by and large untouched. Even so, the shock of the purges to discipline and ideals must have been severe.

The Other Incomparable Max

'When Litvinov comes here, Roosevelt must stand firm on one point. We cannot recognise Soviet Russia until it acknowledges and repudiates its debts in the good, sound, capitalist way.'

—(HOWARD BRUBAKER—before American
recognition of the U.S.S.R.)

This unpluckable burr in the flesh of western Europe, this man who had the temerity to go to a disarmament conference and really suggest disarmament, became such a stable citizen in the past few years—so portly, so well-groomed, so worldly-wise and diplomatically substantial—that one was apt to forget his origins and early years. Maxim Maximovitch Litvinov has not always been Maxim Maximovitch Litvinov. At one time or other he owned the following *noms de révolution*—Papasha; Felike, David Mordecai Finkelstein; Litvinov Harrison; Luvinye; M. G. Harrison; Gustav Graf. And his real name is Moysheev Vallakh.

Litvinov, foreign minister for years until 1939, was born in 1876 in Bialystok, then in Russia, part of Poland thereafter, and now Russia again. He came of a *bourgeois* Jewish family and received a regular high school education. He was drafted into the Czarist army—a little known fact—and served five years as a common soldier. His army experience turned him into a revolutionary, and in 1901 he was arrested and sentenced to exile in Siberia. As slippery physically then as he was diplomatically later, he escaped while *en route* to prison and fled to Switzerland. He met Lenin, and in 1903 joined the party.

For a considerable interval his life was, like that of Stalin, compact of revolutionary adventure, lucky escapes, long and patient hours of research and preparation, political conspiracy, wile and counterwile, and enough colourful episode to fill a movie. He returned illegally to Russia and after the collapse of the 1905 revolution was entrusted with shipping contraband arms to a secret depot on the island of Nargan, near Reval.

1906 he spent more tranquilly editing the legal newspaper *New Life* in St. Petersburg. In 1907 adventure called again; he was the agent sent abroad by the revolutionary party to market the notes and bonds Stalin had procured for the movement in the bank raid at Tiflis. Litvinov got to Paris with the revolutionary booty, disposed of it, and later was expelled from France. He returned to Russia briefly. Then he went to London and lived in exile, close to Lenin, for almost ten years.

His life was brilliantly dual. By day he was a publisher's clerk, seemingly absorbed in the highly *bourgeois* routine of reading manuscript, correcting proof, making out accounts; by night he was a philosopher, a revolutionary. He earned his living first in the publishing house, then as a purchasing agent for—of all things— a German electrical and munitions firm, the Siemens-Schuckert

Company. So came his bread and butter. The food of his soul came from Lenin.

Immediately the Bolshevik revolution occurred in 1917 Litvinov was appointed the plenipotentiary representative of the Soviets in Great Britain. But in August 1918 he was arrested and imprisoned as hostage for Bruce Lockhart, the British Agent whom the Bolsheviks had jailed in Moscow. Lockhart was presently released, and Litvinov returned to the U.S.S.R., becoming a member of the collegium of the Narkomindel (foreign office). He was assistant commissar under Chicherin till 1930, then commissar.

Litvinov's years from 1918 to 1939 were packed with incessant travel, incessant negotiation. The record of his trips and treaties is prodigious. In 1918 he visited Stockholm, in 1919 Tallinn, in 1920 Copenhagen, in 1921 Tallinn again, arranging post-War settlements. He went to Genoa and the Hague in 1922, as member of Soviet delegations, and also made the agreement with the American Relief Commission. In 1925 he concluded commercial treaties with Germany and Norway; in 1926 he began his annual explosive visits to the disarmament *pourparlers* at Geneva, and provoked the successive amusement, indignation, rage, and finally respect of the western powers. He went to Washington in 1933 to negotiate recognition between America and the U.S.S.R.; and in 1934 he saw Soviet Russia into the League of Nations. For five years thereafter, he battled at Geneva for the Russian line.

Litvinov is fat. He speaks English with a heavy accent. His chief quality is an inveterate stubbornness in argument, which arises from his unvaryingly consistent point of view, plus an elasticity in negotiation that few statesmen in Europe can equal. More and more, he was sought on Geneva commissions for all sorts of business, because his stubborn and wary intelligence[1] made him useful in every kind of tangle.

In 1915, while he was in exile in London, Litvinov married the celebrated Ivy, niece of Sir Sidney Low. She became the first lady of the Soviets, hostess at the official receptions which Litvinov gave as foreign minister. It is not an asset to him that his wife is an Englishwoman. She caused a minor tempest when, some years ago, she wrote for a Berlin newspaper a feuilleton describing with admir-

---

[1] Example of his realism: In private conversation during the Locarno crisis in London, deploring the failure of sanctions against Italy as a deterrent towards Germany, he said: 'We thought we were rehearsing for a play, but if there isn't going to be a play why rehearse?'

ation some of the pleasant things about Berlin—the wide clean streets, bright shop-windows, and so forth. The Bolshevik Press in Moscow stormed at Litvinov for harbouring a little *bourgeois* in the home.

Their family life is happy, if record of the telephone conversation he had with her from Washington to Moscow is any indication. Let those who believe that Bolsheviks eat babies for breakfast listen in:

L.   Hello.
Ivy.   Hello, darling. I can hear you beautifully.
L.   Speak slowly, will you?
Ivy.   Where are you?
L.   In the White House. . . . President Roosevelt asked me to give you his regards.
Ivy.   Thank you very much, regards to him. . . . Mischa would like to say a word to you.
L.   Mischa is with you? Hello, Mischa. How are your studies?
Mischa.   Very nice. How are you, papa?
L.   What kind of weather are you having?
Ivy.   Beautiful, clear snow. . . . How is everything in the delegation—all well?
L.   Yes.
Ivy.   When shall we see you? . . .
L.   Love and kisses. Good-bye.

Litvinov, who was considered a kind of technician in foreign policy, almost an engineer, was never as important within Russia as outside. In May 1939 he was suddenly dropped. He had no idea that the axe was going to fall. But he was so closely identified with the League and collective security that he lost his usefulness when Stalin determined to sign up with Germany. Besides, he was a Jew.

Females of the Species

Ivy Litvinov is rather untypical of Soviet women, because she has no job herself. Stalin's wife worked. So do several other important men's wives, and many women, quite in their own right, have established successful careers. In no country in Europe is it so easy for a woman of intelligence and character to make good outside the home.

The wives of Rosengoltz (former head of the foreign trade commissariat), Bubnov (former minister of education in the R.S.F.S.R.), and Krylenko (minister of justice) all have—or had—jobs. The wife of Kalinin, president of the U.S.S.R., is manager of a state farm near Novosibirsk. Molotov's wife, Pauline Semyonova Zhem-chuzhna, was till recently head of the Soviet trust which manu-factures powder, rouge, lipstick.

Naziezda Kroupskaya, Lenin's widow, lived and worked in the Kremlin until her death in 1938; she was assistant commissar of education in the R.S.F.S.R. Madame V. N. Yakovleva is minister of finance in the R.S.F.S.R.—one of the most important jobs in the world to be held by a woman. Pelegeya Yakovlevna Voronova, a party member since 1917 and a former textile worker, is assistant commissar for light industry for the U.S.S.R. A veteran Bolshevik, Klavdiya Ivanovna Nikolaeva, formerly a workwoman in a factory, member of the party since 1909, is chief of division of propaganda and mass work of the central committee of the party. Madame Alexandra Kollontay is Soviet minister to Sweden.

As a rule leading Bolsheviks do not, except among intimates, go out with their wives; for that matter, they seldom entertain or receive formal entertainment themselves. Women do not partici-pate in social activity unless by reason of their own merit of position. No outsider can recall ever having seen Kaganovitch's wife, or Voro-shilov's. No one pays attention. The matter of marriage is not of sufficient importance to be inserted in the party Who's Who.

Kalinin

Michael Ivanovitch Kalinin, born in 1875 in the province of Tver, son of a peasant, was sent off to work for his living at the age of sixteen, as a stable boy and second footman on the near-by estate of a wealthy aristocrat. He migrated to St. Petersburg, became a factory workman there. He joined the party in 1898. To-day he is chairman of the All-Union Central Executive Committee, and thus 'President of Russia'. It is Kalinin who, as formal head of the Soviet Union, receives diplomats when they present themselves at the Kremlin.

His titular importance is greater than his actual power. Yet his influence, particularly on Stalin personally, is apt to be under-estimated; his opinion carries weight, especially in matters concern-ing the peasants. Kalinin, a peasant himself, who still wears peasant clothes, is an authority on agrarian life, and the peasants trust him.

Kalinin was a great friend of Lenin's, and it was he who an-nounced Lenin's death. Duranty's description of his speech and the emotion it evoked should be imperishable.

Molotov

When I was first in Moscow in 1928, Molotov had recently become a member of the Politburo, but scarcely anyone knew his name. He was predominantly a party man, 'Stalin's shadow', and his function in the Politburo seemed to be to watch party affairs. One by one the giants of those days, Rykov and Bukharin and Tomsky, were dismissed and later shot; and in the twinkling of a shadow, it seemed, the inconspicuous Molotov had become chairman of the council of people's commissars, the job he still holds—prime minister.

Rykov, his predecessor as premier, was the single leading Bolshevik with a university education; but Molotov never went even to grammar school. Bukharin was a dazzling theoretician orator, writer of polemics; Molotov, as Lenin said, was 'the best filing clerk in the Soviet Union'. Stalin knew the kind of man he wanted. He was tired of flamboyant theorists; he wanted cool administrators. He liked Molotov for several reasons. For one thing, he had like Stalin himself stuck it out inside Russia during the long underground period, never once having retreated to easy exile.

'Molotov' is a pseudonym, like Stalin; it means 'hammer'. His real name is Vlacheslav V. Skriabin. He was born in 1890 of a workers family, and entered the party in 1906. In February 1917 he was chairman of the Bolshevik faction of the Petrograd soviet. From that time on he has had the full confidence of Stalin. It is quite likely that he might take precedence over Kaganovitch or Voroshilov if Stalin died, and so—behind his back—people called him 'the Czarevitch'.

He has a fine forehead, and looks and acts like a French professor of medicine—orderly, precise, a bit pedantic. He is a vegetarian and a teetotaller. His importance is sometimes not appreciated; he is by no means a mere figurehead, but a man of considerable intelligence and influence. Stalin for a time gave him most of the dirty work to do;[1] for instance he had the nasty job of admitting how many cattle and hogs were killed by the peasants before the famine. In 1939, as Stalin prepared his new orientation in foreign policy, Molotov became foreign minister.

[1] As Hitler, for instance, made Hess give the first apologia for the events of June 30.

Pattern for Leadership

Most leaders in the Soviet Union are cut to the same pattern. Extreme poverty in youth; self-education and manual labour;[1] revolutionary activity from the beginning; punishment before 1917 and success thereafter, plus murderously hard work and untiring obsession to the cause. Any of a dozen men deserve detailed mention. But their careers vary only in minor detail.

Andrey A. Andreyev, one of the most important younger Bolsheviks, a member of the Supreme Council of the U.S.S.R., and secretary of the Central Committee of the party, was born in 1896. His father was a janitor. He had only two years in school. Andrey A. Zhdanov, for years the party boss in Leningrad, was—late in 1939 —closer to Stalin than any man in Russia. When they appear together at party meetings, Stalin bends towards him, listening. Like Andreyev, he is a member of the Supreme Council and a party secretary. He is the son of a schoolteacher.

The Gay-Pay-Oo

A vast lot of nonsense has been written about the G.P.U. Of course, terror played a considerable role in the evolution of the U.S.S.R., and the Gay-Pay-Oo, the secret police, was the instrument of terror. Stalin himself has defined its function in no uncertain terms:

> 'The G.P.U. is the punitive organ of the Soviet government: it is more or less similar to the Committee of Public Safety which existed during the great French revolution. It punishes primarily spies, plotters, terrorists, bandits, speculators, forgers. It is something in the nature of a military political tribunal set up for the purpose of protecting the interests of the revolution from attacks on the part of counter-revolutionary *bourgeoisie* and their agents.'
> —*Leninism*, I. p. 419.

Note well that the G.P.U. has powers, not merely to arrest, but, as Stalin admits, to punish. It is judge, jury, executioner, all in one. But, on the other hand, it is not exclusively a political police. One hears mostly stories of its melodramatic activities. It is much more, however, than a force that engages in espionage and shoots suspects and traitors. The G.P.U. numbers about two hundred thousand picked men, and is in a sense a superior cadre of the Red Army; it guards frontiers, patrols railways, and the like.

[1] Mikoyan was a mechanic for instance, Postyshev an electrician, Eikhe a ship's stoker. Workmen tried to make Russia work.

Especially it watches affairs *within* the party. The law-abiding citizen who is not a party member has less to fear from it than party men.

The terror in Russia is an agent of social aims, as the Bolsheviks put it. Better to kill a few people—even if by chance they are innocent—than risk a counter-revolution in which many thousands may die, and which might kill the Soviet experiment. There is a big streak of the Oriental in Russians, with a concomitant Oriental contempt for the value of individual life. Moreover, one should not forget that the Bolsheviks drew a terrible lesson from the Paris Commune, when thirty thousand communards were executed by the reaction.

The first leader of the G.P.U. was a friend of Lenin's named Dzherzhinsky, a Pole of enormous ability and fanaticism. He was a policeman-mystic, one of the most extraordinary characters of modern times. He died, to be succeeded by a more commonplace man, Menzhinsky. When Menzhinsky in turn died, his place was taken by G. G. Yagoda, a careerist and wire-puller, corrupt and unscrupulous, whom Stalin got rid of in 1937. His successor, Yezhov, was an outrageous fanatic, largely responsible for the purges that followed. He gave way in December 1938 to a much less violent man, L. P. Beria.

The G.P.U. became a bit of a nuisance to the Kremlin during the Yagoda period. It stupidly arrested foreign engineers, and shocked foreign public opinion by wanton slaughter of Russian professors and intellectuals accused of 'sabotage'. It failed to un-cloak for many years the activities of a remarkable spy named Konar, a Polish agent who succeeded in becoming Soviet Assistant Commissar of Agriculture. Stalin decided to curtail the powers of the G.P.U. On July 10, 1934, it was reorganised with considerably restricted authority; the name G.P.U. disappeared; it was no longer allowed to impose the death penalty without trial; and its title was changed to 'Commissariat of Home Affairs'.

Six months later, on December 1, 1934, Stalin's best friend Sergei Mironovich Kirov, member of the Politburo and boss of Lenin-grad, was shot and killed by a communist assassin—the first assas-sination or attempted assassination of a Bolshevik notability since Fanny Kaplan's shooting of Lenin in 1918. This gave the G.P.U. chance to reassert itself—with extreme unpleasantness.

Stalin heard the news and took the first train to Leningrad, Voroshilov accompanying him. Panic struck Moscow. The Soviet

Union had a bad attack of nerves. Kirov's assassin, it was discovered, was not a 'White', but a communist himself, a young man named Leonid Nikolaiev. The heads of the G.P.U. in Leningrad were jailed for negligence. Nikolaiev was questioned, tried, and with thirteen alleged accomplices, shot.

The reason for Kirov's assassination was a confused *mélange* of personal and political forces. Nikolaiev had been dismissed from the communist party in one of its periodic purges, then, after a brief stay in the wilderness, reinstated. He was a theorist, a radical, and apparently he had objected with some heat to the growing development of 'socialist inequality'. Besides he had personal difficulties with Kirov, who, it seemed, did not keep a promise to get him a better job.

Kirov was an extraordinary person. He was an orphan. The legend is that he was suckled by a sow. He was born in 1886, and brought up in an asylum; he joined the party in 1904, and after the revolution became one of Stalin's first henchmen; he was entrusted with the clean-up of Zinovievists in Leningrad, as Kaganovitch swept the Trotskyists out of Moscow. He was harsh, vital, impressive, cunning, uncouth, bold—a great leader of men; and his death removed a powerful figure from the party.

The G.P.U. resumed its usual capers after Kirov's death. It was the 'Commissariat of Home Affairs' in name, but the good old G.P.U. in spirit still. One hundred and three persons were summarily executed, as well as the thirteen said to have been Nikolaiev's accomplices. It was not pretended that the hundred and three had anything whatever to do with the Kirov case. They were, however, not innocent men and women picked off the streets, as was alleged. All were in prison at the time Kirov was shot; all were accused of some crime or other, from conspiracy to assassinate Stalin to espionage on behalf of foreign powers; all had been convicted of some offence.

Stalin then dissolved the Society of Old Bolsheviks, an organisation founded by Lenin's friends in 1922 and including only the party fathers, those with more than eighteen solid years in the revolutionary movement. These Old Bolsheviks, 'radicals', were a nuisance to Stalin. The Kirov murder was a perfect pretext for wiping up old scores. Stalin precisely followed the technique of Hitler after June 30; he made use of an artificial panic in the country to undertake Draconian steps for which otherwise he had small excuse.

Then came the arrest of the veteran dissident-communists Zino-viev and Kamenev, charged with complicity in the Kirov plot. After this—violent crisis all over Russia, as the great treason trials began.

Succession

Kirov was the man being trained by Stalin as his successor. He is dead; and the succession would now seem to be between Kagano-vitch, Voroshilov, and Molotov. Neither is a satisfactory candidate: Kaganovitch is a Jew, Voroshilov is too limited in interests, Molotov not big enough a personality. Another possibility is Zhdanov, who is more and more talked of—in whispers—as the future leader.

If Stalin should die, the *party*, not one man, would of course attempt to take over. Personal rivalries, like those that followed the death of Lenin, are perfectly possible, but it is unlikely that they could disrupt the régime. Discipline is strict, and the party is unanimous within itself on major issues. There is no obvious candidate for power in Russia, like Goering in Germany, simply because no man in the U.S.S.R. can be unduly prominent if he is conspicuously ambitious. The Soviet State could hardly be more affected by the death of Stalin than it was by the death of Lenin.

CHAPTER XXXIX

THE RUSSIAN TRIALS

I N August 1936 a series of treason trials began in the U.S.S.R.
that perplexed and indeed stupefied the western world. Old
Bolsheviks like Zinoviev and Kamenev were tried and shot; so were
important vice-commissars like Pyatakov and generals like Tukhachevsky, who was considered the second military man in the Soviet
Union. Incredibly sensational details were alleged: that Trotsky
was negotiating with Hitler, that such well-known leaders as Radek
and Sokolnikov plotted the overthrow of the Stalinist government,
that generals who had devoted their lives to the Red Army sold out
to Germany and Japan. Those found guilty were given short
shrift. It seemed that friends of the Soviet Union were confronted
with two alternatives equally unpleasant, that (a), the opposition to Stalin was much more serious than anyone had believed,
reaching in fact the very heart of the army and the state, or (b),
Stalin was a ruthless murderer getting rid of Trotskyist or other
opponents and indeed anyone he didn't happen to like, by means
of the most monstrous frame-up of modern times.

Let us dismiss at outset some of the fairy-tales. Stalin, some
whisperers had it, was mortally ill, and was extirpating the last
remnants of opposition while he was still alive; according to other
'reports' he had suddenly gone 'insane'. It was said that the prisoners were tortured, hypnotised, drugged (in order to make them
give false confessions) and—a choice detail—impersonated by
actors of the Moscow Art theatre! But the trials occurred soon
after the preliminary investigations were concluded, and they took
place before hundreds of witnesses, many of them experienced correspondents, in open court. The prisoners testified that they were
well-treated during the investigation. Radek, indeed, says that it
was he who tortured the prosecutor, by refusing to confess month
after month. Pressure there certainly was, in the manner of police
investigation all over the world, but no evidence of torture.

The trials, the Trotskyists assert, were a colossal frame-up. The
prisoners were induced to confess, they say, on a promise of

immunity and a pardon after the trial—if they talked freely—and then double-crossed and shot. This is hardly conceivable from a close reading of the testimony. It could not easily have occurred in the second trial, when the defendants must have known that the first batch, despite their confessions, were sentenced to death and duly executed. On the other hand, the defendants probably hoped that whoever behaved best might get off with a light sentence.

An important point to keep in mind is the peculiarity of Russian legal procedure. It differs drastically from ours, and resembles to some extent the French system, where the real 'trial' is the preliminary investigation; the final court session does not so much determine guilt as decide what penalty shall be attached to the guilty. In Russia, a prisoner is not brought to what we call a 'trial' until he has confessed. Within the circumscriptions of Russian procedure the trials were fair enough. The defendants had the right of legal defence; they had the privilege of cross-examining witnesses; they talked with the greatest vivacity and freedom. The attitude of the court was severe but not coercive. The closing speeches of the prosecutor, A. Y. Vyshinsky, were violent, but during the testimony he treated the defendants with reasonable consideration. For instance:

> Vyshinsky: Accused Pyatakov, perhaps you are tired.
> Pyatakov: No, I can go on.
> The President: I propose to adjourn at three o'clock.
> Vyshinsky: I do not object, but perhaps it is tiring for the accused?
> Pyatakov: How much longer?
> The President: Fifty minutes.
> Vyshinsky then resumes the questioning.

The confessions, in both the first and second trials, bewildered observers because it seemed literally inconceivable (a) that men like Sokolnikov, Smirnov, Radek, Serebryakov, and so on could possibly be traitors, and (b) that they should have so meekly gone to conviction without a struggle. Point (a) we shall come to later on. As to point (b), the defendants *did* struggle. It lasted during all the preliminary examination, which was prolonged. Radek held out two and a half months. Muralov, an old Trotskyist, held out eight months. Radek says of him, 'I was convinced he would rather perish in prison than say a single word.'

The first trial, with the old Bolsheviks Zinoviev, Kamenev, and Smirnov as the chief defendants, opened on August 19, 1936. It was heard by the military collegium of the supreme court, with

V. V. Ulrich as the presiding judge and Vyshinsky as prosecutor. The defendants were accused of forming a terrorist 'Centre' in Leningrad, instigated by Trotsky and devoted to counter-revolution and conspiracy against the U.S.S.R., of planning the assassination of Stalin and other leaders, and actively conniving the murder of Kirov. All sixteen defendants were found guilty and executed.

The high point of this trial was the examination of Zinoviev:

> Vyshinsky: When was the united centre organised?
> Zinoviev: In the summer of 1932.
> Vyshinsky: What were its activities?
> Zinoviev: Its main activities consisted of making preparations for terrorist acts.
> Vyshinsky: Against whom?
> Zinoviev: Against the leaders.
> Vyshinsky: That is, against Comrades Stalin, Voroshilov, and Kaganovitch? Was it your centre that organised the assassination of Comrade Kirov? Was the assassination of Sergei Mironovitch Kirov organised by your centre, or by some other organisation?
> Zinoviev: Yes, by our centre.
> Vyshinsky: In that centre there were you, Kamenev, Smirnov, Mrachkovsky and Ter-Vaganyan?
> Zinoviev: Yes.
> Vyshinsky: So you all organised the assassination of Kirov?
> Zinoviev: Yes.
> Vyshinsky: So you all assassinated Comrade Kirov?
> Zinoviev: Yes.
> Vyshinski: Sit down.

This trial, not the second one, provoked the most natural of the Trotskyist 'frame-up' charges. It seemed odd, for one thing, that the 'centre' was organised in 1932, whereas Kirov was murdered in December 1934 and the trial took place only in 1936. Zinoviev and Kamenev were arrested after the murder and sentenced to exile, then brought back, arrested again, and tried again. And the testimony—of which no verbatim record exists in English—indicated some remarkable contradictions. For instance Smirnov was apparently in jail in 1933, during which time he was supposed to have been plotting with the 'centre'; there seems to be considerable confusion about the false Honduras passport of another defendant; another, Holtzman, testified that he met Sedov, Trotsky's son, in the Hotel Bristol in Copenhagen in 1932, when in fact no hotel by this name existed in Copenhagen. Sedov asserts that he was never in Copenhagen in his life.

The second trial, somewhat more convincing, and of which a full record exists in various languages, occurred January 23–30, 1937, before the same court and the some prosecutor. The defendants, seventeen in all, included Y. L. Pyatakov, the assistant commissar of heavy industry; Gregory Sokolnikov, the assistant commissar of foreign affairs; Y. A. Livshitz, the assistant commissar of railways; such well-known old-line Bolshevists as Muralov and Serebryakov, and of course Radek. Thirteen of the seventeen were sentenced to death and shot; Sokolnikov and Radek got ten years—Radek literally talked himself out of the death penalty in an inordinately fascinating last plea; two dupes, Arnold (an unbelievable character, a sort of cross between the Four Marx Brothers and the people in Gorki's *Lower Depths*) and Stroilov, got lesser sentences.

The indictment was a good deal broader than that of the first trial. The defendants were accused of sabotage and wrecking, of selling information of military importance to Japan and Germany, of plots to murder Molotov and other members of the government, and of conspiracy with Germany and Japan whereby, if the plotters usurped power in the Soviet Union, the Ukraine was to be surrendered to Germany and the Maritime Province to Japan, presumably as a price for non-interference while Stalin was being overthrown. Nothing more sensational or—at first sight—incredible could be imagined.

As unfolded inexorably in the testimony, the story begins when Pyatakov, a well known Trotskyist who had spent long periods in opposition and exile, secretly saw Sedov, Trotsky's son, in Berlin in 1931. Sedov sounded Pyatakov out; Pyatakov returned to Russia and cautiously, with infinite slowness and secrecy, communicated with Radek, Sokolnikov, and the others. Gradually a 'parallel' or 'reserve' centre—first of conspiracy, then of terrorism—was formed, to back up the Zinoviev group and carry on if the Zinovievites were exposed and crushed.

Vyshinsky tried hard to find out how the alleged conspirators disclosed themselves to one another:

> Vyshinsky: What gave Ratachak reasons for disclosing himself to you?
> Pyatakov: Two persons had spoken to me. . . .
> Vyshinsky: Did he disclose himself to you, or did you disclose yourself to him?
> Pyatakov: Disclosure may be mutual.
> Vyshinsky: Did you disclose yourself first?
> Pyatakov: Who first, he or I—the hen or the egg—I don't know.

He tried hard to pin Radek down, to make Radek too disclose more fully the inter-relations of the group.

> Vyshinsky: These actions of yours were deliberate?
> Radek: Apart from sleeping, I have never in my life committed any undeliberate actions.
> Vyshinsky: And this, unfortunately, was not a dream?
> Radek: Unfortunately it was not a dream.

Some of the conspirators seemed desperately unhappy at their own role in the plot, as it tightened and developed. For instance Sokolnikov:

> 'Just imagine. I am conducting official negotiations at the People's Commissariat of Foreign Affairs. The conversation draws to a close. The interpreters have left the room. The official representative of a certain foreign state, Mr.—, suddenly turned to me and asked: Am I informed about the proposals Trotsky has made to his government. . . . How does Trotsky visualise that? How can I, as Assistant People's Commissar, conduct such negotiations? This is an absolutely impossible situation.'

Trotsky, according to the testimony, was the heart and soul of the conspiracy. He sent letters to Radek, concealed in books or shoes; one of the intermediaries was the journalist Vladimir Romm, formerly *Izvestia* correspondent in Washington, who says he met Trotsky in Paris. Pyatakov, unless he was lying, took a secret aeroplane trip from Berlin to Oslo, and there saw Trotsky, in December 1935. But there is no record of an aeroplane having landed at Oslo on the day mentioned. Trotsky, questioned by the John Dewey commission in Mexico, denied flatly either that he met Romm or saw Pyatakov. Trotsky was not in Paris at all when Romm was there, he insists. It is a question of taking the word of one against the other. But it is illuminating to note that in his testimony Trotsky says it is sometimes necessary in modern society for politicians to tell something less than the complete truth. 'Everybody from time to time is obliged not to say the truth,' he confesses.

Pyatakov revealed—according to his testimony—how, among other things, the Trotskyist movement outside Russia was financed. For instance; in his official capacity as assistant commissar of heavy industry, Pyatakov (incidentally Lenin in his will called Pyatakov one of the ablest men in Soviet Russia), gave orders for machinery to German firms and promised to pay more than the normal price; the difference went to the Trotskyists, through Sedov, and other agents. But Pyatakov says the plot was not engineered 'purely for the sake of Trotsky's beautiful eyes'.

Trotsky's close connection with German Fascists was constantly alleged, which seems simply monstrous. Half a dozen times in the testimony Hitler's first aid, Rudolf Hess, was named as the German negotiator. The court was extremely careful to keep mention of compromising diplomatic details from the public sessions. Time and again the defendants were rebuked for mentioning foreigners' names.

> Radek: I informed him (Sokolnikov) of the directives and asked about the specific fact regarding —. (Name cut from the record.)
> The President: Accused Radek, are you trying to provoke us?
> Radek: I am not trying to provoke you: this will not occur again.
> Vyshinsky: Such behaviour on the part of the accused Radek places me in a very difficult position during the course of the investigation.
> The President: Quite so.
> Vyshinsky: You are a man sufficiently well-versed in politics to understand that it is forbidden to speak about certain things in Court; this must be accepted as a demand of the law.
> Radek: I deeply apologise; this will not occur again.
> The President: I consider that if Radek repeats anything of this kind, this question will have to be dealt with *in camera*.
> Radek: I repeat that this will not occur again.

The plot developed although inefficiently. Sabotage did occur. Trains were wrecked, soldiers killed. Details came out in testimony that make the flesh creep; officials of the railways deliberately slowing up car loadings, disrupting freight schedules, stalling trains, (the chief train-wrecker, Knyazev, confessed to getting 15,000 roubles from a Japanese agent); engineers ruining chemical factories by burning out their furnaces and sabotaging work in the mines; one defendant, Shestov, described how he ordered the murder of an honest official who suspected sabotage in the coal industry.

But by the middle of 1935 the conspirators began to lose their enthusiasm. Trotsky himself, according to Radek, saw that they could not bring Stalin down by these means. In the most emotional and moving passages in the trial Radek describes his gradual awareness that he and his colleagues have made a terrible mistake. He debates what to do. It is very difficult for the conspirators to meet; in the whole course of the affair Radek, Pyatakov, and Sokolnikov actually see one another and confer only two or three times. Radek comes finally to a conclusion.

Vyshinski: What did you decide?

Radek: The first step to take would be to go to the Central Committee of the Party, to make a statement, to name all the persons. This I did not do. It was not I that went to the G.P.U., but the G.P.U. that came for me.

Vyshinsky: An eloquent reply.

Radek: A sad reply.

It would be obtuse to deny or gloss over some extreme weaknesses in the testimony. For instance the prosecutor went back to Kirov over and over again, but he could never make Radek or Sokolnikov at least admit they had any connection with the assassination or knowledge of it. Again, it may well be asked why the conspirators, with years to work in, were so inadequate and bungling; aside from sabotage which was after all minor, they accomplished little. The one attempted assassination, that of Molotov, with which they were charged, sounds 'fishy' in the extreme. But the man in charge of it was Arnold, an exceedingly fishy character.

Again, there was very little actual evidence. Prime evidence would have been the letters Trotsky sent to Radek. But Radek says he burned them (as he might prudently have done).

Reasonably neutral observers construct a 'theory' about the trials more or less as follows:

1. Every important defendant in the first and second trials was a Zinovievite or a Trotskyist. Radek, Pyatakov, Sokolnikov, Serebryakov, had been Trotskyists for years. Radek joined the Trotsky faction in 1923, went into exile, and only recanted in 1929; he was readmitted to grace in 1930. Their opposition to Stalin was ingrained and inexpugnable; they were Trotskyists to the bone; when they saw things going badly according to their lights, it was perfectly reasonable for them to turn back to their old leader.

2. Moreover, these old revolutionaries, quite apart from the fact that they were Trotskyists and therefore dissidents, were conspirators by nature, *conspirators* born and bred. From their very earliest days they had breathed the air of plot and counterplot. The day of their eminence passed; Stalin wanted engineers and administrators; they were naturally disgruntled. In a police-run state like Russia, one should remember, discontent can be expressed only by conspiracy. And Radek and company were congenitally incapable of giving conspiracy up.

3. The Trotskyists—outside Russia at least—made no effort to conceal their violent hatred of the Stalinist régime. They were far

beyond such '*bourgeois*' considerations as orthodox patriotism. They were world revolutionaries, and they no longer regarded the U.S.S.R. as a revolutionary or communist state. They had the same aim as pre-1939 Germany and Japan, to overthrow the Stalinist régime. Stalin was as much an enemy to them as Hitler. And they were willing to co-operate even with Hitler, at that time an obvious ally, for their supreme goal—Stalin's destruction.

4. Radek and the others testified over and over again—the central issue of the trial—that they felt war to be inevitable in 1933 or 1934 and that the Russians would be inevitably defeated. They thought that things were going very badly, and that when the crash came the Soviet Union would not survive it. Therefore, as good world revolutionaries, they deemed it their duty to get to work and perfect an underground organisation that would survive the war, so that revolutionary communism would not altogether perish. Also, if war came, they might themselves have had a chance at getting power in Russia, and therefore an attempt to buy the Germans off, buy the Japanese off, was natural.

5. So much for Radek and his friends inside. As regards Trotsky outside, an anti-Trotskyist could probably add two more considerations: (*a*) Trotsky was actively eager for a German war against the U.S.S.R., and he hoped that the U.S.S.R. would lose—therefore he sought to weaken it by sabotage; (*b*) his ambition and his lust for office were such that he was quite willing to give up the Ukraine and the Maritime Provinces as a price for power. One should not forget that Trotsky fought the Czar during the Great War much as he fights Stalin now, that Lenin crossed Germany with German aid in a German sealed train, and that Trotsky signed the Treaty of Brest-Litovsk giving an immense amount of Russian territory to Germany.

Finally and very importantly—it is quite possible that the trials were exploited inside Russia to impress the Russian masses. The government exaggerated the crimes of the victims in order to simplify the issue. The overthrow of capitalism in the U.S.S.R., the partition of the country, were added to the indictment to give the crimes of the conspirators a final and overwhelming smear of black. Stalin was eager to clean out the Trotskyists once for all, they were conveniently in his hands, and he neglected no factor to make the job as thorough and complete as possible.

The third trial, that of the generals, was of a different category; proceedings were secret and the testimony has not been published.

Announcement simply came on June 11, 1937, that eight high officers of the Red Army, including Marshal Tukhachevsky, had been arrested, tried for traitorous behaviour, and promptly shot. Among the eight were General Putna, formerly the Russian military attaché in Berlin and London (he was named as a conspirator in the second trial), General Yakir, the commander of the Leningrad military district, General Uborovitch, former commander in White Russia, General Eidemann, the head of Osoaviakhim, and General Feldman, the chief of the personnel division of the general staff. The generals were accused of treasonable relations with Germany and Japan, and the betrayal of the Red Army in the event of war.

This shocked world opinion warmly. It seemed incredible that men like Tukhachevsky, who had devoted the totality of their lives to the defence of the Soviet Union, could be guilty of wantonly planning its defeat. Tukhachevsky, only forty-four, had a brilliant revolutionary and military career; he was one of the great heroes of the Soviet Union. Dissident careerists like Zinoviev and Kamenev, no longer prominent, were one thing; eight in-the-prime-of-their-powers generals including Tukhachevsky and Yakir were quite another. Many friends of Russia, even if unwillingly, accepted the first two trials; they found it extremely difficult to accept the third.

But investigation, so far as investigation was possible, began to disclose a number of enlightening details. Tukhachevsky, brilliant and ambitious, wanted power for himself; he and Voroshilov were on bad terms, it is said; a general impression in military circles is that Tukhachevsky planned a 'palace' *coup d'état* to get rid of Stalin and set up a dictatorship himself. Stalin got him first.

All eight of the generals had close relations at one time with the German Reichswehr. The Red Army and the German Army worked intimately together before 1932, it should be remembered; every year Russian officers went to Germany for training and study; even after Hitler, the two general staffs had a cordial respect for each other. Generals Kork and Feldman, with obviously German names, were Baltic Germans; General Uborovitch attended the German manœuvres after the Nazi party congress last year; both Kork and Putna had been military attachés in Berlin.

Few people think that Tukhachevsky could have sold out to Germany, or promised the defeat of his own army in the event of war; but it is quite possible that he envisaged some arrangement with the Reichswehr independently of Stalin. He wanted the Red Army and the German Army to work together; politics prevented this. He was known to be an opponent of the Franco-Soviet pact, and the French distrusted him. One suggestion is that the Reichswehr planned to overthrow Hitler just as Tukhachevsky wanted to overthrow Stalin, the two armies to refrain from interference with each other.

Then came the fourth great trial, again a public trial promoted almost like a festival, in March 1938, with Bukharin, Rykov, Yagoda, and Rakovsky as chief defendants. Thus, having eliminated all possible 'left' opposition, Stalin now turned to eliminate the last survivors of the 'right'—Bukharin and Rykov. Yagoda, a policeman in the dock, was a picturesque phenomenon as he sat in court—it was he who had procured the evidence against victims in the previous trials! Rakovsky was an old-line Trotskyist who had had a distinguished career as an ambassador abroad. Bukharin, Rykov, and Yagoda were condemned to death and—presumably—shot; Rakovsky got off with ten years.

During most of 1938 the purge went drearily on, having repercussions almost everywhere in the Soviet Union. The great bulk of Russian citizens were not deeply impressed by the public trials, with which they had only a spectator's contact; but the purges, striking unpredictably in every direction, put terror into every heart. Seven presidents of various Soviet republics were removed, six prime ministers, thirty-one commissars and vice commissars, innumerable army and naval officers, trade union leaders, and party chieftains, down to the smallest local officials. Of the seventy-one members of the Central Committee of the party, its highest organ, appointed as recently as 1934, only sixteen survived in 1939. Some of the best men in Russia, like Mezhlauk, the creator of the Five Year Plan, and Marshal Bluecher, the commanding officer in the Far East, disappeared.

Yet Stalin and the régime—shaken as they undoubtedly were—appeared to have withstood the shock.

CHAPTER XL

'DURANTY'S INFERNO'

' Give me four years to teach the children, and the seed I have sown will never be uprooted.'

—LENIN.

THE things that one most objects to in the Soviet Union are, as as a rule, Russian and not necessarily communist characteristics —cruelty, slovenliness, crudity in mechanical technique, espionage, red-tape, dirt, backwardness, administrative inefficiency. It is interesting to read Baedeker's *Russia*, the 1914 edition. You will find that you had to leave your passport with the police in those days too, and that to depart the country you had to have an exit visa. The communists have done their best to eliminate some of the tedious and cumbersome nuisances that have always disfigured some aspects of Russian life. But even the whole weight of the Kremlin cannot, apparently, make the porter of any Moscow hotel efficient—or his telephone. The late Frank Wise, M.P., brought back a pleasant story from one of his Russian trips; he visited the central head-quarters of the supreme electricity board of the U.S.S.R. and found the electric bell outside the offices marked 'Not Working'. It is the despair of many communists that Karl Marx had his first try-out in, of all countries, Russia; that *Das Kapital* had to undergo its first concrete translation into a language as formidably difficult as Russian.

One point to make regarding the Soviet Union is its colossal and typically Russian vitality. Perhaps the most important single thing about the U.S.S.R. to-day is that it is the only modern dictatorship which has survived a series of tremendous internal crises. Neither Mussolini nor Hitler has suffered such crises yet. And the chief Soviet crisis—the resistance of the peasants to industrialisation— was none the less severe in that it was self-inflicted. The Soviets have survived twenty-two terrible years. Despite civil wars, despite two major famines, the population has *increased* by twenty-three million people since 1918, and is increasing now at the rate of almost three million per year. In a generation, in other words, the Soviet

Union, in its present borders, will contain two hundred million people.

Another point to be noted is the emphatic emergence of Russia, in the view of Russians, as a *national* state. Be it remembered that the official name of the country, adopted after the revolution, was U.S.S.R.—Union of Soviet Socialist Republics—a name with a profoundly centrifugal connotation, a label indicating the permanent possibility of expansion, of merger with other states. This expansion, indeed, began in 1939 with the acquisition of White Russia and part of the Ukraine from Poland. Even so, the predominant forces in Russia became centripetal during the 30's. Russia was taught that it was not merely a nucleus of communist states, but a Russian national state as well. The Red Army may fight—eventually—even beyond Finland, but at the same time it is the Soviet State, the Russian Fatherland, which it must continue to defend. In February 1939 Red Army soldiers were given a new oath, not to the 'workers of the world' but to the Soviet Government. 'Patriotism' in our sense of the term hardly existed in the U.S.S.R. ten years ago. Now even the *Pravda* runs editorials on 'Mother Russia'.

A third preliminary point to make is that the revolutionary phase of Soviet policy has distinctly slowed down. In fact anti-Stalinists would say that the revolution has ceased to exist, and that socialism in Russia—if it ever did exist—is now extinct.

Piatiletka

The Five-Year Plan was not a Five-Year Plan at all. This is the simple gist of it. I have alluded to the plan several times in these chapters; let us spare a paragraph or two in brief description of the way it worked and what it means. The fact is that all economy in Russia is regulated by planning, to infinity and beyond; successive plans, spaced into five-year periods for convenience, are, as Duranty says, part of a single programme, which is continuous.

The Plan was the invention of no single man, though Stalin is fond of pointing out that he suggested an electrification programme to Lenin as far back as 1921; it grew naturally and inevitably out of the nature of the Soviet system; and it was put into effect so gradually that even well-informed correspondents in Russia did not know that the first Plan had begun until it was under way. The theoretician most largely responsible for its origin, as far as any one person can take the credit, was probably Osinski; the practical man of affairs who most decisively executed its workings was Mezh-lauk, once called the 'ablest man in the Soviet Union'.

Stalin announced that the first plan was 93.7 per cent successful. He was referring to industrial results, and probably he exaggerated. Even so, it was a tremendous, unprecedented effort; the only thing in the world quite to be compared to it was the expansion of the United States in the frontier period. Industrial output quad-rupled in four years, an 'outstanding and unsurpassed achievement'. The production of steel increased forty per cent in four years, of pig iron eighty-four per cent. Tractor, automobile, engineering, aviation, industries were created out of nothing. Entire new cities were built on the Siberian steppes, or in the Urals, like Magnito-gorsk, an industrial colossus that will probably become the largest steel plant in Europe. Enough machinery was imported to enable the U.S.S.R. to maintain succeeding five-year plans with diminish-ing amounts of foreign aid. Mines were developed—with the not unimportant result that the U.S.S.R. now possesses the third largest gold reserve in the world. Unemployment ceased. All this, too, at a time when the capitalist powers were ravaged by an economic crisis of unprecedented severity and scope.

The Plan had important political results, because it helped to make Russia a strong national state, and as Chamberlin points out, it thrust the Soviet centre of gravity eastward. The object of the Plan was to industrialise a largely agrarian country. Nicely, the greatest mineral deposits were found in regions hitherto almost inaccessible, tucked away in remote parts of Siberia. Here the heart of new Russia throbs—geographically impregnable. This is important from a military point of view.

The costs of the Plan were of course enormous. Tens of mil-lions of people did not have enough to eat; the cruel hungry bottom of subsistence was reached. Human values were utterly replaced by industrial values; when human beings resisted, they were ruth-lessly destroyed, as we have seen. In communist jargon, the first Five-Year Plan was a period of 'postponed consumption'. Sacrifice, in other words, had to precede sufficiency. Also, great as was the success of the Plan, it by no means produced enough material to satisfy the people. Domestic production was intensified, but Russia still remains the largest market in the world. The standard of liv-ing may have improved slightly, but it is still unbelievably, shock-ingly low.

In the second plan the tempo of activity was a good deal relaxed.

The second plan was not so much publicised as the first. It aimed to complete the collectivisation of agriculture by 1937, and to stress the production of consumers' goods, rather than heavy industrial products, in order to lessen the terrible need in Russia for such items as—to choose at random—nails, decent paper, rope, kitchenware, plumbing utensils, scientific and medical supplies, boots, metal-ware. It hoped to double the food supply in the cities and reduce retail prices something like thirty-five per cent. And it sought to contain provision for housing, because the outrageous and appalling condition of housing in Moscow and the bigger cities is a disgrace to the Soviet Union—and honest sovietites admit it.

'I Contradict Myself? Very Well, I Contradict Myself!'

The basis of Soviet economy is production for use, not profit. 'Each man shall work according to his abilities and receive according to his needs.' The communist party considers itself a sort of central organisation with authority over the whole nation to distribute both activity and rewards according to this formula. It mercilessly extracts profits from labourers and peasants—for instance H. R. Knickerbocker has calculated that the profit of the government on grain is one thousand per cent—but these profits are all ploughed back into the business. There are no private gains. The interests of the country as a whole, as determined by the communist party, are the only criterion. The communists accept nominal managerial salaries for their labour. These salaries are minuscule. Communists, as a rule, get much less that non-communist technicians whom they hire. The theory is that all fruits of production are pooled for redistribution to the common good. Political democracy is extinct. But economic democracy—theoretically—is complete.

Naturally the operation of this process and modifications to it made necessary by temporary contingencies have produced a considerable number of paradoxes, of contradictions. Ferreting them out is a favourite Moscow sport.

For instance, Soviet citizens may inherit private property—although Soviet law[1] limits the heirs-presumptive to direct descendants of the deceased, or persons in direct connection by marriage or adoption. Disinheritance of minors under eighteen is not allowed.

[1] For the background of this section I am indebted to Mr. Ralph Barnes.

The testator may, if he wishes (it doesn't happen very often) leave his property to the state.

Soviet citizens may, another point not generally known, own property in the form of houses—though under severe restrictions. Small houses in town and also *datchas* in the country, may be bought (if there are any buyers) and are absolute individual property of the purchaser, but one person may not own more than one house and one *datcha*. *Land* may not be owned. The land of the U.S.S.R. is nationalised, the property of the state.

A Soviet citizen may buy the ownership to an apartment in a co-operative house, but he is subject to eviction if—I quote Barnes —he 'commits a crime, indulges in illicit private trade, or becomes a priest or counter-revolutionary'. He may, in certain rare cases, lease land from municipal authorities if he uses it for building purposes.

A Soviet citizen may own a library or art collection, if he registers it with the authorities. He may buy an automobile—if he can afford it. He may own a sailing-boat, yacht, or launch. Theoretically, he may own an aeroplane, but in practice it is virtually impossible for a private individual to obtain one.

A Soviet citizen may even hire the services of another. Personal servants—domestics—are allowed. He may, with great risk, go into private business and employ labour (for instance a neighbourhood cobbler may have one assistant) but in such cases his business is so heavily taxed that profits are virtually impossible. A professional man, doctor or lawyer, may have a private practice provided he is not in state service.

There is no limit—in theory—to the salary anyone may receive, nor to the amount of capital anyone may accumulate. There are no opportunities for investment, however, except in state bonds. These bonds pay interest, exactly as do bonds in capitalist countries, and a good rate too—eight per cent. Savings banks are encouraged, and in 1935 no fewer than forty-three million depositors throughout the Soviet Union used them. They pay eight to ten per cent interest.

Above all, sharp differences are possible in earning power. The janitor in Sovkino—the movie company—gets, perhaps, 150 roubles per month; the star may get 15,000. Piece-work exists in factories, in order to encourage production. Artists, literary men, may earn very large sums for Russia, though there is very little they can do with their incomes—in paper roubles—after they get it. A playwright, Vasily V. Shkvarkin, author of a *bourgeois* comedy *Another Man's Child*, which swept the provinces, earned 200,000 roubles in royalties a few years ago. A journalist named Michael Koltzoff, editor of the comic paper *Oganok* (Little Light) is reputed to earn 30,000 roubles per month. *Izvestia*, the chief Soviet newspaper, pays 500 roubles each for feuilletons.

One should keep in mind, however, that big incomes such as these are still extremely rare. Earning power may vary in the Soviet Union, according to artistic or technical proficiency, but the extremes, as Louis Fischer has pointed out, are very close. No such 'spread' is conceivable in the U.S.S.R. as exists in Britain or America between say, a clerk in a factory and its owner. Among all the one hundred and sixty-five million Russians, there are probably not ten men who earn £5,000 per year.

And two vitally important elements in this issue of 'socialist inequality' should never be forgotten.

1. No man in the Soviet Union has any individual control of the means of production. A man may accumulate and transfer wealth, but not the means of producing wealth.

2. No man in the Soviet Union may exploit labour for private profit. Interest may be paid on bonds, yes, but this interest does not represent private profits on the use of labour.

These safeguards, as may readily be seen, are so potent that Stalin has no reason to worry from the 'contradictions', which affect only a comparatively small percentage of the population, and which were, in fact, deliberately introduced as a spur to production.

'Stampede to Common Sense'

Perhaps as a result of relaxation from the extreme ardours of the Five-Year Plans, a considerable revaluation of old Soviet value is going on.

The *Pravda* (shades of Lenin!) has come to print touching editorials about love and motherhood. Divorce is still easy, but a strenuous effort is being made to improve the level of family life. Abortions, formerly encouraged, are now prohibited. Children, once taught to pretend complete independence of their parents, are being encouraged to attitudes of filial duty and devotion. Alimony payments for the support of children of divorced parents are strictly enforced. A new law inflicts imprisonment of one year for desertion of a child, and cases of 'sexual hooliganism' may be strictly punished.

2 P

In education, a movement led by Stalin himself (who has insisted on standardised text-books) has restored examinations in schools and universities; teachers and professors are encouraged to enforce discipline, instead of the opposite; degrees like Ph.D. once abolished, are now granted again. It was impossible ten years ago to get a liberal education in the Soviet Union. The whole emphasis was on economics from a strictly Marxist point of view and on natural science. Now history is being taught (though from a Marxist point of view of course), geography also, and there is a powerful movement to revive interest in study of the classics. The University of Moscow has courses on Shelley and Keats.

In regard to the arts, too, something of a counter-revolution has taken place. In June 1935, a musical conductor of the extremist type now considered old-fashioned cut two movements from a symphony on the ground that they were '*bourgeois*'. He was severely rebuked. Fashion shows came to Moscow; so did masked balls, roller skates, and playthings for children without benefit of propaganda. Shakespeare had several good seasons in Moscow. A company of Bashkirs from Orenburg dazzled the town with a performance of *Othello*. And the Theatre of the Revolution, for the benefit of the Consomols, put on *Romeo and Juliet* to show the youthful audience what true love should be. The text was not mutilated. But servants of the Montagues and Capulets were made to fraternise in the first act—to illustrate proper proletarian solidarity!

What the Boss Thinks

Stalin's own considered definition of the Soviet system is perhaps worth quoting:

'The Soviet economy,' he writes, in *Leninism* (II, p. 307), 'means that:

'1. The power of the capitalist class has been overthrown and has been replaced by the power of the working class.

'2. The tools and means of production, the land, factories, etc., have been taken away from the capitalists and handed over to the working class and to the peasantry.

'3. The development of production is subordinated, not to the principle of competition and the safeguarding of capitalist profit, but to the principle of planned guidance and systematic improvement of the material and cultural level of the toilers.

'4. The distribution of the national income takes place—in the interests of systematically raising the material position of the workers and peasants, and extending socialist production in town and country.

'5. The systematic improvement of the material position of the toilers and the ceaseless growth of their requirements (purchasing power)—guarantees the working class against crises of overproduction, against the growth of unemployment, etc.

'6. The working class is the master of the country, working not for the capitalists, but for its own class.'

Stalin is very eager to point out that the Russian revolution of 1917 differs from all other revolutions in history in that not a mere transfer of political sovereignty occurred, not the substitution of one party for another, but the replacement of one economic order by an entirely different one on an international, not a national, basis. This, Harold Laski has said, is the 'seminal' fact of modern history.

Stalin thinks that a communist society will eventually have the following results:

'*a*. There will be no private ownership of the means of production, but social, collective ownership;

'*b*. There will be no classes or state, but workers in industry and agriculture managing their economic affairs as a free association of toilers;

'*c*. national economy will be organised according to plan, and will be based on the highest technique in both industry and agriculture;

'*d*. science and art will enjoy conditions conducive to their highest development;

'*e*. the individual, freed from bread and butter cares, and of necessity of cringing to the "powerful of the earth", will become really free.'

—*Stalin On Technology*, p. 13.

Stalin considers that the problems of production in both industry and agriculture have been solved. Now facing him are two other issues—distribution and transport.

Soviet 'Democracy'

Radicals enamoured blindly of the Soviet cause do it more harm than good by wantonly inaccurate colouring of information. Recently I read an argument, citing details of the Soviet 'elections', designed to show that the U.S.S.R. was more of a democracy than the U.S.A. All the article omitted to mention was (1) the 'vote' was not by secret ballot, but by show of hands, (2) it 'elected' men to serve on a body which by no conceivable stretch of the imagination could be said to have legislative powers. Another point—in most communist 'elections' there is only one candidate!

But in the summer of 1936 a new and ostensibly serious effort towards the evolution of Soviet democracy was made. This was the publication of the new Constitution, which duly came into force with a ceremonial sitting of the Congress of Soviets in 1937. The Constitution, a potentially important document, was drawn up by a committee on constitutional reform which was set up in July 1935 and of which Stalin himself was chairman. The ten vice-chairmen comprised a formidable list of Soviet chieftains: Litvinov, Radek, Vyshinsky, Voroshilov, Molotov, Bukharin, Akulov (the chief prosecuting attorney, who has theoretical powers even over the G.P.U.), Chubar, Zhdanov, Kaganovitch.[1] For a year the committee worked.

The new Constitution set up a two-chamber parliament much like that of the western democracies. The lower house will eventually be elected by universal popular suffrage (so at least it is asserted), the upper house chosen from representatives of the various national minorities. The parliament will pass laws in the regular manner of such bodies, call new elections, and, in general, be the source of the power of the state. This marks a very broad change from the present system, if it is applied with honest intent.

It is incorrect, incidentally, to repeat the usual assertion that communists form only two per cent of Russia's population. The proper figure is nearer ten per cent. In estimating the total population, one includes babies, children, women; one should do likewise in numbering the communists. There are 3,000,000 full adult party members, and 835,298 candidates. But the Consomols, of whom there are about 4,000,000, the Pioneers, about 6,000,000 and the Octobrists, the children, like Mussolini's Wolf-Cubs, of kindergarten and early school age should be included as communists. The general opinion is that the number of party members is bound soon to be widened, as more and more Consomols reach party age.

Associated with the issue of 'democracy' throughout the broad spaces of the Soviet Union is that of exclusive control by Stalin and his men at the top in Moscow. The ruling directorate is small enough to run a terrible risk of losing touch with the country as a whole, and as the present hierarchy congeals into a permanent pyramidal structure, the chance increases of its isolation from the masses. Russia is ruled by a party machine. It may become, as someone put it, a dictatorship not of—but *over*—the proletariat.

---

[1] Of these, however, Litvinov has lost his job, and Bukharin, Radek, and Chubar have been purged.

Jokes

A peasant queues up to see Lenin's body in the Red Square mausoleum, comes out again. 'What did you think of him?' a friend asks. Reply: 'He's just like us, dead but not yet buried.'

Another peasant watches the construction of a new short-wave radio station. The technician explains that any voice in the microphone will be heard over the entire world. The peasant pleads to be allowed the supreme thrill of trying it. He asks to be permitted to say just one word—only one. Permission granted. The peasant steps up to the microphone and shouts—'Help!'

The G.P.U. was 'liberalised'; all agents were instructed to show the greatest courtesy to the common folk. A man in a street-car sneezed. A G.P.U. agent on the platform, peering into the car, snorted angrily, 'Who did that—who was it who sneezed?' Terror in the car. Friends urge the luckless fellow who sneezed to give himself up, confess his sin, in order to save the whole car from arrest. He speaks up, quavering, '*I* sneezed.' The G.P.U. man bellowed: '*Gesundheit!* Your good health!'

Stalin had lice in his hair. No means, mechanical, medicinal, chemical, could extirpate them. Desperate, Stalin called Radek into consultation. Radek said: 'Simple. Collectivise one louse. The others will run away.'

When the intelligentzia and the old 'technical bureaucracy' were being severely scrutinised and punished the joke ran: 'My wife and I have three sons. One is an engineer. The other is a professor of bacteriology. The third is also in Siberia.'

A horde of rabbits jumped out of the Soviet Union across the Polish border. The Poles expressed surprise and consternation. 'Ah,' the rabbits explained, 'the G.P.U. has issued orders to arrest all giraffes in Russia.' 'But,' remonstrated the Polish customs officers, 'you are not giraffes.' The rabbits replied: 'Yes, but try to prove it to the G.P.U.'

A terrible turmoil was heard outside Stalin's private office. The boss was denouncing someone with a tornado of violent epithets. Fifteen minutes it lasted. The terrified doorman peered within. He looked for the comrade whom Stalin must have been chastising. No one except Stalin was there. 'Where is the man you were denouncing?' timidly inquired the doorman. Stalin replied: 'I have just finished my daily quarter of an hour of self-criticism.'

Foreign Affairs

For a long time the foreign policy of the Soviet Union could be fairly expressed in one word—peace. Liberals the world over and even many conservatives—folk who found it difficult to say a good word for the Bolsheviks in domestic affairs—agreed that Russian policy during the thirties was defensive and pacific. The Soviets adopted a consistently non-aggressive line. They tended to their own business, and made no inroads elsewhere, except in remote Sinkiang and Outer Mongolia. They joined the League, they co-operated vividly in the attempt to make Collective Security work.

As well as anyone, Karl Radek has explained Soviet motives in this period:

> 'The object of the Soviet Government is to save the soil of the first proletarian state from the criminal folly of a new war. To this end the Soviet Union has struggled with the greatest determination and consistency for sixteen years. The defence of peace and of the neutrality of the Soviet Union against all attempts to drag it into the whirlwind of a new world war is the central problem of Soviet foreign policy. The Soviet Union follows the policy of peace because peace is the best condition for building up a socialist society.'
> — *Foreign Affairs*, January 1934.

During most of the last decade it was assumed that the Soviet Union had two potential enemies, Japan and Germany. As to the Japanese, the Russians made every kind of concession to appease and mollify them, for instance the sale of the Chinese Eastern Railway in Manchuria for about one eighth its value. When pressure from Japan was particularly acute, the Soviets offset it by establishing friendly relations with the United States. When the Japanese danger receded, the U.S.S.R., though eager for friendship with America, and delighted at American recognition, tended to neglect the new *rapprochement* with Washington, because it was not so pertinently valuable. Meantime they repeatedly offered the Japanese a non-aggression pact, which Japan refused.

As to Russian relations with Germany, it should be remembered that the phase of acute tension and hostility between the two countries only began *after* 1933, when Hitler took power. Before that, for a long time, the policy of the Soviet Union was predicated on friendship with Germany. The Soviets hoped for communist revolution there; Germany, like the U.S.S.R., was practically an outlaw state; the Russians sympathised with Germany's struggle to free herself from the shackles of Versailles; above all, France and

Poland—back in the neolithic twenties—were allies, and allies presumably against Germany and the Soviet Union. The four countries stretched across Europe, France-Germany-Poland-Russia, mutual and successive checks against each other.

It was very neat. It was too neat. It did not last. Hitler ended it. In 1933, Germany under Hitler seemingly became Russia's enemy, mortal and implacable; therefore the Russians had to make a quick and profound *bouleversement*. First, by surviving the Five Year Plan, they made themselves valuable militarily as allies. Second, by allowing the Communist Internationale to languish forlorn, they achieved a sort of spasmodic respectability. Recognition by the United States, in November 1933, was an important step. Then Litvinov contrived to bring Russia into the League. There followed the treaties with France and Czechoslovakia. Anthony Eden visited Moscow and shook hands with Stalin. Litvinov declared, 'Peace is indivisible,' and Russian commissars drank the health of George V of England. God Save the King! The job was done.

Russia, the outcast, the pariah, the chief of revisionist powers—certainly the idea of world revolution connoted revisionism!—thus became, in the short space of three years, the newest addition to the countries in the status quo group. Not only this. The treaties signed with Laval of France and Beneš of Czechoslovakia were virtually military treaties. Concurrently came the congress of the Communist Internationale in Moscow in 1935, the first one in seven years. At this congress Stalin tossed revolutionary internationalism overboard—temporarily—and the Popular Front phase of communist policy began. Communists everywhere were instructed to co-operate with *bourgeois* parties against threats of war and Fascism.

Collective Security and Popular Frontism persisted till 1939. Then came the immense shock of the Russo-German pact, one of the cardinal events in world history this century. Stalin jumped out of one camp and into the other. The pact helped bring the war. I have already described it briefly in Chapter IX above.

That Russia should return to collaboration—no matter how sketchy—with Germany was sufficiently sensational; that, immediately after the outbreak of the war, Russia should invade Poland, enforce demands on the Baltic states, and attack Finland, was beyond the wildest dreams.

Stalin's speech of March 10, 1939, delivered to the Eighteenth Congress of the communist party, was, however, a clear indication of his dissatisfaction with the democracies, and his impending with-drawal from their front. He pointed out that war—'the second imperialist war'—had been going on since the Japanese invasion of Manchuria in 1931. He pointed out that the non-aggressor democ-racies were beyond doubt stronger than the aggressor states, but that nevertheless the democracies continued to give way to them. They surrendered Spain, Czechoslovakia, parts of China. Why? One reason he adduced was fear of revolution. Another was that the democracies, no longer interested in collective security, found that non-intervention, a policy of isolation and neutrality, served their best interests. Stalin indicated quite clearly that he could play this same game. Britain, he implies, played Germany off against Russia. Very well. Why should not Russia, in turn, play Germany off against Britain?

Stalin's speech, however clearly it forecast the change in policy he was planning, certainly did not on the other hand hint at the Russian invasion of Poland and Russian penetration into the Baltic states. For he said, 'We stand for peaceful, close, and friendly relations with all the neighbouring countries with which we have common frontiers. We stand for the support of nations which are the victims of aggression and which are fighting for the inde-pendence of their country.'

How long Stalin will continue to co-operate with Germany—on which issue the fate of Europe presumably depends—is unknown. It depends on his central aims. If he is still a revolutionary at heart, if he still believes in world communism, then Germany serves him a useful purpose, since Germany is attacking the western capi-talist states. He says in the March speech, 'Never forget that we are surrounded by a capitalist world'. Over and over again, in all his pronouncements, he reiterates his belief that this capitalist world is the ultimate enemy. And he may have come to the conclusion that Hitler, too, is an enemy of capitalism, that Fascism contains much of radical elements, that the two revolutions may be useful to one another and may even—conceivably and eventually—merge.

If Stalin is a simon-pure Russian nationalist, interested in noth-ing whatsoever except Russian security, then logic would compel him to be suspicious of the Germans, in case they should become too strong on his frontier, with hungry eyes on the Ukraine. Even so, it would serve his purpose to co-operate with the Germans at least for a time, since Germany is fighting the British Empire, which from the long range point of view is a basic Russian enemy.

Stalin is a nationalist, certainly. But nationalists easily become imperialists, as we know only too well. Stalin may use Germany to a point, then turn on her. He may turn out to be a 'Marxist imperialist', if that phrase has any meaning.

In any case, no matter what happens, it would seem that the Russians are in a position to gain. If the allies lose the 1939 war, then the British Empire is weakened, western capitalism is weakened. If Germany loses the war, then presumably there will be a revolution in Germany, which would also serve Russia's ends. It would weaken or destroy Germany as a nationalist neighbour, and it might bring communism.

Looking at it in the broadest perspective possible, one can only conclude that Stalin wants, above all, to make nationalist Russia strong, to keep Russia strong, against any possible eventuality. To this end, he co-operates with Germany to a certain extent, but at the same time guards very closely against any shift in the situation that might make Germany his enemy.

THE END

ACKNOWLEDGMENTS AND BIBLIOGRAPHY

ABOUT two-thirds of this book, I should think, is the result of direct evidence accumulated by my own eyes and ears. For the rest I have a hundred sources to thank. It is difficult to list them. If this book dealt with a dead instead of a living period, I should have had merely to consult documents in the regular manner of research. But I have been dealing with very contemporary figures and the best information to be had about them can be collected only by word of mouth. A book may be written about Napoleon purely from written records. A chapter about Mussolini, it is obvious on the other hand, should be based partly on written records, but also on the evidence of people who know him, have talked to him, and can report their observations first-hand.

In every capital I have written about, friends and acquaintances have generously collaborated by giving me a word-of-mouth treasury of intimate material and ideas. I have winnowed and checked this material as carefully as possible. The friends who helped me may be counted by the score. I cannot mention their names, because many are residents of countries ruled by dictatorship, and it would be invidious to mention some, who might be named freely, and not others. In addition, other friends have carefully read and checked every part of the manuscript.

To these loyal and generous colleagues in twenty countries, *salaam!*

As to books and documents, I have referred to hundreds—and I must have read several thousand newspaper and magazine clippings on each important country—but I don't want to burden this long manuscript with a formal bibliography. However, the following books have been particularly valuable, some of them in fact indispensable:

Allen, Jay: *Spain. Speech before the Chicago Council of Foreign Relations,* Chicago 1936.
Anonymous: *Recovery Through Revolution,* New York 1933.
Anonymous: *Not to be Repeated,* New York 1932.
Anonymous: *Heil!* Bristol 1934.
Armstrong, Hamilton Fish: *Europe Between Wars?* London 1934.

Armstrong, H. C.; *Grey Wolf*, London 1934.
Armstrong, Hamilton Fish: *We or They*, London 1937.
Armstrong, Hamilton Fish: *Where There Is No Peace*, London 1939.
Baldwin, Stanley: *On England*, London 1926.
Bauer, Otto: *Austrian Democracy under Fire*, Prague 1934.
Beneš, Eduard: *My War Memoirs*, London 1928.
British Blue Book, *Outbreak of Hostilities Between Great Britain and Germany*, London 1939.
Broad, Lewis and Russel, Leonard: *The Ways of the Dictator*, London 1935
Čapek, Karel: *President Masaryk Tells His Story*, London.
Chamberlin, W. H.: *Russia's Iron Age*, London 1935.
Childs, Marquis W.: *Sweden, the Middle Way*, New Haven 1936.
Churchill, Winston: *My Early Life*, London 1930,
Churchill, Winston: *The World Crisis*, London 1931.
Churchill, Winston: *The Aftermath*, London 1929.
Cole, G. D. H.: *Intelligent Man's Review of Europe To-day*, London 1933.
Crane, John O.: *The Little Entente*, New York 1931.
Cripps, Sir S.: *Problems of Socialist Transition*, London 1934.
Daladier, Edouard: *Defense du Pays*, Paris 1939.
Dalton, Hugh: *Practical Socialism for Britain*, London 1935.
Duranty, Walter: *Duranty Reports Russia*, London 1934.
Duranty, Walter: *Europe—War or Peace*, London 1935.
Dutt, R. Palme: *Fascism and Social Revolution*, New York 1934.
Eden, Anthony: *Places in the Sun*, London 1926.
Finer, Herman: *Mussolini's Italy*, London 1935.
Fischer, Louis: *Soviet Journey*, New York 1934.
Fischer, Louis: *The War in Spain*, New York 1937.
Fodor, M. W.: *South of Hitler*, London 1936.
Fortune, Italian Number (July 1934), New York 1934.
Fox, Ralph: *Portugal Now*, London 1936.
Garratt, Geoffrey T.: *Mussolini's Roman Empire*, London 1939.
Gedye, G. E. R.: *Heirs to the Habsburgs*, Bristol 1932.
Gedye, G. E. R.: *Fallen Bastions*, London 1939.
Harris, H. Wilson: *What the League of Nations Is*, London 1925.
Heiden, Konrad: *A History of National Socialism*, London 1934.
Henri, Ernst: *Hitler Over Europe*, London 1934.
Hitler, Adolf: *My Struggle*, London 1933.
Horrabin, J. F.: *An Atlas of Current Affairs*, London 1934.
Horrabin, J. F.: *An Atlas of European History*, London 1935.
Howe, Quincy: *World Diary, 1929—1934*, New York 1934.
Jackson, J. H.: *The Post-War World*, London 1935.
Jerrold, Douglas: *England*, Bristol 1936.
Kaganovitch, L. M.: *Various Pamphlets*, Moscow 1932-35.
Keyserling, H.: *Europe*, London 1928.
Knickerbocker, H. R.: *Will War Come in Europe?* London 1934
Krutch, J. W.: *Was Europe a Success?* London 1934.
Landau, Rom: *Pilsudski, Hero of Poland*, London 1930.
Laski, H. J.: *Communism*, London 1927.
Laski, H. J.: *Politics*, Philadelphia 1931.

Lefebure, Victor: *Scientific Disarmament*, London 1932.
Livingston, A.: *The Peace Ballot*, London 1935.
Lugwig, Emil: *Talks with Mussolini*, London 1933.
Madariaga, S. de: *Spain*, London 1931.
Markham, R. H.: *Meet Bulgaria*, Sofia 1932.
Marsh, Sir Edward: *A Number of People*, London 1939.
Martin, William: *Europe as I see It To-day*, New York 1931.
Masaryk, T. G.: *The Making of a State*, London 1927.
Messinger, J.: *Death of Dollfuss*, London 1935.
Mirsky, Dmitri: *The Intelligentzia of Great Britain*, London 1935.
Morrison, Herbert: *Practical Socialism in Great Britain*, London 1933.
Mosley, Oswald: *The Greater Britain*, London 1934.
Mowrer, Edgar A.: *Germany Puts the Clock Back*, London 1938.
Mussolini, Benito: *My Autobiography*, London 1937.
Mussolini, Benito: *Political and Social Doctrine of Fascism*, London 1933.
Reed, Douglas: *The Burning of the Reichstag*, London 1934.
Report of Court Proceedings, Case of Anti-Soviet Trotskyite Centre, Moscow 1937.
Report of Court Proceedings, Case of Trotskyite-Zinovievite Terrorist Centre, Moscow 1936.
Rintelen, Capt. von: *The Dark Invader*, London 1933.
Rothery, Agnes: *Denmark, Kingdom of Reason*, London 1937.
Rudlin, W. A.: *Growth of Fascism in Great Britain*, London 1935.
Russell, Bertrand: *Freedom versus Organisation, 1814–1914*, London 1934.
Schachtman, Max: *Behind the Moscow Trial*, New York 1936.
Schevill, F.: *A History of Europe*, London 1939.
Schuschnigg, Kurt: *Farewell Austria*, London 1938.
Siegfried, A.: *France, A Study in Nationality*, London 1930.
Siegfried, A.: *England's Crisis*, London 1933.
Simonds, Frank H. and Emeny, Brooks: *Price of Peace*, London 1935.
Stalin-Wells: *Stalin-Wells Talk*, London 1934.
Stalin and Others: *Socialism Victorious*, Moscow 1934.
Stalin, Joseph : *Leninism*, London 1934.
Stalin, Molotov and Litvinov: *Our Foreign Policy*, Moscow 1934.
Stalin, J.: Various Pamplets, Moscow 1932–35.
Steed, Wickham: *The Real Stanley Baldwin*, London 1932,
Strachey, John: *Menace of Fascism*, London 1934.
Thompson, Dorothy: *I saw Hitler*, New York 1932.
Trevelyan, G. M.: *History of England*, London 1927.
Trotsky, Leon: *Where is Britain Going?* London 1926.
Trotsky, Leon: *History of the Russian Revolution*, London 1934.
Trotsky, Leon: *The Revolution Betrayed*, New York 1937.
Various Authors: *Great Contemporaries*, London 1935.
Various Authors: *What Would be the Character of a New War*, London 1933.
Voigt, F. A.: *Unto Caesar*, London 1938.
Union of Democratic Control: *The Secret International*, London 1932.
Union of Democratic Control: *Patriotism, Ltd.*, London 1933.
Vergin, Fedor: *Subconscious Europe*, London 1932,
'Vigilantes': *Inquest on Peace*, London 1935.
Wells, H. G.: *Outline of History*, London 1932.

Werth, Alexander: *France in Ferment*, London 1935.
Wheeler-Bennett, J. W.: *The Disarmament Deadlock*, London 1934.
White, Freda: *War in Spain, A Short Account*, London 1937.
World Committee: *Brown Book of the Hitler Terror*, London 1933.
Zimmern, A.: *The Third British Empire*, London 1926.

As to pamphlets, those of the Foreign Policy Association (New York), and of the Royal Institute of International Affairs (London) were most valuable. I am particularly indebted to the *Bulletin of International News* published by the latter. Among newspapers, I used most the *Manchester Guardian*, *The Times*, the *Evening Standard,* and the *Daily Telegraph.* The diary columns of the latter two were very helpful. And my debt to the *New Statesman* in the English chapters is manifest.

This book has been written fresh and as a whole, and all from a consistent point of view. I had, of course, covered some of the same ground in magazine articles, as well as in dispatches to the *Chicago Daily News.* Thus I should mention that *Vanity Fair* gave hospitality to some early views of Madame Lupescu, Mr. Eden, General Goering and others; *Foreign Affairs* allowed me to discuss in its pages Dr. Dollfuss and the Habsburg problem; the *Nation* let me say what I thought about Central Europe for many years. *Harper's Magazine* published some of the material in this book on Spain, the Reichstag Fire trial, and the arms traffic, as well as an essay called 'Policy by Murder'. The chapters on Blum and de Valera appeared in the *Strand Magazine.* I have also used a few passages from sections I wrote of an anonymous book on Europe, called *Not to be Repeated.*

I have my newspaper, the *Chicago Daily News,* to thank for the wide opportunity it has given me the past dozen years to work in almost every country in Europe. The *News,* with its admirable tradition of foreign news reporting, gave me a free hand from Scandinavia to Palestine, from Moscow to London and back again, and I spent five eventful years in Vienna as *Daily News* correspondent in Central Europe and the Balkans. Of course the *News* is not responsible for any sentiments or opinions in this book. Nor, except for an occasional sentence, is there any reproduction of *Daily News* material. But, for the opportunities they freely gave me, I have the publisher and editors to thank.

Finally, this book would have been impossible to write except for the patient and generous collaboration of my wife.

INDEX

INDEX

Heavy type distinguishes, where necessary, the most important references